CONTEMPORARY SOCIAL PSYCHOLOGICAL THEORIES

CONTEMPORARY SOCIAL

PSYCHOLOGICAL THEORIES

EDITED BY PETER J. BURKE

STANFORD SOCIAL SCIENCES
An imprint of Stanford University Press
Stanford, California

Stanford University Press
Stanford, California

Printed in the United States of America on acid-free, archival-quality paper

Library of Congress Cataloging-in-Publication Data
Contemporary social psychological theories / edited by Peter J. Burke.
    p. cm.
  Includes bibliographical references and index.
  ISBN 0-8047-5346-6 (cloth : alk. paper)—ISBN 0-8047-5347-4 (pbk. alk. paper)
    1. Social psychology—Philosophy.   2. Social psychology.   I. Burke, Peter J. (Peter James), 1939–
HM1011.C66 2006
302.01—dc22

                                              2006001204

Typeset by G&S Book Services in 10/13.5 Minion

Original Printing 2006

Last figure below indicates year of this printing:
15   14   13   12   11

CONTENTS

CONTRIBUTORS

JOSEPH BERGER is senior fellow at the Hoover Institution and emeritus professor of sociology at Stanford University. He is the 1991 winner of the Cooley-Mead Award from the American Sociological Association for lifetime contributions to social psychology and is the editor, with Morris Zelditch, of *New Directions in Contemporary Sociological Theory*.

PETER J. BURKE is professor of sociology and codirector of the Social Psychology Research Laboratory at the University of California, Riverside. He is a Fellow of the American Association for the Advancement of Science, the 2003 winner of the Cooley-Mead Award from the American Sociological Association for lifetime contributions to social psychology, past chair of the American Sociological Association section on social psychology, and former editor of *Social Psychology Quarterly*.

COYE CHESHIRE is assistant professor at the School of Information Management and Systems at the University of California, Berkeley.

KAREN S. COOK is the Ray Lyman Wilbur Professor of Sociology at Stanford University. She is the 2004 winner of the Cooley-Mead Award from the American Sociological Association for lifetime contributions to social psychology and was elected to the American Academy of Arts and Sciences in 1996. She is the author of *Social Capital*, with Nan Lin and Ronald S. Burt, and *Trust in Society*.

PAMELA EMANUELSON is a doctoral candidate in sociology at the University of South Carolina. She received the Best Graduate Student Paper award for "Flow Networks: An Extension of Network Exchange Theory" from the Rationality and Society section of the American Sociological Association.

ALEXANDRA GERBASI is a doctoral candidate in sociology at Stanford University.

KAREN A. HEGTVEDT is professor of sociology at Emory University. She is a former deputy editor of *Social Psychology Quarterly*.

MICHAEL A. HOGG is an Australian Research Council Professorial Fellow and professor of social psychology at the University of Queensland. His most recent book, coedited with Dominic Abrams and Jose M. Marques, is *The Social Psychology of Inclusion and Exclusion*.

GUILLERMINA JASSO is professor of sociology at New York University. She has published articles on sociobehavioral theory, distributive justice, status, international migration, mathematical methods for theory building, and factorial survey methods for empirical analysis.

EDWARD J. LAWLER is Martin P. Catherwood Professor of Industrial and Labor Relations and professor of sociology at Cornell University. He is the 2001 winner of the Cooley-Mead Award from the American Sociological Association for lifetime contributions to social psychology, has served as chair of both the social psychology section and rational choice section of the American Sociological Association, and was editor of *Social Psychology Quarterly*. He edits, with Shane Thye, volumes in the series Advances in Group Processes.

MICHAEL W. MACY is professor and chair of sociology at Cornell University. He has published articles on collective action, evolutionary game theory, deviance and social control, social psychology, social exchange theory, and rational choice theory.

GEORGE J. MCCALL is emeritus professor of sociology and public policy administration at the University of Missouri, St. Louis. He has written books on self, identity, social interaction, and personal relationships and is the author, with J. L. Simmons, of the much acclaimed *Identities and Interactions*.

LINDA D. MOLM is professor of sociology at the University of Arizona. She is a former editor of *Social Psychology Quarterly* and the author of *Coercive Power in Social Exchange*.

CECILIA L. RIDGEWAY is the Lucie Stern Professor of Social Sciences at Stanford University. She is the 2005 winner of the Cooley-Mead Award from the American Sociological Association for lifetime contributions to social psychology.

DAWN T. ROBINSON is associate professor of sociology and director of the Laboratory for the Study of Social Interaction at the University of Georgia. She is deputy editor of *Social Psychology Quarterly*.

LYNN SMITH-LOVIN is Robert L. Wilson Professor of Arts and Sciences at Duke University. She has served as vice president of the American Sociological Association, president of the Southern Sociological Society, chair of the American Sociological Association sections on social psychology and the sociology of emotion, coeditor of *Social Psychology Quarterly*. She is the 2005 winner of the Lifetime Achievement Award from the American Sociological Association section on the sociology of emotion. She is the author, with David R. Heise, of *Analyzing Social Interaction: Research Advances in Affect Control Theory*.

JAN E. STETS is professor of sociology and codirector of the Social Psychology Research Laboratory at the University of California, Riverside. She is the author, with Jonathan H. Turner, of *The Sociology of Emotions* and coeditor, with Jonathan H. Turner, of the *Handbook of the Sociology of Emotions*.

JONATHAN H. TURNER is Distinguished Professor of Sociology at the University of California, Riverside. He is past president of the Pacific Sociological Association and the California Sociological Association and a fellow of the American Association for the Advancement of Science. He has written more than 25 books, including *On the Origins of*

Human Emotions: A Sociological Inquiry into the Evolution of Human Affect and *Face to Face: Toward a Sociological Theory of Interpersonal Behavior.*

MURRAY WEBSTER JR. is professor of sociology at the University of North Carolina at Charlotte. He is the recipient of the 2003 First Citizens Bank Scholars Medal.

DAVID WILLER is professor of sociology at the University of South Carolina. He is the author of five books and is currently writing, with Henry Walker, *Experimental Design: Developing and Testing Social Theory.*

MORRIS ZELDITCH JR. is emeritus professor of sociology at Stanford University. He is the 2000 winner of the Cooley-Mead Award from the American Sociological Association for lifetime contributions to social psychology. He is the author, with Joseph Berger, of *Status, Power and Legitimacy: Strategies and Theories.*

PREFACE

I have a list of social psychological theories I give to graduate students who are interested in social psychology that contains some 40 different theories ranging alphabetically from affect control theory to the theory of reasoned action. For some of these theories there is much published work, for some others there is very little that has been published. Some are older, like classical conditioning theory, but most are extant in the literature today and could in some sense be considered contemporary social psychological theories. Some limitations had to prevail for including chapters in this volume. The choices were made relatively easy, however, when I limited the selection to sociological social psychology theories for which there are active cumulative research programs.

Within the past decade or two, there has developed a growth and maturity in sociological social psychology among several lines of theory within that "middle range" proposed by Merton (1957). These programs of theory such as expectation states theory, comparison theory, power-dependence theory, social identity theory, identity control theory, and others have developed through cumulative testing and building in systematic agendas of research. These programs of cumulative research have become the dominant mode of theorizing in sociological social psychology.

For too long, theory has been tied to particular people like Marx, Weber, Durkheim, Mead, or Parsons. Now we can point to theoretical ideas that are being developed and tested by many investigators, where the focus is on the ideas and not on the people, where change and development of theory is taken for granted, and where the arguments are not confined to what so-and-so really said or meant. And most importantly, the ideas in these theories are subject to continuous testing through active programs of research. The theories presented in this volume fit this description of cumulative theoretical programs. The theories are not finished, but are under continuous development, often from initially simple statements, becoming more elaborated and expanded statements with well-developed scopes of application that account for a wide variety of social processes.

What do we mean by cumulative theoretical research traditions? To answer this, let me first say that, in general, social research can be divided into the different approaches that people take on the basis of the kinds of questions that they ask. Some research is purely descriptive in that it seeks to identify and describe some social phenomenon or process. For example, studies that describe the process of organizing a social movement or studies that detail the ways gender is managed in interaction are descriptive. Such work provides us with a glimpse or view of some phenomenon that we did not know about or can now see from a different point of view. Such work neither relates the phenomenon to other phenomena of interest nor seeks to explain or understand its relationship to other phenomena.

Beyond that is work that explicitly links one social phenomenon to other social phenomena. Examples might be studies that link drug use to social class or to family structure by examining the correlation between variables that measure each of these concepts. Such studies, sometimes called variable analyses, go beyond the descriptive studies in that they inform us about the relationships between different processes and concepts. Such studies may be framed in causal language, such as children in single-parent families are more likely to use drugs. However, they do not tell us *how* such concepts or processes are related.

For that we need to raise a more complicated question that directly asks how it is that, for example, drug use and family structure are related. How it is, for another example, that status structures emerge in interaction over time? How it is, for a third example, that identity verification leads to stronger bonds between interaction partners? For questions like these to be answered, we need theory. Theories tell us how such linkages occur. Research that builds and tests theories that answer such questions provides the foundation for cumulative theoretical research programs and theory growth today. And when framed in general terms, such theories not only explain the specific connections that may have led to the theory but can offer explanations of any specific instance representing the general classes of phenomena. Status structures, for example, emerge not only in laboratory task groups but in task groups in educational and organizational settings. Cumulative theory provides general principles that can be used to understand a variety of specific social phenomena and can lead us to ask new questions that could not have been asked before. For example, with the discovery of weak power in exchange networks (see Chapter 10), network exchange theory was extended to consider structural properties of networks that had not been addressed in previous theories (Markovsky et al. 1993).

Each of the chapters in the second part of this volume describes a theory and the cumulative research program that has evolved with the theory. Each of the chapters is written by persons who are intimately tied to the development of the theories described. The theories themselves, however, did not spring forth fully formed but grew slowly out of certain general frameworks or viewpoints that formed the contexts in which the theories developed— contexts that frame the issues, provide the basic assumptions, and shape the view of human nature. While these general frameworks are not in and of themselves theories, they might be called theoretical frameworks. The first part of this volume covers four of these frameworks that have been especially useful in generating the ideas out of which these cumulative theoretical research traditions have developed.

Both affect control theory (Chapter 7) and identity theory (Chapter 5), for example, grew out of the ideas about self and identity that were contained in symbolic interactionism (Chapter 1). Social exchange theory (Chapter 2) gave rise to power-dependence theory

(Chapter 9), elementary theory (Chapter 10), and the affect theory of social exchange (Chapter 11), all of which also draw to varying extents upon both rational choice theory (Chapter 4) and notions of justice in exchange contained in the distributive justice framework (Chapter 3). Comparison theory (Chapter 8) also grows directly out of the distributive justice perspective (Chapter 3). Although not explicitly derived from symbolic interactionism (Chapter 1), many of the ideas in status characteristics theory and expectation states theory (Chapter 12) can be seen in the symbolic interaction framework. Status characteristics and expectation states theories also have a special place among the cumulative research traditions as they were the first to develop and they became a model for other areas to emulate. These theories also gave rise to a set of related theoretical research traditions including status construction theory (Chapter 13) and legitimacy theory (Chapter 14). Finally, as Owens (2003) points out, while social identity theory (Chapter 6) had its beginnings in psychological theories of categorization as applied to self-categorization, it has borrowed from the symbolic interaction framework (Chapter 1) and can be seen now as closely tied with both affect control theory (Chapter 7) and identity control theory (Chapter 5).

The connections among these theories are thus many and various, but the larger picture of social life to which they contribute necessitates an ultimate theoretical integration of some sort. The final chapter reviews the many commonalities and connections, but at the same time asks the larger theoretical question about where these theories must eventually take us. What is it that these theories do not do? What are the larger questions that need to be answered? How might these theories be brought together into a larger understanding that bridges the micro, meso, and macro levels that is the promise of social psychology? Thus the book ends with some thoughts that help the reader grasp the larger, integrated picture toward which all of these theories are pointing and toward which all of these researchers and theorists are working: an understanding of the general, abstract social psychological principles underlying human social behavior.

ACKNOWLEDGMENTS

I wish first to thank the authors who contributed to this volume for their willingness to take the time to help put this volume together and to meet the (sometimes very short) deadlines that were imposed. Their contributions to the field and to this volume are very much appreciated. I wish to thank Kate Wahl and Kirsten Oster of Stanford University Press for the support and help they provided in bringing this volume to life. Andy Sieverman of G&S Book Services was very helpful on the production side, able to deal with queries and last-minute changes in a friendly and courteous manner. Finally, I want to thank the graduate student members of the social psychology seminar at UC Riverside for their help in the production of the index for this volume: Seth Abrutyn, Allison Cantwell, Michael Carter, Chrissy Cerven, Michael M. Harrod, Shelley Osborn, and Yvonne Thai. Thank you all.

REFERENCES

Markovsky, Barry, John Skvoretz, David Willer, Michael J. Lovaglia, and Jeffrey Erger. 1993. The seeds of weak power: An extension of network exchange theory. *American Sociological Review* 58:197–209.

Merton, Robert K. 1957. *Social Theory and Social Structure*. Glencoe, IL: Free Press.

Owens, Timothy J. 2003. Self and identity. In *Handbook of Social Psychology*, ed. J. DeLamater, 205–32. New York: Kluwer Academic.

CONTEMPORARY SOCIAL PSYCHOLOGICAL THEORIES

1 | SYMBOLIC INTERACTION

George J. McCall

Symbolic interaction is a rather recent name (dating back to the 1930s) for a very old and persistent social psychological view (dating back to the mid-1700s). That view has been so thoroughly established in sociology that, as one late theorist remarked (quoted in Gusfield 1995, ix), "We didn't think symbolic interaction was a perspective in sociology, we thought it was sociology." The virtually axiomatic themes of symbolic interaction, in their most basic form, are set forth in Figure 1.1.

CORE THEMES OF SYMBOLIC INTERACTION

Symbolic interaction (SI) is fundamentally a theory of *human nature*, a view that developed among the Scottish moral philosophers[1] in reaction against prevailing views of human beings that they felt were wrongly pessimistic and overly individualistic. Thomas Hobbes, for instance, had written that human lives are, in nature, solitary, nasty, brutish, and short. Although quite a number of the writings of the Scottish moralists proved to be of enduring interest to sociologists, it was one groundbreaking book by Adam Smith—*The Theory of Moral Sentiments* (1759)—that most centrally defined their emerging view of human nature.

Original Themes

Axiom A. To locate that "human nature" that so concerned them, the Scottish moral philosophers agreed among themselves that it would be necessary to look behind the ubiquitous effects of environment (history, culture, circumstance) to find a nature common to all human beings. These scholars accordingly read widely in the just-emerging literature on newly documented peoples, such as various natives encountered in North America, and importantly contributed to theories and works of history itself. And as early economists (Adam Smith of economic renown standing at their center), the Scottish moralists were quite sensitive to how poverty, prosperity, and social position can make one individual seem so different from another.

At the same time that they were digging beneath the ever present effects of environment to identify the common nature of human beings, these scholars had also to be concerned

Axiom A: All humans share a common nature that is unique among all animals but
obscured by human social differences.
Axiom B: Humans generally behave in socially proper ways.
Axiom C: Human conduct is self-regulated
    Postulate C-1: A person is a social animal.
    Postulate C-2: Fundamental to society is communication.
    Postulate C-3: Fundamental to person is mental life.
    Postulate C-4: The key link between society and person is the looking-glass self.
    Postulate C-5: Self-regulation is a process.

Figure 1.1   Core Themes of Symbolic Interaction

with humans' similarities with and differences from other species of animals. Their views of human nature were thus always comparative in nature, pondering quite forthrightly all sorts of comparisons with many other creatures.

Axiom B. Against the brutish behaviorism of Hobbes and others, the views of the Scottish moralists emphasized instead the notion of *conduct.* By that they meant behavior that is sophisticated, civilized, polished—in keeping with their abiding interest in the emergence of a civil society.

Axiom C. But how is it, the Scottish moralists asked, that persons generally do the proper thing, at least in the eyes of their fellows? First of all, they argued, a person is fundamentally a social animal (C-1). Against the prevailing social-contract theorists they argued that society is primary and persons are only secondary, rather than the other way around. Second, they contended that society is peopled by selves, i.e., socially conscious actors who are aware of their position in society.

Serving to make individuals aware of their position is the process of communication, so fundamental to the very existence of society (C-2). Without some sort of communication, there could exist only a population rather than a society.

Smith focused on the fact that individuals tend to make moral judgments about the actions (and underlying emotions) of other human beings. Judgments of the propriety or the merit of such actions (and their source feelings) depend on one's sympathy, or fellow feeling, with the feelings of actor or recipient. Sympathy, in this sense, is experiencing an analogous emotion at the thought of the situation the other person faces. The key point for Smith is that this same mechanism can be used also to ensure propriety in judging one's own actions and feelings; impartiality of judgment can result only from looking at one's own actions as though they were those of someone else. Indeed, Smith contended that others serve the individual as a "social looking-glass," a mirror reflecting to the actor how others are reacting to the actor's doings and feelings—reflecting, that is, their moral judgments about the quality of the actor's actions.

Of course, without some sort of mind—an internal, subjective counterpart to society's communication process (C-3)—a person could never even apprehend those moral judgments provided by society. The perceptual theory of mind that prevailed in the 1700s emphasized the role of *images*—pale derivatives of the externally caused perceptions and sensations. Imagination, or the ability to entertain images, was regarded as a distinguishing human capacity, making possible a truly social intelligence.

In a brilliant leap of theorizing, Smith argued that the key link between society and the person is the "looking-glass self" (C-4); the individual acquires moral compass through *internalizing* the social looking glass:

> We suppose ourselves the spectators of our own behavior and endeavor to imagine what effect it would, in this light, produce upon us. This is the only looking-glass by which we can, in some measure, with the eyes of other people, scrutinize the propriety of our conduct. (Smith 1759)

Smith thus postulated the existence of a divided self—one aspect inclined to execute particular actions, while a second aspect imagined how specific other humans would react to those actions:

> When I endeavor to examine my own conduct, I divide myself, as it were, into two persons. . . . The first is the spectator, whose sentiments with regard to my own conduct I endeavor to enter into, by placing myself in his situation, and by considering how it would appear to me, when seen from that particular point of view. The second is the agent, the person whom I properly call myself. . . . The first is the judge; the second the person judged of. (Smith 1759)

An action that seemingly would be badly received by other people important to the individual would presumably be suppressed. Action, then, is (morally) regulated by this process of the functioning of the divided "looking-glass self" (C-5), and self-regulated action amounts to conduct (axiom C). Doing the proper thing, in the eyes of one's fellows (axiom B), is quite a natural consequence of that sort of process of self-regulation.

Yet Smith held that self-regulation through internalization of the social looking glass is a human characteristic that is far from innate:

> Were it possible that a human creature could grow up to manhood in a solitary place, without any communication with his own species, he could no more think of his own character . . . than of the beauty or deformity of his own face. (Smith 1759)

Subsequent Elaborations of Symbolic Interaction

As an intellectual tradition of long standing, SI is much like a pearl, accreting successive layers of development. In describing these layers of development accreting upon the core, I will make selective use of the framework of intellectual development outlined by Colomy and Brown (1995), defining works that either elaborate, proliferate, revise, or reconstruct a tradition. As we shall discover, adaptations of SI (revisions or reconstructions) have generally been occasioned by the fundamentals (postulates C-2 or C-3), that is, by the rise of new (or at least different) theories of communication or of mental life.

EUROPEAN INFLUENCES

SI, like much of social science, strongly reflects two other defining European intellectual traditions: neo-Kantian relativism and evolutionism.

Neo-Kantian Relativism

Living at about the same time as Adam Smith, the German philosopher Immanuel Kant achieved towering intellectual influence through his reconciling of the ancient traditions of rationalism and empiricism. Like the idealistic rationalists, Kant postulated a pregiven but chaotic world that could make human sense only through the imposition of conceptual categories. Like the empiricists, however, he conceded that such conceptual categories are significantly shaped by individual sensory experience of that world. Kant's new perspectival theory of mind retained Smith's notion of a divided self (the knower and the known) but served to introduce a considerably more cognitive, less emotional view of mental life and action.

A hundred years later, still very much in Kant's philosophical shadow, German Romanticism reveled in the increasingly documented cultural differences among all human groupings—races, nations, folks, tribes—to emphasize how conceptual categories themselves are shaped by such group-based differences in lived experience. By emphasizing differences in peoples' conceptual categories, these Romantic scholars effectively revised Kant's view of how conceptual categories are acquired. Such neo-Kantian relativism importantly defined all of the social sciences for decades to come.

Relativism of this sort acquired its sharpest form in the work of the German-American anthropologist Franz Boas (1911), who contended that languages are the primary basis for differences in conceptual categories. This doctrine of "linguistic relativism" (W. Foley 1997) was subsequently perfected by Boas's student Edward Sapir and Sapir's close colleague Benjamin Whorf (1956). Indeed, it was their doctrine (C-2) on how growing up speaking a particular language shapes a person's worldview, and therefore one's world, that effectively put the *symbolic* dimension into SI.

Evolutionism

The idea of evolution had enjoyed a general currency in Europe for a century or more before its applicability was firmly established through the brilliant empirical and theoretical work by Charles Darwin in 1859. Indeed, the Scottish moralists themselves had made important contributions to evolutionary thought, particularly the evolution of societies.

But it was the English developments of evolutionary doctrine (in biology by Darwin, Alfred Russel Wallace, and T. H. Huxley and in sociology by Herbert Spencer) that truly lent new significance to the Scottish moralists' old questions of human nature, by emphasizing that humans are in fact animals. In the latter half of the 1800s, virtually every field of learning was revolutionized by evolutionism and its focus on changes in animal nature and on survival tests of fitness. For the first time we saw the rise of evolutionary psychology and of evolutionary sociology—fields that are even stronger today (Gaulin and McBurney 2004; Kenrick and Luce 2004; Axelrod 1984; Key and Aiello 1999; R. Foley 2001) and that continue to challenge or refine axiom A, thus lending a very modern cast indeed to ancient questions of human nature.

EARLY AMERICAN PHILOSOPHY

Even though these three European traditions (Scottish moral philosophy, neo-Kantian relativism, and evolutionism) essentially established the intellectual context in which SI further developed, it was an American movement in philosophical thought—pragmatism—that truly evoked SI as we know it today (Lewis and Smith 1980). Pragmatism represents a *philosophical* emphasis on adaptation and fitness (from evolutionism) and on experience (from Kantianism). At base, pragmatism is a philosophy of taking seriously the practical consequences of ideas for intelligent, purposive action.

Cambridge-Style Pragmatism

Among the group of philosophers meeting regularly in Cambridge within which the pragmatic movement sprang, the most seminal was surely Charles Sanders Peirce, who is credited with the invention of pragmatism. After all, it was Peirce's (1878) communication theory of signs—that a sign will always involve a tendency to behavior in anyone for whom it is a sign (Morris 1970)—that lay at the heart of the pragmatists' distinctive theory of meaning (C-2), that what a thing means is what actions it involves.

Yet Peirce remained a recondite figure even among technical philosophers, and it was only much later, through the works of his Cambridge colleague William James, that the movement came to achieve appreciable influence. (The latter was, after all, a well-connected humanist with a superior literary style—the brother of novelist Henry James.) James (1907) effectively broadened the appeal of the pragmatic maxim by bending its original emphasis on how ideas function in the community of scientists to his own concern for how ideas function in the lives of particular individuals.

Chicago-Style Pragmatism

The movement soon attained an even wider audience through the works of John Dewey (1908, 1925), one of the first prominent scholars in the field of education. Dewey's educational theories emphasizing problem solving through inquiry obviously struck a deep nerve in American thought and not incidentally established that explicit self-regulation of actions need only be episodic rather than continual (C-5). But beyond Dewey's own substantive ideas, it was his academic leadership that assembled at the University of Chicago a philosophy department centered (after his own departure) on the brilliant George Herbert Mead (Morris 1970).

After Smith, Mead was undoubtedly the central figure in developing SI, owing mainly to the genius with which he united the pragmatists' theory of meaning (C-2) with an appropriate theory of mind (C-3). Key to that unification (Mead 1934) was attention to a particular type of sign—the gesture—in which the earliest stages of an act call out in its beholders subsequent stages of that act. In Mead's view, animals can signal their intentions only through gestures in just this sense, so that animal interactions amount to a "conversation of gestures." Human actors, on the other hand, also employ another class of sign—the symbol—which evokes within them the same response tendencies (i.e., meanings) that it evokes in beholders. This response in common serves to place actor and audience on the same footing, thus enabling the actor literally to "assume the role of other toward one-self" and thereby to have the basis for that self-regulation of conduct that Smith noted (axiom C); humans act toward objects (including self) in terms of the meanings of those objects. And of course, the use of symbols (i.e., language) to communicate entails that the "other" here is not simply specific persons but is instead the "generalized other," thus transcending the actor's imagination of how numerous specific persons might view one.

Like Smith, then, Mead supposed that the looking-glass self operates through individuals responding identically to something; for Smith, that something was the situation, while for Mead it was the linguistic symbol. Yet the difference between Smith's "seeing ourselves as others see us" and Mead's "taking the role of other toward the self" certainly represents a significant intellectual advance.

Mead's symbolic theory of communication fits closely with his representational theory of mental life (C-3), within which speech and language are taken to dominate human consciousness, at least in those situations where habit no longer succeeds and reflection is required of an intelligent actor. Gradually, by stages (C-5), a human being learns to internalize the "conversation of significant symbols," so that the process of self-regulation comes to take place by means of an "inner forum" of internalized debate. Such an inner forum based on linguistic symbols requires that the divided self (C-4) that carries on the debate consists of the "I" (the impulsive side of the actor) and the "Me" (the reactive side, embodying a variety of imported frameworks for response).

EARLY AMERICAN PSYCHOLOGY

While all this was transpiring in the mother field of philosophy, the major academic disciplines (including the social sciences) were struggling to establish themselves as independent entities in the emerging American universities.

In psychology, James Mark Baldwin (1897) was among the earliest scholars to emphasize that a person's human nature actually has to be developed, by society (C-5). In fact, Baldwin contributed a quite specific theory setting forth and explaining the developmental stages through which such capacities are cultivated.

But among early American psychologists, it was William James who was, again, of greatest importance. Attempting to move the older Continental psychology in a more Darwinian, evolutionary direction, James (1890) initiated what we now regard as a functional psychology, in which the self serves as a key factor in adapting the actor to the environment. His theory of mental life (C-3) accordingly emphasized the functions of the stream of consciousness. In his influential treatment of the self, James was perhaps the first to label the Kantian self-as-knower the "I" and the self-as-known the "Me," and he certainly emphasized that the social self (C-4) is not a single entity but rather is multiple:

> A man's social me is the recognition which he gets from his mates. . . . Properly speaking, a man has as many social selves as there are individuals who recognize him and carry an image of him in their mind. . . . We may practically say that he has as many different social selves as there are distinct groups of persons about whose opinions he cares. (James 1892)

EARLY AMERICAN SOCIOLOGY

Though largely dominated by Social Darwinism, early American sociology, in its battle for standing as an independent scholarly discipline, found SI quite appealing by virtue of its insistence on the primacy of society over individuals and its relatively optimistic account of human nature.

University of Michigan

In the lively academic center of Ann Arbor, Charles Horton Cooley (1902) enormously repopularized among sociologists all the basic ideas of the Scottish moral philosophers, especially that of the looking-glass self (C-4):

A social self of this sort might be called the reflected or looking-glass self:

"Each to each a looking-glass
Reflects the other that doth pass."

A self-idea of this sort seems to have three principal elements: the imagination of our appearance to the other person; the imagination of his judgment of that appearance; and some sort of self-feeling, such as pride or mortification. The comparison with a looking-glass hardly suggests the second element, the imagined judgment, which is quite essential. The thing that moves us to pride or shame is not the mere mechanical reflection of ourselves, but an imputed sentiment, the imagined effect of this imagination upon another's mind. . . . We always imagine, and in imagining share, the judgments of the other mind. (Cooley 1902)

Although Cooley added to the framework the (rather Mead-like) proposition that it is the communication process (C-2) that gives rise to mental life (C-3) and thence to self and other, his phenomenological insistence that the latter two entities are personal ideas—and thus can get together only in the mind—has greatly annoyed numerous other sociologists over the years, even though that insistence also underpinned his argument that society and self are twin-born—two sides of the same coin. Turning aside the contemporary advances of the pragmatists, Cooley stuck to the older theory of communication—emphasizing sympathy as the key mechanism (though his view of sympathy was much less emotional and considerably more cognitive than Smith's)—and to the older theory of mind (C-3) that centered on the faculty of imagination. To Cooley, self is Person's imagination of an idea of Other about Person, while Other is Person's image of Other.

More innovative was Cooley's demonstration that self-regulation (C-5) is a process that has to be developed over time through participation in society:

Man does not have [human nature] at birth; he cannot acquire it except through fellowship, and it decays in isolation. (Cooley 1909)

Cooley's studies on the sociability and imagination of young children helped all to see the truth in Smith's claim that human nature is not inborn but has to be socially developed. Taking the lead in that developmental process are not institutions but what he first styled *primary groups*, particularly the family and the peer group (Cooley, 1909).

University of Chicago

Across Lake Michigan, the newly established University of Chicago—based in the Social Gospel movement of *religious* Darwinism—quickly assumed leadership in the newly emerging social sciences. That leadership has often been attributed in part to Chicago's interdisciplinary character; graduate students in sociology took courses in anthropology with Sapir (1921), in linguistics with Leonard Bloomfield (1933), and in philosophy with Mead. Yet such courses always had considerable sociological focus; for example, Mead long taught the course Social Psychology and keenly appreciated the contributions that Cooley had made (Mead 1930).

But the early sociology faculty itself included two giants of SI in Robert E. Park and W. I. Thomas. These two are widely credited with turning sociology—including SI—into an empirical science (Bulmer 1984). Thomas's sprawling cross-national empirical study (with Florian Znaniecki) of the Polish peasant in Europe and America employed multiple methods, including analysis of a variety of personal documents (Thomas and Znaniecki 1918–20). Park, explicitly treating the city of Chicago as a laboratory, supervised a most ambitious program of participant observation field studies that helped to define sociology. But to suppose that their contribution was mainly this empirical *proliferation* of SI (in the terms of Colomy and Brown [1995]) is surely misleading, as each man also contributed classical theoretical formulations.

The more philosophical Park, having been a student of William James and Georg Simmel and a colleague of Mead, served students as something of a linking character, and his essays (Park 1927, 1931) importantly elaborated the SI view of human nature, delineating more precisely the distinction between humans and other animals (A, C-1). In doing so, Park also clarified the sociological meaning of the term *conduct* (B) and linked it enduringly with Simmel's notions of interaction. Finally, Park sociologically elaborated Adam Smith's (1776) old notions of specialization and division of labor to show that it is social roles that provide the framework for the self-conception (C-4) and thus gave new meaning to the traditional axiom B by asserting that humans strive to live up to their self-conceptions:

> One thing that distinguishes man from the lower animals is the fact that he has a conception of himself, and once he has defined his role he strives to live up to it. . . . Under these circumstances our manners, our polite speeches and gestures, our conventional and proper behavior, assume the character of a mask. . . . In a sense, and in so far as this mask represents the conception we have formed of ourselves, the role we are striving to live up to, this mask is our "truer self", the self we would like to be. So, at any rate, our mask becomes at last an integral part of our personality; becomes second nature. (Park 1927)

From James, Park also derived a lifelong emphasis on grasping the subjective perspective of the actor to understand the meaning and motivation of actions.

Thomas, similarly, is best known today as the author of the so-called Thomas theorem on the *definition of situation* (McHugh 1968): "If men define situations as real, they are real in their consequences" (Thomas and Thomas 1928). The theory of mind (C-3) embodied in that theorem cleverly unites Smith's original emphasis on the social situation with the deepest insights of pragmatism in its focus on consequences.

CLASSICAL SYMBOLIC INTERACTION

University of Chicago

Following the eventual departures of Park and Thomas, the Chicago sociology department consolidated its standing as the fountainhead of SI.[2] Herbert Blumer (as an avowed social psychologist and a follower of Mead) and Everett C. Hughes (as the fieldwork heir to Park) assumed faculty leadership in that consolidation. Indeed, it was Blumer who invented the label *symbolic interaction* for this now richly accreted framework. However, somewhat like Cooley, Blumer (1969) exasperated many other interactionists through his strong emphasis on the necessity of interpreting signs and symbols, such that only full access to the mind of a person could underwrite understanding. Meanwhile Hughes, like his predecessors, continued the empirical elaboration of SI and also contributed importantly regarding the occupational core of the self and how the self-concept changes as a function of career movement (1958).

Yet in many ways it was the postwar students of Blumer and Hughes who most directly elaborated SI in its heyday (Fine 1995). Only a few can be singled out here.

Anselm Strauss played a central role in that elaboration, not only through his book on the writings of Mead (Strauss 1956) and his most influential textbook of social psychology (Lindesmith and Strauss [1949] 1956) but also through his own theoretical monograph *Mirrors and Masks* (Strauss 1959), uniting imagery of the mirror from Smith and of the mask from Park.

Erving Goffman's series of publications on the self and interaction (Goffman 1959, 1961, 1967) is largely responsible for moving dramaturgical theory (Brissett and Edgley 1974) from its place on the periphery strongly toward the center of SI.

Gregory P. Stone (1962; Stone and Farberman 1970) detailed a view of personal appearance that was quite different from Goffman's, while Howard S. Becker (1964; Becker and Strauss 1956) developed views of self and career that significantly advanced those of his mentor Hughes.

Not only did Ralph H. Turner similarly advance the views of Park and Blumer on collective behavior (Turner and Killian [1957, 1962] 1987), he contributed important ideas about role taking, role making (Turner 1962), and the role framework of the self (Turner 1968, 1978).

Tamotsu Shibutani similarly contributed to the application of SI to collective behavior (Shibutani 1966) but also attempted to link SI with more psychoanalytic ideas (Shibutani 1961).

Neo-Chicago

Following the forced breakup of the traditional Chicago department, Blumer and Goffman assembled something of a replica on the Berkeley campus of the University of California, where they turned out a number of remarkable students, including John Lofland and

Stanford Lyman, Subsequently, Norman K. Denzin also joined the faculty, where he became thoroughly Blumerian even though working briefly also with Strauss, who was by then himself in the Bay Area.

Beyond Chicago

Of course, had SI remained a Chicago (or even a neo-Chicago) school of thought, it would never have achieved its wide base among sociologists. In its classical period almost every department of sociology, particularly in the Midwest, taught and usefully elaborated SI. Again, only a few can be singled out for mention here, but the interlocking nature of most such departments must be emphasized.

The University of Minnesota, for instance, featured the contributions of Arnold M. Rose (1962) and generations of his students—most notably Sheldon Stryker (1962, 1980). In turn, Stryker joined others at Indiana University to inspire numerous additional cohorts of SI students.

And of course, the University of Iowa department is said (Meltzer and Petras 1970) to have developed its own distinctive version of SI under the leadership of Manford H. Kuhn (1964a; Kuhn and McPartland 1954). Those views of a role-based self assessable via structured instruments were carried forward by his many students, including Carl Couch (1958) and the duo of George J. McCall and J. L. Simmons ([1966] 1978). But again, Couch and his own students at Michigan State (e.g., McPhail and Tucker 1972) and later at Iowa developed yet another major process-oriented variant (Katovich, Miller, and Stewart 2003).

Common Developments

Wherever their academic home, classical SI scholars moved forward more or less together to achieve common developments of several of SI's basic themes, as sociology became more advanced in both theory construction and empirical testing of theories.

For example, the belief that humans generally behave in socially proper ways was put to a severe test through countless studies of social deviants (Lindesmith 1947; Lemert 1951; Cressey 1953; Rubington and Weinberg 1968). Labeling theory (Becker 1963, Schur 1971), by extending the Thomas theorem to the situation where persons are labeled as deviant by others, had achieved great currency among sociologists. Although labeling theory and the idea of social deviance were more than sustained in these numerous studies, their apparent contradiction of Smith's axiom was resolved by the almost universal discovery that even deviants mainly conform—not to mainstream social and cultural expectations but instead to the expectations held by deviant subcultures and deviant peer groups. Central to these repeated findings was the again-popular scholarly notion of the "reference group," holding that humans tend to judge themselves by the standards of those groups that they hold most important to them (Merton and Kitt 1950; Shibutani 1955; Kuhn 1964b).

A second common development of SI reflected a far more advanced and sophisticated understanding of language and communication during the classical period. *Sociolinguistics* (Fishman 1970) emerged in several disciplines to study the uses of language in society. Especially important for SI was the recognition that the practical uses of language (Hymes

1962; Austin 1965) establish contexts that provide levels of meaning that can never be captured by mere semantics. Pragmatics, as a branch of linguistics, examines such contextual or speaker meanings as opposed to semantic meanings (Kasher 1997; Van Dijk 1997). In response to this new branch of sociolinguistics, there arose within SI an "ethnomethodological approach" interested to discover those methods that members of a speech community use to produce and recognize social actions in social situations (Garfinkel 1967).

At the same time, *psycholinguistics* (Saporta 1961) emerged within several fields studying the connections of language with individuals. Particularly vital to SI were studies of lost linguistic capacities (Brain 1961), of shifts in how a child employs language (Piaget 1959; Vygotsky 1962), and of how language serves to regulate the individual's actions (Luria 1961). The communication phenomenon of role taking, so central to the tenets of SI, was subjected to careful measurement of the ability to take the role of another and to empirical testing of Meadian hypotheses about it (Dymond 1949; Cottrell and Dymond 1949; Miyamoto and Dornbusch 1956; Stryker 1962). Given the SI emphasis on the reciprocity of self and other, of role making and role taking (Turner 1962), numerous related studies were undertaken to examine how self-conceptions are influenced by the reactions of others (Videbeck 1960; Backman and Secord 1962; Quarantelli and Cooper 1966). In both areas of hypothesis testing, the core SI notions received considerable empirical support.

A third common development during the classical period reflected the growth of a more proactive view of individuals—a view entirely consistent with pragmatism's focus on the individual's strivings. As an example of this more proactive view, no longer was SI's focus on how appearances are judged but rather on how the individual can influence how he or she appears to others (Goffman 1959; Stone 1962). While that emphasis was especially strong within the developing dramaturgical approach (Lyman and Scott 1975), a definitely proactive view became quite widespread among SI scholars, leading to far greater attention to processes of negotiation more generally (Strauss 1978). Roles were no longer taken as given but rather as being negotiated with others in a process of role making (Turner 1962). Social situations came to be viewed as being socially defined through a process of collective negotiation involving not only presentation of self and role making but other processes as well (McCall and Simmons [1966] 1978). The "definition of the situation" was seen as entailing a negotiated working agreement on the selves of everyone present (Weinstein and Deutschberger 1964), so that even the social self came to be seen as not merely a personal thing but a "social object" negotiated with others in the course of their social act (McCall and Simmons [1966] 1978). A significant result of this view was the implication that the bipartite self is actually tripartite in its structure: the "I," the "Me," and the self as negotiated social object (Goffman 1959; McCall and Simmons [1966] 1978).

As a result of these and other common developments, the following summary statement of the basic, neo-Meadian, pragmatic principles of SI attained considerable acceptance among classical SI scholars:

1. *Man is a planning animal.* Man is a thinker, a planner, a schemer. He continually constructs plans of action (what Mead called "impulses") out of bits and pieces of plans left lying around by his culture, fitting them together in endless permutations of the larger

patterns and motifs that the culture presents as models. This ubiquitous planning is carried on at all levels of awareness, not always verbally but always conceptually.

2. *Things take on meanings in relation to plans.* The meaning of a "thing" (as a bundle of stimuli, in Mead's sense) can be taken as its implications for these plans of action we are always constructing. Its meaning can be thought of as the answer to the question, "Where does it fit in the unfolding scheme of events?" . . .

3. *We act toward things in terms of their meaning for our plan of action.* Or, better stated, the execution of our plan of action is contingent upon the meaning *for that plan* of every "thing" we encounter. If we bend down to pick up a stick and that stick turns out to be a dead snake—or vice versa—the chances are that that plan of action will be suspended and superseded by some other plan.

4. *Therefore, we must identify every "thing" we encounter and discover its meaning.* We have always to be identifying (categorizing, naming) the "things" we encounter and interpreting (construing, reconstructing) them to determine their meanings for our plans of action. . . . Until we have made out the identity and meaning of a thing vis-à-vis our plans, we have no bearings; we cannot proceed.

5. *For social plans of action, these meanings must be consensual.* If a plan of action involves more than one person and we encounter a "thing" whose meaning for this plan of action is unclear—not consensual among those involved—the meaning must be hammered out by collective effort in the rhetoric of interaction. As the consummation of a social act, the resulting attributed meaning is a "social object." It is this process of arriving at a meaning for a problematic "thing," of structuring an unstructured situation, that lies at the core of that fascinating subject we call "collective behavior." This meaning will seldom be clear and identical in the minds of all concerned, yet it will still be consensual, in the pragmatic sense that the understanding will at least be sufficiently common to permit the apparent mutual adjustment of lines of action, whether in cooperation or conflict.

6. *The basic "thing" to be identified in any situation is the person himself.* For each actor there is one key "thing" whose identity and meaning must be consensually established before all else—namely, himself. "Who am I in this situation? What implications do I have for the plans of action, both active and latent, of myself and of the others?" The answers to these questions, if *consensually* arrived at as already described, constitute what we have called the *character* of that person. Self qua character, then, is not alone a personal thing but also a *social object.* (McCall and Simmons 1966, 60–61)

MORE RECENT DEVELOPMENTS IN SYMBOLIC INTERACTION

Of course, SI has continued to adapt to new circumstances since the classical period came to an end with the Vietnam War.

Sociology had become such a popular field of study during the 1960s that sheer numbers allowed serious expansion of SI into nearly every sociological specialty: e.g., deviance (Becker 1963; Rubington and Weinberg 1968; J. Lofland 1969), urban sociology (Karp, Stone, and Yoels 1977; L. Lofland 1973), organizations and occupations (Glaser 1968;

Hall 1975), even the sociology of knowledge (Berger and Luckmann 1966). The spread became geographical as well as substantive, with SI making a belated return to its original home in Great Britain (Harré and Secord 1972; Rock 1979; Yardley and Honess 1987). Both types of spread gave rise to more specialized publication outlets, including the journal *Symbolic Interaction* and the annual *Studies in Symbolic Interaction,* each of which continues today.

As was so common in the social sciences during the late 20th century, SI too (or specifically, its more interpretivist adherents) entered into an extended dalliance with postmodernism (Denzin 1983; Becker and McCall 1990).

An even more serious challenge to SI during these years was a series of empirical studies that called into question how closely and in what respects the looking-glass self does reflect appraisals by others (Tice and Wallace 2003). Beyond the fact that these studies examined only quantitative ratings and rankings as appraisals (unimaginable to Smith, Cooley, or Mead), the findings that perceptions of external appraisals often are less than accurate, skewed to give greater weight to the opinions of significant others and biased by semi-independent self-images, could scarcely prove surprising to modern SI scholars such as Felson (1993). After all, the proactive character of classical SI had already predicted exactly that pattern (McCall and Simmons [1966] 1978).

Despite such challenges, traditional SI persists into yet another century, the 21st, as marked by the appearance of the thousand-page *Handbook of Symbolic Interactionism* (Reynolds and Herman-Kinney 2003).

ELABORATED THEMES OF SYMBOLIC INTERACTION

Reflecting all these developments, the core themes of SI (as depicted in Figure 1.1) have accreted many additional layers of significance over the years since the time of Adam Smith. Though heavily elaborated, those themes are, I submit, consistent with all the leading textbooks of SI, not only those of yesteryear—from Lindesmith and Strauss ([1949] 1956) to Secord and Backman (1974)—but also those of today, including Hewitt (1999) and Charon (2000). More important, those themes continue to accrete further layers of significance as empirical and theoretical advances are made in many fields—not only sociology and psychology, but also anthropology, linguistics, and philosophy. A brief review of the current standing and significance of each theme is thus useful in this account of SI.

With regard to axiom A, exactly what distinguishes humans from other creatures is still hotly debated today (Griffin 1981; Lieberman 1991), though nearly all commentators agree that language (Deacon 1997) and self-awareness (Ferrari and Sternberg 1998) are surely key aspects of human uniqueness. Obscuring the matter of species differences is the enormous variability among humans—not only individual genetic differences manifested physiologically but also numerous social and cultural differences (Aiken 1999), including the shaping influence of languages (Bloom 1981). This variability within the human species has long been a constant theme of both anthropology and medicine, and from its beginnings psychology has regarded the study of "individual differences" as a major subfield.

Axiom B, that humans generally behave in socially proper ways, has today gone well past the original opposition of the Scottish moralists to Hobbes's view of savage individualism bridled only by the force of the state. Although the latter view is still echoed in various conflict theories (Collins 1975), many social scientists today take for granted the Scottish moralists' claim that the primacy of society is not merely temporal but that selves are built in such a way as to facilitate individuals fitting into, and getting ahead in, society. Self and a benign sort of social control fit one another very nicely; even the radical sociologist Alvin Gouldner (1960) sought to demonstrate that a norm of social reciprocity is fundamental to all societies. Only with Rousseau did "self versus society" emerge as the Romantic myth of individualism; if one's position in society is no longer seen as voluntary, then social control must be seen as coercive rather than cooperative.

Concerning axiom C, *conduct* may remain something of a theory-laden term, but the phenomena of self-regulation have become the focus of considerable empirical and theoretical research (Baumeister and Voh 2004). Still prominent within the large body of work on self-regulation are the SI maxims that we act toward objects (including the self) in terms of their meanings (Mead 1934) and that we strive to live up to our social roles (Park 1927).

The more specific postulates that underlie and flesh out that axiom have similarly accreted their own layers of meaning. The first of these (C-1, that a person is a social animal) has been abundantly demonstrated in social psychological studies of isolation (Davis 1947; Shattuck 1980) and socialization (Clausen 1968), to the point that at least one major textbook of social psychology was actually titled *The Social Animal* (Aronson 1984). In fact, classical SI extended the study of socialization from its focus on children to a consideration of adult socialization (Becker 1968), using the notion of careers (Becker and Strauss 1956; Strauss 1959; Becker 1964) to argue the necessity of studying socialization across the entire life cycle (Brim and Wheeler 1966). The primacy of society that was so vital to Smith's views has now mainly taken the form of the primacy of a speech community (Bloomfield 1933; Sapir 1921), and the importance that Smith attributed to the idea that human society is peopled by selves is seconded today by evolutionary theorists (Sterelny 2003). In fact, the latter provide an additional sense of the primacy of society, as they demonstrate the importance of *group* selection in hominid evolution:

> Group selection became very important, and underwrote the evolution of a cooperation explosion, the effects of which include language, the division of labor, and resource sharing. (Sterelny 2003, 172)

Theories of communication (C-2) are no longer confined to theories of animal communication (Rogers and Kaplan 2000) and of the nature of language (Keller 1998) but have had to be broadened to include the communication of humans with intelligent machines (Preece and Keller 1990).

Accordingly, "theories of mind" (C-3) themselves have also had to cover not only human beings but all sorts of intelligent machines (Clancey, Smoliar, and Stefik 1994), as the phenomena of mental life have been attributed by some scholars to lower animals (Griffin 1981) and to at least some of the machines of artificial intelligence (Minsky 1986).

Accordingly, one now speaks of, and often diagrams, the "cognitive architecture" hypothesized of "intelligent systems." The systems model enjoying greatest popularity among SI scholars today (Burke 1991; McPhail 2000) is perception control theory (Powers 1973).

Serving to link these two types of theories ever more closely is the current importance attributed to the communication process of role taking, or *mind reading* as it is currently termed in other fields (lacking mind, other complex entities are only subject to mere *behavior reading*). Interestingly, the very same mechanism proposed by Adam Smith in 1759 is currently the leading candidate to explain the phenomena of mind reading (Nichols and Stitch 2003). In any case, underlying the capacity for role taking is an ability to employ concepts in the process of categorical perception (Murphy 2002; Zerubavel 1991):

> Behavior is said to make sense when a series of actions is interpretable as indicating that the actor has in mind some role which guides his behavior. . . . The isolated action becomes a datum for role analysis only when it is interpreted as the manifestation of a configuration. . . . For example, the lie which is an expression of the role of friend is an altogether different thing from the same lie taken as a manifestation of the role of confidence man. (Turner 1962, 24)

The looking-glass self is still regarded as the key link between the realms of society and individuals (C-4), but contemporary accounts of the structure of intelligent self-awareness emphasize how many voices have to be included as participants in the inner forum—or in more contemporary terms, how many components must be included in the architecture of intelligent systems (Dennett 1991; Minsky 1986).

That self-regulation is a process extended over time (C-5) now implies not only the social development of the child and the cognitive dynamics of an inner forum—both far better documented and understood in cognitive science these days—but also that the idea that regulating the self is an emotional as well as cognitive affair. To be sure, Smith himself had initially focused on the role of emotions in self-regulation, but SI scholars today have returned to that theme (Franks and McCarthy 1989; Scheff 2003), often including an echo of the pragmatists' claim that much human action is "mindless" (Langer 1992) until a breakdown of routine calls into play emotions and then cognitive intelligence. That emotions often serve as a signal of a blocked routine—even of a threatened identity—is now widely accepted among many SI scholars (Smith-Lovin 1990).

ROOT OF SPECIAL THEORIES

A tradition as venerable and as continuing as SI serves, of course, as an important source and backdrop for many of the special theories recounted in later chapters of this volume. Every special theory, after all, makes key assumptions about human nature and about how individuals relate to society. Most directly linked with SI in these respects are identity theory (Chapter 5) and affect control theory (Chapter 7) perhaps, yet other special theories—especially comparison theory (Chapter 8), status construction theory (Chapter 13), and legitimacy theory (Chapter 14)—are also more deeply understood against the backdrop of the SI tradition.

1. This school of thought is usually reckoned to include, at minimum and in alphabetical order, Adam Ferguson, David Hume, Francis Hutcheson, Lord Kames, Lord Monboddo, Thomas Reid, Adam Smith, and Dugald Stewart (Schneider 1967). The social context of their work is discussed in Herman (2001).

2. The magnitude of that stature is difficult to exaggerate when it had already produced such major SI contributors as Willard Waller (1938), Robert E. Faris (1950), and Leonard Cottrell (1950).

REFERENCES

Aiken, Lewis R. 1999. *Human Differences*. Mahwah, NJ: Erlbaum.

Aronson, Elliot. 1984. *The Social Animal*, 4th ed. New York: Freeman.

Austin, J. L. 1965. *How to Do Things with Words*. New York: Oxford University Press.

Axelrod, Robert. 1984. *The Evolution of Cooperation*. New York: Basic Books.

Backman, Carl W., and Paul F. Secord. 1962. Liking, selective interaction, and misperception in congruent interpersonal relationships. *Sociometry* 25:321–35.

Baldwin, James Mark. 1897. *Social and Ethical Interpretations in Mental Development*. New York: Macmillan.

Baumeister, Roy F., and Kathleen D. Voh, eds. 2004. *Handbook of Self-Regulation: Research, Theory, and Applications*. New York: Guilford.

Becker, Howard S. 1963. *Outsiders: Studies in the Sociology of Deviance*. New York: Free Press.

———. 1964. Personal change in adult life. *Sociometry* 27:40–53.

———. 1968. The self and adult socialization. In *The Study of Personality: An Interdisciplinary Appraisal*, ed. E. Norbeck, D. Price-Williams, and W. M. McCord. New York: Holt, Rinehart & Winston.

Becker, Howard S., and Michal M. McCall, eds. 1990. *Symbolic Interaction and Cultural Studies*. Chicago: University of Chicago Press.

Becker, Howard S., and Anselm L. Strauss. 1956. Careers, personality, and adult socialization. *American Journal of Sociology* 62:253–63.

Berger, Peter L., and Thomas Luckmann. 1966. *The Social Construction of Reality*. Garden City, NY: Doubleday Anchor.

Bloom, Alfred H. 1981. *The Linguistic Shaping of Thought: A Study of the Impact of Language on Thinking in China and the West*. Hillsdale, NJ: Erlbaum.

Bloomfield, Leonard. 1933. *Language*. New York: Holt, Rinehart & Winston.

Blumer, Herbert. 1969. *Symbolic Interactionism: Perspective and Method*. Englewood Cliffs, NJ: Prentice-Hall.

Boas, Franz. 1911–38. *Introduction to the Handbook of American Indian Languages*. Washington, DC: Government Printing Office.

Brain, Sir Russell. 1961. *Speech Disorders: Aphasia, Apraxia and Agnosia*. Washington, DC: Butterworth.

Brim, Orville G., Jr., and Stanton Wheeler. 1966. *Socialization after Childhood: Two Essays*. New York: Wiley.

Brissett, Dennis, and Charles Edgley, eds. 1974. *Life as Theater: A Dramaturgical Sourcebook*. Chicago: Aldine.

Bulmer, Martin. 1984. *The Chicago School of Sociology*. Chicago: University of Chicago Press.

Burke, Peter J. 1991. Identity processes and social stress. *American Sociological Review* 56:836–47.

Charon, Joel M. 2000. *Symbolic Interactionism: An Introduction, An Interpretation, An Integration*, 7th ed. Upper Saddle River, NJ: Simon & Schuster.

Clancey, William J., Stephen W. Smoliar, and Mark J. Stefik, eds. 1994. *Contemplating Minds: A Forum for Artificial Intelligence*. Cambridge, MA: MIT Press.

Clausen, John A., ed. 1968. *Socialization and Society*. Boston: Little, Brown.

Collins, Randall. 1975. *Conflict Sociology*. New York: Academic Press.

Colomy, Paul, and J. David Brown. 1995. Elaboration, revision, polemic, and progress in the Second Chicago School. In *A Second Chicago School? The Development of a Postwar American Sociology*, ed. G. A. Fine. Chicago: University of Chicago Press.

Cooley, Charles Horton. 1902. *Human Nature and the Social Order*. New York: Scribner's.

———. 1909. *Social Organization*. New York: Scribner's.

Cottrell, Leonard S. 1950. Some neglected problems in social psychology. *American Sociological Review* 15:705–12.

Cottrell, Leonard S., and Rosalie F. Dymond. 1949. The empathic responses. *Psychiatry* 12:355–59.

Couch, Carl J. 1958. Self-attitudes and degree of agreement with immediate others. *American Journal of Sociology* 63:491–96.

Cressey, Donald R. 1953. *Other People's Money*. Glencoe, IL: Free Press.

Davis, Kingsley. 1947. Final note on a case of extreme isolation. *American Journal of Sociology* 52:432–37.

Darwin, Charles. 1859. *On the Origin of Species by Means of Natural Selection, or the Preservation of Favoured Races in the Struggle for Life*. London: John Murray.

Deacon, Terrence W. 1997. *The Symbolic Species*. New York: Norton.

Dennett, Daniel C. 1991. *Consciousness Explained*. Boston: Little, Brown.

Denzin, Norman K. 1983. Interpretive interactionism. In *Beyond Methods*, ed. G. Morgan. Beverly Hills, CA: Sage.

Dewey, John. 1908. What does pragmatism mean by practical? *Journal of Philosophy* 5:85–99.

———. 1925. *Experience and Nature*. Chicago: Open Court.

Dymond, Rosalie F. 1949. A scale for the measurement of empathic ability. *Journal of Consulting Psychology* 13:127–33.

Faris, Robert E. 1950. *Social Psychology*. New York: Ronald.

Felson, Richard B. 1993. The (somewhat) social self: How others affect self-appraisals. In *The Self in Social Perspective*, ed. J. M. Suls. Hillsdale, NJ: Erlbaum.

Ferrari, Michael, and Robert J. Sternberg, eds. 1998. *Self-Awareness: Its Nature and Development*. New York: Guilford.

Fine, Gary Alan, ed. 1995. *A Second Chicago School? The Development of a Postwar American Sociology*. Chicago: University of Chicago Press.

Fishman, Joshua A. 1970. *Sociolinguistics: A Brief Introduction*. New York: Wiley.

Foley, Robert A. 2001. Evolutionary perspectives on the origins of human social institutions. In *The Origin of Human Social Institutions*, ed. W. G. Runciman. Oxford: Oxford University Press.

Foley, William A. 1997. *Anthropological Linguistics: An Introduction*. Malden, MA: Blackwell.

Franks, David D., and E. Doyle McCarthy, eds. 1989. *The Sociology of Emotions*. Greenwich, CT: JAI Press.

Garfinkel, Harold. 1967. *Studies in Ethnomethodology*. Englewood Cliffs, NJ: Prentice-Hall.

Gaulin, Steven J. C., and Donald H. McBurney. 2004. *Evolutionary Psychology*. Upper Saddle River, NJ: Pearson/Prentice-Hall.

Glaser, Barney G., ed. 1968. *Organizational Careers: A Sourcebook for Theory*. Chicago: Aldine.

Goffman, Erving. 1959. *The Presentation of Self in Everyday Life*. Garden City, NY: Doubleday Anchor.

———. 1961. *Encounters*. Indianapolis: Bobbs-Merrill.

———. 1967. *Interaction Ritual*. Garden City, NY: Doubleday Anchor.

Gouldner, Alvin W. 1960. The norm of reciprocity: A preliminary statement. *American Sociological Review* 25:161–78.

Griffin, Donald R. 1981. *The Question of Animal Awareness: Evolutionary Continuity of Mental Experience*, rev. ed. New York: Rockefeller University Press.

Gusfield, Joseph R. 1995. The second Chicago School? In *A Second Chicago School? The Development of a Postwar American Sociology*, ed. G. A. Fine. Chicago: University of Chicago Press.

Hall, Richard H. 1975. *Occupations and the Social Structure*, 2nd ed. Englewood Cliffs, NJ: Prentice-Hall.

Harré, Rom, and Paul F. Secord. 1972. *The Explanation of Social Behaviour*. Oxford: Blackwell.

Herman, Arthur. 2001. *How the Scots Invented the Modern World*. New York: Crown.

Hewitt, John P. 1999. *Self and Society: A Symbolic Interactionist Social Psychology*, 8th ed. Boston: Allyn & Bacon.

Hughes, Everett C. 1958. *Men and Their Work*. Glencoe, IL: Free Press.

Hymes, Dell. 1962. The ethnography of speaking. In *Anthropology and Human Behavior*, ed. T. Gladwin and W. C. Sturtevant. Washington, DC: Anthropological Society of Washington.

James, William. 1890. *Principles of Psychology*. New York: Holt.

———. 1892. *Psychology: The Briefer Course*. New York: Holt.

———. 1907. *Pragmatism*. Cambridge, MA: Harvard University Press.

Karp, David, Gregory P. Stone, and William C. Yoels. 1977. *Being Urban: A Social Psychological View of City Life*. Lexington, MA: D. C. Heath.

Kasher, Asa. 1997. *Pragmatics: Critical Concepts*. London: Routledge.

Katovich, Michael A., Dan E. Miller, and Robert L. Stewart. 2003. The Iowa School. In *Handbook of Symbolic Interactionism*, ed. L. T. Reynolds and N. J. Herman-Kinney. Walnut Creek, CA: AltaMira.

Keller, Rudi. 1998. *A Theory of Linguistic Signs*, trans. Kimberly Duenwald. Oxford: Oxford University Press.

Kenrick, Douglas T., and Carol L. Luce, eds. 2004. *The Functional Mind: Readings in Evolutionary Psychology*. Boston: Pearson/Allyn & Bacon.

Key, Catherine A., and Leslie C. Aiello. 1999. The evolution of social organization. In *The Evolution of Culture*, ed. R. Dunbar, C. Knight, and C. Power. Edinburgh: Edinburgh University Press.

Kuhn, Manford H. 1964a. Major trends in symbolic interaction in the past twenty-five years. *Sociological Quarterly* 5:61–84.

———. 1964b. The reference group reconsidered. *Sociological Quarterly* 5:5–21.

Kuhn, Manford H., and Thomas S. McPartland. 1954. An empirical investigation of self-attitudes. *American Sociological Review* 19:68–76.

Langer, Ellen J. 1992. Matters of mind: Mindfulness/mindlessness in perspective. *Consciousness & Cognition* 1:289–305.

Lemert, Edwin C. 1951. *Social Pathology*. New York: McGraw-Hill.

Lewis, J. David, and Richard L. Smith. 1980. *American Sociology and Pragmatism: Mead, Chicago Sociology, and Symbolic Interaction*. Chicago: University of Chicago Press.

Lieberman, Philip. 1991. *Uniquely Human: The Evolution of Speech, Thought, and Selfless Behavior*. Cambridge, MA: Harvard University Press.

Lindesmith, Alfred R. 1947. *Opiate Addictions*. Bloomington, IN: Principia Press.

Lindesmith, Alfred R., and Anselm L. Strauss. [1949] 1956. *Social Psychology*. New York: Dryden Press.

Lofland, John. 1969. *Deviance and Identity*. Englewood Cliffs, NJ: Prentice-Hall.

Lofland, Lyn. 1973. *A World of Strangers*. New York: Basic Books.

Luria, Alexander R. 1961. *The Role of Speech in the Regulation of Normal and Abnormal Behavior*, trans. J. Tizard. New York: Liveright.

Lyman, Stanford M., and Marvin B. Scott. 1975. *The Drama of Social Reality*. New York: Oxford University Press.

McCall, George J., and J. L. Simmons. [1966] 1978. *Identities and Interactions*. New York: Free Press.

McHugh, Peter. 1968. *Defining the Situation: The Organization of Meaning in Social Interaction*. Indianapolis: Bobbs-Merrill.

McPhail, Clark. 2000. Collective action and perception control theory. In *Introduction to Collective Behavior and Collective Action*, ed. D. Miller, 2nd ed. Prospect Heights, IL: Waveland.

McPhail, Clark, and Charles Tucker. 1972. The classification and ordering of responses to the question "Who Am I?" *Sociological Quarterly* 13:329–47.

Mead, George Herbert. 1930. Cooley's contributions to American social thought. *American Journal of Sociology* 35:385–407.

———. 1934. *Mind, Self, and Society: From the Standpoint of a Social Behaviorist*, ed. C. Morris. Chicago: University of Chicago Press.

Meltzer, Bernard N., and John W. Petras. 1970. The Chicago and Iowa Schools of symbolic interactionism. In *Human Nature and Collective Behavior*, ed. T. Shibutani. Englewood Cliffs, NJ: Prentice-Hall.

Merton, Robert K., and Alice S. Kitt. 1950. Contributions to the theory of reference group behavior. In *Continuities in Social Research: Studies in the Scope and Methods of "The American Soldier,"* ed. R. K. Merton and P. F. Lazarsfeld. Glencoe, IL: Free Press.

Minsky, Marvin. 1986. *The Society of Mind*. New York: Simon & Schuster.

Miyamoto, S. Frank, and Sanford M. Dornbusch. 1956. A test of interactionist hypotheses of self-conception. *American Journal of Sociology* 61:399–403.

Morris, Charles. 1970. *The Pragmatic Movement in American Philosophy*. New York: George Braziller.

Murphy, Gregory L. 2002. *The Big Book of Concepts*. Cambridge, MA: MIT Press.

Nichols, Shaun, and Stephen P. Stitch. 2003. *Mindreading: An Integrated Account of Pretence, Self-Awareness, and Understanding Other Minds*. Oxford: Clarendon.

Park, Robert E. 1927. Human nature and collective behavior. *American Journal of Sociology* 32:733–41.

———. 1931. Human nature, attitudes, and mores. In *Social Attitudes*, ed. K. Young. New York: Holt.

Peirce, Charles Sanders. [1878] 1934. How to make our ideas clear. In *Collected Papers of Charles Sanders Peirce, Volume V: Pragmatism and Pragmaticism*, ed. C. Hartshorne and P. Weiss. Cambridge, MA: Harvard University Press.

Piaget, Jean. 1959. *Judgment and Reasoning in the Child*. Paterson, NJ: Littlefield, Adams.

Powers, William T. 1973. *Behavior: The Control of Perception*. Chicago: Aldine.

Preece, Jenny, and Laurie S. Keller. 1990. *Human-Computer Interaction: Selected Readings*. Hemel Hempstead: Prentice-Hall.

Quarantelli, Enrico, and Joseph Cooper. 1966. Self-conceptions and others: A further test of Meadian hypotheses. *Sociological Quarterly* 7:281–97.

Reynolds, Larry T., and Nancy J. Herman-Kinney, eds. 2003. *Handbook of Symbolic Interactionism*. Walnut Creek, CA: AltaMira.

Rock, Paul. 1979. *The Making of Symbolic Interactionism*. Totowa, NJ: Rowman & Littlefield.

Rogers, Lesley J., and Gisela Kaplan. 2000. *Songs, Roars, and Rituals: Communication in Birds, Mammals, and Other Animals*. Cambridge, MA: Harvard University Press.

Rose, Arnold M., ed. 1962. *Human Behavior and Social Processes*. Boston: Houghton Mifflin.

Rubington, Earl, and Martin S. Weinberg, eds. 1968. *Deviance: The Interactionist Perspective*. New York: Macmillan.

Sapir, Edward. 1921. *Language: An Introduction to the Study of Speech*. New York: Harcourt, Brace & World.

Saporta, Sol, ed. 1961. *Psycholinguistics: A Book of Readings*. New York: Holt, Rinehart & Winston.

Scheff, Thomas J. 2003. Shame in self and society. *Symbolic Interaction* 26:239–62.

Schneider, Louis, ed. 1967. *The Scottish Moralists on Human Nature and Society*. Chicago: University of Chicago Press.

Schur, Edwin M. 1971. *Labeling Deviant Behavior*. New York: Harper & Row.

Secord, Paul F., and Carl W. Backman. 1974. *Social Psychology*, 2nd ed. New York: McGraw-Hill.

Shattuck, Roger. 1980. *The Forbidden Experiment: The Story of the Wild Boy of Aveyron*. New York: Farrar, Straus & Giroux.

Shibutani, Tamotsu. 1955. Reference groups as perspectives. *American Journal of Sociology* 60:562–69.

———. 1961. *Society and Personality*. Englewood Cliffs, NJ: Prentice-Hall.

———. 1966. *Improvised News: A Sociological Study of Rumor*. Indianapolis: Bobbs-Merrill.

Smith, Adam. 1759. *The Theory of Moral Sentiments.* London: W. Strahan.

———. 1776. *An Inquiry into the Nature and Causes of the Wealth of Nations.* London: Millar.

Smith-Lovin, Lynn. 1990. Emotion as confirmation and disconfirmation of identity: An affect control model. In *Research Agendas in the Sociology of Emotions,* ed. T. D. Kemper. New York: SUNY Press.

Sterelny, Kim. 2003. *Thought in a Hostile World: The Evolution of Human Cognition.* Oxford: Blackwell.

Stone, Gregory P. 1962. Appearance and the self. In *Human Behavior and Social Processes,* ed. A. M. Rose. Boston: Houghton Mifflin.

Stone, Gregory P., and Harvey Farberman. 1970. *Social Psychology through Symbolic Interaction.* Waltham, MA: Xerox Publishing.

Strauss, Anselm L., ed. 1956. *The Social Psychology of George Herbert Mead.* Chicago: University of Chicago Press.

———. 1959. *Mirrors and Masks: The Search for Identity.* Glencoe, IL: Free Press.

———. 1978. *Negotiations: Varieties, Contexts, Processes, and Social Order.* San Francisco: Jossey-Bass.

Stryker, Sheldon. 1962. Conditions of accurate role-taking: A test of Mead's theory. In *Human Behavior and Social Processes,* ed. A. M. Rose. Boston: Houghton Mifflin.

———. 1980. *Symbolic Interactionism: A Social Structural Version.* Menlo Park, CA: Benjamin Cummings.

Thomas, W. I., and Dorothy Swaine Thomas. 1928. *The Child in America.* New York: Knopf.

Thomas, W. I., and Florian Znaniecki. 1918–20. *The Polish Peasant in Europe and America.* Boston: Badger.

Tice, Dianne M., and Harry M. Wallace. 2003. The reflected self: Creating yourself as (you think) others see you. In *Handbook of Self and Identity,* ed. M. R. Leary and J. P. Tangney. New York: Guilford.

Turner, Ralph H. 1962. Role taking: Process vs. conformity. In *Human Behavior and Social Processes,* ed. A. M. Rose. Boston: Houghton Mifflin.

———. 1968. The self-conception in social interaction. In *The Self in Social Interaction,* ed. C. Gordon and K. J. Gergen. New York: Wiley.

———. 1978. The role and the person, *American Journal of Sociology* 84:1–23.

Turner, Ralph H., and Lewis M. Killian. [1957, 1962] 1987. *Collective Behavior.* Englewood Cliffs, NJ: Prentice-Hall.

Van Dijk, Teun A., ed. 1997. *Discourse Studies: A Multidisciplinary Introduction,* 2 vols. Thousand Oaks, CA: Sage.

Videbeck, Richard. 1960. Self-conception and the reactions of others. *Sociometry* 23:351–59.

Vygotsky, L. S. 1962. *Thought and Language,* trans. Eugenia Hanfmann and Gertrude Vakar. New York: MIT Press and Wiley.

Waller, Willard. 1938. *The Family: A Dynamic Interpretation.* New York: Holt.

Weinstein, Eugene A., and Paul Deutschberger. 1964. Tasks, bargains, and identities in social interaction. *Social Forces* 42:451–56.

Whorf, Benjamin Lee. 1956. *Language, Thought, and Reality*, ed. John B. Carroll. New York: MIT Press and Wiley.

Yardley, Krysia, and Terry Honess, eds. 1987. *Self and Identity: Psychosocial Perspectives*. Chichester: Wiley.

Zerubavel, Eviatar. 1991. *The Fine Line: Making Distinctions in Everyday Life*. New York: Free Press.

2 THE SOCIAL EXCHANGE FRAMEWORK

Linda D. Molm

As early anthropologists first recognized (Malinowski 1922), many forms of social interaction outside the economic marketplace can be conceptualized as an exchange of benefits. People depend on one another for much of what they need and value in social life, and they provide these benefits to each other through the process of social exchange. "Neighbors exchange favors; children, toys; colleagues, assistance; acquaintances, courtesies; politicians, concessions" (Blau 1964, 88).

The social exchange perspective takes as its analytic focus this aspect of social life: the benefits that people obtain from, and contribute to, social interaction and the opportunity structures and interdependencies that govern those exchanges. While classical theories of economic exchange typically assumed that exchanges were independent, one-shot transactions between strangers, social exchange theorists are primarily interested in relations of some length and endurance. This emphasis on the history of relations partly reflects the influence of behavioral psychology, the other discipline that played a key role in the theory's development. What distinguishes the contemporary form of the social exchange perspective from both psychology and economics, however, is its emphasis on the *social structures* within which exchange takes place. Whereas early exchange theorists primarily examined two-party relations, contemporary theorists situate those exchanges in the context of larger networks and explore how actors' structural opportunities for exchange with different partners affect such processes as power, coalitions, commitment, and trust.

The social psychological approach to social exchange did not emerge until the late 1950s. The following decade saw the publication of three major statements on social exchange, by George Homans ([1961] 1974), John Thibaut and Harold Kelley (1959), and Peter Blau (1964). Ten years later, influenced by these works and their critics, Richard Emerson (1972a, 1972b) published his own theory of social exchange, which became known as power-dependence theory (see Chapter 9 of this volume). Empirical tests of power-dependence theory by Emerson, Karen Cook, and their students initiated a period of sustained, programmatic research on social exchange that has continued to this day. Other theories of exchange were developed either as challenges to power-dependence theory's analysis of power (see Chapter 10 in this volume) or as theories of different exchange outcomes (see Chapter 11). All of these efforts have contributed to making the social exchange perspective one of the most established yet vibrant approaches in social psychology.

In this chapter I discuss social exchange as a theoretical *framework* or *orientation*. Within that framework a number of specific theories coexist, several of which are covered in greater depth in other chapters in this volume. My aim is to discuss basic concepts and assumptions common to all (or most) social exchange theories, describe the historical evolution of the perspective, and summarize the scope and variation of contemporary theories and research on social exchange.

BASIC CONCEPTS AND ASSUMPTIONS

While the various theories of social exchange differ from one another in numerous respects, they share a common set of analytic concepts and certain assumptions. These comprise the basic elements of social exchange: the actors who exchange, the resources exchanged, the structures within which exchange relations develop, and the dynamic process of exchange. Each of these core topics includes a set of related concepts and associated assumptions.

Actors

The *actors* who exchange can be either individual persons or corporate groups acting as a single unit (e.g., business corporations, neighborhood associations). In addition, they can be specific entities (e.g., your friend Mary, the Kiwanis Club) or interchangeable occupants of structural positions (e.g., your next-door neighbor, the club president). This flexibility allows exchange theorists to span levels of analysis ranging from microlevel interpersonal exchanges to macrolevel networks of organizations.

Individuals and groups can be combined as actors partly because social exchange theories make few assumptions about characteristics of actors. Virtually all exchange theories assume that actors are self-interested, seeking to increase outcomes they positively value and decrease those they negatively value. They differ in the extent to which they assume a rational actor model, derived from microeconomics, or a learning model, adopted from behavioral psychology. In the former, actors cognitively weigh potential benefits and costs and make conscious choices that seek to maximize outcomes; in the latter, actors respond only to consequences of past choices, without conscious weighing of alternatives (and often without maximizing outcomes). These have been described, respectively, as forward-looking and backward-looking models of the actor (Macy 1990).

Both classical and contemporary theories vary in their relative adherence to these two models. Homans, Blau, Thibaut and Kelley, and Emerson all adopted, to some extent, assumptions derived from learning theories. Some contemporary exchange theories, such as network exchange theory, Friedkin's (1992) expected value model, and rational choice theories of exchange (Bienenstock and Bonacich 1992; Coleman 1990; Yamaguchi 1996) explicitly assume rational actors. As power-dependence theory has evolved, it has combined elements of both. Some classical and contemporary theories also assume that affect, emotions, and norms (e.g., justice norms) affect exchange (Blau 1964; Homans [1961] 1974; Lawler 2001). In general, however, the social exchange perspective is strongly associated with a view of actors as self-interested entities whose behavior is motivated by the need or desire to obtain valued benefits.

Resources

When an actor has possessions or behavioral capabilities that are valued by other actors, they are *resources* in that actor's relations with those others. Social exchange resources include not only the tangible goods and services of economic exchange but capacities to provide socially valued outcomes such as approval or status. Because resources depend on their value to others, they are attributes of *relations*, not actors; i.e., what constitutes a resource for an actor in one relation may not in another.

Exchanges of tangible resources involve the transfer of a physical good from one actor to another. Many social exchanges, however, involve no actual transfer of resources. Instead, one actor performs a behavior that produces value for another. Such exchanges occur, for example, when a person comments on a colleague's paper or does a favor for a friend. In either case, an exchange action incurs some form of *cost* for the actor who performs it and produces some kind of valued *outcome* for the partner. All exchange behaviors entail opportunity costs (the rewards forgone from alternatives not chosen), but some also involve other costs, such as investment costs, the loss of a material resource, or costs intrinsic to the behavior itself (e.g., fatigue).[1]

Exchange outcomes can have positive value (gain, reward, utility) or negative value (loss, punishment). For economists, utility refers to the satisfaction or benefit received. Behaviorists, in contrast, define rewards (or reinforcers) and punishments functionally, by their effects on future behavior: rewards increase and punishments decrease the frequency of behaviors on which they are contingent.

Outcomes have no a priori status as rewards or punishments; whether a particular outcome is rewarding or punishing for an actor depends on both the long-term history that creates value and the actor's current situation (Kahneman and Tversky 1979). Thus a move to a small house might be enormously rewarding to a homeless person but punishing to a formerly rich man whose status and wealth have declined.

An actor's recent history also affects value; i.e., outcomes obey a principle of satiation or diminishing marginal utility. This principle can be used to determine classes of outcomes; e.g., because bread and apples both reduce hunger, both may be considered members of the class of "food." Emerson (1972a) called such classes of functionally equivalent outcomes *exchange domains*; economists refer to resources within an exchange domain as *substitutable* (Yamaguchi 1996). The value of exchange can vary both across and within exchange domains. Across domains, value refers to an actor's preference ordering of those domains (e.g., an actor's relative preference for friendship, money, and status). Within a single domain, value refers to the magnitude of outcomes (the *amount* of valued friendship, money, or status) that an actor potentially can receive from a relation.

Although efforts to develop a theory of value within social exchange have been attempted (e.g., Emerson 1987), values are currently exogenous variables in the exchange perspective;

i.e., they are not explained within the theory. Theories of exchange make predictions about behavior *given* information about what people value, and value then enters into predictions through its effects on actors' relative dependencies (Molm, Peterson, and Takahashi 2001). Exchange theorists have little interest in *what* actors value, per se; instead, they are concerned with the relations that are created between actors when they control valued outcomes of any kind. Most important, exchange theories assume that actors' behaviors are unaffected by the domain of value; that is, actors who value money or approval will tend to behave similarly, in the sense that both will behave in ways that produce more of those outcomes within the constraints of available opportunities.

Exchange Structures

The most important distinction between classical and contemporary exchange theories is the contemporary emphasis on *structure*; i.e., on the form of relations between actors rather than on the actors themselves and the content of their interaction. The key to this development was Emerson's (1972b) concept of exchange networks. Networks bridged the gap between dyadic interaction and macro structures, enabling exchange theories to move beyond their original dyadic limitations and to link up with work on social networks.

At a more basic level, all exchange relations, whether dyadic or embedded in larger networks, develop within structures of mutual dependence; i.e., between actors who are dependent on one another for valued resources. Structures of dependence can take several forms: direct exchange, generalized exchange, and productive exchange. In relations of *direct exchange* between two actors, each actor's outcomes depend directly on another actor's behaviors; i.e., A provides value to B, and B to A. In relations of *generalized exchange* among three or more actors, the reciprocal dependence is indirect: A's giving to B is not reciprocated directly by B's giving to A but indirectly by B's giving to another actor in the network (examples include giving wedding gifts and reviewing journal manuscripts). Eventually, A may receive a return on her exchange from some actor in the system, but not from B. Finally, in *productive exchange*, two (or more) actors contribute their individual efforts to produce a joint good that benefits both (or all) of them (e.g., coauthoring a book).

While collective forms of social exchange were of particular interest to early anthropologists, neither generalized nor productive exchange have received much attention from sociological exchange theorists (for exceptions, see Lawler, Thye, and Yoon 2000; Takahashi 2000; Yamagishi and Cook 1993). Instead, relations of direct exchange have dominated research and theorizing. Most of the examples that we commonly think of as exchange are direct: neighbors who exchange tools or dinner parties, colleagues who exchange advice and help, politicians who exchange votes, and so forth.

Structures of direct exchange can consist of isolated dyads (A–B) or networks of connected dyadic relations (e.g., C–A–B). The latter are not only more common in social life but clearly dominant in contemporary work on exchange. Emerson (1972b) defined an *exchange network* as an opportunity structure, comprising a set of three or more actors each of whom provides opportunities for transactions with at least one other actor in the set. Two relations in a network that share a focal actor (e.g., A–B and A–C) are *connected* if exchange in one relation affects exchange in another relation (Emerson 1972b). Emerson defined network connections as *positive* to the extent that exchange in one relation increases exchange in the other relation, and *negative* to the extent that exchange in one relation decreases exchange in the other. Emerson's basis for this typology was the domain of resources: relations in the same domain (e.g., alternative sources of advice for *A*) create negatively connected relations, while relations in different domains create either positive connections (if the benefit obtained from *A*'s exchange with *B* will facilitate *A*'s exchange with *C*) or no connection. Network exchange theorists classify connected relations, instead, by the types of restrictions on actors' efforts to obtain benefits: in an *exclusionary* network, actors with two or more relations cannot exchange in one or more of their relations on the same opportunity; in an *inclusionary* network, actors must exchange in more than one relation to obtain benefit (Markovsky et al. 1993). In both typologies, mixed or compound networks combine the two.

Networks can vary substantially in size and shape, as well as type of connection. These distinctions and their effects on exchange—particularly power—are the focus of many contemporary theories.

The Process of Exchange

The process of exchange describes how interaction takes place within exchange structures. *Exchange opportunities* provide actors with the occasion to *initiate* exchange; when an initiation is reciprocated (or an offer accepted), the mutual exchange of benefits is called a *transaction*. A series of repeated transactions by the same actors constitutes an *exchange relation*.

One of the core assumptions of any exchange theory is that benefits received from exchange are contingent upon benefits provided in exchange. This assumption is necessary to explain both the initiation of exchange and its continuation. But although some contingency between *A*'s giving to *B* and *B*'s giving to *A* is assumed for all social exchanges, that contingency can result from different processes. In direct exchange relations, transactions take two main forms: negotiated and reciprocal (Emerson 1981; Molm, Peterson, and Takahashi 1999).

In *negotiated transactions* (buying a car, dividing household tasks), actors engage in a joint-decision process, such as explicit bargaining, in which they reach an agreement, typically binding, about the terms of exchange. Both sides of the exchange are agreed upon at the same time and constitute a discrete transaction. Most economic exchanges other than fixed-price trades fit in this category, as do some social exchanges. In *reciprocal transactions*, actors individually initiate exchanges by performing a beneficial act for another (e.g., doing a favor or giving advice), without negotiation and without knowing whether, when, or to what extent the other will reciprocate. Exchange relations that develop under these conditions take the form of a series of sequentially contingent individual acts, rather than discrete two-party transactions, with the equality or inequality of exchange emerging over time. Reciprocal transactions are uncharacteristic of most economic exchanges (with the exception of those embedded in social relationships) but typical of many social exchanges between friends and family members.

While the classical exchange theorists were primarily concerned with reciprocal transactions, most contemporary theorists have studied negotiated transactions. Recently, however, reciprocal transactions, and their distinction from negotiated transactions, have begun to receive renewed attention (e.g., Lawler 2001; Molm, Peterson, and Takahashi 1999; Molm, Takahashi, and Peterson 2000).

The process of exchange can also affect the structure of exchange (Molm 1994). Because negotiated exchanges require mutual agreement before either party can obtain benefits, they create a structure with some of the elements of productive exchange: while the product of the exchange is not a single socially produced outcome (such as a coauthored book or a team trophy), both actors' contributions to the exchange are necessary before either obtains benefits. Similarly, in both reciprocal exchange and generalized exchange, the flow of benefits is unilateral. The distinction between the two is that in reciprocal exchange it is possible for *A*'s giving to *B* to be reciprocated directly by *B*, while in generalized exchange it is not. Both the individual decision making and the lack of communication about terms make reciprocal and generalized exchanges riskier than negotiated exchanges. And because reciprocity is indirect in generalized exchange, it is even riskier than reciprocal exchange.

Classical microeconomic theory assumed that successive transactions between actors were independent of one other.[2] The social exchange framework, in contrast, is built on the premise that actors engage in recurring, *inter*dependent exchanges with specific partners (or interchangeable partners in specific positions) over time. The scope of the theory is restricted to such relatively enduring relations between actors.

When the same actors exchange repeatedly with each other, the assumption that their actions are contingent on one another applies not only *within* transactions (i.e., *A*'s benefits to *B* are contingent on *B*'s benefits to *A*), but *across* transactions (e.g., benefits given and received in an earlier *A–B* exchange affect *A*'s subsequent behavior toward *B*). The interdependence of sequential transactions provides the opportunity for actors to influence their partners' behaviors in ways that are impossible when transactions are independent. The interdependence of transactions also means that the unit of analysis in social exchange must be the series of interactions that comprise a continuing exchange relation (Emerson 1972a).

HISTORICAL BACKGROUND

The Classical Statements

The philosophical roots of social exchange include influences from utilitarian economics, early anthropological studies (Lévi-Strauss 1969; Malinowski 1922; Mauss 1925), and behavioral psychology. All of these contributed to the exchange framework that developed in sociology in the 1960s and 1970s and that matured into the approach we see today. Here I briefly review the contributions of George Homans, John Thibaut and Harold Kelley, and Peter Blau, four theorists whose works were published within a few years of each other and whose ideas were particularly influential in the sociological development of the social exchange framework.

Homans first proposed social exchange as a unique perspective in a 1958 essay and then expanded these notions in *Social Behavior: Its Elementary Forms* ([1961] 1974). In this work, he envisioned social behavior as "an exchange of activity, tangible or intangible, and more or less rewarding or costly, between at least two persons" (1961, 13). In contrast to the collectivistic tradition of Lévi-Strauss (1969), Homans believed that individual self-interest provided the motivation for social exchange, and he focused his attention on direct exchanges between individuals rather than generalized exchange systems. His aim was to explain fundamental processes in dyads and small groups, using a small number of general propositions derived primarily from behavioral psychology. Ironically, however, one of his most enduring contributions—the concept of distributive justice (see Chapter 3)—was based not on behavioral psychology but on ideas derived from balance and social comparison theories.

An ardent reductionist, Homans argued that nothing emerges in social groups that "cannot be explained by propositions about individuals as individuals, together with the given condition that they happen to be interacting" (1974, 12). Following this logic, Homans explained social exchange and the forms of social organization that it produced by showing how *A*'s behavior reinforced *B*'s behavior, and vice versa, under structural and historical conditions taken as givens. The problem with this approach was that it assumed many of the conditions in which sociologists are most interested. Nevertheless, Homans's convincing analysis of the ubiquity of exchange processes in social life and his vivid examples paved the way for the theory's further development.

At the same time, psychologists Thibaut and Kelley (1959) were developing a theory of group behavior based on similar ideas. They also started from basic behavioral assumptions but recognized that social interaction must be predicted from characteristics of the social relation rather than merely the other person's behavior. Two of their contributions are particularly important. First is their analysis of power and dependence, which influenced Emerson's (1962) subsequent development of these ideas. Second are the concepts of *comparison level* (CL) and *comparison level for alternatives* (CL$_{alt}$), standards for evaluating outcomes within (CL) and between (CL$_{alt}$) relations. Actors evaluate outcomes from current relationships by comparing them with their CL, a general level of expectation based on recently experienced outcomes, and they decide whether to stay in a current relationship by comparing their outcomes with CL$_{alt}$, the outcomes expected in their best alternative relationship. Although Thibaut and Kelley focused primarily on dyadic relations, their concept of CL$_{alt}$ laid the foundation for the subsequent development of exchange networks by Emerson (1972b) and other theorists.

Blau's (1964) theory of social exchange began, like his predecessors', with an analysis of relatively simple, direct exchange relations in dyads and small groups. Blau's primary interest, however, was in more complex systems of exchange, at the level of organizations and institutions. In contrast to Homans, Blau recognized that social structures have emergent properties not found in the individual elements. His aim was to bridge the gap between elementary exchange processes and these emergent structures; to do so, he proposed that norms and shared values emerge to regulate patterns of indirect exchange in more complex systems. His integration of concepts from functional, conflict, and interactionist theories, in addition to principles of psychology and technical economic analysis, made Blau's approach the most eclectic of the classical theories.

The publication of these three theories stimulated extensive theoretical controversy but little systematic research. Critics charged exchange theorists with tautological reasoning, psychological reductionism, and an overly rational and hedonistic view of people (see Emerson 1976). Most of these criticisms, while valid at the time, were addressed by later, more sophisticated theories.

Emerson's Theory and the Rise of Programmatic Research

In 1972 Richard Emerson published a new theory of social exchange, based on his 1962 work on power-dependence relations, that marked a new phase in the development of the social exchange framework. His theory departed from earlier formulations in three important ways: First, Emerson replaced the narrative style of his predecessors with a rigorously derived system of propositions that were more amenable to empirical test and that encouraged the development of a strong research tradition. Second, Emerson's theory revolved around the dynamics of power, thus establishing power and its use as the major topics of exchange theory—topics that would dominate theory and research for the next 30 years. Third, by integrating principles of behavioral psychology with social network analysis, Emerson developed an exchange theory in which the structure of relations, rather than the actors, became the central focus. These distinctions influenced not only the character of his theory but the continued development of the social exchange tradition. In recognition of Emerson's basic insight that actors' mutual dependence provides the structural basis for their power over each other, the theory came to be known as power-dependence theory.

Like Homans, Emerson based his theory on assumptions derived from operant psychology. He avoided the problems of tautology and reductionism that had plagued Homans, however, by recognizing that the core concepts of operant behavior, reinforcer, and discriminative stimulus form a single conceptual unit; furthermore, their relation to each other is defined only across repeated occurrences of behavior and stimuli. By maintaining the integrity of this unit, Emerson established the *social relation*, rather than the individual actor, as the basic unit of power-dependence theory. Resources were similarly tied to relations rather than actors, and the concept of actors was expanded to include collective actors.

Emerson was the first to link exchange theory with the growing field of social network analysis, a move that fundamentally changed the nature of exchange research. The location of actors within networks of exchange relations determines their power over one another, by determining which actors have greater or lesser access to partners who control valued resources. Actors whose positions in networks connect them to alternative sources of the same resources, and whose alternative partners are more valuable or more available than other actors' partners, are less dependent on any one partner and have more power over other, more dependent actors.

The concepts of exchange networks and collective actors allowed power-dependence theory to bridge the gap between micro and macro levels of analysis more successfully than its predecessors. With these tools, Emerson (1972b) proposed that the theory could explain the emergence and change of social structures, including network expansion and contraction, the effects of power as a structural potential, and such diverse forms of social organization as stratified networks and the division of labor.

Emerson's collaboration with Karen Cook produced, for the first time, a systematic program of research on exchange relations and networks, testing major tenets of power-dependence theory (Cook and Emerson 1978; Cook et al. 1983).[3] Other programs, conducted by other researchers, were soon to follow. Because of the emphasis on testing and constructing theory, nearly all of this work uses experimental methods and standardized laboratory settings. Most settings share several features: subjects interact via computer to assure that their behavior is affected solely by structural characteristics of networks (rather than by personal characteristics of actors), they exchange repeatedly with partners over multiple trials, and they engage in exchanges that produce positive outcomes for each other, operationalized as money.[4]

The setting that Emerson, Cook, and their students constructed was specifically designed for the study of power in negatively connected networks. In contrast to the reciprocal exchanges envisioned by Homans and Blau and implicitly assumed in Emerson's original formulation, subjects in Cook and Emerson's (1978) setting *negotiated* the terms of exchange, through a series of offers and counteroffers, to reach binding agreements about the division of profit. To create the negative connections, a subject's exchange with one partner precluded exchange with another partner on that opportunity.[5] Information about the size and shape of the network structure was restricted to test Emerson's assertion that power leads to power use, regardless of actors' knowledge or intentions, and information about other actors' benefits from exchange agreements was omitted to eliminate equity concerns, which can dampen the effects of structural power. In reality, subjects divided a fixed amount of profit, but they were unaware of the total profit or their partners' gain.

In this setting, the theory itself came to take on more of an economic flavor, with more emphasis on rational actors, comparison of alternatives, and maximization of outcomes (Cook et al. 1983). At the same time, however, Cook introduced concerns with commitment and equity that were not part of the theory's original formulation and that increased the motivational complexity of actors.

CONTEMPORARY DEVELOPMENT OF THE SOCIAL EXCHANGE FRAMEWORK

Beginning in the early 1980s, the rate of both theory development and programmatic research on social exchange accelerated markedly. Most of this work was influenced, in one way or another, by Cook and Emerson's research, which stimulated both competing theories of power in exchange networks and theories that were based, at least in part, on concepts drawn from power-dependence theory. In contrast to the broad frameworks proposed by the classical exchange theorists, these contemporary theories focused on explaining particular exchange outcomes: initially, power and inequality; more recently, trust, commitment, and affective ties.

Theories of Network Exchange and Power

In a 1983 study, Cook, Emerson, and their associates (Cook et al. 1983) explicitly linked power-dependence theory's analysis of power in exchange networks with social network research on power and centrality. At the same time, they acknowledged the theory's inadequacy for analyzing complex networks; i.e., power-dependence theory takes account of the larger network in which actors are embedded, but it predicts the distribution of power within dyadic relations, not the network as a whole. Network-level analysis required a new approach, and in the late 1980s and early 1990s, three new theories of power in exchange networks were proposed: network exchange theory (Markovsky, Willer, and Patton 1988; Willer 1999); expected value theory (Friedkin 1986, 1992); and game theory (Bienenstock and Bonacich 1992, 1997).

The most well-known of these alternative approaches is the network exchange theory developed by Barry Markovsky, David Willer, and colleagues from the basic concepts of elementary theory (see Chapter 10 and also Willer and Anderson 1981) and resistance theory (Heckathorn 1980; Willer 1981). The theory uses two algorithms—a graph-theoretical power index (GPI) based on a network path–counting algorithm and a resistance model based on actors' expectations about outcomes—to predict relative power and profit in exchange networks. Structural power derives from the availability of alternative partners, as determined by the structure of the network. Differences in availability affect the likelihood that some actors will be excluded from agreements, creating what Markovsky et al. (1993) call "strong power" and "weak power" networks. The distribution of power in strong-power networks can be calculated from the GPI, while predictions in weak-power networks rely on a resistance model that considers how actors' beliefs about potential outcomes affect bargaining.

While Markovsky, Willer, and their associates incorporated bargaining processes in later versions of their theory, the interplay between structure and process was the central issue in Noah Friedkin's (1992) expected value approach from its inception. Friedkin developed his expected value approach from a broader model of social power that applies to a variety of social relations, including social exchange (Friedkin 1986). Rather than assuming that exchange outcomes can be predicted solely from network structure, Friedkin argued that the opportunity structure of exchange networks and the process of bargaining jointly determine exchange outcomes. The probabilities of alternative exchange patterns (which are structurally determined) affect actors' bargaining positions and payoffs, which in turn affect the probabilities of future transactions, and so on, in an iterative process. The bargaining model assumes that actors' offers are inversely related to their dependencies, defined by their relative frequencies of exclusion from exchange.

Elisa Bienenstock and Phillip Bonacich (1992, 1997) took a different approach, arguing that no new theory was required to predict the distribution of power in negatively connected exchange networks. As they pointed out, negotiated exchanges in these networks are equivalent to n-person cooperative games. Consequently, it should be possible to apply existing game-theoretic solutions to predict resource distributions. The game-theoretic solution on which Bienenstock and Bonacich focused most of their attention is the *core*: the set of payoffs that satisfies assumptions of individual, coalition (relation), and group (network) rationality. For networks that have no core outcomes, other game-theoretic solutions are possible (e.g., the Shapley value and the Kernel).

In 1992 Cook and Yamagishi also proposed a new power-dependence algorithm, called "equi-dependence," to predict network-level power. This algorithm determines the exchange ratios that will produce equal dependence of actors on each other in all relations throughout a network, based on iterative calculations of the value of their exchanges with each other relative to the value of exchanges with their best alternatives.

All four of these network-level approaches offer sophisticated mathematical models for predicting the distribution of power in negatively connected (or exclusive) networks. The competition that developed among them produced a large body of research (including a special 1992 issue of *Social Networks* devoted to the different approaches), increased the size and range of networks studied, and spurred refinements in the theories that increased the precision and accuracy of their predictions. All of the work was conducted in laboratory settings modeled after Cook and Emerson's (1978) setting; i.e., actors negotiate the terms of binding agreements that specify how much profit each actor receives from a fixed pool.[6]

The emphasis on theory competition and accuracy of predictions has tended to obscure the extent to which the theories agree on central issues. Most of the theories are based on the notion that actors' structural power depends, at least in part, on the *availability* of their alternative partners, as determined by the network structure (Skvoretz and Willer 1993). The availability of alternative partners affects power use in negatively connected (or exclusive) networks by providing opportunities for powerful actors to engage in exchanges with multiple partners. In power-dependence terms, greater availability of alternative partners reduces a powerful actor's dependence on, and frequency of exchange with, any single partner. In network exchange theory terms, greater availability increases the likelihood that some of those available partners will be *excluded* from exchange on any opportunity. It is this structurally induced exclusion of some actors from exchange with valued partners that drives power use, by creating competition among the excluded, disadvantaged actors for exchange with the powerful actor. Faced with the prospect of either a poor deal or no deal, the disadvantaged actors negotiate exchanges in which they receive increasingly less benefit than their advantaged partners. In networks with strong variations in availability of alternatives across positions, power can be predicted from network structure alone. In networks with weak variations in availability, prediction becomes more complex and depends on assumptions about actors' bargaining strategies. Again, the theories are all based on fairly similar assumptions about actors' behaviors but differ in how they model that behavior and, consequently, the specific predictions they make.

One of the most distinctive features of this period of theory development is the focus on a highly specific problem: predicting how actors divide profits in negatively connected networks of direct exchange when transactions are negotiated and agreements are binding. We now know a great deal about power under these conditions, but far less work has been conducted on power in networks with other types of connections (positive, inclusive, or mixed or compound), although some promising efforts have been made (Bonacich 1987; Szmatka and Willer 1995; Yamagishi, Gillmore, and Cook 1988; Yamaguchi 1996). In positively connected networks, power is driven by value and distance from the source. Thus power typically accrues to more central actors who control access to a valued resource and can act as brokers between others (Marsden 1982; Yamagishi, Gillmore, and Cook 1988). Inclusive connections, on the other hand, produce power differences that disadvantage the inclusively connected position—the actor who must complete exchanges in more than one relation to obtain benefit (Szmatka and Willer 1995).

The effect of the relative *value* of alternatives on power also has received little attention as a dimension of network structure (see, however, Bonacich and Friedkin 1998, and Molm, Peterson, and Takahashi 2001). While value was one of Emerson's (1972b) key determinants of dependence (with B's dependence on A increasing with the value to B of the resources that A controls), Markovsky and Willer's elementary theory assumed relations of homogeneous value (Markovsky, Willer, and Patton 1988) and created positions of relative advantage and disadvantage solely through variations in access to alternative partners. Other researchers adopted this practice. Recent work shows, however, that the value of alternatives has at least as strong an effect on power as the availability of alternatives (Molm, Peterson, and Takahashi 2001). Thye's (2000) status value theory of exchange links status to power through its effect on value, proposing that status can influence power by affecting the perceived value of the resources controlled by an actor (see also Lovaglia 1994).

Finally, one of the most neglected topics in research on power in networks is the study of structure and structural change as *dependent* variables. This was Emerson's (1972b) original interest, and his classic analysis of power-balancing processes included two major forms of structural change that can reduce power differences and inequality: network expansion—increasing alternatives for less powerful actors, and network contraction—reducing alternatives for powerful actors through coalition formation by the weak against the strong. The former has received almost no attention (but see Leik 1992) and the latter far less than it deserves. Cook and Gillmore (1984) showed that in a unilateral monopoly—a network structure in which one powerful actor has multiple alternative partners, who have no other alternatives—a coalition of all the power-disadvantaged actors against the sole power-advantaged actor will balance power in the network. Coalitions that do not include all disadvantaged actors will not balance power because the advantaged actor still has at least one alternative. More recently, network exchange theory has also studied coalition formation in exchange networks (Willer and Skvoretz 1997).

Other Theories of Power

As network theorists developed increasingly precise predictions of power in exchange networks, other exchange theorists pursued different agendas. Both Edward Lawler and Linda Molm drew on concepts from power-dependence theory to develop their own theories of power and related processes, focusing more on dyadic relations within exchange networks than on the distribution of power in networks as a whole. Their work explicitly recognized the nonzero-sum character of power-dependence theory, which implies that both the *absolute* power in a relation (what Emerson called *cohesion*) and the *relative* power in a relation (the primary focus of network-level theories) determine exchange behavior. At the same time, their work introduced ideas and concepts that were not part of Emerson's original formulation: greater attention to cognition and affect in exchange, consideration of punitive as well as rewarding actions, analyses of power strategies and tactics, and comparisons of different forms of exchange.

In the late 1970s and early 1980s, Lawler's work with Samuel Bacharach (Bacharach and Lawler 1981) integrated power-dependence theory's analysis of structural power with bargaining theories' analyses of tactical power. Traditional work on bargaining neglected the power structure within which parties negotiate and paid scant attention to the role of power. Lawler and Bacharach used ideas from power-dependence theory to fill that gap and tested their predictions in a series of experiments modeled after intergroup bargaining. Later work by Lawler and Ford (Lawler and Ford 1993) further developed the integration of these two traditions.

Several features distinguish this work from other research on power in negotiated exchanges. First, Lawler and his colleagues were concerned not only with the terms of agreements (the typical measure of power use) but with whether and how actors reach agreement and the tactics they use. Second, Lawler explicitly adopted a tripartite conception of power that included not only the structure of power and the outcomes of power use, but the *tactics* that actors use to reach agreements. Third, in contrast to the strongly structural stance of other theories, Lawler and his colleagues envisioned the use of power as a more conscious choice, and proposed that actors' perceptions of power mediate the relation between structural power and its use.

Different branches of this research program have investigated reward power, conceptualized in power-dependence terms, and punitive power, based on Lawler's (1986) extension of bilateral deterrence theory. The two theories predict similar effects of some dimensions of the two bases of power: when power in a relation is equal, high absolute power on either base should increase positive, conciliatory actions and decrease the use of threats and punishments. Unequal power on either base should increase hostility and conflict. Research has generally supported these predictions (Bacharach and Lawler 1981; Lawler 1986; Lawler, Ford, and Blegen 1988).

Molm's (1997) theory of coercion in exchange also brought more consideration of strategic power use into the exchange framework and expanded it to include punishment and coercion. Her work, conducted within the power-dependence framework, departs from other contemporary work on social exchange in two important ways. First, unlike both classical and contemporary theorists, who excluded punishment and coercion from the study of social exchange, Molm sought to bring the analysis of coercion within the scope of power-dependence theory, arguing that both reward power and coercive power are derived from dependence on others, either for obtaining rewards or avoiding punishment, and potentially can be explained by the same principles. Unlike reward power, however, the use of coercive power is not induced by a structural power advantage but strategically enacted as a means of increasing an exchange partner's rewards. To explain strategic power use, Molm introduced concepts of decision making under risk and uncertainty.

Second, in contrast to the negotiated exchanges studied by other contemporary exchange researchers, Molm's work on coercion examined *reciprocal* exchanges, in which actors individually provide benefits for another without negotiating the terms of an

exchange and without knowing whether or when the other will reciprocate. This conception of social exchange is closer to that of the classical theorists. It also brings to the fore the
role of *risk* in social exchange. While risk is less important in negotiated exchanges with
binding agreements, it is a critical consideration in reciprocal exchanges and generalized exchanges, in which actors make choices of exchange partners and behaviors without knowing the probability of their partner's reciprocity and without any assurance that they will
reciprocate. When faced with risk, actors tend to focus more on minimizing loss than
on maximizing gain (Kahneman and Tversky 1979); this loss aversion can lead to risk-
reduction strategies that also reduce power use. In general, (reward) power use is lower in
reciprocal exchanges than in negotiated exchanges (Molm, Peterson, and Takahashi 1999),
and coercive power is rarely used because of the high potential costs to the actors most
motivated to use it—actors who are disadvantaged on reward power (Molm 1997).

Whether exchange transactions are negotiated or reciprocal also affects the mechanisms
underlying power use and the relation between structural power and power use (Molm,
Peterson, and Takahashi 1999; Molm 2003). Whether benefits can flow unilaterally (as in
reciprocal exchange) or only bilaterally (as in negotiated exchange) affects which exchange
patterns will maximize powerful actors' benefits, the effect of those patterns on the costs imposed on the weaker partner, and the power use that results. In negotiated exchanges, in
which benefits are obtained only through bilateral agreements, actors should make agreements with those who offer greater rewards. More dependent, less powerful partners will
typically offer better deals than less dependent, more powerful partners. But in reciprocal
exchanges, in which benefits flow unilaterally and actors can receive benefits from multiple
partners at the same time, initiating exchange with a partner who is more dependent on an
actor is *not* the best strategy: because more dependent partners should initiate exchange
more frequently (Emerson 1972a), the best strategy for obtaining maximum benefit from
all of a powerful actor's alternative partners is to give more frequently to those partners who
are less dependent and less frequently to those who are more dependent. These differences
mean that theories developed for one form of exchange may not necessarily hold for
the other.

Theories of Affect, Commitment, and Trust in Social Exchange

The most recent contemporary development is the increasing shift away from the study of
power and inequality to the study of integrative outcomes in social exchange: the development of trust, affective ties, and commitment. These are what Blau (1964) called *emergent*
properties of exchange relations: relational characteristics that develop over time as actors
repeatedly engage in exchange with one another.

Commitment as Behavior and Affect. The most common conception of commitment in
the exchange literature is a behavioral one, with commitment defined by the extent to which
pairs of actors exchange repeatedly with one another rather than with alternative partners.
This conception of commitment was originally introduced by Cook and Emerson (1978)
and has also been used by Kollock (1994) and Molm and colleagues (2000). Commitment
has also been conceptualized in more affective terms, as an emotional attachment to the

relation (Lawler and Yoon 1996) or as feelings of liking and commitment for the exchange partner (Molm, Takahashi, and Peterson 2000). Lawler and Yoon's (1996, 1998; Lawler, Thye, and Yoon 2000) theory of relational cohesion combines these, proposing that commitment behaviors—including unilateral gift giving, contributions to joint ventures, and continued exchange with the same partner—are the end product of a process of emotional attachment.

Behavioral commitment varies inversely with structural power and, in turn, reduces power use. Within a given network, low-power actors (who have few or poor alternatives) are more likely to make behavioral commitments than high-power actors (who have more or better alternatives), and commitments are more likely to develop in relations of equal power or low power imbalance than in relations with greater power differences (Cook and Emerson 1978; Lawler and Yoon 1998; Molm, Takahashi, and Peterson 2000). Because commitments reduce power use by curtailing the exploration of alternatives (Cook and Emerson 1978), they are generally beneficial to low-power actors and costly to high-power actors.

Two distinct theoretical mechanisms link structural power with behavioral commitments. Cook and Emerson (1978), Kollock (1994), and Yamagishi, Cook, and Watabe (1998) have all focused on *uncertainty reduction*; i.e., by forming committed relations, actors can reduce the risk and uncertainty inherent in mixed-motive exchange relations. Because low-power actors face greater uncertainty, they are more likely to initiate and display commitment. Kollock (1994) and Yamagishi, Cook, and Watabe (1998) both found significantly higher levels of commitment in exchange relations with greater uncertainty, operationalized by whether actors could deceive one another. In a comparison of reciprocal and negotiated exchange, however, Molm, Takahashi, and Peterson (2000) found that although actors reported greater *feelings* of commitment when exchanges were reciprocal (and therefore riskier), their actual behavioral commitments were no greater than when exchanges were negotiated.

Lawler and Yoon's program of research on relational cohesion theory (Lawler and Yoon 1996, 1998), in contrast, has proposed that structural power and commitment behaviors are linked by *affective processes*. High mutual dependence and equal power promote frequent, successful negotiations between actors, who in turn experience positive emotions—interest and satisfaction—that are attributed, in part, to the relationship itself. As a result, the relationship becomes an object of affective attachment, which in turn increases commitment behaviors. Lawler and Yoon's (1996) results support their model in equal-power networks but also support the role of uncertainty reduction, suggesting that both processes may contribute independently to the development of commitment.

More recently, Lawler has expanded his analysis of the role of emotions in exchange into a more general affect theory of social exchange (see Chapter 11, as well as Lawler 2001). By conceptualizing emotions as internal stimuli that are reinforcing or punishing, the theory maintains a link to the behavioral assumptions of classical social exchange theories, while arguing that the emotions produced by exchanges—and not only the exchanges themselves—are critical to an understanding of how different exchange structures, forms, and outcomes affect the development of solidarity in relations and groups. Lawler (2001) links emotions to solidarity through actors' efforts to determine the source of their positive or negative feelings, arguing that exchange structures that entail a higher degree of task interdependence should produce stronger attributions of emotions to the social unit (the relation, group, or network).

Trust. Risk and uncertainty are also strongly related to the development of trust. As Blau (writing of reciprocal exchanges) noted, "Since there is no way to assure an appropriate return for a favor, social exchange requires trusting others to discharge their obligations" (1964, 94). Other theorists have proposed that exchange under risk and uncertainty not only *requires* trust, but *promotes* trust by providing the opportunity to demonstrate one's trustworthiness (Ekeh 1974; Lévi-Strauss 1969). Without risk, attributions of trustworthiness are impossible (Kelley and Thibaut 1978). Yamagishi and Yamagishi (1994) make this same point by distinguishing between *trust* and *assurance*. Assurance refers to expectations of benign behavior from an exchange partner because an incentive structure (e.g., contracts or warranties) encourages such behavior; trust refers to expectations of benign behavior because of a partner's personal traits. As long as an assurance structure is present, there is no opportunity for trust to develop.

Research supports the role of risk in building trust in exchange relations. Kollock (1994) showed that ratings of partners' trustworthiness were greater when buyers purchased goods of uncertain quality than when quality was known. And Molm, Takahashi, and Peterson (2000) found that reciprocal exchanges produced higher levels of trust than equivalent (but less risky) negotiated exchanges. Of course, risk potentially creates a breeding ground for exploitation as well as trust; both Kollock and Molm found variations in trustworthy behavior, and thus in trust, under conditions of risk. In generalized exchange systems that form a chain or closed circle (e.g., *A* gives to *B*, *B* to *C*, and *C* to *A*), Yamagishi and Cook (1993) caution that participants must have a relatively high level of general trust in others initially or the system will collapse. More recently, Takahashi (2000) has shown that under some conditions, pure generalized exchange systems can develop and persist without high levels of trust or central sanctioning systems, as long as actors selectively give to others whose behavior meets a personal criterion of fairness.

Exchange theorists have always seen trust and commitment as closely linked to one another. Blau (1964) proposed that they evolve together, beginning with minor transactions in which little trust is required because little risk is involved and gradually expanding as partners prove themselves trustworthy and exchange more frequently. Yamagishi, Cook, and Watabe (1998) found that generalized trust in others leads to stronger commitments, especially when uncertainty is high. Molm and colleagues (Molm, Takahashi, and Peterson 2000) also see trust and commitment as closely linked but propose that affective commitment and behavioral commitment are related to trust in different ways. Their theory argues that feelings of affective commitment emerge from the same processes that generate trust; i.e., risky structures that allow actors to attribute their partner's positive behaviors to the partner's personal traits and intentions rather than to external assurance structures. A partner's behavioral commitment, on the other hand, serves as a signal of the partner's trustworthiness, thus encouraging the development of trust. They found that an actor's trust in a partner significantly increased with the partner's behavioral commitment to the actor, even with structure controlled. These findings support the emphasis in much of the sociological literature on the importance of long-term relations and repeated interactions for developing trust.

CONCLUSION

As long as people are dependent on others for meeting their material and social needs, the exchange of valued benefits will constitute an important part of social life. These exchanges take different forms—direct or generalized, negotiated or reciprocal—and they occur within networks of varying sizes, shapes, and connections. As a result, actors vary in their opportunities to obtain benefits and in the control they exert over others' benefits.

By focusing on the benefits that people exchange and the structures within which exchanges take place, the social exchange perspective provides a framework for developing theories of a wide range of social phenomena. Since its earliest formulations, the differences among actors in opportunity and control have led theorists to focus, in particular, on the relations between exchange and power (e.g., Blau 1964; Emerson 1962). Until recently, the study of power and power use dominated contemporary work on social exchange. Increasingly, however, researchers are incorporating power into broader theories that address not only the competition and conflict inherent in exchange networks with positions of varying power, but the development of such integrative bonds as affect, commitment, and trust. It is likely that this work will continue to grow in importance during the next decade, linking social exchange theory with work in the sociology of emotions, social capital, and theories of trust. Investigation of these topics is also likely to focus less on negotiated exchange in competitive (negatively connected or exclusive) networks and more on other forms of exchange that, until recently, have received less attention: reciprocal, productive, and generalized forms of exchange and positively connected and inclusive networks.

These directions should serve the social exchange tradition well, by recapturing some of the breadth and richness of the earlier, more general frameworks but with the added sophistication and rigor that contemporary scholars have brought to the field.

1. Resources can also vary on such dimensions as divisibility, alienability (or transferability), duplicability, and conservation (Coleman 1990). Exchange researchers have yet to explore the theoretical implications and empirical effects of these distinctions; however, research now in progress is studying the effects of transferability and duplicability on power (Schaefer 2004).

2. In contrast, contemporary theorists recognize that even economic exchanges are often embedded in social relationships (Granovetter 1985).

3. The earliest tests of Emerson's theory were conducted by Stolte and Emerson (1977) and used a somewhat different experimental setting.

4. The use of money in exchange experiments often gives the mistaken impression that researchers are studying economic exchange, not social exchange. But researchers use money solely because of its advantages for experimental control: money is widely valued, quantifiable, and resistant to satiation effects (which could reduce value in unknown ways). The resource in exchange experiments is not money (i.e., money is not transferred from one actor to another) but rather the capacity to produce valued outcomes, operationalized as money, for another.

5. *Theoretically*, negative connections between two relations (e.g., A–B and A–C) are created when B and C offer resources in the same domain (i.e., substitutable resources) to A, making B and C alternative sources of those resources and alternative exchange partners for A. According to the principle of satiation, the more A exchanges with B, the less A will exchange with C, and vice versa. *Operationally*, Cook and Emerson (1978) created negative connections in the laboratory by making exchanges in connected relations mutually exclusive; i.e., on each exchange opportunity, A could exchange with B or C but not both.

6. Network exchange researchers instituted a number of changes, however, that reflect some of the different assumptions underlying the theories: the division of profit became explicit, rather than implicit; subjects knew the structure, actions, and outcomes of others in the network; subjects rotated through all network positions during the exchange period; and the number of partners with whom actors could exchange on a single opportunity (which Cook and Emerson restricted to operationalize negative connections) became a variable condition of exchange. All of these differences reflect the most fundamental distinction between the two theories: power-dependence theory is based on a behavioral or learning model, while network exchange theory adopts a rule-based or initial-conditions approach.

Bacharach, Samuel B., and Edward J. Lawler. 1981. *Bargaining: Power, Tactics, and Outcomes*. San Francisco: Jossey-Bass.

Bienenstock, Elisa Jayne, and Phillip Bonacich. 1992. The core as a solution to exclusionary networks. *Social Networks* 14:231–43.

———. 1997. Network exchange as a cooperative game. *Rationality and Society* 9:37–65.

Blau, Peter M. 1964. *Exchange and Power in Social Life*. New York: Wiley.

Bonacich, Phillip. 1987. Power and centrality: A family of measures. *American Journal of Sociology* 92:1170–82.

Bonacich, Phillip, and Noah E. Friedkin. 1998. Unequally valued exchange relations. *Social Psychology Quarterly* 61:160–71.

Coleman, James S. 1990. *Foundations of Social Theory*. Cambridge, MA: Harvard University Press.

Cook, Karen S., and Richard M. Emerson. 1978. Power, equity and commitment in exchange networks. *American Sociological Review* 43:721–39.

Cook, Karen S., Richard M. Emerson, Mary R. Gillmore, and Toshio Yamagishi. 1983. The distribution of power in exchange networks: Theory and experimental results. *American Journal of Sociology* 89:275–305.

Cook, Karen S., and Mary R. Gillmore. 1984. Power, dependence, and coalitions. In *Advances in Group Processes*, vol. 1, ed. Edward J. Lawler, 27–58. Greenwich, CT: JAI Press.

Cook, Karen S., and Toshio Yamagishi. 1992. Power in exchange networks: A power-dependence formulation. *Social Networks* 14:245–65.

Ekeh, Peter. 1974. *Social Exchange Theory: The Two Traditions*. Cambridge, MA: Harvard University Press.

Emerson, Richard M. 1962. Power-dependence relations. *American Sociological Review* 27:31–41.

———. 1972a. Exchange theory, part I: A psychological basis for social exchange. In *Sociological Theories in Progress*, vol. 2, ed. Joseph Berger, Morris Zelditch Jr., and Bo Anderson, 38–57. Boston: Houghton-Mifflin.

———. 1972b. Exchange theory, part II: Exchange relations and networks. In *Sociological Theories in Progress*, vol. 2, ed. Joseph Berger, Morris Zelditch Jr., and Bo Anderson, 58–87. Boston: Houghton Mifflin.

———. 1976. Social exchange theory. *Annual Review of Sociology* 2:335–62.

———. 1981. Social exchange theory. In *Social Psychology: Sociological Perspectives*, ed. Morris Rosenberg and Ralph Turner, 30–65. New York: Basic Books.

———. 1987. Toward a theory of value in social exchange. In *Social Exchange Theory*, ed. Karen S. Cook, 11–46. Newbury Park, CA: Sage.

Friedkin, Noah E. 1986. A formal theory of social power. *Journal of Mathematical Sociology* 12:103–26.

―――. 1992. An expected value model of social power: Predictions for selected exchange networks. *Social Networks* 14:213–29.

Granovetter, Mark. 1985. Economic action and social structure: The problem of embeddedness. *American Journal of Sociology* 91:481–510.

Heckathorn, Douglas D. 1980. A unified model for bargaining and conflict. *Behavioral Science* 23:73–85.

Homans, George C. 1958. Social behavior as exchange. *American Journal of Sociology*. 62:597–606.

―――. [1961] 1974. *Social Behavior: Its Elementary Forms*. Rev. ed. New York: Harcourt, Brace & World.

Kahneman, Daniel, and Amos Tversky. 1979. Prospect theory: An analysis of decision under risk. *Econometrica* 47:263–91.

Kelley, Harold H., and John W. Thibaut. 1978. *Interpersonal Relations: A Theory of Interdependence*. New York: Wiley.

Kollock, Peter. 1994. The emergence of exchange structures: An experimental study of uncertainty, commitment, and trust. *American Journal of Sociology* 100:313–45.

Lawler, Edward J. 1986. Bilateral deterrence and conflict spiral: A theoretical analysis. In *Advances in group processes*, vol. 3, ed. Edward J. Lawler, 107–30. Greenwich, CT: JAI Press.

―――. 2001. An affect theory of social exchange. *American Journal of Sociology* 107:321–52.

Lawler, Edward J., and Rebecca Ford. 1993. Metatheory and friendly competition in theory growth: The case of power processes in bargaining. In *Theoretical Research Programs: Studies in the Growth of Theory*, ed. Joseph Berger and Morris Zelditch Jr., 172–210. Stanford, CA: Stanford University Press.

Lawler, Edward J., Rebecca Ford, and Mary A. Blegen. 1988. Coercive capability in conflict: A test of bilateral deterrence versus conflict spiral theory. *Social Psychology Quarterly* 51:93–107.

Lawler, Edward J., and Jeongkoo Yoon. 1996. Commitment in exchange relations: Test of a theory of relational cohesion. *American Sociological Review* 61:89–108.

―――. 1998. Network structure and emotion in exchange relations. *American Sociological Review* 63:871–94.

Lawler, Edward J., Shane R. Thye, and Jeongkoo Yoon. 2000. Emotion and group cohesion in productive exchange. *American Journal of Sociology* 106:616–57.

Leik, Robert K. 1992. New directions for network exchange theory: Strategic manipulation of network linkages. *Social Networks* 14:309–23.

Lévi-Strauss, Claude. 1969. *The Elementary Structures of Kinship*, rev. ed. Boston: Beacon.

Lovaglia, Michael J. 1994. Relating power to status. In *Advances in Group Processes*, vol. 11, ed. Barry Markovsky, Karen Heimer, Jodi O'Brien, and Edward J. Lawler, 87–111. Greenwich, CT: JAI Press.

Macy, Michael W. 1990. Learning theory and the logic of critical mass. *American Sociological Review* 55:809–26.

Malinowski, Bronislaw. 1922. *Argonauts of the Western Pacific*. New York: E. P. Dutton.

Markovsky, Barry, David Willer, and Travis Patton. 1988. Power relations in exchange networks. *American Sociological Review* 53:220–36.

Markovsky, Barry, John Skvoretz, David Willer, Michael Lovaglia, and Jeffrey Erger. 1993. The seeds of weak power: An extension of network exchange theory. *American Sociological Review* 53:220–36.

Marsden, Peter. 1982. Brokerage behavior in restricted exchange networks. In *Social Structure and Network Analysis*, ed. Peter V. Marsden and Nan Lin, 201–18. Beverly Hills, CA: Sage.

Mauss, M. 1925. Essai sur le don: Forme et raison de l'echange dans les societes archaiques. *Annee Sociology* 1:30–186.

Molm, Linda D. 1994. Dependence and risk: Transforming the structure of social exchange. *Social Psychology Quarterly* 57:163–76.

———. 1997. *Coercive Power in Social Exchange*. Cambridge, UK: Cambridge University Press.

———. 2003. Theoretical comparisons of forms of exchange. *Sociological Theory* 21:1–17.

Molm, Linda D., Gretchen Peterson, and Nobuyuki Takahashi. 1999. Power use in negotiated and reciprocal exchange. *American Sociological Review* 64:876–90.

———. 2001. The value of exchange. *Social Forces* 79:159–85.

Molm, Linda D., Nobuyuki Takahashi, and Gretchen Peterson. 2000. Risk and trust in social exchange: An experimental test of a classical proposition. *American Journal of Sociology* 105:1396–427.

Schaefer, David. 2004. Resources and power in exchange networks. Paper presented at the Group Processes Conference, San Francisco, August 2004.

Skvoretz, John, and David Willer. 1993. Exclusion and power: A test of four theories of power in exchange networks. *American Sociological Review* 58:801–18.

Stolte, John R., and Richard M. Emerson. 1977. Structural inequality: Position and power in network structures. In *Behavioral Theory in Sociology*, ed. Robert L. Hamblin and John Kunkel, 117–38. New Brunswick, NJ: Transaction.

Szmatka, Jacek, and David Willer. 1995. Exclusion, inclusion and compound connection in exchange networks. *Social Psychology Quarterly* 55:123–31.

Takahashi, Nobuyuki. 2000. The emergence of generalized exchange. *American Journal of Sociology* 105:1105–34.

Thibaut, John W., and Harold H. Kelley. 1959. *The Social Psychology of Groups*. New York: Wiley.

Thye, Shane R. 2000. A status value theory of power in exchange relations. *American Sociological Review* 65:407–32.

Willer, David. 1981. Quantity and network structure. In *Networks, Exchange and Coercion: The Elementary Theory and Its Applications*, ed. David Willer and Bo Anderson, 108–27. New York: Elsevier.

———, ed. 1999. *Network Exchange Theory*. Westport, CT: Praeger.

Willer, David, and Bo Anderson, eds. 1981. *Networks, Exchange and Coercion: The Elementary Theory and Its Applications*. New York: Elsevier.

Willer, David, and John Skvoretz. 1997. Games and structures. *Rationality and Society* 9:5–35.

Yamagishi, Toshio, and Karen S. Cook. 1993. Generalized exchange and social dilemmas. *Social Psychology Quarterly* 56:235–48.

Yamagishi, Toshio, Karen S. Cook, and Motoki Watabe. 1998. Uncertainty, trust and commitment formation in the United States and Japan. *American Journal of Sociology* 104:165–94.

Yamagishi, Toshio, Mary R. Gillmore, and Karen S. Cook. 1988. Network connections and the distribution of power in exchange networks. *American Journal of Sociology* 93:833–51.

Yamagishi, Toshio, and Midori Yamagishi. 1994. Trust and commitment in the United States and Japan. *Motivation and Emotion* 18:129–66.

Yamaguchi, Kazuo. 1996. Power in networks of substitutable/complementary exchange relations: A rational-choice model and an analysis of power centralization. *American Sociological Review* 61:308–32.

3 JUSTICE FRAMEWORKS

Karen A. Hegtvedt

Justice, in its many guises, is a fundamental feature of all social groups and is a focus of discourse in many disciplines. Philosophers debate prescriptions for the just society; economists, despite their allegiance to analyzing market efficiencies, discuss justice in terms of the equality of income distributions or welfare functions; political scientists focus on the fairness of individuals and states' rights; sociologists analyze the social injustices wrought by inequality, racism, sexism, and the like. Social psychologists examine the intersection of people's objective circumstances, their perceived realities, their emotional responses, and their behaviors.

For nearly 40 years, three central questions have guided most conceptual and empirical investigations of distributive and procedural justice: What do people believe constitutes justice? How do people perceive injustice? How do individuals and groups respond to perceived injustice? Research during the 1960s and 1970s emphasized distributive justice, defined as the application of a normative rule to the allocation of benefits or burdens to recipients. Studies first focused on the third question, examining primarily reactions to pay inequity in social exchange situations (see Adams 1965; Cook and Hegtvedt 1983), and then, to address the first and second questions, investigators began to examine preferences for allocation rules (see Cook and Hegtvedt 1983; Leventhal, Karuza, and Fry 1980). In the 1980s emphasis shifted toward issues of procedural justice, defined in terms of the fairness in the means by which distribution decisions are made (Thibaut and Walker 1975; Leventhal, Karuza, and Fry 1980; Lind and Tyler 1988) and later in terms of fairness in the treatment of others (Tyler and Lind 1992). Early procedural justice research focused on specifying which decision rules are fair and how people perceive those rules. More recent procedural justice work examines the consequences of unfair procedures or treatment. Some researchers label emphasis on the fairness of treatment as *interactional justice* (Bies 2001). And, in the last 10 years, work on the intersection of distributive and procedural justice has grown. Research in organizational justice epitomizes the convergence of types of justice (Greenberg and Colquitt 2005).

The general parallels in distributive and procedural justice research regarding the central social psychological questions of justice have yet to generate a unified theoretical

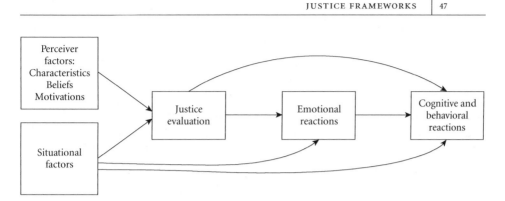

Figure 3.1   Basic Model of Justice Processes

framework. This deficiency may stem from the focused development of discrete theoretical arguments for specific questions, each of which addresses a different phenomenon: beliefs, perceptions, and various types of reactions. Such differential foci underlie the complexity of linking the three central questions, especially across the two primary domains of justice.[1]

In this chapter, I first identify common terms and key assumptions—sometimes disputed—that characterize the core of justice research. Then, to delineate the various theoretical and empirical approaches to justice questions, I organize this chapter around the basic justice model (Figure 3.1). Crosscutting the domains of justice, this model suggests that individual factors (e.g., characteristics, beliefs, and motivations) combine with situational factors to produce perceptions of how fair a distribution or procedure may be. Perceptions of injustice, in turn, affect emotional, cognitive, and behavioral reactions. The context in which perceivers are embedded may also inhibit or facilitate the expression of various responses. The model stresses mediating processes as well as factors that conditionalize the perception of injustice and reactions to it.[2]

BASIC TERMS AND ASSUMPTIONS

Except for the work of Jasso (e.g., 1980, 2002), most justice researchers have yet to formalize their definitions of perceivers, justice evaluations, distribution rules, procedural rules, treatment rules, and reactions. Likewise, the assumptions underlying their explanations are often implicit rather than explicit. Here I identify shared notions of basic terms and assumptions, noting correspondence with Jasso's formalization.

Basic Terms

Fundamental to all justice analyses is the notion of the *perceiver* (or, according to Jasso 2002, the observer). This is the actor who assesses a given outcome distribution, a procedure, or a means to treat individuals. The perceiver may or may not be a *recipient* of the outcomes or a target of the procedure or treatment. Perceivers who are also recipients or targets make first-party assessments. As discussed further below, the perceptions of first-party perceivers may be subject to greater influence by self-interested concerns than those of third-party perceivers who are not also recipients or targets and thus may appear more impartial in their assessments.

A second key concept is that of the *justice evaluation* (also referred to as the perception of justice). The justice evaluation is the result of what individuals believe about the situation, the comparisons that they make, and their perceptions of situational information. Generally, their beliefs encompass what distributions or procedural rules they think are relevant in the situation and other values. Such beliefs may be colored by the perceiver's characteristics and motivations. Their comparisons include whether actual distributions or procedures correspond to those rules as well as specific comparisons of outcomes, procedures, or ratios of outcomes to inputs to past experiences, to other individuals, to other groups, or to more abstract referential standards. And their perceptions of situational factors encompass a wide array of phenomena ranging from characteristics of inputs and availability of outcomes to relationships with group members to group characteristics or situational constraints. Jasso (1980) distills all of this information in her formula of the justice evaluation (JE): $JE = \ln(\text{actual share}/\text{just share})$. The justice evaluation "expresses the observer's [perceiver's] judgment and sentiment that the rewardee [recipient] (possibly him or herself) is justly or unjustly treated, and if unjustly treated, whether over-rewarded or under-rewarded and to what degree" (Jasso 2002, 41). Ultimately, the JE is a *subjective* evaluation of how fair a perceiver thinks the situation is for himself or herself or for others.

Jasso's notion of the just share is a form of shorthand for the beliefs that underlie the assessments, thereby capturing group-level influences and cultural values. The logic of her justice evaluation, however, applies to other justice domains. To evaluate procedural justice requires a comparison between the just procedure and the actual procedure. Similarly, to evaluate interactional or treatment justice requires a comparison between a just treatment and the actual treatment experienced by the perceiver or observed.

Defining the just share, the just procedure, or the just treatment is one of the central questions addressed by justice researchers. Generally agreed upon distribution, procedural, and treatment rules may objectively represent justice insofar as they epitomize general group values. Within distributive justice, three rules are paramount (e.g., Deutsch 1975): equality, equity, and needs. The *equality* rule dictates that each recipient obtain an objectively equal share of the outcomes distributed. The *equity* rule assumes outcomes should be commensurate to contributions, defined broadly to include productivity and effort as well as ability, status, and other characteristics representing individual recipients. Adams's (1965) formulation of equity requires a comparison between the outcome-input ratio of at least two actors. The *needs* rule indicates that outcomes should be commensurate to the needs of potential recipients. Generally, third-party perceivers indicate that equal shares are just when group harmony is the goal, equitable shares when productivity is the goal, and need-based shares when group welfare is the goal (see Leventhal, Karuza, and Fry 1980). Other work (e.g., Jasso 1983) considers the relationship between individual-focused rules like equity and needs and outcome-focused rules like equality that define the shape of a distribution across all recipients.

Leventhal and colleagues (1980) outline broad principles of procedural justice. This work extended the emphasis of procedural justice from its limited concentration on conflict situations (Thibaut and Walker 1975) to decision making more generally. Procedural principles include (1) consistency of procedures across persons and across time, (2) suppression of bias, (3) accuracy of information, (4) mechanisms to correct bad decisions, (5) representativeness of the participants to a decision, and (6) ethicality of standards. Consistency and representativeness, especially as activated by giving voice to the opinions of the individuals affected by the decision, have been judged by third parties to be key to procedural justice judgments (Lind and Tyler 1988).

In their relational model of authority, Tyler and Lind (1992) identify three factors, or rules, that ensure fair treatment because they communicate information about the quality of the relationship between a focal actor and authorities or others in the situation: standing, neutrality, and trust. *Standing* refers to status as communicated through polite behavior, dignified treatment, and respect for one's rights and opinions. *Neutrality* points to equal treatment of all parties and includes honesty and lack of bias. The final factor, *trust*, characterizes the intentions of the decision maker to be fair and ethical in the immediate situation and in the future. Although studies by Tyler and his colleagues (see Tyler et al. 1997) demonstrate the importance of these elements to assessments of procedural justice, these rules also imply just treatment. Bies (2001) identifies respect and neutrality as rules as well as truthfulness and justification (provision of rationale) as guiding principles of interactional justice.

As illustrated in Figure 3.1, emotional, cognitive, and behavioral reactions follow justice evaluations. Jasso (2002) distinguishes mathematically between the perceiver's *experience* of the justice evaluation and his or her *expressed* justice evaluation. She also offers indexes of justice that provide summary measures of the overall injustice in a group or society. Her mathematical approach captures what other scholars refer to as emotional reactions to perceived injustice. Adams's (1965) classic formulation of reactions to inequity highlights the pivotal role of distress. Homans (1974) disassembles distress into specific emotions experienced by those who perceive themselves as under-rewarded, over-rewarded, or equitably rewarded. Negative emotions of anger and guilt, respectively, presumably characterize the first two groups, whereas those who are fairly treated feel satisfaction. That injustice begets negative emotions whereas justice produces positive ones also extends to research in procedural justice (see Tyler et al. 1997).

In addition to emotional reactions, Adams (1965) and Walster, Walster, and Bersheid (1978) in distributive justice and Lind and Tyler (1988; Tyler and Lind 1992; Tyler et al. 1997) in procedural justice draw attention to cognitive and behavioral responses to injustice. Cognitive responses attempt to restore a sense of psychological justice, whereas behavioral responses intend to restore actual justice. Derived from Adams, individual psychological responses to distributive injustice involve (1) cognitive distortion of either own inputs or own outcomes, (2) cognitive distortion of either the inputs or outcomes of another recipient, or (3) changing the object or person used in the comparison. Individual behavioral responses identified by Adams include (1) altering inputs, (2) altering outcomes, and (3) leaving the situation. Many variations on these six core responses exist (see Tyler et al. 1997). For example, cognitive distortion of another recipient's inputs or outcomes may take the form of derogating that actor. Within organizations, lower commitment may imply a cognitive response to unfairness. The notion of altering outcomes may involve actual changes in the actor's own productivity or requests to authorities for higher outcomes. Complaints, in general, may be seen as a behavioral response not fully anticipated by Adams's categories. In addition, responses may extend beyond the individual level to include collective reactions such as coalitions, riots, or social movements.

Behavioral responses to procedural or interactional injustice may take the form of noncompliance or more specific action to change the procedure or the treatment received (e.g., requests, complaints, absenteeism). Tyler and Lind (1992) argue that psychological responses to procedural or interactional injustice, however, may involve more than an alteration in cognitions about the situation. Because of the underlying assumption of group value, which characterizes procedural justice work, such responses may also include feelings of self-worth and value to the group. This assumption distinguishes—at least superficially—procedural justice from that of distributive justice.

Key Assumptions

As distilled from several perspectives (e.g., Adams 1965; Berger et al. 1972; Leventhal, Karuza, and Fry 1980; Lind and Tyler 1988; Walster, Walster, and Bersheid 1978; van den Bos, Lind, and Wilke 2001), the basic framework for most justice models includes several key assumptions. Although the assumptions are typically from a first-party perceiver's viewpoint, they remain relevant to assessments and responses of third parties toward distributions, procedures, or treatments experienced by others.

First, individuals attempt to make sense out of their social experience (see Fiske and Taylor 1991; van den Bos, Lind, et al. 2001) and are thus likely to assess the justice of their outcomes, decision-making procedures, or their treatment—especially when they violate their expectations. In effect, such assessments allow people to address concerns about potential problems associated with social interdependence, including authority and identity processes. These judgments involve taking into consideration a variety of information to produce a justice evaluation.

Second, evaluations of injustice produce the unpleasant sensations of distress and tension (Adams 1965; Walster, Walster, and Bersheid 1978). Observation of others' injustice may also create a similar, though perhaps less intense, feeling. Essentially, the second assumption parallels theoretical perspectives pertaining to relationships (Heider 1958), attitudes (Festinger 1957), and emotions (Smith-Lovin and Heise 1988) that argue that imbalance or inconsistency is disagreeable. Also stemming from these balance models, the third assumption is that people are motivated to relieve the distress or tension by restoring either psychological or actual justice for themselves or for others. Adams (1965) suggests that individuals pursue the least costly means to readdress injustice. Van den Bos, Lind, and Wilke (2001) have recently reiterated his point, explicitly emphasizing the cognitive analysis of material costs and benefits associated with possible reactions. They also argue that fairness judgments act as heuristic guides to interpreting other information and events.

Additional assumptions about social interaction, such as what it is people seek from their contacts with others, help explain why individuals are motivated to assess the justice of their outcomes, procedures, or treatment. Lind and Tyler (1988) contrast instrumental and group-value models, the former focusing on material outcomes and the latter involving identity concerns. Most distributive justice models, with their emergence rooted in social exchange theories, assume instrumental behavior. Individuals seek to maximize positive outcomes with the least expenditure of real or psychological costs. Distributive justice ensures that recipients obtain the outcomes expected based on fair distribution rules. The assumption of instrumental behavior, however, also accounts for the preference for distribution rules that maximize one's own gains or the evaluation of over-reward as fair (see Hegtvedt 1992).

Similarly, Thibaut and Walker's (1975) model of procedural justice takes an instrumental approach with the assumption that people desire fair procedures because they ensure fair distributions. This instrumental orientation leads individuals to seek both decision control and process control (voice) in decision-making situations to secure positive outcomes. Drawing on work demonstrating that concern with procedures is often independent of outcome levels, Lind and Tyler (1988) offer an alternative to the instrumental model. Their group-value model of procedural justice (later extended and referred to as the "relational model" [Tyler and Lind, 1992]) focuses upon individuals' long-term interest in group relationships. Drawing from social identity theory (Tajfel and Turner 1979, 1986), Lind and Tyler argue that people want to be well-regarded within the groups to which they belong and that procedurally just rules and treatment communicates this sentiment. In this model, then, individuals seek to be valued members of their groups, which in turn increases their self-esteem.

On the surface, the instrumental and group-value models seem quite distinct. The instrumental model, akin to a self-interested approach, appears to contradict the notion that "fairness considerations are moral beliefs and rules about right and wrong and what should and what should not be done" (Peters, van den Bos, and Bobocel 2004, 258). Moreover, justice, as distinct from individual deserving, belongs to the collectivity and thus should foster social cooperation (see Hegtvedt 2005; Wenzel 2002). The group-value model emphasizes group relationships and the ties of individuals to their groups by virtue of identity processes. Such ties may underscore particular moral beliefs about right and wrong. In addition, the group-value model resonates more closely with the justice motive, defined in terms of people's need to believe the world is just and to behave accordingly (see Lerner and Lerner 1981). In other words, the pursuit of justice is separate from that of self-interest (see Tyler and Dawes 1993).

Upon closer examination, however, the main assumption of the group-value model is of the same ilk as that of the instrumental model. With the group-value model's focus on decision making or interaction dynamics, the outcome is simply of another type. The group-value model emphasizes maximization of outcomes in the form of intangible, infinite social well-being, whereas the instrumental model presumes that outcomes are tangible, material, and usually finite. To obtain social rewards like those suggested by the group-value model, it is likely that behavior and distributions will also benefit other group members, thereby appearing more just (Hegtvedt 1992). In addition, Wenzel (2000) incorporates identity processes—long the stronghold of procedural justice arguments—more explicitly into a distributive justice framework. By doing so, he calls greater attention to the social context and the meaning of inclusion in the social group for justice evaluations. Those meanings may be dramatically affected by whether the perceiver is also a recipient of outcomes or a target of procedures and treatments.

Recognition of the potential symmetries in motivations and processes of the instrumental and group-value models may allow for greater theoretical integration of issues of distributive, procedural, and interactional justice. Attempts to contrast between pure self-interest and justice per se (e.g., Hegtvedt 2005; Messick and Sentis 1979; Thompson and Loewenstein 1992) require careful consideration of the situational conditions enhancing or mitigating motivations and identity implications of those conditions. The pursuit of individualistic self-interest characterizes a key social value in the developed, Western world, yet the pursuit of justice captures a significant normative element that bears upon social order. Although the contrast between the motivations is most striking for first-party perceivers, the contrast may also remain relevant for third parties whose perceptions and behaviors ultimately ensure justice for others.

The basic terms and assumptions are the building blocks of the basic model of justice. The model is from the viewpoint of a cognitively rational perceiver who uses information about the situation, as colored by his or her own characteristics, beliefs, and motivations, to make a justice evaluation and, if negative, respond to the injustice by eliminating the resulting distress.

ANALYZING THE BASIC MODEL OF JUSTICE PROCESSES

The basic model of justice processes belies a great deal of complexity that hundreds of justice studies have addressed in the last 50 years. The intent here is to amplify the model by examining its constituent relationships without getting lost in a quagmire of intricacies. Specific theoretical paradigms or concepts inform the overview. Reasons emerge for the different ideas about justice; differential perceptions of injustice; and potentially distinct reactions to the same (objectively) unjust distribution, procedure, or treatment.

Analysis of the model begins by examining components identified as perceiver factors and situational factors to reveal patterns about what people perceive as just. Then consideration shifts to the processes underlying how perceiver factors combine with situational factors to produce the justice evaluation. These processes and factors may also impinge on the assumed links between the justice evaluation and emotional, cognitive, and behavioral reactions.

Perceiver Factors

Perceiver factors include individual characteristics, beliefs, and motivations. These factors are interrelated insofar as characteristics may affect beliefs, and both may influence motivations or, alternatively, motivations may affect beliefs. Situational conditions, in turn, may shape aspects of all. This model component incorporates a wide array of factors that are likely to impinge on actors' perceptions of the situation. Early work on allocation or distribution rule preferences addresses these factors, laying the basis for identifying ideas about justice under varying situational circumstances and ultimately revealing the emergence of different justice evaluations. Some work in procedural and interactional justice also focuses on these issues.

Leventhal and colleagues (1980) develop a theory of allocation and procedural preferences. They assume that individuals hold expectancies about how a particular distribution or procedural principle will facilitate or interfere with a given goal. These goals include fairness per se but also self-interest, efficiency, obedience, or other pragmatic concerns. Because individuals may pursue more than one goal, each of varying importance, the combined importance of all relevant goals and the expectancy regarding how well a particular principle will affect attainment of the goal produces a hierarchy of preferences. Although some studies set up conditions that Leventhal and colleagues argue should enhance the pursuit of fairness (e.g., emphasis on fairness, minimization of the importance of other goals), few explicitly test the implications of combined goals or a hierarchy of preferences. In addition, most studies equate individuals' expressions of their preferred principles with what they believe to be just. Individual characteristics and other beliefs affect these empirical beliefs about justice.

Individual Characteristics. Characteristics that describe individuals pertain to statuses such as age and gender, which transcend the situation; performance level, or position more formally; and identity, especially in relationship to other group members. These characteristics affect which distribution or procedural principle individuals are likely to express as a preference or as a just rule.

The effects of age and gender have been examined largely in the distributive justice literature (see Hegtvedt and Cook 2001). The age contrasts between children suggest that different levels of cognitive development and role-taking abilities affect children's preferences, with younger children, whose cognitive structures are less developed, opting for a simple equal distribution or a self-interested allocation. The availability of contextual information, however, disrupts the simple developmental ordering of reward allocations. Similarly, the nature of the allocation context also influences gender differences when the allocator is a corecipient. Although studies that show that female allocators take less for themselves than male allocators, regardless of comparative input levels, confirm stereotypical images of females as communally oriented and males as agency oriented, when females and males work on tasks that are defined as culturally appropriate for their respective genders, both opt for equitable distributions. And when allocations are public, males and females both tend toward equal distributions. Thus age and gender alone hardly specify what is likely to be considered just.

Within a situation, an individual's position in terms of work performance or authority relations may become salient. In impersonal work situations, high performers are likely to prefer equitable distributions and low performers inequitable ones (see Cook and Hegtvedt 1983). Such a pattern is consistent with a materially self-interested orientation. As noted later, under more personal conditions, this pattern alters.

Procedural justice studies examine subordinates' preferences for different rules in the context of authority relationships (but without comparisons to authorities' preferences). Subordinates especially like procedures that allow them to voice their opinions on issues that affect them (see Lind and Tyler 1988) and that provide rationale for an authority's decision (Bies and Shapiro 1987). Providing rationale for decisions signals that subordinates are important group members and thus bolsters their identity within the group.

Although identity processes are fundamental to the group-value model of procedural justice, they are less so to distributive justice models. When identity is analyzed, it is in the form of identification with a particular group. Clay-Warner (2001) notes that people are likely to identify most closely with those with whom they share multiple status identities, although the effect of these identities on justice processes depends upon contextual factors. In allocation studies, results typically indicate that individuals give more to their own groups (often defined by trivial criteria in an experimental setting) and evaluate them more positively than other groups (see Tajfel and Turner 1979). Stronger identification within a group, however, tends to reduce preferences for self-interested allocations within the group (Wenzel 2002). In procedural justice studies, identity is an outcome rather than an impetus to defining procedural justice (see Tyler and Lind 1992). Yet applying Wenzel's (2002) argument, a strong identity within a group may promote fair procedural and interactional rules.

Skitka (2003) draws attention to personal identities, explaining that what people define as fair depends upon the activation of different aspects of the self (e.g., material, social, moral). Clayton and Optow (2003) illustrate this idea by showing that seeing oneself as environmentally aware stimulates greater concerns with environmental injustice. This emphasis on identity represents a new direction in the analysis of the role of personal beliefs in justice processes.

Beliefs. The codification of individual belief systems and their impact on what individuals deem as just has received only minimal attention. There is evidence that individuals who adhere to the Protestant ethic are more likely to award amounts commensurate to worker inputs than those who do not express that ethic (see Hegtvedt and Cook 2001). Attempts to dissect the impact of liberal and conservative philosophies (e.g., Tetlock and Mitchell 1993) demonstrate that justice judgments remain sensitive to contextual factors. Likewise, beliefs about one's self, as captured in self-esteem, interact with other situational elements (see Tyler et al. 1997).

In contrast to individual belief systems, a great deal of research has focused on cultural beliefs (see Morris and Leung 2000). Generally, emphasis rests on the extent to which cultural beliefs, which capture dimensions of values (e.g., collectivistic versus individualistic), affect what people perceive as a just distribution. For example, more collectivistically oriented Chinese tend to opt for equality in distributions with in-group members—a pattern not typically found among Americans. The distinction between in- and out-group members, however, again implies the impact of situational conditions on beliefs. In cross-cultural studies of justice, analysis must indicate how abstract ideas are construed and enacted within particular cultures.

Motivations. The patterns of preferences based on individual characteristics and beliefs denote underlying motivations. Some characteristics or beliefs appear to generate distribution or procedural preferences that reflect material self-interests. Others, like cultural beliefs promoting collectivism, hint at preferences that appear more justice oriented or at least reflect the maximization of social rewards. And as Leventhal and colleagues (1980) contend, multiple goals may operate in a situation and stimulate complex motivations.

When instructed to pursue fairness, first-party allocators' preferences are more like those of impartial third parties. Sometimes, however, the amount that people claim as fair for themselves is distinct from what they perceive as fair for others. This "egocentric bias" (Messick and Sentis 1979) shows that even when trying to be fair individuals judge a larger amount to themselves as fair than the same amount to another. Tyler and Dawes (1993) argue that activation of a prosocial motivation, like that implied by the group-value model, may lead to distributions and procedures that appear less motivated by egoistic concerns. Situational conditions, combined with individual characteristics or beliefs, may stimulate such activation.

Situational Factors

Researchers have investigated a wide variety of situational factors that influence people's beliefs about justice and their evaluations of an actual distribution or procedure. Allocation studies focus on the former, whereas studies addressing justice perceptions per se pertain to the latter. This section examines the former, focusing on situational factors uniquely relevant to distributive justice (e.g., characteristics of what is being distributed, the availability of outcomes) as well as to all types of justice (e.g., interpersonal relationships).

Although most distributive justice research focuses on the distribution of benefits, the distribution of burdens or harms is also fundamental to society (e.g., taxes). While a number of researchers have attempted to distinguish what is fair in the distribution of rewards compared to the allocations of expenses or losses (see Hegtvedt and Cook 2001), no consistent pattern emerges. It appears that actors interpret the distribution of benefits and burdens in the context of other situational factors as well as in terms of their own belief systems and motivations. For example, competitive motivations spur equitable distributions of negative outcomes but other motivations lead to equal distributions.

In contrast, several conditions (see Hegtvedt and Markovsky 1995) inspire prosocial motivations, at least with regard to the distribution of rewards. The inadequacy of rewards to meet all pay expectations increases the responsibility of the allocator and draws attention to the fate of other group members, thus leading to distributions that appear beneficial to others. Increasing an allocator's self-awareness of his or her role or making a public distribution shapes distributions that do not reflect material self-interest. And group discussion may result in the adoption of distribution principles that appear to sacrifice the material self-interest of the one who suggested the rule.

In effect, such conditions personalize the situation. A great deal of research (see Hegtvedt and Cook 2001) confirms different distribution patterns between friends than between strangers. Regardless of performance level, friends tend to prefer equal distributions or ones that appear benevolent to one's partner. The stronger social bond between friends may enhance group identity and suppress material egoism in distributions (Tyler and Dawes 1993). A consequence of increased group identity may be increased emphasis on the importance of the interactional rules of standing, neutrality, and trust (see Tyler and Lind 1992).

Situational conditions thus moderate the effects of perceiver factors and shape motivations that allow, perhaps encourage, deviation from emphasis on material gains. What people believe is just—owing to their characteristics, beliefs, or situational circumstances—

provides the basis for the just share, as previously conceptualized. To produce a justice evaluation, individuals compare their ideas about the just share to their perceptions of the actual inputs and outcomes, decision-making procedures, or interaction.

Producing a Justice Evaluation

Although Jasso (1980, 2002) offers a mathematical formulation for the justice evaluation, most research focuses more informally on perceptions of justice, often measured by responses to an ordinal scale. Individuals indicate to what extent they perceive a particular distribution, procedure, or treatment to be fair or just. Both approaches capture variation in terms of the severity of an injustice. While Jasso's formulation formally represents the magnitude of under- and over-reward, the ordinal measures require other information to indicate the nature of the unfairness. Theorists (Adams 1965; Jasso 1980; Markovsky 1985) recognize that under-reward is likely to be judged as more unfair than over-reward and consequently more distressful. Presumably, the justice evaluation or perception results from trying to make sense out of social experiences, given beliefs about what is just. Such beliefs, coupled with motivations, shape interpretation of situational factors through processes of social cognition and comparison, which ultimately produces a justice evaluation.

Social Cognition Processes. Social cognition involves structures of knowledge, such as those represented in schemas about categories of people, concepts, roles, situations, and the like, as well as processes pertaining to attention, memory, and inferences (Fiske and Taylor 1991; Howard 1995). To varying degrees, the inference process has been integrated into explanations of the development of justice evaluations. Although theoretically perceivers may gather a variety of information, typically they rely upon preexisting expectations, or schemas, to select from all of the available information. Perceivers also tend to take shortcuts—to use heuristics—to reduce complex information to simpler forms to allow for more efficient processing. The final assessments may not reflect rational, objectively accurate strategies but rather the influence of biases owing to motivations, inadequate information, employment of heuristics, and so forth. Given that individuals may differentially process information, the subjective justice evaluation of the same distribution, procedure, or treatment may vary.

Researchers most frequently apply attribution—the process of inferring causes about behavior (see Howard 1995). With regard to distributive justice research, Cohen (1982) argues that if individuals presume external factors like luck are the source of inputs, they are more likely to discount those inputs as a credible basis for allocating rewards. Conversely, when people overcome constraints to ensure high contributions, those inputs are attributed internally, to effort or ability, and thus weigh more heavily in determining outcomes. Receipt of (unexpected) unfavorable outcomes is likely to stimulate a search for an explanation (van den Bos et al. 1999), activating the attribution process and scrutiny of the procedures used to determine the outcome distribution. Ultimately, external attributions about a perpetrator's behavior may attenuate the severity of the perceived injustice, whereas internal attributions have the opposite effect (Utne and Kidd 1980). Mikula (2003) shows this pattern: internal attributions of causality and intention in the absence of justification clearly enhanced the perception of injustice.

Referent cognition theory (Folger 1986) draws attention to the underlying role of more general cognitions in assessments of justice, uniting procedural with distributive justice. Folger focuses on referent cognitions pertaining to (1) the distance between the actual outcome and the referent outcome, (2) the likelihood of remedying the situation, and (3) the extent to which the injustice is justifiable because other, more appropriate procedures cannot be imagined. Individuals are likely to deduce the greatest injustice when they perceive their outcomes to fall short of referent ones, recognize few available remedies, and believe that suitable alternative procedures could have been used. These cognitions also affect the degree of inequity distress and strategies for responses to the injustice.

The recent development of fairness heuristic theory heralds emphasis on cognitions and information processing as well as a new point of departure for linking procedural and distributive justice (e.g., Lind et al. 1993; van den Bos et al. 1997; van den Bos, Lind, and Wilke 2001). The theory argues that procedural information has an advantage over distribution information insofar as procedures carry easily interpretable information about an individual's inclusion in the group. Information about inclusion may reflect on interactional justice as well as affect interpretations about received outcomes. Insofar as evaluations of outcomes require comparison information that may be unavailable, people rely on more readily available procedural information. Van den Bos and colleagues (1997) show that the "fair process effect" (the reliance on procedural justice as a cognitive heuristic) influences distributive justice judgments when people cannot compare outcome levels across group members. Reliance on procedural information diminishes when people have information about the outcomes of others.

Social Comparison Processes. Comparison information has long been touted as key to understanding assessments of distributive justice. It is also implicit in referent cognition theory, thus drawing procedural justice into the fold. With regard to distributive justice assessments, several types of comparisons exist. The internal comparison allows an actor to assess outcomes to himself or herself across time. Adams's (1965) theoretical formulation of equity and subsequent variations emphasizes the local comparison, epitomized by the original formula $O_A/I_A = O_B/I_B$, where O represents the outcomes of an actor, I indicates their inputs (contributions, typically of material value but also potentially of status value), and the subscripts refer to two different actors. But as Berger and colleagues' (1972) formulation of a status-value approach to justice indicates, the equity formula disregards the importance of placing the local comparison in the context of what other similar others receive. Referential comparisons to abstract others with the same social characteristics indicate "what people like us normally get," thereby allowing assessments about whether the two actors represented in the equity formula are both or individually under-rewarded, fairly rewarded, or over-rewarded.

Two forms of group-level comparisons also exist. The first, an extension of the referential comparison, assesses how well one's group fared compared to another group (Markovsky 1985). And the second, implied by fairness heuristic theory, suggests comparisons of one individual across all other group members. Such within-group comparisons may involve aggregating repeated local comparisons to allow a person to determine if he or she is under-rewarded, equitably rewarded, or over-rewarded vis-à-vis each member of the group.

Although studies constrain the choice among comparisons, Törnblom (1977) offers propositions regarding the impact of combinations of internal, local, and referential comparisons. Combinations in which there is the most consistent disadvantageous injustice are likely to spur the motivation to redress the situation. Markovsky (1985) also demonstrates that between-group comparisons are more likely with increasing group identification. And evaluations of justice in social exchange networks often allow for within-group comparisons. Observed inequality of outcomes in a network may constrain subsequent power use by those in power-advantaged positions (Cook and Emerson 1978) and may lead to more severe assessments of injustice by those disadvantaged in the exchanges (Molm, Quist, and Wisely 1994).

Folger and Kass (2000) note that the role of social comparisons diminished as emphasis shifted from distributive justice to procedural justice issues. They argue that individuals employ comparisons as mental constructions of alternative scenarios to understand their outcomes or treatment. They also stress the use of others' opinions as a source of influence on justice perceptions. Such an idea resonates with Hegtvedt and Johnson's (2000) integration of legitimacy and justice processes, in which collective sources of support and approval for a distribution, procedure, or decision maker allow individuals to compare their own assessments with what others—their peers or their superiors—think. Such work reveals how legitimacy in a situation influences fairness perceptions (see Jost and Major 2001).

Although few dispute the underlying role of social cognitions and social comparisons in assessments of justice, little research explicitly studies these processes. More frequently, researchers employ these processes, in varying degrees of explicitness, in their arguments regarding the effects of situational factors on justice evaluations.

Effects of Situational Factors. Some studies emphasize situational factors such as group structure and dynamics. In social exchange studies, for example, variation in structural position produces differences in justice perceptions. Stolte (1983) demonstrates that disadvantaged actors judge outcome distributions as more unfair. Individuals are more likely to judge their partner's behavior as fair under conditions of reciprocal exchange than under conditions of negotiated exchange (Molm, Takahashi, and Peterson 2003). Although negotiation ostensibly involves many of the characteristics of procedural justice (e.g., communication, means to control outcomes), these elements also seem to highlight the potential for conflict, whereas reciprocal exchange requires greater trust. Likewise, Hegtvedt and Killian (1999) show that conflict between the rule preferences of negotiators reduces perceived procedural justice, whereas own outcome levels and bargaining success enhance the perceived fairness of the outcome distribution.

The organizational context also influences perceptions of justice. Schminke, Cropanzano, and Rupp (2002) show that less centralized organizational structures and ones involving higher levels of formalization produce stronger perceptions of distributive, procedural, and interactional justice, although one's hierarchical position moderates the strength of these effects. Mueller and Landsman (2004) demonstrate that the legitimacy of promotion criteria in an organization positively affects perceptions of procedural justice, which in turn mediates the effects of legitimacy on perceptions of distributive justice. In effect, justice evaluations result from the dynamic cognitive and comparison processes that involve information available about the situation—its structure, its people.

Responding to the Justice Evaluation

The heuristic model of justice processes indicates that perceived injustice leads first to emotional reactions and subsequently to cognitive and behavioral responses. Presumably, a negative justice evaluation creates distress, which individuals are motivated to relieve by changing their cognitions about the situation or altering their behavior. As noted previously, theorists have delineated types of reactions that may follow perceived distributive, procedural, or interactional injustice. A great deal of research supports parts of the model and the key assumptions as well as introduces social cognition processes to determine reactions. Despite this, there is some debate about the sequencing of perceptions and emotional reactions and generally too few tests of the fundamental mediation processes implied by the model.

Emotional Reactions. Equity theorists (Adams 1965; Homans 1974; Walster, Walster, and Berscheid 1978) argue that individuals are likely to feel distressed as a result of perceived injustice. This argument presupposes that an evaluation of some sort, involving cognitions and comparisons, occurs before the experience of any emotion. Jasso (1980) contends that the justice evaluation appears to be instantaneous, which to some extent raises the question of whether the cognition or the emotion occurs first. Scher and Heise (1993), in contrast, argue that the emotional reaction may precede the cognitive evaluation of the situation. In other words, individuals feel something that is out of sync with a particular identity and then attempt to determine the source of the feeling to maintain that identity. Empirical research has yet to test this proposition. Theory and research in the sociology of emotions, however, has contributed to a more nuanced understanding of emotional reactions, under various situational conditions.

Early work on emotional responses focused largely on global measures of distress and occasionally employed physiological measures (see Hegtvedt and Markovsky 1995). Although the pattern of responses corresponded to that predicted by equity theory, the measures often failed to take into account the distinct emotional experiences of under-rewarded compared to equitably rewarded and over-rewarded individuals. Subsequent research (e.g., Hegtvedt 1990; Sprecher 1992) shows greater contentment or satisfaction among equitably rewarded individuals than others and greater anger among the under-rewarded than others. Results are more equivocal regarding feelings of guilt among the over-rewarded. Unless the overbenefit is at another's expense in an interdependent relationship (Sprecher 1992), guilt levels rarely vary systematically across reward levels or vary at such low levels as to be relatively meaningless (Hegtvedt 1990). Peters, van den Bos, and Bobocel (2004) suggest that overpayment engenders conflict between egoistic and fairness considerations. When contrasting reactions to an individual's own and others' overpayment, their results show that people think others are more satisfied with being overpaid than they themselves are. This moral superiority may account for the low levels of guilt typically observed.

Situational conditions—like power, interdependence, and so forth—coupled with consideration of the nature of particular emotions provides a basis for extending understanding of emotional responses to injustice. Considering these factors in a bargaining situation, Hegtvedt and Killian (1999) show how procedural and distributive justice perceptions affect distinct negative emotions. While both procedural injustice and distributive injustice to self affect general negative feelings, only the former also influences depression. And only perceptions of another's distributive injustice increase feelings of guilt. The study highlights distinct emotional reactions as well as types and targets of injustice but fails to examine whether perceptions mediate emotional responses.

Younts and Mueller (2001), however, use survey data to examine the mediating role of justice perceptions on satisfaction. Their results demonstrate that the pay comparison, actual pay, autonomy, and justice importance have direct effects on pay satisfaction and, most important, the effects of the first three factors are largely mediated by justice perceptions. Although this study illustrates the crucial role of justice perceptions on one type of emotional response, such mediating models are rarely found in research on other types of reactions. Likewise, little research contrasts experienced and expressed emotions—a contrast that may have implications for understanding other types of reactions.

Cognitive and Behavioral Responses. Although Adams (1965) recognized that responses to distributive injustice may be both cognitive and behavioral, most research focuses on observable, behavioral reactions. The lack of such a response may signal a variety of things: no felt injustice, unobserved cognitive responses, or concerns that a behavioral response may be too costly in terms of time, material expenses, social relations, or the like. Researchers attribute the lack of a response by the disadvantaged to cognitive biases, beliefs in a just world, minimization of personal discrimination, and the need to suppress resentment over deprivation (e.g., Olson and Hafer 2001). In addition, individual characteristics such as equity sensitivity, exchange orientation, and self-esteem (see Hegtvedt and Cook 2001) condition behavioral reactions.

Early experimental work on responses to pay inequity typically constrained the possible behavioral responses and usually measured only one response. Typically, over-rewarded subjects increased their productivity or took less bonus pay whereas under-rewarded actors did not consistently decrease their productivity but would take more bonus pay for themselves if possible (see Cook and Hegtvedt 1983). Utne and Kidd (1980) argue that attributions about an injustice affect reactions. If unjustly treated actors attribute their plight to factors external to a presumed perpetrator, they are less likely to make active responses than when they perceive another person responsible for their injustice. For example, shared perceptions of leader responsibility for inequity result in collective responses (Lawler and Thompson 1978) and provision of rationale for the apparent unfair treatment reduces the likelihood of changes in work performance (Sharpley 1991). Hegtvedt, Thompson, and Cook (1993) demonstrate that attributions to self (but not to the exchange partner, the interaction, or the situation) mediate between situational conditions and anticipated positive reactions to equitable and overpay conditions.

A great deal of research suggests that situational factors such as power, group identity or commitment, and procedural justice moderate reactions. In exchange networks, power-disadvantaged individuals may be unable to respond behaviorally to outcome in-equalities owing to the constraints of their position but power-advantaged individuals—especially those who attribute their higher outcomes externally—may rectify the injustice by giving more to their partners (Cook, Hegtvedt, and Yamagishi 1988). Markovsky (1985) highlights the importance of group bonds in shifting responses from an individual focus to a collective focus. High commitment to a work organization, coupled with perceived unfair-ness, may result in less work effort, lower commitment, and greater turnover intention (Brockner, Tyler, and Cooper-Schneider 1992). Yet to the extent that group members see the system that produced unequal rewards as legitimate, individuals are less likely to com-plain or attempt to change the system (Walker and Zelditch 1993). Also, when procedures are fair, individuals are less likely to respond negatively to an unfair distribution (see Tyler et al. 1997).

In effect, procedural justice leads to the acceptance of outcomes that appear objectively unfair. While people are most offended when both procedures and outcomes are unfair (Greenberg 1987), individuals also respond explicitly to procedural unfairness, indepen-dent of outcomes, in a variety of settings (see Tyler et al. 1997). Reactions to procedural injustice take the form of noncompliance with authorities or decreased self-esteem. Tyler (1990) shows that unfair encounters with legal authorities suppress obedience to laws. Likewise, rejection of nonbinding legal decisions is more likely if procedures are viewed as unfair (Lind et al. 1993). In contrast, people respond to procedural justice with greater willingness to help a group (Tyler and Degoey 1995) and greater cooperation (Tyler and Blader 2000) or, within organizations, greater commitment and lower likelihood of leaving (e.g., Martin and Bennett 1996). And fair treatment—demonstration of respect, neutrality, and trustworthiness—produces positive feelings of self-worth (e.g., Tyler, Degoey, and Smith 1996).

In assessing procedural injustice, individuals may also be likely to ask questions about why the injustice occurred. For example, van den Bos et al. (1999) use attributions to explain why individuals react more negatively when fair, as opposed to unfair, procedures produce an unfavorable outcome. And like research on distributive injustice, behavioral responses to procedural injustice may also be tempered by situational factors (see Tyler et al. 1997).

EXPANDING THE JUSTICE FRAMEWORK: SOME CONSIDERATIONS

The concept of justice embodies what is morally right or good. Few dispute the importance of a just society, a just decision, a just outcome, or the like. But what constitutes that just-ness continues to be debated. The social psychological approach to justice is one among many, generated by different disciplines, encouraged by different agendas. The basic social psychological model of justice processes (see Figure 3.1) heuristically represents the vast number of factors studied under the auspices of various theoretical arguments. In flushing out research germane to the model, it is evident that there are many reasons for people to promote different rules as just; evaluate outcome distributions, procedures, or treatments as differentially fair; and respond in various ways or not at all. Shared conceptions of justice within a moral community (Optow 1990) solidify a group; differential perceptions that justice exists may fuel conflict and inspire social changes (see Deutsch 2000; Mikula and Wenzel 2000). Besides this potential for solidarity and change, analysis of this model suggests themes for further consideration.

First, the analysis indicates that situational factors affect beliefs about what is just, perceptions of injustice, and reactions to injustice. Thus a justice framework must incorporate more explicitly the social context by charting how and why contextual factors influence motivations, shape cognitive processes, and constrain behavioral reactions. Perhaps situational factors increase the costs associated with challenging existing procedures or outcomes. And in considering social factors, it is important to recognize that the theoretically driven model of justice emphasizes mediating processes whereas extant studies pertain largely to the moderating effects of situational, relational, or individual-level factors. Both moderating factors and mediating processes point to reasons for differential perceptions and, especially, reactions to injustice. Distinguishing the two may have implications for resolving marital disputes, ensuring a congenial and productive work environment, and so forth.

Second, elements of the social context may affect the meanings that individuals hold for themselves and for others. While Tyler and colleagues (Tyler et al. 1997) stress the impact of procedural justice on self-esteem, recent work (e.g., Skitka 2003; Stets 2003) draws attention to how identities of individuals may illuminate the meaning of injustice and provide insight into the subjectivity of observed patterns of perceptions and reactions. Moreover, it is necessary to tackle the identity issue at both the individual and group level to reveal how the combination of multiple individual or group identities affects justice processes.

Third, the social implications of justice evaluations and reactions cannot be overlooked. Procedural justice theorists (see Tyler et al. 1997) call explicit attention to such concerns, although largely focused on feelings of self-worth to the group. Distributive justice researchers tend to limit their focus to implications of the outcome distributions for self. What is generally missing is research on justice for others. Yet ironically, some of the most fundamental social changes of the 20th century (e.g., women's voting rights, school desegregation) occurred because people who were unaffected or even advantaged by inequalities took action to ameliorate the disadvantage of others by seeking a more just distribution of opportunities. While injustice for others may or may not be experienced differently (Lind, Kray, and Thompson 1998; van den Bos and Lind 2001) from injustice for self, more explicit theorizing and empirical work might address the role of observers in ensuring justice for others, thereby informing the understanding of social movements, the success of advocacy groups, and the like.

Fourth, the evolution of the study of justice in social psychology has resulted in investigations of at least three types of justice: distributive, procedural, and interactional. Research on fairness heuristic theory examines the relationship between procedural and distributive justice. Tyler and his associates (Tyler et al. 1997) claim that procedural justice often matters more than distributive in predicting satisfaction, compliance, or other reactions. What is largely missing, however, are social conditions that alter the salience of the types of justice on other attitudes or behaviors. Clay-Warner, Hegtvedt, and Roman (2005) attempt to rectify this omission. They show that the experience of downsizing enhances the relevance of distributive justice to organizational commitment in future jobs while procedural justice is most predictive of organizational commitment for those who had not recently been laid off. Thus it is not simply a question of when a type of justice is relevant but of how situations alter the relative impact of distributive, procedural, and interactional justice on other processes.

Indeed, linking justice to other phenomena and extrapolating from basic research on justice to the larger social context is a final theme for consideration. Tyler and colleagues (1997) note the policy implications of procedural justice research in the law enforcement arena. Crosby and Franco (2003) explicitly employ justice theory to analyze affirmative action policy and politics. And organizational justice researchers draw out implications of studies for workplace morale, retention, and productivity (see Greenberg and Colquitt 2005). Far less of the research, however, seems applied to addressing social problems inherent in racism, sexism, environmental battles, and the like even though such issues are often cast as questions of justice. In addition, analysis of concrete social problems may inform theoretical issues within justice.

To pursue many of these themes requires development of a stronger, more inclusive justice framework—one that explicitly identifies assumptions and derivations, links motivations to perceptions and actions, and allows cumulation of knowledge. As the historical record shows, there have been several fashions in justice research. Given the breadth of existing knowledge, systematizing it under a shared rubric seems to be the challenge of the 21st century.

NOTES

I thank the editor and Jody Clay-Warner for their helpful comments on earlier drafts.

1. This chapter focuses primarily on distributive and procedural justice. Interactional and informational justice (see Colquitt et al. 2001) have increasingly obtained attention in the organizational justice literature. They are, however, less developed theoretically.

2. Important reference chapters and books regarding the distributive and procedural justice literatures include Greenberg and Colquitt (2005), Cook and Hegtvedt (1983), Hegtvedt (2005), Hegtvedt and Cook (2001), Hegtvedt and Markovsky (1995), Törnblom (1992), Lind and Tyler (1988), and Tyler and colleagues (1997).

REFERENCES

Adams, J. Stacy. 1965. Inequity in social exchange. *Advances in Experimental Social Psychology* 2:267–99.

Berger Joseph, Morris Zelditch Jr., Bo Anderson, and Bernard P. Cohen. 1972. Structural aspects of distributive justice: A status value formation. In *Sociological Theories in Progress*, ed. J. Berger, M. Zelditch, and Bo Anderson, 119–46. Boston: Houghton Mifflin.

Bies, Robert J. 2001. Interactional (in)justice: The sacred and the profane. In *Advances in Organizational Justice*, ed. Jerald Greenberg and Russell Cropanzano, 89–118. Stanford, CA: Stanford University Press.

Bies, Robert J., and Debra L. Shapiro. 1987. Interactional fairness judgments: The influence of causal accounts. *Social Justice Research* 1:199–218.

Brocker, Joel, Tom R. Tyler, and R. Cooper-Schneider. 1992. The influence of prior commitment to an institution on reactions to perceived unfairness: The higher they are, the harder they fall. *Administrative Science Quarterly* 37:241–61.

Clayton, Susan, and Susan Optow. 2003. Justice and identity: Changing perspectives on what is fair. *Personality and Social Psychology Review* 7:298–310.

Clay-Warner, Jody. 2001. Perceiving procedural injustice: The effects of group membership and status. *Social Psychology Quarterly* 64:224–38.

Clay-Warner, Jody, Karen A. Hegtvedt, and Paul Roman. 2005. Procedural justice/ distributive justice: How experiences with downsizing condition their impact on job commitment. *Social Psychology Quarterly* 68:89–102.

Cohen, Ronald L. 1982. Perceiving justice: An attributional perspective. In *Equity and Justice in Social Behavior*, ed. Jerald Greenberg and Ronald L. Cohen, 119–60. New York: Academic Press.

Colquitt, Jason A., Donald E. Conlon, Michael J. Wesson, Christopher O. L. H. Porter, and K. Yee Ng. 2001. Justice at the millennium: A meta-analytic review of 25 years of organizational justice research. *Journal of Applied Psychology* 86:425–45.

Cook, Karen S., and Richard M. Emerson. 1978. Power, equity, and commitment in exchange networks. *American Sociological Review* 43:721–39.

Cook, Karen S., and Karen A. Hegtvedt. 1983. Distributive justice, equity, and equality. *Annual Review of Sociology* 9:217–41.

Cook, Karen S., Karen A. Hegtvedt, and Toshio Yamagishi. 1988. Structural inequality, legitimation, and reactions to inequity in exchange networks. In *Status Generalization: New Theory and Research*, ed. Murray Webster Jr. and Martha Foschi, 291–308. Stanford, CA: Stanford University Press.

Crosby, Faye J., and Jamie L. Franco. 2003. Connections between the ivory tower and the multicolored world: Linking abstract theories of social justice to the rough and tumble of affirmative action. *Personality and Social Psychology Review* 7:362–73.

Deutsch, Morton. 1975. Equity, equality, and need: What determines which value will be used as the basis for distributive justice? *Journal of Social Issues* 31:137–49.

———. 2000. Justice and conflict. In *The Handbook of Conflict Resolution: Theory and Practice*, ed. Morton Deutsch and Peter T. Coleman, 141–64. San Francisco: Jossey-Bass.

Festinger, Leon. 1957. *A Theory of Cognitive Dissonance*. Evanston, IL: Row, Peterson.

Fiske, Susan T., and Shelley E. Taylor. 1991. *Social Cognition*. New York: McGraw-Hill.

Folger, Robert. 1986. Re-thinking equity theory: A referent cognitions model. In *Justice in Social Relations*, ed. Hans Bierhoff, Ronald L. Cohen, and Jerald Greenberg, 145–63. New York: Plenum Press.

Folger, Robert, and Edward Eliyahu Kass. 2000. Social comparison and fairness: A counterfactual simulations perspective. In *Handbook of Social Comparison: Theory and Research*, ed. Jerry Suls and Ladd Wheeler, 423–41. New York: Kluwer Academic/Plenum.

Greenberg, Jerald. 1987. Reactions to procedural injustice in payment distributions: Do the ends justify the means? *Journal of Applied Psychology* 72:55–61.

Greenberg, Jerald, and Jason A. Colquitt, eds. 2005. *Handbook of Organizational Justice*. Mahwah, NJ: Erlbaum.

Hegtvedt, Karen A. 1990. The effects of relationship structure on emotional responses to inequity. *Social Psychology Quarterly* 53:214–28.

———. 1992. When is a distribution rule just? *Rationality and Society* 4:308–31.

———. 2005. Doing justice to the group: Examining the roles of the group in justice research. *Annual Review of Sociology* 31:25–45.

Hegtvedt, Karen A., and Karen S. Cook. 2001. Distributive justice: Recent theoretical developments and applications. In *Handbook of Justice Research in Law*, ed. Joseph Sanders and V. Lee Hamilton, 93–132. New York: Kluwer Academic/Plenum.

Hegtvedt, Karen A., and Cathryn Johnson. 2000. Justice beyond the individual: A future with legitimation. *Social Psychology Quarterly* 63:298–311.

Hegtvedt, Karen A., and Caitlin Killian. 1999. Fairness and emotions: Reactions to the process and outcomes of negotiations. *Social Forces* 78:269–303.

Hegtvedt, Karen A., and Barry Markovsky. 1995. Justice and injustice. In *Sociological Perspectives on Social Psychology*, ed. Karen S. Cook, Gary Alan Fine, and James House, 257–80. Boston: Allyn & Bacon.

Hegtvedt, Karen A., Elaine A. Thompson, and Karen S. Cook. 1993. Power and equity: What counts in explaining exchange outcomes? *Social Psychology Quarterly* 56:100–19

Heider, Fritz. 1958. *The Psychology of Interpersonal Relationships*. New York: Wiley.

Homans, George C. 1974. *Social Behavior: Its Elementary Forms*. New York: Harcourt, Brace & World.

Howard, Judith A. 1995. Social cognition. In *Sociological Perspectives on Social Psychology*, ed. Karen S. Cook, Gary Alan Fine, and James House, 90–117. Boston: Allyn & Bacon.

Jasso, Guillermina. 1980. A new theory of distributive justice. *American Sociological Review* 45:3–32.

———. 1983. Fairness of individual rewards and fairness of the reward distribution: Specifying the inconsistency between micro and macro principles of justice. *Social Psychology Quarterly* 46:185–99.

———. 2002. Formal theory. In *Handbook of Sociological Theory*, ed. Jonathan H. Turner, 37–68. New York: Kluwer Academic/Plenum.

Jost, John T., and Brenda Major, eds. 2001. *The Psychology of Legitimacy: Emerging Perspectives on Ideology, Justice, and Intergroup Relations.* Cambridge: Cambridge University Press.

Lawler, Edward J., and Thompson, Martha E. 1978. Impact of leader responsibility for inequity on subordinate revolts. *Social Psychology* 41:265–68.

Lerner, Melvin J., and S. C. Lerner, eds. 1981. *The Justice Motive in Social Behavior: Adapting to Times of Scarcity and Change.* New York: Plenum.

Leventhal, Gerald S., J. Karuza Jr., and W. R. Fry. 1980. Beyond fairness: A theory of allocation preferences. In *Justice and Social Interaction*, ed. Gerold Mikula, 167–218. New York: Springer-Verlag.

Lind, E. Allan, and Tom R. Tyler. 1988. *The Social Psychology of Procedural Justice.* New York: Plenum.

Lind, E. Allan, Laura Kray, and Leigh Thompson. 1998. The social construction of injustice: Fairness judgments in response to own and others' unfair treatment by authorities. *Organizational Behavior and Human Decision Processes* 75:1–22.

Lind, E. Allan, C. A. Kulik, Maureen Ambrose, and M. V. de Vera Park. 1993. Individual and corporate dispute resolution: Using procedural fairness as a decision heuristic. *Administrative Science Quarterly* 38:224–51.

Markovsky, Barry. 1985. Toward a multilevel distributive justice theory. *American Sociological Review* 50:822–39.

Martin, Christopher L., and Nathan Bennett. 1996. The role of justice judgments in explaining the relationship between job satisfaction and organizational commitment. *Group and Organization Management* 21:84–104.

Messick, David M., and Kenneth P. Sentis. 1979. Fairness and preference. *Journal of Experimental Social Psychology* 15:416–34.

Mikula, Gerold. 2003. Testing an attribution of blame model of judgments of injustice. *European Journal of Social Psychology* 44:793–811.

Mikula, Gerold, and Michael Wenzel. 2000. Justice and social conflict. *International Journal of Psychology* 35:126–35.

Molm, Linda D., Theron M. Quist, and Phillip A. Wisely. 1994. Imbalanced structures, unfair strategies: Power and justice in social exchange. *American Sociological Review* 59:98–121.

Molm, Linda D., Nobuyuki Takahashi, and Gretchen Peterson. 2003. In the eye of the beholder: Procedural justice in social exchange. *American Sociological Review* 68:128–52.

Morris, Michael W., and Kwok Leung. 2000. Justice for all? Progress in research on cultural variation in the psychology of distributive and procedural justice. *Applied Psychology* 49:100–32.

Mueller, Charles W., and Miriam J. Landsman. 2004. Legitimacy and justice perceptions. *Social Psychology Quarterly* 67:189–202.

Olson, James M., and Carolyn Hafer. 2001. Tolerance of personal deprivation. In *The Psychology of Legitimacy: Emerging Perspectives on Ideology, Justice, and Intergroup Relations*, ed. John T. Jost and Brenda Major, 157–75. Cambridge: Cambridge University Press.

Optow, Susan. 1990. Moral exclusion and injustice: An introduction. *Journal of Social Issues* 46:1–20.

Peters, Suzanne, Kees van den Bos, and Ramona Bobocel. 2004. The moral superiority effect: Self versus other differences in satisfaction with being overpaid. *Social Justice Research* 17: 257–74.

Scher, Steven J., and David R. Heise. 1993. Affect and the perception of injustice. *Advances in Group Processes* 10:223–52.

Schminke, Marshall, Russell Cropanzano, and Deborah E. Rupp. 2002. Organization structure and fairness of perceptions: The moderating effects of organizational level. *Organizational Behavior and Human Decision Processes* 89:881–905.

Sharpley, C. F. 1991. Giving a reason for unfairness: Effects of rationale on Australian students' performances within an implicit reward situation. *International Journal of Psychology* 26:71–81.

Skitka, Linda. 2003. Of different minds: An accessible identity model of justice reasoning. *Personality and Social Psychology Review* 7:286–97.

Smith-Lovin, Lynn, and David R. Heise, ed. 1988. *Analyzing Social Interaction: Research Advances in Affect Control Theory*. New York: Gordon & Breach.

Sprecher, Susan. 1992. How men and women expect to feel and behave in response to inequity in close relations. *Social Psychology Quarterly* 55:57–69.

Stets, Jan E. 2003. Justice, emotion, and identity theory. In *Advances in Identity Theory and Research*, ed. Peter J. Burke, Timothy J. Owens, Richard T. Serpes, and Peggy A. Thoits, 105–22. New York: Kluwer Academic/Plenum.

Stolte, John F. 1983. The legitimation of structural inequality: Reformulation and test of the self-evaluation argument. *American Sociological Review* 48:331–42.

Tajfel, Henri, and John Turner. 1979. An integrative theory of intergroup conflict. In *Psychology of Intergroup Relations*, ed. William G. Austin and Stephen Worchel, 33–47. Monterey, CA: Brooks/Cole.

———. 1986. The social identity theory of intergroup behavior. In *Psychology of Intergroup Relations*, ed. Stephen Worchel, 7–24. Chicago: Nelson Hall.

Tetlock, P. E., and G. Mitchell. 1993. Liberal and conservative approaches to justice: Conflicting psychological portraits. In *Psychological Perspectives on Justice: Theory and Application*, ed. B. A. Mellers and J. Baron, 234–55. London: Cambridge University Press.

Thibaut, John, and Laurens Walker. 1975. *Procedural Justice: A Psychological Analysis*. Hillsdale, NJ: Erlbaum.

Thompson, Leigh, and George Loewenstein. 1992. Egocentric interpretations of fairness and interpersonal conflict. *Organizational Behavior and Human Decision Processes* 51:176–97.

Törnblom, Kjell Y. 1977. Distributive justice: Typology and propositions. *Human Relations* 31:1–24.

———. 1992. The social psychology of distributive justice. In *Justice: Interdisciplinary Perspectives*, ed. Klaus Scherer, 177–236. Cambridge: Cambridge University Press.

Tyler, Tom R. 1990. *Why People Obey the Law*. New Haven, CT: Yale University Press.

Tyler, Tom R., and Steven L. Blader. 2000. *Cooperation in Groups: Procedural Justice, Social Identity, and Behavioral Engagement.* Philadelphia, PA: Psychology Press/Taylor & Francis.

Tyler, Tom R., Robert J. Boeckmann, Heather J. Smith, and Yuen J. Huo. 1997. *Social Justice in a Diverse Society.* Boulder, CO: Westview.

Tyler, Tom R., and Robin Dawes. 1993. Fairness in groups: Comparing the self-interest and social identity perspectives. In *Psychological Perspectives on Justice: Theory and Application*, ed. B. A. Mellers and J. Baron, 87–108. London: Cambridge University Press.

Tyler, Tom R., and Peter Degoey. 1995. Collective restraint in social dilemmas: Procedural justice and social identification effects on support for authorities. *Journal of Personality and Social Psychology* 69:482–97.

Tyler, Tom R., Peter Degoey, and Heather J. Smith. 1996. Understanding why the justice of group procedures matters. *Journal of Personality and Social Psychology* 70:913–30.

Tyler, Tom R., and E. Allan Lind. 1992. A relational model of authority in groups. *Advances in Experimental Social Psychology* 25:115–91.

Utne, M. K., and Robert F. Kidd. 1980. Equity and attribution. In *Justice and Social Interaction*, ed. Gerold Mikula, 63–93. New York: Springer-Verlag.

Van den Bos, Kees, Jan Bruins, Henk A. M. Wilke, and Elske Dronkert. 1999. Sometimes unfair procedures have nice aspects: On the psychology of the fair process effect. *Journal of Personality and Social Psychology* 77:324–36.

Van den Bos, Kees, and E. Allan Lind. 2001. The psychology of own versus others' treatment: Self-oriented and other-oriented effects on perceptions of procedural justice. *Personality and Social Psychology Bulletin* 27:1324–33.

Van den Bos, Kees, E. Allan Lind, Riel Vermunt, and Henk A. M. Wilke. 1997. How do I judge my outcome when I do not know the outcome of others? The psychology of the fair process effect. *Journal of Personality and Social Psychology* 72:1034–46.

Van den Bos, Kees, E. Allan Lind, and Henk A. M. Wilke. 2001. The psychology of procedural and distributive justice viewed from the perspective of fairness heuristic theory. In *Justice in the Workplace*, ed. Russell Cropanzano, 49–66. Mahwah, NJ: Erlbaum.

Walker, Henry A., and Morris Zelditch Jr. 1993. Power, legitimacy, and the stability of authority: A theoretical research program. In *Theoretical Research Programs*, ed. J. Berger and M. Zelditch Jr., 364–81. Stanford, CA: Stanford University Press.

Walster, Elaine, G. William Walster, and Ellen Berscheid. 1978. *Equity: Theory and Research.* Allyn & Bacon.

Wenzel, Michael. 2000. Justice and identity: The significance of inclusion for perceptions of entitlement and the justice motive. *Personality and Social Psychology Bulletin* 26:157–76.

———. 2002. What is social about justice? Inclusive identity and group values as the basis of the justice motive. *Journal of Experimental Social Psychology* 38:205–18.

Younts, C. Wesley, and Charles W. Mueller. 2001. Justice processes: specifying the mediating role of perceptions of distributive justice. *American Sociological Review* 66:125–45.

4 RATIONAL CHOICE

Michael W. Macy

The economist James Duesenberry (1960, 233) wrote that "economics is all about how people make choices; sociology is all about how people don't have any choices to make." Duesenberry's insight is amusing and suggestive, but he got it wrong. If we are to locate the disciplinary boundary using Duesenberry's method, then the difference between sociology and economics is simply this: *sociology is about how people have no choices to make, while economics is about how they have only one.* If we want to learn how people make choices with more than one option, including choices they later regret, a good place to start might be social psychology or the increasingly prominent field of behavioral economics.

Why only one choice? For economists, rational behavior is logically determined by a schedule of preferences and a postulate of full information. The only choice is the one that maximizes utility. Logical determination explains why, until recently, economists have had surprisingly little interest in cognitive or social psychology or in the study of human motivation, bias, or influence.[1]

Game theory provides a compelling illustration of the deterministic model of behavior. Solutions often require the assumption that players know how their partner will behave, which is reasonable if the partner has no choice but to optimize over a set of fixed preferences. This inevitability can transform a game with a definite end point into something akin to Greek tragedy. If the partner's last move in a game is known to all players in iterated Prisoner's Dilemma, there will be no "shadow of the future" as an incentive for cooperation on the last move. If the partner's last move is known, then there is no incentive for cooperation on the next-to-last move, and so on, all the way back to the first move. Both players are trapped from the outset by the inescapable implication of the endgame, no matter how many years into the future that might be. Homer would be impressed.

Experimentalists have tested the endgame hypothesis in the lab and found no experimental evidence for backward induction of more than one or two moves (Selten and Stoecker 1986). Behavioral economists and social psychologists, including those who rely on choice-theoretic assumptions in modeling social exchange (Willer 1999) and collective action (Kollock 1998), have a very different understanding of rationality than the stylized model of *Homo economicus* as a perfect calculating machine with an unfailing ability to locate the global optimum. Among those who study human decision making, rationality is widely recognized as adaptive rather than calculating. Adaptive rationality implies behavior that is shaped by experience and by influence from others. This chapter will compare and contrast these two interpretations of rational choice, the classical *Homo economicus* who has only one choice to make and an alternative based on adaptive rationality that places much greater emphasis on the social psychology of behavior and is attracting growing attention from decision theorists, game theorists, and behavioral and experimental economists.

CAN ACTIONS BE CAUSED BY THEIR CONSEQUENCES?

Rational choice is not a theory but a theoretical framework for consequentialist explanations of purposive individual and collective action. Purposive actions have outcomes to which they are attracted. The consequentialist explanatory framework poses a teleological quandary: how can the future influence the past (Elster 1990, 129–35)? When the feedback loop passes through individual cognition, the ability for outcomes to generate their own causes becomes a problem in the theory of knowledge. This section explores two solutions to this feedback problem in consequentialist models of behavior, one grounded in a rationalist epistemology, the other in an evolutionary alternative.

Calculated Rationality

Orthodox rational choice theory (RCT) assumes forward-looking, purposeful, analytic actors who consciously and deliberately choose among alternatives based on expected outcomes. The analytic ability to forecast returns on competing investments brings the future to bear on the present. The calculus of rational expectations requires cognitive representations of causal relationships that are sufficiently accurate for optimal outcomes to attract the choices that generate them. The ideal type is based on "the neoclassical economic model in which rational agents operating under powerful assumptions about the availability of information and the capability of optimizing can achieve an efficient reallocation of resources among themselves through costless trading" (Axelrod 1997, 4).

Lave and March (1975, 248) have characterized this forward-looking deliberative process as "calculated rationality," in which "the individual uses information about the situation facing him to calculate, according to some rational process, the proper decision." By grasping the logical or mathematical structure of a well-defined problem, the likely consequences of alternative courses of action can be known before the fact. Thus the future can beckon the past.

Back to the Future: An Evolutionary Alternative

Consequentialism is not limited to outcomes that can be predicted from first principles. An alternative "evolutionary epistemology" (Schull 1996) avoids reliance on higher order causal reasoning and instead assumes that knowledge is the distillation of cumulative experience. Through repeated exposure to a recurrent problem, the consequences of alternative courses of action can be iteratively explored, by an individual or population. Recurrence, not prediction, supplies the link to the future by recycling the lessons of the past. Iterative search provides a backward-looking alternative to *Homo economicus* in consequentialist theories of action. The consequences that matter are those that have already occurred, not those the actors intend. Adaptive actors look forward by holding a mirror to the past.

Lave and March (1975, 248) call this "adaptive rationality," which they distinguish from "calculated rationality" in that the actors "learn in a regular manner from trial and error." Trial and error is "based on the principle that what works well for a player is more likely to be used again, whereas what turns out poorly is more likely to be discarded" (Axelrod 1997, 47). The principle can operate at two levels, the individual and the population. Individuals learn through processes like habituation, reinforcement, and Bayesian updating. Populations adapt through evolutionary processes of selective replication, heuristic imitation, and social influence.

Learning alters the probability distribution of beliefs and behavioral responses competing for attention within each individual. Positive outcomes increase the probability that the associated behavior will be repeated, while negative outcomes reduce it. The process closely parallels evolutionary selection, in which positive outcomes increase a strategy's chances for survival and reproduction, while negative outcomes reduce it (Axelrod and Cohen 2000). However, this need not imply that adaptive actors will learn the strategies favored by evolutionary selection pressures (Fudenberg and Levine 1998; Schlag and Pollock 1999). In evolution, strategies compete *between* the individuals that carry them, not *within*. Evolution thus alters the frequency distribution of behavioral responses competing for reproduction within a population. In biological evolution, these responses are genetically encoded in DNA; in cultural evolution, they are encoded in norms, rituals, routines, traditions, mores, protocols, and the like.

Evolutionary models of rational action posit an iterative and stochastic selection process that alters the probability distribution of rules in an ecology characterized by finite resources that constrain propagation. Learning models posit an additional selection mechanism that operates on the probability distribution of rules within the behavioral repertoires of individual actors. These models of adaptive rationality capture the dynamics of interdependent heterogeneous populations in and out of equilibrium. Although behaviors are shaped by the associated payoffs, the payoffs need not be those that were intended by the actors. Hence the responses may be expressive and normative, as well as instrumental.

Adaptive rationality, whether based on learning or evolution, requires recurrent decisions but little cognitive sophistication or information. Iterative search relaxes the highly restrictive cognitive assumptions of calculated rationality, thereby extending applications to highly routinized actors, such as bureaucratic organizations, or boundedly rational individuals whose behavior is based on heuristics, habits, or norms. Adaptive rationality is grounded in action, not calculation. It springs not just from the heads of the actors but also from their hands and feet—from problem-solving, trial-and-error, and other processes of gradient search.

Adaptive rationality applies to behavior based on rules rather than choices (Vanberg 1994). *Choice* refers to an instrumental, case-specific comparison of alternative courses of action. In contrast, *rules* are behavioral routines that "provide standard solutions to re-current choice problems" (p. 19). "The primary mental activity involved in this process," according to Prelec (1991), "is the exploration of analogies and distinctions between the current situation and other canonical choice situations in which a single rule or principle unambiguously applies." Rule-based decision might seem to suggest unthinking pro-grammed behavior, in contrast to the conscious reflection implied by forward-looking calculation. That interpretation would seem to support Duesenberry's conclusion that "economics is about how people make choices" and not about how they follow rules. However, this is only the surface of the matter, for it neglects five important characteristics of heuristic adaptation that support a very different conclusion:

1. *Behavioral rules and heuristics do not work like computer programs.* In ambiguous situations, actors are likely to deliberate over the choice of rules to apply. Rule-based behavior does not require conscious deliberation but neither does it preclude it.

2. *Behavioral rules involve experimentation.* Adaptive rationality assumes actors who relentlessly search but may never find the highest peak on the landscape—the global optimum that is the inevitable destination of rational choice. Adaptive actors grope their way along, making mistakes, trying new paths. Rules can also be modified and combined with parts of other rules to form new rules that are more effective than either predecessor.

3. *Adaptive actors are not black boxes.* Research on heuristic decision, beginning with the seminal studies by Tversky and Kahneman, is concerned with the cognitive limitations and biases that are assumed away in models of calculated rationality (for an overview see Tversky and Kahneman 1990, 140–70).

4. *Rule-based adaptation allows for dynamic equilibrium.* In populations of heterogeneous adaptive actors, equilibrium can be a dynamic balance, in which even highly unstable individuals move about a stable population average. This contrasts with the static game-theoretic equilibrium that persists indefinitely because rational actors have no incentive to unilaterally deviate.

5. *Rule-based behavior need not be instrumentally motivated.* Because the link to the future is recurrence, not prediction, action can be explained by outcomes, intended or unintended, that increase the probability that the action will be repeated.

Unintended consequences, in turn, open up possibilities for noninstrumental behaviors motivated by righteousness or anger. In RCT, only the intended outcomes of action explain the choices that preceded them in time. Unintended outcomes have no explanatory power. Smith's "invisible hand" may produce mutually beneficial market outcomes, but it is not the baker's benevolence that explains the bread.

In contrast, adaptive rationality is not limited to the intended consequences of instrumental choice but applies equally well to the unintended consequences of emotional and expressive behavior that lacks any ulterior instrumental motive. Frank's (1993) evolutionary model of trust and commitment formalizes the unintended rationality of emotions like vengeance and sympathy. An angry or frightened actor may not be capable of deliberate pursuit of self-interest, yet the response to the stimulus has consequences for the individual, and these in turn can modify the probability that the behavior will be repeated, through reinforcement, imitation, or some combination of learning and evolution. Thus adaptive rationality can be applied to righteous participation in symbolic social movements, as well as instrumentally motivated collective actions.

A growing recognition of the limitations of forward-looking calculated rationality has led to increasing interest in backward-looking evolutionary alternatives. The next section reviews criticisms of RCT and the defense based on the as-if assumption that rationality is an emergent property among actors whose choices are constrained.

EMERGENT RATIONALITY

By assuming a set of preferences and sufficient information for actors to calculate the marginal returns on competing investments, RCT can generate rigorously testable, nonautological hypotheses about the behavior of populations. The formal rigor of analytic models has appealed to social scientists outside economics, including many social psychologists interested in using mathematics to build deductive theory. The rigor, parsimony, and analytic power of rational choice has prompted social psychologists to extend the theory beyond market transactions, to exchanges of symbolic and nonfungible resources like social approval, contributions to the public good, and even sex.[2]

These extensions invite considerable skepticism. Critics warn that efforts to accommodate RCT to nonmaterial and nonfungible exchanges may rob the theory of its rigor and falsifiability and lead to "theoretical indeterminacy" (Smelser 1992, 402). The theory may become "an inclusive and universally applicable construct that simultaneously explains everything and therefore nothing" (p. 403).

Other critics have charged that the calculus of expected utility is a prescriptive model of how choices ought to be made, one that bears little resemblance to actual decision making. *Homo economicus* must have the information, cognitive capacity, and temperament to calculate the effects of alternative strategies, including the effects on the choices of others. These conditions are sometimes observed in the behavior of skilled entrepreneurs, legislators, or military strategists. However, it seems clear that these conditions are less than universal. Indeed, "many sociologists find rational choice plausible in only a very small fraction of human interactions" (Hannan 1992, 134).[3]

While the assumptions of perfect information and unlimited calculating ability create "a mathematically elegant world, unfortunately it bears only a faint resemblance to the world that we know" (Young 2003, 1). Experimental studies of decision making have shown that "the axioms of rational choice are often violated consistently by sophisticated as well as naive respondents, and that the violations are often large and highly persistent. In fact, some of the observed biases, such as the gambler's fallacy and the regression fallacy, are reminiscent of perceptual illusions. In both cases, one's original erroneous response does not lose its appeal even after one has learned the correct answer" (Tversky 1977).

In many circumstances, learning is mandated by cognitive limitations and the costs of information (Simon 1992). However, the interactionist school of social psychology points to a much broader and more basic requirement: the possibility of social life (Berger 1966; for a similar view from economics, see Hayek 1973). Among social species, we are unique in our plasticity. Unlike social insects, our genes leave us free to leave the swarm and chart our own individual course. Were we not creatures of habit, routine, and heuristic devices, effective coordination might be impossible—a cacophony of inappropriate responses to unexpected reactions from others. Behavioral rules (including social norms and conventions) make social interaction predictable, so that interdependent individuals can influence one another in response to the influence they receive, thereby carving out locally stable patterns of interaction.

These criticisms of calculated rationality are deflected by economists who argue, following Weber ([1908] 1975), that rational choice describes the end result of market exchange but not the actual decision process by which it obtains (Friedman 1953). The effort to explain the latter is misguided, because the theory is not about the psychology of individual decision but about the equilibrium expected of populations. Within each individual, utility maximization is complicated by a "mass of complex and detailed circumstances surrounding the phenomena to be explained" (Friedman 1953, 13). A good theory aims not to capture the richness of this complexity but to abstract "the common and crucial elements" from the residuals, which in the aggregate, can be dismissed as so much noise (p. 13). The noise gets removed at the macro level as the errors cancel out, leaving a central tendency that conforms closely to the aggregate behavior predicted for fully rational actors (Hedstrom 1994, 19; see also Stinchcomb 1968). What matters, then, is not whether the actors are rational but whether they act *as if* they are.

Friedman defended this as-if assumption on the grounds "that a theory cannot be tested by the 'realism' of its 'assumptions'" but should be tested primarily by the relative accuracy of its predictions (Friedman 1953, 17–23). The market selects optimal solutions through the relentless process of ecological competition (Alchian 1950; Boulding 1981). Suboptimal decisions are removed from the repertoires of the actors by learning and imitation, and any residuals are removed from the population by bankruptcy and takeover. We are then left with rational actions that make their owners look much smarter than they really are, as if the eventual outcome was the one they had intended all along.

Becker offers another variant of the as-if postulate. According to Becker, rational choice is a theory about the efficient allocation of scarce resources among populations who need not even be human. Hence this approach "is a powerful tool not only in understanding human behavior but also in understanding the behavior of other species" (Becker 1991, 307). This "analytical continuity" is possible, according to Becker, because "nonhumans and even most humans do not consciously maximize" (p. 321; see also Becker 1976, 7). Instead, Becker argues that even randomly impulsive actors will find that they have no choice but to be rational under conditions of competition for scarce resources (1976, 164–66). Otherwise, they will exhaust their assets.

The as-if postulate belies Duesenberry's aphorism. *Rational choice* begins to look rather like an oxymoron. Applied to the outcomes of action, *rational* refers not to the capacity for analytic calculation of optimal solutions but to the efficiency of the solutions that can be expected to emerge from a competitive process constrained by finite resources. Simply put, rational choice is no longer about the optimizing calculations of rational actors; it now becomes a theory about how actions are rational because actors do not have any alternative.

From Rational Choice to Rational Action

Elsewhere (Macy 1997) I have suggested that as-if rationality should more appropriately be labeled *rational action*, not *rational choice*. Rational action theory (RAT) uses analytic tools to identify the normative decisions actors ought to make if they want to flourish and then simply assumes that competition over the allocation of scarce resources will eventually select for optimal decisions that converge with the predictions derived from analytic shortcuts.

Although RAT invokes backward-looking logic to justify the heroic behavioral assumptions of RCT, the predicted equilibrium is identical to that in forward-looking theories of rational choice. There is no need to actually model the evolutionary dynamics because the equilibrium outcome can be derived analytically from utility theory. So long as the relentless process of competitive selection converges at equilibrium with the predictions of perfect rationality, we can indulge the theoretical convenience of as-if reasoning.

This convergence is less plausible than it might seem. Kiser and Hechter (1991; see also Elster 1989) contend that gradient climbing is highly vulnerable to becoming trapped in local optima (like the false peaks that can fool naïve mountain climbers). Evolution and learning are highly path dependent and not very good at backing out of culs-de-sac on an adaptive landscape. Both reinforcement and reproduction are biased toward *better* strategies, but they carry no guarantee of finding the best of all possible solutions. Hill climbing thus violates the optimality assumption in RCT. Actors cannot be assumed to attain the highest peak, however relentless the search. In short, RAT rests on convergence postulates that are as problematic as the cognitive assumptions in RCT.

A resurgence of interest in evolution and learning has extended the scope of RAT by replacing the convergence postulate with an "explicit representation of the dynamics of adaptation that result when large populations of boundedly rational agents interact in a partially random manner" (Young 2003, 1). Instead of assuming that competition for scarce resources will ineluctably lead to population behaviors that are individually optimal (as if chosen by perfect calculating machines), evolutionary modelers relax the convergence postulate that course correction and ecological selection pressures will necessarily steer gradient climbers to act as if they were analytically rational. Convergence between calculated and emergent outcomes can then be regarded as empirically variable rather than axiomatic.

Formalization of evolutionary alternatives to orthodox rational choice is most advanced in game-theoretic applications. Evolutionary theory elaborates RAT by relaxing the assumption that emergent outcomes converge with the global optimum predicted for calculated rationality. The next section elaborates the distinction between calculated and adaptive rationality as these principles find expression in analytical and evolutionary game theory.

Game Theory

Game theory is a mathematical tool for modeling conflict and cooperation. A game consists of two or more players, each with a set of strategies and a utility function assigning an individual payoff to each combination of chosen strategies. Game theory assumes that the consequences of an action may depend in part on the actions of others. This strategic interdependence can be represented in several ways: as a payoff matrix (the normal form for simultaneous moves by the players), a decision tree (the extensive form for sequential moves), or as a production function (for n-person games).

Strategic interdependence allows for many types of games. In zero-sum games, a gain for one player is always a loss for the partner, which precludes the possibility of cooperation for mutual gain. In positive-sum games, everyone can gain through cooperation. If cooperation is efficient and both players are rational, why would cooperation ever fail? There are two reasons: the fear of being suckered by the partner and the temptation to cheat. Fear and greed pose a social dilemma (Kollock 1998). Loosely stated, a social dilemma arises when players attempting to maximize their individual well-being arrive at a socially undesirable outcome.[4] In many (but not all) social dilemmas, the game has a Pareto-deficient Nash equilibrium. A Nash equilibrium obtains when every strategy is a best reply to the other strategies played; hence no player has an incentive to unilaterally change strategy. The equilibrium is Pareto deficient when another outcome would make at least one person better off and no one else worse off.

The simplest version of a social dilemma confronts two players with a binary choice: whether to cooperate or defect.[5] These two choices intersect at four possible outcomes, each with an associated payoff: R rewards mutual cooperation, S is the sucker payoff for unilateral cooperation, P punishes mutual defection, and T is the temptation to unilaterally defect. In a social dilemma, mutual cooperation is Pareto optimal yet may be undermined by the temptation to cheat (if $T > R$) or by the fear of being cheated (if $P > S$) or by both. In the game of Stag Hunt the problem is fear but not greed ($R > T > P > S$), and in the game of Chicken the problem is greed but not fear ($T > R > S > P$). The problem is most challenging when both fear and greed are present, that is, when $T > R$ and $P > S$. Given the assumption that $R > P$, this can happen only one way, if $T > R > P > S$, the celebrated game of Prisoner's Dilemma (PD).

Although PD is identical in both normal and extensive form,[6] an interesting variant of the latter is called the "trust game" (Dasgupta 1988; Buskens 2002). The first mover chooses whether to invest resources in a trustee, and if the first mover does so, the second mover chooses whether to betray or reward trust.

Collective Action

Another variant of PD increases the number of players to study the problem of collective action. The problem is twofold. The free-rider problem arises because the benefits of collective action can be enjoyed by all members of the interest group, whether or not they contribute. The efficacy problem arises because the marginal impact of individual contributions is likely to be trivial in large groups. Thus individual members of interest groups reach the same mutually ruinous conclusion: "I will still receive the benefits of collective action, even if I do not contribute, while the benefit may be no greater, even if I do contribute."

Having posed the problem of collective action (Olson 1965), rational-choice theorists then turned their attention to the search for possible solutions. Hechter's (1987) theory of group solidarity points to the capacity of the group to monitor and sanction individual compliance with the obligations of membership. This neo-Hobbesian solution to the problem of social order poses what Oliver (1980) has called "a second-order free rider problem." How can social control explain individual contributions to collective action if the provision of inducements is itself a public good? Members of an interest group know they will benefit from enforcement of member obligations even if they let others bear the cost of the Leviathan. From this angle, neo-Hobbesian theories would appear to have it backward: collective action does not depend on the institutional capacity for social control, rather, it is the other way around.

Heckathorn (1989) has advanced a novel rational-choice solution to the second-order free-rider problem. He argues that enforcement can be much more cost-effective than compliance. Hence rational deviants may be willing to enforce the very norms they violate. He points to the example of corrupt sheriffs in the Old West who nevertheless "increased the level of order" (1989, p. 97).

Other interest-based theories emphasize mobilization rather than sanctioning. Fireman and Gamson (1979), as well as Marwell and Oliver (1993), downplay the free-rider problem and focus instead on the problem of efficacy, the ability to make a difference. Often, the collective-action problem is a game of n-person Stag Hunt, not PD. A member's best payoff may be to cooperate, but only if enough other members of the group choose to cooperate as well. Mobilization of participation in collective action thus requires a critical mass of vanguard contributors who can trigger a chain reaction as the prospects of success begin to snowball. Chong's (1991) case study of the civil rights movement is an important empirical application of the n-person Stag Hunt model.

Finally, Ellickson (1991), Ostrom (1990), and Nee and Ingram (1998) draw on the small-group, exchange-theoretical approach of Homans (1961), Emerson (1972), and Blau (1964) in proposing a solution to the large-group collective-action problem. The core idea is that institutions are permeated with informal mechanisms of social control embedded in local networks and interpersonal relationships. Ellickson showed how informal arrangements, "beyond the shadow of the law," are not only less costly but also more flexible in allowing small transgressions, so long as the books are balanced in the long run. Ostrom pointed to ongoing interactions within a community as an alternative to reliance on central enforcement of environmental regulations. Nee and Ingram see these informal controls as the missing link between networks and institutions as mechanisms that constrain opportunism in social exchange.

Analytical and Evolutionary Game Theory

While the games vary widely, the theory of games provides a solution concept that can be universally applied. The Nash equilibrium predicts mutual defection in PD, unilateral defection in Chicken, and either mutual cooperation or mutual defection in Stag Hunt. There is also a Pareto-deficient mixed-strategy equilibrium in Chicken and Stag Hunt.

Contrary to both advocates and critics, game theory need not assume that these equilibrium strategies are motivated by the pursuit of self-interest. The game's key assumption is not self-interested calculation, it is instead what ought to be most compelling to social psychologists, *the interdependence of the actors*. The game paradigm obtains its theoretical leverage by modeling the social fabric as a matrix of interconnected agents guided by outcomes of their interaction with others, where the actions of each depend on, as well as shape, the behavior of those with whom they are linked. This is known as *strategic interdependence.*

Calculated and adaptive rationality inform alternative ways of formalizing the consequentialist logic of strategic interdependence. Analytical game theory, based on calculated rationality, posits full comprehension of the logical structure of a well-defined problem and cognitive representation of the causal link between outcomes and the actions that produce them.[7] The models typically assume perfect information and may also require the common-knowledge assumption, namely, that "I know x, I know that you know x, I know that you know that I know x," etc. Game contestants may also need to know how to work back from the endgame to anticipate one another's rational choices.[8] Simply put, analytical game theorists study games played by people like themselves.

In contrast, most games in everyday life are played by lay contestants. Informal cooperation and coordination are based on folk strategies—heuristics, habits, conventions, customs, norms, and the like—that evolve through repeated interaction. The emergence and collapse of these folk strategies can be modeled using evolutionary game theory, a method that identifies stable distributions of competing strategies. In evolutionary game theory, "people are rational because they learn in the rough and ready sense that they adjust their strategies in the light of experience so as to move towards the strategy which shows the greatest pay-off in the repeated play of this game" (Hargreaves and Varoufakis 1995, 199).

Limitations of Analytical Game Theory

Nash equilibria in noncooperative games are self-enforcing—no contract is necessary to guarantee compliance. This allows for the possibility that social order can self-organize, even in the absence of a Leviathan. Although this result is clearly of enormous significance across all the social sciences, important limitations have spurred the search for more powerful theoretical extensions. Nash-equilibrium analysis tells us whether any strategic configurations are stable, and if so, how they are characterized. Knowing that a configuration is a Nash equilibrium means that if this state should obtain, the system will remain there forever, even in the absence of an enforceable contract. However, even when Nash can identify a unique equilibrium, this does not tell us whether this state will ever be reached, or with what probability, or what will happen if the equilibrium should be perturbed. Nor does Nash equilibrium explain social stability among interacting agents who are changing strategies individually, yet the changes are countervailing, such that the population distribution remains constant, as in a homeostatic equilibrium. Put differently, the Nash equilibrium explains social stability as the absence of individual change, not as a dynamic balance in a self-correcting distribution of evanescent individual strategies.

Moreover, in most games, Nash cannot identify a unique solution. Both Chicken and Stag Hunt have three equilibria (including one in mixed strategies). Worse yet, if these games are repeated by players who care about future payoffs in an ongoing relation, the number of Nash equilibria becomes indefinitely large (even in PD, which has a unique equilibrium in one-shot play). When games have multiple equlibria, Nash cannot tell us which will obtain or with what relative probability.[9] Nor can it tell us much about the dynamics by which a population of players can move from one equilibrium to another.

These limitations, including concerns about the cognitive demands of forward-looking rationality (Dawes and Thaler 1988; Weibull 1998; Fudenberg and Levine 1998), have led game theorists to explore backward-looking alternatives based on evolution and learning. Evolutionary game theory allows for the possibility that players rely on cognitive shortcuts such as imitation, heuristic decision, stochastic learning, Bayesian updating, best reply with finite memory, and local optimization. Evolutionary models test the ability of conditionally cooperative strategies to survive and reproduce in competition with predators (Maynard-Smith 1979). Biological models have also been extended to military and economic games, in which losers are physically eliminated or bankrupted, and to cultural games, in which winners are more likely to be imitated (Axelrod 1984; Weibull 1998).

However, despite rapid growth in the "science of memetics" (Dawkins 1976; Dennett 1995; Blackmore 1999), skeptics charge that genetics (and genetic analogies) may be a misleading template for models of adaptation at the cognitive level (Aunger 2001). The need for a cognitive alternative to evolutionary game theory is reflected in a growing number of formal learning-theoretic models of cooperative behavior (Roth and Erev 1995; Fudenberg and Levine 1998; Young 1998; Flache and Macy 2002).

Cognitive game theory (a term coined by Roth and Erev [1995]) relaxes three key behavioral assumptions in analytic models based on forward-looking rationality (Flache and Macy 2002):

1. Propinquity replaces causality as the link between choices and payoffs.

2. Reward and punishment replace utility as the motivation for choice.

3. Melioration replaces optimization as the basis for the distribution of choices over time.

Propinquity, Not Causality. Compared to forward-looking calculation, reinforcement learning imposes a lighter cognitive load on decision makers by assuming experiential induction rather than logical deduction. Players explore the likely consequences of alternative choices and develop preferences for those associated with better outcomes, even though the association may be coincident or causally spurious. Anticipated outcomes are but the consciously projected distillations of prior exposure to a recurring problem.

Reward and Punishment, Not Utility. Learning theory differs from expected utility theory in positing two distinct cognitive mechanisms that guide decisions toward better outcomes, *approach* (driven by reward) and *avoidance* (driven by punishment). The distinction means that aspiration levels are very important for learning theory. The effect of an outcome depends decisively on whether it is coded as gain or loss, satisfactory or unsatisfactory, pleasant or aversive.

Melioration, Not Optimization. Melioration refers to suboptimal gradient climbing when confronted with what Herrnstein and Drazin (1991) call "distributed choice" across recurrent decisions. A good example of distributed choice is the decision whether to cooperate in an iterated PD game. Suppose each side is satisfied when the partner cooper- ates and dissatisfied when the partner defects. Melioration implies a tendency to repeat choices with satisfactory outcomes even if other choices have higher utility, a behavioral tendency March and Simon (1958) call "satisficing." In contrast, unsatisfactory outcomes induce search for alternative outcomes, including a tendency to revisit alternative choices whose outcomes are even worse, a pattern Macy and Flache (2002) call "dissatisficing." While satisficing and dissatisficing are suboptimal when judged by conventional game- theoretic criteria, they may be more effective in leading actors out of a suboptimal equilib- rium than if they were to use more sophisticated decision rules, such as testing the waters to see if they could occasionally get away with cheating.

Cognitive and evolutionary game theory can be usefully applied to the equilibrium- selection problem. In repeated social dilemma games there is often an indefinitely large number of Nash equilibria. However, not all these equilibria are learnable, either by indi- viduals (via reinforcement[10]) or by populations (via evolution). Learning theory has also been used to identify a fundamental solution concept for these games—stochastic collu- sion—based on a random walk from a self-limiting noncooperative equilibrium into a self- reinforcing cooperative equilibrium (Macy and Flache 2002).

Growing interest in evolutionary and cognitive game theory has led to increasing reliance on agent-based computational modeling and simulation of artificial life (Simon 1992, 45; Axelrod 1997, 48).[11] The nonlinear and stochastic properties of dynamic systems are much less amenable to analytic modeling. These computational models show how local interaction can affect global population dynamics. Numerous theoretical investigations converge on the conclusion that cooperative strategies benefit from spatial and social em- beddedness of the PD game. The opportunity to interact with similar strategies while min- imizing contact with predators allows strategies based on reciprocity to invade predatory populations. In addition, small "neighborhoods" increase the probability of reencounter- ing a former partner, which increases the "shadow of the adaptive future" (Cohen, Riolo, and Axelrod 2001). Finally, the existence of closed triads facilitates the diffusion of third- party reputational information, allowing cooperators to avoid known predators.

Recent evolutionary extensions of the classical analytic approach address the reasons that game theory has failed to attract interest among social psychologists comparable to the en- thusiasm shown by economists and political scientists. Forward-looking calculation hardly exhausts the range of mechanisms by which payoffs might react back upon choices, as evo- lutionary and learning-theoretic applications clearly demonstrate.

CONCLUSION

RCT assumes that actors calculate optimal strategies based on knowledge of the logical or mathematical structure of a well-defined problem. Analytical game theory formalizes the application of RCT to the problems of coordination and cooperation among strategically interdependent actors. Models based on the assumption of perfect information and unlim- ited calculating ability are most powerful when applied to the equilibrium behavior of populations of homogeneous actors.

Laboratory studies have challenged the behavioral assumptions of forward-looking rationality. In response, the theory has been reformulated around the assumption that actors behave as if they were utility maximizers, allowing for rational action without the need for rational choice. The as-if assumption brings to the surface what is often not apparent in theories of calculated rationality: rational choice is not a theory about individual cognition but a theory of efficient resource allocation. From this angle, it appears that Duesenberry got it backward. Economics is not about how people make choices, it is about the outcomes that obtain in a population of optimizers. This leaves it to others to figure out how the outcomes that emerge from human interaction shape the underlying choices of adaptive actors. In broad strokes, that is a research agenda for social psychology.

The material in this chapter incorporates work previously published in Macy 1997, 1998 and Flache and Macy 2002.

1. Recent Nobel Prizes in Economics indicate growing recognition of the need to replace the assumption of perfect rationality with empirically grounded models of human judgment and decision.

2. Examples of the exchange of approval include social exchange theory (Homans 1961; Emerson 1972; and Blau 1964) and status characteristics theory (Berger et al. 1977; Ridgeway, Chap. 13 this volume). The social psychology of collective action is surveyed by Kollock (1998). For an overview of sexual exchange theory, see Sprecher (1998), and for an empirical test, see van de Rijt and Macy (forthcoming).

3. Simon has warned that the necessary conditions may not even be present where calculated rationality seems most plausible. "The study of actual decision processes (for example, the strategies used by corporations to make their investments) reveals massive and unavoidable departures" from the model (1992, 36).

4. More technically, a social dilemma is a game with a rationalizable outcome that is Pareto dominated by a correlated strategy.

5. More complex variations allow for n players, multiple and continuous choices, and whether to give some or to take some from other players.

6. Since defection is the dominant strategy, it makes no difference whether a player knows what the partner has chosen. That is not true of other types of social dilemmas, where the second mover should do either the same as the partner (Stag Hunt) or the opposite (Chicken).

7. Social psychological applications include both cooperative and noncooperative games. Variable-sum noncooperative games have been widely used to study collective action in social dilemmas (Kollock 1998). Social psychologists have also used cooperative games to model power inequalities in exchange networks (for an overview see Willer 1999).

8. Analytical game theory can be applied to games with incomplete information, but this does not always reduce the cognitive demands. Players may need to know how much information to collect and how to use Bayes's rule to update their probability distributions for choice under uncertainty (Simon 1992, 35). The endgame effect arises when players reason backward from the expected final move in the game to determine the optimal choice on the first (and every succeeding) move, a process called *backward induction*.

9. For solutions to the problem of equilibrium selection, see Selten 1988.

10. Limitation on the number of equilibria requires the assumption that cooperation is reinforced when the partner cooperates and attenuated when the partner defects. An alternative assumption is that players have payoff aspirations that float with experience, in which case, any outcome could be an equilibrium.

11. For an overview of recent sociological applications, including genetic algorithms, neural nets, and cellular automata, see Macy and Willer 2002 and Bainbridge et al. 1994.

REFERENCES

Alchian, A. 1950. Uncertainty, evolution and economic theory. *Journal of Political Economy*, p. 58.

Aunger, Robert. 2001. *Darwinizing Culture: The Status of Memetics as a Science.* Oxford: Oxford University Press.

Axelrod R. 1984. *The Evolution of Cooperation.* New York: Basic Books.

———. 1997. *Complexity of Cooperation.* Princeton, NJ: Princeton University Press.

Axelrod, Robert, and Michael D. Cohen. 2000. *Harnessing Complexity: Organizational Implications of a Scientific Frontier.* New York: Free Press.

Bainbridge, W. S., E. E. Brent, K. M. Carley, D. R. Heise, M. W. Macy, B. Markovsky, et al. 1994. Artificial social intelligence. *Annual Review of Sociology* 20:407–36.

Becker, Gary S. 1976. Altruism, egoism, and genetic fitness: Economics and sociobiology. *Journal of Economic Literature* 14 (3): 817–26.

———. 1991. *A Treatise on the Family.* Cambridge, MA: Harvard University Press.

Berger, P. 1966. *The Sacred Canopy.* New York: Anchor.

Berger, Joseph, M. Hamit Fisek, Robert Z. Norman, and Morris Zelditch Jr. 1977. *Status Characteristics and Social Interaction.* New York: Elsevier.

Blackmore, Susan. 1999. *The Meme Machine.* Oxford: Oxford University Press.

Blau, P. M. 1964. *Exchange and Power in Social Life.* New York: Wiley.

Boulding, K. 1981. *Evolutionary Economics.* Beverly Hills, CA: Sage.

Buskens, Vincent. 2002. *Social Networks and Trust.* Theory and Decision library series C: Game theory, mathematical programming, and operations research, vol. 30. Boston: Kluwer.

Chong, D. 1991. *Collective Action and the Civil Rights Movement.* Chicago: University of Chicago Press.

Cohen, Michael, Rick L. Riolo, and Robert Axelrod. 2001. The role of social structure in the maintenance of cooperative regimes. *Rationality and Society* 13:5–32.

Dasgupta, Partha. 1988. Trust as a commodity. In *Trust: Making and Breaking Cooperative Relations*, ed. Diego Gambetta, 49–72. Oxford: Blackwell.

Dawes, R. M., and R. H. Thaler. 1988. Cooperation. *Journal of Economic Perspectives* 2(3): 187–97.

Dawkins, R. 1976. *The Selfish Gene.* Oxford: Oxford University Press.

Dennett, Daniel C. 1995. *Darwin's Dangerous Idea: Evolution and the Meanings of Life.* New York: Simon & Schuster.

Duesenberry, J. 1960. Comment on "An economic analysis of fertility." In *Demographic and Economic Change in Developed Countries.* National Bureau Committee for Economic Research. Princeton, NJ: Princeton University Press.

Ellickson, R. 1991. *Order Without Law.* Cambridge: Harvard University Press.

Elster, J. 1989. *The Cement of Society.* Cambridge, UK: Cambridge University Press.

Elster, Jon. 1990. Merton's functionalism and the unintended consequences of action. In *Robert Merton: Consensus and Controversy*, ed. Jon Clark, Celia Modgil, and Sohan Modgil. London & New York: Falmer Press.

Emerson, R. M. 1972. Exchange theory: A psychological basis for social exchange. In *Sociological Theories in Progress*, ed. J. Berger et al. 1:38–57. Boston: Houghton Mifflin.

Fireman, B., and W. Gamson. 1979. Utilitarian logic in the resource mobilization perspective. In *The Dynamics of Social Movements*, ed. M. Zald and J. McCarthy, 8–44. Cambridge, MA: Winthrop Press.

Flache, A., and M. Macy. 2002. Stochastic collusion and the power law of learning. *Journal of Conflict Resolution*. 46:629–53.

Frank, R. 1993. The strategic role of emotions: Reconciling over- and undersocialized accounts of behavior. *Rationality and Society* 5:160–84.

Friedman, M. 1953. *Essays in Positive Economics*. Chicago: University of Chicago Press.

Fudenberg, D., and D. Levine. 1998. *The Theory of Learning in Games*. Boston: MIT Press.

Hannan, M. 1992. Rationality and robustness in multilevel systems. In *Rational Choice Theory: Advocacy and Critique*, ed. J. Coleman and T. Fararo. Newbury Park, CA: Sage.

Hargreaves Heap, S., and Y. Varoufakis. 1995. *Game Theory: A Critical Introduction*. New York: Routledge.

Hayek, F. 1973. *Law, Legislation and Liberty, Volume I: Rules and Order*. Chicago: University of Chicago Press.

Hechter, M. 1987. *Principles of Group Solidarity*. Berkeley: University of California Press.

Heckathorn, D. 1989. Collective action and the second-order free-rider problem. *Rationality and Society* 1:78–100.

Hedstrom, P. 1994. Rational choice and social structure: On rational-choice theorizing in sociology. In *Social Theory and Human Agency*, ed. B. Wittrock. London: Sage.

Herrnstein, Richard J., and Prelec Drazin. 1991. Meliorization: A theory of distributed choice. *Journal of Economic Perspectives* 5:137–56.

Homans, G. C. 1961. *Social Behavior: Its Elementary Forms*. New York: Harcourt, Brace & World.

Kiser, E., and M. Hechter. 1991. The role of general theory in comparative-historical sociology. *American Journal of Sociology* 97:1–31.

Kollock, Peter. 1998. Social dilemmas: The anatomy of cooperation. *Annual Review of Sociology* 24:183–214.

Lave, C. and J. March. 1975. *An Introduction to Models in the Social Sciences*. New York: Harper & Row.

Macy, M. 1997. Identity, interest and emergent rationality: An evolutionary synthesis. *Rationality and Society* 9:427–38.

———. 1998. Social order and emergent rationality. In *What Is Social Theory: The Philosophical Debates*, ed. A. Sica. Oxford: Blackwell.

Macy, M., and A. Flache. 2002. Learning dynamics in social dilemmas. *Proceedings of the National Academy of Sciences* 99:7229–36.

Macy, M., and R. Willer. 2002. From factors to actors: Computational sociology and agent-based modeling. *Annual Review of Sociology* 28:143–66.

March, J. G., and H. A. Simon. 1958. *Organizations*. New York: Wiley.

Marwell, G., and P. Oliver. 1993. *The Critical Mass in Collective Action: A Micro-Social Theory*. Cambridge, UK: Cambridge University Press.

Maynard Smith, J. 1979. Game theory and the evolution of behaviour. *Proceedings of the Royal Society of London* 205:475–88.

Nash, John F. 1950. *Non-Cooperative Games*. Princeton, NJ: Princeton University Press.

Nee, V., and P. Ingram. 1998. Embeddedness and beyond: Institutions, exchange, and social structure. In *The New Institutionalism in Sociology*, ed. M. Brinton and V. Nee. New York: Russell Sage.

Oliver, P. 1980. Rewards and punishments as selective incentives for collective action: Theoretical investigations. *American Journal of Sociology* 85:1356–75.

Olson M. 1965. *The Logic of Collective Action*. Cambridge, MA: Harvard University Press.

Ostrom, E. 1990. *Governing the Commons: The Evolution of Institutions for Collective Action*. Cambridge, UK: Cambridge University Press.

Prelec, D. 1991. Values and principles: Some limitations on traditional economic analysis. In *Perspectives on Socioeconomics*, ed. A. Etzioni and P. Lawrence. London: M. E. Sharpe.

Roth, A. E., and I. Erev. 1995. Learning in extensive-form games: Experimental data and simple dynamic models in intermediate term. *Games and Economic Behavior*. Special Issue: Nobel Symposium 8:164–212.

Schlag, K. H., and G. B. Pollock. 1999. Social roles as an effective learning mechanism. *Rationality and Society* 11 (4): 371–97.

Schull, J. 1996. William James and the broader implications of a multilevel selectionism. In *Adaptive Individuals in Evolving Populations*, ed. R. Belew and M. Mitchell. Reading, MA: Addison-Wesley.

Selten, R. 1988. *A General Theory of Equilibrium Selection in Games*. Cambridge, MA: MIT Press.

Selten, R., and R. Stoecker. 1986. End behaviour in sequences of finite prisoner's dilemma supergames: A learning theory approach. *Journal of Economic Behaviour and Organisation* 7:47–70.

Simon, H. 1992. Decision-making and problem-solving. In *Decision Making: Alternatives to Rational Choice Models*, ed. M. Zey. Newbury Park, CA: Sage.

Smelser, N. J. 1992. The rational choice perspective: A theoretical assessment. *Rationality and Society* 4:381–410.

Sprecher, Susan. 1998. Social exchange theories and sexuality. *Journal of Sex Research* 35:32–43.

Stinchcomb, A. 1968. *Constructing Social Theories*. New York: Harcourt, Brace & World.

Tversky, A. 1977. On the elicitation of preferences: Descriptive and prescriptive considerations. In *Conflicting Objectives in Decisions*, ed. D. Bell, R. Kenney, and H. Raiffa. New York: Wiley.

Tversky, A., and D. Kahneman. 1990. Prospect theory: An analysis of decision under risk. In *Rationality in Action*, ed. P. Moser. Cambridge, UK: Cambridge University Press.

Van de Rijt, A., and M. Macy. Forthcoming. Power and dependence in intimate exchange. *Social Forces*.

Vanberg, V. 1994. *Rules and Choice in Economics*. London: Routledge.

Weber, M. [1908] 1975. Marginal utility theory and the fundamental law of psychophysics. *Social Science Quarterly* 56:21–36.

Weibull, J. W. 1998. Evolution, rationality and equilibrium in games. *European Economic Review* 42:641–49.

Willer, D. 1999. *Network Exchange Theory*. New York: Praeger.

Young, H. Peyton. 1998. *Individual Strategy and Social Structure. An Evolutionary Theory of Institutions*. Princeton, NJ: Princeton University Press.

Young, P. 2003. Evolutionary modeling in the social sciences. Santa Fe Institute working paper, http://www.santafe.edu/files/gems/behavioralsciences/peyton.pdf.

5 IDENTITY THEORY

Jan E. Stets

Identity theory grows out of symbolic interaction, particularly structural symbolic interaction (Stryker 1980). The traditional symbolic interactionist perspective, the *situational* approach, sees society as always in the process of being created through the interpretations and definitions of actors in situations (Blumer 1969). Actors identify the things that need to be taken into account, they act on the basis of those identifications, and they attempt to fit their lines of action with others in the situation to accomplish their goals. From this perspective, individuals are free to define the situation in any way they wish with the consequence that society is always thought to be in a state of flux with no real organization or structure. As Stryker (2000, 27) has remarked on this perspective, "[It] tends to dissolve structure in a solvent of subjective definitions, to view definitions as unanchored, open to any possibility, failing to recognize that some possibilities are more probable than others. On the premise that self reflects society, this view leads to seeing self as undifferentiated, unorganized, unstable, and ephemeral."

In the *structural* approach to symbolic interaction, society is not tentatively shaped. It is stable and durable as reflected in the patterned behavior within and between individuals. This patterned behavior has different levels of analysis. At one level, we can look at the patterns of behavior of one individual over time and come to know that individual. By pooling several such patterns across similar individuals, we can come to know individuals of a certain type. At another level, we can look at the patterns of behavior across individuals to see how these patterns fit with the patterns of others to create larger patterns of behavior. It is these larger, interindividual patterns that constitute social structure. At the same time that individuals are creating social structure, they also are receiving feedback from the structures they and others build to change themselves and the way they operate. Thus persons are always embedded in the very social structure that is, simultaneously, being created by those persons.

As society is patterned and organized, so too is the self. The hallmark of selfhood is reflexivity, that is, individuals' abilities to take themselves as an object and reflect back upon themselves. However, the responses of the self as an object to itself come from the point of view of others to whom one interacts. By taking the role of the other and seeing oneself from others' perspectives, individuals' responses come to be like others' responses, and the meaning of the self becomes a shared meaning. Thus the self arises in social interaction and within the larger context of a complex, organized, differentiated society. Since the larger context is complex, organized, and differentiated, so too must we characterize the self, thus the dictum that the "self reflects society" (Stryker 1980).

To see the overall self, we must envision it as comprising many different parts or identities, each of which is tied to aspects of the social structure. This follows James's (1890) notion that there are as many different selves as different positions that one holds in society and different groups who respond to the self. A person has an identity, an "internalized positional designation" (Stryker 1980, 60), for each of the different positions or roles the person holds in society. Thus individuals have *role identities*. Each role identity includes all of the *meanings* that a person attaches to himself while performing a role. These meanings are, in part, derived from culture and the social structure, in that individuals are socialized into what it means to be a worker, wife, or mother, for example. However, persons also bring into the role identity some of their own understandings as to what the identity means to them. In this way, the meanings associated with role identities are both shared and idiosyncratic, and individuals must negotiate the latter with others who may have a different set of understandings about role-identity meanings (McCall and Simmons 1978). Whatever the identity meanings, they are linked to the meanings implied by one's role behavior; in other words, there is correspondence between these self-meanings while in a role and role behavior (Burke and Reitzes 1981). For example, the role identity of mother may involve meanings of being nurturing and caring, and the performance of mothering matches these meanings as in feeding and bathing a child and engaging in warm and intimate interactions with a child. The role identity of husband may include meanings of powerfulness and control, and the behavior of husband should match these meanings as in making the major decisions in the family.

Individuals not only occupy roles in society but are also members of groups. Therefore individuals also have *social identities*.[1] Here individuals identify themselves as members of particular categories such as being an American, a Democrat, a Catholic, and so forth. In the same way that role-identity meanings are defined by culture, culture also defines the meanings of different group memberships and the behavior expected from those memberships. However, there are some differences between role identities and social identities (Stets and Burke 2000). In social identities, people categorize themselves as similar to some, labeled the *in-group*, and different from others, the *out-group*. When individuals take on a group-based identity, there is *uniformity* of perception and action among group members (Oakes, Haslam, and Turner 1994). And groups activate a sense of belongingness and self-worth.

In role-based identities, there are *different* perceptions and action between individuals, as roles interact with counter-roles (Burke 1980). Any role identity that a person claims in an interaction always has a related, alternative identity that is claimed by another. Thus any role identity is always related to a corresponding counter-identity (Burke 1980). For example, the role identity of daughter is enacted as it relates to the corresponding counter-role identity of mother or father. The role identity of student is played out in relation to the counter-role identity of teacher. Further, roles activate a sense of efficacy rather than a sense of self-worth as in group identities. It is *what one does* in one's role identity that is important compared to *who one is* on the basis of one's group identity (Stets and Burke 2000).

Finally, the person is a third basis of identity. These identities are known as *person identities*. A person identity is the set of meanings that are tied to and sustain the self as an individual rather than sustaining a group or role. Like group and role identities, culture influences the important dimensions of meaning that form the basis of person identities (Burke 2004). For example, our society may encourage meanings of who we are in terms of dominance and submissiveness (the control identity; Stets and Burke 1994) or in terms of what is good or bad (the moral identity; Stets and Carter 2006). These meanings that form different person identities operate across various roles and situations; for example, we might have a controlling employer, husband, and father or a worker, wife, and mother who has a high level of morality. As Burke (2004) points out, because person identities figure into many interactions, relationships, and behaviors, they are always on display. Given this constant activation, they are generally salient.

We need to think of social, role, and person identities as simultaneously operating in situations. Within groups, there are roles, and persons play out these roles in different ways. For example, the role identity of teacher is within the larger category or group of academics (the in-group) compared to nonacademics (the out-group). When enacting the role of teacher, some teachers are dominant while others are submissive. Some are kind and compassionate while others are unkind and hardhearted. Which identity we focus on will make salient some issues and not others in the situation. For example, in focusing on the categorical aspect of academics compared to nonacademics, we attend to shared perceptions and uniformity in action among academics and how membership in the academic community facilitates belongingness. In addressing the role identity of teacher, we examine how it relates to the counter-role of student, and we address how the successful performance of a role leads to a feeling of self-efficacy. Finally, in emphasizing the personal aspect of being a teacher, we focus on the individual as a unique entity, distinct from others in how they perform the role of teacher.

THE THEORY

Identity theory has two slightly different emphases and thus two somewhat different programs of research (Stryker and Burke 2000). In the work of Stryker and his colleagues (Serpe 1987; Serpe and Stryker 1987; Stryker 1980, 2004; Stryker and Serpe 1982, 1994), the focus is on how social structure influences one's identity and one's behavior. Thoits's (1983, 1991, 1995, 2003) ongoing research also has this emphasis. The work of Burke and his associates (Burke 1980, 1991, 1997, 2003, 2004; Burke and Cast 1997; Burke and Reitzes 1981, 1991; Burke and Stets 1999; Cast and Burke 2002; Cast, Stets, and Burke 1999; Stets and Burke 1994, 1996, 2000; Tsushima and Burke 1999) emphasizes the internal dynamics within the self that influence behavior.[2] A third form of identity theory is found in the work of McCall and Simmons (1978; McCall 2003). Though a clear program of research has not emerged from this version of identity theory, it does make important theoretical contributions to understanding identities that are important to review here. I will discuss all three perspectives.

A good summary comparison of each version of identity theory comes in the form of how each explains identity performances or behavior. For McCall and Simmons, identity performances are a result of actors attempting to interrelate their identities with those of others in a situation. Every identity is played out in relation to a complementary identity; for example, the identity of doctor is played out in relation to the identity of patient or the identity of clerk is performed vis-à-vis the identity of customer. When conflict between the two identities emerges, negotiation strategies and compromises are employed so that each actor's identity claim can be confirmed and interaction can proceed smoothly. For Stryker, identity performances are a function of how salient an identity is in one's overall hierarchy of identities; a more salient identity is more likely to be invoked in a situation. One important factor that influences the salience of an identity is how committed one is to the identity. Greater commitment to an identity is a function of being tied to a larger social network that is premised on the identity and having deeper ties in that network. Finally, for Burke, identity behavior is a function of the relationship between perceived meanings of the self in a situation and identity standard meanings. When perceived self-in-situation meanings match identity standard meanings, identity verification exists, and the meanings of behavior are consistent with the meanings that have been verified. When self-in-situation meanings do not match identity standard meanings, behavior is modified to restore meanings of the self in the situation to correspond with identity standard meanings, thereby moving the self from a state of identity nonverification to identity verification. The following provides more detail on each of these perspectives.

George McCall and J. L. Simmons

Along with Stryker, McCall and Simmons are the earliest originators of identity theory. At the heart of McCall and Simmons's (1978) work is an emphasis on role identities. A role identity is one's "imaginative view of himself as he likes to think of himself being and acting as an occupant" of a particular social position (McCall and Simmons 1978, 65). McCall and Simmons point out that role identities have two dimensions: (1) a conventional dimension (the role of role identities), which includes the expectations tied to social positions in the social structure that actors try to meet, and (2) an idiosyncratic dimension (the identity of role identities), which involves the unique interpretations that individuals bring to their roles. While Stryker's identity theory, discussed later, focuses more on the normative, conventional aspect of role identities, McCall and Simmons are far more likely to discuss the idiosyncratic dimension of identities, that is, to see identities as improvised, variable, and negotiated.

McCall and Simmons as well as Stryker maintain that individuals typically claim more than one role identity, and given individuals' multiple role identities, these identities can be conceptualized as organized into a hierarchy within the self. McCall and Simmons are principally concerned with what they label a *prominence* hierarchy of identities. This hierarchy reflects how persons like to see themselves given their ideals, what they desire, or what is central or important to them. They argue that the placement of an identity in this hierarchy depends upon how much individuals (1) obtain support from others for an identity, (2) are committed and invested in the identity (that is, how much self-esteem is at stake), and

(3) receive extrinsic and intrinsic rewards from the identity. Essentially, the prominence hierarchy, sometimes called the ideal self, reflects persons' priorities that serve to guide their actions across situations and over time. However, the prominence hierarchy is not the sole determinant of behavior because less prominent identities are sometimes enacted in situations. Consequently, McCall and Simmons identify a second hierarchy of identities, which they label a *salience* hierarchy.

The salience hierarchy of identities reflects the situational self rather than the ideal self. This hierarchy serves as the basis for making predictions as to how persons will behave in a particular situation. The placement of an identity in the salience hierarchy depends upon (1) its prominence, (2) its need for support, (3) a person's need for the kinds and amounts of intrinsic and extrinsic rewards gained through performance of the identity, and (4) the perceived degree of opportunity for its profitable enactment (in terms of cost-reward ratios) in the situation. McCall and Simmons note that the salience hierarchy is rather fluid as role identities become temporarily salient in different situations. In contrast, the prominence hierarchy is more enduring and stable.

For successful enactment of a role identity in a situation, McCall and Simmons highlight the importance of negotiation with others in the situation. Specifically, enacting an identity in an interaction is always done in relation to a corresponding counter-identity of another as in the case of a husband supporting his wife, a mother instructing her child, or a professor teaching a student. One's own expectations (whether conventional or personal) as to how to act given a role identity may differ from the expectations others associate with that role identity in the situation. Thus each actor in an interaction has a view of his or her own identity as well as the identity of the other, and both actors try to enact a role identity that interrelates with the other. This requires a certain degree of coordination between the actors, and when conflict emerges, negotiation and compromises must follow so that role performances can be supported and the interaction can proceed smoothly. When interaction does run smoothly, it aids in the development of durable relationships, which help to stabilize actors' prominence hierarchies. This is not to say that the prominence hierarchy does not change, as some priorities of social actors change over time and relationships end and others emerge.

Emotions enter McCall and Simmons's theory when a prominent identity is threatened in a situation, as when others do not support one's role performance. Under these conditions, individuals will experience negative emotions, and it may prompt them to use any one in a series of mechanisms to eliminate the negative feeling. One mechanism is "short-term credit," in which an identity that is currently not being supported is temporarily accepted by others because it was supported in the past. Essentially, actors draw upon a line of credit they have earned from prior identity support to ride out a current, unsuccessful role performance. Another mechanism is "selective perception," in which actors attend to cues that they think support an identity of theirs, and they do not attend to cues that do not support their identity. Closely related to this is "selective interpretation," in which actors interpret cues as supportive of their identity when these cues are not supportive. Other strategies include blaming others in the situation for not confirming an identity, criticizing and even sanctioning others for their lack of support, disavowing an unsuccessful role performance as not what the actor intended, switching to an identity that can be confirmed, or withdrawing from the interaction. Essentially, these mechanisms help social actors avoid the pain associated with disconfirmed identities.

In identity theory, researchers examine how actors identify themselves in terms of being a particular kind of person, taking on particular roles, and belonging to certain groups. Recently, McCall (2003) has argued that we need to investigate actors' self-disidentifications, that is, who it is that people claim they are not. Rather than answering the question, Who am I? one answers the question, Who am I not? McCall proposes that self-identification and self-disidentification can be regarded as the positive and negative poles of identity—the "Me" and "Not-Me." In a pilot study examining these poles, he finds some interesting differences. For example, he finds that the "Me" is framed more in terms of roles and statuses while the "Not-Me" is framed more in terms of characteristics and dispositions. An interesting issue he raises for future research is how, over time, what is "Me" can become "Not-Me," and correspondingly, how what is "Not-Me" can transform into "Me." While these identity changes can be brought about by expected role transitions through the life cycle, they may also occur unexpectedly. Conceptualizing identity change as a movement between the positive and negative poles of identity serves as fertile ground for the theoretical development of identity theory.

Sheldon Stryker

For Stryker, the many role identities that a person may have are organized in a *salience* hierarchy. For Stryker, a salient identity is an identity that is likely to be played out (activated) frequently across different situations. The salience hierarchy focuses on how social actors will likely behave in a situation. The more salient the identity, the more likely will a person (1) enact role performances that are consistent with role expectations associated with the identity, (2) perceive a situation as an opportunity to enact the identity, and (3) seek out situations that provide the opportunity to enact the identity. One important factor that influences the salience of an identity is the degree of commitment one has to the identity.

Commitment has two dimensions: a quantitative and qualitative aspect (Stryker and Serpe 1982, 1994). In the former, reflecting the individual's ties to the social structure, commitment is the number of persons that one is related to through an identity. The greater the number of persons to whom one is connected through having a particular identity, the greater is the commitment to that identity. Regarding the qualitative dimension of commitment, the stronger or the deeper the ties to others based on a particular identity, the higher the commitment to that identity. Stryker (1968, 1980) suggests that the greater the commitment to an identity, the higher will be the identity in the salience hierarchy. Once again, the relevance of social structure in understanding the self is made clear. Because people live their lives in social relationships, commitment takes these ties into account when explaining which identities persons are likely to invoke in a situation. For example, if a man's social network in terms of the number of others and the importance of those others is largely based on him occupying a particular role, such as father, then the father identity is likely to be invoked across various different situations.

Research strongly supports the link between commitment, identity salience, and behavior consistent with salient identities. For example, Stryker and Serpe (1982) examine the religious role identity. Their six-item commitment scale measures the extensiveness and intensiveness of relations with others in life with regard to the religious role. For example, "In thinking of the people who are important to you, how many would you lose contact with if you did not do the religious activities you do?" (extensiveness), or "Of the people you know through your religious activities, how many are close friends?" (intensiveness). The salience of the religious identity is measured by asking respondents to rank the religious role in relation to other roles they may assume such as parent, spouse, and worker. Their measure of behavior is time in the religious role. Respondents are asked how many hours in an average week they spend doing things related to religious activities. Stryker and Serpe find that those committed to relationships based on religion have more salient religious identities that are associated with more time spent in religious activities.

In another study, Callero (1985) examines the blood-donor role identity. In separate measures of the salience of the blood-donor role identity (in relation to other identities one might claim), commitment to the blood-donor identity (borrowing Stryker and Serpe's 1982 commitment scale), and behavioral measure of the identity (number of blood donations given in a six-month period), Callero reaches similar conclusions to those of Stryker and Serpe. The more one has relationships premised on the blood-donor identity, the higher the blood-donor role identity is in one's identity salience hierarchy and the more this salient role identity is related to donating blood.

Recently, Stryker (2004) has discussed how emotions can be integrated into identity theory. Given his argument that role identities are embedded in social networks, he maintains that affect influences the formation of social networks because persons with similar affective meanings will be more likely to form a social bond. Further, these shared emotions will influence commitment in these social networks. Positive affect will increase commitment and negative affect will decrease commitment. In turn, greater commitment will lead to greater, shared, positive affect among social network members.

Within social networks, individuals behave according to the expectations associated with their roles. For Stryker (2004), emotions importantly influence and are influenced by role behavior in social networks. For example, positive emotions will lead to role behavior that confirms one's identity, and role behavior that meets cultural expectations will produce positive emotions. Emotions will also influence commitment to role identities. For example, intense affect following role behavior will inform individuals that they are committed to the identity.

Commitment importantly influences the salience of identities, but Stryker (2004) discusses how affect also has an influence. Specifically, a strong affective feeling will influence the salience of an identity, with positive emotion increasing the salience and negative emotion decreasing the salience. Affect will also influence the salience of an identity through commitment. For example, positive affect will increase commitment to an identity, and in turn, the salience of the identity, while negative affect will decrease commitment and thus the salience of the identity in the hierarchy.

Finally, Stryker points out that intense and uncontrollable emotion serves to maintain identities, commitment, and the salience hierarchy. For instance, intense emotional responses emerge when role partners do not behave in ways that support one's identity. They also emerge when structural or interactional barriers prevent the playing out of highly positive identities or the denial of highly negative identities. When an emotion emerges spontaneously and uncontrollably, it will influence commitment to the identity, increasing or decreasing it depending upon the valence of the emotional response. It will also influence the salience of the identity, again increasing or decreasing it depending upon the valence of the emotional response. Taken together, Stryker's recent theorizing on the role of emotion in identity theory serves as fertile ground for empirical work. To the extent that his ideas are supported regarding the role of emotions in the formation of networks, role performance, identity salience, and commitment, then we have extended identity theory beyond its current boundaries.

Overall, Stryker's approach to conceptualizing identities is somewhat different from McCall and Simmons's approach. For McCall and Simmons, the salience hierarchy—the situational self—is "the person's own preferences as to the subset of role identities he will enact in a given situation" (McCall and Simmons 1978, 84). Essentially, the salience hierarchy helps predict a person's behavior in the short run. Longer run predictions are determined by the prominence hierarchy—the ideal self—the relatively enduring aspect of the self that focuses on what one is important to the self. More prominent identities influence which identities individuals prefer to enact in a specific situation. In this way, the prominence hierarchy influences the salience hierarchy.

For Stryker, the salience hierarchy—the readiness to act out an identity across situations—directly influences the choices people make among behavioral options. Thus rather than the salience hierarchy predicting short-run behaviors as McCall and Simmons would argue, it predicts longer run behaviors. In this sense, Stryker's salience hierarchy has the same effect as McCall and Simmons's prominence hierarchy; it captures the more enduring rather than fleeting source of behavior. However, McCall and Simmons's prominence hierarchy is different from Stryker's salience hierarchy in that the former assume that individuals are aware of their prominence hierarchy, that is, persons are self-aware of more important identities compared to less important identities. For Stryker, people may not be aware of how salient an identity is in their hierarchy, but their behavior would inform them as to its ranking in their hierarchy (Stryker and Serpe 1994). Additionally, each hierarchy carries different meanings (what is important compared to what one is ready to enact). Thus identity prominence and identity should be kept distinct, theoretically, unlike earlier work that merged the two concepts (e.g., Gecas and Seff 1990; Rosenberg 1979). Future work will want to investigate whether it is fruitful in the development of identity theory to establish a causal ordering between identity prominence and identity salience. Specifically, does the prominence of an identity influence its salience in a situation or does invoking an identity in a situation influence the importance of that identity for the self?

Peter J. Burke

While Sheldon Stryker focuses on the hierarchical arrangement of identities and how identities are tied to the social structure, Peter Burke's work focuses more on the internal dynamics that operate for any one identity (Stryker and Burke 2000). In early work, Burke (1980; Burke and Reitzes 1981; Burke and Tully 1977) argued that identity and behavior are linked through a common system of meaning. When we identify the meanings of an identity for an individual, then we can predict the meanings of the person's behavior. Drawing on the work of Osgood, Suci, and Tannenbaum (1957), Burke and Tully (1977) developed a method for the measurement of the self-meanings of an identity. Essentially, to identify the self-meanings associated with an identity, respondents are given a set of bipolar adjectives, and their responses to themselves as objects along the bipolar dimensions such as good and bad, powerful and powerless, or active and passive help locate their identity meanings.

Since any identity contains a set of multiple meanings (Burke and Tully 1977), multiple bipolar dimensions are provided for any one identity to which one can respond. For example, the gender identity of femininity includes being noncompetitive (competitive–not at all competitive dimension), being passive (very active–very passive dimension), and having feelings easily hurt (feelings not easily hurt–feelings easily hurt dimension; Burke, Stets, and Pirog-Good 1988; Stets and Burke 1996). Further, different persons may have different meanings for the same identity. For example, while one woman may see herself as feminine and in these terms, another woman may also see herself as feminine but closer to the competitive, active, and feelings-not-easily-hurt end of the dimension.

Methodologically, the Burke-Tully procedure uses the meanings of the people in a particular subpopulation to formulate a particular identity rather than meanings from another source, such as the researcher's own intuitive feeling or another population. This method has been used to investigate the meanings associated with a variety of identities such as gender identity (Burke and Cast 1997; Burke, Stets, and Pirog-Good 1988; Stets and Burke 1996), the student identity (Reitzes and Burke 1980), old age (Mutran and Burke 1979), the environment identity (Stets and Biga 2003), and the moral identity (Stets and Carter 2006). What is important about the measurement of identities is that the meanings that individuals have for their identities affect how they will behave. More specifically, their identity meanings influence the meanings that their corresponding behavior implies.

More recent conceptions of identity expand on the notion of a correspondence of meaning between identity and behavior and incorporate the idea of a perceptual control system, a cybernetic model, based on the work of Powers (1973). This is where the internal dynamics of identities are most clearly seen (Burke 1991, 1996; Burke and Cast 1997; Riley and Burke 1995; Tsushima and Burke 1999) and the label *identity control theory* has been applied (Burke 2004). Since an identity is a set of meanings attached to the self, this set of meanings serves as a standard or reference for a person. When an identity is activated in a situation, a feedback loop is established as shown in Figure 5.1. This loop has four components: (1) the identity standard (the self-meanings of an identity), (2) perceptual input of self-relevant meanings from the situation, including how one sees oneself and the meaningful feedback that the self obtains from others (reflected appraisals), (3) a process that compares the perceptual input with the identity standard (the comparator), and (4) output to the environment (meaningful behavior) that is a function of the comparison (difference) of perceptions of self-meanings from the situation with actual self-meanings held in the identity standard. The system works by modifying outputs (behavior) to the social situation in

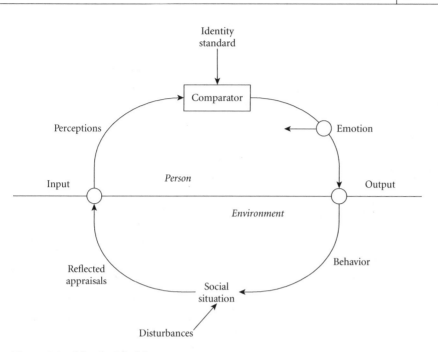

Figure 5.1   Identity Model

attempts to change the input to match the internal standard. In this sense, the identity system can be thought of as having a goal, that is, matching the situational inputs (perceptions) to the internal standards. What this system attempts to control is the perceptual input (to match the standard). When perceptions are congruent with the standard, *identity verification* exists.

What is important about the cybernetic model of the identity process is that instead of seeing behavior as strictly guided by the situation or strictly guided by internal self-meanings, behavior is the result of the relation between the two. It is goal directed in that there is an attempt to change the situation to match perceived situational meanings with meanings held in the identity standard, that is, to bring about in the situation the meanings that are held in the standard. Thus the model has the interesting implication of making different predictions about behavior from the same identity meanings depending upon the (perceived) situation. When self-meanings in the situation match self-meanings in the identity, the meanings of the behaviors correspond to these meanings. However, if the self-meanings perceived in the situation fail to match, behavior is altered to counteract the situational meanings and restore perceptions. Thus, for example, if one views herself as strong and sees that others agree, she will continue to act as she has (strongly). But if she sees that others appear to view her as weak, she will increase the "strength" of her performance in an effort to restore perceptions of herself as strong as seen in the reflected appraisals.

In identity control theory, meanings are tied to resources in that the control of meanings results in the control of resources (Burke 1997, 2004; Freese and Burke 1994). In other words, the activation of an identity in a situation implies the control of resources that correspond to the meanings of the identity standard. These resources should support or verify identity standard meanings.

Resources are of two kinds in identity control theory: active and potential (Burke 1997, 2004; Freese and Burke 1994). Active resources are those conditions and processes that *currently* support the social actor's person identity, role identity, or group identity. Active resources would include air to breathe, a stove on which one is cooking, household products for cleaning when one is housekeeping, current approval from one's spouse, and so forth. Tied to active resources are *signs*. Signs are social actors' responses to resources. Specifically, when active resources are in use, a person has a direct experience in using them that others do not share. For example, the sensations associated with cooking on a stove, such as touching and turning controls, feeling the heat, and smelling the aromas, actors experience as uniquely their own.

Potential resources are *not currently* in use, but they will be used in the future to support a person, role, or group identity such as food that will be later consumed or love that is forthcoming. Tied to potential resources are shared *symbols*. These are responses to anticipated experiences. The responses carry conventional meanings in that everyone responds to them in the same way, compared to the unique responses tied to signs. For instance, the meaning of love is a shared meaning in that culture informs social actors as to how and when this sentiment is to be experienced and who is its target. Individuals can talk about love in an interaction and the communication shores up similar images, thoughts, and feelings.

The cybernetic character of identity theory by Burke has led to a view of the nature of commitment that is slightly different from Stryker's view outlined earlier. In this slightly different view, commitment to an identity is the sum total of the pressure to keep perceptions of self-relevant meanings in the situation in line with the self-meanings held in the identity standard (Burke and Reitzes 1991). One is more committed to an identity when one strives harder to maintain a match between self-in-situation (perceptual input) meaning and the meaning held in the identity standard. Commitment thus moderates the link between identity and behavior, making it stronger (high commitment) or weaker (low commitment). This does not negate the importance of the structural side shown in ties to role partners (Stryker and Serpe 1982, 1994), but it shows how those ties as well as other factors, such as rewards and praise one might receive for being in the role, bring about commitment as defined by Burke and Reitzes (1991) in terms of the strength of the self-verification response. The structural connection is maintained. For example, Burke and Reitzes show that those who are highly committed to a student identity (by having more ties to others, as well as receiving rewards for having the identity) have a stronger link between identity meanings (for example, academic responsibility) and behavior meanings (for example, time in the student role or grade-point average) than those with lower levels of commitment.

As Stryker has, Burke has incorporated emotions into his identity model. Similar to Stryker, Burke argues that a lack of identity verification leads to negative emotion while identity verification produces positive emotion. Some evidence supports this. For example, among newly married couples, verified identities produce positive arousal such as high self-esteem and mastery (Burke and Stets 1999; Cast and Burke 2002) and nonverified identities produce negative emotions arousal such as depression (Burke and Stets 1999) and hostility (Cast and Burke 2002). However, other evidence reveals that in short-term, newly formed interactions in the laboratory, the nonverification of identities in a positive direction, as when one is over-rewarded on a task, produces positive emotions rather than negative emotions (Stets 2003, 2005). It has been suggested that in weak, short-term, uninvolved relationships, people will feel good (and not bad) when they receive nonverifying information in the form of an overevaluation, but when they are in strong, long-term, involved relationships they will feel bad in response to this nonverifying information (Burke and Harrod 2005). In this way, how actors emotionally respond to nonverification may depend upon the context.

Stryker sees identities high in the salience hierarchy as producing stronger emotional reactions than identities low in the salience hierarchy. As Stryker does, Burke (1991) argues that stronger emotions result from the disruption of more salient identities to which a person is committed. While salience of, and commitments to, identities produce stronger emotional arousal, Burke outlines two additional factors that influence the strength of an emotion: how *often* an identity is disrupted and who is the *source* of the identity disruption.

According to Burke (1991), *frequent* interruptions in the identity verification process should lead to more intense negative arousal than infrequent or occasional interruptions. The more intense negative reaction occurs irrespective of the direction of the nonverification. The more negative response is borrowed from Mandler's (1982) interruption theory of stress. According to Mandler, distress is felt when organized action is interrupted or, looked at another way, an expectancy is not confirmed. The distress that is instigated by the interruption signals that something is wrong. An actor responds by attempting to adapt to the interruption. The more repeated the interruption, the more the person is unable to initiate and sustain organized activity and the more distress there will be. In identity control theory terms, an interruption constitutes a break in the smooth flowing cybernetic feedback loop that characterizes the identity process. The hallmark of the identity process is that the meanings held in one's identity standard are congruent with the ongoing meanings of the self in the situation. When an interruption occurs, identity standard meanings become discrepant with self-in-situation meanings and negative emotion is experienced.

While interruptions in the identity system generate more intense negative arousal, Burke further hypothesizes that an interruption in the identity verification process from a significant other should also lead to more intense negative arousal than an interruption from a nonsignificant other. According to Burke, because significant others are those with whom one has built up a set of mutually verified expectations in which past interactions have supported an identity, the meanings that have been built up form a more tightly organized system; and like all tightly woven identities, interruption of the identity control process for one element often poses problems in confirming other elements of the identity. This is consistent with Mandler's (1982) assumption that the interruption of more highly organized processes will lead to higher levels of autonomic arousal.

Research has examined actors' emotional responses to frequent identity nonverification and identity nonverification from a familiar and unfamiliar source (Stets 2003, 2005).

Evidence from data collected in a laboratory study reveals that as participants in the worker identity repeatedly experience nonverification, specifically, being over-rewarded or under-rewarded for average work when they should receive the expected reward, their emotions become less, not more, intense. This pattern suggests that individuals are adjusting their standards to the level of rewards that they are receiving. Since a strong emotional response signals a discrepancy between input meanings and standard meanings, a weak emotional response suggests a closer correspondence between input and identity standard meanings. I have suggested (Stets 2005) two reasons for why people change their identity standards: (1) a low level of commitment to identities created in a short-term study and (2) the inability to take corrective action to alter the feedback or reward they receive.

I also found that the source of the nonverifying information does influence negative emotions, but conditionally. Receiving nonverifying information from a familiar other (compared to unfamiliar other) produces more negative emotions, but only when the nonverification occurs once (compared to more than once) and only when the direction of the nonverification is positive (that is, participants receive an over-reward). These findings suggest that the theoretical relationship between identity processes and the emotions that ensue is conditioned upon certain factors being present.

RECENT RESEARCH AND FUTURE PROSPECTS

A number of areas serve as fertile ground for the development of identity theory. While some research already is under way in these areas, which I will mention, there is still much work to be done in advancing identity theory. Working within these areas will help extend identity theory beyond its current boundaries as well as identify the scope conditions of the theory. Broadly defined, these areas include (1) theory development, (2) methodological innovations, and (3) substantive advances.

Theoretical Development

Theoretical development is needed in several ways. The most obvious involves an integration of Stryker's version of identity theory, which emphasizes how social structures influence the structure of identities, and in turn, social behavior, with Burke's version of identity theory, which focuses on the internal dynamics of self-processes that that influence social behavior (Stryker and Burke 2000). To illustrate, the idea of committed and salient identities from the social structure can be incorporated into the internal dynamics of the identity control model. The identity standard in the identity control model reflects the meanings of particular groups, roles, or persons to which one is committed. The more strongly one is committed to these groups, roles, or persons, the greater the salience of that identity, the greater these identity meanings will be perceived as relevant in a situation, and the greater the motivational force to respond to the nonverification of these identity meanings when they arise. When self-in-situation meanings cannot be aligned with identity standard meanings, the identity should reduce in salience and result in decreased commitment to the relationships on which the identity is premised. Integrating theoretical elements from each version of identity theory such as the preceding can move us toward a more general theory of identity processes.

Another way to develop identity theory is to incorporate into the theory key processes that are the hallmark of alternative social psychological theories. In doing this, the predictive power of identity theory is put to the test, and ideas are examined across theoretical programs. For example, a key process in expectation states theory and status characteristics theory (see Chapter 12 for a review) is the status process. This process is reflected in the idea that when individuals enter interaction, they develop corresponding evaluations and expectations of one another by locating each other's status relative to themselves. Those who are evaluated as having higher status (given the ordering of status value and influence in the social structure) will be evaluated as more competent, expected to contribute more to the interaction, receive more deference from others, and be respected and held in high esteem. Recently, identity theorists have examined the role of status in the identity verification process, arguing that, given their greater influence and esteem, higher status actors should be more likely than lower status actors to induce others to verify their identities (Cast, Stets, and Burke 1999; Stets and Harrod 2004). With more research that applies identity theory to social psychological processes emphasized in other theories, we can determine the limits and possibilities of identity theory as a general theory of social behavior.

Methodological Innovations

In studying identity processes, most of the research has addressed identities in natural groups where individuals are typically committed to the identities they claim, the situation is somewhat predictable, and actors are familiar with the others in the setting. A good example is an analysis of identity processes that emerge in newly formed marriages (Burke and Cast 1997; Burke and Stets 1999; Cast 2003; Cast, Stets, and Burke 1999; Stets 1997; Stets and Burke 1996, 2004). Recently, research has begun to examine identity processes in experimental groups in which individuals are not as committed to the identity they are invoking in the situation, the situation is novel, and actors are generally unfamiliar with one another (Stets 2003, 2004, 2005). We are beginning to find differences in how the identity process operates in these two settings. As mentioned earlier, for example, we find that when individuals experience nonverification in a positive direction (they are overevaluated), people in the laboratory are guided by the enhancement principle and feel good, while people in new marriages are guided by the verification principle and feel bad (Burke and Harrod 2005; Stets 2005). Since identity processes emerge in weak as well as strong relationships, short-term as well as long-term interactions, novel as well as routine settings, we need to identify the conditions under which our predictions hold, and we need to offer alternative theoretical mechanisms when our predictions do not hold.

We also need better measures of our theoretical constructs. For instance, identity salience might be measured by people's response latency. Individuals' greater responsiveness to identity cues should be related to the likelihood of them enacting that behavior in a situation. The cues might be pictures that individuals can identify with. The quicker they identify the pictures, the higher the identity may be in their salience hierarchy and the more likely it may be played out across situations. In a related way, following the idea of

Burke and Reitzes (1991), commitment could be measured by a computer-measured strength of response in bringing disrupted identity descriptions back in line with self-conceptions. Here, not the latency of the response but the strength and persistence of restoring the self-description could be measured. This moves us away from our reliance on measuring identity salience and commitment from self-reports.

Substantive Advances

Investigating Multiple Identities. In identity theory, social actors hold multiple positions in the social structure and, correspondingly, have multiple identities. However, very little research has examined the "'multiple identities' conception of the self" (Stryker and Burke 2000, 291). Although multiple identities have been conceptualized as arranged in a hierarchy with the identity highest in the hierarchy prevailing in a situation, this approach has led to an emphasis, particularly in Burke's identity control theory, on only one identity in a situation. Peggy Thoits (1983, 1986, 2003) is one of the few researchers who has studied multiple identities, primarily focusing on how they are related to psychological well-being. For example, she shows that having multiple identities (that are voluntary as opposed to obligatory) is more beneficial than harmful to individuals because it gives their lives meaning and provides guidance for their behavior.

Some research is beginning to examine multiple identities by studying its relationship to one's position in the social structure. For example, Smith-Lovin (2003) argues that high-status actors will be more likely than low-status actors to develop multiple identities, and thus more complex selves, because they have more diverse social networks that range further through the social system. Stets and Harrod (2004) find that high-status actors, given their greater influence, are more likely than low-status actors to have their identities verified across multiple identities. And Burke (2003) studies how the same two identities play themselves out differently in terms of shared meanings for persons who are in two structurally different locations in a group. He finds that those persons who hold the coordinator role in a group have task and social-emotional identity performances that are highly and positively correlated, whereas those who do not hold the position of coordinator have task and social-emotional identity performances that are relatively independent.

Recently, Burke (2003) offered a number of hypotheses that can be tested in future research. For example, he hypothesizes that given the organization of multiple identities in a salience hierarchy, actors will be motivated to verify those identities that are higher in their salience hierarchy and to which they have higher levels of commitment. Additionally, he anticipates that identities that frequently co-occur will share common meanings and have similar levels of salience and commitment.

A theoretically fruitful way to understand the relationship among multiple identities, which we can more closely examine in future work, is to conceptualize them within the hierarchical structure of the identity control system (Burke 2003). If we think of an identity as the set of all meanings held for oneself in terms of a particular group membership, specific role, or certain personal characteristic, then an identity standard might be thought of as a set or vector of meanings. This set or vector of meanings is part of a single control system. When multiple identities are enacted in a situation, separate control systems have been activated, each of which is acting to control self-in-situation meanings to match the identity standard. Since control systems can be arranged hierarchically, higher, more abstract identities as well as lower, less abstract identities may be activated in a situation.

An identity higher in the hierarchy provides the reference or standard for an identity just below it. Looked at another way, identity standards of lower level control systems are the outputs of higher level control systems. When a higher level identity brings higher level perceptions into alignment with the higher level standard, it does so by changing its outputs, that is, changing lower level standards. Identities operating at higher levels and lower levels must be aligned in their meanings at their respective levels if they are activated at the same time (Burke 2003). If they are in opposition to each other when they are activated simultaneously, for example, when an employer must evaluate an employee who is performing poorly and who also happens to be a close friend, the actor is placed in the impossible position of verifying multiple, incompatible identities. One possible resolution is to change either or both of the identity standard meanings to make them more congruent. This is identity change, which is another area that needs development. This is discussed later.

Linking the Multiple Bases of Identity. Future research needs to examine the interrelationship among the three bases of identities: person, role, and social (group) identities, particularly since they often operate simultaneously in a situation. Recently, Burke (2004) discussed the possible linkages among these identities and provided hypotheses for future testing. For example, Burke maintains that person identities operate like master identities, thus they will influence the content of role and social identities. This theoretical relationship recently has been applied to an analysis of the moral identity (Stets and Carter 2006). Stets and Carter define the moral identity as a person identity, and given the hierarchical structure of the identity control system, they conceptualize it as a higher level control system than role and group identities. Since a higher level control system provides the standard for control systems below it, a person who claims a moral identity that involves meanings of care, kindness, and compassion should be more likely to choose roles that also carry these meanings such as taking on the role of parent, priest, or nurse. Groups that would encompass these roles would include a family, a parish, and a hospital. In this way, we see the interrelationship among person, role, and group identities.

Burke does qualify the influence of person identities on role and social identities by indicating that the influence of person identities should be greater when social actors have a choice in the roles they assume and the groups to which they belong. When there is little choice, the influence will occur in the opposite direction, with role and group meanings influencing the meanings of person identity standards. This suggests that obligatory role identities such as the parent identity, spouse identity, or worker identity will be more likely to influence person identity meanings, whereas person identity standards will be more likely to influence the content of voluntary role identities such as friend or neighbor (Thoits 1992). This could be tested empirically.

Another expectation that Burke discusses is the different consequences that should emerge for the self when person, role, and group identities are verified. Since social (group) identities involve being tied to similar others and being like those others, verification of social identities should lead individuals to feel that they are accepted for who they are. This will increase their feelings of self-worth. Since role identities involve acting in a way that confirms the counter-identity of the other in the situation and, correspondingly, those in the counter-identity behaving in a way that verifies one's own role identity, verification of role identities will be tied to effectively performing one's role. This should lead to feelings of self-competence. Finally, since person identities help establish the self as a distinct entity, unique from others and who others can count on to verify their own person identities, the verification of person identities will foster feelings of authenticity—being who one really is. If these relationships are empirically supported in future research, then linking the different identity bases to different self-esteem bases (self-worth, self-efficacy, and self-authenticity) will develop identity theory further.

Identity Change. While some identity theorists have examined identity change (Burke and Cast 1997; Kiecolt 1994, 2000; Serpe 1987), more generally, this has been a neglected area of research. It is not clear whether this neglect is due to the lack of longitudinal data to capture identity changes, the lack of theory to explain identity changes, or both. Regarding the latter, we may be making some advances. Burke (2006) recently outlined two theoretical mechanisms by which persons' identities change over time, and his findings are consistent with these theoretical processes. The first is the slow change over time in one's identity standard meanings to match the meanings of the self in the situation. This may occur when people take on new roles (as in becoming a parent) or new groups. Because persistent problems emerge with the verification of the existing identity, the identity standard meanings are modified to fit into the new situation rather than trying to change the situation to fit the identity standard meanings.

The second mechanism by which identities may change occurs when individuals hold multiple identities that are related to each other in that they share a common dimension of meaning, and activating the meanings of one identity creates a lack of verification in the meanings for the other identity. An example would be a woman whose gender identity carries meanings of strength and independence while her wife identity carries meanings of less strength and dependence on her husband. Burke argues that the identity meanings for both identities will slowly shift in the direction of the self-in-situation meanings that persons find themselves. In the previous example, the woman's gender identity meanings may become less strong and less independent and her wife identity meanings may become more strong and less dependent. Thus the meanings in each of the identity standards become more like each other in their settings on that dimension when they are activated together. In general, these two mechanisms highlight identity change that is endogenous. The change occurs when there is a lack of verification either because of new situations actors must manage or other identities that are simultaneously being activated and are not being verified.

More recently, Burke (2004) develops several hypotheses for identity change that is exogenous. Here the source of the change is not internal, due to a lack of verification, but external, due to one's location in the social structure and changes in the flow of resources through the structure. These hypotheses include the following: (1) role-identity change due to role making is more likely to occur in new organizations or organizations undergoing restructuring compared to more established organizations, (2) role-identity change is more likely to emerge in organizations where there has been a significant change in resource levels compared to an organization with constant resource levels, and (3) role-identity change is more likely to occur in organizations or groups that significantly change in size compared to organizations or groups that are relatively stable in size. Burke points to identity change as a function of changing connectedness of identities within the social structure and changing resource levels. Hypotheses such as these serve as a source for direct testing with the goal of extending identity theory.

CONCLUSION

This is an exciting time in the development of identity theory. By integrating the different versions of the theory, we are poised to bridge the gap between the individual and society, addressing issues of a more macro concern, such as the origins of the patterns of activity that constitute social structure, as well as addressing issues of a more micro concern, such as the various meanings of the self as a person, in a role, and as a group member and their relationship to individual choice behavior. In advancing identity theory beyond its current boundaries, identity theorists must remain open to new ways of thinking about and testing identity processes. And they must be careful and systematic in these endeavors. Over the past 25 years, identity theory has been formulating a coherent and cumulative theory of social behavior. The next 25 years of theory building can only sharpen and deepen our understanding of self, identity, meaning, and behavior, all of which constitute the very foundation of society.

1. While sociological social psychologists have chiefly focused on role identities, psychological social psychologists have been instrumental in informing us as to the processes involved in social identity formation and activation (Abrams and Hogg 1990; Turner et al. 1987). Role identity theory and social identity theory have developed as separate lines of research. While some have argued that, because these theories are so different, it is inadvisable to integrate them (Hogg, Terry, and White 1995), others have argued that there are substantial similarities between the two theories and they could be linked in fundamental ways (Stets and Burke 2000). See Chapter 6 for an in-depth analysis of social identity theory.

2. Very similar to this version of identity theory is affect control theory, developed by Heise and his colleagues (Heise 1979; MacKinnon 1994; Robinson and Smith-Lovin 1992; Smith-Lovin and Heise 1988), which also focuses on internal dynamics but draws more heavily on the shared cultural meanings of identities as opposed to individual, subcultural, or group meanings. See Chapter 7 for a detailed discussion of this theory.

REFERENCES

Abrams, Dominic, and Michael A. Hogg. 1990. *Social Identity Theory: Constructive and Critical Advances*. London: Harvester-Wheatsheaf.

Blumer, Herbert. 1969. *Symbolic Interactionism*. Englewood Cliffs, NJ: Prentice-Hall.

Burke, Peter J. 1980. The self: Measurement implications from a symbolic interactionist perspective. *Social Psychology Quarterly* 43:18–29.

———. 1991. Identity processes and social stress. *American Sociological Review* 56:836–49.

———. 1996. Social identities and psychosocial stress. In *Psychosocial Stress: Perspectives on Structure, Theory, Life Course, and Methods*, ed. H. B. Kaplan. Orlando, FL: Academic Press.

———. 1997. An identity model for network exchange. *American Sociological Review* 62:134–50.

———. 2006. Identity change. *Social Psychology Quarterly* 69.

———. 2003. Relationships among multiple identities. In *Advances in Identity Theory and Research*, ed. P. J. Burke, T. J. Owens, R. Serpe, and P. A. Thoits. New York: Kluwer Academic/Plenum.

———. 2004. Identities and social structure: The 2003 Cooley-Mead Award Address. *Social Psychology Quarterly* 67:5–15.

Burke, Peter J., and Alicia D. Cast. 1997. Stability and change in the gender identities of newly married couples. *Social Psychology Quarterly* 60:277–90.

Burke, Peter J., and Michael M. Harrod. 2005. Too much of a good thing? *Social Psychology Quarterly* 68:359–74.

Burke, Peter J., and Donald C. Reitzes. 1981. The link between identity and role performance. *Social Psychology Quarterly* 44:83–92.

———. 1991. An identity theory approach to commitment. *Social Psychology Quarterly* 54:239–51.

Burke, Peter J., and Jan E. Stets. 1999. Trust and commitment through self-verification. *Social Psychology Quarterly* 62:347–66.

Burke, Peter J., Jan E. Stets, and Maureen Pirog-Good. 1988. Gender identity, self-esteem, and physical and sexual abuse in dating relationships. *Social Psychology Quarterly* 51:272–85.

Burke, Peter J., and Judy Tully. 1977. The measurement of role/identity. *Social Forces* 55:881–97.

Callero, Peter L. 1985. Role-identity salience. *Social Psychology Quarterly* 48:203–14.

Cast, Alicia D. 2003. Power and the ability to control the definition of the situation. *Social Psychology Quarterly* 66:185–201.

Cast, Alicia D., and Peter J. Burke. 2002. A theory of self-esteem. *Social Forces* 80:1041–68.

Cast, Alicia D., Jan E. Stets, and Peter J. Burke. 1999. Does the self conform to the views of others? *Social Psychology Quarterly* 62:68–82.

Freese, Lee, and Peter J. Burke. 1994. Persons, identities, and social interaction. In *Advances in Group Processes*, ed. B. Markovsky, K. Heimer, and J. O'Brien. Greenwich, CT: JAI Press.

Gecas, Viktor, and Monica A. Seff. 1990. Social class and self-esteem: Psychological centrality, compensation, and the relative effects of work and home. *Social Psychology Quarterly* 53:165–73.

Heise, David R. 1979. *Understanding Events: Affect and the Construction of Social Action.* Cambridge: Cambridge University Press.

Hogg, Michael A., Deborah J. Terry, and Katherine M. White. 1995. A tale of two theories: A critical comparison of identity theory with social identity theory. *Social Psychology Quarterly* 58:255–69.

James, William. 1890. *Principles of Psychology.* New York: Holt, Rinehart & Winston.

Kiecolt, K. Jill. 1994. Stress and the decision to change oneself: A theoretical model. *Social Psychology Quarterly* 57:49–63.

———. 2000. Self change in social movements. In *Identity, Self, and Social Movements*, ed. S. Stryker, T. Owens, and R. White. Minneapolis: University of Minnesota Press.

MacKinnon, Neil J. 1994. *Symbolic Interaction as Affect Control.* Albany: State University of New York Press.

Mandler, George. 1982. Stress and thought processes. In *Handbook of Stress: Theoretical and Clinical Aspects*, ed. L. Goldberger and S. Breznitz. New York: Free Press.

McCall, George J. 2003. The me and the not-me: Positive and negative poles of identity. In *Advances in Identity Theory and Research*, ed. P. J. Burke, T. J. Owens, R. T. Serpe, and P. A. Thoits. New York: Kluwer Academic/Plenum.

McCall, George J., and J. L. Simmons. 1978. *Identities and Interactions.* New York: Free Press.

Mutran, Elizabeth, and Peter J. Burke. 1979. Personalism as a component of old age identity. *Research on Aging* 1:37–64.

Oakes, Penelope J., S. Alexander Haslam, and John C. Turner. 1994. *Stereotyping and Social Reality.* Oxford: Basil Blackwell.

Osgood, Charles E., George J. Suci, and Percy H. Tannenbaum. 1957. *The Measurement of Meaning.* Urbana, IL: University of Illinois Press.

Powers, William T. 1973. *Behavior: The Control of Perception.* Chicago: Aldine.

Reitzes, Donald C., and Peter J. Burke. 1980. College student identity measurement and implications. *Pacific Sociological Review* 23:46–66.

Riley, Anna, and Peter J. Burke. 1995. Identities and self-verification in the small group. *Social Psychology Quarterly* 58:61–73.

Robinson, Dawn T., and Lynn Smith-Lovin. 1992. Selective interaction as a strategy for identity maintenance: An affect control model. *Social Psychology Quarterly* 55:12–28.

Rosenberg, Morris. 1979. *Conceiving the Self.* New York: Basic Books.

Serpe, Richard T. 1987. Stability and change in self: A structural symbolic interactionist explanation. *Social Psychology Quarterly* 50:44–55.

Serpe, Richard T., and Sheldon Stryker. 1987. The construction of self and reconstruction of social relationships. In *Advances in Group Processes*, ed. E. Lawler and B. Markovsky. Greenwich, CT: JAI Press.

Smith-Lovin, Lynn. 2003. The self, identity, and interaction in an ecology of identities. In *Advances in Identity Theory and Research*, ed. P. J. Burke, T. J. Owens, R. Serpe, and P. A. Thoits. New York: Kluwer Academic/Plenum.

Smith-Lovin, Lynn, and David R. Heise, eds. 1988. *Analyzing Social Interaction: Advances in Affect Control Theory*. New York: Gordon & Breach.

Stets, Jan E. 1997. Status and identity in marital interaction. *Social Psychology Quarterly* 60:185–217.

———. 2003. Justice, emotion, and identity theory. In *Advances in Identity Theory and Research*, ed. P. J. Burke, T. J. Owens, R. T. Serpe, and P. A. Thoits. New York: Kluwer Academic/Plenum.

———. 2004. Emotions in identity theory: The effects of status. *Advances in Group Processes* 21:51–76.

———. 2005. Examining emotions in identity theory. *Social Psychology Quarterly* 68:39–74.

Stets, Jan E., and Chris F. Biga. 2003. Bringing identity theory into environmental sociology. *Sociological Theory* 21:398–423.

Stets, Jan E., and Peter J. Burke. 1994. Inconsistent self-views in the control identity model. *Social Science Research* 23:236–62.

———. 1996. Gender, control, and interaction. *Social Psychology Quarterly* 59:193–220.

———. 2000. Identity theory and social identity theory. *Social Psychology Quarterly* 63:224–37.

Stets, Jan E., and Michael J. Carter. 2006. The moral identity: A principle level identity. In *Purpose, Meaning, and Action: Control Systems Theories in Sociology*, ed. K. McClelland and T. J. Fararo. New York: Palgrave-MacMillan.

Stets, Jan E., and Michael M. Harrod. 2004. Verification across multiple identities: The role of status. *Social Psychology Quarterly* 67:155–71.

Stryker, Sheldon. 1968. Identity salience and role performance. *Journal of Marriage and the Family* 4:558–64.

———. 1980. *Symbolic Interactionism: A Social Structural Version*. Menlo Park, CA: Benjamin Cummings.

———. 2000. Identity competition: Key to differential social movement participation? In *Self, Identity, and Social Movements*, ed. S. Stryker, T. Owens, and R. White. Minneapolis: University of Minnesota Press.

———. 2004. Integrating emotion into identity theory. *Advances in Group Processes* 21:1–23.

Stryker, Sheldon, and Peter J. Burke. 2000. The past, present, and future of an identity theory. *Social Psychology Quarterly* 63:284–97.

Stryker, Sheldon, and Richard T. Serpe. 1982. Commitment, identity salience, and role behavior: A theory and research example. In *Personality, Roles, and Social Behavior*, ed. W. Ickes and E. S. Knowles. New York: Springer-Verlag.

———. 1994. Identity salience and psychological centrality: Equivalent, overlapping, or complementary concepts? *Social Psychology Quarterly* 57:16–35.

Thoits, Peggy A. 1983. Multiple identities and psychological well-being: A reformulation and test of the social isolation hypothesis. *American Sociological Review* 49:174–87.

———. 1986. Multiple identities: Examining gender and marital status differences in distress. *American Sociological Review* 51:259–72.

———. 1991. On merging identity theory and stress research. *Social Psychology Quarterly* 54:101–12.

———. 1992. Identity structures and psychological well-being: Gender and marital status comparisons. *Social Psychology Quarterly* 55:236–56.

———. 1995. Identity-relevant events and psychological symptoms: A cautionary tale. *Journal of Health and Social Behavior* 36:72–82.

———. 2003. Personal agency in the accumulation of multiple role-identities. In *Advances in Identity Theory and Research*, ed. P. J. Burke, T. J. Owens, R. T. Serpe, and P. A. Thoits. New York: Kluwer Academic/Plenum.

Tsushima, Teresa, and Peter J. Burke. 1999. Levels, agency, and control in the parent identity. *Social Psychology Quarterly* 62:173–89.

Turner, John C., Michael A. Hogg, Penelope J. Oakes, Stephen D. Reicher, and Margaret S. Wetherell, eds. 1987. *Rediscovering the Social Group: A Self-Categorization Theory*. New York: Basil Blackwell.

6 SOCIAL IDENTITY THEORY

Michael A. Hogg

Social identity theory is a social psychological analysis of the role of self-conception in group membership, group processes, and intergroup relations. It embraces a number of interrelated concepts and subtheories that focus on social-cognitive, motivational, social-interactive and macrosocial facets of group life. The approach is explicitly framed by a conviction that collective phenomena cannot be adequately explained in terms of isolated individual processes or interpersonal interaction alone and that social psychology should place large-scale social phenomena near the top of its scientific agenda.

Social identity theory defines *group* cognitively—in terms of people's self-conception as group members. A group exists psychologically if three or more people construe and evaluate themselves in terms of shared attributes that distinguish them collectively from other people. Social identity theory addresses phenomena such as prejudice, discrimination, ethnocentrism, stereotyping, intergroup conflict, conformity, normative behavior, group polarization, crowd behavior, organizational behavior, leadership, deviance, and group cohesiveness.

Social identity theory was first developed at the start of the 1970s in Britain by Henri Tajfel, out of his scientific and personal interests in social perception, social categorization, and social comparison and prejudice, discrimination, and intergroup conflict. Over the past 30 years social identity theory has attracted many collaborators and followers. It has developed and matured conceptually and has motivated, and continues to motivate, a prodigious quantity of research. Although initially a European analysis of intergroup relations, since the early 1990s it has become accepted around the world as one of mainstream social psychology's most significant general theories of the relationship between self and group. However, this popularity has sometimes brought with it a disjunction between some readings of social identity concepts and the concepts themselves.

This chapter describes the concepts that form the social identity approach. I use the term *approach* because social identity theory is sometimes too narrowly equated with only one aspect—the analysis of intergroup relations and social change as a function of positive distinctiveness (e.g., Tajfel and Turner 1979). In reality the intergroup-relations analysis articulates tightly, beneath a single social identity umbrella, with analyses of social influence, self-categorization, motivation, cohesion, and so forth. The notion of an integrated social identity *approach* is not new. It was explicit in Hogg and Abrams's (1988) integration of social identity concepts, and in their and others' subsequent research, and is consistent with Tajfel's original vision of a multilevel nonreductionist analysis of self and group. It has also been echoed by Turner (1999) and frames recent statements and reviews of social identity theory and research (e.g., Abrams and Hogg 2001; Hogg 2001a, 2003; Hogg et al. 2004).

The chapter opens with a history of the development of the social identity approach and a description of its metatheoretical foundations. I then describe each of the conceptual components, or subtheories, and some associated developments and applications before closing with a discussion of some misunderstandings, controversies, and future directions.

ORIGINS AND DEVELOPMENT

For recent accounts of the development of the social identity approach, see Turner (1999) and Hogg (2000a). The approach has its scientific origins in at least four lines of research by Tajfel: (1) investigations of how categorization causes people to perceptually accentuate similarities among stimuli within the same category and difference between stimuli from different categories (Tajfel 1959), (2) analyses of the role of cognitive processes, specifically categorization, in prejudice (Tajfel 1969), (3) research showing that being categorized, on a minimal or trivial basis, causes people to discriminate in favor of their own group (Tajfel et al. 1971), and (4) a critique of social comparison research, arguing that in intergroup contexts people make comparisons that maximize differences between self (as in-group member) and other (as out-group member) (Tajfel 1974).

The emotional drive for the development of the social identity approach was, however, personal. Tajfel's experiences as a Polish Jew in Europe during the rise of the Nazis, World War II, the Holocaust, and the postwar relocation of displaced Europeans, fueled a personal passion to understand prejudice, discrimination, and intergroup conflict. Tajfel did not believe that these large-scale social phenomena could be satisfactorily explained in terms of personality or interpersonal interactions. Instead, like Sherif (e.g., 1962), writers such as Tolstoy, and political theorists like Karl Marx, he believed that social forces configured individual action. The challenge for social psychology was to theorize how this happened.

His explicit metatheoretical goal (Turner 1996) was to develop an explanation that did *not* reinterpret intergroup phenomena merely as the expression of personality traits, individual differences, and interpersonal processes among a large number of people. In eschewing reductionism Tajfel aligned himself in opposition to the dominant paradigm in social psychology. This is one reason why, from the outset, social identity research often appeared to be conducted as though it were a social movement and social identity theorists were a revolutionary cadre seeking to change the foundations of social psychology from their lair in the Psychology Department at Bristol University.

From the late 1960s until his death in 1982, Tajfel, in collaboration with Turner who joined him in the early 1970s, integrated his social categorization, ethnocentrism, social comparison, and intergroup-relations research around the concept of social identity. Drawing on work by Berger (1966; Berger and Luckmann 1971), Tajfel defined social identity as "the individual's knowledge that he belongs to certain social groups together with some emotional and value significance to him of this group membership" (Tajfel 1972, 292). Groups, defined as collections of people sharing the same social identity, compete with one another to be distinctive in evaluatively positive ways—they compete over consensual status and prestige. The strategies that groups use in this competition are influenced by people's beliefs about the nature of intergroup relations. This analysis, which drew on sources such as Hirschmann (1970), became known as social identity theory and later the "social identity theory of intergroup behavior" (Turner et al. 1987, 42). It was first presented by Tajfel (1974) and then published by Tajfel and Turner in their classic 1979 article, and it also acted as the intellectual springboard for the development by Giles and others of a still burgeoning social psychology of language and intergroup relations (e.g., Giles, Bourhis, and Taylor 1977).

The end of the 1970s through the mid-1980s witnessed a change in focus. Partly in response to the ascendance of American social cognition, Turner and his graduate students at Bristol refocused attention on and elaborated the role and operation of the categorization process in social identity phenomena. These ideas were formalized as self-categorization theory (Turner 1985; Turner et al. 1987)—also called "the social identity theory of the group" (Turner et al. 1987, 42). Self-categorization theory, as the cognitive dimension of the social identity approach, describes how categorization of self and others underpins social identification and associated group and intergroup phenomena. This period witnessed two other major developments. A social identity model of the processes of social influence in groups, called referent informational influence, was elaborated (Turner 1982)—people construct group norms from appropriate in-group members and in-group behaviors and internalize and enact these norms as part of their social identity— and there was growing interest in the motivational bases of social identity processes— self-enhancement seemed to be involved but precisely how was unclear (Abrams and Hogg 1988).

By the mid-1980s social identity research, both conceptual and empirical, had proliferated and was widely distributed—the field was badly in need of integrative focus. This was provided by Hogg and Abrams (1988), who promoted the idea of an integrated social identity approach, within which was embedded specific concepts, theories, or analyses dealing with different aspects of social identity processes and phenomena.

Since the late 1980s there has been a flood of social identity research, and the social identity approach is center stage in the continuing revival of research on group processes and intergroup relations (e.g., Abrams and Hogg 1998; Moreland, Hogg, and Hains 1994). Some of the more substantial conceptual developments have focused on stereotyping, self-conception, motivation, collective behavior, norms and social influence, multiple categorization and diversity, and intragroup phenomena mainly in small groups. Social identity analyses have also become increasingly popular outside mainstream social psychology—in, for example, sociology (e.g., Hogg and Ridgeway 2003; Hogg, Terry, and White 1995; Stets and Burke 2000) and organizational science (e.g., Haslam 2004; Hogg and Terry 2000).

METATHEORETICAL FOUNDATIONS

The social identity approach is framed by an explicit metatheoretical commitment—what the approach should and should not do, what its explanatory scope and range is, what level of explanation is appropriate, and so forth (cf. Abrams and Hogg 2004). Although no longer an exclusively European enterprise, the social identity approach was developed within the metatheoretical framework of postwar European social psychology, and it retains this legacy.

World War II left European social psychology in ruins. For many years it was effectively a satellite of American social psychology. However, by the 1960s European social psychologists fully realized that they had a common European interest in social psychology, which differed from mainstream American social psychology in that it was more concerned with the wider social context of social behavior (e.g., Jaspars 1986) and the development of a more *social* social psychology (e.g., Taylor and Brown 1979). This European emphasis is exemplified by *The Social Dimension: European Developments in Social Psychology*—a two-volume book edited by Tajfel (1984) to portray what was distinctive about European social psychology. In the introductory chapter, Tajfel and colleagues noted that amid the diversity of European social psychology

> there seems to exist a very general common denominator: in a phrase, it can be referred to as *the social dimension* of European social psychology. This is simply described: in much of the work—whatever its background, interests, theoretical approach or research direction—there has been a constant stress on the social and interactive aspects of our subject. Social psychology in Europe is today much more *social* than it was 20 years ago. (Tajfel, Jaspars, and Fraser 1984, 1)

Later, they defined the social dimension as a

> view that social psychology can and must include in its theoretical and research preoccupations a direct concern with the relationship between human psychological functioning and the large-scale social processes and events which shape this functioning and are shaped by it. (Tajfel, Jaspars, and Fraser 1984, 3)

European social psychology attended closely to levels of explanation (e.g., Doise 1986). The aim was to develop concepts and theories that were appropriate to the level of explanation being sought and then to articulate these concepts and theories within a wider conceptual framework, without falling into the trap of reductionism. In conjunction with the emphasis on the social dimension, this interactionist metatheory placed group processes, in particular intergroup relations involving large-scale social categories, high on the European social psychological agenda. The European study of intergroup relations is clearly framed by a distinctive European perspective that focuses on people's interaction with one another not as unique individuals but as members of social groups (Manstead 1990).

The social identity approach was systematically developed within this intellectual milieu. Until the late 1980s, social identity theory, along with research on minority influence and social representations (Moscovici 1980, 1988), epitomized the European approach to social psychology and was a vehicle for the promotion of a European metatheory. The metatheory remains important, but the messianic zeal of the early years is less strident, and the approach is now more inclusive and diverse.

CONCEPTUAL STRUCTURE

The social identity approach has a number of conceptual components that serve different explanatory functions and focus on different aspects of group membership and group life (Hogg 2003; Hogg et al. 2004). They fit together and articulate smoothly with one another to provide an integrated middle-range theory of the relationship between self-conception and group processes—a nonreductionist, interactionist theory linking individual cognition, social interaction, and societal processes.

Social Identity, Collective Self, and Group Membership

Social Identity and Personal Identity. A social group is more than two people who share the same social identity. They identify and evaluate themselves in the same way and have the same definition of who they are, what attributes they have, and how they relate to and differ from people who are not in their group or who are in specific out-groups. Group membership is a matter of collective self-construal—"we" and "us" versus "them." In contrast, personal identity is a self-construal in terms of idiosyncratic personality attributes that are not shared with other people ("I") or personal dyadic relationships with a specific other person ("me" and "you"). Although personal identity has little to do with group processes, group life often frames the development of personal identities and interpersonal friendships and enmities.

People have as many social and personal identities as there are groups they belong to and personal relationships they are involved in. Social and personal identities vary in subjective importance and value and in how accessible they are in people's minds (chronic accessibility) or in the immediate situation (situational accessibility). However, in any given situation only one identity is psychologically salient to govern self-construal, social perception, and social conduct. As the situation or context changes, so does the salient identity, or the form that the identity takes.

Varieties and Dimensions of Selves and Identities. Although social identity theory conventionally distinguishes between social and personal identity, there are some qualifications and alternative views. For example, Reid and Deaux (1996) distinguish between collective selves that reflect social identities and individual selves that reflect personal *attributes* rather than personal *identities*, and Deaux and colleagues (1995) remind us that there are qualitative differences between types of social identity (e.g., ethnicity or religion, stigma, political). Cameron (2004) argues that social identity is not a unitary construct; it has three separate aspects that are related but not isomorphic: centrality, relating to cognitive accessibility of the identity; in-group affect, a self-evaluative feeling that derives from the identity; and in-group ties, reflecting a sense of attachment and belonging to the group that defines the identity (cf. Ellemers, Kortekaas, and Ouwerkerk 1999; Jackson and Smith 1999).

Others have suggested that the social versus personal identity dichotomy is too stark. For example, Brewer and Gardner (1996; Yuki 2003) distinguish between three aspects of the self: *individual self* (defined by personal traits differentiating self from all others), *relational self* (defined by dyadic relationships between self and specific significant other persons), and *collective self* (defined by group membership differentiating "us" from "them"). In another article, Brewer (2001) distinguishes between four types of social identity: (1) *person-based social identities* emphasize how properties of groups are internalized by individual group members as part of the self-concept; (2) *relational social identities* define self in relation to specific other people with whom one interacts in a group context (cf. Brewer and Gardner's [1996] "relational self" and Markus and Kitayama's [1991] "interdependent self"); (3) *group-based social identities* are equivalent to social identity as traditionally defined; and (4) *collective identities* refer to a process whereby group members do not just share self-defining attributes but also engage in social action to forge an image of what the group stands for and how it is represented and viewed by others.

The status of the relational self or relational social identity is particularly interesting. From a social identity point of view, is it a form of social identity or a form of personal identity? One possibility is that it depends on the wider social (e.g., cultural) context of group life. For example, dyadic relational identities in individualistic cultures separate people from the group—for example, married couples working in the same organization. In this case relational identity is clearly personal identity, as described above. However, in collectivist cultures group membership can be defined in terms of people's relationships to one another (Oyserman, Coon, and Kemmelmeier 2002)—your network of relationships locates you within the group and maintains your membership. Here, relational identity is how social identity is expressed.

Because individualist and collectivist cultures differ in people's preferred mode of self-construal—independent versus interdependent or relational self (e.g., Fiske et al. 1998)—we might expect social identity processes in small groups to be more evident in collectivist than individualist societies (e.g., Hinkle and Brown 1990). Collectivist norms prioritize the group over the individual and thus encourage social identity and group-oriented behavior. But is it true that social identity processes are less strong in individualistic societies? The answer is probably no—cultural norms may regulate how people interact and conduct themselves in groups, but groups still provide people with a strong sense of self, social location, and belonging. So people in small groups with a strongly individualistic norm or local culture will, paradoxically, behave more individualistically as a function of increased identification (e.g., McAuliffe et al. 2003).

Dyads, Aggregates, and Groups. How many people make a group? Social identity researchers believe that a dyad is not a group. A group must have at least three people because (1) a dyad is saturated by interpersonal processes, (2) you need at least three people to infer group norms from the behavior of others—in a dyad there is only one other person—and

(3) many group processes can't occur in a dyad—for example, coalition formation, majority social pressure, and deviance processes. This is consistent with the position of many group processes researchers. For example, Forsyth believes that "dyads possess many unique characteristics simply because they include only two members. The dyad is, by definition, the only group that dissolves when one member leaves and the only group that can never be broken down into subgroups (or coalitions)" (1999, 6).

However, from a social identity perspective, two people in the same place at the same time can be a group if they share a social identity defined by a larger collective. For example, two Americans, John and Mary, in Iraq may feel American and act like Americans. In this sense they are a group, but the group they belong to is "Americans," not "John and Mary." From a social identity perspective a person can easily feel and act as a group member when entirely alone—in the Iraqi example, Mary, all alone and abandoned by John, may feel and act American just on seeing the American flag.

What transforms an aggregate of three or more people into a group? From a social identity perspective the critical factor is that they identify with the group. Common fate, interdependence, interaction, shared goals, group structure, and so forth, play a role, but this is because they raise entitativity (Campbell 1958; Hamilton and Sherman 1996) and make the group more grouplike and cohesive. They are factors that facilitate or strengthen identification, but identification is the psychological process underlying group phenomena.

Groups are not all the same—they vary in size, function, longevity, distribution, and so forth (Deaux et al. 1995). One broad distinction is between similarity-based categorical groups and interaction-based dynamic groups (Arrow, McGrath, and Berdahl 2000; Wilder and Simon 1998)—what Prentice, Miller, and Lightdale (1994) call *common-identity* groups (groups based on direct attachment to the group) and *common-bond* groups (groups based upon attachment among members). This distinction has an impressive pedigree going back to a distinction originally made in 1857 by Tönnies (1955) between *Gemeinschaft* (community) and *Gesellschaft* (association)—that is, social organization based on close interpersonal bonds and social organization based on more formalized and impersonal associations. Although these distinctions capture important differences in the nature of a group, social identity theorists believe that the essence of groupness remains identification. People can be in a common-bond or a common-identity group, but if they have no sense of belonging, do not identify, and do not define and evaluate self in terms of the properties of the group, then they are unlikely to think, feel, and behave as group members.

Groups are rarely homogeneous. In almost all cases they are structured into roles, subgroups, nested categories, crosscutting categories, and so forth. Most groups contain generic roles, such as newcomer, full member, and old-timer, which members move in and out of as they enter a group, become socialized, and leave a group (e.g., Levine and Moreland 1994). According to Moreland and colleagues, role occupation is a matter of bilateral commitment between group and member, with commitment resting on how prototypical the member is of the group and of the role within the group (e.g., Moreland and Levine 2003; Moreland, Levine, and McMinn 2001).

Social Categorization, Prototypes, and Depersonalization

Prototypes and Metacontrast. Social categorization is the cognitive basis of social identity processes (Turner et al. 1987)—when we talk of groups we are talking about categories of people, social categories. From a social identity perspective, people cognitively represent a category or group as a *prototype*—a fuzzy set of attributes (perceptions, attitudes, feelings, and behaviors) that are related to one another in a meaningful way and that simultaneously capture similarities within the group and differences between the group and other groups or people who are not in the group.

Prototypes describe categories and also evaluate them and prescribe membership-related behavior. They chart the contours of social groups and tell us not only what characterizes a group but also how that group is different from other groups. Prototypes maximize entitativity (the property of a category that makes it appear to be a cohesive and clearly structured entity that is distinct from other entities—e.g., Campbell 1958; Hamilton and Sherman 1996) and obey the *metacontrast principle*—their configuration maximizes the ratio of perceived intergroup differences to intragroup differences and thus accentuates similarities within groups and differences between groups (cf. Tajfel 1959).

This analysis has a number of implications. (1) The content of a prototype rests on which human attributes maximize metacontrast in a specific context—with the caveat that people are motivated (see later discussion) to emphasize attributes that favor the in-group over the out-group. (2) Because accentuation of intergroup differences is integral to metacontrast, prototypes rarely describe average or typical in-group members—rather they are polarized away from out-group features and describe ideal, often hypothetical, in-group members. (3) Because metacontrast involves both intra- and intergroup comparisons, any change in the social comparative context (e.g., the specific out-group or in-group members present or specific goals embedded in the context) affects the prototype—prototypes are context-specific and can change if the context changes. This variability is relatively modest because of the anchoring effect of enduring and highly accessible representations of important groups we belong to but may be more dramatic in new groups or groups that we know less about. (4) Intra- and intergroup behavior are inextricable—what happens between groups affects what happens within groups, and vice versa.

Categorization and Depersonalization. The act of categorizing someone as a group member transforms how you see them. Rather than seeing an idiosyncratic individual or a close friend, you see them through the lens of the prototype, measuring them against the prototype and assigning prototypical attributes to them. They are perceptually *depersonalized.* Depersonalization is not dehumanization. Dehumanization is the perception of a person as not having qualities that warrant treating him or her as a human being—it justifies and facilitates inhuman actions against that person. Depersonalization means viewing someone as having the attributes of a category—if the attributes are positive (in-group attributes are almost always positive), depersonalization produces favorable perceptions; if they are highly negative and degrading (out-group attributes can sometimes be like this), it may produce dehumanization.

Social categorization depersonalizes both in-group and out-group members. Depersonalized perception of out-group members is more commonly called stereotyping—you view "them" as being similar to one another and all having out-group attributes. When you categorize yourself, exactly the same depersonalization process applies—you view yourself in terms of the attributes of the in-group (self-stereotyping), and since prototypes also describe and prescribe group-appropriate ways to feel and behave, you feel and behave normatively. In this way, self-categorization produces, within a group, conformity and patterns of in-group liking, trust, and solidarity.

Depersonalization of self is not the same as deindividuation. Depersonalization means viewing yourself as a category representative rather than a unique individual and is associated with a change in identity, whereas deindividuation refers to a loss of identity, often under conditions of anonymity, which is associated with primitive antisocial and aggressive impulses (Zimbardo 1970). According to the social identity model of deindividuation (SIDE model), depersonalization can produce antisocial and aggressive behavior but only if people identify with a group that has a prototype prescribing such conduct (Reicher, Spears, and Postmes 1995; Postmes et al. 2001).

An alternative, but generally compatible, emphasis on identification and depersonalization has been proposed by Wright and his associates (e.g., Wright, Aron, and Tropp 2002). Drawing on research showing that people can internalize the properties of other people, and of the in-group as a whole, as part of the self (e.g., Smith and Henry 1996), Wright and his colleagues suggest that strength of identification is a function of the extent to which the group is included in the self.

Psychological Salience. For a social categorization to affect behavior, it must be psychologically salient as the basis for perception and self-conception. The principle governing social identity salience, developed and elaborated by Oakes (1987) from work by Bruner (1957), rests on the two notions of *accessibility* and *fit*. People draw on readily accessible social categorizations (e.g., gender, race, profession)—ones that are valued, important, and frequently employed aspects of the self-concept (they are chronically accessible in memory) or because they are self-evident and perceptually salient in the immediate situation (they are situationally accessible).

People use accessible categories to make sense of their social context—investigating how well the categorization accounts for similarities and differences among people (structural or comparative fit) and how well the stereotypical properties of the categorization account for why people behave as they do (normative fit). If the fit of the categorization is poor (for example, similarities and differences do not correspond to people's gender or race and people do not behave in gender- or race-stereotypical ways), people cycle through other accessible categorizations (e.g., political orientation, religion, profession) until an optimal level of fit is obtained. This process is not entirely automatic. People are motivated to make categorizations that favor the in-group fit and may go to some lengths to do this. Salience is not only a cognitive-perceptual process but is also a social process in which people may compete or "negotiate" over category salience.

The categorization that has optimal fit becomes psychologically salient in that context as the basis of self-categorization, group identification, and prototype-based depersonalization. It accentuates in-group similarities and intergroup differences, enhances perceived entitativity, and underpins context-relevant group and intergroup behaviors.

Social Identity Motivations

Social identity is motivated by two processes, self-enhancement and uncertainty reduction, that cause groups to strive to be both better than and distinct from other groups. A third motivation that plays a role is optimal distinctiveness.

Self-Enhancement and Positive Distinctiveness. One of the most distinctive features of group life and intergroup relations is ethnocentrism (Sumner 1906), or positive distinctiveness—a belief that "we" are better than "them" in every possible way. Groups go to great lengths to protect or promote this belief (see later discussion). Groups and their members strive for positive intergroup distinctiveness because in salient group contexts self, as social identity, is defined and evaluated in group terms, and therefore the status, prestige, and social valence of the group attaches to oneself. This motive for positive social identity may reflect one of the most basic of human motives, for self-enhancement and self-esteem (Sedikides and Strube 1997). Thus positive distinctiveness and the dynamics of group and intergroup behavior may be motivated by self-esteem (e.g., Turner 1982), with the implication that low self-esteem motivates group identification and intergroup behavior and identification elevates self-esteem—the self-esteem hypothesis (Abrams and Hogg 1988).

Conceptual and empirical reviews of the self-esteem hypothesis reveal inconsistent findings, suggesting a distinction between individual and group membership–based self-esteem and that the relationship between self-esteem and group behavior may be affected by other variables such as the extremity of self-esteem, how strongly people identify with the group, and whether the groups and their members feel under threat (e.g., Abrams and Hogg 1988; Crocker and Luhtanen 1990; Rubin and Hewstone 1998). One key finding is that although self-esteem can be raised by group identification it is a much less reliable cause of identification—indeed high-self-esteem people often identify more. This is consistent with the view that rather than motivating behavior, self-esteem is an internal monitor of how well one is satisfying other motivations, such as maintaining rewarding interpersonal relationships (e.g., Leary et al. 1995).

Self-enhancement is undeniably involved in social identity processes. However, the link between individual self-esteem and positive group distinctiveness is not always that tight. Although having a devalued or stigmatized social identity can depress self-esteem, people are exceedingly adept at buffering themselves from the self-evaluative consequences of stigma (e.g., Crocker, Major, and Steele 1998).

Uncertainty Reduction. The other social identity motive is uncertainty reduction (Hogg 2000b). This is an epistemic motive directly associated with social categorization. People strive to reduce subjective uncertainty about their social world and their place within it—they like to know who they are and how to behave and who others are and how they might behave. Social categorization is particularly effective at reducing uncertainty because it furnishes group prototypes that describe how people (including self) will and ought to behave and interact with one another. Such prototypes are relatively consensual ("we" agree that "we" are like this and "they" are like that)—thus one's worldview and self-concept are validated. Social categorization renders one's own and others' behavior predictable and thus allows one to avoid harm and plan effective action. It also allows one to know how one should feel and behave.

The more self-conceptually uncertain one is, the more one strives to belong, particularly to groups that effectively reduce uncertainty—such groups are distinctive, with high entitativity and simple, clear, prescriptive, and consensual prototypes. In extreme circumstances these groups might be orthodox and extremist, possess closed ideologies and belief systems, and have hierarchical leadership and authority structures (Hogg 2004, 2005). Ideological belief systems such as belief in a just world (Furnham and Procter 1989), the Protestant work ethic (Furnham 1990), and right-wing authoritarianism (Altemeyer 1998) are often associated with conditions of social uncertainty and instability. Thus to the extent that such belief systems are tied to group memberships, identification may mediate the link between social uncertainty and ideology (Hogg 2005). Another implication of the uncertainty reduction hypothesis is that subordinate groups may sometimes acquiesce in their subordinate status simply because challenging the status quo elevates self-conceptual uncertainty to unacceptable levels (cf. Jost and Hunyadi 2002).

What is the relationship between uncertainty reduction and self-enhancement, regarding social identity processes? Perhaps uncertainty depresses self-esteem, and it is self-esteem, not uncertainty, that motivates identification via self-enhancement? Although uncertainty can depress self-esteem, it does not have to, and research shows that uncertainty motivates identification independent of self-esteem (Hogg and Svensson 2004). Research also shows that self-enhancement and uncertainty reduction interact (Reid and Hogg 2005). Where people are self-conceptually uncertain, they are motivated by uncertainty reduction to identify equally with low- or high-status groups; where people are self-conceptually certain, they are motivated by self-enhancement to identify more with high- than with low-status groups.

Optimal Distinctiveness. A third motive that may be involved in social identity processes is optimal distinctiveness. According to Brewer (1991), people strike a balance between two conflicting motives, for inclusion or sameness (satisfied by group membership) and distinctiveness or uniqueness (satisfied by individuality), to achieve optimal distinctiveness. Smaller groups oversatisfy the need for distinctiveness, so people strive for greater inclusiveness, while large groups oversatisfy the need for inclusiveness, so people strive for distinctiveness within the group. One implication of this idea is that people should be more satisfied with membership of midsize than very large or very small groups.

Depersonalized Attraction and Group Cohesion

When social identity is salient, the group prototype is the basis of perception, inference, and behavior. Not surprisingly, members pay close attention to the prototype and information about the prototype. They also pay close attention to how well they and others match the prototype. Reactions to and feelings about fellow members are influenced by perceptions of how prototypical they are. If the prototype changes, specific members may become more or less prototypical and feelings for them change accordingly—becoming more favorable if they increase in prototypicality and less favorable if their prototypicality declines.

One implication of this is that as group membership becomes salient the basis of evaluations of and feelings for other people (i.e., liking) is transformed from personal identity–based *personal attraction* (traditional interpersonal attraction) to prototype-based depersonalized *social attraction* (e.g., Hogg 1993). Social attraction is a function of how much one identifies with the group and how prototypical the "other" person is—it is positive regard or liking for the in-group prototype as it is embodied by specific in-group members.

Social attraction is relatively consensual and unidirectional. If membership is salient and there is agreement among group members on the prototype, then more prototypical members tend to be popular (with the consequence that they have more influence and may find it easier to lead—see later discussion of leadership) and less prototypical members tend to be unpopular (with the consequence that they have relatively little influence and may be treated as deviants—see later discussion of deviance). The network of depersonalized prototype-based positive regard and liking within a salient group represents the affective aspect of group cohesiveness—the warm feeling of oneness with fellow members.

Although social and personal attraction are produced by different processes, conditions of group life mean that they can co-occur in groups (e.g., Mullen and Copper 1994)—people like one another as group members and this allows them to develop positive interpersonal relationships. However, social and personal attraction may be associated with different group processes. For example, groupthink, which is generally attributed to excessive cohesiveness in small groups, may be more closely tied to excessive depersonalized social attraction rather than excessive interpersonal attraction (e.g., Hogg and Hains 1998; Turner et al. 1992).

Intergroup Relations

Social identity processes involve people making comparisons among people, including self, based on group membership and group prototypicality. Whereas social comparisons in interpersonal or intragroup contexts are oriented toward similarity, assimilation, and uniformity, intergroup comparisons have a different logic—"social comparisons between groups are focused on the establishment of distinctiveness between one's own and other groups" (Tajfel 1972, 296) and on accentuating that distinctiveness (Turner 1975; Hogg 2000a). Furthermore, because social identity not only describes but also evaluates who one is, intergroup comparisons strive toward in-group distinctiveness that is *evaluatively positive*.

Thus social identity is anchored in valence-sensitive social comparisons that strive for similarity within groups and differentiation between groups. This idea explains the ethnocentrism and in-group favoritism that is characteristic of intergroup relations (Brewer and Campbell 1976; Sumner 1906). It explains why groups compete to be both different and better—why they struggle over status, prestige, and distinctiveness.

Social Belief Structures. Tajfel's (1974) analysis of intergroup behavior and social change integrates the logic of intergroup social comparisons with an analysis of social belief structures—people's beliefs about the nature of intergroup relations and their assessment of the availability and effectiveness of different strategies to achieve or maintain positive intergroup distinctiveness (Tajfel and Turner 1979; also see Hogg and Abrams 1988; Ellemers 1993). Social belief structures have a number of key components: (1) beliefs about the social *status* of one's group relative to an out-group, (2) beliefs about how *stable* this status relationship is, (3) beliefs about how *legitimate* it is, (4) beliefs about how *permeable* the boundary is between one's own group and the out-group and therefore the possibility of psychologically passing from one group to the other, and (5) beliefs about whether an *alternative* status quo is conceivable and achievable.

The combination of these belief variables (status, stability, legitimacy, permeability, and alternatives) generates a wide range of different intergroup behaviors (e.g., Ellemers, Wilke, and van Knippenberg 1993). As an illustration, take the example of lower status groups or their members who believe that the status quo is stable and legitimate and that intergroup boundaries are permeable. These people tend to disidentify from their group and pursue an individual mobility strategy of passing (gaining acceptance) as members of the higher status group. They try to gain psychological entry into the higher status group. The belief that one can pass is consistent with wider beliefs that the world is a just and fair place (belief in a just world) and that if one works hard one can improve one's lot (Protestant work ethic; Furnham 1990; Furnham and Procter 1989).

However, mobility rarely works. This is not surprising. The world is not a fair place, hard work does not necessarily pay off, and subordinate groups' beliefs are ideologically structured by dominant groups to conceal the real nature of intergroup relations. Although wholesale passing is not in the dominant group's interest (if successful, it would contaminate the dominant group and erase the subordinate group—effectively abolishing the comparison group that makes the dominant group relatively superior), the ideology of mobility is very convenient for the dominant group. It prevents subordinate groups from recognizing the illegitimacy of the status quo and pursuing more competitive (and sometimes violent) group-based intergroup strategies that might eventually topple the dominant group and change the status quo. Unsuccessful passing leaves people with a marginal identity (Breakwell 1986)—they are not accepted by the dominant group, and they are rejected by their own group because they have betrayed their identity.

Conflict and Harmony. Presumably, the problems of intergroup behavior can be overcome by integrating warring factions into a cozy single group—thereby transforming conflictual intergroup behavior into harmonious intragroup behavior. From a social identity point of view, recategorization to form a superordinate common in-group identity (e.g., Gaertner and Dovidio 2000) can be difficult to achieve. The main problem is that people have strong attachments to their original groups, and sometimes deep cultural divides exist between groups (Prentice and Miller 1999).

A superordinate group can act as a crucible in which intersubgroup differences are sharpened. In such situations, one group's attributes are almost always better represented in the overarching group, and thus one nested or crosscut group occupies a dominant position (e.g., Mummendey and Wenzel 1999; Wenzel et al. 2003). Subordinate subgroups can therefore feel that their distinct identity within the larger collective is threatened, which can cause them to fight strongly to maintain their independence (e.g., Hewstone 1996; Hornsey and Hogg 2000). This is why many organizational mergers and takeovers fail—members of the newly merged organization struggle to retain their former organizational identity (e.g., Terry, Carey, and Callan 2001).

Theoretically, one way out of this dilemma is for the superordinate identity to structure relations between subgroups such that subgroups thrive as distinct and respected entities that are "playing for the same team" (e.g., Brewer 1996; Hogg and Hornsey, forthcoming), subgroups extend themselves to include each others' attributes as part of themselves (Wright, Aron, and Tropp 2002), and the superordinate identity itself is defined by subgroup diversity (e.g., Roccas and Brewer 2002). But this can be difficult to achieve.

Influence, Conformity, and Norms

From a social identity perspective, norms map the contours of groups and social identities and are cognitively represented as group prototypes that describe and prescribe identity-defining behavior (Turner 1991). Within a given group there is usually substantial agreement on in-group and out-group prototypes—"we agree that we are like this and they are like that." The self-categorization or depersonalization process, previously described, produces conformity to in-group norms (normative behavior) because it assimilates self to the in-group prototype (Abrams and Hogg 1990; Turner 1985; Turner and Oakes 1989). Thus conformity is not surface behavioral compliance but a deeper process whereby people's behavior is transformed to correspond to the appropriate self-defining group prototype.

The social influence process associated with identification-contingent conformity is *referent informational influence* (Hogg and Turner 1987; Turner 1982). In group contexts people attend to information about the context-specific group norm. Typically, the most immediate and best source of this information is identity-consistent behavior of core group members; however, out-groups and marginal in-group members can also provide relevant information ("whatever they are, we are not"). Once the norm has been recognized or established, it is internalized as the context-specific in-group prototype to which people conform through self-categorization.

Contextual norms serve at least two functions—to express in-group similarities and in-group identity and also to differentiate and distance the in-group from the out-group. Because of this, in-group norms tend to be polarized away from out-group norms and are thus more extreme than the average of in-group properties. So, for example, where group norms are polarized away from a salient out-group, then group discussion or decision making will produce group polarization—a postdiscussion group position that is more extreme than the prediscussion position in a direction displaced away from a salient out-group (e.g., Abrams et al. 1990; Mackie 1986).

Group Norms, Individual Behavior, and Social Mobilization. Group norms not only prescribe attitudes and perceptions but also behavior. One feature of group life is that if people identify strongly with a group whose norms prescribe certain actions, then they are more likely to do those things than if they did not identify strongly or the norm did not prescribe behavior (e.g., Terry and Hogg 1996). Groups can also increase people's motivation to exert effort on behalf of the group and its goals. Typically, people exert less effort in collective situations than they would on their own—they loaf (e.g., Karau and Williams 1993). But when they believe strongly in the group and feel they need to compensate for others' poor performance, they may not loaf at all; and when they also identify strongly with the group and the task is identity defining, they may work harder in a group than they do alone (Fielding and Hogg 2000; Williams, Karau, and Bourgeois 1993).

These ideas converge to inform the topic of social mobilization—participation in social protest or social action groups (e.g., Reicher 2001; Stürmer and Simon 2004). The study of social protest is the study of how individual discontents are transformed into collective action. How and why do sympathizers become mobilized as activists or participants? Klandermans (1997) argues that mobilization reflects the attitude-behavior relationship—sympathizers hold sympathetic attitudes toward an issue, yet these attitudes do not readily translate into behavior. Participation also resembles a social dilemma (cf. de Cremer and van Vugt 1999). Protest is generally *for* a social good (e.g., equality) or *against* a social ill (e.g., oppression), and since success benefits everyone irrespective of participation but failure harms participants more, it is tempting to *free ride*—to remain a sympathizer rather than become a participant. The role of leadership (see later discussion) is critical in mobilizing a group to take action. In particular, the leader needs to be viewed as a just person who can be trusted to be acting in the best interest of the group and its members (Tyler and Smith 1998). Ultimately, however, it is social identification that increases the probability of social action and collective protest (e.g., Stürmer and Simon 2004).

Leadership and Influence within Groups. Although norms are the source of influence within groups, some members embody group norms better than others—they are more prototypical and are thus disproportionately influential. This idea is the springboard for the social identity theory of leadership (Hogg 2001b; Hogg and van Knippenberg 2003; van Knippenberg and Hogg 2003).

Where people identify strongly with a group, they pay more attention to and are more influenced by the prototype and perceptions of who is relatively more prototypical. Under these conditions leadership endorsement and leadership effectiveness are significantly influenced by how prototypical the leader is perceived to be. Prototypical members are the focus of depersonalization and conformity and thus appear to exert greater influence than less prototypical members. They are also the focus of consensual depersonalized social attraction, which provides them with status and the ability to gain compliance from others—they appear to have easy influence over members and can be innovative. Because they are figural against the background of the rest of the group their behavior is internally attributed—this constructs in the eyes of the group a leadership persona for them that further facilitates effective leadership.

Prototypical members usually identify more strongly with the group and they therefore quite naturally behave in a group-serving manner. This validates their membership credentials and builds trust for them among fellow members (e.g., Tyler 1997; Tyler and Lind 1992)—they are trusted to be acting in the best interest of the group and are, paradoxically, given greater latitude to be innovative and nonconformist. Leaders who are not highly prototypical still need to prove their membership and therefore are less trusted. They need to behave in a conformist manner that hinders innovation and effective leadership.

Deviance and Marginalization. Less prototypical members, particularly those who are prototypically marginal, are not liked (social attraction) or trusted much by the group and are therefore relatively uninfluential and are cast as deviants (e.g., Hogg, Fielding, and Darley 2005; Marques, Abrams, Páez, and Hogg 2001). Indeed, people on the boundary between in- and out-group are disliked more and are more strongly rejected if they are in-group than out-group members—they are treated as black sheep (Marques and Páez 1994).

Marques and Abrams's subjective group dynamics model (e.g., Marques, Abrams, and Serodio 2001) goes further, to attribute the group's reaction to deviants to the fact that deviants threaten the integrity of group norms. Hogg, Fielding, and Darley (2005) build in a motivational component. They argue that the reaction of members to a deviant depends on (1) whether the deviant occupies a position on the boundary with the out-group or remote from it, (2) whether there is a threat to the group's valence or its distinctiveness, and (3) whether the deviant publicly attributes his or her deviance to self or to the group.

Although marginal members are generally treated negatively by the group, they may also fulfill important social change functions for the group. For example, deviants can serve as in-group critics (e.g., Hornsey and Imani 2004) or as minority groups that challenge the accepted wisdom of the majority (e.g., Nemeth and Staw 1989). In both cases, it can be a struggle for marginal members to be heard, but their contribution to the group is, ultimately, constructive—minorities and critics are effectively trying to change the group's identity from inside.

OUTSTANDING ISSUES AND FUTURE DIRECTIONS

Having described the main components of the social identity approach, in this closing section I discuss some misunderstandings, controversies, and issues and draw together ideas discussed earlier to identify some future directions.

Some Misunderstandings and Unresolved Issues

As is the case with all theories, there are some misunderstandings (or alternative readings) and unresolved issues. One misunderstanding is the belief that the social identity approach is all about intergroup relations and has little to offer small or interactive groups. This was probably true 20 years ago, but over the past 12 years probably the principal area of growth and application has been in the study of intragroup processes and small interactive groups—for example, the study of leadership, deviance, socialization into roles, organizational behavior, and conformity and normative behavior in general. Also, as this chapter shows, social identity theory is a general analysis of the relationship between self-conception and all forms of group and intergroup phenomena.

A second misunderstanding is that the social identity approach places no conceptual value on social interaction and interdependence and therefore speaks only about abstract categories of human beings. From a social identity perspective, a group is psychologically real only if people identify with it. However, interaction, communication, and interdependence are bases for identification, outcomes of identification, and channels for learning about what the group stands for and about one's relative position in the group.

A third misunderstanding is between identification as a generative process and identification as a cognitive structure. We all identify more or less strongly with different groups—some groups are more important, central, accessible, and so forth in our minds. But from a social identity point of view this only increases the probability that in a given context they will become psychologically salient. It is psychological salience that is associated with the social identity processes that generate context-relevant depersonalized behaviors and sense of belonging. For example, knowing I identify more strongly with my professional identity than my nationality will not predict exactly how I behave in a specific context—I will still behave very differently at a conference or when I am watching an international cricket match. One of the most central insights of the social identity approach is precisely that group behavior and self-conception varies from context to context.

There are at least three quite significant unresolved conceptual issues in the social identity literature. One is that although the accessibility × fit formulation of salience makes good sense conceptually, it remains a challenge to operationalize salience reliably as an independent variable in experiments. The second issue has already been alluded to—it is the status of relational identity and the relational self. Is the relational self a social or a personal identity or a quite separate, third kind of identity? One possibility is that the self, defined in terms of relationships, is a personal identity in individualist cultures and a social identity in collectivist cultures. The third issue is whether identities are hydraulically related to one another, so that the more one identity prevails, the less others do (e.g., Mullen, Migdal, and Rozell 2003). Or can multiple identities be simultaneously salient in the same context?

Some Future Directions

This last issue—multiple identities simultaneously salient in the same context—points toward one significant future development in social identity research. In intergroup contexts can people simultaneously identify with a subgroup and a superordinate group—and if so, under what conditions? If dual identification of this type is possible then it may furnish a mechanism for defusing intergroup conflict and constructing groups and identities that celebrate diversity. Related to this is the possibility that people can structure their social identity so that group diversity becomes a defining feature of their in-group.

The current state of our world focuses attention on the harm that rigid and intolerant ideologies can do. The relationship between social identity processes and ideological belief systems relating to social dominance, right-wing authoritarianism, system justification, and belief in a just world is yet to be fully explored. Uncertainty or the specter of uncertainty may play a role in generating powerful identification with groups characterized by orthodox and extreme ideological systems.

The role of different cultural forms of self-construal in social identity processes is still in need of further elaboration—in particular, what is the role of the relational self and how does culture configure social identity and group membership. In this respect culture can of course be defined in terms of East-West but can also be conceptualized on a smaller scale in terms of subcultures within a wider society.

Finally, let me make a plea for language and communication (Hogg and Tindale 2005). In the early days, as noted above, social identity theorists explored the relationship between social identity and language and communication. However a schism has developed—with language scholars, influenced by postmodernism, and social identity theorists, influenced by social cognition, eating at separate tables. Communication is the vehicle for social identity dynamics, and language is one of the most potent symbols of identity. A banquet to launch new integrative directions is called for.

REFERENCES

Abrams, D., and M. A. Hogg. 1988. Comments on the motivational status of self-esteem in social identity and intergroup discrimination. *European Journal of Social Psychology* 18, 317–34.

———. 1990. Social identification, self-categorization and social influence. *European Review of Social Psychology* 1:195–228.

———. 1998. Prospects for research in group processes and intergroup relations. *Group Processes and Intergroup Relations* 1:7–20.

———. 2001. Collective identity: Group membership and self-conception. In *Blackwell Handbook of Social Psychology: Group Processes*, ed. M. A. Hogg and R. S. Tindale, 425–60. Oxford, UK: Blackwell.

———. 2004. Metatheory: Lessons from social identity research. *Personality and Social Psychology Review* 8:98–106.

Abrams, D., M. S. Wetherell, S. Cochrane, M. A. Hogg, and J. C. Turner. 1990. Knowing what to think by knowing who you are: Self-categorization and the nature of norm formation, conformity, and group polarization. *British Journal of Social Psychology* 29:97–119.

Altemeyer, B. 1998. The other "authoritarian personality." In *Advances in Experimental Social Psychology*, ed. M. Zanna, 30:47–92. Orlando, FL: Academic Press.

Arrow, H., J. E. McGrath, and J. L. Berdahl. 2000. *Small Groups as Complex Systems: Formation, Coordination, Development, and Adaptation*. Thousand Oaks, CA: Sage.

Berger, P. L. 1966. Identity as a problem in the sociology of knowledge. *European Journal of Sociology* 7:105–15.

Berger, P. L., and T. Luckmann. 1971. *The Social Construction of Reality*. Harmondsworth: Penguin.

Breakwell, G. 1986. *Coping with Threatened Identities*. London: Methuen.

Brewer, M. B. 1991. The social self: On being the same and different at the same time. *Personality and Social Psychology Bulletin*, 17:475–82.

———. 1996. Managing diversity: The role of social identities. In *Diversity in Work Teams*, ed. S. Jackson and M. Ruderman, 47–68. Washington, DC: American Psychological Association.

———. 2001. The many faces of social identity: Implications for political psychology. *Political Psychology* 22:115–25.

Brewer, M. B., and D. T. Campbell. 1976. *Ethnocentrism and Intergroup Attitudes: East African Evidence*. New York: Sage.

Brewer, M. B., and W. Gardner. 1996. Who is this "we"? Levels of collective identity and self representations. *Journal of Personality and Social Psychology* 71:83–93.

Bruner, J. S. 1957. On perceptual readiness. *Psychological Review* 64:123–52.

Cameron, J. E. 2004. A three-factor model of social identity. *Self and Identity* 3:239–62.

Campbell, D. T. 1958. Common fate, similarity, and other indices of the status of aggregates of persons as social entities. *Behavioral Science* 3:14–25.

Crocker, J., and R. Luhtanen. 1990. Collective self-esteem and ingroup bias. *Journal of Personality and Social Psychology* 58:60–67.

Crocker, J., B. Major, and C. Steele. 1998. Social stigma. In *The Handbook of Social Psychology*, ed. D. T. Gilbert, S. T. Fiske, and G. Lindzey. 4th ed., 2:504–53. New York: McGraw-Hill.

Deaux, K., A. Reid, K. Mizrahi, and K. A. Ethier. 1995. Parameters of social identity. *Journal of Personality and Social Psychology* 68:280–91.

de Cremer, D., and van Vugt, M. 1999. Social identification effects in social dilemmas: A transformation of motives. *European Journal of Social Psychology* 29:871–93.

Doise, W. 1986. *Levels of Explanation in Social Psychology*. Cambridge, UK: Cambridge University Press.

Ellemers, N. 1993. The influence of socio-structural variables on identity management strategies. *European Review of Social Psychology* 4:27–57.

Ellemers, N., P. Kortekaas, and J. W. Ouwerkerk. 1999. Self-categorization, commitment to the group and group self-esteem as related but distinct aspects of social identity. *European Journal of Social Psychology* 29:371–89.

Ellemers, N., H. Wilke, and A. van Knippenberg. 1993. Effects of the legitimacy of low group or individual status on individual and collective identity enhancement strategies. *Journal of Personality and Social Psychology* 64:766–78.

Fielding, K. S., and M. A. Hogg. 2000. Working hard to achieve self-defining group goals: A social identity analysis. *Zeitschrift für Sozialpsychologie* 31:191–203.

Fiske, A. P., S. Kitayama, H. R. Markus, and R. E. Nisbett. 1998. The cultural matrix of social psychology. In *The Handbook of Social Psychology*, ed. D. T. Gilbert, S. T. Fiske, and G. Lindzey. 4th ed., 2:915–81. New York: McGraw-Hill.

Forsyth, D. R. 1999. *Group Dynamics*. 3rd ed. Belmont, CA: Wadsworth.

Furnham, A. 1990. *The Protestant Work Ethic: The Psychology of Work-Related Beliefs and Behaviors*. New York: Routledge.

Furnham, A., and E. Procter. 1989. Belief in a just world: Review and critique of the individual difference literature. *British Journal of Social Psychology* 28:365–84.

Gaertner, S. L., and J. F. Dovidio. 2000. *Reducing Intergroup Bias: The Common Ingroup Identity Model*. New York: Psychology Press.

Giles, H., R. Y. Bourhis, and D. M. Taylor. 1977. Towards a theory of language in ethnic group relations. In *Language, Ethnicity, and Intergroup Relations*, ed. H. Giles, 307–348. London: Academic Press.

Hamilton, D. L., and S. J. Sherman. 1996. Perceiving persons and groups. *Psychological Review* 103:336–55.

Haslam, S. A. 2004. *Psychology in Organisations: The Social Identity Approach*. 2nd ed. London: Sage.

Hewstone, M. 1996. Contact and categorization: Social-psychological interventions to change intergroup relations. In *Stereotypes and stereotyping*, ed. C. N. Macrae, C. Stangor, and M. Hewstone, 323–68. New York: Guilford.

Hinkle, S. W., and R. J. Brown. 1990. Intergroup comparisons and social identity: Some links and lacunae. In *Social identity theory: Constructive and critical advances*, ed. D. Abrams and M. A. Hogg, 48–70. Hemel Hempstead, UK: Harvester-Wheatsheaf.

Hirschmann, A. 1970. *Exit, Voice, and Loyalty: Responses to Decline in Firms, Organizations, and States.* Cambridge, MA: Harvard University Press.

Hogg, M. A. 1993. Group cohesiveness: A critical review and some new directions. *European Review of Social Psychology* 4:85–111.

———. 2000a. Social identity and social comparison. In *Handbook of Social Comparison: Theory and Research,* ed. J. Suls and L. Wheeler, 401–21. New York: Kluwer/Plenum.

———. 2000b. Subjective uncertainty reduction through self-categorization: A motivational theory of social identity processes. *European Review of Social Psychology* 11:223–55.

———. 2001a. Social categorization, depersonalization, and group behavior. In *Blackwell Handbook of Social Psychology: Group Processes,* ed. M. A. Hogg and R. S. Tindale, 56–85. Oxford, UK: Blackwell.

———. 2001b. A social identity theory of leadership. *Personality and Social Psychology Review* 5:184–200.

———. 2003. Social identity. In *Handbook of Self and Identity,* ed. M. R. Leary and J. P. Tangney, 462–79. New York: Guilford.

———. 2004. Uncertainty and extremism: Identification with high entitativity groups under conditions of uncertainty. In *The Psychology of Group Perception: Perceived Variability, Entitativity, and Essentialism,* ed. V. Yzerbyt, C. M. Judd, and O. Corneille, 401–18. New York: Psychology Press.

———. 2005. Uncertainty, social identity, and ideology. In *Advances in Group Processes,* ed. S. R. Thye and E. J. Lawler, 22:203–29. New York: Elsevier.

Hogg, M. A., and D. Abrams. 1988. *Social Identifications: A Social Psychology of Intergroup Relations and Group Processes.* London and New York: Routledge.

Hogg, M. A., D. Abrams, S. Otten, and S. Hinkle. 2004. The social identity perspective: Intergroup relations, self-conception, and small groups. *Small Group Research* 35:246–76.

Hogg, M. A., K. S. Fielding, and J. Darley. 2005. Fringe dwellers: Processes of deviance and marginalization in groups. In *The social psychology of inclusion and exclusion,* ed. D. Abrams, M. A. Hogg, and J. M. Marques, 191–210. New York: Psychology Press.

Hogg, M. A., and S. C. Hains. 1998. Friendship and group identification: A new look at the role of cohesiveness in groupthink. *European Journal of Social Psychology* 28:323–41.

Hogg, M. A., and M. J. Hornsey. Forthcoming. Self-concept threat and multiple categorization within groups. In *Multiple Social Categorization: Processes, Models, and Applications,* ed. R. J. Crisp and M. Hewstone. New York: Psychology Press.

Hogg, M. A., and C. L. Ridgeway, eds. 2003. *Social Identity: Sociological and Social Psychological Perspectives.* Special issue of *Social Psychology Quarterly* 66 (2). Washington, DC: American Sociological Association.

Hogg, M. A., and A. Svensson. 2004. Uncertainty reduction, self-esteem and group identification. Unpublished manuscript, University of Queensland.

Hogg, M. A., and D. J. Terry. 2000. Social identity and self-categorization processes in organizational contexts. *Academy of Management Review* 25:121–40.

Hogg, M. A., D. J. Terry, and K. M. White. 1995. A tale of two theories: A critical comparison of identity theory with social identity theory. *Social Psychology Quarterly* 58:255–69.

Hogg, M. A., and R. S. Tindale. 2005. Social identity, influence, and communication in small groups. In *Intergroup Communication: Multiple Perspectives*, ed. J. Harwood and H. Giles, 141–64. New York: Peter Lang.

Hogg, M. A., and J. C. Turner. 1987. Social identity and conformity: A theory of referent informational influence. In *Current Issues in European Social Psychology*, ed. W. Doise and S. Moscovici. 2:139–82. Cambridge, UK: Cambridge University Press.

Hogg, M. A., and van D. Knippenberg. 2003. Social identity and leadership processes in groups. In *Advances in Experimental Social Psychology*, ed. M. P. Zanna, 35:1–52. San Diego, CA: Academic Press.

Hornsey, M. J., and M. A. Hogg. 2000. Assimilation and diversity: An integrative model of subgroup relations. *Personality and Social Psychology Review* 4:143–56.

Hornsey, M. J., and A. Imani. 2004. Criticising groups from the inside and the outside: An identity perspective on the intergroup sensitivity effect. *Personality and Social Psychology Bulletin* 30:365–83.

Jackson, J. W., and E. R. Smith. 1999. Conceptualizing social identity: A new framework and evidence for the impact of different dimensions. *Personality and Social Psychology Bulletin* 25:120–35.

Jaspars, J. M. F. 1986. Forum and focus: A personal view of European social psychology. *European Journal of Social Psychology* 16:3–15.

Jost, J. T., and O. Hunyadi. 2002. The psychology of system justification and the palliative function of ideology. *European Review of Social Psychology* 13:111–53.

Karau, S. J., and K. D. Williams. 1993. Social loafing: A meta-analytic review and theoretical integration. *Journal of Personality and Social Psychology* 65:681–706.

Klandermans, B. 1997. *The Social Psychology of Protest*. Oxford, UK: Blackwell.

Leary, M. R., E. S. Tambor, S. K. Terdal, and D. L. Downs. 1995. Self-esteem as an interpersonal monitor: The sociometer hypothesis. *Journal of Personality and Social Psychology* 68:518–30.

Levine, J. M., and R. L. Moreland. 1994. Group socialization: Theory and research. *European Review of Social Psychology* 5:305–36.

Mackie, D. M. 1986. Social identification effects in group polarization. *Journal of Personality and Social Psychology* 50:720–28.

Manstead, A. S. R. 1990. Developments to be expected in European social psychology in the 1990s. In *European Perspectives in Psychology*, ed. P. J. D. Drenth, J. A. Sergeant, and R. J. Takens, 3:183–203. Chichester, UK: Wiley.

Markus, H., and S. Kitayama. 1991. Culture and the self: Implications for cognition, emotion and motivation. *Psychological Review* 98:224–53.

Marques, J. M., D. Abrams, D. Páez, and M. A. Hogg. 2001. Social categorization, social identification, and rejection of deviant group members. In *Blackwell Handbook of Social Psychology: Group Processes*, ed. M. A. Hogg and R. S. Tindale, 400–24. Oxford, UK: Blackwell.

Marques, J. M, D. Abrams, and R. Serodio. 2001. Being better by being right: Subjective group dynamics and derogation of in-group deviants when generic norms are undermined. *Journal of Personality and Social Psychology* 81:436–47.

Marques, J. M., and D. Páez. 1994. The black sheep effect: Social categorization, rejection of ingroup deviates, and perception of group variability. *European Review of Social Psychology* 5:37–68.

McAuliffe, B. J., J. Jetten, M. J. Hornsey, and M. A. Hogg. 2003. Individualist and collectivist group norms: When it's OK to go your own way. *European Journal of Social Psychology* 33:57–70.

Moreland, R. L., M. A. Hogg, and S. C. Hains. 1994. Back to the future: Social psychological research on groups. *Journal of Experimental Social Psychology* 30:527–55.

Moreland, R. L., and J. M. Levine. 2003. Group composition: Explaining similarities and differences among group members. In *The Sage Handbook of Social Psychology*, ed. M. A. Hogg and J. Cooper, 367–80. London: Sage.

Moreland, R. L., J. M. Levine, and J. G. McMinn. 2001. Self-categorization and work group socialization. In *Social Identity Processes in Organizational Contexts*, ed. M. A. Hogg and D. Terry, 87–100. Philadelphia, PA: Psychology Press.

Moscovici, S. 1980. Toward a theory of conversion behavior. In *Advances in Experimental Social Psychology*, ed. L. Berkowitz, 13:202–39. New York: Academic Press.

———. 1988. Notes towards a description of social representations. *European Journal of Social Psychology* 18:211–50.

Mullen, B., and C. Copper. 1994. The relation between group cohesiveness and performance: An integration. *Psychological Bulletin* 115:210–27.

Mullen, B., M. J. Migdal, and D. Rozell. 2003. Self-awareness, deindividuation, and social identity: Unraveling theoretical paradoxes by filling empirical lacunae. *Personality and Social Psychology Bulletin* 29:1071–81.

Mummendey, A., and M. Wenzel. 1999. Social discrimination and tolerance in intergroup relations: Reactions to intergroup difference. *Personality and Social Psychology Review* 3:158–74.

Nemeth, C., and B. M. Staw. 1989. The tradeoffs of social control and innovation in groups and organizations. In *Advances in Experimental Social Psychology*, ed. L. Berkowitz, 22:175–210. San Diego, CA: Academic Press.

Oakes, P. J. 1987. The salience of social categories. In *Rediscovering the Social Group: A Self-Categorization Theory*, ed. J. C. Turner, M. A. Hogg, P. J. Oakes, S. D. Reicher, and M. S. Wetherell, 117–41. Oxford: Blackwell.

Oyserman, D., H. M. Coon, and M. Kemmelmeier. 2002. Rethinking individualism and collectivism: Evaluation of theoretical assumptions and meta-analyses. *Psychological Bulletin* 128:3–72.

Postmes, T., R. Spears, K. Sakhel, and D. de Groot. 2001. Social influence in computer-mediated communication: The effects of anonymity on group behavior. *Personality and Social Psychology Bulletin* 27:1243–54.

Prentice, D. A., and D. T. Miller, eds. 1999. *Cultural Divides: Understanding and Overcoming Group Conflict*. New York: Russell Sage Foundation.

Prentice, D. A., D. Miller, and J. R. Lightdale. 1994. Asymmetries in attachment to groups and to their members: Distinguishing between common-identity and common-bond groups. *Personality and Social Psychology Bulletin* 20:484–93.

Reicher, S. D. 2001. The psychology of crowd dynamics. In *Blackwell Handbook of Social Psychology: Group Processes*, ed. M. A. Hogg and R. S. Tindale, 182–207. Oxford, UK: Blackwell.

Reicher, S. D., R. Spears, and T. Postmes. 1995. A social identity model of deindividuation phenomena. *European Review of Social Psychology* 6:161–98.

Reid, A., and K. Deaux. 1996. Relationship between social and personal identities: Segregation or integration. *Journal of Personality and Social Psychology* 71:1084–91.

Reid, S. A., and M. A. Hogg. 2005. Uncertainty reduction, self-enhancement, and ingroup identification. *Personality and Social Psychology Bulletin* 31:1–14.

Roccas, S., and M. B. Brewer. 2002. Social identity complexity. *Personality and Social Psychology Review* 6:88–109.

Rubin, M., and M. Hewstone. 1998. Social identity theory's self-esteem hypothesis: A review and some suggestions for clarification. *Personality and Social Psychology Review* 2:40–62.

Sedikides, C., and M. J. Strube. 1997. Self-evaluation: To thine own self be good, to thine own self be sure, to thine own self be true, and to thine own self be better. In *Advances in Experimental Social Psychology*, ed. M. P. Zanna, 29:209–96. New York: Academic Press.

Sherif, M., ed. 1962. *Intergroup Relations and Leadership*. New York: Wiley.

Smith, E., and S. Henry. 1996. An in-group becomes part of the self: Response time evaluation. *Personality and Social Psychology Bulletin* 22:635–42.

Stets, J. E., and P. J. Burke 2000. Identity theory and social identity theory. *Social Psychology Quarterly* 63:224–37.

Stürmer, S., and B. Simon. 2004. Collective action: Towards a dual-pathway model. *European Review of Social Psychology* 15:59–99. New York: Psychology Press.

Sumner, W. G. 1906. *Folkways*. Boston, MA: Ginn.

Tajfel, H. 1959. Quantitative judgement in social perception. *British Journal of Psychology* 50:16–29.

———. 1969. Cognitive aspects of prejudice. *Journal of Social Issues* 25:79–97.

———. 1972. Social categorization. English manuscript of "La catégorisation sociale." In *Introduction à la Psychologie Sociale*, ed. S. Moscovici, 1:272–302. Paris: Larousse.

———. 1974. *Intergroup Behaviour, Social Comparison and Social Change*. Unpublished Katz-Newcomb lectures, University of Michigan, Ann Arbor.

———., ed. 1984. *The Social Dimension: European Developments in Social Psychology*. Cambridge, UK: Cambridge University Press.

Tajfel, H., M. Billig, R. P. Bundy, and C. Flament. 1971. Social categorization and intergroup behaviour. *European Journal of Social Psychology* 1:149–77.

Tajfel, H., J. M. F. Jaspars, and C. Fraser. 1984. The social dimension in European social psychology. In *The Social Dimension: European Developments in Social Psychology*, ed. H. Tajfel, 1:1–5. Cambridge, UK: Cambridge University Press.

Tajfel, H., and J. C. Turner. 1979. An integrative theory of intergroup conflict. In *The Social Psychology of Intergroup Relations*, ed. W. G. Austin and S. Worchel, 33–47. Monterey, CA: Brooks/Cole.

Taylor, D. M., and R. J. Brown. 1979. Towards a more social social psychology? *British Journal of Social and Clinical Psychology* 18:173–79.

Terry, D. J., C. J. Carey, and V. J. Callan. 2001. Employee adjustment to an organizational merger: An intergroup perspective. *Personality and Social Psychology Bulletin* 27:267–80.

Terry, D. J., and M. A. Hogg. 1996. Group norms and the attitude-behavior relationship: A role for group identification. *Personality and Social Psychology Bulletin* 22:776–93.

Tönnies, F. 1955. *Community and Association*. London: Routledge & Kegan Paul (originally published in German in 1887).

Turner, J. C. 1975. Social comparison and social identity: Some prospects for intergroup behaviour. *European Journal of Social Psychology* 5:5–34.

———. 1982. Towards a cognitive redefinition of the social group. In *Social Identity and Intergroup Relations*, ed. H. Tajfel, 15–40. Cambridge, UK: Cambridge University Press.

———. 1985. Social categorization and the self-concept: A social cognitive theory of group behavior. In *Advances in Group Processes: Theory and Research*, ed. E. J. Lawler, 2:7–122. Greenwich, CT: JAI Press.

———. 1991. *Social Influence*. Milton Keynes, UK: Open University Press.

———. 1996. Henri Tajfel: An introduction. In *Social Groups and Identities: Developing the Legacy of Henri Tajfel*, ed. W. P. Robinson, 1–23. Oxford, UK: Butterworth-Heinemann.

———. 1999. Some current issues in research on social identity and self-categorization theories. In *Social Identity*, ed. N. Ellemers, R. Spears, and B. Doosje, 6–34. Oxford, UK: Blackwell.

Turner, J. C., M. A. Hogg, P. J. Oakes, S. D. Reicher, and M. S. Wetherell. 1987. *Rediscovering the Social Group: A Self-Categorization Theory*. Oxford, UK: Blackwell.

Turner, J. C., and P. J. Oakes. 1989. Self-categorization and social influence. In *The Psychology of Group Influence*, ed. P. B. Paulus, 2nd ed., 233–75. Hillsdale, NJ: Erlbaum.

Turner, M. E., A. R. Pratkanis, P. Probasco, and C. Leve. 1992. Threat, cohesion, and group effectiveness: Testing a social identity maintenance perspective on groupthink. *Journal of Personality and Social Psychology* 63:781–96.

Tyler, T. R. 1997. The psychology of legitimacy: A relational perspective on voluntary deference to authorities. *Personality and Social Psychology Review* 1:323–45.

Tyler, T. R., and E. A. Lind. 1992. A relational model of authority in groups. In *Advances in Experimental Social Psychology*, ed. M. P. Zanna, 25:115–91. New York: Academic Press.

Tyler, T. R., and H. J. Smith. 1998. Social justice and social movements. In *The Handbook of Social Psychology*, ed. D. T. Gilbert, S. T. Fiske, and G. Lindzey, 4th ed., 2:595–629. Boston: McGraw-Hill.

van Knippenberg, D., and M. A. Hogg. 2003. A social identity model of leadership in organizations. In *Research in Organizational Behavior*, ed. R. M. Kramer and B. M. Staw, 25:243–95. Greenwich, CT: JAI Press.

Wenzel, M., A. Mummendey, U. Weber, and S. Waldzus. 2003. The ingroup as pars pro toto: Projection from the ingroup onto the inclusive category as a precursor to social discrimination. *Personality and Social Psychology Bulletin* 29:461–73.

Wilder, D., and A. F. Simon. 1998. Categorical and dynamic groups: Implications for social perception and intergroup behavior. In *Intergroup Cognition and Intergroup Behavior*, ed. C. Sedikides, J. Schopler, and C. A. Insko, 27–44. Mahwah, NJ: Erlbaum.

Williams, K. D., S. J. Karau, and M. Bourgeois. 1993. Working on collective tasks: Social loafing and social compensation. In *Group Motivation: Social Psychological Perspectives*, ed. M. A. Hogg and D. Abrams, 130–48. London: Harvester-Wheatsheaf.

Wright, S. C., A. Aron, and L. R. Tropp. 2002. Including others (and groups) in the self: Self-expansion and intergroup relations. In *The Social Self: Cognitive, Interpersonal, and Intergroup Perspectives*, ed. J. P. Forgas and K. D. Williams, 343–63. New York: Psychology Press.

Yuki, M. 2003. Intergroup comparison versus intragroup relationships: A cross-cultural examination of social identity theory in North American and East Asian cultural contexts. *Social Psychology Quarterly* 66:166–83.

Zimbardo, P. G. 1970. The human choice: Individuation, reason, and order versus deindividuation, impulse, and chaos. In *Nebraska Symposium on Motivation 1969*, ed. W. J. Arnold and D. Levine, 17:237–307. Lincoln: University of Nebraska Press.

AFFECT CONTROL THEORY

Dawn T. Robinson and Lynn Smith-Lovin

How do people know how to react to situations that they haven't encountered before? How do they decide how to respond when someone does something unexpected? Symbolic interactionists posed these questions to role theorists in the 1950s. Affect control theory was an answer.[1]

Role theory, with its roots in structural functionalism, saw actors as learning a set of behavioral expectations associated with a social position. The primary task for society was to socialize its members so that they could competently perform the roles. Symbolic interactionists reacted against this oversocialized view of actors. They pointed out that social behavior—even in well-defined social roles—shows remarkable variability and creativity in response to local circumstances. Social actors are rarely at a loss for action even when confronted with new roles or surprising situations.

The interactionists developed this critique by emphasizing the processual, negotiated nature of all social interaction. They pointed out that structure does not exist except as recreated by the consistent actions of agentic individuals. This processual emphasis led to charges that symbolic interactionists ignored the persistent constraint of institutional structures and of power differentials within situations. So how could one develop a theoretical structure that both (1) showed how cultural knowledge produced consistent, routine patterns of interaction while (2) showing how people generate innovative action and responses to deviations in expected routines? We needed a relationship between role identities and actions that was *both* predictable and creative. David Heise (1977, 1979; Smith-Lovin and Heise 1988) developed affect control theory to answer this challenge.

Affect control theory "predicts" a lot that we already know. It generates the expected role behaviors that occupants of social positions direct toward one another. Wives are expected to Compliment, Adore, and Nuzzle their Husbands and to Entertain their Children[2] (MacKinnon 1994, 102–103). Through its ability to replicate cultural norms, the theory provides a generative model of culture. It uses the cultural meanings that role identities and behaviors have for actors to generate a large matrix of institutionalized role expectations. In addition, identities that are not institutionalized but that still have cultural meaning (like

Mugger and Victim) generate understandable interactions when they maintain these meanings (p. 112). Even cultural entities that do not really exist (like Vampires) but have cultural meanings can generate meaningful lines of action, corresponding roughly to the scripts of myths, folklore, or story plots (Dunphy and MacKinnon 2002).

Affect control theory also allows us to make predictions about what people will do when others violate expectations (perhaps because they are defining the situation differently). In some cases, the prediction of nonrole behavior allows the theory to explain phenomena that have been recognized by other, less formal theoretical traditions. Affect control theory shows that people act to restore the identities of others that have been, in Goffman's (1967) terms, "spoiled." Actors sanction those who violate norms, label those who engage in dramatically unexpected behaviors, and blame the victim of negative acts by others. They expect the worst of those who are negatively labeled, and those others generally fulfill their expectations if the negative labels are accepted by those so labeled.

Why would we need a theory that predicts so much of what we already know? Predicting common cultural knowledge about what people normally do in well-defined role relationships, common features of social life like derogating the victim, or feeling rules that can be described by any competent member of the culture—all of this might seem rather pointless. To the contrary, we argue that having a single, integrated, parsimonious model that predicts a lot of what we already know about social life is immensely valuable. In a sense, it helps define what it means to be a normal social actor, what motivates and shapes our actions toward others. In fact, such a model would be necessary to create an artificial actor that could mimic human motivations and orientations (Heise 2004; Troyer 2004). While more mechanical models can perform some tasks like medical diagnosis, they cannot simulate human actions that require flexibility, creativity, and motivation to choose among alternative courses of action.

In this chapter, we lay out the basic structure of affect control theory, including its scope conditions, measurement model, mathematical model, and computer representation. We then review some empirical work that has been done using the theory thus far and point to directions where we need new research.

STRUCTURE OF THE THEORY

Affect control theory is grounded in symbolic interactionist insights about the primary importance of language and of the symbolic labeling of situations (MacKinnon 1994). Inspired by the pragmatist philosophy of early symbolic interactionists, the theory begins with the premise that people reduce existential uncertainty by developing working understandings of their social worlds. They label parts of social situations, using cultural symbols available to them. After creating this working definition, they are motivated to maintain it.

Affect control theory rests on the idea that our labeling of social situations evokes affective meanings. It is these affective meanings, rather than the specific labels themselves, that we try to maintain during interaction. One of the unique features of affect control theory is that it uses just three specific dimensions to measure the affective meanings of labels. This measurement structure then allows development of a set of equations to describe how events change those meanings and a mathematical function to show what actions will maintain or restore meanings. The theory is fundamentally contained in this three-part formalization—the measurement structure, the event reaction equations, and the mathematical statement of the control process. Consequently, we focus here on describing the mathematical elements of the theory before moving on to a description of research findings. In a real sense, the theory *is* its mathematical structure: the mathematical statement is the formal model that predicts patterns that can then be tested empirically. For readers who prefer a more traditional presentation, MacKinnon and Heise (1993) provide an alternative way of viewing the theory through a propositional structure.

Scope

Scope statements specify the conditions under which a theory applies (Cohen 1989). Heise (1977, 1979) developed affect control theory to describe culturally situated social interactions. Therefore the domain of the theory is quite broad. Specific conditions, however, limit its applicability (Robinson 2006):

There is a directed social behavior. Directed social behavior requires an Actor who generates the behavior, a target of the behavior (called an Object), and a Behavior that is directed toward the object-person.[3] In the case of reflexive behavior, the Actor and Object can be the same person.

There is at least one observer who is a member of an identified language culture. The observer can be the Actor, the Object, or a third party. It is from the perspective of this observer, or labeler, that affect control theory makes its predictions. The theory allows participants to operate under differing definitions of the situation but always makes predictions from a particular person's perspective.

The theory applies only to labeled aspects of social experiences. This scope condition excludes behaviors that are not witnessed or interpreted by observers or participants. Picture a child pointing and laughing at a man who is unaware that he has an unzipped fly. The fact of the open fly would not enter into the man's predicted response unless it became part of his awareness. Picture another child shuffling across the floor to kiss his mother good night. Predictions about the feelings of the mother generated by the event Son Kisses Mother are within the scope of the theory. The startle response that the mother might feel from an electrostatic shock caused by the kiss is outside the scope of the theory.

Now that we have defined the broad conditions under which the theory will apply, we will describe its three-part structure. We begin with the measurement of sentiments, show how these affective meanings are changed by social interaction, and then define the theory's core control principle. Then we will review the research literature that has expanded and tested the theory.

Sentiments

Affect control theory assumes that people respond affectively to every social event (the *affective reaction principle*). The theory describes these affective responses along three dimensions of meaning—evaluation, potency, and activity. These are universal dimensions identified by Charles Osgood and colleagues (Osgood, Suci, and Tannenbaum 1957; Osgood 1962; Osgood, May, and Miron 1975) that describe substantial variation in the affective meaning of lexicons in more than 20 national cultures. These three fundamental dimensions of meaning serve as cultural abbreviations, summarizing important social information about elements of an interaction—identities, behaviors, emotions, and settings.

> *Evaluation.* The evaluation dimension captures the amount of goodness or badness we associate with a concept. It is a bipolar dimension of meaning that ranges from *nice, warm, good* to *nasty, cold, bad.*
>
> *Potency.* The potency dimension captures the amount of powerfulness or weakness we associate with a concept. It is a bipolar dimension of meaning that ranges from *big, strong, powerful* to *small, weak, powerless.*
>
> *Activity.* The activity dimension captures the amount of liveliness or quietness we associate with a concept. It is a bipolar dimension of meaning that ranges from *fast, noisy, lively* to *slow, quiet, inactive.*

All social concepts evoke goodness, powerfulness, and liveliness; these affective meanings are referred to as *sentiments* in the theory. Sentiments are trans-situational, generalized affective responses to symbols that are widely shared in a culture (or subculture). While the dimensions themselves are universal across cultures, symbol sentiments are products of a culture. Mothers come in a wide variety of shapes, sizes, colors, ages, and demeanors. Individuals in a culture may widely vary in attitudes toward their *own* mothers. Nonetheless, all of us in mainstream U.S. culture basically agree that general meaning of the role identity Mother is good, powerful, and moderately active. In contrast, our culturally shared sentiments about Accountants are more neutral on all three dimensions, and our image of Rapists is extremely negative on the evaluation dimension. It is our very agreement about the generalized meanings associated with symbols that allows us to communicate effectively with other members of our culture. Even conflict requires that we share most meanings to communicate the grounds of dispute.

Sentiments can vary cross-culturally, however. Affect control theory researchers have used evaluation, potency, and activity ratings to index meanings in a variety of different cultures, including the United States, Canada, Japan, Germany, China, and Northern Ireland. Within each culture, average evaluation, potency, and activity ratings are compiled into cultural "dictionaries" that contain generalized meanings. There are three-number evaluation-potency-activity profiles for hundreds of identities, behaviors, traits, emotions, and settings in each culture. These sentiment profiles locate these cultural symbols—potential elements of social events—in a three-dimensional affective space. The most important feature of these evaluation-potency-activity profiles is that they represent *all* of the elements of a social interaction using the same metric. It is this feature that allowed Heise (1979) to develop a mathematically specified theory of social interaction.

Impressions

After we define a social situation using culturally meaningful labels, the affective meanings can change as social interaction occurs. Picture a mother with her daughter in a park. The affect generated by the labels—Mother and Daughter—help us know what actions we expect the two people to take. However, now picture the Mother Dragging the Daughter through the park. In response to this event, our feelings about that mother, that daughter, and perhaps even what it means to drag someone, are altered because of our observation of that event (including our labeling of the action). In affect control theory, we call these situated meanings *transient impressions*. These impressions are contextualized affective meanings that come from viewing symbolic labels in specific social events.

In developing affect control theory, Heise used a research tradition developed by Harry Gollob (1968) to create descriptive models of how affective meanings change as a result of social events. Gollob used simple event descriptions of the form the *subject verbs the object*. He analyzed these events by regressing evaluations of the event elements (subject, verb, and object) on evaluations of the subject in the event. Using this technique, he could analyze a set of sentences like "the scholar teaches the pupil" by predicting the evaluation of "scholar" in that context using evaluations of scholar, teach, and pupil outside that event context. Affect control theory uses this subject-verb-object grammar to represent the simplest social event *Actor Behaves* toward *Object*. The regressions have the following general form:

$$A' = c + b_1A + b_2B + b_3O \tag{7.1}$$

where A' is the predicted impression of the Actor (the scholar teaching the pupil in our example), A is the general sentiment toward the actor (scholar), B the general sentiment toward the behavior (teach), and O the general sentiment toward the Object (pupil). In developing affect control theory, Heise (1969b, 1979) elaborated Gollob's technique. He expanded the equations to use all three affective dimensions (evaluation, potency, and activity). In addition, he took all of the basic elements of a social event—actor, behavior, and object—as dependent variables, showing how transient impressions of all three could be changed when an event occurred.

Imagine the event "student corrects the teacher." Impressions of *that particular student* are likely to be somewhat different than our generalized sentiments about students. We can regress our generalized sentiments about "student," "to correct someone," and "teacher" on the situated impressions of that student (the one who corrected the teacher) to learn more about how these social elements combine to form new impressions during social interactions.

Consider the following equation from Smith-Lovin (1987a):

$$A'_e = -.98 + .468A_e - .015A_p - .015A_a + .425B_e - .069B_p$$
$$-.106B_a + .055O_e - .0205O_p - .0015O_a + .048A_eB_e$$
$$+.130B_eO_e + .027A_pB_p + .068B_pO_p + .007A_aB_a - .038A_eB_p$$
$$-.010A_eB_a + .013A_pB_e - .014A_pO_a - .058B_eO_p - .070B_pO_e \quad (7.2)$$
$$-.002B_pO_a + .010B_aO_e + .019B_aO_p + .026A_eB_eO_e$$
$$-.006A_pB_pO_p + .031A_aB_aO_a + .033A_eB_pO_p + .018A_pB_pO_p$$

where A, B, and O represent the Actor, Behavior, and Object, and the e, p, and a subscripts represent the evaluation, potency, and activity ratings of those event elements. Elements with primes (e.g., A'_e) are transient impressions after an event, while nonprime elements are the impressions before an event occurs. Multiplicative terms like B_eO_e represent statistical interactions.

Equation 7.2 uses information about the sentiments associated with all of the elements in a social situation (A_e, A_p, . . ., O_p, O_a) to predict the situated impressions of the goodness (evaluation) of the Actor (A'_e). Note that the largest predictor of how nice an Actor seems in a given situation is the sentiment associated with the Actor's identity. So our impressions about the niceness of the Student who Corrected the Teacher are largely shaped by how nice we think the role identity Student is in general. The large, positive effect of A_e in Equation 7.2 captures the idea that Actors seem nicer when they are occupying identities that the culture evaluates positively. In contrast, someone occupying a negatively evaluated identity like Perpetrator might seem relatively nasty, no matter what he did and to whom.

Similarly, the large, positive B_e coefficient reflects how much nicer an actor seems when he or she is behaving in nice ways. People seem nicer when they Help someone (a very positively evaluated act) than when they Correct them (a mildly negative behavior). The smaller, positive O_e term reflects the idea that the niceness of our interaction partners rubs off on us a bit. We seem somewhat nicer when we act toward nice others, and there is some guilt by association when we act toward those whose identities are generally stigmatized. (Since the equation predicting O'_e [the evaluation of an object-person after an event] also has a significant, positive coefficient for the evaluation of the Actor [A_e], the equations capture the principle that our reputations depend partly on the company we keep.)

The effects of O_e and B_e on A'_e are qualified by a sizable positive interaction between them, captured in the B_eO_e coefficient. This interaction (called the *balance* term, after Heider's [1958] balance theory) captures the idea that social actors seem especially nice when they behave nicely toward good others (or badly toward nasty others). Actors don't seem as good when they are either mean to good others or nice to bad others (i.e., when a negative B_e gets multiplied with a positive O_e or when a positive B_e gets multiplied with a negative O_e).

The negative B_eO_p coefficient captures another feature of our normative culture. This interaction term suggests that actors seem nicer when they behave in nice ways toward weak others or less positively toward strong others. On the one hand, this captures the *social responsibility* norm—that good people should behave in caring, helpful ways to those who are weaker. On the other hand, it captures the idea that if we are *too* nice to powerful others we may appear to be brownnosing or manipulative and thus less good than we would otherwise seem when doing that nice act.

Affect control theory uses a full set of impression-formation equations like Equation 7.2 to predict changes in the impressions of Actors, Behaviors, and Objects on evaluation, potency, and activity (A_e', A_p', A_a', B_e', B_p', B_a', O_e', O_p', O_a') as a result of their combination in social events. Taken as a set, these impression-change equations are empirical summaries of basic social and cultural processes. They capture important information about how social events temporarily transform the meanings of the symbolic labels that we use to define events. Along with the sentiment dictionaries, these equations provide the empirical basis for the theoretical predictions made by affect control theory. Currently, there are impression-formation equations for the United States (Smith-Lovin 1987a), Canada (MacKinnon 1985, 1988, 1998), and Japan (Smith, Matsuno, and Ike 2001).

Control Principle

Sentiments are the culturally shared, fundamental meanings that we associate with social labels. Impressions are the more transient meanings that arise as social interactions unfold. Discrepancies between sentiments and impressions tell us something about how well interactions that we experience are confirming cultural prescriptions.

Recall the pragmatic symbolic interactionist assumption that social actors try to maintain their working definitions of social situations. Inspired by Power's (1973) work on perception control theory, Heise (1977, 1979) developed a control system theory to model this principle. Affect control theory proposes that actors work to experience transient impressions that are consistent with their fundamental sentiments (the *affect control principle*). Fundamental sentiments act like a thermostat setting—a reference level for interpreting what happens in a situation. When impressions vary from that reference level (as the temperature might vary in a room), people do things to bring the impressions back in line with cultural sentiments.

First, affect control theory defines *deflection* as the discrepancy between fundamental cultural sentiments and transient situated impressions (in the three-dimensional evaluation-potency-activity space).[4] Mathematically, we operationalize this as the squared Euclidean distance between the sentiments and impressions (in evaluation-potency-activity space).[4] In a standard Actor-Behavior-Object event, deflection can be operationalized as

$$D = (A_e' - A_e)^2 + (A_p' - A_p)^2 + (B_e' - B_e)^2 + (A_p' - B_p)^2 \qquad (7.3)$$
$$+ (B_a' - B_a)^2 + (O_e' - O_e)^2 + (O_p' - O_p)^2 + (O_a' - O_a)^2$$

This mathematical expression allows manipulation of the impression-change equations to implement the affect control principle. Notice that we can substitute the regression equation (Equation 7.2) for each transient impression (e.g., A'_e) in Equation 7.3. This creates an expression that has only cultural meanings in it (e.g., A_e, B_a, etc.). We can then set the partial derivatives of the deflection to zero. This allows us (or more accurately, a computer program) to solve for a three-number evaluation-potency-activity profile that will minimize deflection.

These equations can predict the optimal behavior (in the form of a three-number profile) for an event that will produce impressions as close as possible to the initial cultural sentiments. These are the expected behaviors for someone in that role relationship. (In practice, all of these calculations are done automatically for researchers by the simulation program INTERACT.) For example, the profile for a behavior that *would optimally* confirm our sentiments for a Student acting on a Teacher is an evaluation of 1.45, a potency of 0.31, and an activity of 1.10, corresponding closest to actions like Applaud, Flatter, and Ask.

After an event that has disturbed meanings, solving for the behavior profile produces the creative response that an actor is expected to generate to repair the situation. The deflection generated by the event Student Corrects Teacher is 2.0, indicating a relatively low discrepancy between the situated impressions and our cultural sentiments about Teachers, Students, and Correcting. After the Correcting, the Student would have to do a new behavior with a cultural meaning like evaluation $= 1.89$, potency $= -0.37$ and activity $= 0.86$ (corresponding most closely to Admire) to bring situated impressions back into line with cultural sentiments. Alternatively, the Teacher could Instruct, Reassure, or Counsel the Student (optimal profile: e $= 1.46$, p $= 1.34$, a $= -0.49$).

Reconstruction Principle

Sometimes events produce deflections that are so large that it is impossible to find a behavioral way to resolve them. Affect control theory's *reconstruction principle* states that inexorably large deflections prompt redefinition of the situation. To implement this principle in the mathematical model, we use the same type of equation used to predict behaviors but solve instead for a new actor identity or a new object identity. Consider the following event: Mother Abandons Child. This event produces a deflection of 29.0, and yields no predicted behaviors; no behavior exists in the sentiment dictionary that could resolve that amount of deflection. In other words, there is nothing that a Mother can do after Abandoning a Child that would fully repair the deflection produced by that event. However, using the reconstruction principle, we can solve for the optimal actor identity that would minimize deflection. In this case, we get a new actor identity evaluation, potency, and activity of -2.85, 1.43, and 1.09. We search the dictionary for identities that match that profile and find that Murderer or Bully are closest. Thus affect control theory can model attribution processes.

Alternatively, we could solve for a new object identity.[5] This approach allows affect control theory to make predictions about our tendencies to blame the victim. What kind of object-person would an Adolescent Accuse? We would expect him to act that way toward a Spendthrift, a Skeptic, or an Egghead.

Traits, Attributions, and Emotions

The impression-change equations tell how events change impressions. The behavioral prediction equations use the affect control principle to tell us how actors are likely to behave, given a definition of the situation. Labeling equations tell us how we might redefine actors or objects as a result of observed interactions. If we take these same labeling equations and hold the actor's *identity* constant, we can solve for a trait that can be added to the actor's identity to make sense of experiences.

Averett and Heise (1987) estimated equations of the form

$$C = c + b_1 I_e + b_2 I_p + b_3 I_a + b_4 C_e + b_5 C_p + b_6 C_a \qquad (7.4)$$

where C is the evaluation, potency, or activity of a trait and identity composite (e.g., an Incompetent Doctor), I is the identity (Doctor), and T is the trait associated with that identity (Incompetent). Once we know what the C_e, C_p, and C_a should be in the event (by producing the actor profile that would minimize deflection), we can solve for the T values in the equation. Both the C's and the I's are known.[6]

What kind of Husband would Accuse his Wife? Affect control theory answers this question by first solving for the optimal actor identity for the event (Actor) Accuses Wife (answer: an Actor with an evaluation of -1.5, potency of 0.0, and activity of 0.37—someone like a Tease or Adulterer). We then hold the identity of Husband constant and solve for the trait that, when combined with Husband, produces a profile that is closest to that optimal identity. These attribution equations tell us what kind of Husband would Accuse his Wife (answer: a Rude or Obnoxious Husband).

The attribution equations solve for traits that, when added to an identity, can make sense of observed behaviors. Heise and Thomas (1989) showed that we can use these same equations to make predictions about the emotions that actors and objects are likely to feel in social interaction. Using information about the identity's original sentiments (I) and the transient identity that is produced by the event (C), we can solve for the emotion that would express the change created by the event (E).

$$E_e = .364 - .871 I_e - .182 I_p - .162 I_a + 1.722 C_e + .317 C_p + .365 C_a$$

$$E_p = .430 - .139 I_e - .117 I_p - .104 I_a + .240 C_e + 1.691 C_p - 0.21 C_a \quad (7.5)$$

$$E_a = .015 - .110 I_e - .174 I_p - .816 I_a + .139 C_e - .159 C_p - 1.326 C_a$$

These equations reveal that emotions are a result of both the transient impressions produced by the event and the deflection. Focusing on evaluation, we can see that the effects of the fundamental sentiments (I) are negative and roughly half the size of the effects of the transient impressions (C). We can simplify this expression to show how positive and negative feelings are a function of the original fundamental sentiment of the identity (f) and its new transient location (t):

$$E_e = (2t - f) = t + (t - f) \qquad (7.6)$$

This shows us that the positivity of emotion is predicted by the positivity of the transient impression (t), as well as the positivity of the deflection produced by that transient impression ($t - f$). In other words, nice events make us feel good. Events that are even better than our identities would lead us to expect make us feel even better. When events are perfectly confirming ($t = f$), then the pleasantness of our emotion should roughly reflect the pleasantness of that fundamental identity.

The potency and activity equations reveal similar dynamics. Both of those equations can be roughly reduced to

$$E_{p,a} = (1.5t - f) = .5t + (t - f) \tag{7.7}$$

As with emotion evaluation, we see that emotion potency and emotion activity are each influenced by both the deflection and the transient impressions. When events push us further upward in potency than our identities suggest, we experience more powerful emotions. Likewise, when events make us seem livelier than our identities suggest, we feel energized. Emotional potency and activation are more sensitive to the direction and amount of deflection than to the transient impression that results. In the case of perfectly confirming events (when $t = f$), we would expect the potency and activity of our emotions to be roughly half the potency and activity associated with that fundamental identity.

Theoretical Elaborations

Researchers have elaborated the basic Actor-Behavior-Object grammar of affect control in several ways beyond the addition of traits and emotions to modify identities. Smith-Lovin (1987b) estimated impression-change equations that explicitly take the behavior setting (S) into account. We can use these A-B-O-S equations to predict behaviors when actors are trying to confirm not only the sentiments of their own and their interaction partners' identities and actions but also the cultural sentiments associated with a socially defined setting (e.g., a church).

Rashotte (2002a, 2002b) incorporated nonverbal behaviors (N) into the event grammar to produce A-N-B-O events. The nonverbal behaviors modify the meanings of the behavior, much like traits, characteristics, or emotions modify the meanings of the actor or object identities. These events allow us to capture the affective difference between Teenager Obeying his Mother and a Teenager Rolling-his-eyes-while Obeying his Mother.

Program INTERACT

Both the logic and the substance of affect control theory are contained in its mathematical specification. The empirically estimated equations contain crucial information about affective processing. They reflect basic social and cultural processes of attribution, justice, balance, and response to deviance. The logic of the theory (for example, the affect control principle and the reconstruction principle) is implemented through mathematical manipulation of these equations. These mathematical manipulations produce predictions about behaviors, emotions, and labeling. A computer program, INTERACT, contains the equations and the dictionaries of culture-specific sentiments.[7] This software allows researchers to work through implications of the theory. Simulation results using INTERACT can be taken as predictions of the theory and subjected to testing through empirical research.

EMPIRICAL WORK ON AFFECT CONTROL THEORY

Research on affect control theory falls into three categories: (1) description of the cultural sentiments that are the reference levels for the control system, (2) tests of the control principle that animates action and labeling within the theory, and (3) applications of the theoretical framework to topics like emotion, deviance, religion, and social movements.

Measuring Culture in an Affect Control Paradigm

Affect control theory, at its core, is a set of cultural meanings, a set of equations that describe how events change those meanings and the control principle. Almost all early work was based on meanings and equations estimated from undergraduates at elite U.S. universities (the University of Chicago and the University of North Carolina at Chapel Hill). On the basis of early studies that Heise (1965, 1966, 1969a) and others (Gordon et al. 1963) did on the meaning of social identities and acts, researchers argued that most people in a language culture shared these meanings. Researchers considered the three-dimensional structure and the equations that transformed meanings within situations to be universal.[8] Since actors learned fundamental sentiments through multiple channels of socialization, these cultural sentiments were reinforced by meaning-maintaining social interactions. Therefore researchers assumed that they changed slowly, if at all, over time.

As a larger circle of researchers became involved, scholars created cultural meaning dictionaries for other national cultures—Northern Ireland Catholics, Canadians, West Germans, Japanese, and mainland Chinese.[9] These new dictionaries allow analyses of institutions across cultures. Researchers often map a domain like emotions (MacKinnon and Keating 1989), occupational titles (MacKinnon and Langford 1994), gendered traits (Langford and MacKinnon 2000), or sexual and erotic identities (Schneider 1999). They can then compare its structure in more than one culture.

Usually the structure is relatively stable across the cultures, and the comparison adds to the strength of its description. For example, potency differentiates negative emotions (sadness versus anger), while positive emotions are more uniform in their (usually high) potency. Activity differentiates intense, overwhelming emotions from milder feelings (Morgan and Heise 1988; MacKinnon and Keating 1989). Gendered traits described in the evaluation-potency-activity meaning space show that, net of potency and activity, the higher the goodness of a trait or characteristic, the more likely it is to be associated with females. Langford and MacKinnon (2000) conclude that there are two status hierarchies that operate in the gendering of traits: a power hierarchy that associates potent traits with maleness and a secondary hierarchy that associates goodness with femaleness. They suggest from the cross-cultural generality of this pattern that a kind of benevolent sexism (or perhaps a recognition of women's caring labor) helps define gender stereotypes. Linking the three-dimensional affective space to occupational prestige ratings shows a more nuanced view than the traditional unidimensional conception of occupational status (MacKinnon and Langford 1994).

Affect control theory researchers also investigate the structure of specialized subcultures, assessing their specialized identities, actions, and meanings. Adam King (2001), for example, examined Internet culture by recruiting respondents through a highly visible Yahoo! advertisement. He found intense (and somewhat gendered) meanings for Internet terms like *Yahoo!*, *spam*, *e-mail*, *cybersex*, and *surf the web* (see King 2001, Table 4). More important, he found that the meanings of the online identities and actions shifted in systematic ways as people spent more time using the Internet. Basically, people learn a new set of cultural labels and meanings when they enter an online subculture.

Heise (1979, 100–102) reported a study of professional socialization carried out by an undergraduate student whose father was a North Carolina highway patrolman. It shows that maintaining undergraduate meanings for the identities State Trooper and Criminal lead to intense, violent interactions: the Criminal would Spit on, Maim, and Ridicule the Trooper, while the Trooper would Handcuff, Refuse, and Punish someone he saw as a Criminal. While this may seem satisfyingly like the script of a television episode, it seems rather extreme for everyday law enforcement. Luckily for the public, trained highway patrol recruits had meanings for their self-identity of State Trooper that were more positively evaluated, more potent, and more lively, while their view of Criminals was that they were less bad and less weak than they were in undergraduates' cultural meanings. Such meanings, when maintained, generate State Trooper expectations that a Criminal will try to Upstage or Evade him, while he will intend to Captivate and Challenge the Criminal. Another study of policemen and police science students showed that the change in law enforcement identity meanings occurred systematically as students entered training and changed from members of the general culture to insiders in a professional law enforcement subculture.[10]

One of the problems with these studies of subculture is that they explore group differences in *meaning*s and their structure, but predictions about what these meanings imply for behavioral norms are speculative. We have to assume that the theory—the mathematical model—is correct and applies to the subculture before any simulations we generate are meaningful as a cultural description. We don't know if the simulations parallel actual behavior in the subculture.

One project that combines quantitative measurement with qualitative field observations is a study of two religious groups by Smith-Lovin and Douglass (1992). They asked the questions, How do gay people who occupy stigmatized identities in the mainstream culture develop a religious interaction ritual (Collins 1990, 2004) that generates positive, rewarding emotions? and How do they create subcultural support for being simultaneously gay and religious? The study contrasted a traditional (and relatively liberal) Unitarian church with the Metropolitan Community Church (MCC), a religious denomination explicitly developed to serve the gay community. Using participant observation, Smith-Lovin and Douglass compiled a list of significant social labels in both religious groups. Church members rated these concepts on the evaluation, potency, and activity dimensions. The data showed large differences between the two groups' ratings of religious and, especially, gay identities

TABLE 7.1
Fundamental Sentiments of Identities in Two Religious Congregations

Identity	METROPOLITAN COMMUNITY CHURCH			UNITARIAN		
	E	P	A	E	P	A
God	3.1	3.6	0.1	1.8	1.8	−0.8
Minister	1.9	1.2	0.4	1.5	0.6	0.0
Worshiper	1.8	0.7	−0.2	0.9	0.1	−0.3
Congregation	1.6	2.1	0.2	1.0	1.0	−0.4
Gay Person	1.9	0.6	1.2	−0.0	−0.5	0.6

SOURCE: Data from Smith-Lovin and Douglass (1992).

(Table 7.1) but not social actions.[11] Unitarians had more negative, less potent meanings associated with gay identities, compared with the MCC. There were also substantial differences in the potency and activity meanings of the religious figures—both symbolic (God) and institutional (Minister). In the MCC context, Gay Person and Worshiper have similar profiles (although Gay Person is substantially livelier), while in the Unitarian church group there are differences on all dimensions, especially on evaluation.

INTERACT simulations using the fundamental sentiments from the two congregations produced hypotheses about the religious rituals expected in both institutional contexts and about the emotions that those interaction rituals would produce (Smith-Lovin and Douglass 1990). The more potent, lively meanings associated with religious identities in the gay church led INTERACT to produce more dramatic, flamboyant interactions. These contrasted markedly with the more staid role relationships among religious figures in the Unitarian church. For example, the expected action of a Minister to a Worshiper in MCC had the affective profile e = 0.9, p = 1.7, and a = 0.7 with labels like Stroke, Visit, and Please. In the Unitarian group, the same role relationship was supported by an action with the profile e = 0.3, p = 1.0, a = 0.2, implying behaviors like Appeal to, Flatter, and Consult. But the institutionalized religious interactions in *both* congregations predicted deep, positive emotions for the groups' members, an important part of the religious experience.

The subcultural meanings of homosexual identities also generated very different predicted behaviors. Using the MCC sentiments about Gay Person, INTERACT predicted positive interactions among gays (e.g., Applaud, Play With, Court). A Congregation would Court, Play With, or Desire Sexually a Gay Person. By contrast, the Unitarian meanings led INTERACT to predict that homosexuals will experience negative, unhappy interactions with one another, with God, and with formal religious figures.

Smith-Lovin and Douglass then tested the validity of these simulation results by having informants from the MCC congregation assess the likelihood of interaction events that were (1) produced by the MCC sentiments, (2) produced by the Unitarian sentiments, or (3) produced through random selection of behaviors from the INTERACT undergraduate dictionary. MCC raters saw the events generated from the MCC sentiments as more likely than events generated from the Unitarian sentiments or the random selections.

Smith-Lovin and Douglass (1992, 243) concluded that affect control theory shows promise as a "generative model of culture."

Thomas and Heise (1995) went "mining error variance" and hit pay dirt, reporting two studies that showed subcultural phenomena in even undergraduate data. In the first study, Thomas and Heise used data from Indiana undergraduates (Heise and Thomas 1989) on 44 emotions and 64 identities. About one-fifth of these concepts produced subgroup differences that could be visually detected. Principal components analyses on the complete sets of emotion and identity concepts consistently produced two meaningful components. The authors concluded that "individual variations in sentiment are somewhat predictable from one concept to another and that there are two main ways that individuals vary in sentiments [in these data]" (Thomas and Heise 1995, 430).

In their second study, Thomas and Heise used the results of the principal components analyses to select concepts that maximally discriminated between the underlying subcultural groups. These stimuli were presented to 55 undergraduate students who rated the concepts. Principal components extracted from these data replicated the results from the first study. To shed light on the subcultures, Thomas and Heise selected nine students who had distinctive patterns of sentiments for in-depth, open-ended interviews. Socially isolated students had less intense sentiments about many concepts. These individuals also reported difficulties in symbolic interaction (e.g., possessing "nebulous opinions," being "irresolute in discourse," and "making jokes that aren't funny"). By contrast, individuals who possessed broad and deep social relations expressed strong sentiments, displayed self-assurance in interpersonal discourse, and projected "intense, confident, and convergent [i.e., nondeviant] opinions." These socially integrated individuals were also apparently less psychologically distressed than the individuals expressing affectively muted sentiments.

Another affect control tradition assessing cross-cultural variations estimates the impression-change equations. The event is the unit of analysis in these studies. Therefore these studies must measure the sentiments for identities and actions and other components *both* in isolation and within the context of events. Luckily, new measurement programs and Internet technology have extended this type of study to several non-U.S. cultures (Heise 2002). Early studies in other English-language cultures like Northern Ireland and Ontario, Canada, found mostly similarities in equation structure (Smith-Lovin 1987a; MacKinnon 1994). More recently, Smith and colleagues did extensive studies in Japan that do show cultural differences (Smith 2002; Smith, Matsuno, and Umino 1994; Smith, Umino, and Matsuno 1998; Smith, Matsuno, and Ike 2001); new studies in mainland China indicate that some of these differences may be pan-Asian while others are culture-specific (Smith, Ike, and Li 2002).

The Japanese impression-change equations appear to be highly similar to the U.S. equations. Japanese reactions to social events appear to be slightly simpler than those of English-speaking cultures, but their structure is quite similar. In contrast, equations that combined social identities and modifiers (traits, status characteristics, moods, or emotions) proved to be quite different across the two cultures (Smith, Matsuno, and Ike 2001). For the Japanese (but not Americans), many of the terms interact with gender, indicating that men and women process the trait-identity and emotion-identity combinations differently.

In addition, the Japanese appeared to contextualize their reactions to a much greater degree; the Japanese equations contain many more interaction terms that qualify the effect of one affective element by the presence of another (Smith, Matsuno, and Ike 2001). These equations function within the affect control model to describe attribution processes (what kind of a person would do such a thing?), emotional response (how would a person feel after experiencing such an event?), and the process through which status characteristics shape behavior (how is a female judge different from a male judge?). Therefore finding that the Japanese are more gendered and contextualized than Americans leads to hypotheses generated by INTERACT about cultural and gender differences in attribution processes. For example, typical traits associated with the role identity Mother are Serious and Studious for Japanese men and women, respectively, while Americans (both male and female) would be more likely to think of Mothers as Persuasive (Smith, Matsuno, and Ike 2001, 192).

Investigating the Control Process

The core principle of affect control theory is that people work to maintain meanings in social interaction. They perceive situations, expect and intend actions, create events, and relabel odd occurrences to sustain culturally given sentiments. Therefore much of the affect control research focuses on hypotheses generated from this core feature of the theory.

Since the theory applies to the perception of social events, many studies use vignettes describing interaction and ask people to respond to them. Researchers typically design the vignettes to represent a variety of combinations of actors, behaviors, and objects. In this way, researchers create variability along the affective dimensions. The central hypothesis is that the perceived likelihood of events will be determined by how well they maintain sentiments. In his original presentation of affect control theory, Heise (1977; 1979, 67–71) calculated deflection of meaning from published impression-formation data and correlated it with subjects' ratings of the perceived likelihood of events; he found strong support for the theory. Later vignette studies also showed strong support, with deflection predicting 30% to 40% of the variance in how probable an event seemed to respondents who read it (Heise and MacKinnon 1987).

Wiggins and Heise (1987) conducted the first experiment that watched participants' behavior in an actual social interaction. Here, naïve participants came into a "communication study" to interact with a young man (actually a confederate) who was labeled as either another University of North Carolina undergraduate (Student) or as a participant recruited from a nearby juvenile delinquent program (Delinquent).[12] The naïve participant sat across from the confederate, who was already completing a questionnaire. The experimenter handed the naïve participant a pen and a questionnaire like the ones the confederate had. After a few moments, a secretary came into the room and collected the completed form from the other "student" or "delinquent" (confederate). In half the sessions, she was polite to both participants, then left the room. In half the sessions, however, she waited impatiently, made rude remarks about the naïve participant's slowness, criticized him sharply for using a pen rather than a pencil for filling out the questionnaire, and interrupted rudely during questions he asked about intentionally confusing instructions. The experiment

TABLE 7.2
Friendliness of Participant Behavior toward Interaction Partner

	Premanipulation	Postmanipulation	Change in Friendliness
Appreciated Participant interacting with another Student	1.01	1.60	0.61
Appreciated Participant interacting with another Student	0.91	1.18	0.32
Appreciated Participant interacting with another Student	0.77	1.05	0.40
Embarrassed Participant interacting with a Delinquent	1.12	0.12	−1.00

SOURCE: Wiggins and Heise (1987).

was a 2 × 2 design: interaction partner as Student or Delinquent crossed with whether the Secretary Criticized the naïve subject. Using INTERACT simulations, Wiggins and Heise (1987) hypothesized that the confederate (Student or Delinquent) would elicit different behaviors from the naïve participant. Specifically, the naïve participant was predicted to be nicer to another Student than to a stigmatized Delinquent. More interestingly, these differences would be much larger *after* the naïve participant had been deflected downward on the evaluation, potency, and activity dimensions by a harsh criticism. In effect, the positively evaluated Student confederate and the negatively evaluated Delinquent confederate presented the naïve participant with different interactional resources to restore the participant's own identity after it had been disturbed by the criticism by the Secretary. Indeed, Wiggins and Heise (1987) found that participants became much friendlier toward another Student than toward a Delinquent after they had been criticized, confirming the hypothesis (Table 7.2).

Robinson and Smith-Lovin (1992) expanded the experimental assessment of the affect control principle to look at emotional responses to deflecting events and at choices of interaction partners. Following closely an experimental paradigm developed by Swann and colleagues (1987), Robinson and Smith-Lovin asked participants to read a 3-minute passage from *Jonathan Livingston Seagull* while (they thought) their performances were being evaluated by two raters behind a two-way mirror. Participants then received feedback from the two raters. Affect control theory predicted a counterintuitive pattern: positive evaluation by a rater would create positive emotion for all participants, but low social-self-esteem participants would choose future interaction with those who *confirmed* their negative self-identities. The hypotheses were confirmed—participants chose future interaction partners who confirmed their self-images even when that confirmation caused them to feel bad.

Research in other theoretical traditions that share the control principle also provides support for the affect control principle. Self-verification theory (e.g., Swann et al. 1987), self-regulation theory (Carver and Scheier 1981), and identity control theory (Burke 1991; see Chapter 5 in this volume) focus on people's attempts to maintain the meanings associated with their self-identities. These impressive bodies of work support the general control system idea introduced by Powers (1973) and its application to social interaction (McClelland and Fararo 2006). In many cases, their hypotheses are consistent with affect control theory since these other research traditions share the control model lineage.

Affect Control Studies of Emotion

Predictions about emotional response are one arena where the control theories differ in their predictions (Smith-Lovin 1990, 1994; Turner and Stets 2005; Turner and Stets, forthcoming; Smith-Lovin and Robinson 2006). Because of this theoretical difference, many recent studies of affect control theory have focused on the emotions component of the model. Robinson and Smith-Lovin (1992) showed that deflections in a positive direction produced positive emotion, even when experimental participants *acted* to reduce that positive deflection by choosing an interaction partner who had evaluated them negatively (consistent with their negative self-image). Some research in other traditions (Stets 2003, 2005) also supports affect control theory predictions, by showing that deflections in a positive direction (over-reward) create positive rather than negative emotion.

While behavioral studies like those conducted by Robinson and Smith-Lovin (1992) or Stets (2003, 2005) are the most compelling examples, they can deal with only a very limited number of situations for ethical reasons. Research using vignettes has demonstrated accurate prediction over a wider range of (imagined) situations. Heise and Calhan (1995) asked students to imagine themselves in 128 situations and report what emotion they felt. This study makes use of the fact that symbolic interactionist theories like affect control theory presume that events are processed symbolically—thinking about being in a situation is expected to arouse the same types of emotions that actually *being* in that situation would evoke (MacKinnon 1994). Half the imagined situations had the student as the actor, and in the other half, the student was the object. For example, students were asked to "imagine that you are flattering a professor. How do you feel at the moment?" Alternatively, they might be asked, "Imagine that an evangelist is condemning you. How do you feel at the moment?" The findings supported the theory.

The studies described above use the theory to predict emotion reactions. A second group of studies show how emotions act as a signal about identities. The first type of study shows that the theory does a good job of predicting what people will feel in what social circumstances. Since emotions indicate *how someone occupying an identity with a particular meaning* is responding to an event, people can use them as signals to help define ambiguous situations. Robinson, Smith-Lovin, and Tsoudis (1994; Tsoudis and Smith-Lovin 1998, 2001; Tsoudis 2000a, 2000b) used this feature of the theory to explore how emotional displays affect judgments made about criminal defendants. The studies follow a common design: they present students with a description of a court case (either a criminal confession or testimony by the victim of a crime), varying the emotions displayed by the perpetrator or victim in the case.[13] INTERACT predicts that people occupying fundamentally good identities should feel remorse after they have committed a negative act toward a good person (e.g., injured an innocent during a drunken driving accident); actors who have fundamentally negative identities would experience more neutral emotions. Similarly, victims who occupy good identities should feel devastated by being the object of such an action, while those occupying stigmatized identities expect negative acts to be directed at them and show less emotional response. In the studies, students gave lighter sentences to perpetrators who showed the negative, angst-filled emotions that INTERACT would predict of fundamentally good actors. They also used the emotional reactions of the victim to shape sentence judgments and the degree of empathy they had for those who had been hurt in the crime.

Since emotional experiences are key to understanding mental health, some affect control research has examined clinical issues. Francis (1997) conducted a qualitative study of two support groups: a divorce support group and a bereavement support group. In both cases, people entered the groups with negative identities and the unpleasant, powerless, low activation emotions that we would expect those identities to evoke. Divorced people saw themselves as failing at marriage and bereaved spouses felt responsible for their partner's pain and ultimate death. Since it was difficult to redefine the event (divorce or death), Francis (1997) found that support group leaders worked on the identities of the group members and their former partners. They reinforced the positively evaluated, potent, and activated identities that the group members could occupy that would generate positive feelings from new events. In addition, they helped relabel the former partners more negatively, giving those partners more responsibility for the divorce or death. In effect, the event became "a bad person does something bad to a good person." Since even this event construction involves some deflection and negative emotion, the group leaders then encouraged the group members to Forgive the former spouse—a good, deep act that helped to support their new positive identity. The most important finding from the Francis study is that the group leaders did *not* focus directly on the negative feelings that the group members had. Instead, the leaders shaped the view of the situation—the identities of self and other—to generate a new set of emotions that would be more productive for continuing life.

Applications of Affect Control to Central Sociological Questions

Social Movements and Politics. Since affect control theory links the framing of a situation to the emotional experiences that the situation evokes, it has found powerful applications to the framing of social movements. Heise (1998) pointed out that we develop emphatic solidarity with other groups if we find ourselves having the same emotional reactions that they do. Berbrier (1998) and Schneider (1999) both discussed the framing and cultural meanings that neoconservative and white separatist movements use to support their positions.

Researchers have applied the theory to more traditional political processes as well. Troyer and Robinson (2006) used INTERACT simulations to show how affect control theory can model political advertisements and voting behavior. MacKinnon and Bowlby (2000) used the theory, with social identity theory (Abrams and Hogg 1990), to explore the affective dynamics of intergroup relationships and the stereotypes that people form about other groups.

While we may not think of nation-states as unitary social actors to which social psychological theories apply, Lerner and colleagues (Azar and Lerner 1981; Lerner 1983) noted that the symbolic processing *can* interpret the cultural understandings that world leaders have about international events. When we process an event like "the United States attacks Iraq," we have affective reactions that guide our cognitive labeling of ambiguous actions, our policy preferences for future events, and our feelings of solidarity (or lack thereof) with other collective actors. Seeing Arab citizens rejoicing in the streets at an event that causes

Americans great distress (e.g., the September 11, 2001, attacks on the World Trade Center) creates U.S. public opinion that Arab people understand the world very differently than Americans do and cannot be trusted to behave in a predictable, "moral" manner.

Networks and Social Structures. The fact that affect control theory is represented in a simulation program allows us to explore a wide range of hypothetical structures. Robinson (1996) developed a social space of all possible types of identity occupants by combining high, medium, and low levels of evaluation, potency, and activity ($3 \times 3 \times 3$) for 27 different affective identity profiles. She then used INTERACT to simulate all *possible* Befriending events. For example, she would use the level of deflection created by the event "a Newsboy Befriends the Invalid" to estimate how likely such a friendship would be, given the two identity occupants. (Notice that these events are asymmetric, in the same way that actual friendship choices would be: "Newsboy Befriends Invalid" produces a different deflection value than "Invalid Befriends Newsboy.") These events were used to fill a 27×27 matrix of friendship choices. Robinson then analyzed the structure of the friendship matrix. She found that evaluation predicted cohesion; homophily resulted as nice people befriended each other and deviants clumped together (albeit less tightly). Power relations formed a structural equivalence pattern, with similarly powerful people having the same types of relationships (either friendly or not) with others who had the same type of identity. This framework could be expanded to examine the structural relations for any type of tie (e.g., Marry, Trust, Attack); the patterns could also be compared to empirical evidence to see if the patterns that are generated by the theoretical model are also found in observations on actual social systems. Indeed, Yelsma and Yelsma (1998) have tested affect control predictions on patterns of social respect among 596 students at a Michigan high school.

Gender. Researchers have applied both affect control theory and related control-based theories to gender and family issues.[14] These applications illustrate the uses the model could have in exploring racial or ethnic, class, and other fundamental divides in our society. Most of these studies begin with a focus on culturally based meanings. Lee (1998), for example, studied 443 talented high school students who attended summer programs in math and science education. He measured boys' and girls' self-concepts, their concepts of gendered identities (Boy, Girl), and scientific identities (e.g., Biologist, Physicist, Psychologist) on the evaluation, potency, and activity dimension. He found that discrepancies between self-identity meanings and meanings associated with scientific identities predicted which scientific interests girls and boys reported. These patterns helped to explain the gender gap in interest in psychology, physics, and mathematics.

Kroska (1997, 2001) has done a series of papers relating the measurement of cultural sentiments to gender ideology. She found that 12 roles among married and cohabiting individuals showed a strong consensus in cultural meanings; gender ideology of the respondent ($N = 309$) did not significantly predict the evaluation, potency, and activity of these role identities. She did find, however, that gender ideology was more effectively measured as an identity (with evaluation, potency, and activity sentiments attached to it) than as an attitude.

Robinson and Smith-Lovin (1990; Smith-Lovin and Robinson 1992; see also Okamoto and Smith-Lovin 2001) have used gendered sentiments to predict conversational behavior.

Since interruptions, topic changes, and talking are all social acts (with evaluation, potency, and activity sentiments associated with them), we can use affect control theory to predict whether men or women (with their gendered identity sentiments) are likely to engage in these behaviors. The studies supported the theoretical predictions, although a paucity of identity information limited the analyses.

FUTURE DIRECTIONS FOR RESEARCH

While a flexible theory of cultural sentiments, social action, and emotion can find application in almost any domain, there are several areas that are clearly ripe for development. First, the early assumption that identity sentiments were widely shared across social groups and subcultures is ready for exploration. The rich studies of subcultures and the application of affect control theory to crime and deviance (Kalkhoff 2002) combine with the availability of Internet measurement tools (Heise 2001) to encourage study of the affective sentiments associated with a much broader population. If the sentiments vary systematically across sociodemographic space (as McPherson [2004] might suggest) or clump in predictable ways along political or ideological lines (e.g., Evans, DiMaggio, and Bryson 1996), we could use the theory to map important framing of institutional logics and the political messages associated with them. In effect, affect control theory has the potential to reunite the study of culture and social psychology—two fields that used to be closely linked through cultural anthropology and research on social values.

Second, there are important issues about which affect control theory makes no firm predictions. Clearly, these areas need development. We know, for example, that people can resolve deflection through actions, through redefinition of the situation, or through seeking out entirely new interactions that will restore sentiments. The current theory, however, gives us little guidance about which of these routes will be chosen (although action is assumed to be primary, if it is feasible). Even when action is not possible and we expect re-identification, we have no clear picture of how people decide *which* event element to relabel. Do we think that a Priest who has Molested a Choirboy is a Fiend? Or is the Molesting an act of Love? Or is the young boy a Seducer? There is no theoretical structure to guide us in these issues involving definition of the situation—yet it is these definitions that invoke the culturally determined affective sentiments that guide our action.

Third, expansions of the basic A-B-O setting are open for exploration. As we noted earlier, there are existing equation estimates for the influence of setting on interaction dynamics as well as the modifying effects of nonverbal behavior. However, these areas remain underexamined in the research literature. Do interactions in a church vary from interactions in a classroom in ways that extend beyond the differences in identities that those settings activate? The setting equations are fully incorporated into the current version of INTERACT and offer a wonderful opportunity for researchers to investigate the importance of physical setting in shaping the affective dynamics of social behavior.

Fourth, one of the few areas where control theories of identity and action disagree is in the domain of emotional experience. Other theories (most notably identity control theory, see Chapter 5 in this volume) regard disruption of identity meanings as leading to stress and unpleasant feelings. In affect control theory, there is a real difference between the sense of unlikelihood, stress, and unreality that may come from deflection and the evaluative valence of emotion. We can be devastated that our interaction partners act negatively toward us (if we have a typically positive self-image), but we can also be dazed and elated by an unexpectedly good fortune (recall Equations 7.4–7.6). To assess which view is more accurate, we will need measures that can differentiate between deflection and emotion—a tall order. Physiological measures may offer some traction on this issue (Robinson, Rogalin, and Smith-Lovin 2004). Research on under- and over-reward represents an important substantive domain for its exploration (Stets 2003, 2005).

Finally, we note that empirical affect control theory research to date has focused heavily on evaluation dynamics—almost to the exclusion of attention to potency and activity dynamics. This is particularly unfortunate because one of affect control theory's distinguishing features is its attention to all three of these fundamental dimensions of social meaning. The theoretical structure of affect control theory could distinguish power dynamics among identities in interaction and discriminate among emotions with different levels of intensity and expressivity. Investigation into these predictions would capitalize on the full structure of the theory and facilitate the exploration of predictions that are unique to affect control theory and nonoverlapping with related theories.

NOTES

Authorship order is alphabetical. The authors thank Alison Bianchi, Kristi Clark Miller, Tiffiny Guidry, David Heise, Neil MacKinnon, Miller McPherson, Linda Molm, Steven Nelson, Shirley Keeton, Amy Kroska, Lisa Rashotte, Christabel Rogalin, Jane Sell, Herman Smith, and Murray Webster for valuable comments on an earlier draft.

1. Sheldon Stryker (1968, 1980) developed identity theory in response to the same intellectual challenge. Identity theory deals more with how people take on role identities than with how they act once occupying role identities within a situation. Peter Burke (1991) developed identity control theory, a direct extension of identity theory, to address the same questions as affect control theory, using a somewhat different measurement structure. For a more complete description of the differences between affect control theory and identity control theory, see Smith-Lovin and Robinson (2006).

2. We capitalize identities, behaviors, emotions, and other social symbols that are used as inputs or produced as outputs in affect control theory analyses using the simulation program INTERACT (described later). All simulation results presented here used female equations and dictionaries from 1978 North Carolina Data in Java INTERACT, accessible at www .indiana.edu/~socpsy/ACT/interact/JavaInteract.html, last updated February 27, 2005.

3. The behavior need not be observable to all: I could Love someone without anyone else knowing about this directed behavior. Also, behaviors can be acts of omission (e.g., Neglect) rather than commission.

4. Sometimes the mathematical operationalization of deflection is offered as a definition. Here we distinguish between the conceptual definition and the operationalization to allow for times when researchers are focused on different event elements (e.g., settings) or even different dimensions.

5. In this case, the event violates our cultural understandings so profoundly that there is no available object-person identity that we would expect a Mother to Abandon. One way to interpret this result is to say that our culture does not expect someone who is a true Mother to ever abandon the person to whom she has that role relationship, no matter *what* kind of person the child is.

6. The *I*'s are the cultural sentiments associated with the original actor identity— Doctor, in this case.

7. See note 2.

8. There were always exceptions to this universality. In her dissertation work on Lebanese and Egyptian Arab students, Bernadette Pelissier Smith (like Osgood before her) found a four-dimensional structure, with the activity dimension decomposed into two distinct types of meaning—frequency and rapidity (Smith 1980, reported in Smith-Lovin 1987a). Similarly, meanings and equations were different enough for male and female university students to make gendered meaning dictionaries and equations useful in the INTERACT simulation program and in most published reports (Heise and Lewis 1978; Smith-Lovin and Heise 1988).

9. Researchers are currently collecting Taiwanese, Korean, and new U.S. dictionaries using the new Surveyor data collection program and the World Wide Web (Heise 2001). All of the currently available dictionaries are available on the affect control theory website, http://www.indiana.edu/~socpsy/ACT/.

10. Other undergraduate subculture projects (reported in Heise 1979, chap. 4, n. 4) involved feminists in a NOW chapter, psychics and their followers, young attorneys clerking at the North Carolina Supreme Court and attorney general's office, and children of isolated black tenant farmers in eastern North Carolina.

11. This pattern supports the common use of the U.S. (undergraduate) behavior dictionary for subcultural analyses and is consistent with Heise's (1966; 1979, 101) suggestion that most social actions will not have different meanings across subcultures. As Kalkhoff (2002) points out, it also gives greater specificity to the claim in the deviance and criminological literature (e.g., Wolfgang and Ferracuti 1967) that subcultures are only partially different from the larger, parent culture.

12. The labeling was accomplished during the description of the purposes of the study to the naïve participant. In both situations, the same young man played the confederate: his dress and demeanor varied to fit the label.

13. The vignette stimuli are designed to correspond to actual court cases but are modified to embed emotion cues that are supposedly transcribed from a videotape to help the research participant imagine the original video.

14. Much of the research using the three-year survey of newly married couples in Washington State supports affect control ideas as well as the identity control theory hypotheses that it was designed to test (see discussion in Chapter 5 of this volume).

Abrams, Dominic, and Michael A. Hogg. 1990. *Social Identity Theory: Constructive and Critical Advances*. New York: Springer-Verlag.

Averett, Christine P., and David R. Heise. 1987. Modified social identities: Amalgamations, attributions, and emotions. *Journal of Mathematical Sociology* 13:103–32.

Azar, Edward E., and Steve Lerner. 1981. The use of semantic dimensions in the scaling of international events. *International Interactions* 7:361–78.

Berbrier, Mitch, 1998. "Half the Battle": Cultural resonance, framing processes, and ethnic affectations in contemporary white separatist rhetoric. *Social Problems* 45:431–50.

Burke, Peter J. 1991. Identity processes and social stress. *American Sociological Review* 56:836–49.

Carver, Charles S., and Michael F. Scheier. 1981. *Attention and Self-Regulation. A Control Theory Approach to Human Behavior*. New York: Springer-Verlag.

Cohen, Bernard P. 1989. *Developing Sociological Knowledge: Theory and Method*. Chicago: Nelson-Hall.

Collins, Randall. 1990. Stratification, emotional energy, and the transient emotions. In *Research Agendas in the Sociology of Emotions*, ed. T. D. Kemper. New York: SUNY Press.

———. 2004. *Interaction Ritual Chains*. Princeton, NJ: Princeton University Press.

Dunphy, Tara, and Neil J. MacKinnon. 2002. A proposal for integrating folklore and affect control theory. *Electronic Journal of Sociology* 6 (3).

Evans, John, Paul DiMaggio, and Bethany Bryson. 1996. Have Americans' social attitudes become more polarized? *American Journal of Sociology* 102:690–755.

Francis, Linda. 1997. Ideology and interpersonal emotion management: Redefining identity in two support groups. *Social Psychology Quarterly* 60:153–71.

Goffman, Erving. 1967. *Interaction Ritual*. New York: Pantheon.

Gollob, Harry F. 1968. Impression formation and word combination in sentences. *Journal of Personality and Social Psychology* 10:341–53.

Gordon, Robert A., James F. Short Jr., Desmond S. Cartwright, and Fred L. Strodtbeck, 1963. Values and gang delinquency: A study of street corner groups. *American Journal of Sociology* 69:109–128.

Heider, Fritz. 1958. *The Psychology of Interpersonal Relations*. New York: Wiley.

Heise, David R. 1965. Semantic differential profiles for 1,000 most frequent English words. *Psychological Monographs* 79 (8) (Whole No. 601).

———. 1966. Social status, attitudes, and word connotations. *Sociological Inquiry* 36:227–39.

———. 1969a. Some methodological issues in semantic differential research. *Psychological Bulletin* 72:406–22.

———. 1969b. Affective dynamics in simple sentences. *Journal of Personality and Social Psychology* 11:204–13.

———. 1977. Social action as the control of affect. *Behavioral Science* 22:163–77.

———. 1979. *Understanding Events: Affect and the Construction of Social Action.* New York: Cambridge University Press.

———. 1998. Conditions for Empathic Solidarity. In *The Problem of Solidarity: Theories and Models*, ed. Patrick Doreian and Thomas Fararo, 197–211. Amsterdam: Gordon & Breach.

———. 2001. Project Magellan: Collecting cross-cultural affective meanings via the internet. *Electronic Journal of Sociology* 5 (3).

———. 2002. Understanding social interaction with Affect Control Theory. In *New Directions in Contemporary Sociological Theory*, ed. J. Berger and M. Zelditch, chap. 2, 17–40. Boulder, CO: Rowman & Littlefield.

———. 2004. Enculturating agents with expressive role behavior. In *Human-Agent Interaction Multi-Cultural World*, ed. S. Payr and R. Trappl. Mahwah, NJ: Erlbaum.

Heise, David R., and Cassandra Calhan. 1995. Emotion norms in interpersonal events. *Social Psychology Quarterly* 58:223–40.

Heise, David R., and Elsa Lewis. 1988. *Programs Interact and Attitude: Software and Documentation.* Dubuque, IA: Wm. C. Brown, Software.

Heise, David R., and Neil J. MacKinnon. 1987. Affective bases of likelihood judgments. *Journal of Mathematical Sociology* 13:133–51.

Heise, David R., and Lisa Thomas. 1989. Predicting impressions created by combinations of emotion and social identity. *Social Psychology Quarterly* 52:141–48.

Kalkhoff, Will. 2002. Delinquency and violence as affect-control: Reviving the subcultural approach in criminology. *Electronic Journal of Sociology* 6 (3).

King, Adam B. 2001. Affective dimensions of internet culture. *Social Science Computer Review* 19:414–30.

Kroska, Amy. 1997. The division of labor in the home: A review and reconceptualization. *Social Psychology Quarterly* 60:304–22.

———. 2001. Do we have consensus? Examining the relationship between gender ideology and role meanings. *Social Psychology Quarterly* 64:18–40.

Langford, Tom, and Neil J. MacKinnon 2000. The affective basis for the gendering of traits: Comparing the United States and Canada. *Social Psychology Quarterly* 63:34–48.

Lee, James Daniel. 1998. Which kids can "become" scientists? Effects of gender, self-concepts and perceptions of scientists. *Social Psychology Quarterly* 61:199–219.

Lerner, Steven Jay. 1983. Affective dynamics of international relations. PhD diss. Chapel Hill: University of North Carolina.

MacKinnon, Neil J. 1985, 1988, 1998. *Final Reports to Social Sciences and Humanities Research Council of Canada on Projects.* 410-81-0089, 410-86-0794, and 410-94-0087. Guelph, Ontario: Department of Sociology and Anthropology, University of Guelph.

———. 1994. *Symbolic Interactionism as Affect Control.* Albany: State University of New York Press.

MacKinnon, Neil J., and Jeffrey W. Bowlby, 2000. The affective dynamics of stereotyping and intergroup relations. *Advances in Group Processes* 17:37–76.

MacKinnon, Neil J., and David R. Heise. 1993. Affect control theory: Delineation and development. In *Theoretical Research Programs: Studies in the Growth of Theory*, ed. Joseph Berger and Morris Zelditch Jr. Stanford, CA: Stanford University Press.

MacKinnon, Neil J., and Leo Keating. 1989. The structure of emotion: A review of the problem and a cross-cultural analysis. *Social Psychology Quarterly* 52:70–83.

MacKinnon, Neil J., and Tom Langford. 1994. The meaning of occupational prestige scores: A social psychological analysis and interpretation. *Sociological Quarterly* 35:215–45.

McClelland, Kent, and Thomas Fararo. 2006. *Purpose, Meaning, and Action: Control Systems Theories in Sociology*. New York: Palgrave-MacMillan.

McPherson, J. Miller. 2004. A Blau space primer: Prolegomenon to an ecology of affiliation. *Industrial and Corporate Change* 13:263–80.

Morgan, Rick L., and David R. Heise. 1988. Structure of emotions. *Social Psychology Quarterly* 51:19–31.

Okamoto, Dina, and Lynn Smith-Lovin. 2001. Gender, status, and the dynamics of topic change. *American Sociological Review* 66:852–73.

Osgood, Charles E. 1962. Studies on the generality of affective meaning systems. *American Psychologist* 17:10–28.

Osgood, Charles E., W. H. May, and M. S. Miron. 1975. *Cross-Cultural Universals of Affective Meaning*. Urbana: University of Illinois Press.

Osgood, Charles E., G. J. Suci, and P. H. Tannenbaum. 1957. *The Measurement of Meaning*. Urbana: University of Illinois Press.

Powers, William T. 1973. *Behavior: The Control of Perception*. Chicago: Aldine.

Rashotte, Lisa Slattery. 2002a. Incorporating Nonverbal Behaviors into Affect Control Theory. *Electronic Journal of Sociology* 6 (3).

———. 2002b. What does that smile mean? The meaning of nonverbal behaviors in social interaction. *Social Psychology Quarterly* 65:92–102.

Robinson, Dawn T. 1996. Identity and friendship: Affective dynamics and network formation. *Advances in Group Process* 13:91–111.

———. 2006. Affect control theory. *Encyclopedia of Sociology*. Malden, MA: Blackwell Publishers.

Robinson, Dawn T., Christabel L. Rogalin, and Lynn Smith-Lovin. 2004. Physiological Measures of Theoretical Concepts: Some Ideas for Linking Deflection and Emotion to Physical Responses During Interaction. *Advances in Group Processes* 21:77–115.

Robinson, Dawn T., and Lynn Smith-Lovin. 1990. Timing of interruptions in group discussions. *Advances in Group Processes* 7:45–73.

Robinson, Dawn T., and Lynn Smith-Lovin. 1992. Selective interaction as a strategy for identity maintenance: An affect control model. *Social Psychology Quarterly* 55:12–28.

Robinson, Dawn T., Lynn Smith-Lovin, and Olga Tsoudis. 1994. Heinous crime or unfortunate accident? The effects of remorse on responses to mock criminal confessions. *Social Forces* 73:175–90.

Schneider, Andreas. 1999. The violent character of sexual-eroticism in cross-cultural comparison. *International Journal of Sociology and Social Policy* 18:81–100.

Smith, Bernadette Pelissier. 1980. Impression formation among Egyptians and Lebanese. PhD diss. Chapel Hill: University of North Carolina.

Smith, Herman W. 2002. The dynamics of Japanese and American interpersonal events: Behavioral settings versus personality traits. *Journal of Mathematical Sociology* 26:1–21.

Smith, Herman W., Takanori Matsuno, and Shuuichirou Ike. 2001. The affective basis of attributional processes among Japanese and Americans. *Social Psychology Quarterly* 64:180–94.

Smith, Herman W., Takanori Matsuno, and Michio Umino. 1994. How similar are impression-formation processes among Japanese and Americans? *Social Psychology Quarterly* 57:124–39.

Smith, Herman W., Shuuichirou Ike, and Ying Li. 2002. Project Magellan redux: Problems and solutions with collecting cross-cultural affective meanings via the Internet. *Electronic Journal of Sociology* 6:3.

Smith, Herman W., Michio Umino, and Takanori Matsuno. 1998. The formation of gender-differentiated sentiments in Japan. *Journal of Mathematical Sociology* 22:373–95.

Smith-Lovin, Lynn. 1987a. Impressions from events. *Journal of Mathematical Sociology* 13:35–70.

———. 1987b. The affective control of events within settings. *Journal of Mathematical Sociology* 13:71–101.

———. 1990. Emotion as the confirmation and disconfirmation of identity: An affect control model. In *Research Agendas in the Sociology of Emotions*, ed. T. D. Kemper, chap. 9. Albany: State University of New York Press.

———. 1994. The sociology of affect and emotion. In *Sociological Perspectives on Social Psychology*, ed. K. Cook, G. Fine, and J. House, 118–48. New York: Allyn & Bacon.

Smith-Lovin, Lynn, and William Douglass. 1992. An affect control analysis of two religious subcultures. In *Social Perspective in Emotions*, ed. V. Gecas and D. Franks, 1:217–48. Greenwich, CT: JAI Press.

Smith-Lovin, Lynn, and David R. Heise. 1982. A structural equation model of impression formation. In *Multivariate Applications in the Social Sciences*, ed. N. Hirschberg and L. G. Humphreys, 195–222. Hillsdale, NJ: Erlbaum.

Smith-Lovin, Lynn, and David. R. Heise. 1988. *Analyzing Social Interaction: Advances in Affect Control Theory*. New York: Gordon & Breach. (Reprint of a special issue of the *Journal of Mathematical Sociology* vol. 13.)

Smith-Lovin, Lynn, and Dawn T. Robinson. 1992. Gender and conversational dynamics. In *Gender, Interaction, and Inequality*, ed. Cecilia Ridgeway, 122–56. New York: Springer-Verlag.

———. 2006. Control theories of identity, action, and emotion: In search of testable differences between affect control theory and identity control theory. In *Purpose, Meaning, and Action: Control System Theories in Sociology*, ed. Kent McClelland and Thomas Fararo. New York: Palgrave-MacMillan.

Stets, Jan E. 2003. Justice, emotion, and identity theory. *Advances in Identity Theory and Research*. New York: Kluwer Academic/Plenum Publishers.

———. 2005. Examining emotion in identity theory. *Social Psychology Quarterly* 68:39–74.

Stryker, Sheldon. 1968. "Identity salience and role performance." *Journal of Marriage and the Family* 4:558–64.

———. 1980. *Symbolic Interactionism: A Social Structural Version*. Menlo Park, CA: Benjamin Cummings.

Swann, William B., J. J. Griffin, S. C. Predmore, and B. Gaines. 1987. The cognitive-affective crossfire: When self-consistency confronts self-enhancement. *Journal of Personality and Social Psychology* 52(5): 881–89.

Thomas, Lisa, and David R. Heise. 1995. Mining error variance and hitting pay-dirt: Discovering systematic variation in social sentiments. *The Sociological Quarterly* 36:425–39.

Troyer, Lisa. 2004. Affect control theory as a foundation for the design of socially intelligent systems. *Proceedings of 2004 American Association for Artificial Intelligence Symposium on Architectures for Modeling Emotion: Cross Disciplinary Foundations*. Menlo Park, CA: AAAI Press.

Troyer, Lisa, and Dawn T. Robinson. 2006. From affect to self to action and back. In *Feeling Politics*, ed. David Redlawsk and G. Robert Boynton. New York: Palgrave-MacMillan.

Tsoudis, Olga. 2000a. Relation of affect control theory to the sentencing of criminals. *Journal of Social Psychology* 140:473–86.

———. 2000b. The likelihood of victim restitution in mock cases: Are the "rules of the game" different from prison and probation? *Social Behavior and Personality* 28:483–500.

Tsoudis, Olga, and Lynn Smith-Lovin. 1998. How bad was it? The effects of victim and perpetrator emotion on responses to criminal court vignettes. *Social Forces* 77:695–722.

———. 2001. Criminal identity: The key to situational construals in mock criminal court cases. *Sociological Spectrum* 21:3–31.

Turner, Jonathan H., and Jan E. Stets. 2005. *The Sociology of Emotions*. New York: Cambridge University Press.

———. Forthcoming. Sociological theories of human emotions. *Annual Review of Sociology* 32.

Wiggins, Beverly, and David R. Heise. 1987. Expectations, intentions, and behavior: Some tests of affect control theory. *Journal of Mathematical Sociology* 13:153–69.

Wolfgang, Marvin E., and Franco Ferracuti. 1967. *The Subculture of Violence*. London: Tavistock.

Yelsma, Paul, and J. Yelsma. 1998. Self-esteem and social respect within the high school. *Journal of Social Psychology* 138:431–41.

8 | THE THEORY OF COMPARISON PROCESSES

Guillermina Jasso

When humans reflect on their attributes and possessions—on their beauty, intelligence, wealth, athletic skill, and so on—they often *compare* their level of an attribute or amount of a possession to some amount or level they expect or deem desirable or think just. These comparisons generate a class of judgments and sentiments that includes self-esteem, satisfaction, relative deprivation, well-being, and the sense of justice. The fundamental relation in comparison processes thus involves three variables: two independent variables—the actual amount or level of a personal characteristic, called the *actual holding*, and the referent to which the actual holding is compared, called the *comparison holding*—and a dependent variable—the *comparison outcome*. Expressed as a template, with each variable in brackets, the relation becomes the following: humans compare the [actual holding] to the [comparison holding], generating the [comparison outcome]. To illustrate, humans compare their actual wealth to their desired wealth, generating well-being.[1]

Early formulations of the foundational idea of comparison processes are found in William James ([1891] 1952, 200), Marx ([1849] 1968, 84–85), and Durkheim ([1893] 1964). These were followed by progressively sharper formulations in the 20th century.[2]

The hallmark of the basic comparison relation is that the actual holding and the comparison holding have opposite effects on the comparison outcome. When the holding is a good—something of which more is preferred to less (for most humans, money and beauty and intelligence are goods)—as the actual holding increases, the comparison outcome increases, and as the comparison holding increases, the comparison outcome decreases. For example, following William James's ([1891] 1952, 200) famous formulation of self-esteem, as the actual amount or level of a good increases, self-esteem increases, and as the comparison holding increases, self-esteem decreases. If the good is knowledge of Greek, then the greater the actual knowledge of Greek, the greater the self-esteem, and the greater the desired knowledge of Greek, the lower the self-esteem.

Of course, comparison processes neither begin nor end with the basic comparison relation. Important elements include (1) the determinants of the actual and comparison holdings, encompassing, even more fundamentally, choice of the goods and bads that will drive the process and (2) the consequences of the comparison outcome. Why some persons value wealth and others beauty, why some retreat into depression and others fight to increase their attainments, where the comparison referents come from—these are all matters within the purview of comparison processes. Indeed, comparison processes appear to have a long reach, touching virtually every area of the human experience, from marriage and religion to crime and war. Thus the comparison relation may be thought of as a bridge between two literatures, literature on its antecedents—such as the literature on reference groups—and literature on its consequences—such as the literature on reactions to injustice.

Meanwhile, *theory* is the lifeblood of a scientific discipline. Theory provides a vocabulary; codifies basic principles; integrates existing knowledge; and yields the questions, models, and measurement procedures for achieving new knowledge. A scientific theory may be thought of as a two-part structure, a small part containing the basic *postulates* and a large and ever growing part containing testable *predictions* deduced from the assumptions. The larger the set of implications and the greater its variety, the more central and far-reaching, potentially, the basic principles.[3]

For all of recorded history, comparison processes have commanded attention, and they are thought to be endemic to the human condition and highly consequential for vast areas of individual and social behavior. The goal of *comparison theory* is to describe the operation of comparison processes and to derive their testable implications. This chapter provides an introduction to comparison theory and to the research agendas it sets in motion.

1. PRELIMINARIES

1.1. Social Science Analysis

The goal of social science is to accumulate reliable knowledge about human behavioral and social phenomena. To that end, we engage in three kinds of activities: (1) developing a framework, (2) building theories, and (3) doing empirical work. Though this book and this chapter are mostly about theory, the theories we describe are connected to the frameworks from which they arise and to the empirical work to which they lead. The frameworks assemble the fundamental questions and provide the fundamental building blocks for addressing them and especially for carrying out both theoretical analysis and empirical analysis.[4]

The central purpose of a theory is to yield testable predictions. And for that reason I take time in this chapter not only to describe techniques of derivation and present a sampling of predictions but also to work through an illustration. As Popper (1963, 221) puts it, "The wealth of [a theory's] consequences has to be unfolded deductively; for as a rule, a theory cannot be tested except by testing, one by one, some of its more remote consequences; consequences, that is, which cannot immediately be seen upon inspecting it intuitively."

There are two sets of criteria for judging a deductive theory, the first theoretical, the second empirical. Theoretical criteria focus on the structure of the theory. A good theory has a minimum of assumptions and a maximum of predictions. The predictions span many topical domains, and they express what the theory requires and what the theory forbids. Moreover, in a good theory, the predictions constitute a mix of intuitive and nonintuitive predictions, and at least some of them are novel predictions. Indeed, novel predictions are the hallmark of deductive theory. Novel predictions are discoveries about the reach of the process. Empirical criteria for evaluating deductive theories focus, of course, on tests of the predictions.

Besides yielding testable predictions, a good theory does much more. A good theory provides a foundation for measurement; it enables interpretation of rare or nonrecurring events; it identifies fundamental constants. Comparison theory, as will be seen, does all these things.

1.2. Comparison Processes—Pervasive but Possibly Not Fundamental

Comparison processes are pervasive and consequential. It is no accident that the first and third recorded social events in Judeo-Christian literature (postcreation) involve comparisons. First, the snake tells Eve, "If you eat this, you will be like gods, knowing good from evil." After a conjugal interlude (the second social event), the third social event again involves a comparison, when Cain compares his reward to Abel's and as a result kills him.

We work hard to understand comparison processes as clearly as possible, to characterize them as sharply as possible, to draw out their myriad consequences as precisely as possible. We write articles that focus exclusively on comparison processes.

But all the while we know that comparison processes are only one set among several basic processes. That is why the predictions of comparison theory are always ceteris paribus predictions. And that is why correct understanding of comparison processes requires parallel correct understanding of other basic processes. We cannot know how strong is the effect of the comparison mechanism without pitting it against other basic mechanisms. Probably one mechanism will dominate in some contexts, a second in other contexts, a third in still others, and so on.[5]

In that spirit, we locate comparison processes within the larger social science enterprise. Our basic premise is that, following the view advanced by Newton for understanding physical nature, observed behavioral and social phenomena may be regarded as the product of the joint operation of several basic forces. We may think of these as fundamental behavioral engines or fundamental drivers (vocabulary has not yet settled). Though we do not know the identity of the basic forces, it is useful to speculate about what they may be. Many years ago, I thought that the sense of justice was a basic force, and for that reason the titles of Jasso (1987, 1989) have the phrase "the theory of the distributive-justice force." When new research showed that the sense of justice was a member of the larger set of comparison processes (Jasso 1990), I shifted to "comparison force." But soon it became clear that neither justice nor the larger class of comparison processes were truly fundamental. As early as Jasso (1989) there had been discussion of the possibility that a deeper set of ultimate forces generates comparison processes, and a set of candidates had been proposed. Subsequently, there was further discussion of the four candidates (especially in Jasso 2001c).

1.3. Fundamental Forces and Middle-Range Forces

A useful approach is thus to distinguish between fundamental forces and middle-range forces; alternative terms might be *fundamental drivers* and *midlevel drivers*.[6] The candidates for fundamental forces are the following:

1. To know the causes of things
2. To judge the goodness of things
3. To be perfect
4. To be free

Operation of the fundamental forces produces the middle-range forces. The middle-range forces include comparison processes, status, power, and identity. Accordingly, the basic-research challenge is to discover the precise ways that the fundamental forces generate the comparison impulse and the other middle-range forces.

1.4. Unified Theory of Middle-Range Forces

Recent work suggests that the middle-range forces of comparison, status, power, and identity all begin with a core of three ingredients and that they can be unified in a synthesis that enriches each component theory while considerably enlarging the sociobehavioral scope. According to this view, four theories—comparison, status, identity, and social identity—have at their core three elements, one from each of three classes: (1) personal quantitative characteristics, such as beauty or wealth, (2) personal qualitative characteristics, such as religion or gender, and (3) sociobehavioral engines, such as status and the sense of justice. This insight is used to start the unification.[7]

The unification would not be possible without substantial advances in the study of each of the component processes. Major advances in the study of identity include the identity models developed in sociology by Stryker and Burke and their colleagues (Burke 1991; Stets and Burke 2000, 2002; Stryker 1968, 2001; Stryker and Burke 2000; Stryker and Serpe 1982) and the social identity models developed in psychology by Tajfel and Turner (1979, 1986); Hogg, Terry, and White (1995); Hornsey and Hogg (2002); and their colleagues (see also Tajfel 1974; Ellemers, Spears, and Doosje 2002). Major advances in the study of status include Zelditch 1968; Sampson and Rossi 1975; Berger et al. 1977; Goode 1978; Nock and Rossi 1978; Sørensen 1979; Berger, Rosenholtz, and Zelditch 1980; Bose and Rossi 1983; Turner 1984, 1995; Ridgeway 1991, 1997, 2001; Ridgeway and Balkwell 1997; and Webster and Hysom 1998. Advances in comparison theory are described in this chapter. Note that other basic processes are ripe for inclusion in the unified theory; these include power.[8]

In the unified theory, a person is viewed as a collection of identities. Each identity, in turn, is a bundle of three elements, one from each of the three classes: (1) personal quantitative characteristics; (2) personal qualitative characteristics; and (3) sociobehavioral engines. In this schema, the personal quantitative characteristics provide the dimensions by which people evaluate their own and others' worth; the personal qualitative characteristics are used to structure groups and subgroups; and the primordial sociobehavioral outcomes (such as status or self-esteem) are generated by reference to the quantitative characteristics (such as schooling or wealth) within the groups and subgroups formed by the qualitative characteristics (such as race, ethnicity, or sex). To illustrate, people may derive status from their rank on schooling or wealth within a particular group. Each identity is labeled to indicate the trio of elements, for example, schooling-sex-status or wealth-country-status.

Individuals have many identities. The configuration of identities can vary enormously across persons, as some individuals fix on one or another element from each of the three classes of elements—e.g., beauty versus wealth, race versus gender, status versus self-esteem. Identities that command large portions of a person's life become associated with that individual's personality; and sometimes special descriptives develop for such persons—power-hungry, gender-obsessed, race-conscious, materialistic, and so on.

Groups, too, become characterized by the configuration of identities among their members. Thus we sometimes speak of a materialistic society—a society whose members construct a substantial portion of their identities by reference to their material possessions—or a justice society—a society in which the salient sociobehavioral engine is the sense of justice, and it is included in a large proportion of the trios that constitute the peoples' identities.

The unified theory incorporates a number of distinct mechanisms that had been studied within the confines of one or another of the component theories, including social distance, individualism and collectivism, internalized oppression, and oppositional culture.

Two immediate reciprocal payoffs are that comparison, status, and power theories can use, in a rigorous way, the identity imagery, and equally, identity theories can use, in a rigorous way, the mechanisms embodied in comparison, status, and power theories.

The scope of vision is immediately enlarged, for now it is seen that the sociobehavioral mechanisms are in competition with each other for the minds and hearts of humans. And because each of the sociobehavioral engines has a distinctive operation, predictions will differ importantly depending on which engine holds sway. For example, two early predictions of the unified theory are that (1) economic inequality is critically important in a comparison society but irrelevant in a status society and (2) culture plays a larger part in a comparison society than in a status society.

1.5. Comparison and Justice

But we are getting ahead of ourselves. Full understanding of the new unified theory of middle-range forces requires full understanding of the component forces. Now that we have located comparison processes within the larger social science enterprise, we can focus on them exclusively.

There remains only one preliminary task, and that is to establish the exact relation between comparison theory and justice theory. In brief, comparison theory is both broader and narrower than justice theory. It is broader because it encompasses all comparison processes, including not only justice but also self-esteem, relative deprivation, satisfaction, and so on. It is narrower because it focuses only on reflexive assessments—the observer reflecting on his or her own beauty, wealth, etc. and experiencing self-esteem, well-being, or the sense of being fairly or unfairly treated—while justice theory also applies to nonreflexive assessments—the observer judging the situation not only of self but also of others.[9]

2. OVERVIEW OF COMPARISON THEORY

2.1. Axiom of Comparison and Logarithmic-Ratio Specification of the Comparison Function

We begin with the basic building blocks. The attributes and possessions that are the subject matter of comparison processes are personal quantitative characteristics (characteristics of which there can be more and less, or higher and lower). They include both *goods*—things of which more is preferred to less—and *bads*—things of which less is preferred to more. As well, they include both *cardinal* things, like land, cattle, and money, and *ordinal* things, like beauty and musical skill.[10]

The fundamental relation in comparison processes, sketched above, may be formalized, yielding the axiom of comparison:

> **AXIOM OF COMPARISON.** There exists a class Z of human individual phenomena that are produced by the comparison of an *actual holding* (A) of a good (bad) to a *comparison holding* (C) of that good (bad), such that Z is an increasing (decreasing) function of A and a decreasing (increasing) function of C:

$$Z^G = Z^G(A,C) \quad \partial Z^G/\partial A > 0 \quad \partial Z^G/\partial C < 0 \tag{8.1}$$
$$Z^B = Z^B(A,C) \quad \partial Z^B/\partial A < 0 \quad \partial Z^B/\partial C > 0$$

As shown in Equation 8.1 and discussed earlier, the comparison function is a function of two independent variables. The axiom specifies the two independent variables and the direction of their effects. But that is all the axiom does. Many important questions remain unanswered: What are the rates at which the Z outcomes increase and decrease with changes in the actual holding and the comparison holding? Do the Z outcomes increase or decrease linearly with changes in A and C? If not, do they increase at an increasing or a decreasing rate? What are the sets of numbers that will be used to represent A, C, and Z? If we knew the amounts of an actual holding and a comparison holding, how would we calculate the Z outcome?

To answer these and other questions, it is necessary to assign a specific functional form to the general comparison function embedded in the axiom of comparison. Thus an important challenge is to find a specific functional form that is faithful to the reality of comparison processes. One approach is to formulate conditions that a desirable functional form should satisfy, state the conditions mathematically, and then search for functional forms that satisfy them. Work along these lines led to one specific form of the comparison function, the logarithmic-ratio form:

$$Z = \theta \ln\left(\frac{A}{C}\right) \tag{8.2}$$

T ABLE 8.1

Key Properties of the Comparison Function

A. Four Properties That a Comparison Function Should Satisfy

1. Additivity. The function $Z = Z(A, C)$ is said to be additive if and only if the effect of A on Z is independent of C and the effect of C on Z is independent of A:

$$Z_{AC} = 0$$

2. Scale-Invariance. The function $Z = Z(A, C)$ is said to be scale-invariant if and only if it is homogeneous of degree zero:

$$AZ_A + CZ_C = 0$$

3. Symmetry. The function $Z = Z(A, C)$ is said to be symmetric if and only if it satisfies the condition

$$Z(A, C) = -Z(C, A)$$

4. Deficiency Is Felt More Keenly than Comparable Excess. The function $Z = Z(A, C)$ is said to satisfy the property that deficiency is felt more keenly than comparable excess if and only if it satisfies the condition

$$|Z_{(A = C_0 - k)}| > Z_{(A = C_0 + k)}$$

where C_0 is the comparison holding and k is a positive constant.

B. Properties of the Logarithmic-Ratio Specification of the Comparison Function

$$Z = \theta \ln\left(\frac{A}{C}\right)$$

1. Log-Ratio Form Satisfies All Four Desirable Properties. The log-ratio form satisfies the additivity, scale-invariance, symmetry, and deficiency aversion properties.

2. Limit of Special Symmetrical, Additive Function. The log-ratio form is the limit of a special symmetrical, additive function:

$$\lim_{k \to 0} \frac{A^k - C^k}{k} = \ln\left(\frac{A}{C}\right)$$

In the log-ratio specification of the comparison function, the actual holding and the comparison holding are represented by positive numbers and the Z outcome by the full real-number line. The Z outcome varies as the logarithm of the ratio of A to C, in the case of a good, and as the negative of that logarithm, in the case of a bad. When A and C are equal to each other, the Z outcome assumes a value of zero—a neutral point. The function includes a multiplicative constant, denoted θ and known as the signature constant; its sign indicates whether the individual regards the holding as a good or a bad, and its absolute value indicates the individual's style of expression. In theoretical work, the signature constant is set at plus or minus unity (for derivations involving goods and bads, respectively), while in empirical work it is estimated for each observer and for each of a class of situations.

The log-ratio form has been intensively studied since its introduction (Jasso 1978), and subsequent mathematical work established that it is the only functional form that satisfies two conditions thought desirable in a comparison function, scale invariance and additivity (Jasso 1990). Other appealing properties include the property that deficiency is felt more keenly than comparable excess—the property that first attracted adherents (Wagner and Berger 1985)—an important symmetry property, and the property that the log-ratio form is the limiting form of a symmetric, additive function. These properties are described and discussed in detail in Jasso (1990, 1996, 1999) and summarized in Table 8.1.

2.2. Postulates of Comparison Theory

The logarithmic-ratio specification of the comparison function is the first postulate of comparison theory.

> POSTULATE 1. (Logarithmic Specification of Comparison Function) The comparison outcome varies with the logarithm of the ratio of the actual holding to the comparison holding,

$$Z = \theta \ln\left(\frac{A}{C}\right) \qquad (8.3)$$

To illustrate, the self-esteem dimension is represented by the full real-number line, with zero a neutral point, degrees of positive self-esteem represented by positive numbers, and degrees of negative self-esteem by negative numbers. If self-esteem is generated by wealth and wealth is regarded as a good, then as actual wealth increases, self-esteem increases, and as expected wealth increases, self-esteem decreases; when actual wealth equals expected wealth, self-esteem assumes a value of zero.

The logarithmic specification was initially proposed for cardinal things; it is easy to measure the actual and comparison holdings of, say, money or hectares of land. But the literature and everyday experience suggest that goods and bads not susceptible of cardinal measurement (beauty, intelligence, athletic skill, heroism) also play important parts in comparison processes. Therefore the second postulate proposes a measurement rule (Jasso 1980):

> POSTULATE 2. (Measurement Rule) Cardinal goods and bads are measured in their own units (the amount denoted by x), and ordinal goods and bads are measured by the individual's relative rank $[i/(N+1)]$ within a specially selected comparison group, where i denotes the rank-order statistic in ascending order and N denotes the size of the group or population:

$$A, C: \begin{cases} x, & \text{cardinal holding} \\ \dfrac{i}{N+1}, & \text{ordinal holding} \end{cases} \qquad (8.4)$$

A substantial portion of theoretical derivation in comparison theory involves drawing out the implications of changes or differences in individuals' actual holdings and societal distributions of actual holdings. Such derivation was hampered by the absence of information about individuals' comparison holdings. The third postulate makes it possible to carry out theoretical derivation even without any knowledge about the comparison holdings and to do so without imposing any additional assumption about how individuals form their notions of the comparison holding (Jasso 1986).

> POSTULATE 3. (Identity Representation of Comparison Holding) The comparison holding C is identically equal to, and can be expressed as, the product of the arithmetic mean of the actual holding in the collectivity and an

TABLE 8.2
Fundamental Postulates of Comparison Theory

A. Individual-Level Postulates

1. Postulate of Logarithmic Specification

$$Z = \theta \ln \left(\frac{A}{C} \right)$$

2. Measurement Rule for Holdings

$$A, C: \begin{cases} x, & \text{cardinal holding} \\ \dfrac{i}{N+1}, & \text{ordinal holding} \end{cases}$$

3. Identity Representation of Comparison Holding

$$C = \phi E(A)$$

B. Social-Level Postulates

4. Social Welfare

$$SW = E(Z)$$

5. Social Cohesiveness

$$SC = -GMD(Z)$$

NOTE: As described in the text, Z denotes the comparison outcome, A the actual holding, and C the comparison holding. The signature constant θ is positive for goods and negative for bads. For both actual and comparison holdings, x denotes the amount of a cardinal holding, i denotes the rank-order statistics arranged in ascending order, and N denotes the population size; ϕ denotes the individual-specific parameter, $E(\cdot)$ the expected value, and $GMD(\cdot)$ the Gini's mean difference.

individual-specific constant, denoted ϕ, which captures everything that is unknown about how the individual chooses his or her own comparison holding:

$$C = \phi E(A) \tag{8.5}$$

Because the arithmetic mean is itself equal to the total sum (S) of a thing divided by the population size (N), the comparison holding in the case of a cardinal holding can be written

$$C = \phi E(A) = \frac{\phi S}{N} \tag{8.6}$$

Thus the identity representation provides a way to incorporate into the basic comparison function two important factors, the group affluence S and the group size N.

The foregoing three individual-level postulates form the heart of the postulate set of comparison theory. For easy reference, they are summarized in panel A of Table 8.2.

Basic Comparison Function Formulas. Combining the three postulates yields the basic comparison formulas (Table 8.3), which express the comparison function for cardinal and ordinal holdings and which can be written in versions for small groups and large collectivities (the small-groups formulas include the population size N; the large-collectivities

TABLE 8.3

Fundamental Formulas of Comparison Theory

A. Comparison Function

  1. When the Comparison Holding Is Known

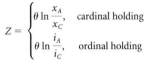

                    Small Groups   **Large Groups**

$$Z = \begin{cases} \theta \ln \dfrac{x_A}{x_C}, & \text{cardinal holding} \\[2ex] \theta \ln \dfrac{i_A}{i_C}, & \text{ordinal holding} \end{cases} \qquad Z = \begin{cases} \theta \ln \dfrac{x_A}{x_C}, & \text{cardinal holding} \\[2ex] \theta \ln \dfrac{\alpha_A}{\alpha_C}, & \text{ordinal holding} \end{cases}$$

  2. When the Comparison Holding Is Unknown

                    Small Groups   **Large Groups**

$$Z = \begin{cases} \theta \ln \dfrac{xN}{\phi S}, & \text{cardinal holding} \\[2ex] \theta \ln \dfrac{2i}{\phi(N+1)}, & \text{ordinal holding} \end{cases} \qquad Z = \begin{cases} \theta \ln \dfrac{x}{\phi E(X)}, & \text{cardinal holding} \\[2ex] \theta \ln \dfrac{2\alpha}{\phi}, & \text{ordinal holding} \end{cases}$$

B. Social Welfare Function

  1. When the Comparison Holding Is Known

                    Small Groups   **Large Groups**

$$Z = \begin{cases} \theta \ln \dfrac{G(X_A)}{G(X_C)}, & \text{cardinal holding} \\[2ex] \theta \ln \dfrac{G(i_A)}{G(i_C)}, & \text{ordinal holding} \end{cases} \qquad Z = \begin{cases} \theta \ln \dfrac{G(X_A)}{G(X_C)}, & \text{cardinal holding} \\[2ex] \theta \ln \dfrac{G(\alpha_A)}{G(\alpha_C)}, & \text{ordinal holding} \end{cases}$$

  2. When the Comparison Holding Is Unknown

                    Small Groups   **Large Groups**

$$Z = \begin{cases} \theta \ln \dfrac{G(X_A)}{E(X_A)} - \ln[G(\phi)], & \text{cardinal holding} \\[2ex] \theta \ln \dfrac{\sqrt[N]{N!}}{N+1} - \ln[G(\phi)], & \text{ordinal holding} \end{cases} \qquad Z = \begin{cases} \theta \ln \dfrac{G(X_A)}{E(X_A)} - \ln[G(\phi)], & \text{cardinal holding} \\[2ex] \theta \ln \dfrac{2}{e} - \ln[G(\phi)], & \text{ordinal holding} \end{cases}$$

NOTE: The relative rank is denoted α. The letter S denotes the total amount of the cardinal good (bad). $G(\cdot)$ denotes the geometric mean.

formulas are the limiting case as N goes to infinity). Formulas for the case in which the comparison holding is known (subpanel A.1) are based on postulates 1 and 2; formulas for the case in which the comparison holding is unknown (subpanel A.2) are based on postulates 1, 2, and 3. The formulas are presented in panel A of Table 8.3.

One of the basic comparison function formulas in Table 8.3 will be used to illustrate theoretical derivation later in this chapter. This is the formula for the comparison function for cardinal holdings in small groups when the comparison holding is unknown (Table 8.3, panel A.2, left column, top branch):

$$Z = \theta \ln\left(\frac{xN}{S\phi}\right) \tag{8.7}$$

Note that in this case the comparison outcome is expressed as a function of the individual's own holding x, the group size N, and the group's total amount S of the holding. Note, moreover, that the logarithmic form enables separating the effects of all factors, thus yielding predictions about the ceteris paribus effects of the individual's actual holding and the group size and group affluence, net of the individual's idiosyncrasy parameter ϕ. This particular formula is the starting point for one of the major techniques for deriving predictions, known as the *micromodel*, which we will use later in the chapter. The micromodel is used to investigate the effects of change in one or more of the three factors in the comparison function, thus enabling derivation of implications for a wide variety of situations involving change in own holding or group affluence or size (such as situations involving gifts, bequests, disasters, war, and so on).

An early insight in justice theory was that a society can be represented by the distribution of justice evaluations among its members and that parameters of this distribution may be importantly related to behavioral and social phenomena (Jasso 1980). Comparison theory inherited this insight and, like justice theory, highlights two parameters of the distribution of comparison outcomes—the expected value (or arithmetic mean) and the Gini's mean difference—forming two postulates around them.

> POSTULATE 4. (Social Welfare) The collectivity's social welfare SW varies with the expected value of the Z distribution:

$$SW = E(Z) \tag{8.8}$$

The social welfare postulate plays a part in some of the implications derived using a second type of strategy for theoretical derivation known as the *macromodel*. Formulas for the social welfare function for both cardinal and ordinal holdings, in versions for small groups and large collectivities (where, as before, the small-groups formulas include the population size N and the large-collectivities formulas are the limiting case as N goes to infinity), are reported in panel B of Table 8.3. As with the formulas for the comparison function, formulas for the case in which the comparison holding is known (subpanel B.1) are based on postulates 1 and 2; formulas for the case in which the comparison holding is unknown (subpanel B.2) are based on postulates 1, 2, and 3. Note that the social welfare is the same as the quantity that in justice analysis is known as the justice index (Jasso 1999).

> POSTULATE 5. (Social Cohesiveness) The collectivity's social cohesiveness SC varies with the Gini's mean difference of the Z distribution:

$$SC = -GMD(Z) \tag{8.9}$$

2.3. Techniques for Theoretical Derivation

As work with comparison theory accumulated, it became clear that the procedures used to derive predictions could be classified into four main techniques. These have come to be called the *micromodel*, *macromodel*, *matrixmodel*, and *mesomodel* strategies.

The micromodel approach begins with investigation of the effects of an event on an individual's Z outcome, where the event may be a human action (such as giving a gift or stealing a radio), the outcome of a human action (such as receiving a gift or having a radio stolen), or an event not traceable to human agency (such as a natural disaster). The objective is to assess the effects of the event on the Z outcome of all individuals in the collectivity. The basic equation in the micromodel approach is an equation that compares the individual at two points in time. The micromodel uses small-groups formulas but, interestingly, yields effects at all levels of analysis. For example, the micromodel yields the macrolevel prediction that a society is more vulnerable to deficit spending as its wealth increases.

The macromodel strategy begins with the distribution of the Z outcome in a collectivity. Interest centers on parameters of that distribution and on a variety of other features, such as substantively pertinent subdistribution structures. For example, two kinds of subdistribution structures are studied: (1) the truncated subdistribution structure associated with three subgroups—those with negative Z, those with zero Z, and those with positive Z; and (2) the censored subdistribution structure associated with splitting the collectivity into subgroups defined by a qualitative characteristic such as race, ethnicity, religion, gender, and the like.[11]

The macromodel strategy uses the large-population formulas, but like the micromodel strategy, it too yields implications at all levels of analysis. For example, it yields the microlevel prediction that the overreward experienced by the most beautiful or most talented person in a collectivity is modest compared to the overreward experienced by the wealthiest person.

The matrixmodel strategy, as the name suggests, begins with the entire matrix of self-other or observer-rewardee magnitudes that arise in the justice subset of comparison processes. The matrixmodel strategy is uniquely suited for studying consensus processes.

The mesomodel strategy begins with an entire small group, characterizing each member by his or her Z outcome, and proceeds to assess the relations among subsets of members. Important areas for investigation include the social distance between adjacent pairs and between the bottom and top members.

All four strategies of theoretical derivation can be used for both cardinal and ordinal holdings. And all appear to yield predictions at all levels of analysis.[12]

Note that mathematics is the power tool for derivation of predictions, for obtaining what Popper (1963, 221) calls the "marvelous deductive unfolding" of the theory. The criterion of fruitfulness, exemplified by novel predictions and by predictions that take the theory far afield from its original domain, is more easily met by the long deductive chains that mathematics enables. Purely verbal arguments tend to tether the deduced consequences to overt phenomena in the assumptions, constraining fruitfulness and destroying the possibility of novel predictions. For example, the popular technique of instantiation by its very nature cannot produce novel predictions, for novel predictions are novel precisely because nothing superficially evident in the assumptions could lead to them.[13]

2.4. Predictions of Comparison Theory

Predictions have been derived for a vast range of individual and social phenomena, from gift giving, marital happiness, parenting, and mourning to crime, disaster, religious institu-

TABLE 8.4

Some Predictions of Comparison Theory

1. A gift is more valuable to the receiver when the giver is present.
2. In wartime, the favorite leisure-time activity of soldiers is playing games of chance.
3. Post-traumatic stress is greater among veterans of wars fought away from home than among veterans of wars fought on home soil.
4. Vocations to the religious life are an increasing function of income inequality.
5. Thieves prefer to steal from fellow group members rather than from outsiders.
6. Informants arise only in cross-group theft, in which case they are members of the thief's group.
7. An immigrant's propensity to learn the language of the host country is an increasing function of the ratio of the origin country's per capita GNP to the host country's per capita GNP.
8. In historical periods when wives tend to predecease their husbands (e.g., due to death in childbirth), mothers are mourned more than fathers; but in historical periods when husbands tend to predecease their wives (e.g., due to war), fathers are mourned more than mothers.
9. Parents of nontwin children will spend more of their toy budget at an annual gift-giving occasion rather than at the children's birthdays.
10. If both spouses work full time, marital cohesiveness increases with the ratio of the smaller to the larger earnings.
11. In a society in which the two-worker couple is the prevailing form of marriage and all husbands earn more than their wives, the societal divorce rate increases with the dispersion in the wives' earnings distribution and with the arithmetic mean of the husbands' earnings distribution and decreases with the dispersion in the husbands' earnings distribution and with the arithmetic mean of the wives' earnings distribution.
12. A society becomes more vulnerable to deficit spending as its wealth increases.
13. Society loses when rich steal from poor.
14. Inequality-reducing schemes arise in societies that value wealth but not in societies that value birth and lineage.
15. In all societies there will arise devices that promote variability in individuals' notions of what is just for themselves.
16. The problem for new groups is to choose the valued goods.
17. Newcomers are more likely to be welcomed by groups that value cardinal goods than by groups that value ordinal goods, and more likely to be welcomed by groups that play games of chance than by groups that play games of skill.
18. Among groups whose valued goods are N ordinal goods, the group's longevity is a decreasing function of group size.
19. In a dispute over revealing salary information, the exact preference structure depends on the distributional pattern of the salaries; if this pattern follows the familiar lognormal or Pareto distribution, then the lowest paid and the highest paid persons prefer to have the information revealed, forming a coalition against those in the middle of the range.
20. In a materialistic society, the greater the economic inequality, the greater the emigration rate, the more severe the conflict between warring subgroups—and the greater the public benefit conferred by the cloister.
21. In a materialistic society, the overall amount of injustice experienced by the population is an increasing function of economic inequality.
22. Inheritance tempers grief.
23. The most advantaged person in a materialistic society experiences far greater overreward than the most advantaged person in a nonmaterialistic society.
24. Societies that welcome immigration must be materialistic societies.
25. In nonmaterialistic societies, the severity of the conflict between two warring subgroups is a decreasing function of the proportion in the disadvantaged group, but in materialistic societies, the effect on conflict severity of the proportion in the disadvantaged group depends on the shape of the income distribution.

tions, and war. Numerous derivations have been published, both as original pieces of research presenting a new derivation and as collections of derivations. For example, Jasso (1991) and Jasso (1993a) derive predictions for religious institutions and social conflict, respectively; Jasso (2001c) presents a collection of predictions derived using the micromodel strategy; and Jasso (2001a) presents a collection of predictions arranged by topical focus.

Table 8.4 provides a sampling of predictions, covering many topical domains and derived via different techniques.

2.5. Further Features of Comparison Theory

Interpretation of Rare or Non-Recurring Events. Comparison theory suggests that the invention in the late 12th century of mendicant institutions (Franciscans, Dominicans) was a response to the switch from valuing birth and nobility to valuing wealth. Similarly, it is no accident that the search for a motive in the murderer-detection enterprise and the associated literary genre seem to have arisen in 19th-century England. Comparison theory also provides an interpretation for the Mariel emigration.[14]

Fundamental Constants. Comparison theory suggests the existence of two sets of fundamental constants. One of these is a critical inequality level, thought to govern the switch between valuing cardinal and ordinal goods.[15]

Foundation for Measurement. Comparison theory provides a foundation for measuring a number of quantities. These include the just reward, framing, expressiveness, impartiality, and the justice indexes, including decompositions into the amount of injustice due to poverty and the amount due to inequality.

2.6. Testing and the Evidentiary Base

2.6.1. Testing Comparison Theory

Two kinds of issues arise in testing scientific theories—philosophical and practical. The philosophical issues received careful and cogent treatment in the 20th century, for example, in the work of Karl R. Popper ([1935] 1959, 1963), Thomas S. Kuhn ([1962] 1970), and Imre Lakatos (1970).[16] If one considers the empirical assessment of a single theory in isolation, then the questions that arise are (1) how many tests? (2) of how many predictions? (3) with what combination of results? There is widespread agreement that rejecting a prediction is not a sufficient condition for rejecting a theory. Moreover, rejecting a prediction is not a necessary condition for rejecting a theory; even if all of a theory's predictions survive the test unrejected, one may still reject the theory—in favor of a better theory, one with "excess corroborated content" (Lakatos 1970). Indeed, the view known as "sophisticated falsificationism" holds that it is not possible to judge the empirical merits of a theory in isolation; falsification requires comparison of the relative merits of two theories (Lakatos 1970, 116).

Consider now the special problem faced by all theories of a single process: it can be difficult to discern whether discrepancies between the theory's predictions and empirical data are due to a defective theory or instead to the operation of another basic process. Of course, design of empirical work usually takes into account the possibility that many other factors may be at work; courses in the empirical methods of the social sciences routinely teach procedures for guarding against omitted-variables bias. Nonetheless, interpreting tests of the predictions of a theory of a single process, given the near certainty that we live in a multifactor world, requires judiciousness and circumspection.

Practical issues that arise in testing scientific theories include (1) selection of predictions to test and the order in which they will be tested; (2) for each prediction to be tested, deciding between designing new explicit tests and conducting meta-analyses of existing studies; and (3) for each prediction to be tested, deciding whether the test is best conducted by the theorist (who may be a general theorist with no special knowledge of the subject matter of the prediction) or by empirical scientists who specialize in the topic of the prediction. When the theory is fruitful and yields many implications for many disparate phenomena, the practical problems are compounded.[17]

2.6.2. The Current Evidentiary Status of Comparison Theory

There are several levels of evidence. First, a few predictions have received rigorous, explicit test. One is the prediction that, ceteris paribus, marital cohesiveness declines the greater the disparity between husband and wife in their holdings of valued goods (deduced in Jasso 1983, tested in Jasso 1988a). The empirical results were consistent with the prediction.

Second, several predictions are consistent with the results of rigorous empirical work that was not designed to test them. These include the prediction that the response to gains is concave and the response to losses is convex (Kahneman and Tversky 1979; Tversky and Kahneman 1986) and the prediction that the rate of vocations to the religious life is higher in societies with greater poverty and inequality, a prediction consistent with Ebaugh's (1993) findings concerning the dearth of religious vocations in the United States and the abundance in third-world countries.

Third, several predictions are consistent with known facts. These include the prediction that parents of two or more children (who do not all have the same birthday) will spend more of their toy budget at a single annual gift-giving occasion (such as Christmas) than at the children's birthdays, a prediction consistent with published toy sales figures (Jasso 1993b).

Fourth, several predictions are consistent with notions that although not rigorously documented appear to be widely believed. These include the prediction that the incidence of gift giving is greater during courtship than after marriage and greater in wartime than in peacetime.

Finally, some predictions are novel, and there seems to be no hint of them in any literature, technical or lay. These include the prediction that post-traumatic stress syndrome is less severe among veterans of wars fought on home soil than among veterans of wars fought away from home. Interestingly, a distinguished journalist, chronicling a trip to Vietnam, observes that Vietnamese veterans of the Vietnam War appear to be better adjusted than American veterans of the Vietnam War (Sheehan 1991) but does not make the connection to the battleground's location. Another novel prediction is that blind persons are less vulnerable to eating disorders than are nonblind persons. Still another novel prediction is the prediction that games of chance are salutary, contrary to the view that gambling is a vice.

Of the foregoing five sets of predictions, only the first two have a rigorous evidentiary status. The rest require rigorous, explicit test. Note that the predictions are amenable to testing via many empirical strategies, including survey research, classical experiments, and comparative historical work.

3. ILLUSTRATION OF THEORETICAL DERIVATION

To illustrate theoretical derivation in comparison theory, we turn to hiring phenomena. The illustration in this section is a small part of a larger project whose aim is to derive implications for the workplace, not only from comparison theory but also from status theory and power theory.

The full workplace project will examine hiring, firing, promotion, and productivity, as well as relationships among workers in the same or different units and hierarchical levels in work organizations. In the illustration in this chapter, we focus on one very special situation—the case in which an *appointment* is to be made to a special position such as executive officer or an endowed chair. For convenience, we will refer to that position as a *top position*, though it need not be the very top position in a hierarchical unit. In the piece of the derivation presented here, we focus on the *members of the unit in which the appointment is to be made*. In general, the new appointee may come from within the unit or may be brought in from the outside; we will refer to these two types of appointments as *insider* and *outsider* appointments.

Comparison theory enables characterization of well-being—that is, of the comparison outcome Z—among the members of the unit both before and after the appointment is made and enables comparison of the change in Z in the insider- and outsider-appointment cases. Thus comparison theory can yield predictions about the preferences of the members of the unit—given that humans typically can imagine their lives under different scenarios—as well as predictions about their well-being in the two cases. Moreover, if members of the unit are also the decision makers—as they often are in the case of making an appointment to an endowed chair—and if they vote to increase their own well-being, then comparison theory also yields predictions for the appointment itself. Of course, comparison processes are not the only factor at work. As always, these predictions are ceteris paribus predictions and their interpretation and test require cognizance of the other factors in play.

Earlier, in section 2.3, we briefly considered the four main methods currently in use to derive predictions from comparison theory. The micromodel method is ideally suited to this application. In the micromodel method, we begin by writing the formula for the individual's well-being at two time points, obtain the formula for the change in Z from time 1 to time 2, and then investigate the effects of the constituent factors of Z. These are the effects, in the cardinal case, of the change in own wealth, group affluence, and group size and, in the ordinal case, of the change in own rank and group size. In the illustration here, we confine the derivation to the cardinal case—the case in which the members of the group value a cardinal good such as wealth—but, of course, the larger workplace project examines the case in which the members of the group value an ordinal good as well as the case in which they value both a cardinal and an ordinal good. For the cardinal case, the basic formula for the comparison function, incorporating the second and third postulates—shown in Equation 8.7 and repeated here—is

$$Z = \ln\left(\frac{xN}{S\phi}\right) \tag{8.10}$$

Whenever there is a change in the individual's own wealth x, in the total group wealth S, or in the group size N, there will be a change in the individual's well-being. Thus, the micromodel method permits assessment of the effects of those changes on the individual's well-being. Note that in general there are many actions and events that can alter the factors in the Z formula. For example, theft affects own wealth and can affect group wealth; murder affects group size; natural disasters can affect all three factors.

To begin, then, the basic equation in the micromodel approach is an equation that compares the individual at two points in time:

$$CZ = Z_2 - Z_1 \qquad\qquad (8.11)$$

where, as before, Z denotes well-being and CZ denotes change in Z. If CZ is zero, then whatever transpired between the two time periods has had no effect on the individual; if, however, CZ is negative, then the individual has become worse off, and, if positive, better off.[18]

Equation 8.10 is the basic expression that will be incorporated into the change equation in 8.11, producing:

$$CZ = \ln\left(\frac{x_2 N_2 S_1 \phi_1}{x_1 N_1 S_2 \phi_2}\right) \qquad\qquad (8.12)$$

The protocol for the micromodel strategy is described in detail in Jasso (2001c). As described there, the first step, after selecting a field of application, is to identify the kinds of actors involved and the kinds of situations and to provide the pertinent special notation. The protocol for the micromodel method includes a special table for collecting the work at each step. Accordingly, as shown in Table 8.5, panel C, in this illustration we identify one kind of actor—*member of the workplace unit*—and two situations—*insider* and *outsider* appointments to the new top position.

Also as shown in Table 8.5, panel C, special notation is introduced. The two situations are called A1 and A2 (where the "A" stands for "appointment"). The total salaries of all the members of the unit are as usual denoted by S. The salary of the new appointee is denoted by s. Finally, if the appointee is an insider, his or her time 1 salary is denoted p. In the illustration here, we restrict the insider appointee's previous salary to an amount smaller than the salary in the new top appointment; that is, $s > p$. This is a mild restriction and follows logically from the illustration's focus on top appointments.

The next step in the micromodel method, shown in panel D of Table 8.5, is to write the formula for CZ for the members of the workplace unit in both the insider- and outsider-appointment situations. Given that S can change only by the amounts s or p or both, we let S without a subscript denote its time 1 value; similarly, given that N can change only by 1, we let N without a subscript denote its time 1 value. Own salary x remains the same for all the group members and thus drops out of the CZ formulas.[19]

The CZ formulas express the change in well-being due to the new appointment. Following the protocol for the micromodel method, there are three main sets of questions to be addressed, each illuminating different aspects of behavior in this appointment situation and singly or in combination yielding a variety of predictions. These three main questions are

1. What is the sign of CZ?

2. In which situation do group members have the higher CZ?

3. What are the effects on CZ of the total salary monies, the salary of the new appointee, the time 1 salary of the insider appointee, and the group size?

TABLE 8.5

Using the Micromodel Strategy to Derive Predictions from Comparison Theory for Hiring Phenomena

A. Write Basic Comparison Function Formula, Cardinal-Good Case.

$$Z = \theta \ln \left(\frac{xN}{S\phi} \right),$$

where Z denotes the comparison outcome, θ is the signature constant, x denotes the individual's own amount of the cardinal good (say, salary), S denotes the total amount of the cardinal good in the collectivity, N denotes the population size, and ϕ denotes the individual-specific parameter capturing idiosyncratic elements in the individual's idea of the comparison holding for himself or herself.

B. Express Change in Z from Time 1 to Time 2.

$$CZ = Z_2 - Z_1$$

$$CZ = \ln \left(\frac{x_2 N_2}{S_2 \phi_2} \right) - \ln \left(\frac{x_1 N_1}{S_1 \phi_1} \right)$$

$$CZ = \ln \left(\frac{x_2 N_2 S_1 \phi_1}{x_1 N_1 S_2 \phi_2} \right)$$

C. Analyze the Top-Appointment Situation.

1. There is one kind of actor: **Member of the Workplace Unit.**
2. Define two top-appointment situations:
(**A1**) The new top appointee is an insider.
(**A2**) The new top appointee is an outsider.
3. Let s denote the top appointee's salary, where s is measured in units of x.
4. Let p denote the top appointee's previous salary if the top appointee is an insider, where p is measured in units of x.
5. The simplest case has the following features: (i) $s > p$; (ii) the group size N remains the same except in A2; and (iii) the amounts of x held by the members remain constant except that of the top appointee in A1.

D. Write the Formulas for CZ in the Two Situations.

Situation A1 Insider Appointee	Situation A2 Outsider Appointee
$\ln \left(\dfrac{S\phi_1}{(S - p + s)\phi_2} \right)$	$\ln \left(\dfrac{S(N + 1)\phi_1}{(S + s)N\phi_2} \right)$

E. Is CZ Positive or Negative? (Assume $\phi_1 = \phi_2$.)

Situation A1 Insider Appointee	Situation A2 Outsider Appointee
negative	negative if $s > \dfrac{S}{N}$

F. In Which Situation Do Group Members Have the Higher CZ?

$$CZ^{A1} \begin{Bmatrix} < \\ = \\ > \end{Bmatrix} CZ^{A2} \quad \text{iff} \quad p \begin{Bmatrix} < \\ = \\ > \end{Bmatrix} \frac{S + s}{N + 1}$$

Result depends on relation between insider-appointee's previous salary
and the new mean in the outsider-appointee case.

Or equivalently,

$$CZ^{A1} \begin{Bmatrix} < \\ = \\ > \end{Bmatrix} CZ^{A2} \quad \text{iff} \quad \ln \left(\frac{S + s}{N + 1} \right) \begin{Bmatrix} < \\ = \\ > \end{Bmatrix} \ln \left(\frac{S - p + s}{N} \right)$$

where result depends on relation between the new means in the two cases.

TABLE 8.5 *(continued)*

G. Obtain First and Second Partial Derivatives of CZ with Respect to Each Factor in the CZ Formulas. (First partial derivatives with respect to S, N, s, and p shown below.)

Derivative	Situation A1 Insider Appointee	Situation A2 Outsider Appointee
CZ_S	$\dfrac{s-p}{S(S-p+s)} > 0$	$\dfrac{S}{S(S+s)} > 0$
CZ_N	0	$-\dfrac{1}{N(N+1)} < 0$
CZ_s	$-\dfrac{1}{S-p+s} < 0$	$-\dfrac{1}{S+s} < 0$
CZ_p	$\dfrac{1}{S-p+s} > 0$	0

The sign of CZ indicates whether the individual is better off, worse off, or unaffected by the appointment. As shown in Table 8.5 (panel D), all the formulas include the ϕ component; and thus it is not possible to know the sign of CZ without making an a priori assumption about ϕ. It is not unreasonable that ϕ, for a given individual, remains constant across the two time periods; that is, there is little a priori reason to suppose that the new appointment or the prospect of the new appointment alters the individual's comparison holding. The most parsimonious assumption is that $\phi_1 = \phi_2$. It can also be argued that even if the comparison holding does change, it does not do so immediately; and hence there is an important period (of unknown duration) when $\phi_1 = \phi_2$. (The duration of this period when $\phi_1 = \phi_2$ becomes an interesting new question.) Panel E of Table 8.5 reports the sign of CZ, assuming $\phi_1 = \phi_2$. As shown, CZ is always negative when an insider is appointed to the new top position; when an outsider is appointed, it is negative only if the appointee's salary s exceeds the time 1 salary mean. In this illustration, given that we are investigating a top appointment, it is unlikely that the new appointee's salary will be less than the current mean; a new top position almost by definition would have a higher salary associated with it. Thus we can conclude that when a new top appointment is made, all the group members—except the new appointee—experience a loss in well-being.[20]

This first set of results indicates that hiring for a new top position is a delicate matter. Whether the new appointee is an insider or an outsider, everyone else loses. In fact, the group may resist the new top position; for example, the group may suggest to a philanthropist who wishes to endow a chair that he or she instead endow a research center, or a lectureship, etc. Even if the offer of an endowed chair is accepted, the group may take years to fill it. And when attention turns to actually searching for the first occupant, a major concern, albeit unspoken and unacknowledged, will be how to attenuate the loss in well-being that every member will experience.

The second set of questions seeks to learn in which situation the group members have the higher magnitude of CZ. Here, CZ is always negative, and thus a higher magnitude indicates a negative number with a smaller absolute magnitude—that is, a smaller loss. To answer this question, we set up and evaluate an inequality whose terms are the situation-specific CZ formulas. In this case, it is not necessary to make any assumptions on the ϕ component, as the ϕ terms drop out.

Thus, we ask whether the loss is greater when the new appointee is an insider (situation A1) or an outsider (situation A2). Evaluating the inequality formed by the members' CZ in A1 and A2, we find that the answer depends on the configuration of factors. Specifically, as shown in panel F of Table 8.5, members are better off with whichever option produces the lower salary mean. As also shown, the critical relation is that between the time 1 salary of the insider appointee and the new salary mean if an outsider is appointed. Members are better off—their loss from the new appointment is attenuated—if an insider appointment is made and the insider's time 1 salary exceeds the new mean if an outsider is appointed. The breakeven point—the point at which the loss in well-being is the same under both the insider- and outsider-appointee scenarios—occurs when the insider's time 1 salary equals the new mean if an outsider is appointed:

$$p = \frac{S + s}{N + 1} \tag{8.13}$$

To put some flesh on this result, let us consider a numerical example. Suppose that the time 1 salary mean in an organization is $100,000; there are 21 members and the total salary budget is $2,100,000. Suppose that a new top appointment is to be made, and the salary of the new appointee will be $300,000. Then if an outsider is appointed, there would be 22 members, the time 2 salary budget would be $2,400,000, and the new salary mean would be $109,091. The breakeven point occurs when the time 1 salary of the insider appointee equals $109,091. Relative to appointing an outsider, appointing an insider with a time 1 salary less than $109,091 intensifies the members' loss in well-being and appointing an insider with a time 1 salary greater than $109,091 attenuates the members' loss in well-being. Thus the ideal appointee—if any appointment can be called ideal, given that it engenders a loss in well-being for everyone else—is an insider with a fairly high salary. If the group members are the decision makers, they are likely to appoint the insider with the highest salary p just under the designated salary s for the new appointment.

The pool of eligible insider candidates, however, may be sparse, as the group may already have a number of special top appointments. Reaching deep into the ranks—that is, appointing an insider with a low salary—would produce a greater loss than appointing an outsider. And thus the choice may be an outsider.

The final set of questions to be addressed involves the effects of each factor on the change function CZ. Panel G of Table 8.5 reports the first partial derivatives for the insider- and outsider-appointee situations. The effect of the time 1 salary budget is to attenuate the loss, in both situations. The effect of the salary for the new appointee is to intensify the loss, again in both situations. The group size has an effect only in the outsider case; the larger the group, the greater the loss from the new appointment. Finally, the time 1 salary of the insider candidate has an effect only in the insider-appointment case, attenuating the loss; the higher the salary of the insider candidate, the smaller the members' loss from the appointment.

TABLE 8.6
Workers' Well-Being When New Top Appointment Is Made

	NEW TOP APPOINTEE	
	Insider	Outsider
A. Change in Well-Being as a Result of New Top Appointment	Loss	Loss
B. Conditioning Factors Total salary budget, before new hire	Attenuates	Attenuates
Group size, before new hire	—	Intensifies
Salary of new hire	Intensifies	Intensifies
Salary of insider candidate	Attenuates	—

The principal results for the change in well-being are summarized in Table 8.6. Although Table 8.6 does not provide any information that is not contained in Table 8.5, it provides a useful verbal summary.

The final step in theoretical derivation is to compile a list of predictions. Here I present an initial list of the predictions obtained from this derivation:

Prediction 1. Making a new top appointment in a workplace group generates a loss in well-being among all the members except the appointee.

Prediction 2. The members' loss of well-being differs according to whether the appointee is an insider or an outsider and the relation between the salary means in the insider and outsider situations.

Prediction 2.1. Relative to the case in which an outsider is appointed, the members' loss of well-being is less when the new appointee is an insider whose time 1 salary exceeds the new mean if an outsider is hired.

Prediction 2.2. Relative to the case in which an outsider is appointed, the members' loss of well-being is greater when the new appointee is an insider whose time 1 salary is lower than the new mean if an outsider is hired.

Prediction 2.3. When the insider candidate's salary is equal to the new mean if an outsider is hired, the members' loss of well-being is the same whether the insider or the outsider is appointed.

Prediction 3. The higher the time 1 salary budget, the smaller the members' loss of well-being.

Prediction 4. In outsider appointments, the larger the time 1 group size, the greater the members' loss of well-being.

Prediction 5. The greater the salary of the new appointee, the greater the members' loss of well-being.

Prediction 6. In insider appointments, the greater the time 1 salary of the new appointee, the lower the members' loss of well-being.

From this basic set of predictions, it is possible to generate many further predictions. For example, if individuals prefer situations that enhance their well-being, then a set of predictions for preferences can be derived. This would include predictions such as "In insider appointments, group members prefer high-salary candidates." Similarly, if the group members are themselves the decision makers, new predictions can be obtained, such as "In a vote to decide between an insider and an outsider candidate, the group will choose the insider candidate if his or her salary exceeds what the new salary mean would be if the outsider is appointed."

In this illustration, taken from a larger project investigating the effects of comparison processes and status processes in the workplace, we have followed the protocol for the micromodel strategy and derived the predictions of comparison theory. We have obtained and reported the principal mathematical results in the special case of a new top appointment and have provided a flavor for their substantive interpretation. The reader will no doubt see many further implications. Avenues of analysis that may prove fruitful include scrutiny of the connections between these implications and further implications for preference formation and decision making. Of course, all the implications are ceteris paribus implications in a multifactor world, and thus testing them will require thoughtful research design.[21]

4. CONCLUDING NOTE

Comparison processes are pervasive and consequential. The key challenge is to obtain accurate understanding of their operation and their relation to other basic processes. To that end, I provided in this chapter a comprehensive overview of comparison theory, including its postulates and predictions, the main techniques of derivation, testing challenges, and the current evidentiary base. I also characterized comparison processes as middle-range forces and located them in a larger framework that includes fundamental forces as well as other middle-range forces.

As a unified theory of the middle-range forces comes into sight, it is all the more important to sharpen comparison theory and the theories of the other middle-range forces and to derive more of their implications. The stage will be set for clever, nuanced tests that enable discernment of the differential strength of their effects across vast areas of the human experience.

1. For discussion of the evolution of the fundamental comparison relation from its predecessors, including the classical statement "Humans compare themselves to others or to previous or envisioned selves," see Jasso (1990, 2001a).

2. Notable contributions include Baldwin (1889–1891); Stouffer et al. (1949); Merton and Rossi (1950); Festinger (1954); Thibaut and Kelley (1959); Merton (1957); Runciman (1961); Homans ([1961] 1974); Wright (1963); Blau (1964); Hyman (1968); Lipset (1968); Sherif (1968); Zelditch (1968); and Berger et al. (1972). A brief history of comparison ideas is found in Jasso (1990) and a summary in Jasso (2001a).

3. For comprehensive characterization of theories and their structure and component parts, see Jasso (1988b, 2001b) and for brief overviews, see Jasso (2003a, 2003b).

4. Comprehensive exposition of the tripartite structure of social science analysis is provided in Jasso (2004).

5. For elaboration of the multifactor nature of sociobehavioral phenomena and the theoretical and empirical challenges it generates, see FAQ 4 in Jasso (2001a, 690–91). Note especially Danto's (1967, 299–300) observation, "Indeed, it is by and large the ability of a theory to permit derivations far afield from its original domain which serves as a criterion for accepting a theory, for in addition to the obvious fruitfulness such a criterion emphasizes, such derivations permit an increasingly broad and diversified basis for testing the theory."

6. The term *middle range* was introduced by Merton ([1949, 1957] 1968).

7. This work is thus in the spirit of Turner (1988, 2002), who has pioneered syntheses of sociological theories.

8. For elaboration of the work on unification, see Jasso (unpubl.), and for further discussion of status theory, see Jasso (2001d).

9. For elaboration and a Venn diagram, see FAQ 1 in Jasso (2001a, 688–689) and Jasso (2001c).

10. Blau (1974, 1977a, 1977b) introduced the distinction between the two main types of personal characteristics, quantitative characteristics and qualitative characteristics, and pioneered analysis of their distinctive operation. Qualitative characteristics are unorderable categorical variables, such as religion, ethnicity, and gender.

11. The macromodel relies heavily on the study of probability distributions (Johnson and Kotz 1969, 1970a, 1970b) and on ideas about truncated and censored subdistributions developed in Gibbons (1988, 355); Johnson and Kotz (1969, 27); Kotz, Johnson, and Read (1982, 396); and Moses (1966). Comprehensive exposition of the macromodel strategy is found in Jasso (1997). For a brief summary of the probability distribution foundation, see Jasso and Liao (2003).

12. Fuller development of the techniques for theoretical derivation will be found in Jasso (1997, 2001c, 2002).

13. Because a fruitful theory is easier to test (Danto 1967), as discussed above, the use of mathematics as a theoretical tool also confers empirical advantages.

14. For elaboration of these instances of comparison theory's interpretive capacity, see Jasso (2001a).

15. For further detail, see Jasso (2001a).

16. For brief discussions of the philosophical issues that arise in testing, see Reynolds (1971) and Jasso (1988b, 3–5; 1989, 139–41).

17. For a brief discussion of these and other practical problems that arise in testing, see Jasso (2001a) and the references cited therein.

18. Note that the change equation refers exclusively to one individual at two points in time. The individual may become better off or worse off relative to his or her own situation at time 1.

19. For the reader interested in working through this derivation, the formulas reported in panels D, E, F, and G of Table 8.5 represent the "answer key."

20. In the larger workplace project, the result that group members gain well-being when the firm hires outsiders at low salaries plays an important part. It has important applications to the study of migration, for example.

21. Parallel predictions for the effects of status theory are reported in Jasso (2004). A task ahead is to derive predictions for the effects of comparison theory when the valued good is ordinal and thence to contrast the three sets of predictions.

REFERENCES

Baldwin, James Mark. 1889–1891. *Handbook of Psychology*, 2 vols. New York: Holt.

Berger, Joseph, Hamit Fisek, Robert Norman, and Morris Zelditch. 1977. *Status Characteristics and Social Interaction: An Expectation States Approach*. New York: Elsevier.

Berger, Joseph, Susan J. Rosenholtz, and Morris Zelditch. 1980. Status Organizing Processes. *Annual Review of Sociology* 6:479–508.

Berger, Joseph, Morris Zelditch Jr., Bo Anderson, and Bernard P. Cohen. 1972. Structural aspects of distributive justice: A status-value formulation. In *Sociological Theories in Progress*, ed. Joseph Berger, Morris Zelditch, and Bo Anderson, 2:119–246. Boston: Houghton Mifflin.

Blau, Peter M. 1964. *Exchange and Power in Social Life*. New York: Wiley.

———. 1974. Presidential address: Parameters of social structure. *American Sociological Review* 39:615–35.

———. 1977a. *Inequality and Heterogeneity*. New York: Free Press.

———. 1977b. A macrosociological theory of social structure. *American Journal of Sociology* 83:26–54.

Bose, Christine E., and Peter H. Rossi. 1983. Gender and jobs: Prestige standings of occupations as affected by gender. *American Sociological Review* 48:316–30.

Burke, Peter J. 1991. Identity processes and social stress. *American Sociological Review* 56:836–49.

Danto, Arthur C. 1967. Philosophy of science, problems of. In *Encyclopedia of Philosophy*, ed. Paul Edwards, 6:296–300. New York: Macmillan.

Durkheim, Émile. [1893] 1964. *The Division of Labor in Society*. Trans. George Simpson. New York: Free Press.

Ebaugh, Helen Rose. 1993. The growth and decline of Catholic religious orders of women worldwide: The impact of women's opportunity structures. *Journal for the Scientific Study of Religion* 32:68–75.

Ellemers, Naomi, Russell Spears, and Bertjan Doosje. 2002. Self and social identity. *Annual Review of Psychology* 53:161–86.

Festinger, Leon. 1954. A theory of social comparison processes. *Human Relations* 7:117–40.

Gibbons, Jean Dickinson. 1988. Truncated data. In *Encyclopedia of Statistical Sciences*, ed. Samuel Kotz, Norman L. Johnson, and Campbell B. Read, 9:355. New York: Wiley.

Goode, William J. 1978. *The Celebration of Heroes: Prestige as a Control System*. Berkeley: University of California Press.

Hogg, Michael A., Deborah J. Terry, and Katherine M. White. 1995. A tale of two theories: A critical comparison of identity theory with social identity theory. *Social Psychology Quarterly* 58:255–69.

Homans, George Caspar. [1961] 1974. *Social Behavior: Its Elementary Forms*, rev. ed. New York: Harcourt, Brace, Jovanovich.

Hornsey, Matthew J., and Michael A. Hogg. 2002. The effects of status on subgroup relations. *British Journal of Social Psychology* 41:203–18.

Hyman, Herbert H. 1968. Reference Groups. In *International Encyclopedia of the Social Sciences*, ed. David L. Sills, 13:353–61. New York: Macmillan.

James, William. [1891] 1952. *The Principles of Psychology*. Chicago: Britannica.

Jasso, Guillermina. 1978. On the justice of earnings: A new specification of the justice evaluation function. *American Journal of Sociology* 83:1398–1419.

———. 1980. A new theory of distributive justice. *American Sociological Review* 45:3–32.

———. 1983. Social consequences of the sense of distributive justice: Small-group applications. In *Theories of Equity: Psychological and Sociological Perspectives*, ed. David M. Messick and Karen S. Cook, 243–94. New York: Praeger.

———. 1986. A new representation of the just term in distributive-justice theory: Its properties and operation in theoretical derivation and empirical estimation. *Journal of Mathematical Sociology* 12:251–74.

———. 1987. Choosing a good: Models based on the theory of the distributive-justice force. *Advances in Group Processes: Theory and Research* 4:67–108.

———. 1988a. Distributive-justice effects of employment and earnings on marital cohesiveness: An empirical test of theoretical predictions. In *Status Generalization: New Theory and Research*, ed. Murray Webster and Martha Foschi, 123–62 (references, pp. 490–93). Palo Alto, CA: Stanford University Press.

———. 1988b. Principles of theoretical analysis. *Sociological Theory* 6:1–20.

———. 1989. The theory of the distributive-justice force in human affairs: Analyzing the three central questions. In *Sociological Theories in Progress: New Formulations*, ed. Joseph Berger, Morris Zelditch Jr., and Bo Anderson, 354–87. Newbury Park, CA: Sage.

———. 1990. Methods for the theoretical and empirical analysis of comparison processes. *Sociological Methodology* 20:369–419.

———. 1991. Cloister and society: analyzing the public benefit of monastic and mendicant institutions. *Journal of Mathematical Sociology* 16:109–36.

———. 1993a. Analyzing conflict severity: Predictions of distributive-justice theory for the two-subgroup case. *Social Justice Research* 6:357–82.

———. 1993b. Choice and emotion in comparison theory. *Rationality and Society* 5:231–74.

———. 1996. Exploring the reciprocal relations between theoretical and empirical work: The case of the justice evaluation function (paper in honor of Robert K. Merton). *Sociological Methods and Research* 24:253–303.

———. 1997. Derivation of predictions in comparison theory: Foundations of the macromodel approach. In *Status, Network, and Structure: Theory Development in Group Processes*, ed. Jacek Szmatka, John Skvoretz, and Joseph Berger, 241–70. Stanford, CA: Stanford University Press.

———. 1999. How much injustice is there in the world? Two new justice indexes. *American Sociological Review* 64:133–68.

———. 2001a. Comparison theory. In *Handbook of Sociological Theory*, ed. Jonathan H. Turner, 669–98. New York: Kluwer Academic/Plenum.

———. 2001b. Formal theory. *Handbook of Sociological Theory*, ed. Jonathan H. Turner, 37–68. New York: Kluwer Academic/Plenum.

———. 2001c. Rule-finding about rule-making: Comparison processes and the making of norms. In *Social Norms*, ed. Michael Hechter and Karl-Dieter Opp. New York, New York: Russell Sage.

———. 2001d. Studying status: An integrated framework. *American Sociological Review* 66:96–124.

———. 2002. Seven secrets for doing theory. In *New Directions in Contemporary Sociological Theory*, ed. Joseph Berger and Morris Zelditch Jr., 317–42. Boulder, CO: Rowman & Littlefield.

———. 2003a. Assumptions. In *The Sage Encyclopedia of Social Science Research Methods*, ed. Michael Lewis-Beck, Alan Bryman, and Tim Futing Liao, 1:33–36. Thousand Oaks, CA: Sage.

———. 2003b. Function. In *The Sage Encyclopedia of Social Science Research Methods*, ed. Michael Lewis-Beck, Alan Bryman, and Tim Futing Liao, 1:407–8. Thousand Oaks, CA: Sage Publications.

———. 2004. The tripartite structure of social science analysis. *Sociological Theory* 22:371–400.

———. 2005. Four theories with a common core. Unpublished manuscript.

Jasso, Guillermina, and Tim Futing Liao. 2003. Distribution. In *The Sage Encyclopedia of Social Science Research Methods*, ed. Michael Lewis-Beck, Alan Bryman, and Tim Futing Liao, 1:276–80. Thousand Oaks, CA: Sage.

Johnson, Norman L., and Samuel Kotz. 1969. *Distributions in Statistics: Discrete Distributions*. New York: Wiley.

———. 1970a. *Distributions in Statistics: Continuous Univariate Distributions—1*. Boston: Houghton Mifflin.

———. 1970b. *Distributions in Statistics: Continuous Univariate Distributions—2*. Boston: Houghton Mifflin.

Kahneman, Daniel, and Amos Tversky. 1979. Prospect theory: An analysis of decision under risk. *Econometrica* 47:263–91.

Kotz, Samuel, Norman L. Johnson, and Campbell B. Read. 1982. Censoring. In *Encyclopedia of Statistical Sciences*, ed. Samuel Kotz, Norman L. Johnson, and Campbell B. Read, vol. 1. New York: Wiley.

Kuhn, Thomas S. [1962] 1970. *The Structure of Scientific Revolutions*, 2nd ed., enlarged. Chicago: University of Chicago Press.

Lakatos, Imre. 1970. Falsification and the methodology of scientific research programmes. In *Criticism and the Growth of Knowledge*, ed. Imre Lakatos and Alan Musgrave, 91–195. Cambridge, UK: Cambridge University Press.

Lipset, Seymour Martin. 1968. Stratification, social: Social class. In *International Encyclopedia of the Social Sciences*, ed. David L. Sills, 15:296–316. New York: Macmillan.

Marx, Karl. [1849] 1968. Wage labour and capital. In *Karl Marx and Frederick Engels: Selected Works*, 74–97. New York: International Publishers.

Merton, Robert K. [1949] 1968. *Social Theory and Social Structure*. New York: Free Press.
———. 1957. Continuities in the theory of reference groups and social structure. In *Social Theory and Social Structure*, ed. R. K. Merton, 2nd ed., revised and enlarged, 281–386. New York: Free Press.
Merton, Robert K., and Alice S. Rossi. 1950. Contributions to the theory of reference group behavior. In *Continuities in Social Research: Studies in the Scope and Method of the American Soldier*, ed. R. K. Merton and P. Lazarsfeld, 40–105. New York: Free Press. Reprinted as *Social Theory and Social Structure*, ed. R. K. Merton, 2nd ed., revised and enlarged, 225–80. New York: Free Press.
Moses, Lincoln E. 1968. Statistical analysis: Truncation and censorship. In *International Encyclopedia of the Social Sciences*, ed. David L. Sills, 15:196–201. New York: Macmillan.
Nock, Steven L., and Peter H. Rossi. 1978. Ascription versus achievement in the attribution of social status. *American Journal of Sociology* 84:541–64.
Popper, Karl R. [1935] 1959. *The Logic of Scientific Discovery*. New York: Basic Books.
———. 1963. *Conjectures and Refutations: The Growth of Scientific Knowledge*. New York: Basic Books.
Reynolds, Paul Davidson. 1971. *A Primer in Theory Construction*. New York: Macmillan.
Ridgeway, Cecilia L. 1991. The social construction of status value: Gender and other nominal characteristics. *Social Forces* 70:367–86.
———. 1997. Where do status-value beliefs come from? New developments. In *Status, Network, and Structure*, ed. J. Szmatka, J. Skvoretz, and J. Berger, 137–58. Stanford, CA: Stanford University Press.
———. 2001. Inequality, status, and the construction of status beliefs. In *Handbook of Sociological Theory*, ed. Jonathan H. Turner, 323–40. New York: Kluwer Academic/Plenum.
Ridgeway, Cecilia L., and James Balkwell. 1997. Group processes and the diffusion of status-beliefs. *Social Psychology Quarterly* 60:14–31.
Runciman, William G. 1961. Problems of research on relative deprivation. *Archives Européennes de Sociologie* 2:315–23.
Sampson, William A., and Peter H. Rossi. 1975. Race and family social standing. *American Sociological Review* 40:201–14.
Sheehan, Neil. 1991. *After the War Was Over: Hanoi and Saigon*. New York: Random House.
Sherif, Muzafer. 1968. Self Concept. In *International Encyclopedia of the Social Sciences*, ed. David L. Sills, 14:150–59. New York: Macmillan.
Sørensen, Aage B. 1979. A model and a metric for the analysis of the intragenerational status attainment process. *American Journal of Sociology* 85:361–84.
Stets, Jan E., and Peter J. Burke. 2000. Identity theory and social identity theory. *Social Psychology Quarterly* 63:224–37.
———. 2002. A sociological approach to self and identity. In *Handbook of Self and Identity*, ed. Mark Leary and June Tangney, 128–52. New York: Guilford.
Stouffer, Samuel A., et al. 1949. *The American Soldier*, 2 vols. Studies in Social Psychology in World War II. Princeton: Princeton University Press.
Stryker, Sheldon. 1968. Identity salience and role performance. *Journal of Marriage and the Family* 4:558–64.

―――. 2001. Traditional symbolic interactionism, role theory, and structural symbolic interactionism: The road to identity theory. In *Handbook of Sociological Theory*, ed. Jonathan H. Turner, 211–31. New York: Kluwer Academic/Plenum.

Stryker, Sheldon, and Peter J. Burke. 2000. The past, present, and future of an identity theory. *Social Psychology Quarterly* 63:284–97.

Stryker, Sheldon, and Richard T. Serpe. 1982. Commitment, identity salience, and role behavior: A theory and research example. In *Personality, Roles, and Social Behavior*, ed. William Ickes and Eric S. Knowles, 199–218. New York: Springer-Verlag.

Tajfel, Henri. 1974. Social identity and intergroup behavior. *Social Science Information* 13:65–93.

Tajfel, Henri, and John C. Turner. 1979. An integrative theory of intergroup conflict. In *The Social Psychology of Intergroup Relations*, ed. W. G. Austin and S. Worchel, 33–47. Monterey, CA: Brooks/Cole.

―――. 1986. The social identity theory of intergroup behavior. In *The Psychology of Intergroup Relations*, ed. S. Worchel and W. G. Austin, 7–24. Chicago: Nelson-Hall.

Thibaut, John W., and Harold H. Kelley. 1959. *The Social Psychology of Groups*. New York: Wiley.

Turner, Jonathan H. 1984. *Societal Stratification: A Theoretical Analysis*. New York: Columbia University Press.

―――. 1988. *A Theory of Social Interaction*. Stanford, CA: Stanford University Press.

―――. 1995. *Macrodynamics: Toward a Theory on the Organization of Human Populations*. ASA Rose Monograph Series. New Brunswick, NJ: Rutgers University Press.

―――. 2002. *Face-to-Face: Toward a Sociological Theory of Interpersonal Behavior*. Stanford, CA: Stanford University Press.

Tversky, Amos, and Daniel Kahneman. 1986. Rational choice and the framing of decisions. In *Rational Choice: The Contrast between Economics and Psychology*, ed. Robin M. Hogarth and Melvin W. Reder, 67–94. Chicago: University of Chicago Press.

Wagner, David, and Joseph Berger. 1985. Do sociological theories grow? *American Journal of Sociology* 90:697–728.

Webster, Murray, Jr. and Stuart J. Hysom. 1998. Creating status characteristics. *American Sociological Review* 63:351–78.

Wright, Georg Henrik, von. 1963. *The Varieties of Goodness*. London: Routledge & Kegan Paul.

Zelditch, Morris, Jr. 1968. Status, social. In *International Encyclopedia of the Social Sciences*, ed. David L. Sills, 15: 250–57. New York: Macmillan.

9 POWER, DEPENDENCE, AND SOCIAL EXCHANGE

Karen S. Cook, Coye Cheshire, and Alexandra Gerbasi

What determines who has power and how power is exercised are central issues in social life as well as in politics. One of the most significant contributions to the analysis of social power was Emerson's (1962, 1964) early theoretical treatise on power-dependence relations. This work became the focus of a major body of work in contemporary social psychology that builds on the contributions of George Homans and Peter Blau to the development of social exchange theory in sociology.

For Blau ([1964] 1986), as for Emerson (1972a, 1972b), there was a clear connection between power and social exchange. The fact that some actors control more highly valued resources than others can lead to inequality in exchange as social debts are incurred and discharged by acts of subordination. Subjugation by the less powerful or domination by the more powerful often become self-perpetuating, forming the foundation of power inequalities in relations of exchange. Inequality and power differentiation were viewed by Blau as emergent properties of social exchange processes. Differences in the nature of the valued resources among actors result in interdependence and thus the need for exchange. They also serve as the basis for emerging inequalities in exchange outcomes as well as power differentials between actors linked by exchange (see Cook and Rice 2003).

For Emerson (1962, 1964) these power differentials derive from the relative dependencies of actors on one another for the resources of value they obtain through exchange. His 1962 paper, "Power-Dependence Relations," is a citation classic. It formed the foundation for a large literature on power relations within social psychology and sociology more broadly. It also formed the primary basis for the analysis of power in exchange networks, the direction his work took in subsequent publications (1972a, 1972b, 1976). Emerson's (1972a, 39) initial reason for beginning the work, set forth in the two chapters written in 1967 and eventually published in 1972, was "to formulate a more encompassing framework around previous work on power-dependence relations." Power and exchange were closely interconnected in all of the subsequent work on social exchange.

THE THEORY AND RESEARCH EXAMPLES

Emerson (1962) analyzed power explicitly in relational terms as a function of the dependence of one actor on another. He later used this general formulation to provide a specific definition of power within an *exchange* relation (Emerson 1972a, 1972b), conceived as a "temporal series" containing opportunities for exchange that evoke initiations of exchange that result in transactions. An *exchange network* is a set of actors linked directly or indirectly through exchange relations. An actor is conceived as "a point where many exchange relations connect" (Emerson 1972a, 57). In an exchange relation between two actors, A and B, the *power* of actor A over B in the Ax–By exchange relation (where x and y represent resources of value) increases as a function of the value of y to A and decreases proportional to the degree of availability of y to A from alternative sources (other than B). These two factors—resource value and resource availability—determine the level of B's dependence on A and thus A's power over B. The more dependent B is on A, the more power A has over B. This postulate, that power is based on dependence, became the defining element of Emerson's formulation: $P_{AB} = D_{BA}$.

This relational conception of power generated a large body of research on social exchange relations and exchange networks.[1] We focus on only that work that has derived explicitly from Emerson's conception of exchange and power. However, we also suggest ways this work ties to other current research on social exchange and exchange networks more generally. Two traditions of work seem most closely linked to Emerson's perspective: work by Linda Molm, especially her work on reciprocal exchange and see Chapter 2 in this volume, and the work of Edward Lawler, primarily his work on power, relational cohesion, and affect and see Chapter 11.

From Dyads to Networks

Although Emerson's original formulation focused on the dyad, the dyadic A–B exchange relation is typically embedded in a network of exchange opportunities with other actors, C, D, . . . , N. This social structure of exchange opportunities formed the basis for Emerson's (1972b, 1976) structural theory of power.[2] One of the two major determinants of power is the structure of the available opportunities for exchange embodied in networks. Networks are composed of exchange relations that are *connected* to the extent that exchange in one relation affects or is affected by the nature of the exchange in another relation. The connection can either be positive or negative. A *negative* connection means that exchange in one relation reduces the amount or frequency of exchange in another exchange relation involving one of the same parties (e.g., the A–B and B–C exchange relations are negatively connected at B if exchange in the A–B relation reduces the frequency or amount of exchange in the B–C relation). A connection is *positive* if the amount or frequency of exchange in one relation increases the amount or frequency of exchange in an exchange relation involving at least one of the parties to both exchanges (e.g., the A–B relation is positively connected to the B–C relation if exchange in the A–B relation increases the frequency or amount of exchange in the B–C relation). More complicated mixed networks may involve both positive and negative exchange connections (Yamagishi, Gillmore, and Cook 1988). The connection between the specific structure of the networks and the distribution of power in the network became the central focus of research in the social exchange tradition beginning with the empirical work of Cook and Emerson (1978).

Emerson initially adopted operant psychology as the behavioral foundation for his theory because he viewed it as a more *social* microlevel theory. This was useful since he focused on the relatively enduring social relations between particular actors rather than what he viewed as the dominant focus in economics, the transaction, in which actors were viewed as interchangeable. Later, Cook and Emerson (1978) included cognitive concepts such as risk, uncertainty, and the rational calculation of benefits and costs in their theory of exchange. The actors could thus be motivated by future gains, avoidance of anticipated losses or costs, or simply pursuit of behaviors that they had learned through past interactions were rewarding (or avoidance of those that had aversive consequences).

The main assumptions of exchange theory, summarized by Molm (1997; Molm and Cook 1995, 210), are that (1) behavior is motivated by the desire to increase gain and to avoid loss, (2) exchange relations develop in structures of mutual dependence (both parties have some reason to engage in exchange to obtain resources of value or there would be no need to form an exchange relation), (3) actors engage in recurrent, mutually contingent exchanges with specific partners over time (i.e., they are not engaged in simple one-shot transactions), and (4) valued outcomes obey the economic law of diminishing marginal utility (or the psychological principle of satiation). On the basis of these core assumptions, predictions are made about the behavior of actors engaged in exchange and the effects of different factors on exchange outcomes. The power-dependence principle, in addition, allows for the formulation of predictions concerning the effects of altering the value of the resources in the exchange and the availability of resources from alternative sources (i.e., the network structure) on power and power use.

In addition to power, several key concepts define factors that are significant in understanding exchange relations. These include reciprocity, balance, cohesion, and power-balancing operations. Reciprocity, for Emerson, was primarily a description of the contingencies intrinsic to all social exchange. Norms of obligation emerge to reinforce reciprocity. Reinforcement principles and their link to initiation of exchange provide sufficient explanation for the continuity or extinction of exchange relations. Emerson, like Homans, focused primary attention on the microfoundations of exchange (see Part I of his formulation [1972a]).

Lack of balance in an exchange relation is typically reflected in differences in initiation probabilities and defined as differences in relative dependencies of the actors. An exchange relation is balanced if $D_{AB} = D_{BA}$, that is, if both parties are equally dependent on the other for exchange. The concept of balance is important in Emerson's formulation since it set the stage for understanding the balancing operations that explain changes in exchange relations and networks. Subsequently, Cook and Yamagishi (1992) developed the notion of equidependence to describe the point at which two actors are equally dependent on the relationship, creating power balance. However, as Emerson made clear, since actors are motivated to maintain or to increase their power in exchange relations to increase benefits and to minimize losses, power conditions are rarely stable. Change is likely to occur even when actors are initially power equals. Today the concept of power balance is used primarily to refer to power equality in exchange relations. It is not used as much as a motivating factor. Even though the concept was generally a cognitive concept when Emerson developed his theory of exchange (based on Heiderian balance theory), Emerson used the concept in a different sense to refer to structural tension or pressures at the system or network level for change stimulated by actors' efforts to gain or to protect power advantage.

Cohesion represents the strength of the exchange relation as well as the propensity of the relationship to survive conflict. Relational cohesion is the average dependence of the two actors in the relation: the higher the average mutual dependence, the higher the relational cohesion (Emerson 1972a). Subsequently, Molm (1985) and others (e.g., Lawler, Ford, and Blegen 1988) refer to cohesion as average total power (or simply total power). The concept represents how much is at stake in the relation (not the relative power of each actor within the exchange relation, which is treated separately in further developments in the theory). Molm and Lawler have examined the impact of total power, as well as relative power, on exchange relations.

Emerson, as did Blau ([1964] 1986), viewed the fundamental task of exchange theory to be building a framework in which the primary dependent variables were social structure and structural changes. Social structures were viewed as emergent properties of exchange processes as well as factors that constrained and enabled specific types of exchange. While Cook and Emerson (1978) investigated other exchange outcomes, particularly commitment formation, it was the connection between power and the structure of social networks that became the main focus of the experimental work in the 1980s and 1990s. More recently, theorists have turned back to the study of the dynamics of power and the variables that alter the nature of the exchange outcomes: commitment, cohesion, and collective action. We turn to work on these topics that derives from Emerson's perspective after summarizing his collaborative work with Cook and others on the determinants of the distribution of power in exchange networks.

Power in Networks

Interactions that extend beyond the dyad form *social networks* that contain nodes (i.e., individuals) interconnected by ties (i.e., relationships). Two nodes have a tie if an exchange relation is possible. Cook and Emerson (1978) describe a specific type of social network, the *exchange network*, as a system that connects three or more individuals who exchange goods or services. In fact, a meaningful discussion of power requires *networks* rather than dyads— precisely because dyadic relationships lack the alternatives central to Emerson's conception of power (Cook and Emerson 1978).

The existence of power in exchange relationships depends on more than just the presence of three or more actors. In a three-person network with relations *A–B* and *B–C*, the exchange network *A–B–C* does not exist unless the exchange relationships are contingent on each other—positively or negatively (Yamagishi, Gillmore, and Cook 1988). As described earlier, negative relationships reduce exchange frequency with alternative partners, while positive relationships increase exchange frequency with at least one other alternative partner. The convergence of investigations regarding negatively connected networks is likely due to the fact that these systems involve the principle of competition that can lead to exclusion. Competition is fundamental to many types of economic and market relationships.

Network location clearly affects power for exchange relations connected negatively, positively, or a combination of both (mixed networks). As Yamagishi, Gillmore, and Cook (1988) demonstrate, the factors that create power differentials in networks with these three connection types are distinct. In negatively connected networks, access to alternative exchange partners with valued resources decreases dependence on others and therefore increases individual power. In positively connected networks, however, alternative partners are not competitive. In these systems, alternative partners facilitate one or more additional exchanges in the network. Using empirical research and computer simulations of positively connected networks, they find that local scarcity of valued resources determines relative power. In mixed-type networks, positive and negative exchange relations exist in the same exchange system. In these hybrid networks, the combined function of scarce resources and network position determines an individual's relative power.

Cook and Yamagishi (1992) identify three classes of relations in exchange networks that can emerge from a potential set of exchange opportunities: (1) *exchange relations* (connected in various ways to form networks) that represent ongoing exchanges, (2) *latent relations*, which are links in the network opportunity structure that remain unused (hence "latent"), and (3) *nonrelations*, which are potential links within the network that are never used. The difference between the latter two categories is that latent relations affect the predicted distribution of power when they are removed from the network. Nonrelations have no such effect. Cook and Yamagishi (1992) demonstrate through simulations (and subsequently empirically) the significance of latent relations that can modify the distribution of power in the network if they are ever activated as an alternative source of valued resources.

The relative position of actors in an exchange network is the main factor producing differences in the use of power. Changes in the relative position of nodes and ties alter the distribution of rewards throughout the network. Subsequent empirical work by Willer (1991), Markovsky and colleagues (1988), Skvoretz and Willer (1993), Friedkin (1992, 1993), and Bienenstock and Bonacich (1992, 1993) has developed more precise predictions concerning features of networks and exchange relations that determine the exact distribution of power in networks of different types (Willer, Chapter 10 in this volume).

Much of the work following from Emerson's power-dependence formulation focused on the effects of variations in the network structure and in the types of connection as determinants of power, specifically, power inequality. However, Whitmeyer's research was the first to investigate the importance of *individual preferences* for power dynamics in exchange networks. His research shows that varying the interests (or values) of the actors can have effects on the distribution of power independent of the network structure (1999a) and power inequalities are created when individual preferences are convex (1999b). The role of value and preference ordering is a key topic for theoretical and empirical development. Only recently has there been a return to the topic of power dynamics and associated mechanisms that alter the very structure of the networks under study.

Power Dynamics. An important part of Emerson's theory was his identification of power *balancing operations*, though there has been less empirical work on this topic. Balance is used to refer to factors that alter features of the dyadic exchange relation or the structure in which it is embedded. An exchange relation in which power (and conversely dependence) is unequal was defined by Emerson as *unbalanced*. Power imbalance creates strains in exchange relations and provides an impetus for structural change as noted above. He claimed that four distinct balancing operations existed that might stabilize relationships, though perhaps not for long.

Focusing on the two variables that affect dependence, Emerson proposed four processes that would make power more equal in unbalanced relations in which, for example, A is more powerful than B (i.e., $P_{AB} > P_{BA}$ and $D_{BA} > D_{AB}$). To balance this relation, (1) B can reduce motivational investment in goals (or value of the resources) mediated by A (a form of withdrawal from the relation); (2) B can locate alternative sources (e.g., actor C) for the goals mediated by A (referred to as "network extension"); (3) B can increase A's motivational investment in goals B mediates (e.g., through status giving to A); and (4) B can work to eliminate A's alternative sources for the goals B mediates (e.g., engaging in coalition formation or another form of collective action with other actors, particularly other suppliers of the resources A values).

With these power-balancing principles Emerson was able to predict the types of changes in exchange networks produced by actors attempting to gain power or to maintain power in the network. For example, a division of labor could occur if actors who were once competitors in a negatively connected network specialize in the production of different resources of value to the powerful actor. Or they could coalesce and bargain collectively with the more powerful actor to gain advantage in setting the terms of trade (see later discussion). Other network-level processes were also predicted to result from the strategic use of positional power. Various researchers, including Emerson, later noted that the coalition of the powerful with the less powerful could also occur to thwart the collective action or power-balancing efforts of the power-disadvantaged.

Differences in types of exchanges occurring in a network might alter the power dynamics in the network. Different levels of commitment may translate into more stable dyadic exchange relations within networks, which has implications for those connected to these relatively committed dyads. In the extreme, strongly committed dyads might become isolated from the network over time, changing the structure of the alternatives for those remaining in the network. Recent work on generalized exchange (Cheshire 2005) and productive exchange (Lawler and Yoon 1993, 1996, 1998; Lawler, Ford, and Blegen 1988) may provide new insights into the nature of power dynamics in networks involving other modes of exchange. Negotiated exchange has been the primary focus of much of the existing empirical research.

Emerson predicted other network-level changes to be a function of the types of resources involved in the exchanges (Whitmeyer and Cook 2002). For example, he predicted that network closure was more likely to occur when one dominant type of resource is exchanged (e.g., approval). He referred to this as intracategory exchange, as when friends exchange approval with one another. Social circles form in this way and tend to become closed, maintaining their boundaries. Examples include exclusive social clubs. The logic behind closure is vague, involving pressures to maintain exchange relations and levels of appropriate exchange. With too large a group the process breaks down and the group loses the status it might gain as an exclusive network.

Emerson also discussed the emergence of stratified closed classes within intracategory networks. For example, subgroups based on different ability levels or levels of exchange might emerge as in tennis when actors tend to associate only with those of similar ability levels over time. Networks form into stratified elements based on resource magnitude as well. Exchange stratification also occurs with intercategory exchange. Emerson notes, for example, the tendency for initiations to flow upward in interclass exchange and for transactions within such relations to be initiated from above. Many of these theoretical insights in Part II of Emerson's (1972b) formulation have never been fully developed theoretically.[3]

Coalitions and Collective Action in Exchange Networks. In power-imbalanced networks, coalitions of the power-disadvantaged occur under various circumstances to create a more equal distribution of power. Those with power, however, may thwart such collective action, while those who stand to gain work to create a sense of shared fate and cooperation to promote coalition formation. This is only one strategy that actors with a power disadvantage may use to gain power. Cook and Gillmore (1984) demonstrate that such coalitions of the power-disadvantaged can form, especially in relatively simple networks in which several powerless actors coalesce against a more powerful actor to balance the power differential. Coalitions in this case bring about a balance of power and a more equal distribution of exchange profits. However, in larger networks in which there are more power-disadvantaged actors to bring into the coalition, collective action is less effective because of the transaction costs required to coordinate the activity of a larger number of actors. Coalitions that did not include all of the disadvantaged actors in the networks failed to attain power balance because the powerful actors retained access to alternative sources of the resources they valued when some potential members of the coalition did not join. This factor mitigates the gains that coalitions might produce in some circumstances as free riding occurs or there is a failure of coordination of the relevant parties due to the costs involved. Such factors clearly undermine the potential effectiveness of coalition formation as a power-balancing mechanism. Cook and Gillmore (1984) demonstrated that coalitions in simple networks that did include all of the power-disadvantaged actors were relatively stable, whereas those that did not tended to deteriorate over time since actors competed for access to the more powerful party. Such results reproduce findings obtained in organizational settings outside the laboratory and replicate what we know about the difficulties of collective action in general.

More often the tensions generated by power inequality can result in network extension as actors seek new exchange partners. Power-disadvantaged actors, rather than banding together to form coalitions to balance power, may seek out new relations, thus reducing their dependence on a given actor. This solution to power imbalance has been investigated relatively recently. Leik (1992) proposed a theory of network extension and contraction based on principles derived from network exchange theory formalized by Markovsky, Willer, and

Patton (1988). Recent empirical work by Lawler and Yoon (1998), however, suggests that emotional responses to inequality may be an important factor motivating network extension (see also Cook and Rice 2003). In the Lawler and Yoon (1998) study, after exchanging with a limited number of partners, actors are allowed to interact with all other participants in their network. Actors in power-balanced relationships continue to solicit exchange with their previous partners. In power-imbalanced relationships, however, the power-advantaged actors seek out their previous disadvantaged partners, but those disadvantaged actors tried to find new partners who had not behaved opportunistically. Thus low levels of reward coupled with negative affect regarding the power-advantaged actor appear to motivate network extension.

Before discussing specific applications of power-dependence and exchange network theory, we discuss work derived from Emerson's formulation on generalized exchange, a topic that has received less attention. Work on generalized exchange connects to Molm's research on reciprocal exchange since the structure of generalized exchange is similar to reciprocal exchange networks, although in Molm's work the relations are typically dyadic and not chain generalized across a larger network as in the classic case of the generalized exchange of necklaces and armbands in Malinowski's Trobriand Islands (see Bearman 1997).

GENERALIZED EXCHANGE AND PROBLEMS OF COLLECTIVE ACTION

Unlike negotiated direct exchange, in *generalized exchange* "the reward that an actor receives . . . [is] not directly contingent on resources provided by that actor" (Yamagishi and Cook 1993, 235). Generalized-exchange systems are a type of indirect exchange (Emerson 1972a, 1972b; Blau 1964). In these exchanges, one actor gives resources to another, but resources are reciprocated not by the recipient but rather a third party (Molm and Cook 1995). Thus generalized-exchange systems inherently involve a minimum of three actors. From the perspective of the recipient, the obligation to reciprocate is not necessarily directed to the benefactor but instead to one or more actors who are "implicated in a social exchange situation with his benefactor and himself" (Ekeh 1974). Inspired by early descriptions of generalized exchange by anthropologists (e.g., Malinowski 1922; Lévi-Strauss 1969), Emerson (1981) suggested the importance of generalized exchange, but he never had the opportunity to pursue it. His colleagues and former students, e.g., Gillmore (1987) and Yamagishi and Cook (1993), conducted the initial studies that became the foundation for laboratory research on generalized exchange.

Ekeh (1974) identifies two main types of generalized exchange. The first type he calls *chain-generalized exchange*, which is synonymous with network-generalized exchange (Yamagishi and Cook 1993). In this type of exchange, each individual gives goods or services directly to other individuals, and they can receive goods or services from others in the same network. The Kula Ring trade studied by Malinowski (1922) is the most famous example. The Kula Ring involved the exchange of necklaces of red shells in a clockwise fashion between islands, while bracelets of white shells were exchanged in a counterclockwise direction. Another empirical example of a near-perfect cyclic chain is the exchange of women in a 1940's Aboriginal population (Bearman 1997).

The second major type of generalized exchange involves individuals who contribute to a public good and receive benefits from this public (or collective) good. Ekeh (1974) calls this *group-focused generalized exchange*. Yamagishi and Cook (1993) refer to this type of system as "group-generalized" exchange, in which individuals pool their resources centrally (in contrast to the decentralized nature of network-generalized exchange). Examples include villagers who pool resources to build a school or construct a bridge (Yamagishi and Cook 1993), combining resources for business ventures (Ruef 2003), and sharing digital music in peer-to-peer Internet systems (Cheshire 2005).

Generalized exchange, like coalitions, presents a collective-action problem. That all generalized-exchange systems require a minimum of three actors means that coordination issues are likely to emerge. Since rewards are not reciprocated directly, individuals must rely on the goodwill of a third party. And because receiving is not conditional on one's own giving, it becomes possible to free ride (i.e., to receive without giving). Thus generalized-exchange systems produce *social dilemmas* (Yamagishi and Cook 1993; Cook and Rice 2003). In generalized exchange, people do better by not giving to others while receiving from others, but if all refuse to give, everyone does worse than if they all gave (Yamagishi 1995). Several authors have attempted to explain how such complex exchange systems emerge (Bearman 1997; Takahashi and Yamagishi 1996, 1999; Ziegler 1990; Takahashi 2000; Mark 2003; Cheshire 2005) and how they differ from other types of exchange networks.

The production of collective action is difficult in generalized exchange because the interests of individuals and that of the collective persistently diverge. One solution to this problem is to allow individuals to pass along reputation information about previous exchanges. For example, networks that allow individuals to be held accountable by sharing information about previous interactions can successfully produce cooperative behavior in repeated Prisoner's Dilemma games (e.g., Axelrod 1984; Macy and Skvoretz 1998). Using a series of simulations, Takahashi (2000) shows that when self-interested actors can pass along information about the behaviors of others, network-generalized exchange does emerge. This occurs when individuals employ a fairness-based selective-giving strategy (see also Mark 2002). He assumes individuals in generalized exchange want to give more often to those with higher ratios of giving or receiving. Although this explanation works in situations in which reputations exist, it does not apply when individuals are anonymous or when reputation information cannot be transferred to others. Also, it only applies to network-generalized exchange.

Recent research that attempts to explain the emergence of a type of group-generalized exchange is the study of digital goods exchanged on the Internet (Shah and Levine 2003; Cheshire 2005). This research focuses on how digital information goods (Kollock 1999b) are pooled as a collective good from which individuals receive benefits. Shah and Levine (2003) and Cheshire (2005) argue that digital goods have near-pure jointness of supply (i.e., they are nonrival goods). Specifically, digital goods can be enjoyed by many, and contributors need not lose much (if any) of their value when they make a contribution, because digital goods can be perfectly *replicated*, so the contributor keeps a copy when she makes a contribution (Kollock 1999b; Cheshire and Cook 2004; Cheshire 2005). This line of research demonstrates how important the *nature of the good* is in the development of this and other types of exchange systems.

Commitment, Relational Cohesion, and Trust

Recently, research on social exchange has focused more attention on the effects of important factors such as uncertainty and risk on the nature and structure of social exchange. Facing uncertain environments, actors involved in exchange are more likely to form committed exchange relations (Cook and Emerson 1978; Kollock 1994; Lawler and Yoon 1996) or networks of trusted exchange partners. A significant effect of the emergence of commitment is that it reduces the extent to which actors seek exchange with alternative partners and thus reduces power inequalities within the exchange relation and the network in which it is embedded (Rice 2002). Kollock (1994) demonstrates that uncertainty not only results in commitment as a means of reducing uncertainty but also tends to be correlated with perceptions of trustworthiness of the actors involved in the exchange. Recent work on trust (Cook 2005) in social exchange relations treats trust as an emergent property in certain types of exchange settings.

Cook and Emerson first studied commitment in exchange relations and its impact on power inequality in 1978. They found that under conditions of relatively low uncertainty some actors formed commitments (measured as the extent to which two actors engaged in repeat exchange with one another in the face of more profitable alternatives) over time. More interesting, they found that dyadic commitment reduced power use by the high-power actors in power-imbalanced networks. Commitment in this situation reduced the economic exchange outcomes of the high-power actors because they reduced their exploration of alternatives. The exchange outcomes of the low-power actors increased as a result, suggesting that commitment was advantageous for them. This finding provided some support for the argument of Leik and Leik (1977) that low-power actors foster commitment to reduce outcome disparities that derive from power imbalance.

Cook and Emerson (1984) explicitly explored the role of uncertainty in exchange networks. They conceived uncertainty as the subjective probability of concluding a satisfactory exchange with any partner. They found that commitment varied directly with uncertainty, increasing when uncertainty was high. As the likelihood of concluding a transaction decreased, an actor was more likely to exchange with one partner exclusively, ignoring possible alternatives. They also found that commitment formation reduced this uncertainty. Cook and Emerson (1984, 13) argue that commitment behavior in this context is rational because it increases the frequency of exchange and thus improves benefits for those within the relationship.

Kollock (1994) subsequently investigated commitment formation under low uncertainty and high uncertainty. He conceptualized uncertainty in terms of the unknown quality of the goods being exchanged, thus focusing on a different source of uncertainty than Cook and Emerson (1978, 1984). Kollock (1994) argued that committed relationships were more likely to form under conditions of high uncertainty about quality to reduce risk and assure

profit. Kollock's work (and subsequent research) viewed commitment as a strategy for reducing uncertainty in exchange situations, testing the argument posed originally by Cook
and Emerson (1978, 1984). In addition, Kollock investigated the role of trust. He found that
perceived trustworthiness of a partner was directly related to increased rates of commitment
(under uncertainty) and reduced rates of malfeasance.

Yamagishi, Cook, and Watabe (1998) report that trust emerges in exchange relations under conditions of high uncertainty when actors begin to form commitments to exclusive exchange relations in an attempt to avoid the possibility of exploitation by unknown actors
who enter the exchange opportunity structure. Given low uncertainty, actors are more
likely to continue to play the market and avoid forming commitments to specific partners
to maximize access to valued resources. Uncertainty in these experiments refers to the likelihood of being exploited by a new partner in a network of exchange opportunities that
changes over time. Uncertainty and vulnerability to exploitation are often defined as two
key elements in situations in which trust becomes paramount (Heimer 2001).

Recently, Lawler and his colleagues (e.g., Lawler and Yoon 1993, 1996, 1998) and Molm
and her colleagues (e.g., Molm, Takahashi, and Peterson 2000) have explored commitment
between exchange partners in greater depth. In his theory of relational cohesion, Lawler
builds on the notion of *cohesion* derived from Emerson's work (1962, 1972a, 1972b). He
defines cohesion as the total mutual dependence of both partners in an exchange relation;
the stronger the mutual dependence, the more cohesive the relation. He also investigates the
emotional processes that derive from positive and successful exchange that form the basis
for affective commitment. This research extends Emerson's original formulation emphasizing the exchange relationship as the focus of analysis.

A key feature of Lawler's theory of relational exchange is the idea that instrumental
exchange relations become transformed over time based on the nature of the exchange dynamics so that the relationship itself becomes a valued object worthy of commitment. In his
studies of gift giving, for example, he measures this transformation by testing the strength
of the commitment between the exchange partners. Commitment, if it is meaningful, is
expected to precipitate gift giving as a symbolic gesture.

Molm and her colleagues (Molm, Takahashi, and Peterson 2000) examine the effect of
type of exchange (reciprocal or negotiated) on affective commitment and trust. They argue
that reciprocal exchange is inherently more uncertain than negotiated exchange. Because
exploitation is always possible, actors in reciprocal exchange risk giving benefits unilaterally
while receiving little or nothing in return. Moreover, Molm, Takahashi, and Peterson
(2000) emphasize that affective commitment is more likely to form in reciprocal exchange
than in negotiated exchange. Because of the inherent uncertainty, actors are likely to attribute a partner's positive behaviors to personal traits and intentions, which results in the
emergence of stronger positive feelings in reciprocal exchange than in negotiated exchange.
Molm, Takahashi, and Peterson (2000) also argue that trust should be higher in reciprocal
exchange compared with negotiated exchange, precisely because the fear of exploitation
should be stronger in reciprocal exchange. In these current lines of research Lawler, Molm,
and their colleagues explicitly incorporate emotions into the theory, an aspect that is
distinctly missing in Emerson's early work on exchange but much less so in the work of the

anthropologists who studied more primitive forms of exchange (e.g., Mauss [1950] 1990; Malinowski 1922). Before discussing future directions we comment on some of the applications of exchange theory, in particular those based on power-dependence principles derived from Emerson's research program.

SUBSTANTIVE APPLICATIONS OF POWER-DEPENDENCE AND EXCHANGE NETWORK THEORY

Emerson's work on power, dependence, and exchange networks has been applied to a wide variety of social phenomena. Interactional dynamics in all types of settings frequently involve exchange and power. To the extent that power and power use is responsible for outcomes, Emerson's approach proves useful in analysis and explanation. Substantive areas of study in which exchange theory has been applied include the study of personal and family relations and, more broadly, organizations and economic relations. There is clear overlap with developments over time in social network theory and research (Cook and Whitmeyer 1992) and economic sociology. We will briefly mention only a few areas of application given space constraints. We begin with some of the earliest applications in organizational theory and research before examining some of the uses of exchange theory in economic sociology.

Power-dependence theory is the basis for an important theoretical approach in the field of organizational studies, known as the *resource dependence* perspective (e.g., Pfeffer and Salancik 1978). According to this perspective, organizations have a fundamental need for resources from both outside and within the organization. Those entities—individuals, subunits, or other organizations—that exclusively provide the most needed or valued resources will have the most power in the organization. This key postulate comes directly from the main principle in power dependence theory concerning the relationship between dependence and power. Resource dependence theorists note that for power actually to be exerted other factors come into play. Molm, Lawler, and others have studied the specific determinants of power use[4] that extend beyond structural sources of power. They include the strategic use of power, commitment, type of power (reward or punishment power), and normative considerations (e.g., fairness concerns).

Since organizations are not self-sufficient they must engage in exchanges with other organizations and entities in their environments to assure survival. Organizations thus spend much of their time and energy involved to manage these "strategic dependencies." As Scott (1992, 115) argues, "One of the major contributions of the resource dependency perspective is to discern and describe the strategies—ranging from buffering to diversification and merger—employed by organizations to change and adapt to the environment." The application of power-dependence theory to the analysis of organizational exchange and interorganizational relations was pursued by Cook (1977) and subsequently by Cook and Emerson (1984). This work is reflected in more recent developments within the field of organizations. Many of the strategies available to organizations to manage their critical dependencies can be understood in terms of the balancing operations spelled out in power-dependence theory, since the goal is to acquire necessary resources without increasing dependence. Such strategies include, under different circumstances, joint ventures, long-term contracting, specialization, consolidation, reduction in production arenas, and vertical integration of various types, among others. As Scott (1992, 193) puts it, "Unequal exchange relations can generate power and dependency differences among organizations, causing them to enter into exchange relations cautiously and to pursue strategies that will enhance their own bargaining position."

The work of Emerson and his colleagues also informs research and theory in the field of organizations beyond the resource dependence perspective. In particular, it has contributed to the network perspective on organizations (e.g., Mizruchi 1993, 2000; Knoke 1990; Knoke and Guilarte 1994).[5] A number of organizational theorists have extended the analysis of exchange networks to examine network processes within and between organizations in addition to investigating the role of networks more broadly in the economy (e.g., Powell 1990; Powell et al. 1999; Lincoln, Gerlach, and Ahmadjian 1996; Lincoln, Gerlach, and Takashi 1992). Much of this research is consistent with power-dependence principles. Networks have been examined as significant determinants of labor practices, informal influence, and the organization of business groups and networks of companies that cross national boundaries (Powell and Smith-Doerr 1994). Central to these efforts is the attempt to analyze the relative power of the economic actors in the network and the strategies used to enhance network-wide power or to alter the distribution of power within the network. The focus of attention is on the structural location of the actors in the network and how that influences strategy. Exchange theory and the resource-dependence perspective (e.g., Pfeffer and Salancik 1978) based on power-dependence arguments are commonly used for analysis in these investigations of economic impact. Other topics of investigation include strategic alliances, collaborative manufacturing enterprises, vertical integration of firms, interlocking directorates, network diffusion of innovative practices, and mergers.

IMPLICATIONS OF EXCHANGE THEORY FOR ECONOMIC SOCIOLOGY

Work on power, dependence, and exchange networks also has significant implications for economic sociology (Cook and Rice 2003; Cook and Gerbasi 2005). Uzzi and Gillespie (1999), for example, examine how firms hierarchically stratify their dependence on different sources of financial capital to reduce uncertainty. They use network theory to explain how the organization's network of exchange relationships to outside suppliers of capital affects the firm's capital structure. The pecking order predicted by economic models can be modified, depending on the firm's network ties. All relationships are not equal. Certain ties are viewed as more dependable, thus firms use these ties more often. These ties also affect the dispersion of capital sources within tiers of the pecking order. The uncertainty inherent in the market serves to structure an organization's networks and thus modifies its market choices, underscoring the importance of recent research on the effects of uncertainty and risk on social exchange, discussed earlier.

Uzzi's (1996) research on the apparel industry demonstrates that network ties in the industry are clearly embedded in an exchange system involving social relations that create unique opportunities in contrast to the standard vision of purely economic markets. Importantly, firms embedded in networks involving personal relations have higher chances for survival than do firms that maintain arm's-length, more asocial market relationships. The positive effect of embeddedness, however, reaches a threshold after which the positive effect reverses, becoming negative. This finding suggests the wisdom of maintaining a diverse set of relationships: up to a point it is wise to rely on one's personal relations, but it is equally wise to maintain some arm's-length ties to secure access to more diverse opportunities.

Moving from organizations to individuals engaged in economic transactions, DiMaggio and Louch (1998) use exchange network theory to explain why and to what extent people make significant purchases from others with whom they have prior noncommercial relationships. They argue that engaging in transactions with social contacts is effective because it embeds commercial exchanges in a web of obligations and holds the seller's network hostage to appropriate role performance in the economic transaction, especially under uncertainty. They find that in-network exchanges are more common for risky transactions that are unlikely to be repeated and in which uncertainty is high.

Biggart and Castanias (2001) similarly argue that under uncertainty social relations provide assurance that an economic transaction will proceed as agreed by the parties involved. Commitment (Rice 2002) between exchange parties helps to provide this assurance, especially when there is risk of opportunism or malfeasance. Committed social relations may be more effective than actual contracts in this respect (see Malhotra and Murnighan 2002). DiMaggio and Louch (1998) also find that, in terms of preferences for exchanges within one's social network, uncertainty about product and performance quality leads people to prefer sellers with whom they have noncommercial ties. The converse is true as well; people prefer to avoid selling to social contacts under the same conditions that lead buyers to seek such transactions. Thus there is an interesting asymmetry. Under conditions of uncertainty (especially when the quality of the good is of concern), buyers prefer to interact with a known seller, but under those same conditions, sellers prefer to exchange with an unknown buyer.

When risks increase, commitment and trust become even more important (Heimer 2001). Under high risk people will often engage in exchange only with those they trust. Cook, Rice, and Gerbasi (2004) identify the types of economic uncertainty that lead to the formation of trust networks for exchange. Trust networks, if they become closed networks, actually may retard the transition to market economies under high economic uncertainty such as that characteristic of eastern European countries and other countries making the transition from socialist to capitalist economies. Other implications of social exchange theory for economic relations are explored in Cook, Rice, and Gerbasi (2004). Applications of social exchange theory to macrolevel social structures and processes reflect Blau's enduring influence on the development of exchange theory, despite his subsequent skepticism about linking microlevel theories of exchange and macrolevel social structures and processes.

Applications of exchange theory in fields like health care at the organizational and network level are less common. As early as 1974 Shortell used exchange theory to analyze physician referrals when fee-for-service was the primary mode of financing physician services. Grembowski et al. (1998) more recently have examined physician referrals using an exchange model to analyze referral decisions and the network of providers involved in the delivery of health services under varying types of managed care in comparison with fee-for-service (a much smaller segment of the health-care market currently). Issues of power and dependence are investigated as they apply to physician-patient relations, the relations between various categories of providers (e.g., physician to physician, primary care provider to specialist, physician to alternative health care provider, and physicians to hospital administrators or other managers within the health care system), as well as relations between organizations involved in the delivery of health-related services (e.g., insurance carriers, suppliers of goods and services, other health and community agencies).

Grembowski et al. (2002) developed a general model of the power relations between purchasers, managed care organizations, providers, and patients in the health-care system in the United States at three levels: exchanges between purchasers (primarily large health insurance policy buyers) and managed care organizations, exchanges between managed care organizations and physicians, and exchanges between physicians and patients. Their research supports Emerson's (1972) hypothesis that imbalanced exchanges tend to move toward power balance. Grembowski and his colleagues find that collective action is one of the most common strategies for reducing dependence, thus increasing power in the exchange relations at stake.

Research based on models of exchange and power-dependence principles in the arena of health care holds the promise of providing a more general theory of the processes involved than is currently available. The major shifts that have occurred over the last decade in the delivery of health care have involved significant changes in the distribution of power among the key players in that organizational system. For example, there has been a shift in power from relatively autonomous physicians to the hospitals in which they practice and, more significant, the insurers that pay them, and who now exercise a great deal of control over the nature of the practice of medicine as well as remuneration and working conditions. New applications of exchange theory and power-dependence principles in arenas such as the health-care industry may offer important directions for future theoretical development. In addition, a number of directions for theory development and research derive from unanswered questions and lines of inquiry, many derived from Emerson's fruitful formulation, and have never been fully explored.

FUTURE DIRECTIONS OF THEORY DEVELOPMENT
AND EMPIRICAL RESEARCH

We have identified a number of areas of research for further development. These include power dynamics, additional determinants of power such as differential values or preferences, exploration of more complex forms of exchange, analysis of mechanisms of network change beyond the strategic use of power, and continued investigation of emotions in exchange relations and the networks they form. In addition, exploring further possibilities for applications of exchange theory outside the laboratory is important to extend the range and scope of the theory. New methodologies for studying exchange networks and emerging markets on the Internet should make this possible. For example, the study of systems of buying and selling on various Internet sites, in addition to other forms of Internet exchange, may allow the collection of large data sets on the emergence and maintenance of exchange relations and network connections. Let us comment briefly on some of these opportunities for further theoretical development and research.

The significance actors give to resources, services, or other outcomes is central to understanding the behavior of individuals in social exchange networks and power-dependence relationships. Emerson's (1987) last published paper, though unfinished, emphasizes the importance of developing a more comprehensive understanding of actors' preferences and values. As power-dependence and social exchange theories continue to be expanded to apply to real-world exchange systems (in which value is not as easily controlled or measured as in the laboratory), there is a clear need for a more complete theoretical treatment of the social origins of value and the role of individual preference evaluations in social exchange. Recent developments, such as Hechter's (1992) call for the endogenous use of values in behavioral explanations and Thye's (2000) status value theory of power in exchange relations, signal new developments in the sociological analyses of values and preferences in social exchange.

Most experimental research on social exchange involves one or perhaps two types of pure exchange (usually binding *negotiated* exchange or *reciprocal* exchange), but real-world examples (such as Uzzi's work [1996] on the apparel industry) show us that exchange relationships are not always that simple. Often relationships start out as one type of exchange (for example, as a contractual relationship), and as the parties get to know one another, the relationship changes. For example, the same individuals may begin exchanging favors or gifts, transforming the negotiated exchange relationship by including elements of reciprocal exchange. On the other hand, some relationships begin with the exchange of favors, such as picking up mail for a neighbor who is away for a weekend in exchange for having one's cat fed. Eventually this relationship might involve formal, direct negotiation over other goods or services (such as lending tools or the loan of a car for a short time). Several factors may increase or decrease the likelihood of these transitions occurring between different types of exchange, including perceived trustworthiness, the emergence of obligation, and considerations of fairness. Relationships are dynamic, and social exchange theory is in a good position to examine the changes in relationship trajectories over time.

In addition to transitions or the evolution from one type of exchange to another, social exchange systems can also overlap and interact to produce more complex structures. Social roles and interpersonal interactions in the real world are often multiplex—that is, they may involve different intersecting modes of exchange (for different goods and services and among positively, negatively, or mixed types of exchange). The real world is dynamic, such that an exchange relationship between individuals in one small network may affect one or more other exchange relationships among the same (or different) actors embedded in a larger system. For example, managers within an organization might lobby to produce a collective good such as billets for new hires. This creates a positively connected, group-generalized-exchange system in which the collective good is a limited number of new employees. As new billets become available, the same individuals who lobby for them may also engage in negotiated exchanges with each other to acquire one of these scarce resources.

Thus a portion of the same system simultaneously takes the form of a negatively connected negotiation network where favors and resources are exchanged for billets. Much like the mixed-type exchange systems explored by Yamagishi, Gillmore, and Cook (1988), the relative power of the managers to obtain the billets may be determined by a number of interrelated factors such as the network position relative to scarce resources as well as the number of alternative exchange partners. Furthermore, behavioral reputation from one exchange system (such as the lobby for new employees) may affect one's exchange success in the other negotiated exchanges. Clearly, such complex systems are taken for granted in everyday life. Much of the future of social exchange theory and power-dependence theory may involve the investigation of these complex systems and the specification of the determinants of power within overlapping and compound forms of exchange.

Computer-mediated interaction situations, such as those that emerge on the Internet, have become a particularly relevant area for theoretical development and empirical research in social exchange and power-dependence relationships. As discussed earlier, one avenue of empirical research on generalized-exchange networks involves the exchange of digital goods (music, movies, software, etc.) in Internet peer-to-peer systems (Shah and Levine 2003; Cheshire 2005). These types of exchange systems are contemporary real-world examples of group-generalized exchange. Because these systems are positively connected, the structure of power differentials may have less to do with the numerous exchange partners in the system than with the relative scarcity of valuable goods throughout the networks. Understanding how such systems emerge, overcome the inherent social dilemmas (and potential power differentials), and produce persistent structures of exchange represents an area ripe for continued research.

Finally, pure economic exchange on the Internet is another arena in which Emerson's conception of exchange and power has renewed significance. Online auction sites (such as eBay) are interesting to sociologists and economists, especially with respect to the nature of reputation systems in these networks (e.g., Kollock 1999a; Houser and Wooders 2000; Yamagishi and Matsuda 2003; Resnick et al. 2000). The focus on reputation systems is due to the fact that they serve to *reduce the risk and social uncertainty* that are created when individuals interact anonymously across the Internet. The role of reputation in online social exchange relationships is, however, just one of many possible ways that anonymity can be reduced in online interactions. The reduction in anonymity (and hence risk) largely depends on the continuity of the online exchange system (i.e., whether one's partners are fixed or random) and the frequency of the interactions (i.e., iterated or one-time interactions; Cheshire and Cook 2004). While widely described in the popular media and increasingly so in academia, Internet trading, virtual communities, and other forms of computer-mediated social interactions are still largely uncultivated arenas for research on social exchange processes, trust formation, collective action, and power dynamics. "Back to the future" is a good motto for the future of exchange theory. In many ways the world itself has now become a fertile laboratory for the study of social exchange networks.

1. Emerson was the first exchange theorist in sociology to extend the theory to networks of connected exchange relations. Homans's theoretical work remained at the dyadic and group level. Blau's framework extended into the macro realm of social life and more complex forms of association, but he did not propose networks as the basis for the extension of exchange concepts beyond the micro level as Emerson did. The significance of this theoretical move is that it connects exchange theory directly to important developments in the analysis of social networks.

2. The relationship between social structure and power is broader than the concern with relations of exchange. Willer and his collaborators (e.g., Willer and Anderson 1981; Willer 1999), for example, deal with exchange as well as other types of social process (e.g., coercion) in what they view as a more general theory of social structure and social process often referred to as the "elementary theory of social behavior." We limit our concern to relations of exchange.

3. As a part of his theory of structural change and group formation, Emerson speculated on norm formation. The link between types of exchange (negotiated or productive) and the emergence of norms of fairness was empirically examined by Stolte (1987).

4. See also Cook and Emerson (1978) on commitment and fairness as constraints on power use in exchange networks.

5. Knoke acknowledges the significance of laboratory research on exchange and power for research on organizational relations, but he argues that application of the theory has been hindered by the complexities inherent in naturally occurring networks.

REFERENCES

Axelrod, Robert. 1984. *The Evolution of Cooperation*. New York: Basic Books.

Bearman, Peter. 1997. Generalized Exchange. *American Journal of Sociology* 102:1383–1415.

Bienenstock, Elisa Jayne, and Phillip Bonacich. 1992. The core as a solution to exclusionary networks. *Social Networks* 14:231–43.

———. 1993. Game-theory models for exchange networks: Experimental results. *Sociological Perspectives* 36:117–35.

Biggart, Nicole Woolsey, and Richard P. Castanias. 2001. Collateralized social relations: The social in economic calculation. *American Journal of Economics and Sociology* 60(2): 471–500.

Blau, Peter. [1964] 1986. *Exchange and Power*. New York: Wiley.

Cheshire, Coye. 2005. A sociological analysis of generalized information exchange. PhD diss. Stanford, CA: Stanford University.

Cheshire, Coye, and Karen S. Cook. 2004. The emergence of trust networks: Implications for online interaction. *Analyse and Kritik* 26:220–40.

Cook, Karen S. 1977. Exchange and power in networks of interorganizational relations. *Sociological Quarterly* 18:62–82.

———. 2005. Networks, norms and trust: The social psychology of social capital. *Social Psychology Quarterly* 68:4–14.

Cook, Karen S., and Richard M. Emerson. 1978. Power, equity and commitment in exchange networks. *American Sociological Review* 43:721–39.

———. 1984. Exchange networks and the analysis of complex organizations. *Research in the Sociology of Organizations* 3:1–30.

Cook, Karen S., and Alexandra Gerbasi. 2005. Trust in the economy. In *Encyclopedia of Economic Sociology*, ed. Jens Beckert and Milan Zagiroski. London: Routledge.

Cook, Karen S., and M. R. Gillmore. 1984. Power, dependence and coalitions. In *Advances in Group Processes*, ed. Edward J. Lawler, 1: 27–58. Greenwich, CT: JAI Press.

Cook, Karen S., and Eric R. Rice. 2003. Social exchange theory. In *Handbook of Social Psychology*, ed. John Delamater, 53–76. New York: Kluwer Academic/Plenum.

Cook, Karen S., Eric R. W. Rice, and Alexandra Gerbasi. 2004. The emergence of trust networks under uncertainty: The case of transitional economies—Insights from social psychological research. In *Problems of Post Socialist Transition: Creating Social Trust*, ed. Susan Rose-Ackerman, Bo Rothstein, and Janos Kornai. New York: Palgrave-Macmillan.

Cook, Karen S., and Joseph W. Whitmeyer. 1992. Two approaches to social structure: Exchange theory and network analysis. In *Annual Review of Sociology*, ed. Judith Blake and John Hagan, 18:109–27. Palo Alto, CA: Annual Reviews.

Cook, Karen S., and Toshio Yamagishi. 1992. Power in exchange networks: A power-dependence formulation. *Social Networks* 14:245–66.

DiMaggio, Paul, and Hugh Louch. 1998. Socially embedded consumer transactions: For what kinds of purchases do people most often use networks? *American Sociological Review* 63:619–37.

Ekeh, Peter. 1974. *Social Exchange Theory: The Two Traditions*. Cambridge, MA: Harvard University Press.

Emerson, Richard M. 1962. Power-dependence relations. *American Sociological Review* 27:31–41.

———. 1964. Power-dependence relations: Two experiments. *Sociometry* 27:282–98.

———. 1972a. Exchange theory, part I: A psychological basis for social exchange. In *Sociological Theories in Progress*, ed. Joseph Berger, Morris Zelditch Jr., and B. Anderson, 38–57. Boston: Houghton Mifflin.

———. 1972b. Exchange theory, part II: Exchange relations and network structures. In *Sociological Theories in Progress*, ed. J. Berger, M. Zelditch, and B. Anderson, 2:58–87. Boston: Houghton Mifflin.

———. 1976. Social exchange theory. *Annual Review of Sociology* 2:335–62.

———. 1981. Social exchange theory. In *Social Psychology: Sociological Perspectives*, ed. Morris Rosenberg and Ralph Turner, 30–65. New York: Basic Books.

———. 1987. Toward a theory of value in social exchange. In *Social Exchange Theory*, ed. Karen S. Cook, 11–58. Newbury Park, CA: Sage.

Friedkin, Noah E. 1992. An expected value model of social power: Predictions for selected exchange networks. *Social Networks* 14:213–29.

———. 1993. An expected value model of social exchange outcomes. In *Advances in Group Processes*, ed. Edward J. Lawler, 163–93. Greenwich, CT: JAI Press.

Gillmore, Mary R. 1987. Implications of generalized versus restricted exchange. In *Social Exchange Theory*, ed. Karen S. Cook, 170–89. Newbury Park, CA: Sage.

Grembowski, David, Karen S. Cook, Donald Patrick, and Amy Roussell. 1998. Managed care and physician referral: A social exchange perspective. *Medical Care Research and Review* 55:3–31.

———. 2002. Managed care and the US health care system: A social exchange perspective. *Social Science and Medicine* 54:1167–80.

Hechter, M. 1992. Should values be written out of the social scientist's lexicon? *Sociological Theory* 10:214–30.

Heimer, Carol. 2001. Solving the problem of trust. In *Trust in Society*, ed. Karen Cook, 40–88. New York: Russell Sage.

Houser, Daniel, and John Wooders. 2000. Reputation in auctions: Theory, and evidence from eBay. Working paper, Department of Economics, University of Arizona.

Knoke, David. 1990. *Political Networks: The Structural Perspective*. Cambridge, UK: Cambridge University Press.

Knoke, David, and Miguel Guilarte. 1994. Networks in organizational structures and strategies. *Current Perspectives in Social Theory* 14(1): 77–115.

Kollock, Peter. 1994. The emergence of exchange structures: An experimental study of uncertainty, commitment, and trust. *American Journal of Sociology* 100:313–45.

———. 1999a. The production of trust in online markets. In *Advances in Group Processes*, ed. Edward J. Lawler, 99–123. Greenwich, CT: JAI Press.

————. 1999b. The economies of online cooperation: Gifts and public goods in cyberspace. In *Communities in cyberspace*, ed. Marc A. Smith and Peter Kollock. London: Routledge.

Lawler, Edward J., Rebecca Ford, and Mary A. Blegen. 1988. Coercive capability in conflict: A test of bilateral deterrence versus conflict spiral theory. *Social Psychology Quarterly* 51:93–107.

Lawler, Edward J., and Jeongkoo Yoon. 1993. Power and the emergence of commitment behavior in negotiated exchange. *American Sociological Review* 58:465–81.

————. 1996. Commitment in exchange relations: A test of a theory of relational cohesion. *American Sociological Review* 61:89–108.

————. 1998. Network structure and emotion in exchange relations. *American Sociological Review* 63:871–94.

Leik, Robert K., and Sheila K. Leik. 1977. Transition to interpersonal commitment. In *Behavioral Theory in Sociology*, ed. Robert L. Hamblin and John H. Kunkel, 299–322. New Brunswick, NJ: Transaction.

Leik, Robert K. 1992. New directions for network exchange theory: Strategic manipulation of network linkages. *Social Networks* 14:309–23.

Lévi-Strauss, Claude. 1969. *The Elementary Structures of Kinship*, rev. ed. Boston: Beacon.

Lincoln, James R., Michael L. Gerlach, and Christina L. Ahmadjian. 1996. Keiretsu networks and corporate performance in Japan. *American Sociological Review* 61:67–88.

Lincoln, James R., Michael Gerlach, and Peggy Takashi. 1992. Keiretsu networks in the Japanese economy: A dyad analysis of intercorporate ties. *American Sociological Review* 57:561–85.

Macy, Michael W, and John Skvoretz. 1998. The evolution of trust and cooperation between strangers: A computational model. *American Sociological Review* 63:638–60.

Malhotra, Deepak, and J. Keith Murnighan. 2002. The effects of contracts on interpersonal trust. *Administrative Science Quarterly* 47:534–59.

Malinowski, Bronislaw. 1922. *Argonauts of the Western Pacific*. New York: E. P. Dutton.

Mark, Noah. 2002. Cultural transmission, disproportionate acquisition, and the evolution of cooperation. *American Sociological Review* 67:323–44.

Markovsky, Barry, D. Willer, and T. Patton. 1988. Power relations in exchange networks. *American Sociological Review* 53:220–36.

Mauss, Marcel. [1950] 1990. *The Gift: The Form and Reason for Exchange in Archaic Societies*. New York: Norton.

Mizruchi, Mark S. 1993. Managing with power: Politics and influence in organizations. *American Journal of Sociology* 99:483–85.

————. 2000. Social networks and interorganizational relations: An illustration and adaptation of a micro-level model of political decision making. *Research in the Sociology of Organizations* 17(1): 225–65.

Molm, Linda D. 1985. Relative effects of individual dependencies: Further tests of the relation between power imbalance and power use. *Social Forces* 63:810–37.

————. 1997. *Coercive Power in Social Exchange*. Cambridge, UK: Cambridge University Press.

Molm, Linda D., and Karen S. Cook. 1995. Social exchange and exchange networks. In *Sociological Perspectives on Social Psychology*, ed. Karen S. Cook, Gary A. Fine, and James S. House, 209–35. Boston: Allyn & Bacon.

Molm, Linda, N. Takahashi, and Gretchen Peterson. 2000. Risk and trust in social exchange: An experimental test of a classical proposition. *American Journal of Sociology* 105:1396–1427.

Pfeffer, Jeffrey, and Gerald R. Salancik. 1978. *The External Control of Organizations: A Resource Dependence Perspective*. New York: Harper & Row.

Powell, Walter W. 1990. Neither market nor hierarchy: Network forms of organization. In *Research in Organizational Behaviour*, ed. L. L. Cummings and B. M. Staw, 12:295–336. Greenwich, CT: JAI Press.

Powell, Walter W., and Laurel Smith-Doerr. 1994. Networks and economic life. In *The Handbook of Economic Sociology*, ed. Neil Smelser and Richard Swedberg, 368–402. Princeton: Princeton University Press/New York: Russell Sage Foundation.

Powell, Walter W., Kenneth W. Koput, Laurel Smith-Doerr, and Jason Owen-Smith. 1999. Network position and firm performance: Organizational returns to collaboration in the biotechnology industry. *Research in the Sociology of Organizations* 16(1): 129–59.

Resnick, Paul, Richard Zeckhauser, Eric Friedman, and Ko Kuwabara. 2000. Reputation systems: Facilitating trust in Internet interactions. *Communications of ACM* 43:45–48.

Rice, Eric R. 2002. The effect of social uncertainty in networks of social exchange, PhD diss. Stanford, CA: Stanford University.

Ruef, Martin. 2003. Norms of generalized exchange in formal organizations. Working paper. Stanford Graduate School of Business.

Scott, W. Richard. 1992. *Organizations: Rational, Natural, and Open Systems*, 3rd ed. Englewood Cliffs, NJ: Prentice Hall.

Shah, S. K., and Sheen S. Levine. 2003. Towards a theory of large-scale generalized exchange. American Sociological Association, Theoretical Issues in Economic Sociology Session. Atlanta, GA. August 2003.

Shortell, S. M. 1974. Determinants of physician referral rates: An exchange theory approach. *Medical Care* 12:13–31.

Skvoretz, John, and David Willer. 1993. Exclusion and power: A test of four theories of power in exchange networks. *American Sociological Review* 58:801–18.

Stolte, John F. 1987. Legitimacy, justice and productive exchange. In *Social Exchange Theory*, ed. Karen S. Cook, 190–208. Newbury Park, CA: Sage.

Takahashi, N. 2000. The emergence of generalized exchange. *American Journal of Sociology* 105:1105–34.

Takahashi, N., and Toshio Yamagishi. 1996. Social relational foundations of altruistic behavior. *Japanese Journal of Experimental Social Psychology* 36:1–11.

———. 1999. Voluntary formation of a generalized exchange system: An experimental study of discriminating altruism. *Japanese Journal of Psychology* 70:9–16.

Thye, Shane R. 2000. A status value theory of power in exchange relations. *American Sociological Review* 65:407–32.

Uzzi, Brian. 1996. The sources and consequences of embeddedness for the economic performance of organizations: The network effect. *American Sociological Review* 61:674–98.

Uzzi, Brian, and James J. Gillespie. 1999. Interfirm relationships and the firm's financial capital structure: The case of the middle market. *Research in the Sociology of Organizations* 16(1): 107–26.

Whitmeyer, Joseph M. 1999b. Convex preferences and power inequality in exchange networks: An experimental study. *Rationality and Society* 11:419–42.

———. 1999a. Interest-network structures in exchange networks. *Sociological Perspectives* 42:23–48.

Whitmeyer, Joseph, and Karen S. Cook. 2002. Social structure and social exchange. In *Structure, Culture and History: Recent Issues in Social Theory*, ed. Sing C. Chew and J. David Knottnerus, 271–302. New York: Rowman & Littlefield.

Willer, David. 1999. *Network Exchange Theory*. Westport, CT: Praeger.

Willer, David, and Bo Anderson. 1981. Networks, exchange and coercion: The elementary theory and its applications. New York: Elsevier.

Yamagishi, Toshio. 1995. Social dilemmas. In *Sociological Perspectives on Social Psychology*, ed. Karen S. Cook, Gary A. Fine, and James S. House, 311–54. Needham Heights, NY: Allyn & Bacon.

Yamagishi, Toshio, and Karen S. Cook. 1993. Generalized exchange and social dilemmas. *Social Psychology Quarterly* 56:235–48.

Yamagishi, Toshio, Karen S. Cook, and M. Watabe. 1998. Uncertainty, trust and commitment formation in the United States and Japan. *American Journal of Sociology* 104:165–94.

Yamagishi, T., M. R. Gillmore, and K. S. Cook. 1988. Network connections and the distribution of power in exchange networks. *American Journal of Sociology* 93:833–51.

Yamagishi, Toshio, and M. Matsuda. 2003. The role of reputation in open and closed societies: An experimental study of online trading. Center for the Study of Cultural and Ecological Foundations of Mind Working Paper Series, No. 8.

Ziegler, R. 1990. The Kula: Social order, barter and ceremonial exchange. In *Social Institutions: Their Emergence, Maintenance and Effects*, ed. M. Hechter, K-D. Opp, and R. Wippler, 141–68. New York: Aldine de Gruyter.

10 ELEMENTARY THEORY

David Willer and Pamela Emanuelson

Elementary theory (ET) is a formal theory of action in social relations such as exchange and coercion. Its orienting perspective flows from the classical theories of Marx, Weber, Simmel, and Michels. It shares with them the realization, basic to all understanding of human activity in society, that the interests that actors pursue are embedded in social relations. And those interests are *reflected* in actors when acting in that relation.

Interests are valued states of social relations that actors seek. For example, all four of the classical theorists understood that, when masters exploit slaves and capitalists profit from workers, they are acting on values and beliefs embedded in master-slave and capitalist-worker relations. Nevertheless, classical theorists also understood that, at times, values and beliefs acquired at one social location are carried by actors to another. Thus economic structures can be reflected in religious beliefs, and religious ethics can frame economic rationality.

In ET social relations are embedded in social structures. To conceptualize relations in structures, graphic models are built in the following way. Fundamental concepts are given by interpreted network points and arcs like those of Figure 10.1. Derived concepts are constructed by combining fundamental concepts and also by combining fundamental concepts with concepts already derived.[1] For example, the fundamental concepts of *preference system*, *belief system*, and *decisions* combine to generate the derived concept of *social actor*. Actors are then located in social structures as at the positions *A* and *B* of Figure 10.1a. Then the *sanction* displayed in Figure 10.1a is an act that positively affects the preference state of *B*, the actor receiving it. By contrast, the sanction of Figure 10.1b negatively affects the preference state of *B*. Sanctions may also affect the preference states of transmitting actors. As shown in Figure 10.2, these fundamental concepts are combined to build derived concepts. In each diagram two sanctions are paired, resulting in the three basic types of social relationships: exchange, coercion, and conflict.

As does classical theory, ET builds its simplest explanations by inferring (what Marx called "reflecting") actors' values and beliefs from relations and structures. Unlike the classics, formulations for actors in relations in structures are modeled as shown in the figures.

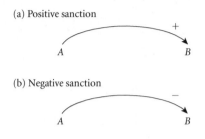

Figure 10.1 Types of Sanctions

For example, in the coercive relationship of Figure 10.2, *C* has an interest in gaining *D*'s positive sanction by threat of the negative sanction and *D* has an interest in avoiding *C*'s negative sanction. When sanctions are given a quantitative interpretation, ET seeks to relate the size of the positive sanction that *D* sends to the size of negative sanction in *C*'s threat. The interests in seeking positives and avoiding negatives are embedded in the signs used to display the relation.

Classical theory also understands that the conditions under which actors pursue interests are given by the *social structures* in which relations are embedded. Using concepts as simple and few in number as possible, ET builds models for social structures as shown in Figure 10.3. These modeled structures are not static. They are dynamic in two senses. First, actors decide and act within them. Those decisions and actions are produced by applying the two principles and resistance equations that are introduced later. The dynamics of action in structures are well understood, having been investigated using ET for more than two decades. Second, modeled structures are dynamic in that actors can seek to alter the structure. Investigations of dynamics of the second kind have only recently begun (Willer and Willer 2000).

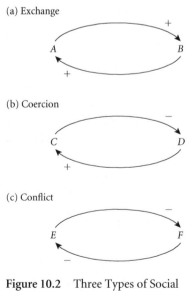

Figure 10.2 Three Types of Social Relations

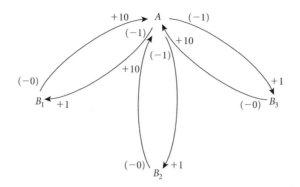

Figure 10.3 An Exchange Branch Connected at *A*

Since its inception, ET has extended its scope in a number of directions. For example, though much work has been done on exchange structures, coercion and conflict structures have also been studied. Discussed here are seven structural conditions. By "structural conditions" we mean the qualities of social structures, which advantage some positions at the expense of others. Interestingly, of the seven, only one structural condition was recognized by classical theory. ET also applies to different types of structures. In some structures resources move through positions and in others they do not. The problems of prediction in these two types are quite different. Yet both are within the scope of ET.

The scope of ET has been extended because broad scope is essential for any theory to pass beyond the limits of the laboratory. Within the confines of the laboratory, scope matters little insofar as the application of theory is concerned. Even the narrowest of theories can be applied in the lab—and have been—but only when the ideal and pure conditions they require can be realized. Outside the lab, when applying theory to historical and contemporary social structures, an array of relations and structures are found mixed together. In the face of such complexity, theories of narrow scope theory cannot be applied. Or worse, they are applied and offer faulty explanations and imprecise predictions.

This chapter is organized to reflect ET's scope. We begin with the seven structural conditions that affect activity. For that discussion, we consider only simple centralized networks in which a single central position is connected to a number of peripherals who are not connected to each other. Both exchange and coercive structures are examined so that qualities of the two can be highlighted. We continue by examining two kinds of social structures that differ in resource movement. We first consider "flow networks," which are social structures in which resources flow through one or more positions. Next we take up discrete networks, ones in which resources flow only between and not through positions. We conclude by looking toward further scope extensions.

MODELING ACTORS' DECISIONS

ET applies to relations with mixed motives and to social structures composed of those relations. Two actors' motives are mixed in any relation containing at least one state in which both prefer agreement over disagreement. For example, exchange is a mixed-motive relation because both gain more when exchange occurs than when the two disagree and fail to exchange. The capitalist seeks the labor of the worker but wants to pay as little as possible for it. The worker seeks as large a wage as possible and exchanges labor for it. Said somewhat differently, both capitalist and worker want to exchange but seek different and opposed terms of that exchange. Conversely, exchange is possible only when there is at least one exchange ratio for which both benefit more than when not exchanging. A wage, which is price per unit of labor, is an exchange ratio.

Coercion is also a mixed motive relation for analogous reasons. The coercer gains a positive sanction at agreement but gains nothing at disagreement when negatively sanctioning the coercee. The coercee loses less when agreeing and sending the coercer a positive sanction than when receiving the negative. Weber referred to mixed-motive relations as ones in which the actors' interests are opposed but complementary ([1918] 1968). Undoubtedly, many social relations are mixed motive.

When actors choose among relations and structures in which to act, Principle 1 applies and asserts that all social actors act to maximize their expected preference state alteration. Principle 1 is a rationality principle and can be thought of as bringing actors to the relations in which they face each other. That principle alone is not enough to explain or predict behavior in relations like coercion and exchange where motives are mixed, however. For example, when capitalists and workers negotiate over wages, Principle 1 asserts that workers seek to receive the highest possible wages and capitalists seek to pay wages as low as possible. But that principle alone cannot predict the wage at which the two will reach agreement. To generate that prediction, ET uses resistance.

The resistance factor to the right of Equation 10.1 captures the mixed motives of an actor who (1) *competes* to gain higher payoffs as given by the factor in the numerator but (2) *cooperates* to arrive at agreements as given by the factor in the denominator. Let P_i be actor i's payoff from a possible agreement, $P_{i\max}$ be i's best possible outcome, and P_{icon} be i's payoff at confrontation, when no agreement occurs. For example, in exchange the payoff at confrontation is frequently zero. The numerator, $P_{i\max} - P_i$, is i's interest in gaining a better payoff, and the denominator, $P_i - P_{icon}$ is i's interest in avoiding confrontation. The resistance of i, R_i, is

$$R_i = \frac{P_{i\max} - P_i}{P_i - P_{icon}} \qquad (10.1)$$

Principle 2 asserts that agreements occur at the point of equal resistance for undifferentiated actors in a full information system. Principle 2 calls for us to set A's and B's resistance equal to each other, giving

$$R_A = \frac{P_{A\max} - P_A}{P_A - P_{Acon}} = \frac{P_{B\max} - P_B}{P_B - P_{Bcon}} = R_B \qquad (10.2)$$

Resistance will now be applied to Figure 10.3, where three exchange relations are connected at A. The three are identical so consider any one. B has a resource worthless to B but worth 10 to A. Said somewhat differently, B's resource has exchange value only. By contrast, A's resources are valuable to A and to B. When transmitted as sanctions, for each of A's resources there is a loss of one to A and a gain of one when received by B. Importantly, each of these valuations is asserted for the designated actor only. For example, A's resource is valued at 1 to A and also at 1 to B, but the utility associated with that valuation for A and B can be quite different. That utilities can be quite different matters not because the utilities of actors are never compared. Instead, all that is compared in resistance equations are *ratios* of valued flows and, because they are ratios, the utility dimension cancels out.[2]

Now resistance will be used to solve for x, the number of resources transmitted by A in exchange for B's single resource. Let $P_B = x$ and $P_A = 10 - x$. When one resource is the smallest unit, $P_{Bmax} = 9$ when $x = 9$ and $P_{Amax} = 9$ when $x = 1$. $P_{Acon} = 0$ and $P_{Bcon} = 0$ when no sanctions flow. Therefore

$$R_A = \frac{9 - P_A}{P_A - 0} = \frac{9 - P_B}{P_B - 0} = R_B$$

and

$$R_A = \frac{9 - (10 - x)}{10 - x} = \frac{9 - x}{x} = R_B$$

Then $P_A = 5$ and $P_B = 5$ when A pays 5 for B's sanction.

For ET all *mixed-motive relations*, including the exchange relation just solved, are by definition *power relations*.[3] Here we have a theoretically pure and fully isolated exchange relation where nothing advantages one actor over the other. Therefore, this *equiresistance* solution is *equipower*. In coercive relations like those of Figure 10.4, there is an equiresistance point, which is the predicted point of agreement between coercer and coercee. But at that point C, the coercer is advantaged at the expense of D, the coercee. Therefore in coercion, equiresistance is not equipower because at equiresistance C is exercising power by threat of the negative over the coercee Ds.

In Figure 10.4 there are three coercive relations to which resistance is now applied. Since the three are identical, apply resistance to any one. Let x be the number of sanctions sent by D in response to C's threat. Therefore at agreement, $P_C = x$ and $P_D = -x$. Since the strength of the negative sanction is -10, D will send at most 9 positives to C. Therefore $P_{Cmax} = 9$. Sending the negative is costly. Thus it is possible that C will not send it even when no positives are received. Therefore $P_{Dmax} = 0$ when no sanctions flow. At confrontation the negative sanction is transmitted and, from Figure 10.4, $P_{Ccon} = -1$ while $P_{Dcon} = -10$.

$$R_C = \frac{9 - x}{x - (-1)} = \frac{0 - (-x)}{-x - (-10)} = R_D$$

Therefore $x = 4.5$. That result means that D, the coercee, transmits 4.5 positive sanctions to C such that $P_C = 4.5$ and $P_D = -4.5$. Because $x = 4.5$ is at equiresistance, it is the predicted compromise point. Nevertheless, as already explained, $x = 4.5$ is not equipower. To the contrary, at the $x = 4.5$ equiresistance agreement, since the relation is coercive, C is exercising power over D.

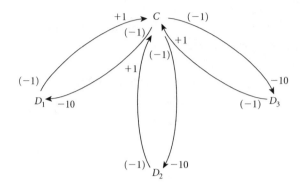

Figure 10.4   A Coercive Branch Connected at C

STRUCTURAL CONDITIONS

Structural conditions are contingencies across relations connected at a node that advantage some actors at the expense of others. In experiments, structural conditions are set as initial conditions. In the field, historical and contemporary power structures reproduce themselves by reproducing the structural conditions producing power in them. For example, capitalism reproduces itself, at least in part, by reproducing a surplus of workers over jobs—what Marx called the "reserve industrial army." In ET the surplus of workers over jobs is an example of exclusion, a structural condition that is introduced in the following. Bureaucracies reproduce themselves and their relations of domination by reproducing structured hierarchies through which people are mobile. This structural condition, hierarchy/mobility, is also introduced in the following.

To introduce structural conditions, we will initially consider only simple networks. Simple networks are ones in which N positions are connected to a single central position and not to each other. Later sections generalize the discussion to complex structures. Here five structural conditions that are types of connection are introduced as are two further structural conditions that, though not themselves types of connection, are derived from two of those types.

Types of connection are defined by the quantities N, M, and Q. Those three define the number of others to which the actor is connected and the maximum and minimum numbers of relations in which the actor can benefit. N is degree, the number of relations connected to the node. M is the maximum number of relations in which the actor can benefit. Q is the minimum number of relations in which agreement must be concluded for the actor to benefit from any one. Let i be any actor: by definition $N_i \geq M_i \geq Q_i \geq 1$ and

i is inclusively connected if $N_i = M_i = Q_i > 1$.

i is exclusively connected if $N_i > M_i \geq Q_i = 1$.

i is null connected if $N_i = M_i > Q_i = 1$.

i is inclusive-exclusively connected if $N_i > M_i \geq Q_i > 1$.

i is inclusive-null connected if $N_i = M_i > Q_i > 1$.

i is singularly connected if $N_i = M_i = Q_i = 1$.

The six types are exhaustive for N, M, and Q.

Null and exclusive connections are defined by comparing N, the number of relations incident at a node, to M, the largest number of relations in which the actor at the node can benefit. When the two are equal, the connection is null. Null connected relations are independent in that exchange or coercion goes forward in each relation exactly as it would were the other relations not present. It immediately follows that resistance is applied to null connected exchange and coercive structures exactly as it was earlier to individual exchange and coercive relations.

By contrast, as will be shown shortly, resistance finds that, in simple networks, exclusively connected nodes are advantaged. For example, outside the laboratory an array of circumstances determines the sizes N and M. When a firm has exactly M suppliers, one each for N components, it is null connected and neither firm nor suppliers is advantaged. But if it has a surplus of suppliers, $N > M$, the connection is exclusive, and the firm is advantaged over the suppliers. That advantage may result in better prices, more favorable contractual conditions, and/or other advantages.

Inclusive connection occurs when Q, the minimum number of relations that must be completed, is larger than 1. $Q > 1$ may result when all of a set of diverse resources is needed for any to be of value or may result from a division of labor in which each part of the labor is useful only when combined with the others. Alternatively, in experiments and in the field, $Q > 1$ may be the result of a threshold effect. For example, when moving a piano requires the work of three, $Q = 3$ and, when only two show up to move it, the work cannot be done. Threshold effects can be produced in the lab where Q may be set at any value such that subjects must complete at least that number to benefit from any exchange. Importantly, when $N = M = Q > 1$, in simple structures, and regardless of the reason for Q being larger than 1, the inclusively connected central node is disadvantaged.

RESISTANCE IN STRUCTURES

We now show how resistance factors are modified for each type of connection. Both structures with exchange relations and those with coercive relations will be modeled. Not to be discussed here is null connection, which, as explained, was already covered when resistance was applied to isolated relations. When both actors are singularly connected, they are in a dyad and that too has already been covered. The structures discussed will be simple 3-branch structures of Figure 10.3 or 10.4. ET's application to complex exchange structures is covered in later sections.

Exclusion

The Figure 10.3 branch network is exclusively connected when A can exchange with one or two of the Bs; then $N = 3$ and $M = 1$ or $M = 2$ and $Q = 1$. Consider the latter and call the structure Br321. Br321 is a *strong exchange structure*, where A is the high power position. The Bs become low power in the following way. All Bs are motivated to exchange and will make offers that are A's exclusive alternatives. Once A has received two offers, A's P_{con} for the third is not zero as in the dyad but increases to the best of the two offers in hand.

Furthermore, the most that the third B can hope to gain is just less than that offered by the other Bs. Therefore $P_{\max}$ for the third B is deflated. Both effects shift the point of equiresistance in a direction favoring the high power position at the expense of the low power positions.

Those effects are modeled in the following way. Let P_A^{t-1} be the payoff to A from one of A's exclusive alternatives at time $t-1$. Then $P_{A\text{con}} = P_A^{t-1}$, the cost of confrontation for A at t, is the alternative payoff already offered at $t-1$. $P_{\max}$ for B now has a lower upper bound: $P_{B\max} = P_B^{t-1}$, which is the payoff to B of an offer just better for A than A's alternative to that B. Thus the resistance expression for a strong power structure, where R_A^H is the resistance of the high power A and R_B^L is the resistance of any low power B, is

$$R_A^H = \frac{P_{A\max} - P_A}{P_A - P_A^{t-1}} = \frac{P_B^{t-1} - P_B}{P_B - P_{B\text{con}}} = R_B^L \tag{10.3}$$

Taking the calculations from Equation 10.2 as the outcome at $t-1$,

$$R_A = \frac{9 - (10 - x)}{(10 - x) - 5} = \frac{4 - x}{x} = R_B$$

and $P_A = 7.5$ and $P_B = 2.5$. Those values are the first step of a power process, for at $t+1$ there are new negotiations, and plugging in the values just calculated gives $P_A = 8.5$ and $P_B = 1.5$. At $t+2$, the iterative process ends, and $P_A = P_{A\max} = 9$ while $P_B = 1$.

The analogous *strong coercive structure* is formulated in the following way. Figure 10.4 is a Br321 strong coercive structure when C receives positive sanctions from two Ds and negatively sanctions the third. *The strong coercive structure is analogous to the strong exchange structure because the high power position reaches agreements with two of those low in power and is in confrontation with the third.*

As already mentioned, unlike exchange where confrontation is the absence of sanction flows, for coercion, at confrontation the negative sanction is transmitted by the coercer. As in exchange, those who are low in power make a series of better offers to the high power position. Here that means that the coercees are making better and better offers to the coercer. Treating the calculations for the coercive dyad previously modeled as the first step, at t the C has two offers of 4.5 and

$$R_C = \frac{9 - x}{x - 4.5} = \frac{-5 - (-x)}{-x - (-10)} = R_D$$

Now $x = 7.1$, $P_C = 7.1$, and $P_D = -7.1$. As in exchange, the power process in the coercive structure goes forward until $P_C = P_{C\max} = 9$.

Strong coercive structures are as easy to construct in the lab as are strong exchange structures, but are they found in the field? Are there strong coercive structures in which the coercer routinely sends negative sanctions, thereby producing the competition that maximizes power in the strong coercive structure? There is good reason to suppose that they have existed. For example, Marx's discussion of slavery in Jamaica links high profits to the "reckless sacrifice" of slaves' lives ([1867] 1990, 377ff)—a linkage that suggests strong coercive structures. Similarly, Weber's discussion of Roman slavery where, "The ancient slave estate devours human beings as the modern blast furnace devours coal" ([1916] 1963, 346), implies that those coercive structures were strong.

Nevertheless, strong coercive structures are by no means as frequently encountered historically as are strong exchange structures, and the reason lies in this. The confrontations necessary for an exchange structure to be strong can be costless because, for them, no sanctions flow. By contrast, for strong coercive structures, confrontation always has a cost because confrontation is the transmission of the negative sanction.

There is a second kind of coercive structure, and for it, instances of the strong power are well known. Imagine the Figure 10.4 structure with the three relations reversed such that there is a single coercee and three coercers. Then a *strong coercee structure* is one in which only one of three Cs can benefit from the D's positive sanction while the others are excluded. Since D is advantaged, the Cs compete such that x, the size of the sanction sent by D, declines toward zero. Let states be coercers and mobile corporations the coercees. Corporations can choose the state in which to locate, and the coercee central structure explains the oft-observed fact that, when selecting a location, corporations come to pay no taxes. Location and its effects are not new. Weber noted that it was the mobility of capital between the small states of early modern Europe that was decisive for capitalist development ([1918] 1968, 352).

Hierarchy/Mobility

While not a type of connection, people's mobility in hierarchies, ET finds, is analogous to exclusive connection. When higher positions are advantaged by high pay and perquisites, as they always are in bureaucracies, subordinates will compete to move up, but only some will be selected. The rest will be excluded from mobility. Then competitive mobility in hierarchies is identical to exclusion in the strength of its effects.

Recognizing hierarchy/mobility allows the theorist to infer that organizational hierarchies have centralized control and to locate in competitive mobility the reason for that centralization. Importantly, mobility can occur only when people are *separated* from ownership of their positions—a condition used by Weber ([1918] 1968) to distinguish structures where power is centralized from structures where it is not. For example, in feudal structures, where all owned their positions, subordinates were not mobile and power was not centralized. Of course, there were power differences in feudalism, but they can be traced to differential ownership of land and the military forces consequently supported. Experimental studies that contrasted hierarchies with and without mobility support these inferences about historical power structures (Willer 1987).

Inclusion

The Figure 10.3 exchange network is *inclusively connected* when A must exchange with all three Bs to benefit from any of its exchanges. Call that network Br333. In fact, any simple network in which $N = M = Q$ for the central position is inclusively connected. Examples include the manufacturer who needs all of an array of parts from single suppliers and the boss with irreplaceable subordinates working in highly interdependent jobs. Assume that A exchanges first at equipower such that $P_{Ab} = 5$. Since A loses the value of its first exchange if its second exchange is not completed, for the second exchange, $P_{Abcon} = -P_{Ab} = -5$ and

$$R_A^I = \frac{P_{A\max} - P_A}{P_A - (-P_{Ab})} = \frac{P_{B\max} - P_B}{P_B - 0} = R_B \qquad (10.4)$$

Since for the first exchange $P_{Ab} = 5$, for the second

$$R_A^I = \frac{9 - (10 - x)}{(10 - x) - (-5)} = \frac{9 - x}{x} = R_B$$

$P_A = 4.13$ and $P_B = 5.87$ and the peripheral B is exercising power over the central A.

More generally, the effect of inclusion increases with Q, the number of inclusively connected relations. For example, for the third exchange of the preceding example, the payoffs from the first two could be lost. Therefore $P_{Abcon} = -(5 + 4.13)$ and $P_A = 3.65$. When exchanges in this structure are repeated, soon all will realize that the peripheral exchanging last gains the best payoff. With all seeking to exchange last, exchanges approach simultaneity and A's payoffs across exchanges become increasingly similar. Then Equation 10.5 is used for all exchanges:

$$R_A^I = \frac{P_{A\max} = P_A}{QP_A} = \frac{P_{B\max} - P_B}{P_B - 0} = R_B \qquad (10.5)$$

Coercive structures are inclusively connected for the same conditions, as are exchange structures, and with the same kind of effect. An inclusively connected C in Figure 10.4 will still exercise power by force-threat, but to a lesser degree due to inclusion. If agreements are simultaneous, use Equation 10.5 together with the initial conditions for coercive relations to calculate C's payoffs. When $Q = 3$, as it does in Figure 10.3, $P_C = 3.37$ and $P_D = -3.37$.

Ordering

Very frequently the relations in which we engage occur in a fixed sequence. For example, I have an infection, but I cannot go directly to the druggist for the antibiotic. Instead, I must first visit my physician and pay her a fee for access to the drug I need. Due to ordering, the physician, acting as a gatekeeper, benefits because I pay a fee. A gatekeeper controls access to value that she or he does not own. When I am ill, I value drugs that will make me well. The physician gatekeeps me. Alternatively, I want to open a business, but, to do so, I must first have my building approved by the fire marshal. The fire marshal is a gatekeeper. So that I can open my business on time, I am more than willing to pay the fire marshal a fee even though the law interprets my payment as corruption of a public official. Examples of gatekeeping range from the patrons of antiquity, through your departmental secretary, to the corrupt officials of today.

More generally, the order in which exchanges must occur, though not a type of connection, is a structural condition. If A of Figure 10.3 must exchange with B_1 before B_2 and with B_2 before B_3, then A is most disadvantaged in the first exchange, less so in the second, and exchanges at equipower in the third. In each case, A's disadvantage stems from fear of loss of future benefits; thus P_{Acon} is the sum of losses resulting from failure to exchange now. In fact, the effects in ordering are identical to those of inclusion, but in reverse. More precisely, the effects of the two are the same except in flow networks (see later discussion). Thus Equation 10.4 is applied such that the largest effects come first and the last exchange is at equipower.

Inclusion-Exclusion Connection

The 3-branch structure of Figure 10.3 is the smallest network in which inclusive-exclusive connection can occur. Called Br322, A exchanges maximally with two Bs and must complete exchanges with both to benefit from either. A has three opportunities to exchange and needs make only two; therefore the first exchange is not affected by inclusion. With the completion of that exchange, $Q = 1$ and the last two relations are not inclusively connected. Therefore inclusion does not affect the second exchange. By contrast, exclusion affects all three exchanges. It follows that, in Br322 and all inclusive-exclusively connected simple networks, the central inclusive-exclusively connected position is high power and gains maximally exactly as it does when only exclusively connected.

ET asserts that if C in Figure 10.4 is a strong power coercer, the coercive structure, though inclusively connected, is unaffected by inclusion. In coercion, as in exchange, the competition produced by strong power eliminates the effect of inclusion. Thus the strong power coercer benefits maximally.

Inclusion-Null Connection

The 3-branch structure of Figure 10.3 is also the smallest network in which inclusive-null connection can occur. Called Br332, A can exchange with all three Bs but must complete at least two of the three exchanges to benefit from any. Since A has three opportunities to exchange and must make only two, the first exchange is not affected by inclusion. With the completion of that exchange, $Q = 1$ and inclusion does not affect the second exchange or third exchange. Thus A is equipower with the Bs exactly as any null connected A—and similarly for all inclusive-exclusively connected central positions in simple networks. An inclusive-null connected coercer in Figure 10.4 must complete two of three agreements but is unaffected by inclusion. That C will gain payoffs as a consequence of threats to transmit negatives in each relation. And the payments thereby received are predicted to be of exactly the same size as those gained by a coercer with no inclusive connection.

When Ordering Occurs with Other Structural Conditions

Since ordering shares qualities with inclusion, it should not be surprising that its effects are similarly eliminated by either exclusive or null connection. For example, two competing gatekeepers will bid against each other, thus eliminating the effect of ordering (Corra and Willer 2002). Similarly, two gatekeepers who are alternatives that are not exclusive will also not benefit from ordering: they will not gain fees. Why then is the social world full of multiple gatekeepers who yet gain fees? They are able to do so by controlling competition, frequently through state licensing boards.

Finally, consider the combined effect of ordering and inclusion. The effects of ordering and inclusion are combined when a node must complete all of Q exchanges in a fixed order and has no alternatives that can be substituted. Surprisingly, the joint effect of the two appears to be larger than twice the effect of either condition taken individually. Exactly why remains to be seen.

Conformational Scope

Resistance predictions for all seven power conditions just discussed have been supported in experimental tests—with one exception (Willer 1999). The exception is the impact of inclusion and ordering on coercive structures that has yet to be studied. ET is an evolving theory and that evolution has now reached the point that, with the exception just noted, experimental tests cover *all* structural conditions thus far discovered. Equally important, experimental tests cover all of the joint effects just discussed. Since no other social theory has discovered more than two structural conditions, the support for ET is substantially broader than other theories to which it has been compared.[4] These formulations for power conditions now form a set of tools awaiting use in the natural settings for institutional and historical-comparative investigations.

FLOW NETWORKS

Flow networks contain resources that move through one or more positions. For instance, A–B–C is a flow network if A sends resource w to B and B sends w to C. That is to say, because w has flowed through B, A–B–C is a flow network. The distribution of power in flow networks is affected by (1) the sequence in which exchanges occur and (2) the interdependence of exchanges within the network. Exchanges are sequential so that resources can flow through the network and are interdependent because the outcomes of all previous exchanges affect the outcome in the current exchange.

Since exchanges in flow networks are sequential and interdependent, the effects of power exercise in one relation should extend to adjacent exchange relations and beyond. As a result, positions are able to exercise power at a distance over positions to which they are not directly connected (Willer 2003). For instance, in the A–B–C network previously discussed, power can be exercised not only between A and B and between B and C positions but also across A and C positions.

As a result of sequentiality, inclusion and ordering are always initial structural conditions in flow networks. Consider again the smallest possible flow network, A–B–C (Figure 10.5), under the following initial conditions. A has a resource w, C wants w, B and C have multiple units of the resource $, and A and B want $. In this structure, B is the middleman, a position that appropriates (buys) a resource with the purpose of alienating (selling) that resource to another position for a profit. To realize a profit, B must participate

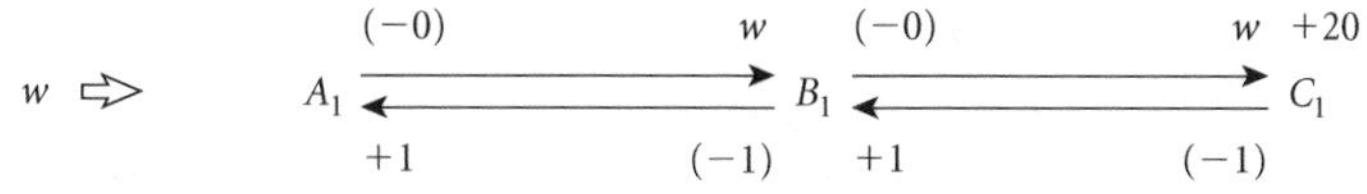

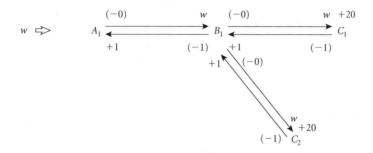

Figure 10.5 A Three-Position Flow Network

Figure 10.6 A Flow Network Where Exclusion Masks the Effects of Inclusion

in two exchanges in the following sequence. First, B must buy w from A using units of \$. Second, B must sell w to C for more units of \$ than it used to appropriate w. Because B must buy w before it can sell to C, A is B's gatekeeper and B is disadvantaged by ordering in the A–B exchange. Furthermore, B is disadvantaged by inclusion in the second exchange because B needs to recover the units of \$ it invested in buying w.

Except under conditions discussed later—when negotiations and exchanges do not occur together—middlemen are structurally disadvantaged in flow networks. Like B in the above network, middlemen will always be disadvantaged by ordering in their first exchange and by inclusion in their second exchange. Since all flow networks contain at least one middleman, all flow networks will contain positions that are connected by ordering and inclusion.

Because exclusion eliminates the effects of inclusion and ordering, it is the only structural condition that can advantage the middleman. Nevertheless, when exclusion is present in flow networks, it is never the only power condition. Instead, either ordering or inclusion will also be present. As seen in the previous section, however, ET asserts that, when exclusion occurs in conjunction with either ordering or inclusion, the effects of exclusion eliminate the effects of the other structural conditions. For example, examine the B–C exchange in the network of Figure 10.6 where B, as a middleman, is disadvantaged by inclusion. Because B has two exclusive alternative Cs to whom it can sell resource w, B is advantaged by exclusion, an advantage that eliminates the effect of inclusion.

Willer (2003) offered the first extension of resistance to predict exchange ratios in flow networks. The simultaneous mode of solution presented by Willer (2003) accounted for the interdependency of exchanges across a flow network. Since, in flow networks, each exchange is dependent on what occurs in other exchanges, Willer's model, here called the interdependency exchange model (IEM), forms and solves simultaneously a series of resistance equations, one for each subnetwork. We will now examine how exchange ratios are predicted in flow networks, first applying that model and then applying a model recently introduced by Emanuelson.

Within flow networks, the payoff to a position takes into consideration all the flows to and from it. In the flow networks of Figures 10.5 and 10.6, as in networks just discussed, the resource flowing from left to right is called w and the resource flowing from right to left is called \$. Exchange occurs when one w is exchanged for a quantity of \$. The quantity of \$ that flows in the first exchange is X and the quantity of \$ in the second exchange is Y. The resource w is valued only by C: it is worth \$20. In the A–B–C network of Figure 10.5, first, w flows from A to B at no cost to A while X \$ units flow from B to A. Since A receives X, A's payoff is $P_A = X$. Next, w flows from B to C at no cost to B while Y \$ units flow from C to B. P_B sent X and received Y so $P_B = Y - X$. Finally, since C sent Y \$ units in exchange for w, $P_C = 20 - Y$.

Although there is no flow network that does not contain at least inclusion and ordering, it is possible to create equations that reflect what would happen in the absence of any structural power condition. The equal power equations for flow networks are written to provide an equipower baseline to be compared to exchanges under other structural conditions. For the IEM, P_{max} for the equipower baseline resistance equation equals the total value available in the network minus one times the number of other positions in the network. In the preceding example, the total value available is \$20, the value of w to C. For example, assume that no structural conditions are in the A–B–C network and that the total value available for negotiation equals 20. As will be remembered, actors exchange only when gaining a positive payoff. Here the minimum positive payoff is 1. A should get its maximum payoff when all the other positions in the network, B and C, receive that minimum payoff of 1. The minimum payoff to A, $P_A = 1$, occurs when B buys the widget for one \$ unit. The minimum payoff to C, $P_C = 1$, occurs when B sells the widget for 19 \$ units. Therefore $X = 1$ and $Y = 19$. $P_B = Y - X$ and $P_{Bmax} = 19 - 1 = 18$. In fact, $P_{max} = 18$ for A and C as well. Furthermore, at equipower, P_{con}, which occurs at no exchange, equals zero for all actors.

Using the aforementioned payoffs, IEM writes two equal power resistance equations, one for the A–B exchange and one for the B–C exchange. When R_{Ab} is the resistance of A relative to B and similarly for the other expressions,

$$R_{Ab} = \frac{18 - X}{X - 0} = \frac{18 - (Y - X)}{(Y - X) - 0} = R_{Ba} \qquad (10.6)$$

$$R_{Bc} = \frac{18 - (Y - X)}{(Y - X) - 0} = \frac{18 - (20 - Y)}{(20 - Y) - 0} = R_{Cb} \qquad (10.7)$$

We now have two equations with two unknowns. Solving simultaneously, IEM finds that, at equal power, the payoffs to all positions are equal, $P_A = 6.67$, $P_B = 6.67$, and $P_C = 6.67$.

Nevertheless, for the A–B–C network of Figure 10.5, ordering creates power differences in the A–B exchange, and inclusion creates power differences in the B–C exchange. Therefore the preceding equations, while they can be solved for the equipower baseline, do not offer realistic predictions for the network. For example, in the A–B exchange, if B does not complete exchange with A, B will not gain Y from C. Without Y, B cannot gain its $Y - X$ payoff. Therefore $P_{Bacon} = -(Y - X)$, making B lower in power than A. Equation 10.8 finds the point of equiresistance in the A–B exchange.

$$R_{Ab} = \frac{18 - X}{X} = \frac{18 - (Y - X)}{2(Y - X)} = R_{Ba}^0 \qquad (10.8)$$

In the B–C exchange, B is lower power relative to C because, if exchange does not take place, B will lose its payoff, $Y - X$. Therefore $P_{Bccon} = -(Y - X)$. Similar to ordering, the middleman is disadvantaged by its need to engage in two exchanges before gaining its payoff. IEM attributes the same resistance factor to disadvantaged positions connected by ordering and inclusion in that the only change made from the equipower baseline equation is to increase the P_{con} for the disadvantaged position. Equation 10.9 finds the point of equiresistance for the B–C exchange.

$$R_B^l = \frac{18(Y - X)}{2(Y - X)} = \frac{18 - (20 - Y)}{20 - Y} = R_{Cb} \qquad (10.9)$$

Solving the preceding equations simultaneously for the A–B–C network, IEM predicts that $X = 7.6$ and $Y = 12.4$.

As previously mentioned, in the network of Figure 10.6, exclusion eliminates the effects of inclusion. Still, in the A–B relation, ordering disadvantages B, so Equation 10.8 is used. In the B–C relation, B is connected to two exclusive alternative Cs with which to exchange. Therefore unlike in the earlier A–B–C network, the resistance equation written for the B–C relation is not for inclusion but for exclusion. As seen in the previous section, for exclusive connection the values for P_{con} and P_{max} change across exchanges: P_{con} increases for the advantaged actor and P_{max} decreases for the disadvantaged actor. These changes occur because outcomes from previous exchanges alter P_{con} and P_{max}, continuing until equilibrium is reached at the extreme, favoring the high power actor.

In Figure 10.6, B is high power in subnetwork C–B–C because B has two exclusive alternative Cs.[5] P_B^{t-1} represents the payoff to B from one of the Cs at $t - 1$. At t, B will never get less than P_B^{t-1} and, therefore, $P_{Bcon} = P_B^{t-1}$. Either of the Cs cannot gain more from the high power actor than offered by the other C. Consequently, P_{Cmax} for both Cs has an upper bound that equals the payoff of the offer of opposing C at $t - 1$ (P_C^{t-1}). More generally, B's worst world, P_{Bcon}, will progressively get larger and C's best world, P_{Cmax}, will progressively get smaller until the system is driven to its extreme in favor of the B. In Equation 10.10, the resistance factor for the high power B in the strong power subnetwork is on the left and the resistance equation for the low power C in the strong power subnetwork is on the right. Reflected in Equation 10.10 is P_B^{t-1}, the improving worst world for the high power position, and P_C^{t-1}, the declining best world for the low power position.

$$R_B^H = \frac{18 - (Y - X)}{(Y - X) - P_B^{t-1}} = \frac{P_C^{t-1} - (20 - Y)}{(20 - Y) - 0} = R_C^L \qquad (10.10)$$

Solving equations 10.8 and 10.10 for the network of Figure 10.6 yields $X = 12.44$ and $Y = 19$.

IEM's predictions are accurate for some but not all flow networks. IEM's predictions are most accurate in networks that contain strong power subnetworks (i.e., exclusion). In the network of Figure 10.6, IEM predicts that $Y = 19$. The observed mean for Y is 18.74, and 18.74 does not significantly differ from 19. Unfortunately, IEM has trouble predicting networks where power is produced by inclusion and ordering. Out of 10 networks for which data was gathered, IEM's prediction is the worst for the $A–B–C$ network previously discussed, where only ordering and inclusion determine the distribution of payoffs within the network (Emanuelson and Willer 2003). IEM predicts that $X = 7.60$ and $Y = 12.40$ and the observed mean flows are $X = 13.78$ and $Y = 16.23$. With t values of 12.11 and 6.76, respectively, the predictions made by IEM are not close to observations.

Identifying the power of positions is also problematic using IEM. A position can be identified as more or less powerful to the extent that its payoff deviates from what it would receive in the absence of power exercise. To find that deviation, payoffs are compared to the equipower baseline. However, IEM's predictions concerning equal power are not supported by evidence. In the experiments reported by Emanuelson and Willer (2003), an $A–B–C$ network was discussed where the resource w was valued not just by C but also by the middleman B. In this network, IEM would expect to find flows that approach its equal power solution, but it did not. In fact, this network was the second worst predicted by IEM. These results suggest that IEM's solution for equal power is wrong. If so, IEM cannot determine which positions are exercising power and which are subject to that exercise.

To solve the problems of IEM, a new model has been devised by Emanuelson that takes into consideration not only interdependency but also sequentiality of exchanges in flow networks. The new model, the sequential exchange model (SEM), writes equations for each subnetwork and solves them in order. The order of solution matches the order of exchanges across the network.

SEM makes several assumptions not made by IEM. One assumption refers to the treatment of value across a flow network. SEM assumes that value is used up as exchanges are completed across a network. For instance, in the $A–B–C$ network, once A appropriates the X flow after the completion of the $A–B$ exchange, B and C have X fewer units of value over which to negotiate in the $B–C$ exchange than did A and B in the $A–B$ exchange. More generally, every subsequent exchange in a flow network negotiates over less value than did previous exchanges.

Furthermore, SEM asserts that value available for negotiation in each subnetwork is also affected by actors' projections of what is necessary for the completion of exchanges to follow. Actors are modeled as making the assumption that, for all actors in the network who have yet to exchange, enough value must remain for a minimal payoff of one for each. Then that amount is set aside and is not part of the value being negotiated.

SEM also assumes that actors act as if they take into consideration only the gain and loss of flows, in contrast to IEM where actors act as if they consider only payoffs. Therefore for IEM in the $A–B–C$ network, when B is disadvantaged by inclusion, $P_{con} = -(Y - X)$. By contrast, in the $A–B–C$ network SEM assumes that B's $P_{con} = -X$. This mode of solution as used by SEM will differentiate the impacts of inclusion and ordering. Since ordering occurs before inclusion, it occurs in the subnetwork in which there is more value. Thus

SEM implies that ordering will always have a stronger effect than inclusion—an implication supported by empirical evidence.

As a result of these contrasting formulations, the equipower baseline calculated for SEM is distinct from the equipower baseline calculated for IEM. For IEM, when power is equal, P values across subnetworks are equal, an equality that follows from the assumption that value available for negotiation is the same for all subnetworks. By contrast, SEM assumes that value available for negotiations is reduced across the network as exchanges are completed. Since each subsequent subnetwork is dividing less value than did previous subnetworks, payoffs to positions in flow networks at equal power are not equal. For example, in the A–B–C flow network where the total value available for negotiation is 20, A and B negotiate over 19 (1 is subtracted from 20 to ensure that C will get at least a payoff of 1 in the B–C exchange). A and B split 19 equally, so $P_A = 9.5$. And B and C negotiate over $20 - 9.5 = 10.5$, because 9.5 was already appropriated by A and is not available for B–C negotiations. There are no further exchanges in the network so nothing needs to be set aside. Thus at equipower, B and C equally split 10.5, so $P_B = 5.25$ and $P_C = 5.25$; but P_A is substantially larger at 9.5. Flows at equipower are $X = 9.5$ and $Y = 14.75$.

SEM's predictions are strongly supported by evidence. When all subnetworks contain exclusion, predictions made by SEM and IEM are identical. Consequently, since IEM is a good predictor for strong power subnetworks, so is SEM. Furthermore, unlike IEM, SEM makes accurate predictions for many networks in which power is due to inclusion and ordering. In the A–B exchange of the network of Figure 10.6, SEM predicts that X, a flow influenced by ordering, equals 12.44 and IEM predicts that $X = 11.05$. The observed mean is $X = 12.76$. SEM's prediction does not significantly differ from the observed mean, while IEM's prediction does differ at the $<.001$ level.

The greater accuracy of SEM is reflected in its predictions for both A–B–C networks, the one with power differences and the one where w is valued by B such that rates approach equal power. In the A–B–C network with power differences, SEM's prediction of $X = 11.93$ is much closer to the observed mean flow $X = 13.78$ than is IEM's prediction of $X = 7.60$. Although still significantly different from the observed mean at $<.001$, SEM's prediction with a t value of 3.62 is much more accurate than IEM's prediction with a t value of 12.11. A comparison of the predictions for the A–B–C network that approaches equal power with the observed mean flows of $X = 11.45$ and $Y = 15.01$ shows strong support for SEM's predictions.[6] SEM's prediction that $X = 10.56$ differs from the observed mean only at the $<.05$ level and SEM's prediction that $Y = 15.16$ is not significantly different from the observed mean Y. In contrast, as previously mentioned, both predictions made by IEM are significantly different at the $<.001$ level. Importantly, these results also support SEM's conception of equipower flow rates.

As our understanding of flow networks evolves and improves, so does our ability to apply ET to empirical phenomena. For instance, the study of organizations has a long and honored tradition in sociology; however, until recently, few if any mathematical models have been developed that can make predictions for organizations. Because organizations engaged in interorganizational exchanges can be thought of as being in flow networks, we suggest that our SEM model applies. For the future, we expect to extend the SEM model inside organizations to the power relations of hierarchies.

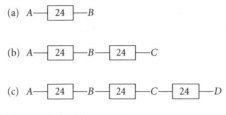

Figure 10.7   Discrete Lines

DISCRETE NETWORKS

This section takes up ET's understandings of power and the effects of power in discrete networks like those first studied by Stolte and Emerson (1977). Discrete networks are networks in which no resources flow through any position. In the ones studied by Stolte and Emerson, subjects did not exchange. Instead, they divided a pool of resources set between each pair of positions as in Figure 10.7. Because resources could flow only to the two positions dividing them and could not flow through those positions, their networks were discrete. We also follow Stolte and Emerson by adopting the rule that each position can divide at most one resource pool for a given time period, called the 1-exchange rule by Markovsky, Willer, and Patton ([1988] 1999). That time period was a round for negotiation. Finally, resource pools are all the same size, and following Cook and Emerson (1978), that size is set at 24 units. Though actors are dividing pools, not exchanging, we will follow the convention that refers to those activities as exchanges.

Resource Pools and Knotty Problems

Resource pool networks have been more extensively investigated by sociologists than any other type of structure. This focus is not because of their empirical significance: it is doubtful that resource pool networks exist outside the laboratory. Nevertheless, the study of resource pool networks can be defended both empirically and theoretically. Empirically, resource pool networks are easily created in the laboratory and, once created, easily understood by experimental subjects. Theoretically, resource pool networks pose difficult problems for theory, perhaps surprisingly difficult given their simplicity. For example, unlike exchange relations where two distinct resources flow in opposite directions, resource pools are completely symmetrical and have no direction whatsoever. That lack of directionality poses problems for theory because it gives no clues concerning who is advantaged or who will exchange with whom.

Furthermore, though resource pools may be found only in the lab, they have important commonalities with exchange relations. For example, the two actors who divide resources gain nothing when they cannot agree on the terms of the division just as do the two who cannot settle on the terms of an exchange. Further, for any division, the more resources gained by one, the fewer gained by the other. Thus for all agreements, the interests of the two are opposed, just as they are in exchange. Taken together, like exchange, resource pools are a mixed-motive game. Furthermore, outside the lab there may be no resource pool networks, but there are mixed-motive discrete social structures. For example, a structure in which all resources are services is discrete because services are consumed as they are received and thus cannot flow through positions. From these similarities, it follows that there are practical reasons to study resource pool networks.

Moreover, much can be learned—and has been learned—about developing a general theory of structures from studying resource pool networks. For instance, all of the structural conditions that occur in flow networks were studied first in discrete networks. When studied there, each condition could be investigated in isolation from the others and, as a result, theory predicting the size of the effects could be readily and precisely tested. Had those conditions not been previously studied and understood in discrete networks, flow networks may have posed such difficult problems that predicting their flows might yet be impossible.

This section addresses three related problems for theory posed by 1-exchange resource pool networks: distal effects, the shape of power, and network breaks. A structure has distal effects when change in one part affects relations at one or more steps removed. Distal effects are discussed, albeit briefly, in the subsection to follow. "The shape of power" refers to the significance of configuration in 1-exchange resource pool networks. In these networks, only exclusion determines power and only configuration determines who is and is not excluded. Therefore configuration is the only condition determining power differences. As will be seen, strong, weak, and equal power are three distinct kinds of network configurations with three distinct power levels. How the three are distinguished and why they produce different degrees of power are discussed in the second subsection to follow. Because all three types of networks are treated extensively elsewhere (Willer 1999), this discussion will also be relatively brief.

Network breaks is the third problem posed by discrete networks. Discussed in the third subsection to follow, breaks are relations that are never used. Network breaks are important because only when they are accurately located can subnetworks be broken out and analyzed to determine whether they are strong, equal, or weak power. Breaks are also important because they are barriers limiting the distance through which distal effects can occur. Furthermore, breaks are produced by power conditions that are by no means obvious from the configuration of the network—as in Figure 10.9. Thus the problems posed by network breaks interact with the problems posed by distal effects and by network configurations to form a single complex problem. But here the three are taken up one at a time. Because breaks are not well understood yet should be, they will be discussed in more detail than the other two problems.

Distal Effects

The lines of Figure 10.7 are now used to explain distal effects. In those networks resource pools are drawn between each pair of positions. (In fact, Figures 10.8, 10.9, and 10.10 are also of resource pool networks, but there the pools are understood, not drawn.) The network in Figure 10.7a is a dyad and, of course, equipower. A and B will divide their resource pool equally. But the Figure 10.7b 3-Line is not equal power, both because B has two exchange partners, A and C, and because it is limited to a single exchange. Since only one will exchange with B, the other will be excluded and gain nothing. In fact, the connection at B is

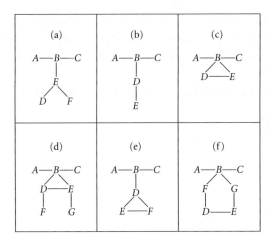

Figure 10.8   When Breaks Do and Do Not Occur

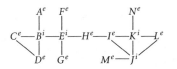

Figure 10.9   Complex Discrete Network

Figure 10.10   Discrete Network with Breaks

exclusive, as are all connections of two or more relations in 1-exchange networks. Seeking to avoid exclusion, *A* and *C* will make better and better offers to *B*. In fact the network in Figure 10.7b is a strong power structure. In it *B*, the high power position, gains maximally, either *A* or *C* exchanges to gain very little, and the other is excluded and gains nothing.

Distal effects can be discerned by comparing the dyad and 3-Line. In the dyad, *A* and *B* exchange at equipower, but in the 3-Line *B* exercises power over *A* and gains almost all of the resource pool. This difference is due wholly to the addition of *C*. That is to say, *A*'s fate in exchanging—whether *A* gains 12 resources all the time or 1 resource half the time—is not determined within the *A*–*B* relation but by whether there is a *C* at one step removed.

The third network of Figure 10.7c shows that distal effects are by no means limited to a single step. There *D* has been added to form a 4-Line where power differences occur but only at medial levels. Now *A* is by no means as powerless as in the triad. Of course, *B* can still exclude *A*, but power is not extreme because *C*, having *D* as an exchange partner, will not bid against *A*. Therefore the addition of *D* two steps from *B* and three steps from *A* reduces *B*'s power over *A*. As a result, *B* is higher power and *A* is lower—and similarly for *C* and *D*. As explained later, the 4-Line is a weak power network.

As can be seen from the examples, distal effects are quite different from power-at-a-distance effects of the flow networks discussed in the previous section. For power-at-a-distance, a position exercises power beyond adjacencies, a phenomenon that cannot occur in discrete networks. It cannot occur here because power exercise can occur only among positions that are linked by common resource flows, but in discrete networks flows occur only between adjacencies. Conversely, distal effects cannot occur in flow networks, a postulation that we leave to the reader to prove.

Configuration and Power

In this section we distinguish strong, weak, and equal power networks and explain how power is predicted in each. Strong power networks contain two and only two kinds of positions: (1) high power positions, which are never excluded, and low power positions, at least one of which must always be excluded. Low power positions are connected only to high power positions (Simpson and Willer 1999). The 3-Line of Figure 10.7b and the 5-Line *A–B–C–D–E* network are both strong power. In the first, it is the central position that is high power, but in the 5-Line *B* and *D* are high power while one of *A*, *C*, or *E*—the low power positions—must be excluded.

Once a strong power structure has been identified, predicting power and thus exchange ratios is quite easy. Generalizing the discussion of the 3-Line above, low power positions engage in a bidding war, the result of which is to move the exchange ratio to the extreme favoring the high power position(s).

In equal power networks all positions have exactly the same degree (Girard and Borch 2003). That is to say, all are connected to the same number of others, and as a result, all positions in the network can be distinguished only by the labels we give them. Since positions are identical, none are advantaged. Therefore all exchange at equal power. In resource pool networks, when exchanges are equipower, each actor receives the same number of resources.[7]

All other networks are weak power and exchanges between higher and lower power positions occur at medial divisions that are neither equal as in equal power networks nor extreme as in strong power networks.[8] ET predicts these unequal resource divisions in the following way. First, the exchange-seek likelihood that the position is included (1 − likelihood of exclusion) is calculated. The exchange-seek likelihood assumes that all positions seek exchange equally with all partners and calculates the joint probability that they will exchange. For example, in the 4-Line of Figure 10.7c, *A* always seeks exchange with *B* but *B* seeks exchange half the time with *A* and half the time with *C*. *C* seeks exchange half the time with *B* and half the time with *D*. Thus the joint probability that *B* and *C* will exchange is $.5 \times .5 = .25$. *A* and *D* are included and exchange except when *B* and *C* exchange with each other. Therefore the probability that *A* is included is .75 and similarly for *D*, while *B* and *C* are included in all exchanges.

Following Lovaglia et al. ([1995] 1999), in weak power networks P_{max} equals one half the pool plus one half the pool times the probability of being included. Thus $P_{Amax} = 12 + 12 \times .75 = 21$ while $P_{Bmax} = 12 + 12 \times 1 = 24$. And P_{con} equals one half the pool times the probability of being included. Thus $P_{Acon} = 12 \times .75 = 9$ and $P_{Bcon} = 12 \times 1 = 12$. Plugging these values into Equation 10.2 yields

$$R_A = \frac{21 - P_A}{P_A - 9} = \frac{24 - P_B}{P_B - 12} = R_B \qquad (10.11)$$

$P_A = 10.5$ and $P_B = 13.5$, both of which are supported experimentally (Emanuelson and Willer 2004; Emanuelson 2005).

While quite simple in conception, the prediction of weak power exchange ratios is not as simple as just shown for networks other than the 4-Line. It is not because the calculation of exchange-seek likelihoods becomes more complex for larger, denser networks, a complexity that explodes as the number of nodes and relations increases. Fortunately, a program to calculate likelihoods for networks up to approximately 20 positions is included as an applet on Willer's University of South Carolina website at http://www.cas.sc.edu/socy/faculty/willer/index.html. We will return to that size-related scope limit in the next subsection.

Breaking Networks and Finding Substructures

Look over the networks of Figure 10.8. Of the six networks displayed, none is readily comprehended in light of the concepts presented in this section. Looking again, the Figure 10.8a network actually does fit the definition of strong power. *B* and *E* are certainly high power positions, for each has two partners one of which is always excluded. Nevertheless, *B* and *E* are connected to each other. While that connection seems odd, the definition of strong power is silent about connections between high power positions (see preceding discussion). The remaining networks do not appear to be tractable, however. What are these networks? Who exchanges with whom? Who is advantaged?

These are compound networks. Compound networks are composed of two or more subnetworks, and each of those subnetworks is one of the three types: strong, weak, or equal power. Some compound networks break into their component parts. Some do not. Figure 10.8 displays examples of both. We begin with compound networks that break.

Simpson and Willer (1999) have shown that breaks occur only between high power positions and positions that are never excluded. This is a simple rule, but in its application there is one complication. The rule does not refer to excludability in the compound network. Instead, the rule refers to whether the position is excudable after all breaks have been located and removed. As will be seen, some positions that are excludable in the compound are not excludable when subnetworks are broken out. Therefore some breaks will be initially hidden and can be uncovered only by tentatively removing relations that are possible breaks.

Fortunately, *suboptimality* is a clue that helps to find all possible breaks. A relation is suboptimal if exchanging in that relation reduces the number of exchanges that can occur in the network. Breaks occur only at suboptimal relations, but only some suboptimal relations are breaks. Therefore all *possible* breaks are suboptimal.

The procedure for finding breaks follows steps introduced by Simpson and Willer (1999) but benefits from an innovation introduced by Girard and Borch (2003). Whereas Simpson and Willer used exchange-seek likelihoods, Girard and Borch point out that using likelihoods sharply limits the procedure's scope to networks of approximately 20 or less. Beyond that size, the time needed to calculate likelihoods sharply increases with network size and density blocking calculation. Instead of likelihoods, Girard and Borch use the binary distinction of excludable versus nonexcludable, which are readily found by inspection.

Here are the three steps to find breaks:

1. Label each position, either e if it is excluded for any configuration of exchanges or i if not.

2. Label relations s if suboptimal.

3. Remove and replace suboptimal relations determining excludability at disconnection.

We now apply this procedure to the 4-Line of Figure 10.7c. Because the B–C relation is suboptimal, it is a possible break. (It is suboptimal because when B and C exchange with each other, only one exchange occurs, but when exchanging with A and D, two exchanges occur.) But neither B nor C is a high power position: thus B–C is not a break. Nor should it be. B and C must occasionally exchange with each other to exclude A and D. Having been excluded, future offers of A and D will be more favorable to B and C. Since the B–C relation advantages B and C, they will assuredly not break from each other.

Now the three-step procedure is applied to the Figure 10.8 networks. For all networks, label the positions and find and label the suboptimal relations, if any. It is immediately obvious in Figure 10.8a that both B and E are high power positions. Remove B–E, which is suboptimal, and find that both are not excludable. Therefore, B–E is a break. It can now be seen that the network in Figure 10.8a was a compound of two strong power structures that are now separated. And the parts should be separated because B and E, making profitable exchanges with their low power positions, will not exchange equally with each other.

In Figure 10.8b, B is high power and D is never excluded after the suboptimal B–D relation is removed. Thus the network was a compound of a strong power substructure, A–B–C and the D–E dyad. In Figure 10.8c the breaks are hidden because D and E are excludable. But there is a clue: B–D and B–E are suboptimal. Remove those relations and we find that D and E are not excludable in their dyad while B is high power. Therefore Figure 10.8c, like Figure 10.8b, is a compound of strong power and dyadic substructures now broken into their component parts. The network in Figure 10.8d is also a compound and its two breaks, B–D and B–E, are easily found. D–E, though suboptimal, is not a break. Once broken it is found that the compound was composed of the strong power A–B–C substructure and the F–D–E–G 4-Line.

The last two networks are not like the first four because, though compound, their component parts do not break. In Figure 10.8e, B–D does not break because D, facing exclusion when E and F exchange, prefers to exchange with B than to be excluded. Therefore D will make equipower offers to E and F and low power offers that are highly favorable to B. In Figure 10.8f, there are two suboptimal relations, but neither is a break. There is no break because, when both are removed, both F and G are excludable. Since they are, they would prefer to exchange with B than to be excluded. Thus Figure 10.8f does not break.

How general is the three-step procedure? Figure 10.9 shows that it can be readily applied to sizable networks. The positions are already labeled. Having found the suboptimal relations, we are sure that the reader can locate the breaks. Once they are found, compare your findings with Figure 10.10.

Earlier it was asserted that breaks limit distal effects. Looking at Figure 10.10 it can be seen that there will be no distal effects beyond subnetworks as long as they remain broken. For example, connecting another node to B, C, or D has no effect on any subnetwork to the right—and similarly for an array of further changes across the subnetworks.

CONCLUSION

ET, by building up from elementary concepts to more complex concepts, predicts and explains action within social structures. ET has continuously expanded its scope through incorporating and testing new ideas. As explained in this chapter, ET now identifies seven structural conditions that produce power differences in exchange and coercive structures. These seven conditions can now be applied, along with resistance equations, to make predictions for both discrete and flow networks. Of the seven conditions, one condition, exclusion, determines the power distribution in strong, equal, and weak power network types. For complex discrete networks, distal effects and network breaks are explained. Not discussed here is ET's theory of property (Gilham 1981, Willer 1985).

In addition to expanding scope, ET also bridges to theories of other scopes. One bridge connects power, as understood by ET, to status and influence, as understood by status characteristics theory (Thye, Willer, and Markovsky, 2006). A second bridges through game theory to generate formulations for collective action (Willer and Skvoretz 1997; Simpson and Macy 2001). A third links across ET–status characteristics–game theory to explain cohesion and solidarity (Willer, Borch, and R. Willer 2002). Sadly, discussion of these bridges and of future directions for the development of ET are both precluded by space considerations.

1. For details on building complex out of simpler formulations, see Willer and Anderson (1981) or Willer (1999).

2. For a discussion of why ET avoids interpersonal utility comparisons, see Willer (1999).

3. By that definition, almost all social relations are power relations because all but limiting cases are mixed motive.

4. For example, power dependence has discovered only two conditions. See Cook et al. (1983).

5. In flow networks an embedded actor's payoff is a cumulative total of the flows in all the actor's exchanges, while in discrete networks, actors receive a payoff from each exchange in which they are involved. As a result, in a discrete network, $A–B–C$, where B can exchange with A and C, B's payoff in the $A–B$ exchange is P_{Ba} and B's payoff in the $B–C$ exchange is P_{Bc}.

6. The predictions presented here are not identical to the predictions for equal power. Changing the worth of w for the middleman, B, causes the network to approach equal power; however, it does not completely eliminate the effects of inclusion and ordering. Rather, making the resource of value to the middleman only reduces the effects of inclusion and ordering such that values approach but do not reach equal power.

7. That exchanges are equal power is not because both receive the same number of resources, but because they exchange at equiresistance *and* there is no power condition affecting the exchanges. It happens then that equiresistance is an equal division in all resource pool networks.

8. Some exchanges in weak power networks are equipower, as between B and C in the 4-Line of Figure 10.7c. These can be readily found because the positions, like B and C, are identical but for their labels.

Cook, Karen S., and Richard M. Emerson. 1978. Power, equity, and commitment in exchange networks. *American Sociological Review* 43:721–39.

Cook, Karen S., Richard M. Emerson, Mary R. Gillmore, and Toshio Yamagishi. 1983. The distribution of power in exchange networks: Theory and experimental results. *American Journal of Sociology* 89:275–305.

Corra, Mamadi, and David Willer. 2002. The gatekeeper. *Sociological Theory* 20:180–205.

Emanuelson, Pamela. 2005. Improving the precision and parsimony of network exchange theory: A comparison of three network exchange models. *Contemporary Research in Social Psychology* 10, http://www.uiowa.edu/%7Egrpproc/crisp/crisp.10.11.html.

Emanuelson, Pamela, and David Willer. 2003. The middleman. Presented at the Annual Meeting of the American Sociological Association, Atlanta, GA.

———. 2004. The use of sub-optimal exchanges and the development of power in weak power networks. Presented at the Annual Meeting of the American Sociological Association, San Francisco, CA.

Gilham, Steven A. 1981. State, law, and modern economic exchange. In *Networks, Exchange and Coercion*, ed. David Willer and Bo Anderson. New York: Elsevier/Greenwood.

Girard, Dudley, and Casey Borch. 2003. Optimal seek simplified. *Contemporary Research in Social Psychology* 8, http://www.uiowa.edu/%7Egrpproc/crisp/crisp.8.16.html.

Lovaglia, Michael, John Skvoretz, David Willer, and Barry Markovsky. [1995] 1999. Negotiated outcomes in social exchange networks. In *Network Exchange Theory*, ed. David Willer, 157–84. Westport, CT: Praeger.

Markovsky, Barry, David Willer, and Travis Patton. [1988] 1999. Power relations in exchange networks. In *Network Exchange Theory*, ed. David Willer, 87–107. Westport, CT: Praeger.

Marx, Karl. [1867] 1990. *Capital: Volume I*. New York: Penguin Classics.

Simpson, Brent, and Michael W. Macy. 2001. Collective action and power inequality: Coalitions in exchange networks. *Social Psychology Quarterly* 64:88–100.

Simpson, Brent, and David Willer. 1999. A new method for finding power structures. *Network Exchange Theory*, ed. David Willer, 270–84. Westport, CT: Praeger.

Stolte, John, and Richard M. Emerson. 1977. Structural inequality: Position and power in exchange structures. In *Behavioral Theory in Sociology*, ed. R. Hamblin and J. Kunkel, 117–38. New Brunswick: Transaction.

Thye, Shane, David Willer, and Barry Markovsky. 2006. From status to power: New models at the intersection of two theories. *Social Forces*. Forthcoming.

Weber, Max. [1916] 1963. *Economy and Society: Volume I*. Los Angeles: University of California Press.

———. [1918] 1968. *Economy and Society: Volume II*. Los Angeles: University of California Press.

Willer, David. 1985. Property and Social Exchange. In *Advances in Group Process: Theory and Research. Vol.* 2, ed. Edward Lawler, 123–42. Greenwich, CT: JAI Press.

———. 1987. Theory and the experimental investigation of social structures. New York: Gordon & Breach.

———, ed. 1999. *Network Exchange Theory*. Westport, CT: Praeger.

———. 2003. Power-at-a-distance. *Social Forces* 81:1295–1334.

Willer, David, and Bo Anderson, eds. 1981. *Networks, Exchange, and Coercion*. New York: Elsevier.

Willer, David, Casey Borch, and Robb Willer. 2002 Building a model for solidarity and cohesion using three theories. *Advances in Group Process: Group Cohesion, Trust and Solidarity* 19:67–107.

Willer, David, and John Skvoretz. 1997. Games and structures. *Rationality and Society* 9:5–35.

Willer, Robb, and David Willer. 2000. Exploring dynamic networks: Hypotheses and conjectures. *Social Networks* 22:251–72.

11 | THE AFFECT THEORY OF SOCIAL EXCHANGE

Edward J. Lawler

The affect theory of social exchange places emotion and feelings at the center of social exchange theorizing (Lawler 2001). It posits that exchange generates emotions and that emotions are internal responses that reward and punish actors. Emotions that occur regularly in exchange processes include feeling good about successful exchange, feeling shame about the terms accepted, feeling gratitude toward a conciliatory exchange partner, and feeling anger at a difficult or hostile exchange partner. The theory argues that such emotions and feelings have important consequences for the relations, networks, and groups within which they occur.

The affect theory of social exchange asks how and when social exchange gives rise to or sustains a stable social order. Emotions are an integral part of the answer. A stable order occurs to the degree that the emotions and feelings are attributed to relevant social units— relations, groups, networks, organizations. This occurs in part because of the jointness of social exchange tasks or activities. Social exchange is a quintessential joint task, because it succeeds only with the consent and collaboration of one or more other actors. If a joint task (exchange) is accomplished, individual actors generally feel uplifted or good; when it is not accomplished, they feel downcast or bad. The affect theory of social exchange analyzes structural conditions that generate variations in the *jointness* of the exchange task and shows how the simple, everyday emotional effects of social exchange lay the foundation for stronger or weaker affective ties to social units (e.g., a relation, network, or group). Person-to-unit ties are fundamental to the larger problem of social order, as Parsons (1951) and others (Kanter 1968) have theorized.

In broader terms, the theory connects a fundamental idea about order from Durkheim (1915) with a fundamental idea from Emerson (1972b). Durkheim (1915) argued, in his examination of preliterate societies, that joint activities among a group of people give rise to and sustain a social order. This occurs because the emotions of uplift and excitement from such activities are objectified in the group or society (see also Collins 1975). The idea from Emerson's (1972b) exchange theory is that mutual dependencies or interdependencies are the structural foundation of cohesion in exchange relations. This occurs because mutual interests are stronger and cooperation more prevalent under high levels of mutual dependence. My theory assumes that structural interdependencies are the foundation for ongoing interactions and group affiliations but argues that joint activities and emotional consequences mediate the effects of structural interdependencies on social order.

The terms *emotion* and *feeling* are used interchangeably. Emotions are defined as a positive or negative evaluative state with physiological and cognitive components (Kemper 1978; Izard 1991; Clore and Parrott 1994). They have a visceral, nonvoluntary foundation and the potential to generate a consciousness of the connection between self and an object (Damasio 1999). A key idea adopted from psychology is that emotions are both a response to stimuli (i.e., others' behavior, nature of exchange) and a stimulus that generates cognitive or interpretive processes (Izard 1991). This suggests an internal, self-reinforcement dynamic (see Bandura 1997). The implication is that social exchange produces a primary emotional response, and this emotional response in turn generates further responses, cognitive and emotional. These internal dynamics contain the mediating mechanisms through which social structures (interdependencies) strengthen or weaken affective attachments to social units.

In brief, the affect theory of social exchange connects different structures of social exchange with the joint tasks involved, the common emotions felt, and the strength of person-to-unit ties. Person-to-unit attachments are interpreted as a dimension of micro order and solidarity, and behaviorally these are reflected in commitment, trust, and group formation. The following section overviews the intellectual context in which the affect theory of social exchange was formulated.

BACKGROUND

The Social Exchange Tradition

Social exchange theory articulates a transactional view of social interaction and an instrumental view of human behavior (e.g., Thibaut and Kelley 1959; Homans 1961; Blau 1964; Emerson 1972a; Molm and Cook 1995). Two or more actors interact with each other to the extent that they receive valued rewards or profits that are not available from others or by acting alone. They form social relations, i.e., patterns of regular, repeated interaction, with those from whom they expect and receive repeated flows of reward over time. The transactional quality of social interactions is based on the fact that individual actors are self-interested and instrumental. Actors are motivated to enhance their own rewards, and their concern about others' rewards is contingent on whether that concern serves their own self-interest. The confluence of an instrumental view of actors and a transactional view of social relations gives social exchange theory a distinctive place in sociological theorizing and important ties to rational choice theory and economic sociology.

The central phenomena to be explained in social exchange theorizing is who gets what at what price or cost and what implications does this have for social relations and networks. The central explanatory constructs are social structural dimensions such as power and dependence. Sociological exchange theory has spawned traditions of research on the fairness, equity, or justice in exchange (Homans 1961; Hegtvedt and Markovsky 1995; Jasso 1980); on how structures of power dependence shape negotiation processes or reciprocal exchanges (Bacharach and Lawler 1981; Molm 1997); and on how network structures affect the division of profits and the accumulation of resources across network positions (Molm and Cook 1995; Willer 1999). Beyond theory testing in the laboratory, exchange-theory notions have brought to light important transactional elements of parent-child relationships, coworker relationships, and person-organization relations.

Any theory requires simplifying assumptions and principles that direct attention to some phenomena and away from others; extant social exchange theories are no exception. The focus on the instrumental and transactional has a firm theoretical foundation in both reinforcement theory from psychology (see Emerson 1972a) and rational choice theory from economics (see Coleman 1990). Reinforcement and rational choice theories constitute the two primary microfoundations of social exchange. In both these perspectives, however, emotions and emotional processes play little or no role. From reinforcement theories, emotional responses are epiphenomal; they correspond so closely with the experience of reinforcement or punishment that they add little or no explanatory value beyond operant reinforcement and punishment (Skinner 1938; Homans 1961). In rational choice theories, there has been some growth in attention to emotions but the focus is limited to when emotions distort information processing and account for departures from rational-choice predictions (Hechter 1987).

The affect theory of social exchange is a response to the relative neglect of emotional and affective processes in the social exchange tradition but also to the growing evidence from neuroscience (see Damasio 1999; Turner 2000), psychology (Forgas 2000), and sociology (Kemper 1978; Hochschild 1983; Lawler and Thye 1999) that emotions are fundamental to and mediate many rational and cognitive processes. Damasio (1999), for example, suggests that human consciousness occurs when visceral internal nonvoluntary feelings are sensed by actors, i.e., when actors feel feelings. Rational and cognitive processes start here and, in this sense, inherently have an emotional basis. Jonathan Turner (2000) provides an evolutionary argument for the centrality and foundational nature of emotions to the human species. He argues that visual emotional cues were prelinguistic, adaptive mechanisms of solidarity. The evolution of human capacity to communicate and read such cues was critical to the development of strong communities. Lawler and Yoon (1996) experimentally demonstrate that, whereas actors enter exchange situations for instrumental purposes, repetitive exchange with the same others generates positive feelings that enhance the cohesion of and commitment to the resulting exchange relation. An important implication is that the emotional process transforms exchange relations from purely instrumental to partly expressive (Lawler and Yoon 1996; Lawler and Thye 1999).

The affect theory of social exchange specifies structural conditions under which the emotions unleashed by social exchange give rise to enduring affective attachment or detachment (sentiments) to relevant social objects, such as a relation, group, network, or organization. As currently formulated, the theory analyzes two structural dimensions central to the social exchange tradition: (1) How the *form of exchange* interconnects the behaviors of the parties to exchange. Exchange theorists have distinguished four forms of social exchange—reciprocal, negotiated, productive, and generalized (Ekeh 1974; Emerson 1981; Molm 1994; Molm and Cook 1995)—and these are a key focus of the affect theory of exchange. (2) How the *type of network connection* links possible exchanges or exchange relations. The theory contrasts positively connected networks, where one exchange or relation promotes others, with negatively connected networks, where one exchange or relation precludes others (Emerson 1981). These structural dimensions bear on the cohesion and solidarity of social units.

In the affect theory of social exchange, solidarity is defined as "the strength and durability of person-to-group and person-to-person relations" (Parsons 1951; Hechter 1987). Solidarity is manifest in the degree that behaviors take account of and weigh the interests and welfare of others and the group itself. Examples include unilateral gift giving, expanding areas of collaboration, forgiving periodic instances of opportunism, and remaining in an existing relation despite equal or better benefits elsewhere (Lawler 2001). The affect theory of social exchange aims to explain person-to-unit ties and theorize how these develop from person-to-person interactions.

Relation Cohesion Theory

Emerson (1981) defined an exchange relation as a pattern of repetitive exchange among the same actors over time. Thus if actors repeatedly exchange with each other, they are presumed to have some sort of relationship. That relationship, however, varies in resilience or strength and this will be particularly evident when actors have viable alternatives to one another. Because of the transactional nature of exchange relations, one would expect significant instability, as actors continually pursue better alternatives. This raises an important question: what conditions or processes generate stability within or among a set of relations? The answers of exchange theorists focus on commitment, defined broadly as the proclivity to continue exchanging with those exchanged with in the past. Exchange relations, as Emerson (1981) defined them, are essentially self-reproducing.

Answering the commitment question gives us information on why and when actors in exchange relations may be prepared to sacrifice individual rewards to maintain or strengthen the exchange relation or a larger unit in which it is nested (see Cook and Emerson 1984; Lawler 1992). The standard exchange-theory explanation for commitment is uncertainty reduction—namely, that commitment between two actors in repeated exchange is most likely to develop under conditions of high uncertainty. Commitment enables actors to reduce uncertainty and produce more predictable and stable results for themselves (Cook and Emerson 1984; Kollock 1994). The underlying mechanism or process here is quite simple: as two actors exchange more frequently, they learn more about each other and become more confident they can anticipate each other's behavior and predict more accurately the terms of exchange.

In an innovative study of this process, Kollock (1994) did an experiment in which multiple parties were involved in a spot market for one of two products (rice or rubber). With one of the products, the quality was standardized and therefore prospective buyers faced low uncertainty about what exactly they were buying; with the other product, the quality was unknown and unknowable until after a buy had been made. Comparing these two conditions, Kollock found that commitments were more likely to form in the high-uncertainty condition than in the low-uncertainty condition. The explanation is that by exchanging with the same others, the quality and value of what was being bought would be more predictable. The Kollock (1994) study is a basic demonstration of the uncertainty-reduction explanation for commitment.

The theory of relational cohesion was developed to provide an alternative, yet complementary, emotional and affective explanation for commitment. This theory interweaves some basic ideas of exchange theory (Emerson 1972b, 1981) with ideas from Berger and Luckmann's (1966) social construction theory and Randall Collins's theory of interaction-ritual chains (1981, 1989). From Emerson (1972), relational cohesion theory is built on a passing reference he made suggesting that actors who are more dependent on each other develop more cohesive exchange relations. That is, cohesion is a function of mutual dependence. From Berger and Luckmann (1966), relational cohesion theory adopts the principle that it does not take many repetitions of exchange for a relation to begin to emerge. In fact, Berger and Luckmann argue that "all actions repeated once or more tend to be habitualized to some degree" (p. 57). The reason for this is that actors give meaning to their repeated interaction by inferring a relationship. Through habitualization (repetition, recurrence), the relation or other social unit becomes a third force in the situation, i.e., it becomes an object distinct from self and other. Actors, therefore, orient themselves in part to the social unit.

Collins's (1981, 1989) theory of interaction-ritual chains explicitly argues that recurrent interaction is the microfoundation for social order (cohesion, commitment, solidarity) and that emotions play a central role. Social interactions (conversations) create the feelings of uplift and confidence that people carry from one interaction episode to another. A successful, uplifting conversation at time 1 with person *A* will carry over to a subsequent conversation at time 2 with person *B*. Through such emotional dynamics, group affiliations or memberships become more salient (Collins 1989).

According to Collins's theory, the sense of a group and its solidarity increase, especially under certain conditions: (1) actors have a common focus, (2) they are aware of their common focus, and (3) they experience common emotions that (4) grow stronger as they are shared and regenerated over time. Under these conditions, group memberships become more real as objects to actors, along the lines suggested by Berger and Luckmann, and actors come to develop moral obligations to one another. Collins's theory suggests that the moral or normative impact of a group affiliation can be traced to fundamental emotions generated repeatedly in social interaction.

By integrating ideas from these different theoretical perspectives, relational cohesion theory aims to connect structural power to commitment through a mediating emotional and affective process. Figure 11.1 presents the theory in the form of a theoretical model (Lawler and Yoon 1996). The theory contends that the frequency of exchange between two actors is greatest to the degree that their relationship entails greater mutual dependence, because here the incentives to exchange are stronger. Frequencies of exchange also are greater under equal power than they are under unequal power, primarily because equity or

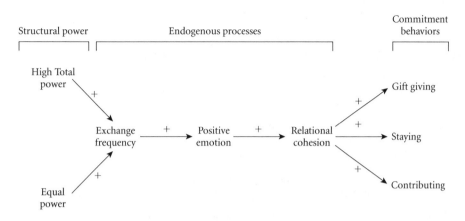

Figure 11.1 Model for the Theory of Relational Cohesion
SOURCE: Reprinted from Lawler and Yoon (1996).

justice issues tend not to complicate the exchange agenda. Structural power (dependence) generates relational commitment through a series of indirect steps. More repetitive or frequent exchange generates stronger emotional responses (positive or negative) and these emotional responses promote perceptions that the relation is a unifying third force in the situation (Lawler and Yoon 1996). Relational cohesion, in turn, promotes various forms of commitment behavior: unilateral token gifts, staying in the relation despite alternatives, and cooperating with another despite risk of exploitation (i.e., in a social dilemma). The heart of relational cohesion theory is the endogenous process—*exchange to emotion to cohesion.* This is the mechanism linking exchange structure to commitment behavior.

The evidence for relational cohesion theory is quite strong (for a review see Thye, Yoon, and Lawler 2002). In fact, all links in the theoretical model shown in Figure 11.1 have received significant support across several studies (see Lawler and Yoon 1993, 1996, 1998; Lawler, Thye, and Yoon 2000; Lawler and Thye 1999; Thye, Yoon, and Lawler 2002). The following summarizes these points: (1) Power-dependence conditions have the predicted, indirect effects on commitment behavior through the endogenous mechanism. Equal and high total power generates more commitment by fostering more frequent exchange, stronger positive emotions, and greater perceived cohesion (Lawler and Yoon 1993, 1996; Lawler et al. 1995). (2) If a network produces both equal- and unequal-power relations with similar frequencies of exchanges, stronger commitments develop in the equal-power relation than in the unequal-power relation (Lawler and Yoon 1998). This indicates that the emotional impact of exchange is stronger under equal power than it is under unequal power. (3) If the exchange relation is structurally induced, rather than structurally enabled (i.e., promoted), the commitment process is weaker (Lawler, Thye, and Yoon, 2006). (4) In multiactor, productive exchange, group formation develops through the relational cohesion process, but our research also revealed a role for uncertainty reduction. The emotional and affective process operated to generate more stay behavior and gift giving, and the uncertainty reduction process explained cooperation rates in an *N*-person social dilemma

(Lawler, Thye, and Yoon 2000). Overall, research on relational cohesion confirms the important role of emotions. The endogenous process—exchange to emotion to cohesion—is strongly established. When it operates, commitment is stronger and more resilient.

THE AFFECT THEORY

The affect theory of social exchange takes off from the theory of relational cohesion, without displacing or superseding it. Relational cohesion theory is dyad-focused, whereas the affect theory is network-focused. The endogenous process previously described is assumed and incorporated into the affect theory, but the emphasis is structures of exchange and effects on solidarity. The theory argues that structural dimensions create variations in the jointness of exchange; the jointness of exchange takes precedence over repetitive or frequent exchange as a source of order and solidarity. The theory distinguishes the primary social objects in exchange contexts—task, self, other, social unit—and specifies the conditions under which positive or negative emotions are attributed to social units rather than to self or other.

The affect theory consists of five elements: (1) Scope conditions that identify the general properties of the social context to which the theory applies; (2) assumptions about the role of emotions, based primarily on relational cohesion theory; (3) a conceptual framework for linking different emotions to different social objects; (4) two core principles on the sources of jointness in the exchange task or activity; and (5) a series of testable propositions derived from these principles (Lawler 2001). This section provides a synopsis of the theory organized around these five elements.

Scope of the Theory

The affect theory of social exchange applies to social contexts with the following properties: (1) a network of three or more actors; (2) actors have the opportunity to engage in exchange with one or more other actors in the network; (3) there are repeated opportunities for exchange in the same structure; (4) actors make decisions about whether to exchange, with whom, and with what terms; (5) actors are motivated to improve their rewards or profits, which may or may not involve maximization (Molm and Cook 1995); and (6) exchanges are dyadic but (7) the dyads are interconnected such that exchange in one dyad has an effect on exchange in other dyads (Emerson 1981).

These conditions all stem from the exchange-network tradition of research, initiated in the 1970s by Emerson and Cook (e.g., Cook and Emerson 1978). The first condition, requiring three or more actors, reflects Emerson's (1972a, 1972b) assumption that dyads do not exist alone but always are connected in some way to other dyads in a network. This was a departure from the dyadic focus of earlier exchange theories (Thibaut and Kelley 1959; Homans 1961; Blau 1964). A fixed, unchanging network structure is the basis for repeated opportunities for exchange with the same others. This repetition, however, raises the possibility that cohesive relations or groups may develop endogenously and thereby transform particular relations or the network into a recognized unit, a third force in the situation. Overall, the scope conditions indicate that the theory can apply to a wide variety of social contexts.

Theoretical Assumptions

Five assumptions of the theory are the following (Lawler 2001, 327):

1. That social exchange generates global emotions and feelings (along a positive or negative dimension)

2. That such global emotions constitute internal self-reinforcing or punishing stimuli

3. That actors strive to reproduce global positive emotions and avoid global negative emotions

4. That global emotions from exchange trigger cognitive efforts to understand the sources or causes of global emotion or feelings

5. That actors interpret and explain their global emotions with reference to social units (e.g., relations, groups, networks) within which they experience the emotions

To summarize, assumptions 1 and 2 of the affect theory indicate that social exchange generates global feelings and that these are special classes of reinforcement and punishment. Global emotions are immediate, internal, involuntary events generated by exchange. They take the general form of "feeling good or pleasant" or "feeling bad or unpleasant" (Lawler 2001; Russell, Weiss, and Mendelsohn 1989). Assumptions 3 and 4 portray global emotions as motivational forces (Izard 1991). When activated, they organize action or interaction and unleash cognitive efforts to interpret where they come from. Following Weiner (1986), these interpretations lead to specific emotions directed at objects in the situation. Specific emotions result from the interpretation and attribution of sources or causes of global or primitive emotions to social objects. The fifth assumption indicates that, in the context of joint tasks, actors interpret global emotions as produced in part by social units. This leads to stronger or weaker affective attachments to relations, networks, groups, or organizations. The affect theory of social exchange is the first effort to theorize the structural conditions under which actors make social-unit attributions of emotion and thereby strengthen (or weaken) affective attachments.

Attributing Emotions to Social Objects

The affect theory offers a classificatory scheme that identifies a key emotion for each of four social objects relevant to social exchange: task, self, other, and social unit (Table 11.1). This scheme borrows heavily from Weiner's (1986) attribution theory, Izard's (1991) differentiated emotions theory, and Russell, Weiss, and Mendelsohn's (1989) affect grid. The global emotions, resulting from the task activity, are termed *pleasantness* or *unpleasantness*. This object-to-emotion connection captures the immediate, involuntary response to success or failure at consummating an exchange. Examples of such global emotions and feelings from the psychological literature are interest (i.e., excitement, uplift) and joy (i.e., comfort, satisfaction; Izard 1991), and sadness or stress (Russell et al. 1989).

The remaining emotions are specific. They are directed at a particular social object, and they arise from an actor's interpretation of pleasant or unpleasant feelings from exchange. If positive global feelings are attributed to self, the specific emotion is *pride*; if attributed to

TABLE 11.1
Emotions Directed at Each Object

Social Object	VALENCE OF EMOTION	
	Positive	Negative
Task	Pleasantness	Unpleasantness
Self	Pride	Shame
Other	Gratitude	Anger
Social unit	Affective attachment	Affective detachment

SOURCE: Reprinted from Lawler (2001).

the other, the specific emotion is *gratitude*. If negative emotions are attributed to self, the specific emotion is *shame*; if attributed to the other, the result is *anger* toward the other. If the emotions are attributed to the social unit, the specific emotions are *affective attachment* or *affective detachment*. Such relational or group attributions of emotion are the central mechanism by which emotions, experienced individually, strengthen or weaken order and solidarity at the group level.

The attribution process, assumed by the affect theory, differs in important ways from theory and research on attribution in psychology. In psychology the focus is on inferences about individuals from their individual behavior (Kelley 1967; Weiner 1986); the standard contrast is between dispositional (internal to the person) attributions and situational (external to person) attributions. A behavior, therefore, may be perceived as caused by a quality of the person or by an aspect of the situation. In these terms, social-unit attributions are a type of situational attribution. However, the rubric *situational attributions* is a catch-all category for most anything that falls outside the individual. The affect theory of social exchange contends that the dispositional-situational contrast breaks down in group or interaction settings, especially where the group or interaction entails joint tasks and individual contributions are difficult to distinguish.

From extant attribution theory and research, however, it is well-known that individuals tend to make self-serving attributions for success or failure at a task, i.e., giving credit to self for success and blaming the situation (or others) for failure. If self-serving attributions are dominant in social exchange, each actor credits self for the success at exchange and blames the other for failures. Pride in self and anger toward the other would occur more frequently than shame or gratitude, and social unit attributions would be weak or nonexistent (Lawler 2001). The main principles and propositions of the theory specify the conditions under which social-unit attributions of emotion can override self-serving attributions. We now turn to these principles and propositions.

Core Theoretical Principles

The core question for the affect theory of social exchange boils down to the following: under what conditions do actors perceive the social unit as the primary source of global emotions? This depends on the *jointness of the exchange task or activity*. Greater task jointness generates a greater propensity to attribute individual emotions or feelings to the social unit. Examples of highly joint tasks include child rearing by a couple, a work group on an assembly line, and an organizational merger. These tasks can be structured and defined in a variety of ways by actors, and the theory identifies structural and perceptional dimensions to address this.

The structural dimension is the degree that each actor's contributions to task success (or failure) are separable (distinguishable) or nonseparable (indistinguishable). This contrast is adopted from Oliver Williamson's (1985, 245–47) analysis of governance structures. He argues that, in a work setting, when contributions are nonseparable, workers cannot assign individual credit or blame to each other for work-group success or failure, and this generates relational teams as a governance mechanism. Relational teams become important structures of control to the degree that collective responsibility for group success is more salient to actors than their individual responsibility.

However, the structure of tasks is often complicated as is the capacity to trace success or failure to individual effort and performance. Child-rearing in a family may be a joint task, yet the degree that the contributions of mother and father are separable or nonseparable vary with how they distribute the subtasks involved and how they define and perceive the allocation of these tasks. Child rearing can be undertaken with clearly separable contributions (i.e., with a well-defined and understood division of labor) or with nonseparable contributions (i.e., overlapping, rotating, substitutable responsibilities). Thus the meaning and implications of task separability or nonseparability are subject to interpretation by the actors, making the subjective or perceptual dimension of jointness important.

The key perceptual dimension of jointness is the degree that the task fosters a sense of shared responsibility for its success or failure and for the emotions produced as a result. The argument of the theory is that if exchange produces a sense of shared responsibility, actors are more likely to interpret their individual feelings also as jointly produced (Lawler 2001, 2002) and therefore more likely to attribute those feelings to their relationship or group. For example, a high-performing work group generates greater cohesion and solidarity than otherwise if they perceive responsibilities for the group performance as shared rather than individually based. Similarly, if the child-rearing activities of parents foster a sense of shared responsibility, their child-rearing activities ostensibly strengthen their relationship more than otherwise. Thus the core principles are as follows (Lawler 2001, 334):

> Core Principle 1: The greater the nonseparability of individuals' impact on task success or failure, the greater the perception of shared responsibility.

> Core Principle 2: The greater the perception of shared responsibility for success or failure at a joint task, the more inclined individuals are to attribute resulting global and specific feelings to social units.

Self-serving attributions in either the work-group or family context have the potential to weaken or even tear apart those relationships. If members of the high-performing work group attribute their positive feelings to their own individual contributions, they will feel pride in self but little gratitude toward others, reducing solidarity effects, e.g., "I did most of the work and made this happen." If they fail at a group task, they may direct anger toward others and little shame toward self, e.g., "I did my part; they didn't do theirs." These processes may help to explain why some marriages are strengthened by children and some are weakened.

A sense of shared responsibility has positive consequences in the case of both success and failure at the task. Shared responsibility for success generates social-unit attributions of positive emotion but also specific emotions of pride in self and gratitude toward the other. Failure generates both shame directed at self and anger directed at others. Sharing blame entails a social-unit attribution of emotion that could mobilize joint efforts to succeed in the future, though it also could lead actors to seek other partners with whom they might succeed at exchange.

To conclude, these core principles indicate when self-serving or social-unit attributions dominate interpretations of emotions and feelings: (1) Self-serving attributions dominate when the exchange task entails low nonseparability and little sense of shared responsibility. (2) Social-unit attributions dominate when the exchange task entails high nonseparability and generates a strong sense of shared responsibility. An important implication is that when social-unit attributions are made, exchange generates *both* pride in self *and* gratitude toward the other; actors can feel gratitude toward the other without diminishing pride in self, and vice versa. Self-serving attributions would lead these feelings to be inversely related, i.e., to take a zero-sum form. Social-unit attributions not only strengthen person-to-unit ties but also indirectly strengthen person-to-person ties by promoting mutual feelings of pride and gratitude. In this manner, the affect theory suggests a particular way that affective ties to groups influence interpersonal affective ties between exchange partners (see Lawler 2002, 2003).

Structures of Social Exchange

The core principles provide explanatory propositions for understanding how and when different social exchange structures generate different degrees of cohesion and solidarity at relational or group levels. As noted earlier, the theory addresses two basic dimensions of exchange structure: the *form of exchange* (Molm 1994; Molm and Cook 1995) and the *type of network connection* among three or more exchange relations. The form of exchange treats the link between actors' behaviors in exchange, whereas network connections deal with the link between different exchange relations in a network. The theory predicts that the strength of global emotional responses to an exchange is stronger under some structures than others, as is the tendency to attribute these emotions to the social unit. Under such conditions, specific emotions are positively correlated, i.e., actors feel both pride in self and gratitude toward the other.

Forms of Social Exchange. Sociological theories of exchange contrast four structural forms of exchange: productive, negotiated, reciprocal, and generalized (Ekeh 1974; Emerson 1981; Molm 1994; Molm and Cook 1995). In *productive exchange*, actors coordinate their behaviors to produce a joint private good; in *negotiated exchange*, actors make an explicit agreement specifying the terms of a trade or the division of a fixed pool of profit; in *reciprocal exchange*, actors sequentially provide to each other valued goods or services; in *generalized exchange*, an actor provides benefits to one member of a group or network and receives benefits from another member, rather than from the one given to. A productive form of exchange is essentially a person-group exchange; negotiated and reciprocal forms involve direct person-person exchange; and a generalized form involves indirect exchanges between persons, e.g., A gives to B, B gives to C, and C gives to A.

To illustrate, apply the four forms to intellectual exchanges among three graduate students, A, B, and C. A joint research project is an example of productive exchange; each contributes to the joint effort and receives something in return from that joint effort. A negotiated exchange occurs if A and B are working on different projects but get together to give each other comments on their work. The terms of the trade are the time and attention to each others' work. The form of exchange would be reciprocal if A asks for and receives statistical advice on a project from B, without expectations that A will provide assistance to B in the future; but later B asks for and receives feedback from A. Generalized exchange occurs if A, B, and C each receive helpful comments on their work but whom they give comments to and whom they receive comments from are different. The affect theory of social exchange is unique in its effort to analyze and compare the emotional dynamics of the four forms of social exchange.

Network Connections. Sociological theories of social exchange also distinguish various types of connection among pairs in a network—for example, in a fully connected three-actor network, how does an exchange between A and B affect prospective exchanges between A and C and B and C? Emerson (1972b, 1981) was the first to address this issue, and he distinguished two types of network connection: positive and negative. If a three actor network is positively connected, an A–B exchange increases the probability that A–C and B–C exchanges will occur; if the network is negatively connected, an A–B exchange reduces the probability that A–C or B–C exchanges will occur. The affect theory of social exchange draws out the group formation implications of these network connections.

To understand network connections, it is important to examine the incentives actors have to exchange with one or more partners in the network. Willer (1999) elaborates and refines Emerson's (1972b) approach by distinguishing inclusive, exclusive, and null connections. Inclusive and null can be considered different varieties of a positive connection. An inclusive connection is one where all relations must form for any given relation to receive benefit. With null connections, all exchanges do not have to occur, but each exchange produces benefit and these benefits accumulate across relations. Thus actors have an incentive to exchange with as many others as they can, given the network structure. In a negatively or exclusively connected network, actors have an incentive to exchange with only one other at a time. The original formulation of the affect theory focused on the simple contrast of positively and negatively connected networks, but it can be extended to address the tripartite contrast offered by Willer (1999).

Theoretical Propositions

The theoretical propositions of the affect theory are derived by applying the core principles to forms of social exchange and to positive or negative types of network connection. This section offers a synopsis of these propositions.

TABLE 11.2
Comparison of Effects of Exchange Structures

	Nonseparability	Perception of Shared Responsibility	Social-Unit Attributions of Global Emotions
Productive	High	High	High
Negotiated	Medium	High	Medium to high
Reciprocal	Low	Medium to high	Medium
Indirect	Low	Low	Low

SOURCE: Reprinted from Lawler (2001).

Forms of Social Exchange. The four forms of social exchange involve different degrees of nonseparability and separability and, therefore, are likely to generate different degrees of shared responsibility. These effects are summarized in Table 11.2 and discussed in the following for each form of exchange.

In productive exchange there is a single, jointly produced, private good, a good shared only by members of the group. The main problems are how to coordinate behaviors to produce that good and how to share or allocate the resulting benefits. There is higher structural interdependence here than in other forms of exchange, and the exchange processes are likely to make this interdependence salient to actors. Prototypes include a business partnership, coauthoring scholars, and a home-owner association working to solve a community problem that individual members cannot solve alone or in smaller groups. Productive exchange generates higher nonseparability than other forms of exchange, given cooperative incentives and a joint good. Individuals indeed may make distinguishable contributions, but these are so interwoven in the result that the sense of shared responsibility also should be high. Thus global emotions are stronger here and they are attributed to the social unit, thereby producing increases or decreases of cohesion and solidarity, contingent on the valence of the emotions.

In negotiated exchange, actors seek to arrive at a contractual agreement on the terms of a trade. This typically develops from a negotiation process in which each makes offers or counteroffers reflecting their own individual interests. Actors' contributions to exchange (i.e., their explicit offers) are distinguishable, yet there is a joint result produced by the negotiation. The joint outcomes are essentially the average of negotiators' offers. In negotiated exchange the jointness of the exchange task is salient, and the sense of shared responsibility should be relatively high. Overall, nonseparability and shared responsibility should result in global emotions being attributed in part to the social unit, though not to the degree found in productive exchange.

In reciprocal exchange, tacit understandings replace explicit agreements or trades. Rewards are sequential and given unilaterally, i.e., without explicit expectations of reciprocity. Yet patterns of reciprocity emerge over time, because if *A* receives a unilateral benefit from *B*, *A* feels obligated to provide benefits to *B* sometime in the future. Giving advice, providing a favor, and invitations to dinner exemplify behaviors that may give rise to or be a part of reciprocal exchanges. Each exchange behavior (giving) is distinct and separated in time from the reciprocal behavior. Thus the degree of nonseparability is low. A sense of shared responsibility develops from repeated exchange over time, but it should be lower than in the case of negotiated or productive exchange where the jointness of the exchange is more explicit and salient.

The notion that reciprocal exchange contains less potential for cohesion and solidarity than negotiated exchange seems counterintuitive. In fact, research by Molm indicates that reciprocal exchange generates more positive feelings about and commitment to the exchange partner than negotiated exchange (Molm 2003). The affect theory resolves this apparent contradiction by indicating that reciprocal exchange fosters cohesion primarily through an interpersonal process in which the social objects of greatest import are self and other, rather than the social unit as such. This is consistent with Molm's interpretation of her research (see Molm 2003). Negotiated exchange, on the other hand, renders the person-to-unit tie most salient. Thus actors involved in recurrent negotiated exchange with each other may become committed to their relation or common group affiliation without directing much affect (e.g., liking or disliking) toward one another (See Lawler 2001, 338; 2002, 10–11, for relevant discussion). Social identity theory and research takes a similar position, distinguishing interpersonal from intergroup identities or interactions and demonstrating that interpersonal attraction is not necessary for group formation (Hogg and Turner 1985; Brewer and Gardner 1996).

Unlike negotiated and reciprocal exchange, generalized exchange is indirect and impersonal. Everybody presumably receives and everybody presumably gives, but actors do not give to those they receive from. In an academic department, a structure of generalized exchange produces a collegial environment in which everybody receives feedback on their research, but dyadic or pairwise relations remain weak. The person-to-group ties are stronger here than the relational ties. Similar to the productive form, generalized exchange fosters high levels of interdependence among the actors, and coordination is a key problem. The prime difference is that the individual giving or contributions are highly separable, and the exchange behaviors are unlikely to generate much sense of shared responsibility.

Five interrelated propositions capture the logic and implications of Table 11.2 and the surrounding discussion:[1]

> PROPOSITION 1. Productive exchange generates stronger perceptions of shared responsibility and stronger global emotions than direct or indirect (generalized) exchange relations.

> PROPOSITION 2. Direct exchange produces stronger perceptions of shared responsibility and stronger global emotions than indirect (generalized) exchange.

> PROPOSITION 3. Stronger perceptions of shared responsibility produce stronger relational or group attributions for emotions felt.

> PROPOSITION 4. Stronger relational and group attributions produce stronger affective attachments to the social unit.

The theory treats person-to-group affective attachments as the fundamental solidarity effect of relational and group attributions. Thus the main prediction is the following:

PROPOSITION 5. The strength of person-to-group affective attachments (solidarity) should be ordered as follows across forms of social exchange:

Productive > Negotiated > Reciprocal > Generalized

The theory argues further that enduring sentiments (attachment or detachment) about the relations or groups tend to form if (1) the relation or group is perceived as a *stable* source of the particular emotions or feelings and (2) the relation or group also enables actors to *exercise control* over the events that produce positive or negative emotions (see Weiner 1986). The first condition obtains if actors expect the relation or group to continue to provide exchange opportunities to actors, and the second obtains as long as the relation or group promotes voluntary giving and a sense of control or efficacy. Relations and groups can be stable, controllable sources of positive experiences and emotions, and if so, the differences in solidarity across the four forms of social exchange will be greater than otherwise (see Lawler 2001, 342–43 for more detail).

Most any social context includes multiple social units, some nested within others. Academic departments are nested within colleges, companies within corporations, and neighborhoods within communities. Interacting or exchanging within multiple, nested social units is a universal human experience. Lawler (1992) argues in a choice-process theory of commitment that actors form stronger affective attachments to social units perceived by actors as giving them a greater sense of control. More proximal units tend to receive more credit for positive feelings and less blame for negative feelings, because these are the context for actors' immediate experience. Local or proximal units have a social interaction advantage, and thus we should expect a bias toward relational (local) attributions in social exchange. Collins's (1981, 1989) theory of interaction-ritual chains adds theoretical weight to this argument.

The affect theory of social exchange indicates that this local bias is contingent on the form of exchange. In direct exchange—negotiated or reciprocal—the immediate experience is with a particular other and it is not clear that the larger group or network is sufficiently salient to be perceived as a cause of their local experiences. Generalized and productive exchange make salient a larger social unit, though in different ways. Generalized exchange does so, *structurally*, by virtue of the fact that benefit flows at the dyadic level are all one way and the form of exchange transcends any particular dyadic (direct) relation. Productive exchange does so, *cognitively*, by revealing benefits of collaboration and coordination. The theory offers the following proposition:

PROPOSITION 6. Direct-exchange structures—negotiated and reciprocal— generate relational rather than group attributions of emotions; whereas productive or generalized (indirect) exchange structures generate group rather than relational attributions of emotion.

The logic of this inference is tied to both Lawler's (1992) choice-process theory of commitment and Collins's (1981) theory of interaction-ritual chains.

Network Connections. Group attributions of emotion presuppose that actors perceive a group or grouplike unit, i.e., that a unit exists cognitively as a third force in the social situation (Berger and Luckmann 1966). In social identity theory, a group is said to exist if actors "share a conception of themselves as belonging to the same unit" (Brown 2000, 4). Perception or cognition is sufficient, and it leads group members to treat each other more favorably than those outside the group (Tajfel and Turner 1986; Brown 2000). Group formation, in this cognitive sense, can be produced exogenously by common group affiliations or meaningful social categories (e.g., gender, ethnicity) or it can be produced endogenously by interaction processes unleashed by a social structure (Gaertner et al. 1990). The affect theory of social exchange suggests that network connections are a structural basis for such an endogenous process.

In a positively (inclusively) connected network, actors have incentives to exchange with all or as many others as possible. At the network level, this implies relatively high potential for shared responsibility to develop. In a negatively connected network, actors have an incentive to choose one exchange partner at a time; partners can be different or rotate over time, but they tend to settle into a pattern of exchanging with the same other. Negative connections are not likely to generate a sense of shared responsibility beyond dyadic ties. These structural differences promote *group formation* in positively connected networks and *relation formation* in negatively connected networks. The affect theory of social exchange offers an emotional and affective explanation for group formation.

The theory assumes that emotions spread or diffuse across relations that are interconnected in a network (Markovsky and Lawler 1994). If *A* feels good in an interaction with *B* and then interacts with *C*, *A*'s positive feelings tend to carry over to the *A–C* interaction; if *A* feels bad in an interaction with *B* and then interacts with *C*, *A*'s negative feelings carry over. This is a reasonable assumption because psychological research on emotion and mood indicate that global feelings (good or bad) from one situation (or actor) carry over to other situations (or actors), even if these situations (or actors) have no connection. If positive emotions diffuse from one relation (*A–B*) to another (*A–C*), the result for the *A–C* relation is likely to be greater cooperation, more use of group categories to organize perceptions, more inclusive perceptions of the group, more willingness to take risks, and more use of heuristics in processing information (Isen 1987; Forgas 2000; Bless 2000); the opposite effects occur for negative emotions. Thus in a positively connected network, it is easy to see how positive emotions in each relation would reinforce and strengthen those in other relations.

The valence of the emotions (positive versus negative) has different effects under different types of network connection. In negatively connected networks, positive emotions from repeated exchange in a given relation generates continued exchange and a sense of shared responsibility at the relational level. Such networks therefore create pockets of relational cohesion between pairs of actors who exchange most frequently (Lawler and Yoon 1998). In contrast, negative emotions from a given relation produce a search for better agreements from other possible exchange partners in the network. Affective attachment or affective detachment occurs, as predicted by the affect theory, but the relevant social units are the exchange relations that form. In positively connected networks, both positive emotions (from successful exchange) and negative emotions (from unsuccessful exchange) strengthen group formation, because interdependencies become more apparent and actors make group attributions for both positive and negative emotions. However, the spread of positive emotions promotes unity across relations, whereas the spread of negative emotions promotes disunity. The general implication of the affect theory of social exchange is as follows.

> PROPOSITION 7. In positively connected exchange networks, dyadic exchanges generate group formation and strengthen affective attachments (solidarity) to the network as a group; whereas in negatively connected net-works, exchanges in dyads strengthen affective attachments (solidarity) to the relation rather than the network as a group.

Recent Theoretical Developments

Since the original publication of the affect theory of social exchange, ideas of the theory have been developed in two ways. First, I have shown how the theory could be applied to social interaction in general (Lawler 2002). Second, with this broader interpretation of the theory, I addressed the question of how and when collective identities emerge or become salient, and how they are connected to role identities (Lawler 2003). Each of these theoretical efforts is briefly summarized below.

Generalizing the Theory. Underlying the affect theory is an implicit theory about the role of emotion in social interaction (Lawler 2002). The first step in this direction involves substituting the term *social interaction* for *social exchange* in the theory. Nearly all of the principles of the affect theory still apply. Social interaction inherently involves joint activity; there is variation in the degree that the activities are joint; joint activities with others often generate positive (or negative) emotional experiences; individuals tend to interpret the meaning of these feelings in broader terms (Durkheim 1915; Collins 1981); and finally, affective attachment to (or detachment from) groups, organizations, communities, or societies develops in part from these processes. If the joint activities interweave individual behaviors and foster a sense of shared responsibility for the activities and results, these in-dividual feelings produce affective attachments to the social unit. This emotional process is not the only basis for micro social order but it can be construed as one of several ways that people in repeated social interaction create groups that they value highly and are strongly tied to. In this context, interpersonal relations among members of the group are shaped in part by their person-to-social-unit ties (see Lawler 2002, 11–14, for more discussion). A simple causal chain (Figure 11.2) captures this generalization of the theory.

Figure 11.2   Basic Causal Sequence: Micro Solidarity
SOURCE: Reprinted from Lawler (2002).

Collective Identities. Another paper uses this broader interpretation of the theory to analyze collective and role identities. Collective identities are shared beliefs about a person's group affiliations or ties; these beliefs emerge from social interactions. Role identities are tied to structural positions and associated cultural definitions (Stryker 2000). Collective identities define the "we" in social interaction, whereas role identities define the "me" for each actor (Thoits and Virshup 1995). In accord with the affect theory of social exchange, collective identities are grounded in joint tasks or activities that involve nonseparability and a sense of shared responsibility; role identities distinguish responsibilities and define them in individual terms.

My argument is that in the context of multiple identities, actors enact those identities that are most likely to promote positive emotional experiences (Lawler 2003). When collective identities are salient, the sense of shared responsibility and social-unit attributions of emotion should be stronger; when role identities are salient, the sense of individual role responsibility and self-other attributions of emotion should be stronger. Thus collective identities strengthen, whereas role identities weaken the propensity of actors to structure and interpret individual contributions in nonseparable ways (see Lawler 2003). The question of how collective and role identities are interrelated is similar to the question of how social-unit and specific self-other emotions are intertwined in the affect theory, and it can be answered in those terms (see Lawler 2001, 2003). If self-efficacy is mediated by collective efficacy, collective identities strengthen social-unit attributions of emotion and role identities foster a positive correlation between pride in self and gratitude toward the other.

CONCLUSION

The affect theory of social exchange builds an emoting actor into social exchange theorizing. The actors of the theory respond emotionally in exchange relations; these emotions are internal, reinforcing or punishing, events; actors interpret these emotions to understand how to reproduce the positive and avoid the negative ones in the future. Central to the theory is the idea that these emotions, while felt individually, are often interpreted in relational or group terms, i.e., as stemming from relations with others or group affiliations. The theory contends that, insofar as this happens, the emotions bear on actors' affective attachments to (or detachments from) relations or groups. Affective attachments are construed as a key component of order and solidarity (Parsons 1951).

The emphases on emotions and social-unit unit attributions are distinguishing features of the theory. Another distinguishing feature is the explicit emphasis given to conceptualizing exchange as a joint task or activity. It is jointness that generates a sense of shared responsibility for the global feelings produced in social exchange and that makes social-unit attributions of emotion possible or likely. Jointness is the construct that enables a theoretical link to be made between structural conditions (network connections, forms of exchange) and micro social order in relations, networks, or groups.

The affect theory of social exchange has not yet been subjected to empirical test. Its underlying assumptions are well established in the line of research on relational cohesion theory (e.g., Lawler and Yoon 1993, 1998; Lawler and Thye 1999), and a study of productive exchange has demonstrated group-formation effects that are consistent with the theory (Lawler, Thye, and Yoon 2000). Experiments in the planning stage will comprehensively test the theory, comparing (1) the four forms of social exchange and (2) positive and negative network connections (Lawler and Thye 2003).

To conclude, the fundamental message of the affect theory of social exchange is that while actors enter exchange for instrumental reasons, endogenous emotional and affective processes result in social units taking on expressive value. i.e., becoming valued in themselves. The theory explains group solidarity or micro social order by interrelating the rational and the nonrational. The rational brings actors together in the first place (mutual interest), but their interaction or exchange produces a result that is nonrational (global emotions). This nonrational result (emotion) generates a rational response in the form of cognitive work to interpret the source of the emotions, and under conditions specified by the theory, this leads relations or groups to take on value in themselves, a nonrational result. In this manner, the affect theory of social exchange offers an explanation for micro order, cohesion, and solidarity that bridges rational choice and emotion-based perspectives in sociology.

NOTES

The author gratefully acknowledges the financial support of several grants from the National Science Foundation in support of this program of work: SBR-9022192, SES 9222668, SBR 9614860, and SES 0350221. Communications should be sent to the author at EJL3@cornell.edu or School of Industrial and Labor Relations, Cornell University, Ives Hall, Ithaca, NY 14853.

1. Compared to the original theoretical formulation (Lawler 2001), the propositions are restructured slightly to communicate as clearly and comprehensively as possible in light of space constraints.

REFERENCES

Bacharach, Samuel B., and Edward J. Lawler. 1981. *Bargaining: Power, Tactics, and Outcomes*. San Francisco: Jossey-Bass.

Bandura, Albert. 1997. *Self Efficacy: The Exercise of Control*. New York: W. H. Freeman.

Berger, Peter L., and Thomas Luckmann. 1966. *The Social Construction of Reality*. New York: Doubleday.

Blau, Peter. 1964. *Exchange and Power in Social Life*. New York: Wiley.

Bless, Herbert. 2000. The interplay of affect and cognition: The mediating role of general knowledge structures. In *Thinking and Feeling: The Role of Affect in Social Cognition*, ed. J. Forgas, 201–22. Cambridge, UK: Cambridge University Press.

Brewer, Marilyn B., and Wendi Gardner. 1996. Who is this "we"? Levels of collective identity and self representations. *Journal of Personality and Social Psychology* 71:83–93.

Brown, Rupert. 2000. *Group Processes*. 2nd ed. Oxford, UK: Blackwell.

Clore, Gerald L., and Gerald W. Parrott. 1994. Cognitive feelings and metacognitive judgments. *European Journal of Sociology and Psychology* 24:101–15.

Coleman, James S. 1990. *Foundations of Social Theory*. Cambridge, MA: Harvard University Press.

Collins, Randall. 1975. *Conflict Sociology*. New York: Academic Press. Collins, Randall. 1981. On the microfoundations of macrosociology. *American Journal of Sociology* 86:984–1014.

———. 1989. Toward a neo-Meadian sociology of mind. *Symbolic Interaction* 12:1–32.

Cook, Karen S., and Richard M. Emerson. 1978. Power, equity, and commitment in exchange networks. *American Sociological Review* 27:41–40.

———. 1984. Exchange networks and the analysis of complex organizations. In *Research on the Sociology of Organizations*, ed. Samuel B. Bacharach and Edward J. Lawler, 3:1–30. Greenwich, CT: JAI Press.

Damasio, Antonio. 1999. *The Feeling of What Happens*. New York: Harcourt Brace.

Durkheim, Emile. 1915. *The Elementary Forms of Religious Life*. New York: Free Press.

Ekeh, Peter. 1974. *Social Exchange Theory: The Two Traditions*. Cambridge, MA: Harvard University Press.

Emerson, Richard M. 1972a. Exchange theory part I: A psychological basis for social exchange. In *Sociological Theories in Progress*, ed. J. Berger, M. Zelditch Jr., and B. Anderson, 2:38–57. Boston, MA: Houghton Mifflin.

———. 1972b. Exchange theory part II: Exchange rules and networks. In *Sociological Theories in Progress*, ed. J. Berger, M. Zelditch Jr., and B. Anderson, 2:58–87. Boston, MA: Houghton Mifflin.

———. 1981. Social exchange theory. In *Social Psychology: Sociological Perspectives*, ed. M. Rosenberg and R. H. Turner, 30–65. New York: Basic Books.

Forgas, Joseph. 2000. Affect and information strategies. In *Thinking and Feeling: The Role of Affect in Social Cognition*, ed. J. Forgas, 253–80. Cambridge, UK: Cambridge University Press.

Gaertner, Samuel L., Jeffrey Mann, John F. Dovidio, Audrey J. Murrell, and Marina Pomare. 1990. How does cooperation reduce intergroup bias. *Journal of Personality and Social Psychology* 59:692–704.

Hechter, Michael. 1987. *Principles of Group Solidarity*. Berkeley and Los Angeles: University of California Press.

Hegtvedt, Karen, and Barry Markovsky. 1995. Justice and injustice. In *Sociological Perspectives on Social Psychology*, ed. K. S. Cook, G. A. Fine, and J. S. House, 257–80. New York: Allyn & Bacon.

Hochschild, Arlie R. 1983. *The Managed Heart: Commercialization of Human Feeling*. Berkeley and Los Angeles: University of California Press.

Hogg, A. Michael, and John C. Turner. 1985. Interpersonal attraction, social identification and psychological group formation. *European Journal of Social Psychology* 15:51–66.

Homans, George L. 1961. *Social Behavior: Its Elementary Forms*. New York: Harcourt, Brace, Jovanovich.

Isen, A. M. 1987. Positive affect, cognitive processes, and social behavior. *Advances in Experimental Social Psychology*, ed. L. Berkowitz, 20:203–53. New York: Academic.

Izard, Carroll E. 1991. *The Psychology of Emotion*. New York: Plenum.

Jasso, Guillermina. 1980. A new theory of distributive justice. *American Sociological Review* 45:3–32.

Kanter, Rosabeth M. 1968. Commitment and social organization: A study of commitment mechanisms in utopian communities. *American Sociological Review* 33:499–517.

Kelley, Harold H. 1967. Attribution theory in social psychology. In *Nebraska Symposium on Motivation*, ed. Donald Levine, 15:220–66. Lincoln: University of Nebraska Press.

Kemper, Theodore D. 1978. *A Social Interactional Theory of Emotions*. New York: Wiley.

Kollock, Peter. 1994. The emergence of exchange structures: An experimental study of uncertainty, commitment, and trust. *American Journal of Sociology* 100:315–45.

Lawler, Edward J. 1992. Choice processes and affective attachments to nested groups: A theoretical analysis. *American Sociological Review* 57:327–39.

———. 2001. An affect theory of social exchange. *American Journal of Sociology* 107:321–52.

———. 2002. Micro social orders. *Social Psychology Quarterly* 65:4–17.

———. 2003. Interaction, emotion, and collective identities. *Advances in Identity Theory and Research*, ed. P. J. Burke, T. J. Owens, R. Serpe, and P. A. Thoits, 135–49. New York: Kluwer Academic/Plenum.

Lawler, Edward J., and Shane R. Thye. 1999. Bringing emotions into social exchange theory. *Annual Review of Sociology* 25:217–44.

———. 2003. Collaborative research on the affective basis of social disorder. Proposal to National Science Foundation. Cornell University and the University of South Carolina.

Lawler, Edward J., Shane R. Thye, and Jeongkoo Yoon. 2000. Emotion and group cohesion in productive exchange. *American Journal of Sociology* 106 (3): 616–57.

———. 2006. Commitment in structurally enabled and induced exchange relations. *Social Psychology Quarterly.*

Lawler, Edward J., and Jeongkoo Yoon. 1993. Power and the emergence of commitment behavior in negotiated exchange. *American Sociological Review* 58:465–81.

———. 1996. Commitment in exchange relations: Test of a theory of relational cohesion. *American Sociological Review* 61:89–108.

———. 1998. Network structure and emotion in exchange relations. *American Sociological Review* 63:871–94.

Lawler, Edward J., Jeongkoo Yoon, Mouraine R. Baker, and Michael D. Large. 1995. Mutual dependence and gift giving in exchange relations. In *Advances in Group Processes*, ed. B. Markovsky, J. O'Brien, and K. Heimer, 12:271–98. Greenwich, CT: JAI Press.

Markovsky, Barry, and Edward J. Lawler. 1994. A new theory of group solidarity. In *Advances in Group Processes*, ed. B. Markovsky, K. Heimer, J. O'Brien, and E. J. Lawler, 11:113–34. Greenwich, CT: JAI Press.

Molm, Linda. 1994. Dependence and risk: Transforming the structure of social exchange. *Social Psychology Quarterly* 57:163–89.

———. 1997. *Coercive Power in Social Exchange*. Cambridge, UK: Cambridge University Press.

———. 2003. Power, trust and fairness: Comparisons of negotiated and reciprocal exchange. *Advances in Group Processes*, ed. S. Thye and J. Skvoretz, 20:31–65. Oxford, UK: Elsevier.

Molm, Linda, and Karen Cook. 1995. Social exchange and exchange networks. In *Sociological Perspectives on Social Psychology*, ed. K. S. Cook, G. A. Fine, and J. S. House, 209–35. Boston: Allyn & Bacon.

Parsons, Talcott. 1951. *The Social System*. New York: Free Press.

Russell, J. A., Anita Weiss, and G. A. Mendelsohn. 1989. Affect grid: A single-item scale of pleasure and arousal. *Journal of Personal and Sociology Psychology* 57 (3): 493–502.

Skinner, B. F. 1938. *The Behavior of Organisms*. New York: Appleton-Century Crofts.

Stryker, Sheldon. 2000. Identity competition: Key to differential social movement. In *Self, Identity, and Social Movements*, ed. Sheldon Stryker, Timothy J. Owens, and Robert W. White, 21–40. Minneapolis: University of Minnesota Press.

Tajfel, Henri, and John C. Turner. 1986. The social identity theory of intergroup behavior. In *Psychology of Intergroup Relations*, ed. S. Worchel and W. G. Austin, 7–24. Chicago, IL: Nelson-Hall.

Thibaut, John W., and Harold H. Kelley. 1959. *The Social Psychology of Groups*. New York: Wiley.

Thoits, Peggy, and Lauren K. Virshup. 1995. Me's and We's: Forms and functions of social identities. *Self and Identity: Fundamental Issues*, ed. Richard Ashmores and Lee Jussim, 106–33. New York: Oxford University Press.

Thye, Shane R., Jeongkoo Yoon, and Edward J. Lawler. 2002. The theory of relational cohesion: Review of a research program. In *Advances in Group Process*, ed. Shane R. Thye and Edward J. Lawler, vol. 19. Oxford, UK: Elsevier.

Turner, Jonathan H. 2000. *On the Origins of Human Emotions*. Stanford, CA: Stanford University Press.

Weiner, Bernard. 1986. *An Attributional Theory of Motivation and Emotion*. New York: Springer-Verlag.

Willer, David. 1999. *Network Exchange Theory*. Westport, CT: Praeger.

Williamson, Oliver E. 1985. *The Economic Institutions of Capitalism*. New York: Free Press.

12 | EXPECTATIONS, STATUS, AND BEHAVIOR

Joseph Berger and Murray Webster Jr.

Sociologists and social psychologists studying interpersonal behavior have investigated a wide range of phenomena. In this chapter we describe the theoretical understandings and the empirical investigations by many different scholars within a single program of research called expectation states theory. Consider the following questions:

- When members of a committee, a work group, or a team differ in gender, race, and occupation, how do those differences affect their behavior in groups?

- A study of all-male and all-female police teams in a large city found that the least senior member of the team was described as more expressive and interpersonally oriented *regardless of whether that person was male or female*. How can we explain this?

- Under what conditions can the inequalities produced by status differences be overcome?

- Why do women and members of minority groups often have difficulty in being openly directive in their behavior when occupying a leadership position?

- When are the expectations that another holds for you most likely to determine the expectations that you hold for yourself?

- In what kinds of status situations are you most likely to see double standards being used?

Scholars working within the expectation-states program have dealt with all of these questions and many more. Expectation states theory is a *theoretical research program*. As such it consists of a set of interrelated theories, bodies of relevant research concerned with testing these theories, and bodies of research that use these theories in social applications and interventions. What are the different ways these theories are interrelated? In some cases later theories are extensions (or elaborations) of earlier theories. In other cases, later theories represent integrations of different theories in the program, and in still other cases they are formulations (proliferations) that attack new problems by building on the established concepts and principles in the program.

Expectations is a key concept in the program and the program deals with different types of expectations. *Performance expectations* are anticipations on the part of an individual of the abilities and task capacities of self and others, *reward expectations* are anticipations of the rewards (or goal objects) to be possessed by self and others, and *valued status expectations* are anticipations of the status positions to be held by self and others.

The different theories in the program that we consider in this chapter are concerned with the *sources* of such expectations, whether they be interaction patterns, status differences, reward levels, or cultural beliefs; the *combining* (or aggregation) of such expectations if multiple ones exist in a situation; and the *consequences* of such expectations—for instance, how participation rates and influence patterns change among individuals as expectations form and change.

In section I, we describe the initial research in the expectation-states program on the development of power and prestige orders. In section II, we present the core status characteristics theory and in sections III and IV, respectively, theoretical extensions of that theory and theoretical integrations of that theory with other theories in the program. In section V, we describe a theory concerned with the use of multiple standards, and in section VI, we conclude with brief descriptions of current research developments and an assessment of the theoretical growth in the program.

I. THE INITIAL RESEARCH: POWER AND PRESTIGE THEORY

The original research concern of expectation state theory was with the emergence of inequalities in power and prestige behaviors in small problem-solving groups. These processes were most evident in Bales's observations of small, informal task groups whose members were presumably initially similar in status. (See Bales et al. 1951; Bales 1953; Bales and Slater 1955; Heinicke and Bales 1953). Bales found that inequalities in the initiation of activity, in the receipt of activities, on ratings of best ideas, and in group guidance regularly emerged in such groups. Once they emerged, these inequalities tended to be stable. And with the possible exception of sociometric rankings, the various inequalities studied by Bales were highly intercorrelated. Research by others (e.g., Harvey 1953; Sherif, White, and Harvey 1955; Whyte 1943) has shown that established inequalities in power and prestige are also correlated with members' evaluations of specific performances. Independent of actual performance level, high-status members are seen as performing better than low-status members.

Berger (1958) and Berger and Conner (1966, 1969) conceptualized the behavioral inequalities observed in these groups as the components of a one-dimensional power-prestige order. They argued that this order consists in (1) chances to perform (action-opportunities); (2) attempts to solve the group's problem (performance outputs); (3) communicated evaluations of such problem solving attempts (reward actions); and (4) changes of opinion when confronted with disagreement (influence). Collectively these inequalities are referred to as the *observable power and prestige order of the group*.

Berger and Conner were interested in accounting for (1) the emergence of observable power and prestige orders in groups; (2) the intercorrelation of the component inequalities of these orders; and (3) the stability of the observable power and prestige orders in the groups. The groups they were concerned with are also small, informal groups whose members are similar in terms of external status. Further, these groups operate under certain conditions: first, the members of the group are task oriented in the sense that they are committed to solving a problem whose outcome is valued, and second, the members of the group are collectively oriented in the sense that it is necessary and legitimate for them to take each other's behavior into account in working on the group's task. These are thought of as *scope conditions*; they define the situational conditions under which a theory was expected to hold.[1]

Given these conditions, Berger and Conner assumed that individuals who begin as similar in external status develop, in the course of collectively working on their group task, differences in underlying performance expectations for self and other. These performance expectations are stabilized anticipations of future task performances and are based on the evaluations of past performances that individuals make and communicate to each other. Hence as expectations form, evaluations of specific past behavior give rise to generalized anticipations of future behavior.

In accounting for the intercorrelation of the components of the observable power and prestige order, Berger and Conner argued that this resulted from the fact that they were all functions of the same underlying performance-expectation structure. Imagine, for example, a two-person group where higher performance expectations are held for individual *A* as compared to *B*. They reasoned that in such a situation *A* was more likely to initiate performance outputs than *B*, *A* is more likely to have those performances positively evaluated by *B* than those of *B* by *A*, and *A* was more likely to exercise influence over *B* than *B* over *A*.

In accounting for the stability of power and prestige orders, Berger and Conner argued that the power and prestige behaviors, which are functions of differences in performance expectations, also operate to maintain these performance expectations. Therefore, barring changes in the initial conditions of the group's action, such as the input of external evaluations or a shift to less task orientation with the passage of time (see Heinecke and Bales 1953), the observable power and prestige is expected to be stable.

Subsequently, this theory was generalized by Berger and Conner (1974). They started out by analyzing what they called unit sequences of interaction that lead to consensual acceptance or consensual rejection of problem-solving attempts (performance outputs). Sequences were composed of different patterns of power and prestige behaviors; for example, *A* initiates a performance output to *B*, *B* rejects that output, and *A* exercises influence on *B* so that *B* accepts the performance output of *A*.

They argued that in a group where individuals start out similar in external status, performance expectations emerge out of sequences involving accepted performance outputs. In a two-person group, say, if the rate of accepted performance outputs of *A* is greater than *B*, then there is a likelihood that at some subsequent point the performance expectations for *A* will be greater than those for *B* and that subsequent power and prestige behaviors will be functions of these expectations.

Under this formulation differences in the rate of accepting performance outputs are not only affected by differences in the evaluations of performances but also differences, say, in the rate at which an individual initiates performance outputs or differences in the likelihood of an individual being influenced by others. Thus an interesting consequence of this theory is the argument that *differences in any of the components* of the observable power and prestige order such as receipt of action-opportunities, initiation of performance outputs, received reward actions, or exercise of influence can affect the rates at which performance outputs are accepted. If so, these differences can determine expectation relations in the group and the particular power and prestige ordering that emerges.

II. STATUS CHARACTERISTICS THEORY: THE CORE FORMULATION

The power and prestige theory was concerned with how individuals formed performance expectations that determined their behavior in situations where they were initially similar with respect to status. The status characteristics theory was formulated to account for how individuals formed performance expectations that determined their behavior in situations in which they initially differ on such status distinctions as gender, race, or occupational positions.

Already by the 1950s and early 1960s it was well-known that the external statuses that individuals possessed had a major impact on their behavior in face-to-face task-oriented groups (Hurwitz, Zander, and Hymovitch 1960; Strodbeck, James, and Hawkins 1958; Torrance 1954; Zander and Cohen 1955). However, it was also known, as the sociologists Strodbeck and colleagues (1958) pointed out, that we did not understand *how* this differentiation arises from such status elements. Reviewing this literature and seeking to formulate an abstract statement of their findings, Berger, Cohen, and Zelditch (1966) concluded that when the members of task groups are differentiated in terms of status characteristics external to the task situation, this differentiation determines the observable power and prestige order in the group. This relation apparently held whether or not the external characteristics had a prior, established association with the goal or task of the group. However, it did depend somewhat on how well members of the group knew each other; the effect decreased as the acquaintance of the members of the group increased (Heiss 1962; Leik 1963).

The initial status characteristics theory (Berger, Cohen, and Zelditch 1966, 1972) was formulated to provide, among other things, a theoretical explanation for this important relation. Subsequently, this theory was elaborated and formalized (Berger and Fisek 1974; Berger et al. 1977). In the following we present a nonmathematical description of the theory. (For a mathematical presentation see Berger et al. 1977.)

A. Concepts and Assumptions of the Core Theory

The theory of status characteristics describes the evolution of a status-organizing process. A *status-organizing process* is one in which evaluations and beliefs about the characteristics of actors become bases of observable inequalities in face-to-face interaction.

A central concept in describing such a process is that of a status characteristic. A *status characteristic* is any characteristic around which beliefs and expectations about actors come to be organized. We distinguish two kinds of status characteristics, specific and diffuse.

The distinction hinges on the difference between specific and general expectations. Expectations are *specific* if they are applicable to clearly defined situations. Expectations are *general* if they are not restricted to any specified situation but are applicable to an unlimited range of situations. *Reading ability* carries specific expectations while *intelligence* carries general expectations. A characteristic is a *specific status characteristic* if it involves two or more states that are differentially evaluated; and associated with each state is a distinct expectation state. For example, mathematical ability may function as a specific status characteristic. We can distinguish different levels of the characteristic that are differentially evaluated, and we associate beliefs on how individuals possessing the different states will perform on specific tasks. A characteristic is a *diffuse status characteristic* if the following three things are true: (1) it involves two or more states that are differentially valued; (2) associated with each state are distinct sets of specific expectations, each itself evaluated; and (3) also associated with each state is a similarly evaluated general expectation state. Thus gender may be a diffuse status characteristic for a given population at a given time if the members of that population hold differential status evaluations for males and females, hold distinct specific expectations about the behavior of males and females, and they assume, say, that males in general are more capable on a wide (and typically unspecified) range of valued tasks and activities.

In this theory, status characteristics are pregiven cultural elements that frame any particular situation of action. They are part of the *larger social (or global) framework* of taken-for-granted social categories and cultural beliefs within which actors operate, and they initially structure any particular encounter for the actors involved. Established diffuse status characteristics such as those involving race, ethnicity, and gender already exist in the social framework, becoming information structures for actors when those characteristics become salient.

The theory assumes a situation of action in which a status-organizing process can occur. A *situation of action* consists of goals that drive the action in a particular setting and the contextual conditions of that action, such as the number of actors, whether they are face-to-face, and the status information they possess.

As in the Berger and Conner formulations, this theory applies to group situations in which individuals are collectively oriented to achieving a shared goal. We assume that this shared goal is a valued task with outcomes of success or failure and that individuals are motivated to succeed on the task. We again assume that the actors understand that it is both necessary and legitimate to take the behavior of others into account in achieving the group's goal.

The core theory consists of five assumptions; the first of these addresses the question of under what conditions do status characteristics become *salient* to the actors? The assumption claims that such status information becomes salient if it is initially defined as relevant to the task, as would be the case with gender, for example, if the task were culturally defined as masculine or feminine. It also claims that status characteristics will become salient if they are a basis of discrimination among the actors, as would be the case in a mixed-gender or biracial group.

Assume that a status characteristic that is not initially relevant to the task becomes salient; how will actors treat this information? The theory argues that actors tend to generalize status advantages to ever new situations. High-status individuals, for example, behave and are treated as if they have greater performance capacities than low-status individuals to deal with the task. The *burden of proof is on the interactants to dissociate such status advantages from their immediate situation, not on establishing their relevance.* As a consequence status advantages are generalized from one situation to the next as part of normal interaction unless their applicability is called into question (dissociated) or challenged.

The third assumption states that if new status information becomes salient or new actors enter the group, those already in the group will restructure their situation in *sequence*. They will further develop their structure of the situation through the salience and burden-of-proof processes, while previously completed parts of their structure remain as long as they are in the situation.

The fourth assumption claims that actors combine all the status information that is salient and relevant to the task in forming their performance expectations. While in all likelihood the process by which this occurs is outside the individual's awareness, we can construct a model to describe it. According to this model, known as the *principle of organized subsets*, all information leading to positive performance expectations is combined into a subset to determine its positive value and all information leading to negative performance expectations is combined into a subset to determine its negative value. This combining process is subject to an attenuation effect in that the more information of a given sign in a subset, the less the incremental effect of additional like-signed information. This combining also takes into account the possibility that status distinctions differ in their relevance to the immediate task, that is, in how closely they are connected to the group's goal. By this subset combining principle, the aggregated expectations for an actor are given by summing the values of the positive and negative subsets. The actor's *expectation advantage (or disadvantage)* relative to another is equal to the aggregated expectation for self less that formed for the other.

The fifth assumption, the *basic-expectation assumption*, builds on the work of Berger and Conner and argues that the specific behaviors, those collectively referred to as observable power and prestige behaviors, are direct functions of an actor's expectation advantage relative to another. Subsequently, Berger et al. (1986) elaborated this assumption by arguing that certain verbal and nonverbal task cues that provide information on an actor's competence on the group's immediate task are also functions of an actor's expectation advantage relative to another. These include such behaviors as an actor's rate of gesturing, rate of maintaining eye gaze with others while speaking, and ratio of fluent to nonfluent speech.

B. Applications to Different Status Distinctions

The status characteristics theory is an abstract formal theory. It is not a theory of gender, race, or occupational status. It is a theory about status characteristics, diffuse and specific; goal objects; referential structures; and behavioral interchange patterns (see later discussion). Thus it can be used in the study of status processes involving gender, race, occupation, and many other socially significant concrete status distinctions provided these distinctions operate as status characteristics for a given population at a given time.

The status characteristics theory has been used to describe the status-organizing effects of, among other status distinctions, educational attainment (Moore 1968; Zelditch, Lauderdale, and Stublarec 1980; Markovsky, Smith, and Berger 1984); occupational position and sexual orientation (Webster, Hysom, and Fullmer 1998); race (Cohen and Roper 1972; Webster and Driskell 1978; Brezina and Winder 2003); gender (Lockheed and Hall 1976; Lockheed 1985; Meeker and Weitzel-O'Neill 1977); physical attractiveness (Webster and Driskell 1983); ethnic identities, including Anglo American versus Mexican American (Rosenholtz and Cohen 1985), Sephardic versus Ashkenazic Jews (Cohen and Sharan 1980), and Anglo Australian versus Greek Australian (Foddy and Riches 2000); and organizational ranks and positions (Berger, Cohen, and Zelditch 1972; Johnson 2003). It also has been used to theoretically integrate research on the status effects of gender (Carli 1991; Ridgeway and Diekema 1992; Wagner and Berger 1998) and to theoretically integrate research on the effects of physical attractiveness as a status distinction (Jackson, Hunger, and Hodge 1995).

C. Empirical Consequences[2]

The literature on empirical tests of the status characteristic theory is extensive. Among other findings this research shows that the magnitude of inequality in power and prestige behaviors is a direct function of the consistency of status distinctions, of their number (given consistency), and the relevance of a status distinction to the group's task. Further, Fisek, Norman, and Nelson-Kilger (1992), reporting on 27 experiments, find that overall there is a good fit between theory predictions and the results of these experiments. (See also the research reported in Webster and Foschi 1988 and in Balkwell 1991.) We illustrate the nature of this work by examining studies on three of the many issues dealt with in this research: on the status typing of tasks, on overcoming status inequalities, and on the relation of status to personality conceptions.

The core theory provides a set of arguments that explains the effect on power and prestige behaviors of the status typing of tasks. The theory argues that the greater the relevance of a status distinction to the task goal, the greater its impact on behavior. Thus the immediate task characteristic should have more impact than one that is relevant to the task characteristic, and a relevant characteristic should have more impact than a status characteristic that is not initially relevant to the task. If a task is gender typed—say, for example, that it involves mechanical ability—then gender is a status characteristic that is relevant to the task characteristic of mechanical ability. These and other arguments in the theory predict that when individuals in two-person, mixed-gender groups are working on a gender-neutral task (no initial relevance of gender to the task) males will be advantaged over females, that this advantage will be increased when they are working on a male-typed task, and this advantage actually will be reversed—so as to favor females—when they are working on a female-typed task. An experiment by Dovidio and colleagues (1988) provides a direct test of these arguments. Mixed-gender, two-person groups worked on neutral tasks and male- and female-typed tasks. It was found that when working on a gender-neutral task, males initiated more speech, spoke more, made more eye contact when speaking, and gestured more than females. These inequalities favoring males increased on the male-typed task, and as predicted, they were reversed when the group worked on the female task.

Another important claim of the status theory is that the inequalities generated by a diffuse status characteristic can be overcome by the introduction of inconsistent status information. Further, since a task characteristic has greater relevance to the group's goal than either a relevant or initially nonrelevant diffuse status characteristic, a task characteristic that is inconsistent with either type of diffuse status characteristic is predicted to reverse status inequalities. An inconsistent task characteristic might be one that establishes that the lower status individual has greater task competence than the higher status individual. This prediction has been directly tested in experiments by Zelditch and colleagues (1980) and Wagner, Ford, and Ford (1986). In each case where there is an experimentally created inconsistency between the task characteristic and a diffuse status characteristic it has been found that the lower status individual was less influenced by the behavior of the higher status individual than the higher status individual by the behavior of the lower status individual.

The last study we consider in this section is both an application and extension of status theory. Gwendolyn Gerber (2001) was interested in the attributions that are made of dominating and expressive traits in two-person police teams, some of which were mixed gender, others all male, and still others all female. On same-gender teams, Gerber regarded the individual with greater experience as having higher status.[3] On mixed-gender teams, males were regarded as having the higher status.

The status theory implies that high- and low-status individuals will have different behavioral profiles in these two-person teams. The higher the status of the actor, the more he or she is expected to engage in task behaviors relative to his or her rate of reacting to others' task performances; the lower the status of the actor, the more that actor is expected to react to another's task performance relative to his or her rate of task performances. Such performer-reactor differences should lead to stereotyping attributions that are consistent with the actors' behavioral profiles. Therefore Gerber predicted that low-status team members are more likely to be characterized with expressive traits *independent of* whether they were male or female; this is what she found. Further, she predicted that high-status team members, whatever their gender, were more likely to be characterized with dominating traits. In general, this is also what she observed (although this relation was not statistically significant).

Assuming that such attributions come to be treated as dispositional properties of the individual ("that is the type of person this individual really is"), Gerber's research shows how the construction of personality conceptions by the individual and others can arise out of the operation of status-organizing processes.

III. THEORETICAL EXTENSIONS

A. The Reward Expectation States Theory

The reward expectation states theory is an extension of the core status characteristics theory, which also builds on the status value theory of distributive justice (Berger, Zelditch, Anderson, and Cohen 1972). It is formulated to apply to situations in which differential rewards are allocated as a condition of action in the situation. The theory is concerned with describing how actors form reward expectations in status situations. The basic argument of the theory is that the pattern of status distinctions that have become salient in a group and the prevailing cultural beliefs on how rewards are typically distributed, which are activated from the actor's encompassing social framework, play major roles in the formation of reward expectations. The theory uses the concept of referential beliefs (or structures) introduced in the status value theory of distributive justice, and it distinguishes different types of such belief structures.

Referential structures are sets of socially validated beliefs held in common by actors. These beliefs describe what is thought to be the usual association between a valued characteristic and levels of rewards. As in the case of status characteristics, the source of such beliefs is the culture that is part of the larger collectivity of which interactants are part, such as an organization, a subculture, or the larger society. The theory distinguishes three types of referential structures—categorical, ability, and outcome structures—and describes conditions under which each is activated.

In *categorical structures*, the valued characteristics that are associated with different reward levels are broad social categories such as diffuse status characteristics (e.g., race, gender, occupational position, educational attainment, or age). These beliefs involve criteria of "who you are" in determining the distribution of rewards. If actors hold referential beliefs with respect to a given status characteristic, those beliefs are activated if the status characteristic becomes salient in an immediate situation.

Ability structures associate different reward levels with the ability characteristic that is directly relevant in the task situation. These beliefs relate rewards to criteria of "what can you do" or "what are your capacities" in the immediate situation. If referential ability beliefs are held by the actors and are not explicitly prohibited, they will be activated when the actors are in a task-oriented situation.

Outcome structures relate reward levels to actual performances and accomplishments in the situation. They invoke criteria of "what have you done" and "what have you actually accomplished" in the immediate situation. Such beliefs are activated when task accomplishments are evaluated by an external source or interactants in terms of agreed-on standards.

In any given situation these beliefs, when activated, become bases for the allocation of rewards. Status situations differ in terms of what referential structures are activated. There are situations where only performance capacities matter; situations where capacities, accomplishments, and status categories matter; and situations where only status category matters—for example, a seniority system. This theory uses the principles of the core theory—salience, burden of proof, organized subsets—conjoined with these new ideas on referential structures and their activation to describe the formation of reward expectations.

A basic consequence from this theory is the claim that if multiple referential beliefs are activated in a situation, actors will combine these structures in forming their reward expectations. Similarly if multiple status distinctions exist in a situation, actors will combine information from these characteristics to form their reward expectations.

Surveys by Jasso and Rossi (1977) and Alves and Rossi (1978) show that a high degree of consensus exists in U.S. society over the norms and standards to be applied to the distribution of earned income. Further, these standards are used in evaluating one's income expectations, and people combine several criteria in arriving at these evaluations. We inter-pret these studies to show that multiple referential structures exist and have a combined effect in determining reward expectations.

In a situation where a single status distinction exists in the group, the differentiation in reward expectations should be directly related to the differentiation on that status distinc-tion. Wagner (1995) conducted a direct test of this argument. He differentiated individuals in a two-person group on a specific status characteristic that was instrumental to the group's task and found that they differentiated their proposed reward allocations in accord with their status differentiation. In groups where he equated actors on the specific status charac-teristic, their proposed allocations for the self and the other tended to be equal. He found no significant differences in proposed allocation behaviors in all-male groups and all-female groups.

Another consequence of reward expectations theory is that if a differentiated status dis-tinction (or a consistent set of status distinctions) exists in a group, the greater the relevance of these status distinctions to the group's task, the greater the differentiation in proposed re-ward allocation. In a second set of studies, Wagner (2000) composed mixed-gender, two-person task groups. In one condition where gender initially was neither related to nor dis-sociated from the task, he found that women's proposed allocation of rewards for self was less than proposed by men for themselves. In a second condition where the diffuse status characteristic of gender was made initially relevant to the task, he found, as predicted, that the magnitude of differentiation in proposed reward allocations was even greater; women allocated even less for themselves, while men allocated more in this condition. However, in a third condition where task-ability status was made inconsistent with gender status, he found, also as predicted, that this effect of reward allocations favoring men was eliminated. In this connection, a study by Hogue and Yoder (2003) also shows that the effect of women allocating less rewards to themselves than do men for the same quality work can be elimi-nated by enhancing the status of women in a given situation. (For further research on the allocation of rewards as a function of status, see Fisek and Hysom 2004.)

One of the most interesting arguments from the rewards theory, which was originally proposed in the status value theory of distributive justice, is what is called the *reverse process*. This is the argument that the allocation of differentially evaluated goal objects (or rewards), in and of itself, will lead to the formation of high- and low-performance expectations con-sistent with the allocated rewards and that these task expectations in turn will determine be-havior. We now have extensive empirical support for the existence of this reverse process in studies by Lerner (1965); Cook (1975); Harrod (1980); Bierhoff, Buck, and Klein (1986); and Stewart and Moore (1992).

This reverse process of reward allocations leading to performance expectations can be particularly important in accounting for the stability of diffuse status characteristics. If differential rewards are allocated in a group that are consistent with, for example, gender differences, then the reverse process will operate to reinforce the differential performance expectations that are typically associated with gender differences. If that is so, the reverse process enables us to identify conditions under which well-established status distinctions are particularly stable.

Finally, we note that this theory argues for an interdependence of task and reward expectations. In situations where differentially valued goal objects (or rewards) are distributed as a condition of action, the theory claims that expectations for rewards will be formed *simultaneously* with expectations for task performances. Further, it claims that if status distinctions in a group are consistent, changes in task expectations, say, by introducing new status characteristics, will produce corresponding changes in reward expectations. In turn, changes in reward expectations, for example, by activating a new referential standard, will produce changes in task expectations. A study by Parcel and Cook (1977) provides some evidence that bears on this interdependence argument. They found that when changes in task expectations were produced by informing subjects how well they actually performed, that gave rise to reward expectations consistent with such changes. However, the full implications of the interdependence of task and reward expectations are still to be explored.

B. The Evolution of Status Expectations

The core version of the status characteristics theory is restricted to describing status-organizing processes as they occur in situations in which actors are confronted with a single group task. But this restriction leaves open an unanswered set of important theoretical and empirical questions. What happens to actors' status expectations and behaviors if upon the completion of an initial group task they move on to a second task, a third task, or still further tasks? How are the expectations actors have formed on an initial task affected by the introduction of new and different partners as they move from one task to another? How do evaluations of success or failure on an initial task affect expectations and behaviors on a succeeding task? What happens to status interventions that are introduced on an initial task as the sequence of successive tasks evolves?

To provide answers to these questions and still others, Berger, Fisek, and Norman (1989) constructed a formulation that allows us to apply the core theory to situations involving a sequence of group tasks. To do this they introduce an assumption that is in addition to those in the core status theory. This assumption argues that, on the completion of an initial task, actors behave as if success or failure on that task is relevant to success or failure, respectively, on the succeeding task. It is assumed that the tasks in this sequence are not dissociated from each other (on the basis of cultural or other information) and are not inversely related to each other.[4]

Most of the empirical research that is directly relevant to this formulation has been concerned with whether different types of status interventions transfer across (1) different status occupants, e.g., male to male or female to female, (2) across different tasks, and (3) across different status characteristics, e.g., gender to educational attainment. In general, this extension argues that status interventions will transfer across status occupants, across tasks, and across status characteristics but that there will be a decrease (or an attenuation) in the effectiveness of these interventions in the course of these transfers.

In a series of studies on the status effects of gender, Lockheed and Hall (1976) provided females with the opportunity to develop performance expectations by first interacting in gender-homogeneous groups and then interacting in mixed-gender groups. Females who had this experience were more likely to occupy high-status positions in mixed-gender groups than those who had not had such prior experience. When members of these mixed-gender groups subsequently interacted on a different task, those who were highly or less active on the first task tended, respectively, to be highly or less active on the second task. However, the researchers also note what they call a tendency for females to hold more low-status positions on the new task. These results are consistent with our formulation. We interpret this situation as one in which females developed specific competencies in gender-homogeneous groups that affected their status position in a mixed-gender group operating on a different task and that also showed some evidence of an attenuation effect.

After first demonstrating that gender operates as a status characteristic by showing that women are more likely to defer to men than men to women when they disagree while working on a collective group task, Pugh and Wahrman (1983) introduced status interventions. They provided information to both males and females that the specific female in each group is highly competent and the specific male is not competent on an ability that is relevant to the task ability. This information sharply reduced the effect of gender differences on deferring behaviors. Then they were able to show that their status intervention continued to operate without diminution of effect when the specific female interacted with a second male (and the specific male interacted with a second female) on the same task.[5] While the results of this study are consistent with the evolution extension in that it shows that the intervention transfers across status occupants, the study does not provide us with evidence of the predicted attenuation effect.

Building on the work of Pugh and Wahrman (1983), Markovsky, Smith, and Berger (1984) were able to mitigate the effect of differences in educational attainment on deferring behaviors by informing the relatively low-education participant that he was high on an ability relevant to the task ability while the relatively high-education participant was low on that ability. Markovsky and colleagues then found that this intervention carried over in determining a participant's behavior when he interacted on a new task with a new partner with similar educational status as his partner on the initial task. At the same time, Markovsky and colleagues found that the effect of the intervention in determining the participant's behavior on the second task with the new partner was reduced. This study is fully consistent with the extension, including providing evidence on the weakening of the status intervention in the course of transfer.

Building on previous research, Prescott (1986) investigated the transfer of an intervention across status characteristics. Male subjects who were college freshmen interacted with similarly educated females on a task that was defined as one on which females were superior to males. Under these conditions males deferred to females at a much higher rate than when they were working with females on a gender-neutral task. Males then worked on a second and different task that was defined as gender neutral with new female partners who were identified as high school dropouts. The rate of deferring for males went down but the rate of deferring for those males who initially interacted on the gender-typed task was higher than that for males who initially interacted on the gender-neutral task. We interpret this experiment as providing evidence for what is a strong prediction from the evolution extension, namely, that the effect of the status intervention, i.e., the gender typing of the task, can transfer across status occupants, different tasks, and different status characteristics.

While the results of most of the research that is directly relevant to the evolution extension are supportive of this extension, there are important arguments that are still to be tested. These include predictions on the long-term status behaviors of interactants and predictions concerning the very special conditions under which status interventions are predicted to have a lasting effect.

C. Status Legitimation Theory

It has long been recognized that important changes occur when a power and prestige structure becomes legitimated. But exactly how does this occur? While we have interesting theories in sociology about legitimation, these have been largely concerned with consequences of legitimation rather than with the process by which legitimation emerges. To address this problem, Berger and colleagues (1998), building on earlier work by Ridgeway and Berger (1986), have constructed a theory that describes processes and conditions under which a nonlegitimated order can become a legitimated order. This theory builds on the core status theory as well as its reward expectation and status-evolution extensions.

The theory starts with the idea that as part of the cultural framework within which a group operates there may exist referential beliefs that associate the possession of high- and low-valued status positions with the possession of different states of diffuse status characteristics, different levels of task ability, or different levels of task achievement. One such referential structure, for example, is the commonly held belief (whatever its validity) that males ordinarily occupy higher valued status positions in U.S. society than females. These referential beliefs become salient under the conditions described in the reward expectation theory for the activation of categorical, ability, and outcome structures.

Given that such beliefs are activated, actors use them to form expectations as to who will occupy high- and low-status positions *within their immediate group*. These valued status expectations, in turn, determine the actors' generalized deferential behaviors—the respect, the esteem, the honor, and the social support they will accord to others in the group. Given that such deferential behaviors, for example, to a high-status individual, are validated by others and that expectations for valued status positions coincide with those of task performances, then the probability exists that the power and prestige becomes a legitimated order. Generalized deferential behaviors are *validated* if others engage in similar behaviors or do not engage in behaviors that contradict the initial deferential behaviors.

With legitimation, expectations become normatively prescriptive. The high-status individual *should* be shown more generalized deference and support by others in the group than lower status individuals. In addition, these normative expectations are applied to the power and prestige behaviors in the group. High-status individuals have the *right* to control more of the group's time and attention than the lower status members in order to present their ideas and proposals. However, the ideas, proposals, and decisions of high-status individuals should be more valued, more effective, and more successful group contributions than those from lower status members. In addition, with legitimacy comes a *presumption of collective support* in the sense that other members of the group will act to maintain the power and prestige ordering. For high-status actors this can imply the right to employ (presumably in the service of the group's goals) directive and dominating behaviors with the anticipation of group support for such behaviors.

This formulation accounts for certain common observations about legitimacy in task settings, for example, that legitimate power and prestige orders tend to be stable (Michener and Burt 1975; Thomas, Walker, and Zelditch 1986). It also accounts for observations that states of legitimacy affect an actor's ability to engage in directive, leaderlike behaviors or domineering behaviors (Burke 1968; Driskell, Olmstead, and Salas 1992; Ridgeway 1987). Such research supports the relationship that is posited in the theory to exist between legitimacy and the effective use of directive and domineering behaviors.

There is also evidence that leaders with low external status—women or minorities—are confronted with resistance that restricts their ability to engage in effective assertive behaviors and therefore limits their capacity to be successful leaders (Butler and Geis 1990; Eagly, Makhijani, and Klonsky 1992; Eskilson and Wiley 1976). The legitimation formulation can account for such findings. Status characteristics bring with them referential beliefs that provide varying amounts of cultural support for different types of people in leadership positions. Given that individuals form expectations for valued status positions on the basis of these referential beliefs, this leads them to treat individuals who occupy high-status positions differently depending on their external status. Specifically, those with low external status may often be treated as normatively inappropriate occupants of high-status positions.

Aside from being consistent with evidence on legitimacy effects in informal hierarchies, there are also direct tests of this formulation. One of the consequences of the formulation is the argument that there is a greater probability that the power and prestige order in a consistent status structure will become legitimated than that in an inconsistent status structure. Ridgeway, Johnson, and Diekema (1994) created two types of power and prestige orders. In one type, leaders (the most influential members) were advantaged over other members on two consistent status characteristics—age and educational attainment. In the second type, an inconsistent structure, leaders had demonstrated special expertise at the task but possessed a diffuse status disadvantage on educational attainment. In accord with predictions from this formulation, group members were more compliant with directive dominance behaviors—an indicator of legitimacy—in the first type of power and prestige order than in the second. These results held for both male and female groups.

Another consequence of this formulation is the argument that if the performance evaluations of the members of a group in terms of task success or task failure that occur at the end of their problem-solving session are consistent with their expectation advantage, then there is an increase in the likelihood that the power and prestige order of the group will become legitimated as the group moves to the next problem-solving session. Evaluations are consistent if a success evaluation is assigned to the actor with an expectation advantage and a failure evaluation to the one with an expectation disadvantage. In a recent study, Munroe (2001) conducted an experiment to test for this process and found as predicted that the rate of an actor's compliance to dominating behaviors was more likely to be maintained or increased after the consistent evaluations of task success and failure were assigned to the members of their group.

In terms of this theory, a crucial component in the emergence of a legitimated power and prestige order is the validation by others in the group of the generalized deferential behaviors accorded to high-status individuals. In another recent study, Kalkhoff (2003) has found some support for the argument that the likelihood of such validation is itself related to the magnitude of status differentiation that exists in a group. In addition, he found that judgments of the appropriateness of status behaviors were directly related to an individual's validating behaviors.

The legitimation theory highlights sharply the multilevel nature of theories in the program. Cultural beliefs begin the process of legitimation by affecting the likelihood that one actor treats another with honorific deference. But to result in legitimacy, the process depends on the contingent reactions of others who can provide consensual validation and who collectively construct a local reality that makes the power and prestige order prescriptive.

IV. THEORETICAL INTEGRATIONS

A. Behavior-Status Theory

Fisek, Berger, and Norman (1991) proposed a new theory, called behavior-status theory, that seeks to integrate research in which individuals are similar in terms of external status and research on status-heterogeneous groups in which individuals are differentiated in terms of external status distinctions. The former are situations dealt with in the power and prestige theory and the latter are situations dealt with in the status characteristics theory.

Fisek, Berger, and Norman's (1991) theory builds upon the concept of unit sequences as developed in Berger and Conner (1974; see previous discussion). Since such sequences determine whose performances are accepted and whose performances are rejected, such sequences have both decision-making consequences and expectation-formation consequences. The authors introduce the concept of *behavior interchange pattern*, which is a set of unit sequences in which all the sequences in the set have the same ordering in terms of expectation differences for the actors involved. Once these expectation orderings have emerged, actors combine them along with other status information in the immediate situation in forming their aggregated expectation states.

Using this formulation, the authors construct a specific model to predict participation rates in open-interaction, status-heterogeneous groups and status-homogeneous groups. (For a critical exchange on this model see Robinson and Balkwell 1995; Fisek, Berger, and Norman 1997; Balkwell 1991.)

While previous models in this area describe the power and prestige *outcomes* of a structure-formation process (Fisek, Berger, and Norman 1991; Balkwell 1991), recently Skvoretz and Fararo (1996) have formulated a model that describes how the structure-formation process actually *evolves* through time in addition to describing the power and prestige outcomes of such a process.

These authors are concerned with small, newly constituted face-to-face groups whose members are task and collectively oriented. These groups can consist of different combinations of members who are either similar or differentiated on status characteristics. In constructing this model Skvoretz and Fararo make use of Fisek, Berger, and Norman's (1991) concept of *behavior interchange patterns* to describe how expectation states (or E-states in their terminology) can emerge out of the ongoing interaction process, as well as Ivan Chase's concept of the *bystander*. Chase (1980) has argued that a bystander, while observing the interaction of two others who themselves may be forming expectations for each other, can also form expectations that relate the bystander to each of the actors in the interacting pair.

The model that Skvoretz and Fararo have developed is a probabilistic one. They present a set of axioms that describes the possibilities and probabilities of interactants forming E-states given their behavior toward each other and the possibilities and probabilities that bystanders form E-states based on their observations of the behaviors of these interactants. As the interaction evolves, tie relations are established between actors. Each tie relation represents a symmetrical pair of E-states, where one actor expects to be ascendant to a second and the second expects to defer to the first. In the formation of these E-states between actors, their external status differences, if they exist, play an important role. For example, an E-state in which A is ascendant to B is not possible if B is superior to A in terms of a diffuse status characteristic that is activated (which can occur with a certain probability) in the situation.

The tie relations that evolve may be complete in the sense that they link all actors to each other and they may be strongly hierarchical in the sense that all triadic relations are transitive.[6] Once these ties are established they are stable and they determine the individual's behavior in the group. However, because of the probabilistic nature of this model it is possible to realize the development of hierarchies that are not complete and that are only partly transitive structures.

Skvoretz, Webster, and Whitmeyer (1999) report a study involving 60 four-person open interaction discussion groups. Their data provide evidence that triads were more transitive in these groups than would be expected by chance. This provides favorable evidence for the bystander effect that is built into the model. In addition they found that individuals who were initially higher on external status rank higher in the internal participation distribution of the group. This provides support for the status activation effect that is part of this model.

Finally, we observe that the particular way in which Skvoretz and Fararo have conceptualized the structure-formation process is of special interest. They describe this formation process from the standpoint of each actor involved in the situation. Each actor contributes to the emergence of E-state structures by his or her behavior with another as an interactant or through his or her observations of the behaviors of others as a bystander. However, the processes that are involved in the structure formation process are in all likelihood outside the actor's conscious awareness. Nevertheless, out of these processes an E-state structure emerges that provides opportunities for performances for higher status individuals while creating constraints on behavior for lower status individuals. Thus, while *neither intended* nor *consciously engineered*, a social structure is created that in the end determines the power and prestige behaviors of the actors involved.

B. Evaluations and Expectations

Expectation theorists have long known (see discussion of Berger 1958 and Berger and Conner 1969 and the previously discussed behavior-status theory) that one of the ways expectations states form during interaction is out of patterns of positive and negative unit evaluations. That is, if someone's performance attempts consistently receive positive evaluations (for instance, "That's correct"), high expectations are likely to form for that person, and vice versa for negative evaluations and low expectations.

Many of the early theories relied on empirical situations where someone who was highly credible, such as an experimenter administering a test of some ability, evaluated the performances of individuals. Such evaluations are, almost by definition, reliable and true. Of course, in many natural settings, individuals receive evaluations of performances with less than certainty of their being credible. In classrooms, teachers evaluate students' answers, and most students treat those evaluations as highly reliable, while the evaluations by fellow students may be treated as less reliable. How can we extend the theory to understand what happens to performance expectations in cases where evaluations are from evaluators of uncertain credibility?

1. Source of Evaluations and Expectations for Performance. Webster and Sobieszek (1974) constructed a theoretical formulation, source theory, just for those situations where an evaluator may be less than perfectly credible. Their approach was to define a new term, a *source*, someone whose evaluations will be accepted by the person being evaluated, and to focus on conditions under which an evaluator can become a source. A basic argument in this theory is that if an actor holds higher performance expectations for an evaluator than for self, then the evaluator becomes a source for the actor. If the evaluator is a source to the actor, the actor's evaluations of his or her own performances and those of another will coincide with the source's evaluations of these performances. Those evaluations in turn will determine the performance expectations for self and other formed by the actor. On the other hand, if an actor holds lower performance expectations for an evaluator than self, the evaluator will not become a source, his or her evaluations will be ignored, and they will not affect the actor's expectations.

Webster and Sobieszek conducted several sets of experiments to test and develop source theory. The first set confirmed the basic ideas just discussed. A second set of experiments assessed newer ideas about what happens when someone is confronted with two evaluators who may either agree or disagree in their evaluations. A third set looked for an interesting phenomenon, a negative source, someone whose own ability is so low that people believe the opposite of his or her evaluations. (These experiments found no evidence for the negative-source phenomenon.) Finally, Webster and Sobieszek studied what happens when an evaluator's skill level is unknown but the evaluator's status position is known. Ideas from the status branch of expectation states theories led to a prediction that in those cases individuals will form expectations for an evaluator based on his status position relative to their own, and that is what happened in the experiments.

The theory and experiments on sources of evaluations established the following:

- An evaluator's likelihood of being accepted as a source can be predicted from knowing the evaluator's expectation advantage over the person he or she evaluates. The greater the evaluator's expectation advantage, the more likely he or she is to become a source.

- Evaluations from an accepted source are treated as reliable; that is, they get incorporated into a person's aggregate expectations.

- If a person holds lower expectations for the evaluator than for himself or herself, that evaluator will not become a source and the person will ignore his or her evaluations.

- If multiple sources exist, information from all of them affects a person's expectations, whether they agree or disagree. Two agreeing sources have greater effects than either of them alone, and two disagreeing sources weaken or cancel each other's evaluations.

- If an evaluator's skill level is unknown, those evaluated may form performance expectations for the evaluator from status generalization processes based on the evaluator's relative-status position. Then the first four of the preceding processes will occur just as if the evaluator's skill level were known.

2. Integrating Source and Status Characteristics Theories. Fisek, Berger, and Norman (1995) formulated a theory that integrates source theory with the latest version of status characteristics theory and its extensions. This integration enables us to use concepts and principles developed in these status theories to describe and explain evaluation processes.

The integration introduces the notion of an *imputed possession*, which is an attribution of the task ability of an actor made by an evaluator. The theory assumes that an evaluator will become a source to an actor if the actor holds positive expectations for the evaluator. To capture the idea that evaluators can differ in their credibility, it is argued that the higher the expectations that an actor holds for the evaluator, the greater the strength of those evaluations and therefore the greater their impact on the actor's behavior. The theory also introduces the idea of a *valued role* as a status-evaluated position that involves defined rights and responsibilities in a given situation of action. The argument is made that the evaluator in the Webster and Sobieszek research has been given the right to evaluate and therefore possesses a positively valued role.

Using the concepts and principles in the latest version of the status characteristics theory, Fisek, Berger, and Norman (1995) are able to derive specific predictions for the experimental conditions investigated by Webster and Sobieszek and for a second set of experimental conditions investigated by Ilardi and McMahon (1988). They find a good fit between these predictions and observed results.

The Fisek, Berger, and Norman (1995) integration enables us to describe and explain the five kinds of situations described earlier for source theory. Further, it enables us to make precise predictions of the actor's behavior that are created from the many possible combinations of expectations that actors can hold for themselves and those they hold for evaluators. It also relates source phenomena to phenomena dealt with in the general theory of status characteristics and expectation states.

3. Second-Order Expectations and Status Claims. Approaching the problem of the formation of expectations from a different perspective, Moore (1985) posed the question, Under what conditions do the expectations that another holds for an actor and some other become the expectations that the actor holds for himself and this other? Moore referred to the expectations that another holds for the actor and some other as *second-order expectations* to distinguish them from the expectations that the actor holds, which he regarded as *first-order expectations*. Assuming that the actor knows the second-order expectations of the other, Moore proposed answering this question with the argument that, given that the actor holds no initial expectations, if his or her behavior accords with (or enacts) the second-order expectations of another, then the actor's first-order expectations will coincide with the other's second-order expectations. Based on results from a carefully designed experiment, Moore (1985) obtained evidence that supports this argument.

Interpreting second-order expectations as imputed ability evaluations and using the concepts and principles of the evaluation-expectation theory, Fisek, Berger, and Moore (2002) have reanalyzed Moore's original study plus four additional studies conducted by him and report a good fit between theory and data. Among the results of particular interest in this research is that *even when an actor's behavior is forced and determined by conditions in the situation, such as role demands,* if that behavior accords with the other's expectations, it can determine the actor's expectations and behavior. This result provides insight on how structures that are externally imposed on interaction situations can determine the expectations and behavior of actors in such situations.

Research by Troyer and her colleagues (Troyer and Younts 1997; Troyer, Younts, and Kalkhoff 2001) has shown that second-order expectations can also affect the actors' interaction in the absence of behavior that enacts those expectations. An important idea in this research is that actors assume that first- and second-order expectations are consistent unless they learn otherwise. For example, if an actor, p, is in a status-advantaged position over another, o, and forms higher expectations for self in relation to other, then p assumes that o's expectations are lower for self and higher for p unless p learns otherwise. This equates the situation where there is only first-order information with one where there is consistent first- and second-order information and implicitly argues that second-order information is effective when it is *inconsistent* with first-order information (or when there is no first-order information).

Working within Fisek and colleagues' evaluation-expectation theory, Webster and Whitmeyer (1999) have constructed a model for second-order expectations. To begin with, they suggest that publicly asserted second-order expectations may be thought of as *status claims* on the part of interactants, and they assume that (1) all such claims whether consistent or inconsistent with first-order expectations affect behavior in the situation and (2) the strength of the claim on an actor's behavior is directly related to his or her expectations for the imputing actor—whether those are positive or negative. Their first assumption differs from that of Troyer and Younts's theory that focuses on inconsistent information, and their second differs from Fisek and colleagues who argue that the strength of second-order expectations varies directly with the imputing actor's expectation *given that those expectations are positive*.

Webster and his colleagues have designed a set of experiments to discriminate among these theoretical arguments. Recently, Webster, Whitmeyer, and Rashotte (2004) and Whitmeyer, Webster, and Rashotte (2005) have shown that their model, which uses Webster and Whitmeyer's two assumptions, predicts the results from experiments they have conducted better than one that uses the inconsistency argument and one in which the actor takes account of information only from those imputing others for whom he or she holds positive expectations.

While a final discrimination between specific models probably awaits further empirical results, it would appear from what already has been done that we may have the concepts and principles that we need to deal effectively with problems that concern the global evaluation of an actor's abilities and, in particular, with issues involving the credibility of the evaluators of these abilities.

V. MULTIPLE STANDARDS

In deciding whether a particular performance is good, adequate, or failing, individuals use *standards*. The standards may be lenient or strict; for instance, a grade of 90 out of 100 may seem excellent to a student but only fair to her parents. Martha Foschi and her colleagues (Foschi 1989, 2000; Foschi, Enns, and Lapointe 2001) developed a research program investigating when and why individuals use different standards for assessing similar performances.

The program investigates situations where individuals are judged differently depending on who they are—even though all of them provide the same evidence regarding the attribute being assessed. The core process of using multiple standards has the following elements:

- a status characteristic differentiates individuals into two or more categories;
- at the same time, objective evidence shows that individuals from the different categories possess an attribute to the same extent;
- individuals invoke multiple standards to interpret that evidence; and thus
- individuals demand higher performances from members of socially devalued groups.

In Foschi's studies, multiple standards appear in cases where some objective measure such as a test score already exists. The standards affect how one *interprets* the objective measure—whether a given score is seen as good enough, or whether a particular SAT score merits acceptance into college. Standards change as a function of the status of the individual who is being evaluated. Multiple standards are an order-preserving mechanism, making it harder for a low-status person to be assigned positive categories and easier to be assigned to negative categories.

In an early experiment (Foddy and Graham 1987), men and women received identical scores in different conditions of this experiment and were asked to tell whether those scores indicated having ability or lacking ability. Sometimes gender was said to be relevant to the task—e.g., "Men usually do better at this task"—and sometimes relevance was unspecified. Either way, the gender-status difference would lead to assigning lower performance expectations to women than to men and, hence, to using stricter standards for the women. As expected, women set stricter standards for themselves than men did when relevance of gender was unspecified. When gender was said to be relevant with men doing better at the task, the women set even stricter standards for themselves and the men set standards that were even more lenient for themselves.

Two experiments reported by Foschi (1996) again showed women held to stricter standards than men. In the first, mixed-gender pairs of individuals worked at a task said to be one at which men usually did better than women. However, both individuals received about the same scores on the test. Investigators then asked them to set ability standards. Both women and men demanded a higher test score of a woman before concluding that a performance was adequate. The second experiment showed effects of accountability; that is, having to justify the assessments and standards used for judging different actors. When participants were told they would *not* have to justify the standards, they applied stricter standards to women, as before. However, when investigators told them they *would* have to justify the standards, they used similar standards for both men and women. This suggests that participants may not see that sort of gender discrimination as legitimate when they must think about justifying it.

Studies reported by Foschi, Lai, and Sigerson (1994) show other results of multiple standards, this time in selecting applicants for jobs. Here, respondents were not asked directly about the standards they used but revealed them through their recommendations. Men and women saw files of two purported finalists, one man and one woman who had similar, average academic records. They were asked to recommend one of them for a position. Male respondents more often chose the male candidate and said he was better suited for the job and more competent. Female respondents in this study, however, did not display use of a double standard. A follow-up study by Foschi, Sigerson, and Lembesis (1995) showed that when respondents judged one job candidate at a time, double standards did not come into play. Double standards were significant when respondents were asked to compare two candidates.

The pattern of results from these studies provides an understanding of conditions under which multiple standards appear and affect individuals' beliefs and behaviors. It also shows the mechanism by which the process operates: observers form performance expectations for individuals through status generalization from characteristics such as gender. Then multiple standards are invoked to interpret new performance information such that performances are seen as consistent with the high or low expectations produced by status generalization. If low expectations are attached to an actor because of her gender-status disadvantage, then new performance information may be interpreted by a strict standard so that judgment is consistent with the low expectations already formed. If high expectations are attached to another actor because of his gender-status advantage, then lenient standards may be invoked to keep judgments consistent with high expectations.

VI. CURRENT RESEARCH AND GROWTH

The expectation-states program continues to grow. There currently is extensive research in two branches of the program, one dealing with the social construction of status character- istics and the second dealing with the relation of sentiments to status processes. In addition, those working in the program are also undertaking research on completely new theoretical problems.

Cecilia Ridgeway (1991) formulated a theory describing processes by which status char- acteristics can come to be constructed. She imagines situations where individuals are con- sistently discriminated on an initially nonvalued characteristic and the possession of high and low resources (rewards). She argues that possessing high or low rewards will lead to oc- cupying, respectively, high or low positions on the group's power and prestige order (for ex- ample, by the reverse process previously described). In turn, high and low evaluations of an individual's ability and competence will be based on his or her power and prestige position. If such situations are repeated and generally consistent (same states of nonvalued charac- teristic associated with high and low rewards), these high- and low-ability evaluations will become status beliefs associated with the initially nonvalued characteristic. The processes described by this theory have been experimentally investigated (Ridgeway and Erickson 2002) and the theory itself has been elaborated by Ridgeway (2000) and others (Webster and Hysom 1998; Berger, Ridgeway, and Zelditch 2002). For further information on this theory, see Chapter 13.

It is well-known that sentiment structures such as patterns of likes and dislikes that exist among members of a group can affect status relations (Shelly 1993; Lovaglia and Houser 1996; Driskell and Webster 1997). Of particular interest in this research is the question of what pattern of sentiment relations *dampen or reduce* the inequalities produced by status re- lations and what pattern of sentiment relations *accentuate* those inequalities.

Lovaglia and Houser (1996) argue that in a two-person group if the low-status individ- ual likes the high-status individual and the high-status individual dislikes the low, sentiment and status relations are consistent, and the effect of sentiment relations is to accentuate the inequalities produced by status. On the other hand, if the high-status individual likes the low-status individual and the low dislikes the high, sentiment and status relations are in- consistent, and the effect of sentiment is to reduce the inequalities due to status. These predictions were found to hold in their study of two-person groups conducted by these investigators.

The studies by Lovaglia and Houser as well as that by Driskell and Webster (1997) indi- cate that effects of sentiment relations are combined with status relations in determining status inequalities. If this is so, what is the mechanism involved? Fisek and Berger (1998) identify two possible mechanisms—what they call a mediational mechanism and a consti- tutive mechanism. In the case of the *mediational* mechanism, sentiment mediates the trans- lation of expectations to behavior. This is akin to the situation of holding high performance expectations for a status superior but being less influenced because of one's dislike of the person. In a *constitutive* mechanism, sentiments become part of the expectations the actor forms for the other. This is akin to a situation in which one is influenced less by the disliked status superior because performance expectations for him have been reduced. Current research by Shelly (2001) and by Bianchi (2004) may allow us to discriminate between these mechanisms or determine under what conditions each of them operates. An answer to this question will enable us to develop a theoretical formulation that relates sentiment to status processes.

There are also completely new research problems being investigated within the program. Among the many interesting examples of such work are Lucas's research on the institutionalization of female leadership roles (Lucas 2003); Correll's research on how different career aspirations of men and women can be explained in terms of status characteristics theory and Foschi's theory of multiple standards (Correll 2004); Lovaglia and colleagues' research on how status-based expectations affect performances on mental ability tests (Lovaglia et al. 1998); Kalkoff and Barnum's research on the relation of social identity processes to status characteristic processes (Kalkoff and Barnum 2000); Thye's research on how status value spreads from valued status elements to initially nonvalued social objects (Thye 2000); and Johnson's research applying status characteristic theory to problems of legitimacy in organizational settings (Johnson 2003). In addition, there is work by Willer and his colleagues on interrelating arguments in the expectation-states program with those in his elementary theory (see Chapter 10).

It is clear that expectation states theory has been an evolving research program.[7] Our current theories say more, and what they say is more discriminating and precise than what they said at an earlier stage. They also rest on a more extensive body of empirical tests and a more extensive body of social applications and interventions than they did at an earlier stage in the program.[8] It is reasonable to conclude that, in any real sense of the idea of growth, the theories in this program have grown. However, it should be immediately added that given the many important problems that sociological social psychologists are interested in and that expectation-state researchers have not even begun to tackle, expectation states theory is still very much an evolving theoretical research program.

Joseph Berger's preparation of this chapter was partially supported by the Hoover Institution at Stanford University. Murray Webster Jr.'s preparation was partially supported by NSF award SES 0351020. We gratefully acknowledge this support. Of course, the content of the chapter does not reflect the views or policy of either of those institutions, and any errors in the chapter are our own.

1. On the concept of scope conditions and its applications, see Berger 1974 and Walker and Cohen 1985.

2. To promote comparability among different experimental studies of expectation-state processes, a standardized experimental situation was developed in the early 1960s. This included procedures for obtaining influence measures on an individual's behavior, experimental techniques for manipulating an individual's expectations, novel tasks constructed so that ability levels could be randomly assigned, and detailed scenarios to make experimental situations socially meaningful. For the initial status research in this situation, see Berger and Conner 1966, 1969. For information on this situation, see Berger et al. 1977, chap. 4.

Aside from the standardized experimental situation, status-characteristic theories have been tested in a variety of observational situations, including (1) open interaction situations (Skvoretz, Webster, and Whitmeyer 1999); (2) controlled interaction settings (Balkwell and Berger 1996); (3) hypothetical vignette situations (Balkwell et al. 1992; Shelly 2001); and (4) situations involving questionnaire response data (Webster and Driskell 1983; Gerber 2001; Fisek and Wagner 2003).

3. If there was no difference in experience, educational level was used to determine status position. If there were no differences on both of these characteristics, age was used to determine status position.

4. Two tasks are dissociated if by cultural convention the abilities involved in each are so defined that it is not possible to predict the level of one ability from information about the second. Two tasks are inversely related to each other if by cultural definitions high ability on one task is associated with low ability on the second and low ability on one is associated with high ability on the other.

5. In this and the subsequent intervention studies, subjects' second partners were believed to be not involved in the initial status intervention.

6. A triadic relation is *transitive* if, for example, actor A is ascendant to B and B is ascendant to actor C, then A is also ascendant to C.

7. Due to limitations of space, two of the branches of the program have not been discussed in this chapter. These are the branch of the status value theory of distributive justice and that of status cues. For research on the former, see Berger, Zelditch, Anderson, and Cohen (1972), and for that on the latter branch, see Berger et al. (1986) and Fisek, Berger, and Norman (2005).

8. In this context, it is important to note that aside from the studies in the United States, expectation-state processes also have been investigated in other cultures and countries. These include Israel (Yuchtman-Yarr and Semyonov 1979); Germany (Bierhoff, Buck, and Klein 1986); France (Lambert and Ehrlich, 1980); Holland (Wilke, van Knippenberg, and Bruins 1986; De Gilder and Wilke 1990); Canada (Foschi and Buchan 1990); Australia (Foddy and Riches 2000), and Turkey (Fisek and Hysom 2004).

REFERENCES

Alves, Wayne, and Peter Rossi. 1978. Who should get what? Fairness judgments of the distribution of earnings. *American Journal of Sociology* 84:561–64.

Bales, Robert F. 1953. The equilibrium problem in small groups. In *Working Papers in the Theory of Action*, ed. Talcott Parsons, Robert F. Bales, and E. H. Shils, 111–61. Glencoe, IL: Free Press.

Bales, Robert F., and P. Slater. 1955. Role differentiation in small decision making groups. In *Family, Socialization and Interaction Process*, ed. Talcott Parsons and Robert F. Bales. Glencoe, IL: Free Press.

Bales, Robert F., F. L. Strodbeck, T. M. Mills, M. E. Roseborough, 1951. Channels of communication in small groups. *American Sociological Review* 16:461–68.

Balkwell, James W. 1991. From expectations to behavior: An improved postulate for expectation states theory. *American Sociological Review* 16:461–68.

Balkwell, James W., and Joseph Berger. 1996. Gender, status, and behavior in task situations. *Social Psychology Quarterly* 59:273–83.

Balkwell, James W., Joseph Berger, Murray Webster Jr., Max Nelson-Kilger, and Jacquelin Cashen. 1992. Processing status information: Some tests of competing theoretical arguments. In *Advances in Group Processes*, ed. E. J. Lawler, B. Markovsky, C. Ridgeway, H. A. Walker, 9:1–20. Stamford, CT: JAI Press.

Berger, Joseph. 1958. Relations between performance, rewards, and action-opportunities in small groups. PhD diss. Harvard University.

———. 1972. Status characteristics and expectation states. *American Sociological Review* 37:241–55.

———. 1974. Expectation states theory: A theoretical research program. In *Expectation States Theory: A Theoretical Research Program*, ed. Joseph Berger, Thomas L. Conner, and M. Hamit Fisek, 3–22. Cambridge, MA: Winthrop.

Berger, Joseph, Bernard P. Cohen, and Morris Zelditch Jr. 1966. Status characteristics and expectation states. In *Sociological Theories in Progress*, ed. Joseph Berger, Morris Zelditch, and Bo Anderson, 1:29–46. Boston: Houghton Mifflin.

Berger, Joseph, and Thomas L. Conner. 1966. Performance expectations and behavior in small groups. *Technical Report No. 18*. Stanford, CA: Laboratory for Social Research, Stanford University.

———. 1969. Performance expectations and behavior in small groups. *Acta Sociologica* 12:186–98.

———. 1974. Performance expectations and behavior in small groups: A revised formulation. In *Expectation States Theory: A Theoretical Research Program*, ed. Joseph Berger, Thomas L. Conner, and M. Hamit Fisek, 85–109. Cambridge, MA: Winthrop.

Berger, Joseph, and M. Hamit Fisek. 1974. A generalization of the theory of status characteristics and expectation states. In *Expectation States Theory: A Theoretical*

Research Program, ed. Joseph Berger, Thomas L. Conner, and M. Hamit Fisek, 163–205. Cambridge, MA: Winthrop.

Berger, Joseph, M. Hamit Fisek, and Robert Z. Norman. 1989. The evolution of status expectations: A theoretical extension. In *Sociological Theories in Progress: New Formulations*, ed. Joseph Berger, Morris Zelditch Jr., and Bo Anderson, 100–30. Newbury Park, CA: Sage.

Berger, Joseph, M. Hamit Fisek, Robert Z. Norman, and Morris Zelditch Jr. 1977. *Status Characteristics and Social Interaction: An Expectation States Approach.* New York: Elsevier.

Berger, Joseph, Cecilia Ridgeway, M. Hamit Fisek, and Robert Z. Norman. 1998. The legitimation and delegitimation of power and prestige orders. *American Sociological Review* 63:379–405.

Berger, Joseph, Cecilia Ridgeway, and Morris Zelditch Jr. 2002. Construction of status and referential structures. *Sociological Theory* 20:157–79.

Berger, Joseph, Murray Webster Jr., Cecilia L. Ridgeway, and Susan Rosenholtz. 1986. Status cues, expectations, and behavior. In *Advances in Group Processes*, ed. Edward J. Lawler, 3:1–22. Greenwich, CT: JAI Press.

Berger, Joseph, Morris Zelditch Jr., Bo Anderson, and Bernard P. Cohen. 1972. Structural aspects of distributive justice: A status value "formulation." In *Sociological Theories in Progress*, ed. Joseph Berger, Morris Zelditch Jr., and Bo Anderson, 2:119–46. Boston: Houghton Mifflin.

Bianchi, Alison. 2004. Rejecting others' influence: Negative sentiment and status in task groups. *Sociological Perspectives* 47 (4): 339–55.

Bierhoff, Hans W., Ernst Buck, and Renate Klein. 1986. Social context and perceived justice. In *Justice in Social Relations*, ed. Hans W. Bierhoff, Ronald L. Cohen, and Jerald Greenberg, 165–85. New York: Plenum.

Brezina, Timothy, and Kenisha Winder. 2003. Economic disadvantage, status generalization, and negative racial stereotyping by white Americans. *Social Psychology Quarterly* 66:402–18.

Burke, Peter J. 1968. Role differentiation and the legitimation of task activity. *Sociometry* 31:404–11.

Butler, Dore, and Florence J. Geis. 1990. Nonverbal affect responses to male and female leaders: Implications for leadership evaluations. *Journal of Personality and Social Psychology* 58:48–59.

Carli, Linda L. 1991. Gender, status, and influence. In *Advances in Group Processes*, ed. E. J. Lawler, B. Markovsky, C. L. Ridgeway, and H. A. Walker, 8:89–114. Greenwich, CT: JAI Press.

Chase, Ivan. 1980. Social process and hierarchy formation in small groups: A comparative perspective. *American Sociological Review* 45:903–25.

Cohen, E. G., and S. Roper. 1972. Modification of interracial interaction disability: An application of status characteristics theory. *American Sociological Review* 37:643–55.

Cohen, E. G., and S. Sharan. 1980. Modifying status relations in Israeli youth. *Journal of Cross-Cultural Psychology* 11:364–84.

Cook, Karen S. 1975. Expectations, evaluations, and equity. *American Sociological Review* 40:372–80.

Correll, Shelley J. 2004. Constraints into preferences: Gender, status, and emerging career aspirations. *American Sociological Review* 69:93–113.

De Gilder, D., H. A. M. Wilke. 1990. Processing sequential status information. *Social Psychology Quarterly* 53:340–51.

Dovidio, John F., Clifford E. Brown, Karen Heltmann, Steve L. Ellyson, and Caroline F. Keating. 1988. Power displays between women and men in discussions of gender-linked tasks: A multichannel study. *Journal of Personality and Social Psychology* 55:580–87.

Driskell, James E., Beckett Olmstead, and Eduardo Sales. 1992. Task cues, dominance cues, and influence in task groups. *Journal of Applied Psychology* 78:51–60.

Driskell, James E., and Murray Webster Jr. 1997. Status and sentiment in task groups. In *Status, Network, and Organization*, ed. Jacek Szmatka, John Skovertz, and Joseph Berger, 179–200. Stanford, CA: Stanford University Press.

Eagly, Alice H., Mona G. Makhijani, and Bruce G. Klonsky. 1992. Gender and the evaluation of leaders: A meta-analysis. *Psychological Bulletin* 111:915–28.

Eskilson, Arlene, and Mary Glenn Wiley. 1976. Sex composition and leadership in groups. *Sociometry* 39:183–94.

Fisek, M. Hamit, and Joseph Berger. 1998. Sentiment and task performance expectations. In *Advances in Group Processes*, ed. John Skvoretz and Jacek Szmatza, 15:23–40. Greenwich, CT: JAI Press.

Fisek, M. Hamit, Joseph Berger, and James C. Moore. 2002. Evaluations, enactment, and expectations. *Social Psychology Quarterly* 65:329–45.

Fisek, M. Hamit, Joseph Berger, and Robert Z. Norman. 1991. Participation in heterogeneous and homogeneous groups: A theoretical integration. *American Journal of Sociology* 97:114–42.

———. 1995. Evaluations and the formation of expectation. *American Journal of Sociology* 101:721–46.

———. 1997. Two issues in the assessment of the adequacy of formal sociological models of human behavior. *Social Science Research* 26:153–69.

———. 2005. Status cues and the formation of expectations. *Social Science Research* 34:80–102.

Fisek, M. Hamit, and Stuart J. Hysom. 2004. Status characteristics and reward expectations: Test of a model. Paper presented at the Annual Meeting of the American Sociological Association, San Francisco, August 14–17.

Fisek, M. Hamit, Robert Z. Norman, and Max Nelson-Kilger. 1992. Status characteristics and expectation states theory: *A priori* model parameters and test. *Journal of Mathematical Sociology* 16:285–303.

Fisek, M. Hamit, and David G. Wagner. 2003. Reward expectations and allocative behaviors: A mathematical model. In *Advances in Group Processes*, ed. Shane R. Thye and John Skvoretz, 20:133–48. New York: Elsevier/JAI Press.

Foddy, Margaret, and H. Graham. 1987. Sex and double standards in the inference of ability. Paper presented at the annual meeting of the Canadian Psychological Association. Vancouver, BC, June.

Foddy, Margaret, and Phoebe Riches. 2000. The impact of task and categorical cues on social influence: Fluency and ethnic accent as cues to competence in task groups. In *Advances in Group Processes*, ed. Shane R. Thye, Edward J. Lawler, Michael W. Macy, and Henry A. Walker, 17:103–30. Stamford, CT: JAI Press.

Foschi, Martha. 1989. Status characteristics, standards, and attributions. In *Sociological Theories in Progress: New Formulations*, ed. Joseph Berger, Morris Zelditch Jr., and Bo Anderson, 58–72. Newbury Park, CA: Sage.

———. 1996. Double standards in the evaluation of men and women. *Social Psychology Quarterly* 59:237–54.

———. 2000. Double standards for competence: Theory and research. *Annual Review of Sociology* 26:21–42.

Foschi, Martha, and S. Buchan. 1990. Ethnicity, gender, and perceptions of task competence. *Canadian Journal of Sociology* 15:1–18.

Foschi, Martha, Sandra Enns, and Vanessa Lapointe. 2001. Processing performance expectations in homogeneous task groups: Feedback and gender effects. In *Advances in Group Processes*, ed. Shane R. Thye, Edward J. Lawler, and Michael W. Macy, 18:185–216. Stamford, CT: JAI Press.

Foschi, Martha, Larissa Lai, and Kirsten Sigerson. 1994. Gender and double standards in the assessment of job applicants. *Social Psychology Quarterly* 57:326–39.

Foschi, Martha, Kirsten Sigerson, and M. Lembesis. 1995. Assessing job applicants: The relative effects of gender, academic record, and decision type. *Small Group Research* 26:328–52.

Gerber, Gwendolyn L. 2001. *Women and Men Police Officers: Status, Gender, and Personality*. Westport, CT: Praeger.

Harrod, Wendy J. 1980. Expectations from unequal rewards. *Social Psychology Quarterly* 43:126–30.

Harvey, O. J. 1953. An experimental approach to the study of status relations in informal groups. *American Sociological Review* 18:357–67.

Heinecke, C., and R. F. Bales. 1953. Developmental trends in the structure of small groups. *Sociometry* 16:7–38.

Heiss, J. S. 1962. Degree of intimacy and male-female interaction. *Sociometry* 25:197–208.

Hogue, Mary, and Janice D. Yoder. 2003. The role of status in producing depressed entitlement in women's and men's pay allocations. *Psychology of Women Quarterly* 27:330–37.

Hurwitz, J. I., A. F. Zander, and B. Hymovitch. 1960. Some effect of power on the relations among group members. In *Group Dynamics*, ed. D. Cartwright and A. Zander, 448–56. New York: Harper & Row.

Ilardi, Barbara, and Anne M. McMahon. 1988. Organizational legitimacy and performance evaluation. In *Advances in Group Processes*, ed. Edward J. Lawler and Barry Markovsky, 5:217–44. Greenwich, CT: JAI Press.

Jackson, Linda A., John E. Hunger, and Carole N. Hodge. 1995. Physical attractiveness and intellectual competence: A meta-analytic review. *Social Psychology Quarterly* 58:108–22.

Jasso, Guillermina, and Peter H. Rossi. 1977. Distributive justice and earned income. *American Sociological Review* 42:639–51.

Johnson, Cathryn. 2003. Consideration of legitimacy processes in teasing out two puzzles in the status literature. *Advances in Group Processes* 20:251–84.

Kalkoff, William. 2003. Collective validation in multi-actor task settings: Extending the Berger et al. theory of legitimation. PhD diss. University of Iowa.

Kalkoff, William, and Christopher Barnum. 2000. The effects of status-organizing and social identity processes on patterns of social influence. *Social Psychology Quarterly* 63:95–115.

Lambert, Roger, and Marianne Ehrlich. 1980. Statut scolaire et influence sociale au cours d'une tache de discrimination perceptive. Recherches de psychologie sociale 57–68.

Leik, Robert K. 1963. Instrumentality and emotionality in family interaction. *Sociometry* 26:131–45.

Lerner, M. 1965. Evaluation of performance as a function of a performer's reward and attractiveness. *Journal of Personality and Social Psychology* 1:355–60.

Lockheed, M. E. 1985. Sex and social influence: A meta-analysis guided by theory. In *Status, Rewards, and Influence: How Expectations Organize Behavior*, ed. Joseph Berger and Morris Zelditch Jr., 406–29. San Francisco: Jossey-Bass.

Lockheed, M. E., and K. P. Hall. 1976. Conceptualizing sex as a status characteristic: Applications to leadership training strategies. *Journal of Social Issues* 32:111–24.

Lovaglia, Michael J., and Jeffrey A. Houser. 1996. Emotional reactions and status in groups. *American Sociological Review* 61:867–83.

Lovaglia, Michael J., Jeffrey W. Lucas, Jeffrey A. Houser, Shane R. Thye, and Barry Markovsky. 1998. Status processes and mental ability test scores. *The American Journal of Sociology* 104:195–228.

Lucas, Jeffrey W. 2003. Status processes and the institutionalization of women as leaders. *American Sociological Review* 68:464–80.

Markovsky, Barry, Roy F. Smith, and Joseph Berger. 1984. Do status interventions persist? *American Sociological Review* 49:373–82.

Meeker, Barbara F., and P. A. Weitzel-O'Neill. 1977. Sex roles and interpersonal behavior in task-oriented groups. *American Sociological Review* 42:91–105.

Michener, H. Andrew, and Martha Burt. 1975. Components of "authority" as determinants of compliance. *Journal of Personality and Social Psychology* 31:606–14.

Moore, James C., Jr. 1968. Status and influence in small group interactions. *Sociometry* 31:47–63.

———. 1985. Role enactment and self-identity. In *Status, Rewards, and Influence: How Expectations Organize Behavior*, ed. Joseph Berger and Morris Zelditch Jr., 262–316. San Francisco: Jossey-Bass.

Munroe, Paul. 2001. Creating a legitimated power and prestige order: The impact of status consistency and performance evaluations on expectations for competence and status. PhD diss. Stanford University.

Parcel, Toby L., and Karen S. Cook. 1977. Status characteristics, reward allocation, and equity. *Sociometry* 40:311–24.

Prescott, W. S. 1986. Expectation states theory: When do interventions persist? Unpublished manuscript, Dartmouth College.

Pugh, Meredith D., and Ralth Wahrman. 1983. Neutralizing sexism in mixed-sex groups: Do women have to be better than men? *American Journal of Sociology* 88:736–62.

Ridgeway, Cecilia L. 1987. Nonverbal behavior, dominance, and the basis of status in task groups. *American Sociological Review* 52:683–94.

———. 1991. The social construction of status value: Gender and other nominal characteristics. *Social Forces* 70:367–86.

———. 2000. The formation of status beliefs: Improving status construction theory. In *Advances in Group Processes*, ed. Shane Thye, Edward J. Lawler, Michael W. Macy, and Henry A. Walker, 18:77–103. Stamford, CT: JAI Press.

Ridgeway, Cecilia L., and Joseph Berger. 1986. Expectations, legitimation, and dominance behavior in task groups. *American Sociological Review* 51:603–17.

Ridgeway, Cecilia L., and David Diekema. 1992. Are gender differences status differences. In *Gender, Interaction, and Inequality*, ed. Cecilia Ridgeway, 157–80. New York: Springer-Verlag.

Ridgeway, Cecilia L., and Kristan G. Erickson. 2002. Creating and spreading status beliefs. *American Journal of Sociology* 106:579–615.

Ridgeway, Cecilia L., Cathryn Johnson, and David Diekema. 1994. External status, legitimacy, and compliance in male and female groups. *Social Forces* 72:1051–77.

Robinson, Dawn T., and James W. Balkwell. 1995. Density, transitivity, and diffuse status in task-oriented groups. *Social Psychology Quarterly* 58:241–54.

Rosenholtz, S. J., and E. G. Cohen. 1985. Activating ethnic status. In *Status, Rewards, and Influence: How Expectations Organize Behavior*, ed. Joseph Berger and Morris Zelditch Jr., 430–44. San Francisco: Jossey-Bass.

Shelly, Robert K. 1993. How sentiments organize interaction. In *Advances in Group Processes*, ed. Edward J. Lawler et al., 10:113–32. Greenwich, CT: JAI Press.

———. 2001. Predicting performance expectations from sentiments. Paper presented at the American Sociological Association Meeting, Anaheim, CA.

Sherif, M., B. J. White, and O. J. Harvey. 1955. Status in experimentally produced groups. *American Journal of Sociology* 60:370–79.

Skvoretz, John, and Thomas Fararo. 1996. Status and participation in task groups: A dynamic model. *American Journal of Sociology* 101:1366–414.

Skvoretz, John, Murray Webster Jr., and Joseph Whitmeyer. 1999. Status orders in task discussion groups. In *Advances in Group Processes*, ed. Shane R. Thye, Edward J. Lawler, Michael W. Macy, Henry A. Walker, 16:199–218. Stamford, CT: JAI Press.

Stewart, Penny, and James C. Moore. 1992. Wage disparities and performance expectations. *Social Psychology Quarterly* 55:78–85.

Strodbeck, F. L., R. M. James, and C. Hawkins. 1958. Social status in jury deliberations. In *Readings in Social Psychology*, ed. E. E. Maccoby, T. M. Newcomb, and E. L. Hartley, 3rd ed., 379–88. New York: Holt.

Thomas, George M., Henry A. Walker, and Morris Zelditch. 1986. Legitimacy and collective action. *Social Forces* 65:379–404.

Torrance, E. P. 1954. Some consequences of power differences on decision making in permanent and temporary three-man groups. *Research Studies State College Washington* 22:130–40.

Thye, Shane. 2000. A status value theory of power in exchange behaviors. *American Sociological Review* 65:407–32.

Troyer, Lisa, and Younts, C. Wesley 1997. Whose expectations matter? The relative power of first-order and second-order expectations in determining social influence. *American Journal of Sociology* 103:692–732.

Troyer, Lisa, C. Wesley Younts, and Will Kalkhoff. 2001. Clarifying the theory of second-order expectations: The correspondence between motives for interaction and actors' orientation toward group interaction. *Social Psychology Quarterly* 64:128–45.

Wagner, David G. 1995. Gender differences in reward preferences: A status-based account. *Small Group Research* 26:353–71.

———. 2000. Status inconsistency and reward preference. Unpublished manuscript. Department of Sociology, SUNY, Albany.

Wagner, David G, and Joseph Berger. 1998. Gender and interpersonal task behaviors: Status expectation accounts. In *Status, Power, and Legitimacy: Strategies and Theories*, ed. Joseph Berger and Morris Zelditch Jr., 229–61. New Brunswick, NJ: Transaction.

Wagner, David G., Rebecca S. Ford, and Thomas W. Ford. 1986. Can gender inequalities be reduced? *American Sociological Review* 51:47–61.

Walker, Henry A., and Bernard P. Cohen. 1985. Scope statements: Imperatives for evaluating theory. *American Sociological Review* 50:288–301.

Webster, Murray, Jr., and J. E. Driskell. 1978. Status generalization: A review and some new data. *American Sociological Review* 43:220–36.

Webster, Murray, Jr., and James E. Driskell Jr. 1983. Beauty as status. *American Journal of Sociology* 89:140–65.

Webster, Murray, Jr., and Martha Foschi. 1988. *Status Generalization: New Theory and Research*. Stanford, CA: Stanford University Press.

Webster, Murray, Jr., and Stuart J. Hysom. 1998. Creating status characteristics. *American Sociological Review* 63:351–78.

Webster, Murray, Jr., Stuart J. Hysom, and Elise M. Fullmer. 1998. Sexual orientation and occupation as status. In *Advances in Group Processes*, ed. J. Skvoretz and J. Szmatka, 15:1–21. New York: JAI Press.

Webster, Murray, Jr., and Barbara L. Sobieszek. 1974. Sources of evaluations and expectation states. In *Expectation States Theory: A Theoretical Research Program*, ed. Joseph Berger, Thomas L. Conner, and M. Hamit Fisek, 115–58. Cambridge, MA: Winthrop.

Webster, Murray, Jr., and Joseph Whitmeyer. 1999. A theory of second-order expectations and behavior. *Social Psychology Quarterly* 62:17–31.

Webster, Murray, Jr., Joseph Whitmeyer, and Lisa Slattery Rashotte. 2004. Status claims, performance expectations, and inequality in groups. *Social Science Research* 33:724–45.

Whitmeyer, Joseph, Murray Webster Jr., and Lisa Slattery Rashotte. 2005. When status equals make status claims. *Social Psychology Quarterly* 68:179–86.

Whyte, William F. 1943. *Street Corner Society*. Chicago University: Chicago Press.

Wilke, H. A. M., A. F. M. van Knippenberg, and J. Bruins. 1986. Conservation coalitions: An expectation-states approach. *European Journal of Social Psychology* 16:51–63.

Yuchtman-Yarr, E., and M. Semyonov. 1979. Ethnic inequality in Israeli schools and sport: An expectation-states approach. *American Journal of Sociology* 85:576–90.

Zander, A., and A. R. Cohen. 1955. Attributed social power and group acceptance: A classroom experimental demonstration. *Journal of Abnormal Social Psychology* 51:490–92.

Zelditch, Morris, Jr., Patrick Lauderdale, Steve Stublarec. 1980. How are inconsistencies between status and ability resolved? *Social Forces* 58:1025–43.

13 STATUS CONSTRUCTION THEORY

Cecilia L. Ridgeway

How do apparently nominal social differences between people become status differences? A society's status distinctions have social histories after all. While some status distinctions in our society, such as gender, have ancient histories, others such as educational attainment developed more recently. Yet others, like Irishness in the United States, have lost their status significance in recent years while new status distinctions emerge. It may be, for instance, that the "digital divide" between the computer literate and nonliterate is currently being transformed into a status distinction. How can we account for the development and persistence of status distinctions?

This is a question of some importance for those interested in social inequality. Status is social esteem and respect that typically yields influence. As Weber (1968) pointed out, it is a fundamental basis of inequality along with power and wealth. Weber (1968) focused on status as an evaluative hierarchy between social groups in society, but status can also be understood as a hierarchy of esteem and deference between individuals (Ridgeway and Walker 1995; Goffman 1967). Status between groups and status between individuals are connected by *status beliefs*. Status beliefs are cultural beliefs that people presume are widely held in the society that associate greater social esteem and competence with people in one category (e.g., men or whites) than another category (women, people of color) of a group distinction (e.g., gender or race; Berger et al. 1977). The association of difference with competence is especially significant because it legitimates the inequality in esteem, particularly in an achievement-oriented society.

Years of research in expectation states theory has established that status hierarchies among individuals are largely organized by the way that people's distinguishing attributes evoke shared status beliefs about the social categories or groups to which they belong (Berger et al. 1977; Wagner and Berger 2002). Most of the social differences that form significant axes around which social relations are organized, including occupation, education, race, gender, age, and ethnicity, are associated in U.S. culture with widely shared status beliefs (see Fiske et al. 2002; Webster and Foschi 1988 for evidence). Widely shared status beliefs are key to the organization of status inequality, whether it be between social groups or among individuals.

The question for us here, then, is how status beliefs about a social difference develop and become widely shared in a society or collectivity. Status construction theory is an effort to address this question. While there are likely to be many ways that status beliefs develop, the theory proposes one set of social processes that it argues are sufficient to create status beliefs about a socially recognized but not consensually evaluated social difference (Ridgeway 1991, 2000; Ridgeway and Erickson 2000). The theory argues that, since these processes are sufficient to create status beliefs, if they are currently acting in regard to a given social difference, these processes will maintain and continually recreate status beliefs about that difference whether or not they played a role in the actual historical origin of those status beliefs.

To explain how status beliefs are created and spread in a population, status construction theory focuses on the *local contexts of action* in which people from different categories of a social difference (e.g., men and women or different ethnic groups) encounter one another. The theory argues that, under certain conditions, these local encounters create experiences for their participants that induce them to form status beliefs about their social difference. Furthermore, such local encounters spread status beliefs as those who hold the belief teach it to others in the context by treating those others in accord with the belief. Thus local contexts in which people routinely encounter those who differ from them in some socially recognized way are social "factories" in which status beliefs can be created, spread, interrupted, or maintained, according to the theory.

To specify when beliefs formed in local contexts are likely to spread widely in a population and which category of the social difference will be cast as higher status in the beliefs, the theory turns to the *social structural conditions* that frame the local contexts of action. Such conditions include factors such as the distribution of material resources between people from one category of the social difference compared to the other. Like many social psychological theories, then, status construction theory is a micro-macro theory that focuses on the aggregate effects that emerge from local events that are framed and constrained by macro structural conditions (Coleman 1986). Before examining the theory's argument in detail, it will be helpful to first consider more carefully the nature of status beliefs themselves.

STATUS BELIEFS

The mere recognition of social difference evokes an evaluative response in people to favor their own categorical group, as research on social identity theory has clearly shown (Brewer and Brown 1998; Turner and Tajfel 1986). Simple in-group favoritism, however, does not create a status belief since it results in competing perspectives about which group is better. In contrast, when a status belief forms, both those in the social category favored in the status belief and those in the disfavored category *agree*, as a matter of social reality, that those in the favored group are more respected and assumed to be more competent in society than are those in the disfavored group (Jost and Banaji 1994; Berger, Rosenholz, and Zelditch 1980). The resulting shared evaluative hierarchy between the categorical groups is the hallmark of status beliefs. The formation of a status belief, then, requires that those in one categorical group overcome their tendency to favor their own group and accept, or at least concede, that those in the other group are seen in society as better than are those in their own group. A theory of the development of status beliefs must explain how this occurs.

As beliefs about which group is more respected in society, status beliefs are a type of social reputation. Consequently, they are necessarily beliefs about what most people (i.e., the generalized other) believe or would believe about the groups. If an individual's personal evaluative ranking of two groups is a first-order belief ("I respect this group more than that one") and an individual's perception of a particular other's ranking is a second-order belief ("my partner respects this group more than that one"), then status beliefs are distinguished by being third-order beliefs ("most people respect this group more than that one") (Ridgeway and Correll 2005; Troyer and Younts 1997; Webster and Hysom 1999).

People who hold status beliefs as third-order beliefs frequently personally endorse them as well (i.e., also hold them as first-order beliefs). In many cases, people likely do not distinguish between their personal beliefs and what they assume most people believe (Marks and Miller 1987). Such personal endorsement of a status belief may be most likely when the belief is flattering to a person's own group but occurs even when the belief is relatively unflattering. There is evidence, for instance, that men and women hold largely similar gender stereotypes that include status beliefs favoring men (Fiske et al. 2002; Eagly, Wood, and Diekman 2000). This third-order consensus, however, does not mean that everyone similarly endorses or approves of these gender-status beliefs (see Eagly, Wood, and Diekman 2000 for a review of evidence).

Status beliefs' character as third-order beliefs about what most people think is what gives them force in social relations. If I assume that most people share a status belief, then I expect that they will act in accord with that belief themselves and that they will judge me according to it as well. As a consequence, I must take that belief into account in shaping my own behavior whether or not I personally endorse the belief. In this way, the presumption that status beliefs are widely shared shapes people's mutual expectations for behavior in ways that tend to become self-fulfilling, as expectation-states research has documented (Wagner and Berger 2002; Webster and Foschi 1988). Those advantaged by the status belief are implicitly emboldened by the social presumption of their greater status worthiness and competence to speak up and act assertively. Those disadvantaged by the belief are held back by the social presumption of their lesser worthiness and competence.

In this manner, then, status beliefs act as the cultural rules of the game that organize social relations between those they advantage and those they disadvantage. Research supports the argument that these instrumental social effects of status beliefs depend crucially on their nature as third-order beliefs about what most people think. The extent to which people's behavior is guided, even in a private or unconscious fashion, by their personal group stereotypes (i.e., their first-order beliefs) is strongly affected by their presumption that their stereotypes are shared by most people (Seachrist and Stangor 2001). Note that this is more than a classic conformity process since it affects private behavior that is not under the surveillance of others. Similarly, learning that most others do not share one's personal stereotypes has been shown to change those stereotypes even at an implicit cognitive level more than exposure to a counterstereotypic experience (Stangor, Seachrist, and Jost 2001). Clearly, the perception that most people hold a status belief gives that belief a force that shapes its impact on individuals' behavior in social relations.

To function as a status belief with significant implications for social relations, then, the belief must have the character of a third-order assumption about what most believe. Such status beliefs usually but need not necessarily also have the character of personal, first-order beliefs for the individual. It is possible, as a result, for people to assume that most others esteem one group more than another when few at a personal level actually do (yet or still). While this situation of pluralistic ignorance is likely to be fragile, it hints at the processes through which status beliefs might develop in the first place. In general, however, status beliefs are likely to be sustained most easily when, in addition to being nearly consensually shared as third-order beliefs, they are also endorsed as first-order beliefs by a majority of the population.

When status beliefs form, they become part of the cultural stereotypes of the groups that they evaluatively rank. They add a distinctive, common content to those group stereotypes by depicting one group as more esteemed and generally more competent and agentic than another group (Berger, Ridgeway, and Zelditch 2002; Berger, Rosenholz, and Zeldtich 1980; Conway, Pizzamiglio, and Mount 1996; Fiske et al. 2002). In the United States, race and gender stereotypes, for instance, differ in many ways, but each describes one group (men, whites) as more respected, competent, and agentic than another (women, African Americans).

In addition to differences in status and general competence, status beliefs, as they are defined by expectation-states theory, also depict differences between the groups in specific skills, such as cooking versus car repair for gender (Berger, Rosenholz, and Zeldtich 1980). Interestingly, these specific skills typically depict the lower status group as more expressive or communal than the more generally competent and agentic higher status group (Conway, Pizzamiglio, and Mount 1996; Fiske et al. 2002). Conway, Pizzamiglio, and Mount (1996) speculate that this aspect of status beliefs arises from cultural schemas for interpersonal status relations in which high-status actors are proactive and influential and lower status actors are reactive and responsive. While status beliefs are defined by their status and competence content, then, they frequently carry with them complementary beliefs in the greater socioemotional skills of the lower status group. With this fuller understanding of the distinctive qualities of status beliefs, we can now turn to an account of their development.

STATUS CONSTRUCTION THEORY

Status construction theory takes as a starting point the existence of a socially recognized but not yet consensually evaluated distinction that divides the population into at least two categorical groups. The theory assumes as a scope condition that there is some degree of interdependence among these categorical groups in that members from the groups must regularly cooperate to achieve what they want or need. Under this condition, the theory argues, the local contexts in which people from different social categories encounter one another become potent arenas for the formation and maintenance of status beliefs about categorical difference (Ridgeway 1991, 2000; Ridgeway and Erickson 2000; Webster and Hysom 1998). The theory's basic arguments can be summarized simply.

In interdependent encounters between categorically different people, hierarchies of influence and esteem are likely to develop among the participants just as they do in virtually all cooperative, goal-oriented encounters (Ridgeway and Walker 1995). Such interpersonal hierarchies develop implicitly, through multiple small behaviors that the participants rarely scrutinize. Since the actual origins of their influence hierarchy are obscure to them but their categorical difference is salient, the theory argues that there is some likelihood that the participants will associate their apparent difference in esteem and competence in the situation with their categorical difference. If this association is repeated for them in subsequent intercategory encounters, the theory argues that it will eventually induce them to form generalized status beliefs about the categorical distinction. Once people form such status beliefs, they carry them to their next encounters with those from the other group and act on them there. By treating those others according to the status beliefs, they induce at least some of the others to take on the belief as well. This, in turn, creates a diffusion process that could potentially spread the new status belief widely in the population.

Whether the fledgling status belief does spread widely and which group it casts as higher status depend on the structural conditions that shape the terms on which people from each categorical group encounter one another (Ridgeway 1991, 2000; Ridgeway and Balkwell 1997). Of central concern is whether structural conditions give people from one categorical group a systematic advantage in some factor such as material resources or technology that is helpful in gaining influence in intercategory encounters. The theory argues that if such a biasing factor exists, status beliefs favoring the structurally advantaged group will emerge and spread to become widely shared in society.

In its initial formulation, status construction theory focused on a specific structural condition, a correlation between superior material resources and membership in a particular categorical group, and sought to delineate the processes through which this condition would give rise to status beliefs about the group distinction (Ridgeway 1991). Sociologists have long observed that a common precondition for the development of status beliefs about two social groups is that people in one group become materially richer than those in the other group (Weber 1968). Subsequently, however, the logic of the theory has been shown to imply that an inequality in the distribution between two groups of *any* factor, not just material resources, that biases the development of influence hierarchies in encounters will lead to the emergence of status beliefs about the group distinction (Ridgeway et al. 1998; Webster and Hysom 1998). Using this argument, Webster and Hysom (1998) show how the social distribution of moral approval based on sexual orientation acts as such a structural factor that fosters the formation of status beliefs about homosexuality.

As this summary suggests, status construction theory contains two types of arguments. One set describes the social psychological processes through which intercategory encounters induce their participants to form status beliefs. The second set describes the diffusion processes that result from belief formation in local encounters under different structural conditions. Since the social significance of the theory's arguments about belief formation in local encounters depends on its arguments about structural conditions, preliminary investigation of the theory began there. Ridgeway and Balkwell (1997) used computer simulations to show that if people do form status beliefs from encounters as the theory argues, then the emergence of widely shared status beliefs is indeed a plausible outcome under many structural conditions. Bolstered by this logical support for the theory's structural arguments, empirical investigation turned to the arguments about belief formation in local encounters.

In what follows, I focus first on the process of belief formation in local contexts of action. I describe empirical tests of the theory's arguments and subsequent elaborations that broaden the scope of the contexts to which the arguments apply. I conclude this section with a set of propositions that summarize the theory's current arguments about belief formation in local contexts. Then I return to the arguments about structural conditions and describe in greater detail how and when such conditions result in the emergence of widely shared status beliefs.

BELIEF FORMATION IN LOCAL CONTEXTS

The theory describes two general types of local contexts that induce their participants to form status beliefs about a social difference. Both have in common that they are goal-oriented encounters in which a socially recognized categorical distinction is salient for the participants, usually because the participants differ on it (Berger et al. 1977; Cota and Dion 1986). In the first type of these intercategory encounters, the participants associate standing in the local influence hierarchy with their salient categorical difference and form a status belief directly. In the second type of such encounters, participants acquire a status belief from someone who holds the belief already and acts on it in the context. Belief formation in the first type of situation allows new status beliefs to develop; belief formation in the second context allows them to spread.

Interestingly, however, the underlying social psychological processes by which each of these contexts induce their participants to form status beliefs is just the same. In each, categorically different actors, say, As and Bs, work together on a mutual goal and an influence hierarchy emerges between an A and a B. The development of this hierarchy creates a shared reality for the participants in which a person from one category, say the A, is more active, influential, and apparently more competent, while the B is cast into the role of reacting to the A. The hierarchy develops through implicit, small behaviors so that its origins are unclear for the participants. Instead, they simply find it revealed to them, through the unfolding of events, that the A is proactive, influential, competent, and in some sense, important, while the B is more reactive and apparently less competent and important.

Since both As and Bs participate in these events, the social validity of what they reveal about the A and the B becomes difficult for the participants to deny. If subsequent encounters repeat for a participant a similar association between influence, competence, and the A–B difference, the apparent social validity of the pattern is further strengthened. Eventually, even the Bs who participate in these encounters are forced to concede, as a matter of social reality, that most people would rate the typical A as higher status and more competent that the typical B. According to the theory, then, it is the power of the repeated, seemingly valid local realities that the person has participated in that induces the person to presume that most people and often he or she personally would judge As and Bs as different in status and competence (Ridgeway 2000). As a result it is in the person's interest, even if he or she is a B, to take on a generalized status belief about As and Bs as a means of anticipating the behavior of others.

In this way, the apparently consensual and socially valid correspondence between the A–B difference and esteem and competence in repeated local contexts induces participants to form a belief that has three characteristics. It is not about specific As or Bs that the person has dealt with but rather a categorical generalization about As and Bs as social groups. It is also a third-order belief about how most see As and Bs that the person usually but not always personally endorses. Finally, it is accepted, at least as a third-order belief, even by those it disadvantages.

Contexts in which people infer a status belief, de novo, and those in which they are taught the belief by actions of another both induce beliefs by drawing the participant into an apparently valid local reality in which As appear more esteemed and competent than Bs. The difference between these contexts lies only in the means by which the emergent influence hierarchy in the situation takes the shape that it does. In the first type of context, in which participants infer a status belief from their interactional experience that none of them previously held, the influence hierarchy may develop by chance and favor either As or Bs. Alternatively, the hierarchy may be shaped by some biasing factor that As (or Bs) are advantaged in by structural conditions.

Since the presence of a structural biasing factor plays an important role in determining whether widely shared status beliefs will predictably emerge from events in local contexts, the theory pays special attention to so-called doubly dissimilar encounters that embody these structural conditions (Ridgeway 1991; Ridgeway et al. 1998). These are encounters in which participants differ not only on the categorical distinction but also in a factor, such as material resources, that has a systematic effect on the development of influence in goal-oriented encounters. An example would be encounters between people who differ in riches as well as the A–B distinction. If more As than Bs in the population are resource rich, then doubly dissimilar encounters will systematically foster the formation of status beliefs favoring As rather than Bs.

In the second type of belief-formation context, a person who holds a status belief treats another according to it by either deferring to the other or asserting influence over the other. While the other who does not yet hold the belief might resist such treatment, research suggests that people most often fall into line with implicit behavioral expectations others cast toward them (Miller and Turnbull 1986; Moore 1985; Troyer and Younts 1997). Consequently, in many situations the deferential or assertive actions of the belief holder will cause an apparently valid influence hierarchy to arise that corresponds to the holder's status belief and that teaches the belief to the other. In effect, the status belief of the holder acts as a systematic biasing factor that shapes emergent influence hierarchies between As and Bs in a way that propagates the status belief.

Empirical Tests of Belief Formation and Spread in Local Contexts

Do people form and spread status beliefs in encounters, as status construction theory argues? With colleagues, I conducted four experiments to answer this question (Ridgeway et al. 1998; Ridgeway and Erickson 2000). Since doubly dissimilar encounters, in which participants differ in a structural biasing factor (e.g., material resources) as well as on a categorical distinction, are pivotal to the development of widely held status beliefs, the first experiment examined belief formation in this context. This experiment was designed to create all aspects of doubly dissimilar encounters that are indicated in the theory to be important for the construction of status beliefs and examine their combined sufficiency to create such beliefs. It was particularly important to ascertain whether such encounters have the power to induce people to take on status beliefs that disadvantage their own group since this must occur for shared status beliefs to emerge.

Expectation-states research has shown that when interactants differ in material resources such as pay, these differences shape the influence hierarchies that develop between them (Harrod 1980; Stewart and Moore 1992). Actors seem to infer that if valued rewards such as pay are typically distributed on the basis of perceived esteem and competence, those who possess more of such rewards can be expected, other things being equal, to be more competent (Berger et al. 1985). These expectations shape assertiveness or deference in the situation, giving rise to an influence hierarchy that corresponds with pay differences. Although the studies here focus on pay differences, the logic of this argument implies that not just pay but any socially valued reward (called "goal objects"), such as a corner office, will shape competence expectations and influence in a similar manner (Berger et al. 1985; Troyer 2003; Webster and Hysom 1998).

Study 1. The first experiment drew on this research to create the conditions hypothesized by status construction theory to induce the formation of status beliefs in doubly dissimilar encounters (Ridgeway et al. 1998, study 1). These conditions require repeated goal-oriented encounters in which participants differ on a salient but unevaluated categorical distinction and also differ in resource (i.e., pay) levels and in which an influence hierarchy develops that corresponds to participants' pay levels.

To enact these conditions, male and female subjects worked via an audio link with a same-sex partner, actually a confederate, on two rounds of a cooperative decision-making task. Round two repeated the conditions of round one with a different confederate-partner. Before beginning the task, subjects completed a brief background-information form with employment history and other such factors. To create a categorical distinction, subjects then completed a task adapted from social identity studies in which they chose between pictures by Klee and Kandinsky (Tajfel et al. 1971). They were told that this "test" of "personal response style" differentiates between two types of people, S2s and Q2s, whose distinct response styles are stable aspects of their selves. Supposedly, there are about equal numbers of S2s and Q2s in the world.

While waiting for the "results" of their personal response style test, subjects were told that "based on the information that the laboratory has about you" they and their partners had been assigned different pay levels. To maintain ambiguity about the basis for these pay differences, subjects only then learned that they and their partners also differed in response style. Finally, to simulate the structural condition of a general, but not perfect, association between the categorical distinction and resource differences, subjects signed a pay sheet on which previous simulated signatures revealed a general tendency for S2s and Q2s to be paid differently, but with some overlap in their pay levels.

Subjects then worked with their round one and then their round two partners on the multitrial task. In task discussions, confederate-partners on both rounds followed a script that treated the subject deferentially when the subject was better paid and confidently and assertively when the subject was lower in pay, mimicking the typical effects of pay differences on interaction (Harrod 1980; Stewart and Moore 1992). These behaviors resulted in the development of clear influence hierarchies on both rounds that corresponded to pay differences, as required by the theory. When subjects were paid less, they changed choices to agree with their confederate-partner (a measure of influence) more than three fourths of the time. When subjects were paid more, they changed to agree with their partners less than half the time.

After two such doubly dissimilar interactions, subjects completed a series of semantic differential items asking how most people and, on a separate sheet, how they personally, see the typical S2 and the typical Q2 in terms of status (respected–not respected, high status–low status, leader-follower, powerful-powerless), competence (competent-incompetent, knowledgeable–not knowledgeable, capable-incapable), and social considerateness (considerate-inconsiderate, cooperative-uncooperative, likable-unlikable, pleasant-unpleasant). The "most people" scales for status and competence provide the primary measure of status beliefs since these capture the distinctive third-order nature of such beliefs, while the personal status and competence scales measure first-order beliefs.

The formation of status beliefs in this experiment can be seen most clearly by examining the difference between the way subjects thought most people would rate the typical member of their own and the other response-style group. As the results for experiment 1 in Figure 13.1 show, subjects who were repeatedly better paid and more influential than a member of the other group formed beliefs that most people see their own groups as higher status, more competent, but less considerate than the other group. Even more striking, subjects who were poorly paid and less influential than a different other came to believe that their own group is lower status, less competent, yet more considerate than the other group in the eyes of most people. All these differences are significant at $p < .001$ (Ridgeway et al. 1998, study 1). In this and in subsequent studies, results for personal ratings of the two groups were very similar to those for most people except that subjects in the low-pay conditions resisted the personal belief that their own group was actually less rather than similarly competent than the other group, even though they conceded that most would see them that way.

This experiment showed that the many factors involved in doubly dissimilar encounters are together sufficient to induce the formation of shared status beliefs about a social difference. However, this experiment alone does not indicate which aspects of such encounters are crucial for the formation of status beliefs. The theory argues that it is the repeated association between an apparently consensual influence hierarchy and the categorical

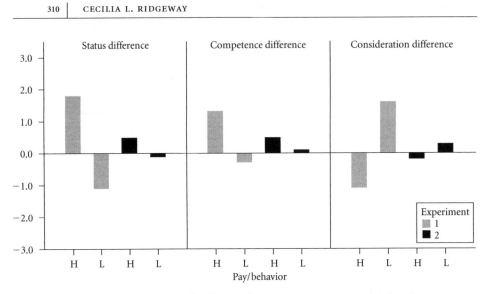

Figure 13.1 Subjects' Evaluation of Difference between Own Group and Other Group: Experiments 1 and 2

distinction that actually induces the participants to form status beliefs. The effect of resources on status beliefs, then, is *mediated* by the local reality created by the influence hierarchy that resources shape. This is an important point since, if such mediation occurs, any factor, not just pay differences, that biases the development of influence hierarchies will have a similar effect on belief formation. This point, then, has implications for the generality of conditions under which status beliefs might form through the processes that status construction theory describes.

Study 2. A second experiment examined whether the influence hierarchies subjects experienced in the first experiment were central to their formation of status beliefs, as the theory argues (Ridgeway et al. 1998, study 2). It is possible, after all, that subjects in the first experiment simply inferred their status beliefs from the simple knowledge of their pay differences alone. The second experiment replicated the first without the experience of the influence hierarchy. As in the first, subjects found that they would be paid differently than their partner and that they also differed in personal response style. Then, before beginning the task with their partner, they were asked to complete a measure of their first impressions that contained the status beliefs scales. As Figure 13.1 shows, the results of experiment 2 demonstrated that the mere knowledge of a pay difference between categorically different participants was not sufficient to induce full status beliefs. While high-paid subjects thought most people would rate their own group as higher status and more competent (an in-group favoritism effect), low-paid subjects did not think most would rate their group as significantly different than the other group in status and competence. As a result, the shared evaluation of one group compared to the other that is the hallmark of status beliefs did not develop in this context.

These two experiments suggest that doubly dissimilar encounters can indeed begin the process by which widely shared status beliefs form by systematically inducing their

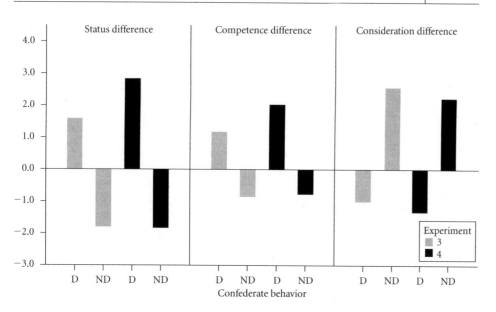

Figure 13.2 Subjects' Evaluation of Difference between Own Group and Other Group: Experiments 3 and 4

participants to develop status beliefs favoring the structurally advantaged categorical group. However, beliefs formed in these local contexts will mean little in the end unless people can spread those beliefs through subsequent encounters with those from the other group. For the beliefs to spread widely, people must be able to teach the beliefs to those from the other group even when those others do not differ from them in resources.

Study 3. A third experiment took up this question of whether people can spread status beliefs by acting on them in intercategory encounters (Ridgeway and Erickson 2000, study 1). As in the first experiment, subjects worked over an audio hookup with a different same-sex partner for each of two rounds of a cooperative decision-making task. As before, subjects differed from each of their partners in personal response style, but this time there were no pay differences. Partners were confederates who acted on both rounds as though they held status beliefs about the response-style difference by either behaving deferentially toward the subject or behaving confidently and nondeferentially. As expected, the confederate's deferential behavior created influence hierarchies favoring the subject while nondeferential behavior led to hierarchies favoring the confederate.

After two rounds in which an influence hierarchy consistently developed between them and a categorically different other, subjects formed clear status beliefs about the difference, as the results for experiment 3 in Figure 13.2 show. Subjects who were treated deferentially and became influential in repeated encounters thought that most people attribute substantially greater status and competence to their own group than the other group ($p < .001$). Those who were treated nondeferentially and ceded influence to the different other believed that their own group is seen by most people as lower status and less competent than the other group ($p < .001$). Thus the confederate-partner had taught his or her apparent status belief to the subject even when the belief disadvantaged the subject's own group. This study shows, then, that intercategory encounters can spread beliefs from one participant to another, as the theory argues.

By showing that people develop status beliefs from the simple, repeated association of influence with social difference without supporting resource differences, this experiment also strengthens the theory's claim that any factor that systematically biases the formation of influence hierarchies between socially different actors will foster status beliefs about the difference. This in turn lends credence to Webster and Hysom's (1998) account of the way differences in moral approval for homosexuals and heterosexuals foster status beliefs about sexual orientation. It further suggests that a large range of structural conditions between groups in addition to material resource differences may foster status beliefs.

Study 4. Status construction theory argues that intercategory encounters induce their participants to form status beliefs by creating for them repeated experiences of shared, apparently valid social realities in which actors' esteem and apparent competence consistently corresponds to their categorical difference. If this argument is correct, then when an *A* consistently becomes more influential than a *B* in repeated encounters, not only the particular *A* and *B* involved but also other participants in the encounter who witness these events should form status beliefs. After all, these bystanders to the assertion of influence by the *A* over the *B* also enter into and participate in the local reality that is constructed in the encounter. As a result, the apparently consensual nature of the revealed correspondence between the *A–B* distinction and esteem and competence should make that correspondence seem socially valid to these bystander participants as well. If it is the case that bystander participants in such intercategory encounters acquire status beliefs as well, then the power of such encounters to create and spread status beliefs is greatly enhanced. Computer simulations suggest that encounters of two to six people will become social engines that drive the spread of status beliefs throughout the population (Ridgeway and Balkwell 1997).

To test this implication of the theory, a fourth experiment examined whether bystander participants can acquire status beliefs by repeatedly observing the status-evaluated treatment (i.e., the assertion of influence over or deference to) of someone of their own category by someone of a different category (Ridgeway and Erickson 2000, study 2). Subjects were told that they would be part of three-person, same-sex decision teams with all team members paid the same. The personal response style "test" revealed subjects to be similar in response style to one of their teammates but different from the other one. The teammates were actually taped confederate-subject interactions from the third experiment. The taped confederate was always the opposite response style from the live subject. In half the conditions, subjects heard the confederate treat someone like them deferentially; in the other half they heard nondeferential treatment that asserted influence over someone like them. Subjects were instructed to listen to their teammate discussions before all three members made a combined decision on each trial. A second round repeated round one with different taped teammates.

As the results for experiment 4 in Figure 13.2 show, subjects did indeed take on status beliefs from repeatedly witnessing a different other treat someone like them as though their difference had status value. When they witnessed their own group repeatedly deferred to, they formed beliefs that most people consider their group to be higher status, more competent, but less socially considerate than the other group. When a different other consistently asserted influence over a member of their own group (nondeferential conditions), subjects thought most see their own group to be lower status, less competent, but more considerate than the other groups. These differences were all significant ($p < .001$). It appears that intercategory encounters are indeed potentially powerful propagators of status beliefs.

These four studies, taken together, provide support for several key arguments of social construction theory. They show that people do indeed form status beliefs about a categorical distinction from repeated encounters that present their participants with an apparently valid social correspondence between that distinction and esteem and competence. These beliefs form in both doubly dissimilar encounters and in encounters in which participants differ only on the categorical distinction. Furthermore, the studies show that people can spread status beliefs by treating others according to the belief in subsequent encounters. All participants of such encounters, including witnesses to this treatment, appear to acquire the status beliefs of the "teacher."

Social Validity and the Formation of Status Beliefs

Although the studies I have described show that encounters between people from different categorical groups can foster status beliefs, they do not directly test status construction theory's argument about *how* these encounters create such beliefs. The social validity argument is important because it sets a limit on the range of conditions under which local contexts will create status beliefs. After all, not all social differences become status differences and axes of social inequality. We need to understand the necessary conditions for the formation of status beliefs in local contexts to understand not only how status beliefs are formed but how the formation of status beliefs might be disrupted so that some differences do not become status differences.

What does it mean to say that a local context presents a participant with a *socially valid* correspondence between a categorical distinction and esteem and competence? The concept of social validity comes from Weber's (1968, 31–33) analysis of legitimacy. It refers to the collective dimension of legitimacy that is captured by the sense that others will accept something (e.g., a social pattern or event) in a situation, whether or not the actor approves of it (Zelditch and Floyd 1998). Research shows that something will seem socially valid to people in a situation if it appears to be consensually accepted in that local context or if it is authorized by a legitimate authority in the context (Zelditch 2001).

In the everyday encounters that are the focus of status construction theory, authoritative support for a correspondence between a categorical distinction and esteem and competence is not necessarily or typically present. Instead, social validity derives from the apparent consensual acceptance by participants of the social pattern in which actors of one category rather than the other display behavioral markers of higher status and competence, such as assertively making task suggestions and becoming influential. Those in the other category display markers of lower status, such as acting hesitantly and accepting influence (Ridgeway 2000; Ridgeway and Correll 2006).

In the absence of authoritative backing, then, the correspondence between the categorical distinction and esteem and competence acquire validity from the apparent consensual acceptance of the influence hierarchy between categorically different actors. This is why the consensual influence hierarchy mediates the effect of biasing factors such as pay differences on the formation of status beliefs in contexts in which authoritative support for a link between the categorical distinction and status is lacking. In effect, the appearance of consensus about the correspondence in the local context bootstraps the formation of status beliefs by causing participants to presume that most others even outside the local context would also accept it, creating a third-order belief about the perspective of most people. Note that this is not a conformity process in which participants acquire beliefs espoused by a majority, but rather a process in which participants similarly form from their shared reality a belief that none of them held before (Ridgeway and Correll 2006).

Two of the experiments discussed previously offer indirect support for the social validity argument. In the fourth experiment, participants who repeatedly experienced a consensually accepted correspondence between a categorical distinction and esteem and competence formed status beliefs even though they were not personally treated in a status-evaluated way (Ridgeway and Erickson 2000, study 2). Even more suggestive, in the second experiment, participants were not presented with a socially valid correspondence in that they did not experience a consensual influence hierarchy between themselves and their categorically different partners and did not receive authoritative information that they were paid differently because of their categorical difference. As the validity argument predicts, these participants did not develop fully formed, shared status beliefs (Ridgeway et al. 1998, study 2).

The importance, however, of consensual acceptance of the influence hierarchy for social validity in most intercategory encounters suggests a means for directly testing the theory's social validity argument. It is a clear implication of the argument that challenges to the apparent consensual acceptance of the correspondence between a categorical distinction and status and esteem will undermine the formation of differentiated status beliefs.

A recent experiment tested this prediction (Ridgeway and Correll 2006). In this study, after participating in two same-sex encounters in which an enacted correspondence between response-style category and greater or lesser influence and apparent competence was supported and apparently consensual, subjects formed clear status beliefs favoring the more influential group, as in previous studies. As predicted, however, after two such encounters in which one team member made brief nonsupportive comments about the influence hierarchy that corresponded with response style, subjects formed substantially weaker status beliefs ($p < .001$). In particular, the legitimating competence dimension of status beliefs collapsed for these subjects in that they did not believe that most people would rate those in one response-style category as any more competent than those in the other category. Not surprisingly, those who were pressured in the encounters to form status beliefs that disadvantaged their own response-style group rejected status beliefs most strongly in the nonsupportive conditions, even though they, too, accepted such beliefs in the supportive conditions (Ridgeway and Correll 2006).

This study clarifies how intercategory encounters create status beliefs by demonstrating the importance of social validity to the process. In so doing, it helps explain why not all differences become status differences. It is as though the appearance of social validity establishes a relevance bond, as expectation states theory would call it, between the categorical difference and markers of status and competence that allows the status implications of those markers to spread to that categorical distinction (Berger, Ridgeway, and Zelditch 2002; Thye 2000). Challenges to consensus weaken or break that bond of social relevance. A clear implication is that resistance to an implied status difference between categorical groups counts in that it can interrupt the formation of status beliefs about the categorical difference. Of course, structural conditions may constrain the ability of those in a categorical group to easily display such resistance in everyday encounters.

In addition to clarifying how local contexts induce status beliefs, the social validity argument also suggests an account for why people would *transfer* a status belief formed in one situation to a subsequent context and act on it there, as the theory claims they will. Although this claim has not yet been directly tested, it is based on expectation-states research that shows that people do transfer modifications of existing status beliefs (e.g., gender) from the context that induced the modification to later encounters (Markovsky, Smith, and Berger 1984). But why should a person transfer a newly acquired status belief that disadvantages his or her group to a new situation and act on it there?

If an encounter convinces someone through social validity that most do or would see those in one social category as more respected and competent than those in another, that newly formed status distinction has an apparent social instrumentality that the person must take into account. The status distinction appears useful for anticipating how people from the other category will act; it also appears useful for anticipating how others will judge the person. Both forms of social instrumentality implicitly constrain the person to transfer the belief to the next encounter and take it into account in behaving toward someone of the other category.

Validity in Other Local Contests

The social validity argument has a further implication as well. Status construction theory has focused on interactional encounters in which influence hierarchies arise among categorically different people as the primary contexts for belief formation. However, the validity argument suggests that *any* local context, whether an interactional encounter or not, that creates a socially valid correspondence between a salient categorical distinction and esteem and competence will foster status beliefs. There is some evidence to support this prediction. Jost and Burgess (2000) showed that when students were given apparently authoritative (and therefore valid) data on the social and economic success of graduates of their own university compared to another, the students formed beliefs that graduates of the more successful university were more intelligent, hardworking, and skilled, but not as friendly as those from the less successful university. In the classic indication of status beliefs, students formed such beliefs even when the beliefs disadvantaged graduates of their own university.

Note that these status beliefs were created in a situation without interaction in which the link between university and signs of status was made valid through authoritative support rather than local consensus. Note as well that indicators of esteem and competence in the context that lead to status beliefs were not behaviors in an influence hierarchy but socially valued rewards, or goal objects. It appears, then, that status construction theory could be expanded to incorporate belief formation in a broader range of local contexts than it has addressed thus far. In an example of such an extension, Troyer (2003) used arguments from the theory to account for the development of status distinctions based on substantive educational background (e.g., engineering versus finance) in newly founded business firms.

Belief Formation Propositions

As we have seen, status construction theory's arguments about belief formation in local contexts have developed through an interacting series of conceptual elaborations and empirical studies. The theory's current account of the belief formation process in such contexts can now be stated in a set of propositions. In the first proposition, indicators of esteem and competence in the situation are called "status markers." Status markers include both goal objects and status typifications. Goal objects are any valued social reward, from a corner office to a BMW to the social success used by Jost and Burgess (2000) in their study (Webster and Hysom 1998). Status typifications are cultural schemas of the behaviors through which people enact interpersonal status and influence hierarchies (Berger, Ridgeway, and Zelditch 2002; Conway, Pizzamiglio, and Mount 1996). These are the assertive versus deferential behaviors employed in status-construction experiments.

1. Local contexts that create a socially valid correspondence between a salient categorical distinction and status markers create a likelihood that their participants will form correspondent status beliefs about the categorical distinction.

2. Subsequent local contexts in which the categorical distinction is salient (typically, encounters with others who differ on the distinction) and that confirm the correspondence between the distinction and status markers increase the social validity of the correspondence for the participant, while inconsistent, disconfirming experiences undermine its social validity.

3. The greater the apparent social validity for a participant of a correspondence between a categorical distinction and status markers, the more likely that the participant will form strongly differentiated correspondent status beliefs about the distinction.

4. Actors transfer status beliefs formed in one context to future encounters with others who differ on the categorical distinction.

5. In a context in which participants differ on the categorical distinction, an actor can spread status beliefs to other participants by treating another according to the status belief.

STRUCTURAL CONDITIONS AND THE EMERGENCE
OF WIDELY SHARED STATUS BELIEFS

The social significance of the status beliefs that individuals form in local contexts depends on the likelihood that these status beliefs will eventually spread to become widely held in the society or population of interest. Only when status beliefs about a social difference are widely held do they become a significant axis around which social relations are organized. The structural conditions that frame the terms on which people from different categorical groups encounter one another in local contexts shape the emergence of widely shared beliefs in two ways. First, structural conditions constrain the frequency with which various sorts of intercategory encounters occur. Second, as we have seen, they constrain who becomes more influential than whom in these encounters (Ridgeway 1991; Ridgeway and Balkwell 1997; Ridgeway 2001).

The structural condition of greatest interest to the theory is an inequality in the distribution between categories of a social difference of some tipping or biasing factor, such as material resources or technology, that systematically biases the formation of influence hierarchies in intercatgory encounters. In effect, a correlation exists between the categorical distinction and advantages in the biasing factor. For instance, it might be that 60% of As but only 40% of Bs are resource rich rather than poor. Two other structural conditions also have an impact, however. One is the relative distribution of the population among categories of the social difference. Is the population evenly divided between As and Bs, as, for instance, with gender, or is one of the categorical groups a distinct minority? The last structural condition is the strength of homophily bias in the population on either the categorical distinction or the biasing factor. This last condition captures people's well-established tendencies to associate more frequently with similar others (McPherson, Smith-Lovin, and Cook 2001).

Since intercategory encounters are arenas in which status beliefs are formed and spread, the diffusion of status beliefs is affected by the frequency of such encounters in the population. To calculate how structural conditions shape this frequency, status construction theory draws on Blau, who predicts rates of intercategory association as a joint function of the strength of homophily bias on the categorical distinction and the availability of categorically similar and different others in the population (Blau 1977; Blau and Schwartz 1984; Skvoretz 1983).

Calculations based on Blau show that intercategory encounters are generally less than half the encounters occurring at any given time under most structural conditions (see the example in Ridgeway 1991, 371–73). Doubly dissimilar encounters between those who differ on both the categorical distinction and the biasing factor will be even less likely, usually comprising a small minority of all encounters. How then might widely shared status beliefs emerge from intercategory encounters? Although at any given time less than half of encounters are intercategory, status construction theory points out that people in the population circulate in and out of these encounters over time so that most at some time participate in such encounters. It is a scope condition of the theory, after all, that there is some degree of interdependence among the categorical groups so that they must regularly interact. When people acquire a status belief from their experience in an intercategory encounter, they carry that belief to subsequent encounters and potentially spread it to others, making a broad diffusion process possible.

Whether a diffusion process actually emerges that leads to a widely shared status belief depends on additional events. In intercategory encounters in which participants do not also differ in the biasing factor (i.e., singly dissimilar encounters), participants may well develop status beliefs about the categorical distinction, but the category (say, As or Bs) that is favored in their beliefs will be governed by chance. In some such encounters people will form beliefs favoring As and in others they will form beliefs favoring Bs in an unpredictable fashion. As people transfer their new status beliefs to future such encounters, the presence of so many conflicting beliefs in the population increases the likelihood that their new beliefs will be undermined by disconfirming experiences and dissipate in a cultural confusion of idiosyncratic beliefs.

This problem shows why doubly dissimilar encounters, although a small minority of encounters, are so important to the emergence of predictable status beliefs. Because the biasing factor, say, resources, is unequally distributed among the categorical groups, there will always be more doubly dissimilar encounters between rich As and poor Bs than between poor As and rich Bs. As a result, doubly dissimilar encounters will continually foster more status beliefs favoring As than Bs. As people circulate out of doubly dissimilar encounters, they carry a surplus of beliefs favoring As to other intercategory encounters. Some of these new status beliefs will dissipate in conflicting experiences as well, but others will survive and be successfully spread to others. Furthermore, as new people circulate in and out of doubly dissimilar encounters, these encounters act as a steady force that continually pumps more beliefs favoring As than Bs into the population. Consequently, the theory predicts that, eventually, status beliefs favoring As will diffuse broadly and become widely held in society.

Ridgeway and Balkwell (1997) conducted simulations of these processes that captured the dynamics previously described. The simulations confirmed that the emergence of widely held status beliefs is indeed a plausible outcome under most structural conditions. These simulations showed, for instance, that homophily bias does not stop the eventual spread of status beliefs in the population; it can only slow it. The emergence of widely shared beliefs is driven most powerfully by the strength of the association between membership in a particular categorical group and being advantaged in the biasing factor. However, even a relatively weak association is likely to produce widely shared beliefs over time.

Mark (1999) has also used simulations to explore the emergence of widely shared status beliefs under differing social structural conditions. These simulations show that broadly shared status beliefs actually can emerge even without an inequality in the distribution of a biasing factor between categorical groups. This occurs when by chance alone an initial string of intercategory encounters produces a cluster of status beliefs favoring one particular category rather than others. This accidental surplus of beliefs favoring one group, which develops out of contingent events, then propagates through the population just as beliefs fostered by doubly dissimilar encounters do. Without such an inequality in a biasing factor, however, the categorical group that is favored by the emergent status belief cannot be predicted in advance.

These examinations of the conditions under which status beliefs created in local contexts spread to become widely held in a population suggest the following additional theoretical propositions:

6. Given a correlation between the distribution of an influence biasing factor and a categorical distinction in a society, interactional processes will be sufficient to create widely shared status beliefs about that distinction that favor the categorical group advantaged by the factor.

7. In the absence of a correlation between a categorical distinction and an influence biasing factor, interactional processes may create widely shared status beliefs about the distinction through stochastic processes, but the categorical group favored by the emergent status beliefs will be a result of chance.

Implications: The Example of Gender

At the beginning of this chapter, I noted that status-construction processes are sufficient to produce status beliefs but, according to the theory, are not the only means by which such beliefs might arise. As a result, status-construction processes can be involved in the maintenance of contemporary status beliefs whether or not they were involved in the historical origin of those beliefs. This is actually an implication of proposition 6. Consider the example of gender. The actual origins of male dominance in Western society and elsewhere are lost in the past. Many theories of these origins, however, posit some factor, such as differences in physical strength or the mobility constraints faced by lactating mothers, that is likely to have provided men with a systematic advantage in gaining influence over women in their shared endeavors either directly or via a resulting division of labor that gave men a resource advantage over women (see, for instance, Eagly and Wood 2002; Eagly, Wood, and Johannesen-Schmidt 2004). Status construction theory implies that such factors, in addition to their other effects, would also have fostered the development of shared status beliefs that associate greater esteem and competence with men. Such status beliefs locate gender inequality in the sex category itself rather than in physical strength or motherhood status. As a result, the emergence of gender-status beliefs consolidates male dominance by providing men with a status advantage even over women who are their equals in physical strength and who are not themselves lactating mothers.

Status construction theory, via proposition 6, also implies that interactional processes are likely to play a role in the maintenance of gender-status beliefs in contemporary society as long as men continue, on average, to have higher levels of resources and social rewards than do women (Ridgeway 1997; forthcoming). Gender inequality in Western society has persisted over major transformations in the socioeconomic organization of gender relations, including industrialization, the movement of women into the paid labor force and, most recently, the movement of women into formerly male occupations. At the edge of social change, the contexts in which people take the first steps that lead to new ways of organizing economic relations are local, interpersonal contexts that are, in turn, shaped in some degree by existing gender-status beliefs. As a result, such contexts are likely to rewrite gender inequality into the new social and economic forms that they create, conserving gender inequality as they do so (Ridgeway 1997; forthcoming).

CONCLUSION

Status construction theory, then, is a social psychological theory that helps us understand how social differences in society become axes along which social inequality is organized. By connecting local contexts of action with structural conditions, it highlights the role that social psychological processes play in the creation and re-creation of inequality in the society.

It is closely linked in this regard with expectation states theory (Berger et al. 1977; Wagner and Berger 2002). That theory explicates how macrolevel cultural features such as taken-for-granted status beliefs organize interpersonal relations in a manner that enacts and reproduces inequality based on social difference. Status construction theory closes the circle by suggesting how interpersonal contexts, constrained by structural conditions, create and maintain widely shared status beliefs about social difference.

REFERENCES

Berger, Joseph, M. Hamit Fisek, Robert Z. Norman, and David G. Wagner. 1985. The formation of reward expectations in status situations. In *Status, Rewards, and Influence*, ed. J. Berger and M. Zelditch, 215–62. San Francisco: Jossey-Bass.

Berger, Joseph, M. Hamit Fisek, Robert Z. Norman, and Morris Zelditch Jr. 1977. *Status Characteristics and Social Interaction*. New York: Elsevier.

Berger, Joseph, Cecilia L. Ridgeway, and Morris Zelditch Jr. 2002. Construction of status and referential structures. *Sociological Theory* 20:157–79.

Berger, Joseph, Susan Rosenholz, and Morris Zeldtich Jr. 1980. Status organizing processes. *Annual Review of Sociology* 6:479–508.

Blau, Peter M. 1977. *Inequality and Heterogeneity: A Primitive Theory of Social Structure*. New York: Free Press.

Blau, Peter M., and Joseph E. Schwartz. 1984. *Crosscutting Social Circles: Testing a Macrostructural Theory of Intergroup Relations*. New York: Academic.

Brewer, Marilyn B., and Rupert J. Brown. 1998. Intergroup relations. In *The Handbook of Social Psychology*, ed. D. T. Gilbert, S. T. Fiske, and G. Lindzey, 4th ed., 2:554–94. New York: McGraw-Hill.

Coleman, James. 1986. Social theory, social research, and a theory of action. *American Journal of Sociology* 91:1309–35.

Conway, Michael, M. Teresa Pizzamiglio, and Lauren Mount. 1996. Status, communality, and agency: Implications for stereotypes of gender and other groups. *Journal of Personality and Social Psychology* 71:25–38.

Cota, Albert, and Kenneth Dion. 1986. Salience of gender and sex composition of ad hoc groups: An experimental test of distinctiveness theory. *Journal of Personality and Social Psychology* 50:770–76.

Eagly, Alice. H., and Wendy Wood. 2002. A cross-cultural analysis of the behavior of women and men: Implications for the origins of sex differences. *Psychological Bulletin* 128:699–727.

Eagly, Alice. H., Wendy Wood, and Amanda B. Diekrnan. 2000. Social role theory of sex differences and similarities: A current appraisal. In *The Developmental Psychology of Gender*, ed. T. Eckes and H. M. Trautner, 123–73. Mahwah, NJ: Erlbaum.

Eagly, Alice. H., Wendy Wood, and Mary C. Johannesen-Schmidt. 2004. Social role theory of sex differences and similarities: Implications for the partner preferences of women and men. In *Psychology of Gender, Second Edition*, ed. A. H. Eagly, A. E. Beall, and R. J. Sternberg, 269–95. New York: Guilford.

Fiske, Susan T., Amy J. C. Cuddy, Peter Glick, and Jun Xu. 2002. A model of (often mixed) stereotype content: Competence and warmth respectively follow from perceived status and competition. *Journal of Personality and Social Psychology* 82:878–902.

Goffman, Erving. 1967. *Interaction Ritual*. Garden City, NY: Doubleday.

Harrod, Wendy J. 1980. Expectations from unequal rewards. *Social Psychology Quarterly* 43:126–30.

Jost, John T., and Mazarin R. Banaji. 1994. The role of stereotyping in system-justification and the production of false consciousness. *British Journal of Social Psychology* 33:1–27.

Jost, John T., and Diana Burgess. 2000. Attitudinal ambivalence and the conflict between group and system justification in low status groups. *Personality and Social Psychology Bulletin* 26:293–305.

Mark, Noah. 1999. The emergence of status inequality. Paper presented at the annual meeting of the American Sociological Association, Chicago, August.

Markovsky, Barry, LeRoy F. Smith, and Joseph Berger. 1984. Do status interventions persist? *American Sociological Review* 49:373–82.

Marks, G., and Norman Miller. 1987. Ten years of research on the false-consensus effect: An empirical and theoretical review. *Psychological Bulletin* 102:72–90.

McPherson, Miller, Lynn Smith-Lovin, and James M. Cook. 2001. Birds of a feather: Homophily in social networks. *Annual Review of Sociology* 27:415–44.

Miller, Dale T., and W. Turnbull. 1986. Expectancies and interpersonal processes. In *Annual Review of Psychology*, ed. M. R. Rosenzweig and L. W. Porter, 37:233–56. Palo Alto, CA: Annual Review.

Moore, James C., Jr. 1985. Role enactment and self-identity. In *Status, Rewards, and Influence*, ed. Joseph Berger and Morris Zelditch, 262–316. San Francisco: Jossey-Bass.

Ridgeway, Cecilia L. 1991. The social construction of status value: Gender and other nominal characteristics. *Social Forces* 70:367–86.

———. 1997. Interaction and the conservation of gender inequality: Considering employment. *American Sociological Review* 62:218–35.

———. 2000. The formation of status beliefs: Improving status construction theory. In *Advances in Group Processes*, Ed. E. J. Lawler, M. Macy, S. R. Thye, and H. A. Walker, 17:77–102. Greenwich, CT: JAI Press.

———. 2001. Inequality, status, and the construction of status beliefs. In *Handbook of Sociological Theory*, ed. J. H. Turner, 323–40. New York: Kluwer/Plenum.

———. Forthcoming. Gender as an organizing force in social relations: Implications for the future of inequality. In *The Declining Significance of Gender?* ed. F. D. Blau, M. C. Brinton, and D. B. Grusky. New York: Russell Sage.

Ridgeway, Cecilia L., and James W. Balkwell. 1997. Group processes and the diffusion of status-value beliefs. *Social Psychology Quarterly* 60:14–31.

Ridgeway, Cecilia L., Elizabeth Heger Boyle, Kathy Kuipers, and Dawn T. Robinson. 1998. How do status beliefs develop? The role of resources and interactional experience. *American Sociological Review* 63:331–50.

Ridgeway, Cecilia L., and Shelley J. Correll. 2006. Consensus and the creation of status beliefs. *Social Forces* 85(1).

Ridgeway, Cecilia L., and Kristan G. Erickson. 2000. Creating and spreading status beliefs. *American Journal of Sociology* 106:579–615.

Ridgeway, Cecilia L., and Henry A. Walker. 1995. Status structures. In *Sociological Perspectives on Social Psychology*, ed. K. Cook, G. Fine, and J. House, 281–310. New York: Allyn & Bacon.

Seachrist, Gretchen B., and Charles Stangor. 2001. Perceived consensus influences inter-group behavior and stereotype accessibility. *Journal of Personality and Social Psychology* 80:645–54.

Skvoretz, John. 1983. Salience, heterogeneity and consolidation of parameters: Civilizing Blau's primitive theory. *American Sociological Review* 48:360–75.

Stangor, Charles, Gretchen B. Seachrist, and John T. Jost. 2001. Changing racial beliefs by providing consensus information. *Personality and Social Psychology Bulletin* 27:486–97.

Stewart, Penni A., and James C. Moore Jr. 1992. Wage disparities and performance expectations. *Social Psychology Quarterly* 55:70–85.

Tajfel, Henri, M. G. Billig, R. P. Bundy, and Claude Flament. 1971. Social categorization and intergroup behavior. *European Journal of Social Psychology* 1:149–77.

Thye, Shane R. 2000. A status value theory of power in exchange relations. *American Sociological Review* 65:407–32.

Troyer, Lisa. 2003. The role of social identity processes in status construction. *Advances in Group Processes* 20:149–72.

Troyer, Lisa, and C. Wesley Younts. 1997. Whose expectations matter? The relative power of first-order and second-order expectations in determining social influence. *American Journal of Sociology* 103:692–732.

Turner, John C., and Henri Tajfel. 1986. The social identity theory of intergroup behavior. In *The Psychology of Intergroup Relations*, ed. S. Worchel and W. C. Austin, 7–24. Chicago: Nelson-Hall.

Wagner, David G., and Joseph Berger. 2002. Expectation states theory: An evolving research program. In *New Directions in Contemporary Sociological Theory*, ed. J. Berger and M. Zelditch, 41–76. New York: Rowman & Littlefield.

Weber, Max. 1968. *Economy and Society*. Ed. G. Roth and C. Wittich and trans. E. Frischoff et al. New York: Bedminster.

Webster, Murray, and Martha Foschi, eds. 1988. *Status Generalization: New Theory and Research*. Stanford, CA: Stanford University.

Webster, Murray, and Stuart J. Hysom. 1998. Creating status characteristics. *American Sociological Review* 63:351–79.

Zelditch, Morris, Jr. 2001. Theories of legitimacy. In *The Psychology of Legitimacy*, ed. J. T. Jost and B. Major, 33–53. New York: Cambridge.

Zelditch, Morris, Jr., and Anthony S. Floyd. 1998. Consensus, dissensus, and justification. In *Status, Power, and Legitimacy: Strategies and Theories*, ed. J. Berger and M. Zelditch, 339–68. New Brunswick, NJ: Transaction.

14 | LEGITIMACY THEORY

Morris Zelditch Jr.

Legitimacy means that something is natural, right, proper, in accord with the way things are or the way things ought to be. Anything can be said to be legitimate: acts, persons, positions, relations, the rules governing them, or any other feature of a group, including the group itself. The distinguishing feature of legitimacy is that if something is natural, right, proper, in accord with the way things are or ought to be, it is accepted not only by those who in some way gain from it but also those who do not.

This chapter is almost entirely about the legitimation of power.[1] *Power* means control over the allocation of resources, in particular over the allocation of rewards and penalties: the control by one actor, say *A*, over rewards and penalties that matter to another, say *B*, is one way of controlling the behavior of *B*. There are many kinds and conditions of compliance by *B*, but compliance in the case of power is involuntary in the sense that, whether induced by promise of a reward or coerced by threat of a penalty, *B* does something *B* would not otherwise have done only because *B* had to. But the legitimation of power transforms it into *authority*, a claim by *A*, accepted by *B*, that *A* has a right to expect compliance by *B* with any directive by *A*, say *X*, that is within the scope of *A*'s authority, whether or not *B* would have done otherwise. Compliance with authority is voluntary, in the sense that *B* willingly does *X* because it is a duty, because *B* recognizes the obligation to do *X*, an obligation that does not depend on *B*'s own preferences for or against *X*. It is legitimacy that explains why I did not refuse to pay my taxes just because the candidate I voted for lost the election.

It is the impotence of pure power that motivates the effort political regimes put into legitimating it. The advantages of authority are its economy and stability. Pure power is perilous, costly, and unstable. It is perilous because, absent legitimacy, the use of force is as dangerous to the power that uses it as it is to the population it is used to control. Power is impotent to control its own instruments of coercion—arms, armies, police—by coercion alone. It is costly because, although the threat of force costs nothing, arms, armies, police, and prisons do. Furthermore, the compliance they coerce is only public, not private. It isn't observed if it isn't observable. But continually monitoring it magnifies its costs. They are magnified also by the reactivity of coercion: coercion increases private resistance as much as it increases public compliance, breeding the need for ever more coercion, magnifying even further the burden of maintaining a regime by coercion alone. Finally, it is unstable because its perils, its costs, and especially its reactivity make it prone to civil disorder, to coups, riots, and rebellions. Side payments may mitigate its perils. They may buy the loyalty of some of the led, who may suffice to coerce the rest of the led. But compliance motivated only by inducements, even though it is voluntary, still depends on the preferences of mercenaries, which are sometimes capricious, as much as it does on the preferences of their leader. Costs too may be mitigated: loyalty can be based on sentiments of attachment. But like side payments, compliance motivated by sentiment, though voluntary, is potentially fickle. Every political regime therefore attempts to create a belief in its own legitimacy. Legitimacy is a more economical, stable foundation of a political regime than force, side payments, or sentiment. If a regime is legitimate, even the disaffected, no matter how much they dislike the regime, tend, for a time at least, to willingly comply with it; they even support the mobilization of a regime's resources to counter challenges to it. Legitimacy inoculates it for a time, protecting it from paying for its failures, creating a sometimes considerable lag between its failures and its actual downfall.

There have been many theories of the legitimation of power. (For a review see Zelditch 2001a.) This chapter refers to a particular theory of it, which it calls simply "legitimacy theory." (For reviews of this particular theory at various stages of its development see Zelditch et al. 1983; Zelditch and Walker 1984, 2000; Walker et al. 1991; Walker and Zelditch 1993; Zelditch 2001b.) This theory addresses three questions about the legitimation of power: (1) What is the nature of the process? (2) What are its consequences? and (3) What are its causes and conditions? The chapter is therefore divided into three parts, each of which addresses one of these questions.

I. THE NATURE OF THE PROCESS

A. The Problem

The nature of the process has been a puzzle for centuries: the definition of authority presupposes that B believes that A has a right and therefore B has a duty to comply with any directive within the scope of A's authority, hence B's compliance with it is (1) voluntary and (2) does not depend on either the promise of a reward nor the threat of a penalty. But this way of conceptualizing authority raises a puzzling question about the nature of the legitimacy of power. On the one hand, it makes it entirely internal to B, entirely voluntary, its motives entirely noninstrumental. Legitimate power does not itself depend on the power legitimated by it. On the other hand, legitimacy empowers authority. It gives authority the capacity to enforce its directives. Having the capacity to enforce its directives, it has the capacity to compel B to do whatever A wants whether or not it is within the scope of A's authority. But if legitimate authority is capable of controlling the behavior of B purely by inducements and coercion, how can B's compliance with it be entirely internal, voluntary, its motives entirely noninstrumental?

Of course, most authority structures are made up of more than one relation. A hierarchy of authority is typically a set of relations, say, $A > B > C$. It is the task of B, whose position is superior to C, to direct and control the performance of C. Because legitimacy empowers authority, evaluations and sanctions also flow from B to C. At the same time, B is directed, evaluated, and controlled by a higher level of authority, A. Therefore directives, evaluations, and sanctions typically flow from A to B and B to C, C complying with B, B with A.

But none of this unriddles the nature of legitimate authority. On the one hand, compliance is voluntary, noninstrumental; but because legitimacy empowers authority, there is another hand—legitimate authority is capable of compelling compliance even if it is involuntary, of inducing it for purely instrumental reasons even if it is voluntary.

That such a well-ordered hierarchy as $A > B > C$ actually oversimplifies the authority structure of many groups only complicates the puzzle further. It oversimplifies it because many groups divide the labor in authority. There are a number of authority rights: the right to allocate tasks, to make final decisions about them, to direct their performance, to set the criteria by which their performance is evaluated, to monitor their performance, to evaluate it, and to allocate sanctions to the people who perform them (Dornbusch and Scott 1975). These rights can be divided among different positions in a group. If the labor in authority is divided among different positions, any particular position depends on the cooperation of a complex system of other positions for its authority, as Nixon depended on his attorney general, Richardson, or later Bork, to fire his Watergate special prosecutor, Cox. A control attempt is meaningless if these other positions do not support it, either by not executing authority's commands, as Richardson's refusal to fire Cox, or by not backing them up when challenged, as the Judiciary Committee of the House recommended Nixon's impeachment.

Thus at each level of the hierarchy $A > B > C$ there typically corresponds a position A', B', and C' at the same level as A, B, and C, the cooperation and support of which is a necessary condition of the exercise of the authority of A over B and of B over C. Each of the positions A', B', and C' cooperates with and supports the authority of any position A, B, and C equal to or higher than itself in the hierarchy of authority over any position equal to or lower than itself in the hierarchy. (C' is included because it makes a difference whether C's peers do or do not support the authority of A or B, or both, over C.) Thus the system of authority, taken as a whole, establishes a pattern in which some control others but are themselves subject to control, embedding authority in the mechanisms of social control of the group as a whole. At the same time, because the exercise of authority depends on the cooperation and support of others, the exercise of authority is accountable to others.

A more encompassing view of systems of authority does make a difference to how one understands the nature of legitimate authority. For one thing, it means that one must think beyond the dyadic relation $A > B$. Every act of authority and every act of compliance with it implicates an entire system of actors in it. The exercise of authority is not dyadic, it is a group process (Dornbusch and Scott 1975). But in some ways it only complicates the riddle further, because to the puzzle of consent it adds another puzzle, the normative regulation of power. Normative constraint is supposed to be the price power pays for legitimacy. Authorities have no right to expect compliance, or to negatively sanction noncompliance, with directives outside the scope of their authority (Barnard 1938). But having less power than A, what is there in the relation of A to B that gives B the capacity to enforce the norms if they are abused by A? In a dyad, the only restraints on the abuse of power by A are voluntary, internal to A, motivated by a belief by A in the rightness of the rules rather than sanctions for noncompliance with them. But in more complex systems of authority the accountability of A or B to A', B', and even C' means that they are constrained by the sanctions of others, hence by involuntary as well as voluntary constraints. Thus the compliance not only of the powerless but also of the powerful is, on the one hand, voluntary, internal, a matter of noninstrumental motives but at the same time also involuntary, external, a matter of inducement and coercion.

Although the puzzle turns out to have a fairly simple, straightforward solution, it has nevertheless persisted for centuries (Zelditch 2001a). Centuries of cynics have understood legitimacy purely as power. In their view, might makes right. Law is made in the interests of the stronger. It is the interests of the stronger that explain what the law says, the power of the stronger that makes what it says law. Legitimacy is therefore nothing more than a mask concealing interest. It is entirely a matter of power, it is external rather than internal to the actor, the actor's orientation to it is entirely instrumental, compliance with it entirely a matter of rewards for compliance and penalties for noncompliance, rather than a belief in what is "right." (This view has often been called a "conflict" theory of legitimacy. Although often associated with Marx—see, particularly, Marx and Engels [1845–1847] 1976—it probably originates with Machiavelli [1517] 1940a, [1532] 1940b.)

But is it might that makes right or right that makes might? The cynics' argument has sometimes been turned on its head: on this view, absent legitimacy, authority has no power. It depends for its power on mobilizing the resources of the members of a group over whom it exercises its power (e.g., by taxation). But the mobilization of resources depends on the legitimacy of its claims. Hence authority has power only if it is legitimate. Its legitimacy, in turn, is grounded in the norms, values, and beliefs of the group. Legitimacy is therefore entirely a matter of consent, entirely a matter of belief in what is right, entirely internal to the actor rather than external, oriented entirely by noninstrumental motives, compliance with its authority entirely voluntary. (This view has often been called a "consensus" theory of legitimacy. Although often associated with Parsons [1958] 1960, an early form of it can be found in Aristotle [335–323 BC] 1946.)

There has of course been a third view, a middle course, for which the puzzle is not really a puzzle. Like the mind-body problem, it is merely a pseudo problem created by a false dichotomy. There is no reason to suppose that legitimacy is either all might or all right, all power or all belief, its motives all instrumental or all noninstrumental, compliance with it all voluntary or all involuntary. Nor is it that difficult to see how it could be both. If one distinguishes between individual and group levels of legitimacy one admits the possibility that something is legitimate to others in a group that is not legitimate to a particular individual in it, say p. If others in the group back up legitimacy at the group level by negatively sanctioning behavior by p that is not in accord with it, then it is prudent of p to comply with what is legitimate at the group level whether or not p personally believes in it. In this view, there are many motives for compliance, some internal, a matter of belief, and some external, instrumental, a matter of expedience; some compliance is voluntary, some involuntary. The entire house of cards is founded on legitimacy because, without legitimacy somewhere, it remains true that power is perilous, costly, unstable. But it does not require legitimacy everywhere for it to confer stability on the structure of authority of a group. (Though this view has never had a widely accepted label, it might be called a "mixed" or a "conflict-consensus" view, originating with Weber [1918] 1968.)

B. The Two Faces of Legitimate Power

Legitimacy theory is simply an elaboration of this mixed view of the nature of legitimate power. It discovers in the legitimation of power a more complex process than either conflict or consensus theories find in it—multiple levels of legitimacy, multiple levels of authority, multiple levels of support for it, multiple motives for compliance with it. The theory's conceptualization of the process mirrors its complexity. First, it distinguishes between legitimacy at the individual level, which it refers to as "propriety," and legitimacy at the group level, which it refers to as "validity." Second, it distinguishes between the levels of the hierarchy of authority that supports its legitimacy, a level of an authority's peers and superiors that "authorizes" it, and a level of subordinates that "endorses" it.

The distinction between "validity" and "propriety" is a distinction between recognizing that a normative order exists and personally believing in it. *Validity* refers to whether an individual acknowledges the existence of a normative order (Dornbusch and Scott 1975, 39, following Weber [1918] 1968, 31–33). The recognition that norms, values, beliefs, purposes, practices, or procedures exist does not depend on whether a particular individual willingly approves of them. *Propriety*, on the other hand, refers to whether an individual personally approves of them (Dornbusch and Scott 1975, 39, following Cohen 1966, 17).

Thus a smoker may recognize that a city has an enforceable ordinance against smoking in restaurants, whether or not believing it fair to smokers. Recognizing the ban on smoking in restaurants, even a smoker may accept a duty not to smoke in them, even accept that the manager, host, and waiters in the restaurant not only will but also ought to enforce the ban if someone else in the restaurant violates it.

How does one come to recognize that something is valid? From the point of view of any particular actor in a group, say p, one can say that the behavior of others in the group is an object of orientation to p. Saying that a norm, value, belief, purpose, practice, or procedure exists in a group means that it observably governs the behavior of the group (from Weber [1918] 1968). Saying that it observably governs the behavior of the group, in turn, means that participants in the group act in accord with it, do nothing that contradicts it, and act to support it. In particular, acts not in accord with it are negatively sanctioned for noncompliance. Thus one may or may not know a city's ordinances, but one can observe that no one smokes in its restaurants and is asked to go outside if they do.[2]

If an element of the structure of a group is valid, it is normative in the everyday practice of the group, because validity embeds it in the group's mechanisms of social control. This is as true of values, beliefs, purposes, practices, customs, and habits as it is of norms. Whether or not they are *musts*, *shoulds*, or *oughts*, if they are valid, they must, should, or ought to be valued, believed in, or done in the everyday practices of a group. On the other hand, whether or not they are *musts*, *shoulds*, or *oughts*, if they are invalid, they are not normative in the everyday practice of a group. If they are valid, it becomes a matter of duty that p enforce them, whether or not p personally believes in them. If they are invalid, p has no such duty, whether or not p personally believes in them, and is unlikely to be backed by anyone else if, because p does personally believe in them, p tries to enforce them.

But validity also means that, whether or not p personally believes them proper, p presupposes that there is consensus with respect to them among others in the group. Hence p not only observes that others act in accord with and support them but p comes to *expect* that in the future others will act in accord with and can be expected to support them. In particular, p expects that if p does not behave in accord with them, others will negatively sanction p's behavior. Compliance is therefore prudent, whether or not p believes in them. Thus before ever eating out in a city that bans smoking in restaurants, p already anticipates that no one will smoke, that if anyone does they will be asked to smoke outside, that if p does want to smoke, the place to do it is outside, and whether or not p is a smoker, p is unlikely to smoke inside the restaurant unless p intends civil disobedience.

The distinction between validity and propriety holds whether or not a group has an authority structure, but if it has an authority structure, it is also useful to distinguish between two sources of support of the authority of A over B and B over C. Support of the authority of A over B or B over C is *authorization* if it is support by A' or B', peers at the same levels of authority as A and B, the more powerful positions in the system of authority, or their superiors. It is *endorsement* if it is by C', a peer at the same level of authority as C, the least powerful position in the system of authority.

Thus legitimate power has two faces, one a matter of belief in its propriety, the other a matter of prudence, an effect of its validity, authorization, and endorsement.

II. THE EFFECTS OF LEGITIMACY

Legitimacy theory is largely concerned with the interrelations of validity, propriety, authorization, and endorsement and how the way they are interrelated affects (1) the stability of authority and (2) the normative regulation of power. Part II is therefore itself divided into two parts.

Part A studies the stability of authority, although what legitimacy theory actually defines is its instability. By the *instability* of authority, it means (1) tensions attributed by the participants in a group to its structure, (2) pressures created by these tensions to change it, and (3) actual change due to these pressures. In section 1, part A studies how the way authority is structured is itself a factor in its propriety or impropriety and how its propriety or impropriety is a factor in its stability. But although empirical research testing this part of the theory has found that impropriety is a factor in the instability of authority, it has found much more impropriety than instability. This is due to the effect of validity, studied in section 2. Validity, a collective property that has other sources besides individual-level propriety—operating both directly and indirectly, through propriety, authorization, and endorsement—dampens pressures toward change due to impropriety, often (though not always) canceling them.

Part B studies the normative regulation of power. Again the starting point is propriety, but section 1 finds propriety insufficient to regulate the use of, particularly the abuse of, power. Section 2 studies how validity, operating through the same mechanisms studied in part A, to some extent constrains the abuse of power by making its abuse imprudent. This depends on validity's direct effects on authorization and endorsement, which are studied in section 3. But section 3 finds the same frailties in the social control of power that section 1 had found in the regulation of its use. Section 4 therefore studies what legitimacy theory implies about the conditions under which norms in fact regulate the use and abuse of power.

A. The Stability of Authority

1. Propriety. Many factors affect the stability of authority. One cannot really claim that a structure of authority will be stable if it is proper because propriety is only one of these factors. But one thing one can say is that the pressure to change a structure of authority is inversely proportional to its propriety. The more improper it is, the more likely it is to create pressures to change it. But one of the more interesting and important sources of the impropriety of a structure of authority is the structure itself—that is, the way rights in authority are divided among its positions. Rights in authority cannot be randomly divided among them. It matters how compatible they are (Dornbusch and Scott 1975).

From the point of view of a particular actor p, a particular distribution of the rights in authority is *compatible* if and only if its consequences for evaluation of the performance of p justly attributes causality for its outcome to p. A distribution of the rights in authority is *incompatible* if it requires of p that p do X at the same time that it prevents p from doing it— the directives given to p or the criteria by which p is evaluated are contradictory or the facilities provided by the organization to do X are inadequate to satisfactorily accomplish it. In an incompatible system of authority, p does not get credit for the good things p does but is subject to blame for performances over which p has no control. Maxims like the unity of command or the need to match authority to responsibility are concrete instances of this compatibility principle.

Incompatibility undermines individual beliefs in the propriety, and therefore the stability, of a group's authority structure. The basic social psychology of the compatibility principle is that no one wants to be faulted for something that isn't their fault. It is important to emphasize that incompatibility is a property of a system of authority, not the person who feels it. It refers to the existence of certain problems in the authority system that would affect any other occupant of the same position. To the extent that p perceives the structure of authority itself to be the cause of the incompatibility, the propriety of the structure is undermined, inducing pressures by p to change it. Pressure by p may not suffice to actually change the structure of authority, but if there is no actual change in the structure of authority, there is likely to be a great deal of unresolved tension. If there *is* change, it is in the direction of compatibility.

Tests of the compatibility principle have confirmed that incompatibility undermines beliefs in the propriety of authority, which in turn induces pressures to change the structure of authority in the direction of greater compatibility (Dornbusch and Scott 1975, chap. 10). But Dornbusch and Scott find considerably more tension than attempts to actually change the structure of authority and considerably more attempts to change the structure of authority than actual change in it. In a field study of five formal organizations, they found that if a structure of authority was incompatible, 72% of those working in it were dissatisfied with their work arrangements. But only 60% of those who were dissatisfied made any attempt to change it, and only 16% of attempts to change it actually succeeded in making any change in the structure of authority (Dornbusch and Scott 1975, 330).

In other words, the empirical findings show more stability than one would predict simply from the distribution of individual-level impropriety. But subsequent research has shown that there are other sources of legitimacy that act to resist the pressures to change induced by impropriety.

2. Validity. One of these other sources of legitimacy is validity, which, because incompatibility does not undermine it to the same extent that it undermines propriety, resists pressures to change a structure of authority. Once it emerges, legitimacy at the collective level has a life of its own, independent of propriety. It acquires the capacity to maintain itself because, once emerged, it has its own mechanisms of social control—authorization and endorsement. Its maintenance is further facilitated by the fact that validity is a property of the system of authority as a whole, whereas Dornbusch and Scott found incompatibility more likely to be position-specific. Not only did different organizations have different frequencies and patterns of different types of incompatibility but, within organizations, different positions also had different frequencies and patterns of different types of incompatibility (Dornbusch and Scott 1975, 262–64). Different positions don't necessarily share the same pressures to change; even when they do, they don't necessarily share the same agendas for change. For example, p may believe the structure of authority improper; others in the same position may even share p's view; but other positions often do not. And even when they do, they nevertheless often believe it their obligation to enforce the validity of the system of authority.

When a structure of authority is improper but nevertheless valid, legitimacy theory thinks of the two as countervailing factors, impropriety acting to destabilize it but validity counteracting impropriety, stabilizing it. But it thinks of the battle as often unequal: legitimacy theory implies that the effect of validity is greater than the effect of propriety.

Actually, it thinks this whether or not the authority system is improper. When validity and propriety are consistent, each has an independent effect on each element of the authority system's observed order of compliance and control, on attempts to change it, and on support for or resistance to them. Hence the effects of the two are additive. But legitimacy theory also argues that, in addition to their additive effect, the two interact such that an actor p is more likely to follow his or her personal conscience (i.e., propriety) when it is backed by validity. Hence validity accentuates the effect of propriety—propriety is more likely to have an effect when validity is present than when it is absent. When the two are inconsistent, each again has an independent effect but, because they are now countervailing, validity dampens the effect of impropriety. But validity has a greater effect than impropriety because it has more paths connecting it to the stability of authority.

When validity is inconsistent with impropriety, there are four mechanisms accounting for its countervailing effect on the stability of authority. First, validity has a direct effect on each element of the observed order of compliance and control, on attempts to change it, and on support of or resistance to them. In part this is because of unthinking mimesis of things as they are, but more important, also because by definition validity is a binding obligation on the members of a group, independent of any individual's personal belief in it.

But it also has direct effects on propriety and on expectations of authorization and endorsement, through each of which, in turn, it has indirect effects on each element of the observed order of compliance and control, on attempts to change it, and on support of or resistance to them.

While the effect may be small, there is some chance that, because p believes that others act in accord with and support the validity of authority, p comes to personally believe that authority's rights are in fact right. Thus a second mechanism of validity's countervailing effect on the stability of authority—i.e., in addition to its direct effect—is through its effect on propriety.

But even without an effect on propriety, the belief that others act to support valid authority induces expectations of its authorization and endorsement. The fact that validity has a direct effect on authorization and endorsement is fundamental to the theory's understanding of the fact that there is less instability than there is impropriety, but they have their effect more tellingly before than after the fact of p's behavior. Because p presupposes that validity is consensual, p expects authorization and endorsement of it, hence, whatever p's personal beliefs, it becomes expedient to behave in accord with it. It is not only that there will be negative sanctions for noncompliance and attempts to change the structure of authority but, if p attempts to change it and others do not act in concert, p's attempts will be futile even without any sanctions. The presupposition of consensus becomes a self-fulfilling prophecy that maintains the structure of authority and, with it, the appearance that belief in it is in fact consensual. Thus a third mechanism of validity's countervailing effect on the stability of authority is through its effect on expected authorization; a fourth is through its effect on expected endorsement.

Therefore legitimacy theory implies that, even if a structure of authority is incompatible, there will be less instability than there is impropriety. If validity and propriety are inconsistent, there will be pressures to change a hierarchy of authority due to the impropriety of authority, but three of the four mechanisms through which validity delays or prevents change do not depend on propriety. Even if validity and propriety are consistent, the effect of validity is greater than the effect of propriety because validity accentuates the effect of propriety. Thus the effect of validity is greater than the effect of propriety if the two are consistent because validity accentuates the effect of propriety; it is greater if the two are inconsistent because, if they are inconsistent, validity attenuates the effect of propriety.

The empirical findings of tests of these hypotheses come mostly from experiments in a standardized experimental setting that made the structure of a communication network improper but made change of the structure possible by majority vote. The setting employed a network comprising five positions. Subjects (Ss) worked in separate rooms and communicated by written messages only. Their task required communication among all five positions. It was a problem-solving task whose solution depended on coordinating information distributed among the members of the network at the beginning of each problem in such a way that each position had some but no position had all the information required to solve it. The network created by most of the experiments in this setting was highly centralized. It consisted of four channels of communication, each connecting one of four peripheral positions with one central position—a hub with four spokes often referred to as a "wheel," although the wheel had no rim. The center could communicate directly with all other positions, but the four peripheral positions could communicate directly only with the center. All communication between peripheral positions was indirect, through the center (from Bavelas 1950).

The Ss solved a series of 10 problems. Experimental instructions made a centralized network improper by inequitably awarding a bonus to the first position transmitting a correct solution to each of the 10 problems to the experimenter (E). In a centralized network the center will always complete the problem first. This was uniformly seen by all Ss as unfair and was typically blamed on the structure of the network. But the experimental instructions established procedures that permitted network members to change its structure by majority vote. Ss had the opportunity to propose an election to change the structure of the network at the end of each problem.

In any one experiment, Ss were placed in only one position in this structure. S could occupy a peripheral position, the central position, or assist E in E's office as part of E's staff. All other positions played roles preprogrammed by E so that each role in the process could be studied controlling for the behavior of all other roles.

When S was in a peripheral position, each S was stopped and interviewed at a point at which S proposed a change in the structure of the communication network. If S was not stopped, S continued until 10 problems were completed. Thus the dependent variable of experiments in which S was in a peripheral position of the network was the timing of S's initiation of a procedure to change its structure. (See Zelditch et al. 1983 or Walker et al. 1991 for a complete description of the basic setting.)

The timing of a change-response is best represented by a curve reflecting the proportion of Ss surviving at the end of each trial of the experiment. The baseline rate of change in the setting is the rate of change when legitimacy is undermined by inequity but nothing else is done to manipulate legitimacy or power. The results for the baseline condition of five experiments in which S was in a peripheral position were that almost a third of the 111 Ss in the condition made a change-response by the end of the 2nd trial of the experiment. Almost half made a change-response by the end of the 3rd trial. Only a fifth were still in the experiment by the time the 10th trial was completed.

From the survival curve of any experimental treatment in this setting, it is possible to compute a statistic that compares the ratio of the relative rates of change in the treatment condition to this baseline. Table 14.1 shows the effect of any of the several ways we manipulated legitimacy in these experiments as the percentage of change in the baseline condition that was delayed or prevented by the treatment in the experimental condition. For example, by this measure, validity delayed or prevented 45% of the change taking place in the baseline condition of the setting.[3]

Thus as Dornbusch and Scott predicted, other things being equal, impropriety induced substantial pressures to change the structure of a centralized network in this setting. But

TABLE 14.1
Proportion of the Baseline Rate of Change Initiated by Peripheral Positions That Is Delayed
or Prevented by Various Manipulations of Legitimacy[a]

Source or Type of Support for Legitimacy	N	Proportion of Baseline Rate of Change delayed/ Prevented	p
Validity[b]	51	.45	< .005
Propriety[c]	21	.63	< .005
Authorization[d]	24	.60	< .05
Endorsement[e]	40	.51	< .01

[a]Adapted from Zelditch et al. (1983), Table 2. The rate of change includes both individualistic and collective change-responses. The major concern of almost all these experiments was with collective action, but a small number of attempts to directly bargain with the central position occurred even in the baseline condition because collective action entailed small but measurable costs, referred to by Ss as the "hassle of renting." See note 3 for the method for computing the proportion of change delayed or prevented. There were small changes in procedure from experiment to experiment, but each comparison is made to an exactly similar baseline.

[b]Pooled data from Thomas et al. (1986) and two conditions that replicate it in Walker et al. (1988). The manipulation of validity was embedded in the experiment's instructions, which described the purpose of the experiment as the investigation of detailed patterns of information flow that became stable only after eight problems had been completed. Thus change before the eighth problem had been completed would damage the objectives of the experiment.

[c]From Lineweber, Barr-Bryan, and Zelditch (1982). Unequal rewards were justified by instructing Ss that the person in the central position had been chosen for merit demonstrated in a previous experiment.

[d]From Ford and Zelditch (1988). E authorized the use of power by the center and reported results of previous experiments in which the center had in fact frequently penalized change attempts. Three individualistic change-responses were added to the data published in Zelditch et al. (1983), which did not change the proportion of the baseline rate of change delayed or prevented by authorization but did change N. The results also differ slightly from Ford and Zelditch (1988), which did not study individualistic change-responses.

[e]Pooled data from two experiments in which Ss answered a questionnaire after two practice trials, the results of which were used by E to inform Ss that three of their peers believed a centralized network appropriate. After being run with males, the same condition was replicated with female Ss. There were no differences by gender. See Walker et al. (1986). There was an error in the proportion of the baseline rate of change delayed or prevented ("49%") published in Zelditch et al. (1983) that is corrected here.

validity, other sources of propriety, authorization, and endorsement all delayed or prevented a substantial amount of this change. (See the notes to Table 14.1 for operational definitions of the theoretical variables.) No attempt was made to test the hypothesis that validity created expectations of authorization and endorsement. In these experiments, E directly manipulated them. But as the results for Ss in other positions in the network will show (later), validity itself is a factor affecting propriety, authorization, and endorsement. The significance of these findings is therefore that the effects of validity, authorization, and endorsement substantially counter the effect of impropriety on the baseline rate of change-responses, which explains why Dornbusch and Scott (1975) found more impropriety than instability.[4]

B. The Normative Regulation of Power

1. Propriety. In theory, normative regulation of its use is the price power pays for legitimacy. No authority has the right to expect compliance with a directive outside its legitimate scope. To a considerable extent, empirical authority structures depend on internal constraints—on an authority's own sense of propriety—to prevent abuse of power by authority. But propriety is a frail reed on which to rest the normative regulation of power. A study of the effects of gain from the existing structure of an information-exchange network on transmission of motions to change the structure by Ss at the center of the network—who, because all messages had to pass through them, effectively controlled the agenda of group decisions—found that half the Ss at the center of a network made unauthorized use of their control over the flow of information to prevent elections that could have changed the structure of the network.

Not all of this was greed: the size of the bonus was so large that virtually all Ss in virtually every experiment we have ever run thought it was inequitable in a centralized network. Half the Ss who did not forward the change-proposals they received found other (also unauthorized) means of redressing the inequity. But half of them simply took the money and ran.

Thus a quarter of Ss at the center of a network who gained from the fact that it was centralized allowed self-interest to override normative constraints on abuse of their power. Postsession questionnaires found that many who had prevented change in their networks did so because they thought that, because it was efficient, a centralized network was proper. But even their sense of its propriety was to some extent self-serving: the more Ss gained from the network, the more likely they were to think it proper.

2. Validity. But normative regulation of power does not depend only on propriety. An authority system is a system in which some control others but are themselves subject to control. To the extent that the control to which they are subject backs authority only if it is valid, external as well as internal constraints normatively regulate power.

In legitimacy theory, authorization and endorsement are functions of validity. Validity is independent of propriety, but propriety itself should have little independent effect on authorization and endorsement. However, if the exercise of authority is proper *and* valid, validity accentuates the effect of propriety on each of them—*p* is more likely to sanction noncompliance by authority if *p*'s own conscience is backed by validity.

If authorization and endorsement are functions of validity, then the mechanisms of the normative regulation of power are the same as the mechanisms of the stability of authority. First, authorization and endorsement aside, validity will have a direct effect on the use of power by authority, partly because anything else is unthinkable, partly because it is obligatory. Second, validity will have an effect on the use of power through its effect on an authority's sense of what is proper. Furthermore, as in the case of authorization and endorsement, an authority is more likely to follow his or her conscience if it is backed by validity. Third, validity will have an effect on expectations of authorization and therefore an indirect effect on an authority's use of power through the effect expected authorization has on it. Fourth, validity will have an effect on expectations of endorsement and therefore an indirect effect on an authority's use of power through the effect expected endorsement has on it.

The empirical findings of tests of these hypotheses come from the standardized experimental setting already described except that S was at the center of the wheel and the behavior of all other positions of the network was preprogrammed. But one important difference in procedure was that at the end of the 3rd trial, E had preprogrammed one of the peripheral positions to send a change-response to another peripheral position. The center of the wheel, of course, entirely controls the flow of communication in a centralized network

TABLE 14.2

Odds of a Subject in the Central Position Not Forwarding a Change-Proposal by a Peripheral Position by Source or Type of Support for Legitimacy[a]

Source or Type of Support for Legitimacy	N	Odds Ratio	p
Validity[b]	88	4.50	< .01
Propriety[c]	307	2.17	< .001
Validity × Propriety	88	8.68	< .10
Authorization[d]	40	7.43	< .01
Endorsement[e]	41	1.08	n.s.

[a] Adapted from Zelditch and Walker (2000), 165, Table 1. There were small changes in procedure from experiment to experiment, but each comparison is made to an exactly similar control group.

[b] Change would have damaged the objectives of the experiment.

[c] Aggregated over five experiments with S at the center of the wheel. A bonus made the wheel improper; without it, the wheel was proper. There was a typographical error in the odds ratio (the "4.50" in row two) published in Zelditch and Walker (2000) that is corrected here.

[d] In one condition, E authorized the use by S of the center's capacity to control the agenda of the election. In the other, E deauthorized S's use of the center's agenda power. The odds ratio of 4.56 published in Zelditch and Walker (2000) was for authorization vs. all other conditions.

[e] In one condition, manipulated feedback from three peripheral confederates endorsed the wheel. In the other, they endorsed an all-all network.

and therefore has the capacity to control the agenda of group decisions, including whether the group votes to change its structure. The dependent variable of these experiments was whether S forwarded the preprogrammed change-response. (In one experiment, the change-response was repeated four times. In this experiment, the dependent variable was whether S ever forwarded a change-response.)

A bonus was almost as inequitable from the point of view of an S at the center of the wheel as it was if S was in a peripheral position. Thus even though S had something to gain from the bonus, other things being equal, S still was more likely to forward a change-response than not. The odds of not forwarding a change-response were .40; i.e., S was 1.5 times more likely to forward a change-response by one peripheral position to another than not forward it.[5]

Absent manipulation by E of the validity of the wheel, the fact that there was a valid procedure for changing its structure was a considerable constraint on the use of the center's agenda power by S. But validity of the structure, operationalized by framing the objectives of the experiment in such a way that change would damage them, appeared to empower S to prevent change, significantly increasing the rate at which S did not forward change-responses. Independent of validity, to the extent that the wheel was proper, its propriety also appeared to empower S to prevent change, also significantly increasing the rate at which S did not forward change-responses. But to the extent that propriety was backed by validity, S was more likely to follow his or her own conscience (though the probability does not quite achieve significance). Finally, if E authorized the center's use of the agenda power, S was 7.4 times more likely not to forward a change-response than if E deauthorized its use. But endorsement had no significant effect. A subsequent experiment found that its effect depended on how aware the center was of the periphery's power (Zelditch 1999).

3. Authorization and Endorsement. Norms regulate power only if authorization and endorsement depend only on validity. Authority ought to be authorized or endorsed if it is valid; it ought to be deauthorized or disendorsed if it is not; and propriety ought to have little or no effect on them unless backed by validity (Zelditch and Walker 2000).

But an important finding of experiments on the normative regulation of external constraints on authority's use of power is the regress of the frailties of its internal constraints: the same frailties found in its internal constraints are found in its external constraints. Self-interest, self-serving beliefs, and eccentric beliefs about what is proper all affect the behavior of an authority system's mechanisms of social control. Validity does have significant effects on authorization and endorsement. But both self-interest and propriety also affect them, and the effect of propriety is not always constrained by whether it is backed by validity.

The standardized experimental setting used to test legitimacy theory up to this point is inadequate to test hypotheses about authorization of the behavior of its central position. To study authorization of the behavior of the center, a two-team variant of the standardized experimental setting placed S in E's office, with responsibility for monitoring the conduct of two teams. One of S's functions was to authorize or deauthorize each team leader's recommendations for how to distribute team earnings. In half the teams, S heard E tell team leaders to reward everyone equally. In this experiment there was no bonus, but half the teams were centralized information-exchange networks, in which equality is not equitable. The other half were all-to-all networks, in which equality is equitable. In this experiment, validity significantly increased authorization of recommended distributions of team earnings and backing by validity significantly increased the effect of propriety (Table 14.3). But contrary to hypothesis, propriety had an effect on authorization independent of validity. In fact, if S's personal beliefs in equity were inconsistent with the equality norm backed by E, fully a third of Ss followed their own conscience rather than the norms of the experiment (Walker et al. 1997). The same sort of anomaly was also found in an experiment in the one-team setting in which, again, S assisted E in E's office. In this experiment, S had the agenda power. When the wheel was made improper by a bonus and change was valid, the odds were 19 to 1 that Ss in E's office authorized a change-response made by a confederate in a peripheral position in the wheel. But if change was invalid, the odds were only 1.6 to 1 that S authorized a change-response. Furthermore, the effect of validity was independent both of interests in gain from the bonus, also manipulated in the experiment, and measured propriety. But holding validity constant, interest in gain had an independent effect on S's authorization of change-responses (Zelditch, Gilliland, and Thomas 1984).

Studies of endorsement are equally equivocal. In the case of endorsement, the dependent variable is whether a subject in a peripheral position in the standardized experimental setting seconds the motion of a confederate, also in a peripheral position, to change the wheel. In these experiments, propriety was experimentally manipulated by awarding a bonus to only half the teams. Validity had a significant effect on endorsement, but contrary to hypothesis, propriety also had an effect independent of validity and the interaction of validity with propriety, although in the right direction, was not significant (see Table 14.3). Furthermore (not shown in Table 14.3), if endorsement rather than validity was directly

TABLE 14.3

Odds of Authorization or Endorsement by Source and Type of Support for Legitimacy

Source of Legitimacy	Type of Support	N	Odds Ratio	p
Validity[a]	Authorization[a]	43	30.43	< .001
Propriety[b]	Authorization	166	2.71	< .001
Validity × Propriety[c]	Authorization	166	2.61	< .05
Validity[d]	Endorsement[d]	88	2.50	< .05
Propriety[e]	Endorsement	168	5.26	< .001
Validity × Propriety	Endorsement	88	1.67	n.s.

[a]Rows one through three are from data analyzed by Walker and Zelditch (1985) and Walker et al. (1997). Validity was operationalized as an instruction to distribute earnings equally. Authorization was operationalized as acceptance by S, assisting E in E's office, of pay recommendations made by team leaders.

[b]Propriety was operationalized by varying network structure, assuming that unequal rewards were proper if the network was centralized but improper if it was decentralized.

[c]Because propriety was experimentally created by the interaction of network structure and the allocation of rewards recommended by team leaders, the interaction of validity by propriety is actually a three-way interaction of rule, structure, and pay recommendation. Instead of computing it directly, the significance of the odds ratio was inferred from the three-way interaction in a more complex repeated-measures analysis of variance of the amount actually paid to team leaders by S. See Walker et al. (1997).

[d]Rows four through six are from data analyzed by Walker et al. (1989). Validity was operationalized as an instruction that change would damage the objectives of the experiment. Endorsement was operationalized as a seconding by an S in a peripheral position of a centralized network of a change-response by a confederate in another peripheral position in the network.

[e]A bonus made the wheel improper; without it, the wheel was proper.

manipulated, there was no effect of peer endorsement of the wheel on endorsement of a change-response by S (Walker et al. 1989).

Similar anomalies were found in the study of sanctions. In the two-team setting, Ss also had the responsibility of deciding whether to replace team leaders at the midpoint of the experiment. In support of legitimacy theory, it was found that validity had a significant effect on sanctions of team leaders by S. Similarly, in studies of endorsement, Ss were asked if they were willing to work in a follow-up experiment with the individuals in each of the other positions in their network. Again, validity had a significant effect on sanctions. Furthermore, propriety did not significantly affect sanctions of peers unless backed by validity. Nevertheless, propriety did have an independent effect on sanctions of team leaders by Ss who were their supervisors in E's office, and its effect did not depend on backing by validity. And when endorsement, rather than validity, was directly manipulated by E, endorsement decreased rather than increased sanctions (an effect apparently unique to punishment power—cf. Molm 1997).

4. Conditions under Which Norms Regulate Power. Such anomalies raise serious questions about the conditions under which norms in fact regulate power. The question is not the conditions under which there are frailties in the external constraints on the abuse of power by authority. But if there *are* frailties, under what conditions do norms regulate them? What follows is a series of as yet untested hypotheses (from Zelditch and Walker 2000). They are based either on the theories behind the experiments—not only legitimacy theory but also two other theories, power-dependence theory (Emerson 1972) and the theory of structural holes (Burt 1992), with which it is interrelated in the particular experimental settings in which legitimacy theory has been studied—or on the ex post facto interpretation of its results. Taken together, they imply three conditions on which the normative regulation of power depends: (1) consensus, (2) the extent to which authority depends on others for the resources that empower it, and (3) the density of the network that backs it up.

Validity presupposes consensus. Absent consensus, there are fewer sanctions for non-compliance with the norms that govern the use of power, they depend less on validity, and agents of social control are more likely to act on their own sense of what is proper. Furthermore, authority's perception that there is no consensus decreases the effect that expected authorization and endorsement have on its use of power and increases the effect that its interests or its own sense of what is proper have on its use of power.

But even if there is consensus, the effect of external constraints on the use of power by authority depends on the extent to which authority is dependent on others for the resources on which its power depends. The less it depends on others for resources, the less their sanctions matter. The less their sanctions matter, the less validity, expected authorization, or expected endorsement constrains its abuse of its power and the less validity conditions the effects of its own interests or its own eccentric sense of what is proper or improper.

But authority systems also presuppose accountability. Anything that weakens accountability weakens external constraints on the use of power by authority. This has an effect both on particular positions in authority, such as A, and on particular positions in support of A's authority, such as A'. The less the density of the network of ties to A, on which cooperation with A's authority depends, the greater A's structural autonomy. The greater A's structural autonomy, the fewer the sanctions for its noncompliance with the norms that govern the use of its power, and, quite as important, the fewer of them A expects. The latter effect weakens the association between validity and expected support on which the normative regulation of the use of power by A depends. It also weakens the conditional effect of validity on the extent to which A's use of power is governed by its own interests or sense of propriety.

But there is also the question of who guards the guardians. The frailties in external constraints on the abuse of power by A only regress if ties to A are dense but A' is structurally autonomous. The normative regulation of power depends as much on the density of ties to A' as to A. In fact, only to the extent that agents of social control are densely interconnected are the interests of any one agent of social control, or the eccentricities of any one agent's sense of what is proper, constrained by the system's mechanisms of social control.

III. CAUSES AND CONDITIONS OF LEGITIMACY

Legitimacy theory is largely a theory of the consequences, not the causes or conditions, of legitimacy. Its theory of the causes and conditions of legitimacy is simply a digest of previous theory and research (Zelditch 2001a), and its empirical findings about them are simply a by-product of investigations of their effects. Almost all of these investigations presupposed, rather than investigated, its causes and conditions. But the successes and especially the failures of their attempts to create legitimacy in a laboratory give some insight into its causes and conditions (Zelditch and Walker 2003).

A. Causes

1. The Legitimacy of Acts, Persons, and Regimes. A system of authority claims legitimacy by appealing to norms, values, beliefs, purposes, practices, or procedures that are already widely accepted. The claim that it makes is that the already accepted elements to which it appeals either logically or empirically imply it, or it logically or empirically implies them.

The claim can be made for anything from regimes as a whole—their positions, relations, and the rules that govern them, such as democracy—to particular authorities, such as a president, to particular acts, such as the invasion of Iraq. For example, to legitimate a regime, in many of the studies that legitimacy theory has made of centralized networks, E has justified the structure of the network by claiming that previous research had shown it was the most effective way to achieve the goal of the group. This way of legitimating a centralized network succeeds to the extent that the Ss who volunteer to participate in them already understand and value the goals of experiments and already believe in the legitimacy of science.

To legitimate a person, in some of these studies E justified the powers of a particular confederate at the center of a particular network by claiming she or he had been selected for competence at the task, displayed in previous experiments. In this case, E relied on S's pregiven beliefs in competence as a justification for task leadership.

But studies by legitimacy theory found that Ss themselves deployed the same logic of legitimation to legitimate their own acts. Naïve Ss (as opposed to confederates) at the center of centralized networks often justified not forwarding motions to change the structure made by peripheral confederates by saying they believed a centralized network was instrumental to achieving the goal of the group.

Each of these claims either creates the legitimacy of regimes, authorities, or acts that lack it or strengthens the legitimacy of regimes, authorities, or acts if they are contested.[6] But precisely the same formula can be used to de-legitimate as to legitimate them. Thus in most of legitimacy theory's experiments, E's instructions led Ss to attribute the cause of their inequity to the centralization of their networks, de-legitimating them. In many, E's instructions de-legitimated change-attempts by implying that they damaged the objectives of the experiment.

That a claim to legitimacy succeeds to the extent that whatever it appeals to has already been accepted has a corollary, the conservation of legitimacy. Undefined or contested elements of a social situation can neither create nor strengthen it—legitimacy cannot be created de novo, out of nothing. It requires a pregiven structure of socially accepted values, norms, beliefs, purposes, practices, or procedures. There are instances mostly requiring only agreement of particular individuals in a particular situation about the particular goals of the group. But even in these cases the beliefs that connect a particular regime to attainment of particular goals must themselves be pregiven. New bases of legitimacy do emerge, as science, for example, displaced religion as the grounds for natural law in the enlightenment or, as Stryker shows, came to compete with legal rationalities in legitimating contemporary legal acts, authorities, and institutions (Stryker 1994). But before science can ground a belief as a matter of unquestioned fact it must itself have been accepted as an element of a society's pregiven structure. To legitimate undefined or contested elements of a regime, something must already be accepted somewhere. But this implies a second corollary, the spread of legitimacy. A claim to legitimacy creates a relation between the already accepted and the as yet undefined or contested elements of a situation: the legitimacy of the already accepted elements spreads across the relation to any undefined or contested elements to which it relates them. A third corollary is a variant of the second: to the extent that a group accepts a goal, any regime or any act of it that is instrumental to achieving its goal is accepted as legitimate by the group (Lipset 1959; Linz 1978).

2. Empirical Findings. Legitimacy theory's empirical findings support all this as far as it goes. But it turns out that it does not go far enough. It says nothing about multiple sources of legitimacy. But the causes of legitimacy turn out to be just as complex as its effects. It has multiple sources, such as the purposes of the group, the effectiveness of its arrangements, the justice of its procedures, and the justice of its rewards. They legitimate multiple objects, such as groups, regimes, persons, and acts. Extending the theory to multiple sources and objects of legitimacy requires some idea of how they all combine.

The formulation most consistent with the evidence is that both multiple sources and multiple objects of legitimation have independent, and therefore additive, effects on creating and strengthening legitimacy (Zelditch and Walker 2003). For example, one of the ways E attempted to manipulate the legitimacy of the wheel in legitimacy theory's standardized experimental setting was to emphasize its efficiency, a value in which Ss typically already believed. This invariably had the effect of increasing its measured propriety. But Ss also already believed in fairness. The fact that a bonus would always be won by whoever was at the center of the wheel was sufficient to de-legitimate the wheel. This invariably had the effect of decreasing its measured propriety. Thus both sources of legitimacy—one legitimating the wheel, the other de-legitimating it—affected its propriety. Post hoc analysis of variance of the results of eight of these experiments found that each source of legitimacy spread independently along a distinguishable path of causal implication, multiple paths combining additively in their effects on the propriety of the wheel (Zelditch and Walker 2003).

To investigate how multiple objects of legitimation combine, a more complex experimental setting was required. A three-level hierarchy made it possible to separate the legitimacy of a regime from that of its authorities and that of its authorities from the legitimacy of their acts. A confederate of E who was a midlevel supervisor in this hierarchy was responsible for maximizing the productivity of a four-person team competing with another team in the same organization. One of the supervisor's methods was to penalize a team for underachievement. Payment of the penalty was anonymous, beyond the surveillance of the team's supervisor or, as far as Ss were aware, of E. The experiment manipulated the legitimacy of the institution of a penalty, of the manager, and of the amount of the penalty imposed by the manager in such a way that all were legitimate, each independently of the others was illegitimate, or all were illegitimate. The legitimacy of each object had an independent, additive effect on the amount of the penalty S actually paid (Walker et al. 2002).

All of these results support the "spread" of legitimacy that is a corollary of the basic logic of legitimation—that in connecting accepted norms, values, beliefs, purposes, practices, or procedures with the undefined or contested elements of regimes, persons, or acts, what one creates is a relation across which the legitimacy of the one spreads to the other.

On the other hand, none of legitimacy theory's experiments offer any evidence that directly supports the conservation of legitimacy—that no undefined or contested element of a situation can create or strengthen the legitimacy of an act, person, or regime. What they do offer is evidence that Ss asserting claims to the legitimacy of new wines typically pour them into old bottles. In this case, what legitimacy theory was actually studying was the fate of claims to legitimacy. This required yet another experimental setting, a computerized version of the tragedy of the commons, in which two Ss each represented local communities sharing a common source of water. Each was responsible for releasing water to its own community from a finite general reserve that was replenished after every trial by a water monitor (WM), preprogrammed by computer. Ss were awarded points for maximizing their own community's water resources but were explicitly asked to balance two conflicting interests, their own community's interest and the larger collective interest in conserving the general reserve for as long as possible. Ss expected WM to obey a general rule, agreed on in advance, that replenished each local reserve at a fixed rate. But WM violated the rule on 4 of the 10 trials of the experiment, justifying himself or herself on 2 of the 4 trials. After each of the 10 trials, S was asked whether the behavior of WM was appropriate, justified, legitimate, and fair. (See Massey, Freeman, and Zelditch 1997 for a complete description of the basic setting.) In a variant of this setting, Ss were asked how each would justify WM's behavior. (See Zelditch and Floyd 1998 for a complete description of this setting.) Finally, a vignette experiment simulating this setting asked Ss to justify WM's justifications. To elicit such meta-justifications, Ss were asked to offer the best defense they could think of in response to three challenges to either a valid or invalid justification of WM's behavior—challenges to WM's rights to discretionary powers, rights to disregard an agreed-on rule, and the importance of conservation.

Supporting the conservation of legitimacy, Ss in the vignette simulation of the tragedy of commons offered justifications for WM's justifications that were highly stereotyped (Zelditch and Floyd 1998). While there was no evidence that their justifications of WM's justifications would have failed had they deployed new bottles, when offering regime-legitimating formulas Ss deployed mostly old bottles.

But experiments in the information-exchange setting and the multilevel hierarchy did find strong support for the effectiveness hypothesis. A regime that was effective in attaining goals accepted by S was legitimate. A regime that was ineffective was not. In the information-exchange setting, a change in the instructions that made network-stability instrumental to the purposes of the experiment undermined the legitimacy of a change-response, substantially increasing S's resistance to change (Thomas, Walker, and Zelditch 1986; Zelditch and Walker 2003). In the multilevel hierarchy, almost half the Ss illegitimately penalized by a supervisor nevertheless voluntarily paid the penalty. Postsession interviews found that Ss' most frequent explanation of their unexpected compliance appealed to the effectiveness of the penalty for the purposes of the group (Erlin and McLean 1989; Walker et al. 2002; Zelditch and Walker 2003).

B. Conditions

1. Four Conditions of Legitimation. But not just anything goes. Centuries of thought about legitimacy suggest that an authority's claims to legitimacy will be unsuccessful unless (1) there is general consensus on the norms, values, beliefs, purposes, practices, or procedures to which it appeals; (2) any benefits to which it appeals are either in the common interest or can be made universal; (3) any beliefs to which it appeals are believed to be matters of objective fact; and (4) the values, norms, beliefs, purposes, practices, or procedures to which it appeals are consonant with the nature, conditions, and consequences of the structure of authority they are supposed to legitimate (Zelditch and Walker 2003).

The hypothesis that legitimacy depends on consensus dates at least to Aristotle ([335/-323 BC] 1946) and is found in all theories of legitimacy since, whether consensus theories such as Parsons ([1958] 1960), conflict theories such as Machiavelli ([1517] 1940a, [1532] 1940b), or hybrids of them such as Weber ([1918] 1968) or Habermas (1975).[7] But the claim must also be in the group interest, rather than any special interest, unless, if self-interest is appealed to at all, it can be made universal—i.e., if interchanging actors would make no difference, hence the playing field would be level. A corollary is the mystification of the motives for making a claim to legitimacy: if the motive for making a claim to legitimacy is in fact self-interest, the claim will fail if its motive is transparent; it legitimates only if the motive is masked (from Machiavelli [1517] 1940a, [1532] 1940b). Hence also, demystification of a claim, unmasking the interest that lies behind it, is a way of de-legitimating an act, person, or regime. But the claim will also fail if it is merely a matter of opinion, merely a matter of the personal, possibly unwarranted beliefs of a few. It will succeed only to the extent that any beliefs to which it appeals are thought to be matters of objective fact (from Berger and Luckmann 1966). Finally, it will fail if it appeals to conditions irrelevant to those it claims to legitimate—a hypothesis due to Habermas (1975), whose example is legitimating monopoly capitalism by appeal to 19th-century free-market liberalism.

2. Empirical Findings. While broadly supporting all four of these conditions, the empirical findings of legitimacy theory's experiments required minor elaborations of two of them. With respect to consensus, it was necessary to refine both the definition of consensus and the scope of its application. *Consensus* has always been a troublesome concept: it is not always clear just how many have to agree, how many issues they have to agree about, or how intensely they have to believe in something before it counts as consensus. Tests of the consensus hypothesis found that in the population from which the Ss of legitimacy theory's experiments were drawn consensus was mixed. In the experiments, issue-specific, near consensus was sufficient for legitimacy and validity was sufficient whether or not it was proper.

In a study of the acceptance of justifications for WM's offenses in the tragedy of the commons setting, there was almost perfect consensus with respect to some justifications but a substantial amount of disagreement with respect to others. To manipulate the validity of the justifications used by WM in the experiment, a sample of Ss had first been drawn from the same population as the Ss in the experiment and asked to offer the best and worst justifications they could think of for WM's offense. A second sample drawn from the same population rated the justifications they offered from best to worst. The second sample's ratings were transformed into a rank order of justifications from best to worst, rank depending on the extent to which Ss agreed. The experiment operationalized validity as the consensually best justification, invalidity as the consensually worst justification, but it also studied the effect of an ambiguous justification about which there was substantial disagreement. It found that ambiguous justifications created significantly more legitimacy than invalid justifications but not much less legitimacy than valid justifications, implying considerable latitude in Ss' sense of the group's consensus (Massey, Freeman, and Zelditch 1997). But of equal interest is the fact that there was a great deal of disagreement in the second sample of Ss about many of the justifications that Ss in the first sample had offered as the best and worst justifications of WM's offense. Whatever consensus there was, it was issue-specific. Furthermore, in the tragedy of the commons setting, acceptance of WM's justification was again directly proportional to its validity. But if WM's justification was not valid, even if Ss therefore doubted consensus, they still searched for, expected to find, and thought they had found another justification that they thought *was* valid (Zelditch and Floyd 1998). But legitimacy did not require perfect consensus. Near consensus was sufficient. E varied agreement between S and his or her partner, but the fact that one person did not agree with S did not lead S to question consensus elsewhere in the group and had no effect on the legitimacy of WM (Zelditch and Floyd 1998). Finally, belief that others believed in consensus, even if S did not, was sufficient for legitimacy. In the vignette simulation of the commons setting, many Ss said they did not themselves believe in the justification that they offered as a valid justification for WM's offense. They merely believed that others believed in it (Zelditch and Floyd 1998).

Thus unless the pregiven structure of values, norms, beliefs, purposes, practices, and procedures on which a claim to legitimacy draws for its premises is so well integrated that dissensus anywhere in it is dissensus everywhere, near, collective, issue-specific consensus is all that is necessary for legitimacy.

With respect to the impartiality condition, it was found that where self-interests were involved, at least in a commons dilemma, a level playing field was not sufficient for impartiality. It also required that self-interest be justified as in the group interest.

There *was* strong support for the hypothesis that transparent self-interest de-legitimated rather than legitimated a centralized network in the information-exchange setting. Where S in the information-exchange setting was in E's office, had the agenda power, and had much to gain from a centralized network, validity (operationalized as damage to the objectives of the experiment) significantly decreased authorization of change-responses by a peripheral confederate. But the effect of validity, which ought to have concealed self-interest, had less, not more, effect on resistance to change if it was combined with an interest in gain from the wheel. Postsession interviews revealed that validity had done nothing to mask interest (Zelditch, Gilliland, and Thomas 1984).

The test, however, is only partial; none of legitimacy theory's experiments have tested the principle's corollary, that mystification would have legitimated interest. But a study of justifications offered by Ss for the WM's offense in the tragedy of the commons setting did find that the justifications Ss offered appealed to the group interest even when E's instructions claimed that the playing field was level. If either or both of the communities acted in their own self-interest it would, in the case of a finite reservoir of water, have been illegitimate no matter how level the playing field (Zelditch and Walker 2003). Absent a commons dilemma, a level playing field may legitimate self-interest, but not if it threatens a collective interest.

There was general support, however, for the objectification and consonance conditions. With respect to objectification, the hypothesis that it is a necessary condition of legitimation wasn't tested, but study of valid versus invalid justifications offered by Ss both in the validation phase of the tragedy of the commons experiments and the vignette study of defenses of them found that use of the personal pronoun *I*, implying personal opinion rather than objective fact, was inversely proportional to the validity of the justifications offered (Zelditch and Walker 2003).

With respect to consonance, again the hypothesis that consonance is a necessary condition of legitimation was never tested, but attempts to manipulate the propriety of the wheel in the information-exchange setting found that appeal to neither ability nor effort was sufficient to legitimate the bonus because Ss thought the task too simple for ability to matter (Lineweber, Barr-Bryan, and Zelditch 1982) and too easy for effort to matter (Zelditch and Walker 2000).

C. A Basic Legitimation Assumption

Consensus, impartiality, objectivity, and consonance are necessary conditions of legitimacy, not causes of it. But given a legitimating formula that links the undefined or contested elements of an act, person, or regime to accepted values, they are jointly sufficient and can be thought of as a single basic principle in terms of which the previous findings can be summarized.

This principle presupposes a legitimating formula, say F, consisting of (1) one or more elements of an act, person, or regime the legitimacy of which is undefined or contested; (2) one or more elements of the act, person, or regime the legitimacy of which is defined and uncontested; and (3) one or more implication relations (in either or both directions) between them.

Given F, the undefined or contested elements of the act, person, or regime acquire the legitimacy of the defined, uncontested elements of it if and only if the following conditions are met:

1. *Consensus.* There is near, issue-specific, collective acceptance of the defined, uncontested elements of F.

2. *Impartiality.* Any benefit of the act, person, or position to which F appeals is (a) in the group interest, under cooperative conditions, (b) universalizable, under competitive conditions, or (c) both in the group interest and universalizable under mixed-motive conditions.

3. *Objectification.* Any belief to which F appeals is consensually accepted as a matter of objective fact.

4. *Consonance.* Any defined, uncontested element to which F appeals is consonant with the nature, conditions, and consequences of the act, person, or regime.

5. Given two or more Fs, the effect of each is independent of any other F.

CONCLUSION

The legitimation of power is a complex process. There are multiple levels of legitimacy, multiple sources of it, multiple objects of it, multiple levels of authority, and multiple levels of support for it. Legitimacy theory's conceptualization of it is correspondingly complex, distinguishing, in the first instance, between collective and individual levels of legitimacy—validity versus propriety—and between support of it by other authorities and support of it by peers of those over whom authority is exercised—authorization versus endorsement.

Neither of these distinctions plays any role in its causes. The basic logic of legitimation is a matter of relating undefined or contested elements of any object—act, person, regime, or group—to elements of it that a group already accepts as legitimate. Some norm, value, belief, purpose, practice, or procedure must already be accepted before it can legitimate anything else. Its legitimacy spreads to any object the legitimacy of which is undefined or contested across the paths that link them. (A special case is the claim, ubiquitous in the legitimacy program's experiments, that an act, person, or regime is effective in attaining some agreed-on goal of a group.) What complicates its causes are multiple sources and objects of it. But if there is more than one source or object of legitimation, each has an independent effect, hence their joint effects are additive.

But only if they satisfy four fairly stringent conditions: the undefined or contested elements of an object acquire the legitimacy of its defined, uncontested elements only if: (1) There is a near, collectively shared consensus specifically with respect to its accepted legitimating elements (consensus). (2) Any benefit appealed to is (a) in the group interest, if the situation is cooperative; (b) universalizable, if it is competitive; or (c) both in the group interest *and* universalizable, if it is a mix of the two (impartiality). (3) Any belief appealed to is consensually accepted as a matter of objective fact (objectification). (4) Any defined, uncontested element appealed to is consonant with the nature, conditions, and consequences of the situation to which it is applied (consonance).

Because the rights that make up a system of authority can be divided in various ways, the structure of a system of authority can itself be one of the causes of its legitimacy or illegitimacy. But in this case, the distinctions between validity and propriety, authorization and endorsement, play an important role in understanding legitimacy's effects. The propriety of an authority structure is directly proportional to the compatibility of its rights. The pressures to change it are directly proportional to its propriety. But field studies have found considerably less instability than impropriety because propriety is not the only source of an authority structure's legitimacy. Once it emerges, legitimacy at the collective level has a life of its own, independent of propriety. It acquires the capacity to maintain itself because, once emerged, it has a direct effect on compliance and attempts to change the structure of authority. But it is itself a source of propriety, over and above any other source, hence indirectly increasing compliance and decreasing pressure to change in a way that does not depend on social controls. In addition, it has its own mechanisms of social control, author-ization, and endorsement, expectations of which increase compliance with authority and decrease attempts to change it and actual change in it. Overall, the effect of validity tends to be greater than that of propriety: when validity and propriety are consistent, validity accen-tuates the effect of propriety. When they are inconsistent, validity attenuates the effect of propriety.

Under certain conditions, the normative regulation of power also depends more on validity than propriety. Absent validity, propriety is a frail reed on which to found the nor-mative regulation of power. But on the assumption that authorization and endorsement are functions of validity, the mechanisms of the normative regulation of power are the same as the mechanisms of the stability of authority. Validity does have a significant effect on authorization and endorsement. But self-interest, self-serving beliefs, and sometimes ec-centric beliefs in what is proper also affect them, and the effect of propriety is not always constrained by validity. Whether authorization and endorsement depend on validity itself depends on three conditions: (1) consensus, (2) the extent to which an authority depends on others for the resources that empower it, and (3) the density of the network that backs it up. Only to the extent that agents of social control are themselves densely interconnected are the interests or eccentricities of any one of them constrained by the authority system's mechanisms of social control.

In all this, legitimacy is only an auxiliary process—a secondary factor in the emergence and maintenance of power structures, however important it is to how power actually be-haves. This is probably true of many other social processes, such as status and reward pro-cesses, in fact almost any other process that creates and maintains the structure of a group (see note 1). Nevertheless, legitimacy is a fundamental social process: it is fundamental to understanding the relation between pregiven structure and the structure of specific, con-crete situations. The norms, values, beliefs, purposes, practices, or procedures that legiti-mate power (or status or rewards or . . .) are pregiven. But they are typically too abstract, general, and incomplete to define specific, concrete situations. A specific consensus is some-thing that is interactively constructed by specific actors in specific, concrete situations out of whatever structure is pregiven and the specific circumstances of the situation. But what is constructed de-legitimates as well as legitimates, creating pressures for change as well as stability and regulation. Legitimation is fundamental not only to our understanding of how pregiven structure is interpreted in specific, concrete situations but also to what changes come to be accepted as future pregiven structure and how they are institutionalized in it.

NOTES

1. Many other structures and processes also involve legitimacy, such as justice or status. In fact, the emergence of virtually any kind of structure raises the question of how it becomes and remains stable, a process in which legitimacy is almost always an important factor. Because the dependent variable differs from process to process, there is no unique dependent variable associated with legitimacy except that it is always a matter of voluntarily accepting that something is or is not right and its consequence is always the stability or instability of whatever structure emerges in the process. No general theory of legitimacy has yet emerged that applies to it in every process in which it is known to be auxiliary (Zelditch 2001a).

2. Aside from its observable behavior, one can look for the validity of a rule in a group's pregiven norms, values, beliefs, purposes, practices, or procedures. If it is rational-legal (see Weber [1918] 1968), many of them will be explicit, even written; for example, one can learn which moves are valid in chess by looking at the rules inside the cover of the box the pieces come in.

3. The essential feature of methods for treating survival curves is that observed change is compared to expected change at each trial, which in turn depends only on the number exposed to risk at the beginning of each trial. If m Ss make a change-response at trial t and a proportion p of all Ss were in condition i when trial t began, then the expected number of change-responses in condition i should be $p_i m$, assuming there is no true difference between conditions. The quantity $r_i = O_i/E_i$, the ratio of the observed to the expected number of change-responses, gives the relative rate of change in the ith condition, i.e., the rate of change in the ith condition compared to that in the population as a whole. The quantity $R = r_i/r_j$ gives the ratio of the relative rate of change in the ith condition to that in the jth condition—reflecting the shape of the two curves because the expected values are computed trial by trial and are based on the number surviving up to the time each trial begins. The quantity $1 - R$ provides essentially the same information but has a more natural interpretation as the rate at which change in the baseline is delayed or prevented by any given experimental treatment. The statistic $(O - E)^2/E$, furthermore, is distributed as chi square with, in this case, 1 degree of freedom, which is the basis for the significance levels in Table 14.1. For a comprehensive survey of methods of analyzing survival curves, see Elandt-Johnson and Johnson 1980. An especially clear and nontechnical treatment based on the (nonparametric) log-rank statistic that is used here can be found in Peto et al. 1977.

4. Legitimacy theory is a theory of the structure of authority in a closed system. If this system is opened to its environment, legitimacy processes external to it may affect its internal legitimacy processes. The more it depends on its environment for some or all of the resources on which it depends for its survival, the more internal pressures to change the system depend on its external validity, external authorization, and external endorsement. Because environments too can be multiple, the number of environments, their

types, the extent of dependence on each type of environment, and how each type of environment is organized, all have an effect both on internal pressures toward the instability of authority and the internal pressure to resist them (Zelditch 2004).

5. The odds of not forwarding a change-response are given by the ratio of the probability of not forwarding it to the probability of forwarding it. Thus if the probability of not forwarding a change-response is .40, the odds of not forwarding it is .40/.60 = .67. Another, possibly more natural, way of saying the same thing is that S is 1/.67 = 1.5 times more likely to forward than not forward the change-response. Proportions are easily inferred from odds because $p = o/(o + 1)$. The advantages of odds are due to the ease of interpretation of odds ratios as a measure of association. Thus the effect of a treatment compared to its control condition is the ratio of the odds of the treatment's effect on the forwarding rate divided by the control's effect. For example, Ss are 4.5 times more likely to not forward a change-response if the network is valid than if it is not (Table 14.2). Had the treatment had no effect, the odds ratio would have been 1.00. In other words, the odds would be the same in both the treatment and control conditions. Had the odds ratio of the validity treatment been .22, Ss in the validity condition would be 4.5 times more likely to forward a change-response than not forward it—the mirror opposite of not forwarding it (see earlier discussion) except for the direction of the effect. In other words, odds ratios greater than 1.00 measure increasing amounts of association as they get larger, odds ratios less than 1.00 measure increasing amounts of association as they get smaller, but both depart to the same degree from independence. Because the sampling distribution of the odds ratio is highly skewed, its significance is estimated by transforming it to log odds and computing a likelihood chi square, which is the source of the probabilities in Table 14.2.

6. If the norms, values, beliefs, purposes, practices, or procedures appealed to by a claim to legitimacy are proper, the legitimacy they create is propriety. If they are valid, the legitimacy they create is validity. But our understanding of the causes of legitimacy does not depend on the distinction between them, and we refer simply to "legitimacy" for the rest of part III.

7. Easton 1965, in which little consensus is required, is an exception.

REFERENCES

Aristotle. [335–323 BC] 1946. *Politics.* Oxford: Oxford University Press.

Barnard, Chester. 1938. *Functions of the Executive.* Cambridge, MA: Harvard University Press.

Bavelas, Alex. 1950. Communication patterns in task-oriented groups. *Journal of the Acoustical Society of America* 22:725–30.

Berger, Peter, and Thomas Luckmann. 1966. *The Social Construction of Reality.* New York: Doubleday.

Burt, Ronald S. 1992. *Structural Holes: The Social Structure of Competition.* Cambridge, MA: Harvard University Press.

Cohen, Albert K. 1966. *Deviance and Control.* Englewood Cliffs, NJ: Prentice-Hall.

Dornbusch, Sanford M., and W. Richard Scott. 1975. *Evaluations and the Exercise of Authority.* San Francisco: Jossey-Bass.

Easton, David. 1965. *A Systems Analysis of Political Life.* New York: Wiley.

Elandt-Johnson, Regina C., and Norman L. Johnson. 1980. *Survival Models and Data Analysis.* New York: Wiley.

Erlin, H. Christopher W., and Bonnie J. McLean. 1989. Normalizing illegitimate acts. Department of Sociology, Stanford University, Stanford, CA. Unpublished honors thesis.

Emerson, Richard M. 1972. Exchange theory. In *Sociological Theories in Progress,* ed. Joseph Berger, Morris Zelditch Jr., and Bo Anderson, 2:38–87. Boston: Houghton Mifflin.

Ford, Joan Butler, and Morris Zelditch Jr. 1988. A test of the law of anticipated reactions. *Social Psychology Quarterly* 51:164–71.

Habermas, Jürgen. 1975. *Legitimation Crisis.* Boston: Beacon Press.

Lineweber, David Charles, Dorine Barr-Bryan, and Morris Zelditch Jr. 1982. Effects of a legitimate authority's justification of inequality on the mobilization of revolutionary coalitions. *Technical Report 84.* Stanford, CA: Laboratory for Social Research, Stanford University.

Linz, Juan J. 1978. Crisis, breakdown, and re-equilibration. In *The Breakdown of Democratic Regimes,* ed. Juan J. Linz and Alfred Stepan, vol. 1. Baltimore: Johns Hopkins University Press.

Lipset, Seymour M. 1959. Some social requisites of democracy: Economic development and political legitimacy. *American Political Science Review* 53:69–105.

Machiavelli, Niccolo. [1517] 1940a. *Discourses on the First Ten Books of Titus Livius.* New York: Modern Library.

———. [1532] 1940b. *The Prince.* New York: Modern Library.

Marx, Karl, and Frederick Engels. [1845–47] 1976. *The German Ideology.* In *Karl Marx, Frederick Engels: Collected Works,* 5:19–539. New York: International.

Massey, Kelly, Sabrina Freeman, and Morris Zelditch Jr. 1997. Status, power, and accounts. *Social Psychology Quarterly* 60:238–51.

Molm, Linda D. 1997. *Coercive Power in Social Exchange.* New York: Cambridge University Press.

Parsons, Talcott. [1958] 1960. Authority, legitimation, and political action. In *Structure and Process in Modern Societies,* ed. Talcott Parsons, 170–98. Glencoe, IL: Free Press.

Peto, R., M. C. Pike, P. Armitage, N. E. Breslow, D. R. Cox, S. V. Howard, N. Mantel, K. McPherson, J. Peto, and P. G. Smith. 1977. Design and analysis of randomized clinical trials requiring prolonged observation of each patient. *British Journal of Cancer* 35:1–39.

Stryker, Robin. 1994. Rules, resources, and legitimacy processes: Some implications for social conflict, order, and change. *American Journal of Sociology* 99:847–910.

Thomas, George M., Henry A. Walker, and Morris Zelditch Jr. 1986. Legitimacy and collective action. *Social Forces* 65:378–404.

Walker, Henry A., Larry Rogers, Katherine Lyman, and Morris Zelditch Jr. 1989. Legitimacy and the support of revolutionary coalitions. Working Paper 89-3. Stanford, CA.: Center for Sociological Research, Stanford University.

Walker, Henry A., Larry Rogers, George M. Thomas, and Morris Zelditch Jr. 1991. Legitimating collective action: Theory and experimental results. *Research in Political Sociology* 5:1–25.

Walker, Henry A., Larry Rogers, and Morris Zelditch Jr. 1988. Legitimacy and collective action: A research note. *Social Forces* 67:216–28.

———. 2002. Acts, persons, positions and institutions: Legitimating multiple objects and compliance with authority. In *Structure, Culture, and History: Recent Issues in Social Theory,* ed. Sing C. Chew and J. David Knottnerus, 323–39. Lanham, MD: Rowman & Littlefield.

Walker, Henry A., George M. Thomas, and Morris Zelditch Jr. 1986. Legitimation, endorsement, and stability. *Social Forces* 64:620–43.

Walker, Henry A., and Morris Zelditch Jr. 1985. Legitimacy and the exercise of authority: The effects of validity and propriety. Working paper 85-1. Stanford, CA: Center for Sociological Research, Stanford University.

Walker, Henry A., and Morris Zelditch Jr. 1993. Power, legitimacy, and the stability of authority: A theoretical research program. In *Theoretical Research Programs: Studies in the Growth of Theory,* ed. Joseph Berger and Morris Zelditch Jr, 364–81. Stanford, CA: Stanford University Press.

Walker, Henry A., Morris Zelditch Jr, Paula S. Taylor, and Valerie C. Montoya. 1997. Choosing standards: Validity, propriety, and pay equity. Unpublished manuscript. Stanford, CA.: Center for Sociological Research, Stanford University.

Weber, Max. [1918] 1968. *Economy and Society.* Ed. G. Roth and C. Wittich. Berkeley: University of California Press.

Zelditch, Morris Jr. 1999. Legitimacy, expected value, and the strength of peripheral power. Paper presented at the meeting of the West Coast Group Processes Conference, April, Stanford, CA.

———. 2001a. Theories of legitimacy. In *The Psychology of Legitimacy,* ed. John Jost and Brenda Major, 33–53. New York: Cambridge University Press.

———. 2001b. Processes of legitimation: Recent developments and new directions. *Social Psychology Quarterly* 64:4–17.

————. 2004. Institutional effects on the stability of organizational authority. *Legitimacy Processes in Organizations. Research in the Sociology of Organizations* 22:25–48.

Zelditch, Morris Jr, and Anthony S. Floyd. 1998. Consensus, dissensus, and justification. In *Status, Power, and Legitimacy*, ed. Joseph Berger and Morris Zelditch Jr, 339–68. New Brunswick, NJ: Transaction.

Zelditch, Morris Jr, Edward Gilliland, and George M. Thomas. 1984. The legitimacy of redistributive agendas. Working Paper 84-9. Stanford, CA.: Center for Sociological Research, Stanford University.

Zelditch, Morris Jr, William Harris, George M. Thomas, and Henry A. Walker. 1983. Decisions, nondecisions, and metadecisions. *Research in Social Movements, Conflict, and Change* 5:1–32.

Zelditch, Morris Jr, and Henry A. Walker. 1984. Legitimacy and the stability of authority. *Advances in Group Processes: Theory and Research* 1:1–25.

————. 2000. The normative regulation of power. *Advances in Group Processes* 17:155–78.

————. 2003. The legitimacy of regimes. *Advances in Group Processes* 20:217–49.

15 | THE STATE OF THEORIZING IN SOCIOLOGICAL SOCIAL PSYCHOLOGY: A GRAND THEORIST'S VIEW

Jonathan H. Turner

I read the excellent chapters in this volume from the perspective of a general theorist rather than as a social psychologist. As a general theorist—grand theorist, if truth be told—my concern has always been to develop models and principles on generic social processes operating at the micro, meso, and macro realms of social reality. In my view, distinctions among micro, meso, and macro reality are more than analytic conveniences; they are *the way reality actually unfolds*. There is a face-to-face level of interaction, best captured in Erving Goffman's (1961, 1983) analysis of the "encounter" and Randall Collins's (2004) similar formulation about the dynamics of interaction rituals. There is a meso-level of reality that unfolds around what Amos Hawley (1986) has termed *corporate units* (revealing a division of labor in pursuit of goals) and *categoric units* (generated by the classification of people in terms of distinctive characteristics or, in Peter Blau's [1994] terms, *parameters*). And finally, there is a macro-level realm of social reality composed of institutional domains (e.g., economy, polity, religion, science, and the like built from corporate units), stratification systems (built around such categoric units as classes, ethnicity, gender, and age), societies as a whole (composed of institutional domains and stratification systems), and ultimately, systems of societies (involving relations among a set of society's respective institutional domains and stratification systems).

These levels of social reality are, on the one side, built from the structural units below them. Thus, corporate units are sustained by micro-level encounters; similarly, categoric units are created and maintained in encounters; and macro units are constructed from corporate and categoric units. On the other side, levels of reality are embedded in each other. Encounters of face-to-face interaction are almost always embedded in corporate and categoric units that, in turn, are embedded in institutional domains, stratification systems, and even inter-societal systems. For the most part, social psychology studies the dynamics of embedding by viewing the cognitions, emotions, and behaviors of individuals as being constrained by corporate and categoric units. Less often, social psychologists theorize on the effects of individual-level cognitions, emotions, and behaviors on the formation, change, or maintenance of corporate and categoric units and, by extension, more macro structures.

Theorizing in social psychology has not, however, fully conceptualized the relationships between psychodynamics—i.e., cognitions, emotions, and behaviors—and various levels of social structure. Part of the reason for this failing is the tendency for much social psychology to use experimental designs that, for all their strong points, tend to impose scope conditions that narrow inquiry. In particular, the theories presented in this volume have generally employed experimental designs on a specific process or small set of processes. The result is for theory and research, from a grand theorist's perspective, to be too focused. Even for theoretical research programs that have expanded over the years—e.g., expectation-states research—the broadening is incremental and does not address meso- and macro-level issues in any detail. Hence, the strength of the chapters in this book—clear theories backed up by a considerable amount of empirical research—is also a weakness because each theory tends to develop its own set of concepts and experimental research designs, with surprisingly little integration across these narrow theories, to say nothing of broader concerns of general theorizing in sociology.

In my overview of the state of theory in social psychology, this criticism will be a recurring theme. It could be argued, of course, that I am simply imposing my theoretical bias on bodies of highly cumulative theorizing and research; and this criticism would be fair and correct. Still, if I am to bring anything to the table in this volume, it is a push for integration across theories in social psychology and between these specialized theories and the more general theories outside social psychology proper.

To anticipate my argument, I think that theorizing in social psychology requires a more robust conceptualization of social structure (the *social* half of social psychology) and the psychodynamic forces connecting individuals to social structures (the *psychology* portion of social psychology). Integration among theories in social psychology must begin with a more complete conception of social structure and the actor because, without a more robust conception of these two elements of social psychology, theories will remain narrow, and new integrative conceptual and research questions will not be posed. Each theory will remain in its intellectual niche, slowly accumulating empirical findings and only incrementally expanding its explanatory reach. While this kind of gradual theorizing and research is cumulative, to be sure, there is another way that knowledge cumulates: through theoretical integration. Indeed, most big breakthroughs in science involve someone asking broader questions and providing answers. I do have not have the answers, but I do intend to ask questions that, I believe, need to be posed if social psychological theorizing in sociology is to move forward.

I adopt a simple conceptualization that contains the potential for much complexity. I follow my outline of social structure, enumerated above, and then ask two related questions: (1) What are the fundamental properties of social structure and individuals? And (2) what psychodynamic processes link individuals to social structures? Let me begin with the conceptualization of social structure.

CONCEPTUALIZING AND RECONCEPTUALIZING SOCIAL STRUCTURE

Social Structure as Networks

Several theories in social psychology—particularly those in exchange theorizing—conceptualize social structure as a network. This view of structure has a number of strengths, including a well-developed system of notation and algorithms, a precise view of structure as a pattern of relations generated by resource flows, a formal way to conceptualize properties of social structures (e.g., relations revolving around power, hierarchy, subgroup formation, inclusion, exclusion, and ordering of resource flows), and a capacity to conceptualize dynamic relations about both individual and collective actors (thus extending the theory to relations among meso- and macro-level units of social organization). There is, then, much to recommend this view of social structure because particular psychodynamics can be linked to varying types of networks. For example, those following Richard Emerson (1962) have a clear conception of power as a function of dependence of one actor on another for resources (in a unilateral monopoly) or in elementary theory as the exclusion of an actor from an exchange network distributing valued resources. Moreover, particular psychodynamic states like commitments can also be seen to follow from particular types of exchange networks, as is illustrated by the affect theory of exchange, which views positive emotional arousal and commitments as arising from dense networks revealing high levels of mutual dependence and revolving around productive exchanges. Or as is the case with power-dependence theorizing, commitments to suboptimal exchange relations are seen as a function of uncertainty reduction in established networks, coupled with the introduction of a new resource—the positive emotions accompanying commitments—into the exchange network.

The problem with this view of social structure is that it leans heavily on only one of many more general theoretical orientations in sociology (exchange theorizing) while tending to undertheorize the larger social structures that generate networks. Networks are almost always part of a meso-level corporate unit—a group at the smallest end to large-scale organizations and communities at the larger end of meso-level structures. These meso structures reveal their own dynamics that generate not only networks but also other important properties of social structures that have independent effects (beyond the effects working through networks) on individuals' cognitions, emotions, and behaviors. Fortunately, other theories in social psychology pick up some of these lost effects of social structure on psychodynamics, as I explore below.

Social Structure as Status Systems

Several theories in social psychology emphasize *status* as the key structural property affecting, and being influenced by, psychodynamics. Status is conceptualized in several ways, as (1) power and authority; (2) prestige, honor, and rights to deference; and (3) membership in a social category or, in Hawley's terms, a "categoric unit" (or in expectation-states theorizing, a *diffuse status characteristic*). These three views of status are not mutually exclusive because high-power persons generally are members of highly evaluated categoric units and, by virtue of power and categoric-unit membership, are entitled to prestige and deference. Of course, some of the more interesting psychodynamics ensue when there is a low correlation among these three conceptions of status in a local encounter or when individuals low on one or more of these status hierarchies seek to move up the hierarchy.

Unfortunately, since this view of status is studied primarily in experimental task groups, the connection to the larger division of labor in meso units is often underemphasized in theorizing and research. The dynamics analyzed are, no doubt, easily transferred to hierarchies of authority in natural settings, but with the focus on the micro status order within a contrived experimental group (and in some cases, only a virtual group or simulation of group processes), the meso-level dynamics generating a status hierarchy are not incorporated into the theory; these dynamic forces are simply excluded by boundary conditions. As a result, several related theories—expectation-states theorizing, status-characteristics theorizing, status-construction theorizing, and legitimacy theorizing—tend to focus on status *at the level of the encounter*, taking as a given the meso structure in which the status order resides. True, status construction theory seeks to explain how status beliefs, once generated, spread out to meso and macro structures; expectation states theory assumes that the status is lodged in a meso structure and involves use of referential structures; legitimacy theory emphasizes group-level validity, endorsement, and authorization; and status characteristics theory recognizes that diffuse status is part of larger systems of categories and their differential evaluation. Still, the dynamic interplay of the meso structural properties is subordinated to the analysis of status, per se, at the level of face-to-face interaction, often in isolation from the very meso and macro forces that establish a status hierarchy. While it is fair to say that a theory cannot explain everything all at once, the structure of status systems is too minimalist in these theories. To extend the reach of these theories, status structures must be conceptualized in more robust terms.

Structure as Distributional Systems

Another approach in theories of social psychology is to view social structure as a distribution system. Network approaches, for instance, see actors in a network as possessing varying amounts of valued resources that, in turn, set into motion a variety of exchange processes. Comparison theories of justice also view individuals as responding to the distribution of goods, bads, and other valued or devalued resources in terms of their perceived fairness or justness. Expectation-states theorizing and related approaches such as status characteristic and status construction theories all conceptualize status structures as both an effect and cause of the differential distribution of prestige, power, and evaluations; moreover, status itself is conceptualized as a distributional process whereby power and prestige are unequally distributed across a set of interacting individuals.

Comparison theory is one of the few to make a more direct link of distributional processes to macro-level concepts of distributions, such as Gini coefficients. Moreover, this theory, along with other work using a justice framework, also sees actors as comparing their holdings of a given resource to a reference point, which is the holdings of goods and resources among members of specific social units, ranging from a group at the more micro end of the continuum to ever more macro-level reference points, such as a society-wide or even inter-societal distribution of resources (as measured by indexes of inequality like Gini coefficients). Out of such comparisons come justice evaluations that, in turn, activate other psychodynamic processes, such as positive and negative emotions, that lead to behaviors that can reaffirm or work to change the distribution of resources and, hence, social structures.

The limitation of this view of social structure is fairly obvious. If distributions of resources are used as a comparison reference point, the structural forces that have created the more meso or macro distribution are not examined; they are simply givens. Similarly, if elements of structure such as status or holders of resources in a network are viewed as a distributional system, theorizing generally begins with an existing distribution and explores the status and power dynamics that ensue; and in so doing, the theory focuses only on distribution and potential redistribution of resources at the micro level rather than on the larger social structural forces that initially generated the distribution. Again, a social psychological theory cannot explain macro-level processes alone, but the attention to the individual as the unit making comparisons among resource shares of diverse actors or the individual as responding to distributions of resources in local situations fails to adequately incorporate the forces generating distributions in the first place. These forces, I believe, will have large effects not only on a person's sense of how just and legitimate a given distribution is but also on the individual's thoughts, emotions, and behaviors. To the degree that the existing theories address this issue—as is illustrated by legitimacy theory's emphasis on validation, status construction theory's analysis of how status beliefs are spread to a more macro level of society, and comparison theory's use of ideas from welfare economics—the emphasis is still on the individual's response to an existing system of distribution rather than the individual's reaction to the operation of meso- and macro-level forces generating the distribution of power, prestige, or any resource.

Structure as Cultural Systems

Several theories in social psychology emphasize cultural systems, such as beliefs and norms, as an element of social structure. Affect control theory, for example, seeks to account for people's thoughts, emotions, and actions in terms of *deflections*, or discrepancies between fundamental sentiments (or beliefs) and transient impressions about actors, self, objects, behaviors, or situations. Status construction theory takes a somewhat different view, emphasizing that status processes are reinforced or changed by status beliefs containing conceptions and evaluations about what individuals revealing particular status characteristics can and should do. Such beliefs set up expectation states for how individuals will and should act in micro encounters; status-construction theory moves in the direction of affect control theory by viewing status beliefs as potentially spreading across a larger social structure, including a whole society, by virtue of consistent reinforcement of the relationship between status characteristics and performances in micro situations. As this process of cultural transmission ensues (often accelerated by sequences of explicit teaching of beliefs to others), something akin to fundamental sentiments about categoric units emerges, serving as a basis for expectations for, and evaluations of, persons. Yet, unlike affect control theory, when status beliefs are challenged or are not confirmed by actual performances, the incongruity can work to change or undo status beliefs. True, in affect control theory, fundamental sentiments can be changed in the face of deflection, but the theory argues that changes in other elements—impressions of others, objects, behaviors, and situations—represent a more likely response to deflections.

Social identity theorizing adds to status construction theory a basic Gestalt argument that individuals are motivated to note differences and to make comparisons between themselves and those in another category, thereby codifying beliefs about the characteristics of outsiders. Moreover, individuals internalize the norms of behavior for their own category, formulating a general prototype for how they are supposed to behave; and they use this prototype to judge their own and others' behaviors. In so doing, the characteristics among members of a categoric unit are reinforced for both those within the category and those looking at its members from the outside. From this perspective, then, social structure is seen as a process whereby individuals categorize themselves and others, and as a result, develop normative prototypes for the typical ways that people in categories behave. Such norms and beliefs will, in turn, lead to stable expectation states for behaviors and performances. Social structure thus becomes a system of norms and beliefs about how members of social categories are likely to behave (often coupled with an evaluation of this behavior); and once these norms and beliefs are in place, they become expectation states in micro-level encounters.

Other theories also contain a conception of social structure as a system of cultural norms or beliefs. Within the Blumer (1969) wing of symbolic interactionism, for instance, norms and beliefs are objects that individuals perceive and use as a frame of reference for self-evaluations and behaviors, but true to Blumer's emphasis on the flexibility of behavior and social structure, these objects can be discarded or reinterpreted. At the more structural end of symbolic interactionism (Stryker 1980), social relations are seen to have a more obdurate character, and the norms and beliefs attached to positions and guiding role behaviors in this structure have the power to constrain the identities that individuals can present, the standards by which these identities are evaluated, and the behaviors that are emitted in roles. Indeed, structure exerts its greatest force on individual thought, emotion, and action via the normative and belief systems that inhere in status positions and that direct role behaviors.

Distributive justice theories in social psychology also contain a normative element. When individuals compare their receipt of resources to those of others and various reference structures, they also invoke beliefs and norms about what is fair. In fact, understandings of what constitutes a just reward is regulated by norms about appropriate procedures to realize rewards and by norms about the appropriate level of payoffs (relative to the investments and costs in securing payoffs for self and others). These norms are ultimately defined by beliefs about fair procedures and just outcomes. Exchange theories make much the same argument, as do rational choice theories. Thus, the calculations of individuals about what they should receive in exchanges and in payoff situations in general, the emotions that are aroused when payoffs are seen as just or unjust, and the resulting propensities to behave in particular ways in the face of perceptions of justice and injustice are all mediated by belief and normative systems. What is missing from much of this analysis, however, is a clear conceptualization of how such beliefs and norms are generated at the more meso and macro levels of social structure. Moreover, none of the theories adequately explains *which* norms and beliefs at *which* level of social structure are used to frame judgments of what is fair and just in payoff situations where resources are distributed.

Structure as Social Categories

Several theories, particularly status characteristics theory, status construction theory, and social identity theory, suggest a vision of social structure as a system of differentially evaluated social categories or categoric units (Hawley 1986; Turner 2002) and nominal parameters (Blau 1994). From a more macro perspective, the meso level of social reality involves not just corporate units revealing a division of labor that sets status hierarchies in place but also social categories that distinguish individuals from each other and that are differentially evaluated. This latter axis of social differentiation is ultimately the building block of macro-level stratification systems that distribute resources unequally to various categories of persons who can be distinguished by their class location, gender, age, ethnicity, and other bases for marking categoric distinctions.

Status characteristics theory argues that diffuse status characteristics create expectation states for individuals' performances in task situations. This narrow focus can be easily generalized beyond tasks in corporate units to virtually all situations where individuals interact and coordinate their respective behaviors. Status construction theory adds the key notion that beliefs emerge and spread across ever more macro domains of social structure when members of distinctive categories reveal habitual levels of performance, and each time the correlation between categoric unit membership and performance is reinforced in micro encounters, status beliefs are ever more likely to develop and spread—unless challenged by individuals. Status beliefs bias expectation states; and once in place, these expectations can be generalized from one type of situation to another. And, as legitimacy theory would argue, they can be validated and endorsed, especially when others are believed to hold to beliefs about the characteristics and competence of individuals in various social categories. Thus, status beliefs become third-order in status-characteristic theorizing because individuals perceive that most people—perhaps a type of Meadian generalized other—share beliefs about the characteristics of people in particular social categories.

Status-construction theorizing also converges with Blau's (1994) conception of macro-structures and Miller McPherson's conceptualization of *Blau-space*, where individuals are differentially distributed across nominal and graduated parameters (McPherson and Ranger-Moore 1991). As Blau argues, the distribution at the macro level of social organization affects micro-level interactions, or at least rates of interaction. There are tipping points in distributions that bias expectations, especially when membership in categories is correlated with inequalities in valued resources. Moreover, the relative size of categoric units has important effects on rates of interaction and homophily, as is the case when one category has many members while another has few, with the result that the rates of intra-category interaction among those in the larger categoric unit will be much higher, and moreover, inter-category interaction between members of large and small categories will represent a greater percentage of all interactions for those in the smaller compared to those in the larger category. Status construction theory thus moves toward a much more robust formulation that cuts across micro, meso, and macro levels of social organization and, in so doing, presents the potential for integration with more general theories of macrostructure.

Social identity theory adds to this conceptualization a better sense for the internal dynamics among those in social categories. As Gestalt theorizing emphasized, individuals always note differences or develop contrast-conceptions, and they will generally engage in a comparison process of assessing their situation relative to those in another category. Individuals are motivated to make contrasts and comparisons because, as noted earlier, once individuals can be categorized, the expectation states for behavior become clear. In fact, as social identity theory emphasizes, categorization reduces uncertainty for both inter- and intra-category interactions. Social identities represent more than a mechanism for facilitating interaction, however; they also can become part of each individual's personal identity structure, with actors evaluating self in terms of the normative prototype of their social identity (or categoric-unit membership). And, the more prominent in the hierarchy of identities is the self arising from a social identity, the greater will be the power of the expectation states contained in the normative prototype for a social category. Individuals thus internalize the normative prototype of their categoric-unit memberships, and the more they do so, the greater the power of these meso-level units over psychodynamic processes of cognition, emotion, and behavior.

As is evident, then, social psychological theorizing develops a number of conceptions about the properties of social structure that, taken together, present a more robust conception than the individual theories alone. If we cobble together these conceptions, the vision of social structure that emerges emphasizes the following:

1. Social structure, as it impinges upon individuals in micro-level social settings, is composed of categoric units and corporate units, with each revealing its own properties.

2. Categoric units are composed of individuals who are seen to possess distinctive characteristics; and the more discrete these characteristics, the more readily are individuals categorized. Key properties of categoric units include the following:

   a. the inequalities of resources among members of various categoric units

   b. the differential evaluation of members of various categoric units

   c. the beliefs, including evaluative beliefs, about the capabilities and behavioral propensities among members of varying categoric units

   d. the clarity of normative prototypes that develop and that are used to direct behavior among members and outsiders of categoric units

   e. the clarity of expectation states arising from (a) through (d) above that impinge upon individuals in local encounters

   f. the degree to which categoric membership becomes part of an individual's identity, with individuals evaluating their respective selves in terms of the standards contained in (b) through (e) above

g. the distribution of individuals across differentiated categoric units, with this distribution affecting likely rates of interaction and homophily for members of different categoric units

3. Corporate units are composed of vertical and horizontal divisions of labor organized to pursue goals of varying degrees of explicitness; and the more explicit are the divisions of labor and clarity of goals, the more salient will status dynamics become. These status dynamics revolve around the following:

   a. the level of inequality in power and prestige in the hierarchical division of labor

   b. the clarity of expectation states for performances among those in both the vertical and horizontal division of labor

   c. the degree of correlation between status in the division of labor and membership in categoric units (or the correlation between diffuse status characteristics and other dimensions of status)

   d. the degree of consensus over beliefs about status distinctions, whether those in the division of labor or those brought to the division of labor by members of diverse categoric units

   e. the degree of legitimacy arising from status beliefs that are perceived to be validated and endorsed

   f. the rates and scope of interaction among individuals at different locations in the division of labor

   g. the properties of the networks—e.g., density, positive or negative, inclusion-exclusion, power-dependence, equivalence—created by the division of labor

   h. the distribution, flow, and exchange of resources across nodes in the networks generated by the division of labor

4. Episodes of behavior and interaction are embedded in corporate and categoric units, with the specific properties of corporate and categoric units having effects on the cognitions, emotions, and behaviors of individuals.

5. Corporate and categoric units are, in turn, embedded within institutional domains, stratification systems, societies, and potentially, systems of societies, with the structure and culture of these macro-level formations imposing constraints of the structure and culture of meso-level units that, in turn, constrain interpersonal behavior at the micro level of face-to-face interaction.

This simple enumeration captures points of emphasis in all of the theories presented in this volume. I have arrayed the list so that a more unified view of structure emerges that can perhaps encourage theorists to see the relevance of an expanded view of social structure. Each theory could, I believe, develop a better conceptualization of the *social* side of social psychological theorizing if the preceding were used as a checklist of relevant properties of social structure.

CONCEPTUALIZING THE INDIVIDUAL

The other side of the *social* in social psychology is the individual who is viewed by various theories as revealing particular characteristics and behavioral propensities. We need not delve into concerns about human nature to ask a basic question: What is the nature of the individual who engages in social behavior? Each theory captures a somewhat different facet of the individual, and so, before moving on to an analysis of the psychodynamic processes that connect the actor to social structure, we should at least pause for a moment to reflect on the propensities of individuals—portrayed by theories of social psychology in sociology.

Humans as Decision Makers

Rational choice and exchange theories posit a vision of the individual as seeking rewards or utilities while trying to avoid costs and punishments. Added to these assumptions is a view of humans as revealing preferences for particular kinds of utilities and rewards, and these can be conceptualized as hierarchies of preferences or as domains of value. As the fine chapters on rational choice and symbolic interactionism both document, there is overlap among utilitarianism, philosophical pragmatism, Darwinian evolutionism, and behaviorism on how individuals make decisions. Humans are adaptive animals attempting to adjust to their environment, and as symbolic interactionists emphasize, this environment is composed primarily of patterns of social organization or social structure. People will, in general, find cooperation with others rewarding and, at the same time, adaptive; and hence, they will, as pragmatism and behaviorism would argue, retain those patterns of behavior that facilitate adjustment and adaptation to social structure, and in so doing, bring rewards to themselves.

Decision making is, therefore, guided by the socially defined preference structures of individuals as they seek to secure rewards and utilities (and avoid costs and punishments) that facilitate adjustment and adaptation to the environment, which for humans is largely social. The big sticking point in conceptions of human decision making is over the degree of rationality in human decision making; and consideration of this issue leads to debate over whether or not humans are utility-maximizing creatures who try to gain as much reward or utility for the least cost and investment (accumulated costs) as possible. There is no debate over the assumption that humans try to make a profit (rewards or utilities less costs and investments) in their exchanges with others and that decisions are greatly influenced by this need to make a profit. But, the question of maximization is more problematic, and except for extreme rational-choice theorizing, it is unnecessary (although the mathematics work better with this assumption of resource maximization). True, if theorizing simply wants to predict the distribution of decisions at some equilibrium point in a population, assumptions of rationality can be useful, although alternative models using evolutionary theory can now provide better ways to conceptualize population-level equilibrium points. Moreover, the actual elements of informal cooperation and coordination—elements like heuristics, habits, conventions, norms, customs, and beliefs—can also be modeled by evolutionary approaches. These kinds of models can predict which elements are likely to dominate decision making in a population, and in a sense, they provide new ways to expand social psychology into important areas of theoretical development in biology, philosophy, psychology, and to a lesser degree, sociology. At the same time, these new evolutionary modeling approaches provide yet another view of macro and meso social structures as equilibrium points in various population-level distributions.

Most critiques of rationality assumptions emphasize that other attributes of humans subvert pure rationality. Human decisions are constrained by emotions, self and identity, power, norms, expectation states, beliefs and values, and many other social and psychological forces. Of course, rational choice theories can counter that these elements simply load the preference structure of a person and define the range of options as individuals seek to make rational decisions and realize rewards and utilities at as low a cost as is possible. All we can conclude, then, is that humans are decision makers in the sense that they will choose among options in most situations, seeking to gain some rewards and utilities while reducing costs and investments. Rewards, utilities, costs, punishments, and investments will all be constrained, if not defined, by social structures and the other properties of humans.

Humans and Emotions

Curiously, it was not until relatively recently that emotions have been conceptualized within social psychology. Even today, as a reading of the chapters in this volume reveals, only some theories address the question of emotions head on. And, when emotions are analyzed, the range of emotions examined is rather limited. Affect control theory and the affect theory of social exchange explicitly examine emotions, but in somewhat different ways. For affect control theory, negative emotions arise from deflections between fundamental sentiments and transient impressions, while positive emotions ensue with consistency between sentiments and impressions. For affect exchange theory, the emotions aroused during interaction are influenced by particular types of structural situations, including network density, network reachability, relational cohesion or high levels of mutual dependence leading to frequent exchanges, productive activities where individual contributions cannot be so easily separated, and salience of identities, especially collective or social identities.

Most theories that introduce emotions in sociological social psychology appear to borrow heavily from the Gestalt tradition. Positive emotions arise when there is congruence among cognitions, whereas negative emotions emerge when there is deflection, incongruence, and inconsistency among cognitions. This general line of argument from Gestalt theory is taken in a number of interesting, if limited, directions by specific theories. Symbolic interactionist theories emphasizing self and identity argue that humans will experience positive emotions when self or identity is confirmed or negative emotions when self is not verified. Expectation state theories stress that positive emotions will be aroused when individuals behave in accordance with expectations, while negative emotions will be generated when individuals violate or challenge expectation states associated with status. Status construction theory makes a similar point, but argues that expectations are enshrined in status beliefs that, when violated, arouse negative emotions. Rational choice and exchange theories argue that when individuals do not receive expected rewards or utilities and/or must incur unexpected costs, they will experience negative emotions; and conversely, when expected rewards are forthcoming, individuals will feel positive emotions. Justice theories make a similar point when they argue that if individuals' shares of resources are perceived as just in terms of comparisons to the resources of various potential reference points, they will experience negative emotions at the injustice, and conversely, when actual rewards are consistent with what is considered just, positive emotions will ensue.

Thus, there is a clear Gestalt line of argument on the basic conditions increasing the flow of either negative or positive emotions in humans. Humans are seen as seeking consistency, congruence, and balance between a range of cognitions about self, expectations, justice, sentiments, and beliefs, on the one side, and the actions of individuals, payoffs, and resource shares, on the other. Theories such as affect exchange theory introduce additional Gestalt ideas—like attribution processes—to explain the nature of emotions aroused and their targets, as will be examined later.

Nonetheless, my sense is that all of these and other theories in social psychology have a long way to go in explaining emotions beyond a simplified continuum of negative and positive emotions. Specific emotions across the full spectrum of human affect need to be connected to specific social structural conditions and psychodynamic processes. I will come back to this point later when trying to tease out in more detail the psychodynamic processes evident in the various theories. Still, most theories tend to underemphasize what is obviously one of humans' most unique characteristics: the capacity to generate a wide range of emotions of widely varying levels of intensity. Since social structures are ultimately held together by an expanded range of positive emotions, or conversely, torn apart from intense arousal of varying types of negative emotions, the affective capacities of humans need further conceptualization in all of social psychological theorizing in sociology (see Turner and Stets 2005, for a review of approaches to emotions in sociology).

Humans as Information Gatherers

Each theory sees humans as disposed to gather particular types of information. For symbolic interactionists, individuals seek information on the extent to which self or identity has been confirmed or verified. For rational choice or exchange theories, people look for information on the resources available and their potential costs in getting them; and in network variants of exchange theory, individuals assess their relative dependence on others for resources or their exclusion or inclusion in exchange networks. For theories within the expectation-states tradition, individuals are attuned to information on the relative status of self and others, along with associated expectation states (as often dictated by status beliefs). For social identity theories, individuals search for information relevant to categorizing both self and others. For justice theories, individuals evaluate information on their shares of resources compared to the shares of a number of potential reference points, including justice norms and resource shares of others, corporate units, or social categories. For affect control variants of symbolic interactionism, persons seek information on the degree to which self, other, behavior, and situation correspond to fundamental sentiments or norms and beliefs about what should transpire in a situation.

It is fairly obvious that humans, with their big brains and cognitive capacities, are information gatherers, but it is interesting to note the types of information that sociological theories in social psychology emphasize. Curiously, information on the emotional states of others is not given great emphasis, despite the fact that it is crucial to the flow of interaction, behavior, and self-evaluation. If we were to extract the generic types of information that individuals are conceptualized to seek, the following list emerges: (1) the relative resources of self and others, (2) the degree to which self is verified by the responses of others, (3) the relative status (power and prestige) and categoric-unit membership (social identity) of self and others, (4) the expectation states associated with status in corporate and categoric units, and (5) the beliefs and norms that direct the formation of expectation states, prototypes for behavior, emotions and sentiments, standards for self-evaluation, and criteria for justice.

CONCEPTUALIZING PSYCHODYNAMICS

I am using the term *psychodynamics* to denote the processes that connect individuals and social structure. Ultimately, social psychology seeks to explain how social structural conditions affect individual thought, emotion, and behavior, and vice versa. The processes by which social structure impinges on the individual, and conversely, how the thoughts, emotions, and actions of persons affect social structure are dynamic because they are always in play; and theories of social psychology attempt to highlight a specific set of these dynamic processes. Taken together, sociological theories offer a fairly robust, though still somewhat incomplete, conceptualization of psychodynamics. Let me begin with the Gestalt processes that sociologists emphasize.

Gestalt Dynamics

Although Gestalt theorizing no longer dominates social psychological inquiry, if it ever did, many of the specific theories clearly owe at least some of their inspiration to basic Gestalt ideas, including contrast-conception, comparison, cognitive consistency and balance, and attribution. Each of these is examined in the following.

Contrast-Conception Dynamics. Gestalt theorizing emphasized that individuals are disposed—presumably by their biology—to seek out contrasts and to conceptualize the environment in terms of differences in form. Several social psychological theories begin with this basic insight. Social identity theories all make the assumption that individuals perceive differences and are disposed to classify self and others into contrasting categories. Once these distinctions are made, they are elaborated by high rates of intra-category interaction, construction of normative prototypes, self-evaluation in terms of how well these prototypes are realized, and identification with the members of a category. At the same time, individuals are disposed to see others outside their category as members of another category and to infer the normative prototypes guiding their conduct. Individuals also evaluate the standing of their social identity relative to those of others in a comparison process that further solidifies the contrast conception. Indeed, the comparison process highlights and legitimates the beliefs, normative prototypes, and evaluation of individuals' social identity.

This line of theorizing has many points of convergence with other theories in social psychology. The processes of forming a social identity and imputing an identity to others work to institutionalize diffuse status characteristics, as these influence expectation states for competence and performance in micro situations. In essence, social identities operate as diffuse status characteristics, setting into motion all of the dynamic processes specified in status characteristics theory. As these processes unfold, they generally reinforce the evaluations and expectations for performance contained in the social identity, although individuals can often seek to challenge and change the expectations (and the implied evaluation of competencies) in a social identity. Social identity theorizing also merges with status-construction theorizing because much of what makes a social identity viable is a set of cultural beliefs and norms about the characteristic of individuals who are members of a particular social category, thereby biasing expectation states. Moreover, as status beliefs spread, they become increasingly third order in that they are no longer about persons but abstract and prototypical persons as a social category, thus reinforcing the contrast conceptions contained in social identities and the expectation states that arise from the perceived characteristics of individuals who belong to particular categoric units.

Another potential avenue for cross-fertilization comes from legitimacy theory. While legitimacy theory is primarily concerned with legitimation of power hierarchies, the processes examined by this theory—propriety, validity, authorization, and endorsement—can work to legitimate not only power differences but also *any* perceived difference. In fact, in order for a contrast-conception denoting categoric-unit membership to persist, legitimization of differences is critical, and especially so when categories are differentially evaluated or receive varying shares of valued resources.

Finally, social identity theorizing has great potential for adding additional concepts to identity theorizing within the symbolic interactionist tradition, since a social identity and the status beliefs contained in this social identity can become a major source of identity standards for individuals' behavioral outputs and self-evaluations. Social identities are thus one of many identities in an individual's repertoire of identities, and it should be possible to determine the structural conditions under which these identities are salient or prominent in a person's hierarchy of identities. Indeed, when role identities are fused with social identities, the latter will direct behavior and self-evaluation in ways that reinforce the salience of individuals' membership in particular categoric units.

Comparison Dynamics. Several theories in sociological social psychology highlight comparison processes, whereby individuals cognitively assess their situation with reference points to be found in others, groupings of others, categories of others, or cultural codes. Humans have, it is implicitly argued, an innate propensity to assess self in relation to comparison or reference points. Identity control theory, for example, conceptualizes this process as intra-psychic, revolving around the use of an identity standard as a reference point for whether or not an identity presented to others has been verified. When individuals see that the identity standard has been met, they experience positive emotions, whereas when they perceive through reflected appraisals that the standard has not been realized, they will experience distress and other negative emotions.

Affect-control theorizing also invokes a comparison process between fundamental sentiments and transient impressions about selves, others, behaviors, and situations. Fundamental sentiments operate as a reference point for determining if transient impressions are consistent with fundamental sentiments; and when they are, the person experiences positive emotions, whereas when there is deflection, negative emotional arousal leads individuals to pursue cognitive and behavioral strategies to bring sentiments and situational impressions back into line.

Comparison theorizing makes this Gestalt dynamic even more explicit, as do other justice theories. In comparison theorizing, individuals always assess their shares of goods and bads in relation to what is considered just and fair; and when they perceive that their shares are just, they experience positive emotions, while feeling negative emotions when they believe that their shares do not match those contained in their standards of justice. Justice theories seek to specify the nature of the comparison standard, with individuals comparing their shares of resources to varying normative standards of justice, especially norms about procedures, equity, and equality.

The emphasis on equity as a standard of justice can be found in various exchange theories emphasizing distributive justice whereby individuals compare their costs, investments, and payoffs to those of others; and when they perceive that payoffs are proportionate to their and others' relative costs and investments, they will perceive that justice prevails and, as a result, will experience positive emotions and engage in positive sanctioning (Homans 1961). Other exchange theories emphasize that when an exchange between individuals has habitually involved a particular ratio of resources exchanged, this ratio becomes institutionalized into norms of fairness that, when violated, will invite negative emotional arousal and sanctioning (Blau 1964). The free-rider problem in rational-choice models also addresses these dynamics, with individuals monitoring others' contributions to a joint activity to be sure that the latter's effort (costs) is sufficient to justify their share of payoffs. Affect-exchange theorizing also emphasizes this comparison process in various types of exchange relations. In productive exchanges where it is often difficult to sort out each person's respective contribution, individuals will develop perceptions of shared responsibility, and if they perceive that contributions have been shared, they will make attributions to self and others that increase solidarity; and if the productive group has been unsuccessful in realizing its goals, individuals will make external attributions about the failings of the group as a whole. Thus, anytime resources are distributed, individuals will make comparisons to a variety of potential yardsticks, including others, corporate and categoric units, and cultural norms and beliefs.

Expectation-states theorizing and such variants as status-construction and status-characteristics theorizing all invoke a comparison dynamic. Expectations create a standard by which the behaviors of others are assessed, and when performances match expectation states, positive emotions ensue; and the status order is reaffirmed. When performances do not match expectations, and particularly when individuals challenge the expectation states generated by the status order, negative emotions are aroused, and efforts are made to assure that expectations and performances are realigned.

As argued earlier, social identity theories all posit a comparison dynamic through the process of contrast-conception. The boundaries of a group or social category are often defined in comparison to those of another group or category, with individuals assessing and evaluating their own conduct not only by the normative standards of their group or category but also by the standards that distinguish them from members of another group or category. Indeed, corporate-unit and categoric-unit boundaries are often sustained primarily by comparison to another corporate or categoric unit.

The ubiquity of comparison processes across a range of psychodynamics suggests a need to clarify conceptually the dimensions along which comparisons occur. At a minimum, comparison processes work along the following: (1) intra-self comparison of identities with identity standards; (2) comparison of resource shares to those of others, corporate units, or categoric units; (3) comparison of resource shares to evaluative and normative standards of what is just and fair; (4) comparison of a person's costs, investments, and payoffs of resources to the relative costs, investments, and payoffs of others within the same corporate or categoric unit and different corporate and categoric units; (5) comparison of a corporate or categoric unit's overall resources, evaluations, normative standards, and behaviors to those of another corporate or categoric unit. Each of these five types of comparisons has been theorized by sociological theory, but as of yet, no theory has integrated these varying bases of comparison into a more general social psychological theory.

Consistency, Congruity, and Balance Dynamics. Many of the social psychological theories presented in this volume posit a need for humans to experience consistency, congruity, and balance among cognitions about self, others, situations, norms, and beliefs. When individuals feel that cognitions are out of balance, they experience negative emotional arousal and are motivated to restore a sense of consistency. All symbolic interactionist theories, in general, for example, argue that individuals seek to have their self confirmed and verified; and when the responses of others or introspection indicate that self is not verified in a situation or that behaviors have violated expectations, individuals are motivated to bring self-presentations, responses of others, and expectations back into line. Identity theories, as a branch of symbolic interactionism, make a similar argument but recast the propensity for consistency as a need to have identities high in a prominence hierarchy verified; and when individuals cannot achieve confirmation, they will readjust role behaviors, re-present self, offer a different role identity, move the unsuccessful identity to a lower place in the prominence hierarchy, or leave the situation in an effort to achieve congruity. Identity control theory adds a cybernetic argument (Powers 1973), viewing self as a control system in which identity standards guide the emission of gestures to others in an effort to present a role identity, coupled with a feedback system whereby the responses of others are read and interpreted in reflected appraisals for signals that identity standards have been met; and when there is inconsistency between the standard and reflected appraisals, a person will experience distress and adjust behavioral outputs to achieve congruity between the identity presented and the responses of others to this presentation.

Affect control theory, as yet another variant of symbolic-interactionist theorizing, also presents this Gestalt dynamic. Individuals are motivated to achieve congruity between their fundamental sentiments or beliefs about actor, behavior, other, and situation (or ABOS).

When there is a deflection or inconsistency between these fundamental sentiments and transient impressions about any aspect of ABOS, individuals will experience negative emotions and seek to adjust behaviors; reinterpret situation, other, and other's behaviors; or assign a new self to other in order to bring fundamental sentiments and transient impressions into line.

Expectation states and related theories such as status characteristics theory, status construction theory, and legitimacy theory also posit this kind of Gestalt process. When expectation states and the performances or behaviors of individuals in a situation are not consistent, negative emotions are aroused, with individuals sanctioning those who violate expectation states. The underlying argument is that individuals seek consistency between expectations and behaviors, and when there is incongruity between the two, they are motivated to bring the two back into line. If they cannot do so, however, the situation may be breached or expectations states may be readjusted to achieve congruity.

Power-dependence exchange theories offer yet another version of this Gestalt process by emphasizing that actors will seek to mitigate their dependence on an actor for resources (and, hence, the latter's power over them) through a series of balancing operations: seeking alternative sources for valued resources, decreasing the value of resources provided by the power-advantaged actor, shutting off the alternative sources of resources to the power-advantaged actor (and thus increasing the dependence of the power-advantaged on the power-disadvantaged actor), offering the power-advantaged actor new types of valued resources (thereby increasing this actor's dependence on the power-disadvantaged), or doing without the resources. Power-dependence is, therefore, an imbalanced situation, and actors are motivated to achieve a balance in all exchange relationships, if they can.

Distributive justice theories similarly present an implicit consistency argument. Individuals are motivated to compare their shares of resources and their costs and investments in securing these resources against various kinds of reference points, including conceptions of what is fair and just, assessments of others' relative costs and investments to secure resources, the resource shares of salient corporate or categoric units, and justice norms. When there is incongruity between a person's share of resources and the just share that should be given, as determined by the reference points invoked, the individual will experience negative emotions and be motivated to bring resource shares and reference points into line.

Across a range of social psychological theories, then, can be found a consistency dynamic from the Gestalt tradition. Yet, there has been little effort to bring these diverse strands of theorizing together into a more robust conception of why and how humans seek consistency, congruity, and balance in their cognitions about a variety of issues, such as self and identity, beliefs, expectations, exchanges, and distributive justice. By focusing on the Gestalt ideas that various theories invoked and hold in common, one avenue for theoretical integration is opened.

Attribution Dynamics. Another concept that comes from the Gestalt tradition is attribution. Individuals are viewed as motivated to make causal attributions about their experiences. Earlier formulations of attribution theory (Weiner 1986) stressed internal and external attributions, with the former denoting the internal states of others and the latter situational factors outside the individual and others that have causal effects. Affect exchange theory as well as other theories in sociology (Turner 2002) recast the attribution argument somewhat, emphasizing that individuals will make attributions about their experiences to a variety of potential objects, including self, other, corporate units, and categoric units. Affect exchange theory argues that positive emotional experiences have a proximal bias, with individuals most likely to perceive self as the cause of positive outcomes, whereas negative experiences have a distal bias and lead individuals to make external attributions to others and social structures. Attribution thus mediates individuals' attachments and commitments to groupings, and as affect exchange theory seeks to do, the conditions under which individuals make various kinds of attributions not only have large effects on their emotions and behaviors but also on the viability of social structures.

Status construction theory and expectation state theories in general also invoke an attribution dynamic. High-status individuals will generally make self-attributions for their success and believe that their status is due to their competence, whereas lower status individuals will make self-attributions if the status order has been legitimated, or if legitimation is not in place, they make external attributions to the corporate unit as a whole or to higher-status individuals who are seen either as operating or acting in an unfair and unjust manner. When expectations are violated or disagreements emerge, high-status individuals will generally blame lower status persons and express variants of anger toward them, whereas lower status individuals, especially if fellow lower status persons negatively sanction them, will tend to make self-attributions and feel negative emotions toward themselves. Thus, many of the dynamics in theorizing about expectation states, status characteristics, status construction, and legitimacy invoke an attribution process that mediates between the status order and individuals' emotional responses to this order. Again, as is the case with other Gestalt dynamics, there is potential for theoretical integration by focusing on the attribution processes that are common to the theories.

I have highlighted these underlying Gestalt dynamics in various theories because, as noted earlier, they represent one entry point for integrating theories. Because the theories all develop somewhat unique vocabularies and concepts, it is often difficult to see what they have in common. One thing that many have in common is the use of old Gestalt ideas— obviously in sophisticated and elaborated forms—and this commonality could serve as a wedge to get theorists considering how their use of Gestalt ideas compare with those in other theories. From this simple shift in focus to what theories have in common, the potential for theoretical integration and the production of more robust—semi-grand, if you will—theories increases.

Other Dynamic Processes

Of course, theories in social psychology go far beyond the Gestalt tradition, and so, I would be remiss if I did not highlight other key processes. I have, to a degree, already discussed these processes, but some should be mentioned again as key psychodynamics that link persons to social structures.

Rationality. All exchange theories and, of course, rational choice theories make at least this claim: humans seek to gain an excess of rewards and utilities over their costs and investments incurred in securing these rewards and utilities. People are, in this minimal sense, rational because, if a situation is problematic, they will weigh alternatives and choose one that allows them to realize a profit in social exchanges. Symbolic interactionists, beginning with the pragmatists, also make a similar claim. George Herbert Mead's (1934) conception of *mind* captures a kind of rationality, with individuals "imaginatively rehearsing alternatives" (John Dewey's famous phrase) in order to pursue that line of conduct that facilitates adaptation and adjustment (with adaptation being the ultimate reward and utility for humans who must cooperate to survive). Indeed, as noted earlier, evolutionary modeling in some versions of rational choice theory makes a similar claim.

Emotionality. For a long period in the Western philosophical tradition, rationality and emotionality were seen as opposite ends of a continuum. It is now clear, however, that rationality cannot occur without the capacity to tag alternative lines of conduct with emotional valences (Damasio 1994). Thus, as Randall Collins (1993) once argued, emotions are the common denominator of rationality, and so the two fields need to be studied together; and yet, except for affect-exchange theorizing, they still remain apart. In fact, emotions as a topic in social psychology and, indeed, sociology in general, remained a secondary concern until the last two decades of the 20th century.

This fact of human emotionality—which seems so obvious that it is hard to believe that sociologists ignored it for so long—should push all theorists in social psychology to incorporate emotions into their theories. Most do, at least in an implicit and still rather limited way. For symbolic interactionists, and variants like identity theory, emotions are aroused when self and identity are confirmed or disconfirmed. For other variants of symbolic interactionism like affect control theory, any deflection between fundamental sentiments (about actor, other, behavior, or situation) and transient impressions produces emotions. For exchange theorists, as well as rational choice theories, emotions are generated when individuals do not do well in exchanges, when they experience negative externalities, when game strategies do not yield expected payoffs, when they are excluded, or when they are in power-dependent relations. Still, most exchange theories gloss over the emotional dynamics inhering in all exchange relations—save to affect exchange theory. For distributive justice theories and sophisticated variants like comparison theory, emotions are aroused when individuals experience justice or injustice, but the range of emotions addressed—anger, sadness, guilt—is rather narrow. Expectation-states theorizing clearly posits—sometimes explicitly but always implicitly—an emotional dynamic that is set into motion when expectations are realized or violated; and in some theories, the emotional content of a situation becomes the basis for another kind of emotional expectation state. Yet, with a few exceptions (e.g., Ridgeway 1994; Hauser and Lovaglia 2002; Shelly 2004), emotions are not fully integrated into these theories. Moreover, even granting that this book is devoted to theoretical research traditions with cumulative findings, it is rather surprising that only one of the many new theories of emotions is included in these pages. Hence, there is a clear need for the most cumulative theoretical research traditions in sociology to bring emotions into their theories in a more explicit and systematic way.

Self-Regulation. Emotions are part of the larger system of self-regulation. As identity control theory emphasizes, people regulate their presentations of identities by attending to feedback from the responses of others to see whether or not behavioral outputs have met an identity standard. Mead's concepts of role taking, mind, self, and "I-Me" interchanges capture the basic cybernetic nature of human conduct (see Shibutani 1968 for the first explicit statement on this contention). Identity control theory sees distress (a combination of fear and anger) as emerging from the failure to verify self, but clearly the nature of the specific emotion aroused has large effects on self-regulation. Shame, guilt, fear, anger, sadness, and the many variants and combinations of emotions that humans can generate will have entirely different consequences for how humans see self, others, and situations and how they will respond in an effort to regulate conduct so as to cooperate with others while, at the same time, verifying self, meeting justice standards, gaining profits from exchanges, adhering to expectations, making rational decisions, and performing other processes that are all part of self-regulation.

In fact, I see self-regulation as an idea that can be used to integrate theories in social psychology. This integration would begin by asking how each theory conceptualizes humans as self-regulators. For example, exchange theory and rational choice theory would emphasize rational decisions to secure resources, justice theories to realize a sense of fairness, symbolic interactionist theories to confirm self, and so on. Specifying just how regulatory dynamics work in each theory and, further, denoting more precisely the emotions that are aroused would go a long way to producing a more robust theory in sociology of social psychological dynamics.

Expectations. I have come to see expectations as a much more general dynamic than is portrayed in the variants of expectation-states theorizing (Turner 2002). Virtually every social psychological process involves expectations—for profitable or unprofitable exchange payoffs, for confirmation of self, for outcomes of decisions, for flows of resources in networks, for justice, for confirming fundamental sentiments and other beliefs, for sanctions, for emotions, and for any process postulated by social psychological theories. When individuals have expectations, the emotional stakes are raised because, if expectations go unrealized, negative emotions are aroused and attributions made. Thus, another way to integrate theories of social psychology in sociology is to make explicit the expectation dynamics involved. Expectations are aroused for a great deal more than status considerations in task groups, and it would be useful to theorize about the nature of the expectations posited implicitly by theories, the emotions aroused when expectations are realized or unrealized, the cognitive processes that ensue, and the effects of resulting behaviors on social structures.

Expectation states theory has, therefore, been too modest, at least in this sense: it has only incrementally branched out and has been reluctant to theorize beyond what can be tested in controlled experiments. It is time, I think, for greater conceptual leaps to be made and for other theorists within and outside of social psychology proper to adopt the core ideas of this research tradition to a new range of social processes.

CONCLUSION

This volume has presented essays from scholars active in the most cumulative wing of sociological social psychology—cumulative in the sense that the theories are explicit, generally formal, and tested systematically with research. The only negative to this criterion of cumulation is that these theories tend to be narrow. When theorists must also be researchers who test out their own theories, the theories will almost always impose relatively restrictive scope conditions. Such is the case with most of the approaches presented in these pages. As I noted in the introduction, there is another way by which theorizing can be cumulative: integration of specialized theories into a more robust theory. Incremental steps can perhaps get us there, but as a grand theorist, I find it frustrating that these steps are often baby steps. In my view, we need to take some big steps and make a bold effort to look beyond the narrow scope conditions of theories and seek common ground with other theories, even those that are more speculative and imprecise.

Sociology has increasingly become partitioned into specialties; and even our theories, which are supposed to provide the explanatory engine for the discipline, are now highly specialized. Each has a name, which creates a boundary and encourages further partitioning; and this partitioning gets in the way of theoretical integration, especially if theorists are unwilling to alter the vocabularies and focus in searching for common ground. Moreover, I believe that more effort should be made to assess each of these specialized theories in more naturalistic settings. The laboratory is a very good place to gain control, but the real world is a better way to assess the plausibility of theories in their more robust form. Even with the obvious loss of precision, each theory's generalizability can be demonstrated in real-world settings. I am not sure that *timid* is the right term to describe the current state of theorizing in social psychology—perhaps *precision* is better—but there appears to be a "fear of flying" from the comfort of scope conditions and the experimental laboratory. I think that theorists would get needed input by taking their theories on the road, as it were, where real people (rather than subjects and actors) in real situations (rather than the lab) reside.

The theories in this volume are among the very best in the discipline, despite their narrow scope. And even those like elementary theory or power-dependence theory that can conceptualize actors as individuals or collectivities do not fully realize their potential because of the lack of attention to naturalistic settings where theories show their mettle. I am sure that my suggestions will seem vague to scholars accustomed to precision, but these suggestions seem vague because they are only guidelines, not theory itself. They offer ideas for how to break out of the tyranny of scope conditions (for all their other merits) and to extend, expand, and integrate theories so that a more comprehensive conception of social structure, the individual, and the psychodynamics connecting the two can be forthcoming.

REFERENCES

Blau, Peter. 1964. *Exchange and Power in Social Life*. New York: Wiley.

———. 1994. *Structural Context of Opportunities*. Chicago: University of Chicago Press.

Blumer, Herbert. 1969. *Symbolic Interaction*. Englewood Cliffs, NJ: Prentice-Hall.

Collins, Randall. 1993. Emotional energy as the common denominator of rational action. *Rationality and Society* 5:203–30.

———. 2004. *Interaction Ritual Chains*. Princeton, NJ: Princeton University Press.

Damasio, Antonio. 1994. *Descartes' Error: Emotion, Reason, and the Human Brain*. New York: G. P. Putman.

Emerson, Richard. 1962. Power-dependence relations. *American Sociological Review* 17:31–41.

Goffman, Erving. 1961. *Encounters: Two Studies on Face-to-Face Behavior*. Garden City, NY: Anchor.

———. 1983. The interaction order. *American Sociological Review* 48:1–17.

Hauser, Jeffrey A., and Michael J. Lovaglia. 2002. Status, emotion, and the development of solidarity in stratified task groups. *Advances in Group Processes* 19:109–37.

Hawley, Amos. 1986. *Human Ecology: A Theoretical Essay*. Chicago: University of Chicago Press.

Homans, George C. 1961. *Social Behavior: Its Elementary Forms*. New York: Harcourt.

McPherson, Miller, and J. Ranger-Moore. 1991. Evolution on a dancing landscape: Organizations and networks in Blau-space. *Social Forces* 70:19–42.

Mead, George Herbert. 1934. *Mind, Self, and Society*. Chicago: University of Chicago Press.

Powers, William T. 1973. *The Control of Perception*. Chicago: Aldine.

Ridgeway, Cecilia L. 1994. Affect. In *Group Processes and Sociological Analysis*, ed. Marta Foschi and Edward J. Lawler. Chicago: Nelson-Hall.

Shelly, Robert. 2004. Emotions, sentiments, and performance expectations. *Advances in Group Processes* 21:141–65.

Shibutani, Tamotsu. 1968. A cybernetic approach to motivation. In *Modern Systems Research for the Behavioral Sciences: A Sourcebook*, ed. Walter Buckley. Chicago: University of Chicago Press.

Stryker, Sheldon. 1980. *Symbolic Interactionism*. Menlo Park, CA: Benjamin-Cummings.

Turner, Jonathan H. 2002. *Face-to-Face: Toward a Theory of Interpersonal Behavior*. Stanford, CA: Stanford University Press.

Turner, Jonathan H., and Jan E. Stets. 2005. *The Sociology of Emotions*. New York: Cambridge University Press.

Weiner, Bernard. 1986. *An Attributional Theory of Motivation and Emotion*. New York: Springer-Verlag.

INDEX